# Professional Post-Graduate Diploma in Marketing

## PAPER 10:
## STRATEGIC MARKETING DECISIONS

For exams in December 2007 and June 2008

**Study Text**

### In this August 2007 edition

- A new **user-friendly format** for easy navigation
- Regular **fast forward** summaries emphasising the key points in each chapter
- Recent examples of marketing practice
- Fully revised
- A full **index**

LEARNING MEDIA

Fourth edition August 2007

ISBN  978 0 7517 4176 6 (Previous edition 0 7517 2705 9)

British Library Cataloguing-in-Publication Data
A catalogue record for this book
is available from the British Library

Published by

BPP Learning Media
BPP House, Aldine Place
London W12 8AA

www.bpp.com/learningmedia

Printed in Great Britain by

WM Print
45-47 Frederick Street
Walsall
WS2 9NE

We are grateful to the Chartered Institute of Marketing
for permission to reproduce in this text the syllabus,
tutor's guidance notes and past examination
questions.

Your learning materials, published by BPP Learning Media
Ltd, are printed on paper sourced from sustainable,
managed forests.

# Contents

# The BPP Study Text

## Aims of this Study Text

To provide you with the knowledge and understanding, skills and application techniques that you need if you are to be successful in your exams

This Study Text has been written around the **Strategic Marketing Decisions** syllabus.

- It is **comprehensive**. It covers the syllabus content. No more, no less.

- It is targeted to the **exam**. We have taken account of the pilot paper, guidance the examiner has given and the assessment methodology.

To allow you to study in the way that best suits your learning style and the time you have available, by following your personal Study Plan (see below)

You may be studying at home on your own until the date of the exam, or you may be attending a full-time course. You may like to (and have time to) read every word, or you may prefer to (or only have time to) skim-read and devote the remainder of your time to question practice. Wherever you fall in the spectrum, you will find the BPP Study Text meets your needs in designing and following your personal Study Plan.

To tie in with the other components of the BPP Effective Study Package to ensure you have the best possible chance of passing the exam

**BPP**
LEARNING MEDIA

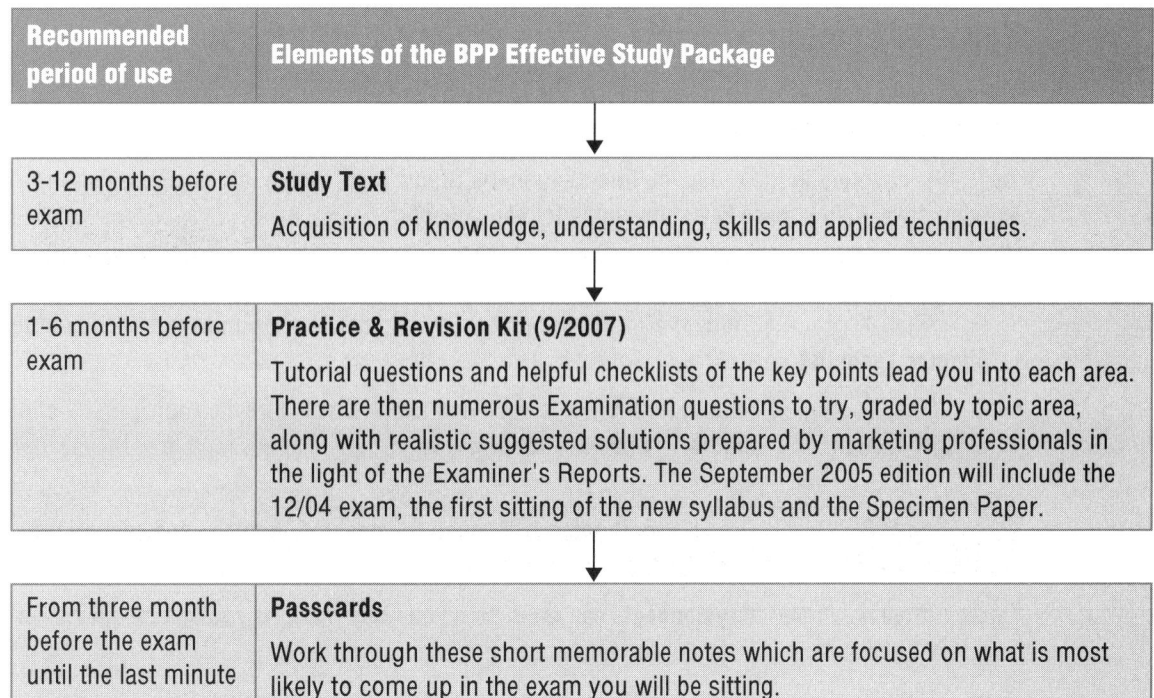

| Recommended period of use | Elements of the BPP Effective Study Package |
|---|---|
| 3-12 months before exam | **Study Text**<br>Acquisition of knowledge, understanding, skills and applied techniques. |
| 1-6 months before exam | **Practice & Revision Kit (9/2007)**<br>Tutorial questions and helpful checklists of the key points lead you into each area. There are then numerous Examination questions to try, graded by topic area, along with realistic suggested solutions prepared by marketing professionals in the light of the Examiner's Reports. The September 2005 edition will include the 12/04 exam, the first sitting of the new syllabus and the Specimen Paper. |
| From three month before the exam until the last minute | **Passcards**<br>Work through these short memorable notes which are focused on what is most likely to come up in the exam you will be sitting. |

## Settling down to study

By this stage in your career you may be a very experienced learner and taker of exams. But have you ever thought about *how* you learn? Let's have a quick look at the key elements required for effective learning. You can then identify your learning style and go on to design your own approach to how you are going to study this text – your personal Study Plan.

| Key element of learning | Using the BPP Study Text |
|---|---|
| Motivation | You can rely on the comprehensiveness and technical quality of BPP. You've chosen the right Study Text – so you're in pole position to pass your exam! |
| Clear objectives and standards | Do you want to be a prizewinner or simply achieve a moderate pass? Decide. |
| Feedback | Follow through the examples in this text and do the Action Programme and the Quick Quizzes. Evaluate your efforts critically – how are you doing? |
| Study Plan | You need to be honest about your progress to yourself – don't be over-confident, but don't be negative either. Make your Study Plan (see below) and try to stick to it. Focus on the short-term objectives – completing two chapters a night, say – but beware of losing sight of your study objectives. |
| Practice | Use the Quick Quizzes and Chapter Roundups to refresh your memory regularly after you have completed your initial study of each chapter. |

These introductory pages let you see exactly what you are up against. However you study, you should:

- **Read through the syllabus** – this will help you to identify areas you have already covered, perhaps at a lower level of detail, and areas that are totally new to you

- **Study the examination paper section**, where we show you the format of the exam (how many and what kind of questions and so on)

# Key study steps

The following steps are, in our experience, the ideal way to study for professional exams. You can of course adapt it for your particular learning style (see below).

Tackle the chapters in the order you find them in the Study Text. Taking into account your individual learning style, follow these key study steps for each chapter.

| Key study steps | Activity |
|---|---|
| Step 1<br>**Chapter Topic list** | Study the list. Each numbered topic denotes a **numbered section** in the chapter. |
| Step 2<br>**Introduction** | Read it through. It is designed to show you **why the topics in the chapter need to be studied** – how they lead on from previous topics, and how they lead into subsequent ones. |
| Step 3<br>**Explanations** | Proceed **methodically** through the chapter, reading each section thoroughly and making sure you understand. |
| Step 4<br>**Key Concepts** | **Key concepts** can often earn you **easy marks** if you state them clearly and correctly in an appropriate exam. |
| Step 5<br>**Exam Tips** | These give you a good idea of how the examiner tends to examine certain topics – pinpointing **easy marks** and highlighting **pitfalls**. |
| Step 6<br>**Note taking** | Take **brief notes** if you wish, avoiding the temptation to copy out too much. |
| Step 7<br>**Marketing at Work** | Study each one, and try if you can to add flesh to them from your **own experience** – they are designed to show how the topics you are studying come alive (and often come unstuck) in the **real world**. You can also update yourself on these companies by going on to the World Wide Web. |
| Step 8<br>**Action Programme** | Make a very good attempt at each one in each chapter. These are designed to put your **knowledge into practice** in much the same way as you will be required to do in the exam. Check the answer at the end of the chapter in the **Action Programme review**, and make sure you understand the reasons why yours may be different. |
| Step 9<br>**Chapter Roundup** | Check through it very carefully, to make sure you have grasped the **major points** it is highlighting |
| Step 10<br>**Quick Quiz** | When you are happy that you have covered the chapter, use the **Quick Quiz** to check your recall of the topics covered. |
| Step 11<br>**Illustrative question(s)** | Either at this point, or later when you are thinking about revising, make a full attempt at the **illustrative questions**. You can find these at the end of the Study Text, along with the **Answers** so you can see how you did. |

# Developing your personal Study Plan

Preparing a Study Plan (and sticking closely to it) is one of the key elements in learning success.

First you need to be aware of your style of learning. There are four typical learning styles. Consider yourself in the light of the following descriptions. and work out which you fit most closely. You can then plan to follow the key study steps in the sequence suggested.

| Learning styles | Characteristics | Sequence of key study steps in the BPP Study Text |
|---|---|---|
| Theorist | Seeks to understand principles before applying them in practice | 1, 2, 3, 7, 4, 5, 8, 9, 10, 11 (6 continuous) |
| Reflector | Seeks to observe phenomena, thinks about them and then chooses to act | |
| Activist | Prefers to deal with practical, active problems; does not have much patience with theory | 1, 2, 8 (read through), 7, 4, 5, 9, 3, 8 (full attempt), 10, 11 (6 continuous) |
| Pragmatist | Prefers to study only if a direct link to practical problems can be seen; not interested in theory for its own sake | 8 (read through), 2, 4, 5, 7, 9, 1, 3, 8 (full attempt), 10, 11 (6 continuous) |

Next you should complete the following checklist.

| | | |
|---|---|---|
| Am I motivated? | (a) | |
| Do I have an objective and a standard that I want to achieve? | (b) | |
| Am I a theorist, a reflector, an activist or a pragmatist? | (c) | |
| How much time do I have available per week, given: | (d) | |

- The standard I have set myself
- The time I need to set aside later for work on the Practice and Revision Kit
- The other exam(s) I am sitting, and (of course)
- Practical matters such as work, travel, exercise, sleep and social life?

**Now:**

- Take the time you have available per week for this Study Text (d), and multiply it by the number of weeks available to give (e)  (e)
- Divide (e) by the number of chapters to give (f)  (f)
- Set about studying each chapter in the time represented by (f), following the key study steps in the order suggested by your particular learning style

This is your personal **Study Plan**.

## Short of time?

Whatever your objectives, standards or style, you may find you simply do not have the time available to follow all the key study steps for each chapter, however you adapt them for your particular learning style. If this is the case, follow the Skim Study technique below.

### Skim Study technique

Study the chapters in the order you find them in the Study Text. For each chapter, follow the key study steps 1–2, and then skim-read through step 3. Jump to step 9, and then go back to steps 4–5. Follow through step 7, and prepare outline Answers to the Action Programme (step 8). Try the Quick Quiz (step 10), following up any items you can't answer, then do a plan for the illustrative question (step 11), comparing it against our answers. You should probably still follow step 6 (note-taking).

## Moving on...

However you study, when you are ready to embark on the practice and revision phase of the BPP Effective Study Package, you should still refer back to this Study Text:

- As a source of **reference** (you should find the list of key concepts and the index particularly helpful for this)

- As a **refresher** (the Chapter Roundups and Quick Quizzes help you here)

## A note on pronouns

On occasions in this Study Text, 'he' is used for 'he or she', 'him' for 'him or her' and so forth. Whilst we try to avoid this practice it is sometimes necessary for reasons of style. No prejudice or stereotyping accounting to sex is intended or assumed.

# Syllabus

## Aims and objectives

The *Strategic Marketing Decisions* module covers the second part of strategic marketing in a global context by building on the skills and knowledge gained from the study of the Analysis and Evaluation module. The focus of this module is on the nature of competitive strategy in a global context. It examines how, in such a dynamic environment, competitive advantage might be developed through strongly differentiated positioning and exploited in a cost-effective manner. Its emphasis is on where and how the organisation competes and, in doing this, highlights the strategic marketing significance of brands, innovation, alliances and relationships and e-marketing. An important theme running through the module is the development of the capability to develop innovative solutions that enhance an organisation's competitive position in its chosen markets.

## Learning outcomes

Participants will be able to:

- Appraise a range of corporate and business visions, missions and objectives and the processes by which they are formulated, in light of the changing bases of competitive advantage across geographically diverse markets.

- Identify, compare and contrast strategic options and critically evaluate the implications of strategic marketing decisions in relation to the concept of 'shareholder value'.

- Evaluate the role of brands, innovation, integrated marketing communications, alliances, customer relationships and service in decisions for developing a differentiated positioning to create exceptional value for the customer.

- Demonstrate the ability to develop innovative and creative marketing solutions to enhance an organisation's global competitive position in the context of changing product, market, and brand and customer life cycles.

- Define and contribute to investment decisions concerning the marketing assets of an organisation.

- Demonstrate the ability to re-orientate the formulation and control of cost-effective competitive strategies, appropriate for the objectives and context of an organisation operating in a dynamic global environment.

## Knowledge and skill requirements

| Element 1: The changing dimensions of competitive advantage (10%) | |
|---|---|
| 1.1 | Examine the role of life cycles in strategic decisions to manage competitive advantage across global, international and domestic markets. |
| 1.2 | Examine the influence of market position on strategy and performance. |
| 1.3 | Critically appraise the changing dimensions of strategic decisions made to sustain competitive advantage in today's global markets. |
| 1.4 | Assess how product/market/brand/customer life cycles can be managed strategically across markets. |
| 1.5 | Examine the role of competitive relationships and how organisations compete to achieve customer preference. |

| Element 2: Challenging traditional strategic thinking: innovation and the reorientation & reformulation of competitive marketing strategies (25%) | |
|---|---|
| 2.1 | Examine the significance and application of new marketing thinking to strategic decisions. |
| 2.2 | Explain the nature of innovation in marketing and the factors affecting its development in decisions to create competitive advantage and customer preference. |
| 2.3 | Evaluate the role of innovation management and risk-taking in achieving competitive advantage. |
| 2.4 | Examine the issues in creating an innovative marketing culture within an organisation. |
| 2.5 | Determine drivers for realignment in strategic thinking. |
| 2.6 | Explore the alternative approaches to strategic marketing decisions (e.g. formal/analytical approach v transformation approaches). |
| 2.7 | Explore competitive marketing strategy as an emergent /learning process. |
| 2.8 | Examine the role of knowledge management in sustaining competitive advantage. |
| 2.9 | Evaluate the incorporation of customer-led internet marketing into marketing strategies. |
| 2.10 | Examine issues in strategic marketing decision making in SMEs. |

| Element 3: Strategic marketing decisions for the global marketplace (25%) | |
|---|---|
| 3.1 | Examine the issues of decisions to build competitive capability and approaches to leveraging capability to create advantage across geographically diverse markets. |
| 3.2 | Evaluate Porter's three generic strategies in the context of today's competitive environment. |
| 3.3 | Critically appraise strategic marketing decisions for pioneers, challengers, followers and niche players. |
| 3.4 | Identify and critically evaluate strategic options in relation to shareholder value, using appropriate decision tools. |
| 3.5 | Describe the formulation and evaluation of competitive strategies. |
| 3.6 | Determine the lessons of best practice from strategic decisions made by successful global companies. |
| 3.7 | Evaluate the use of e-technology to build and exploit competitive advantage. |
| 3.8 | Critically appraise innovative marketing strategies in small and large companies operating on global markets. |
| 3.9 | Appreciate the value of effective knowledge management in creating competitive advantage. |
| 3.10 | Leverage individual and corporate learning across geographically diverse markets for competitive advantage. |

| Element 4: Strategic marketing decisions in the management of the portfolio (25%) | |
|---|---|
| 4.1 | Explain and evaluate the contribution of value-based marketing. |
| 4.2 | Assess the nature and dimensions of branding /brand decisions, their role in the development of advantage and their significance in global markets. |
| 4.3 | Examine product strategies and the role of new product development in competitive strategy. |
| 4.4 | Evaluate the role of integrated marketing communications in competitive global strategy. |
| 4.5 | Understand the concept of relationship marketing and the role of long term customer relationships in creating and delivering value. |
| 4.6 | Determine the importance of managing marketing relationships in generating customer commitment. |
| 4.7 | Examine the role of alliances and the creation of competitive advantage through supply chain development and marketing partnerships. |
| 4.8 | Examine how pricing policies and strategies can be used to build competitive advantage. |
| 4.9 | Explain the strategic management of the global portfolio and the expanded marketing mix. |
| 4.10 | Assess the issues of corporate and social responsibility (CSR), sustainability and ethics in achieving competitive advantage, enhancing corporate reputation and creating stakeholder value. |

| Element 5: Investment decisions and control (15%) | |
|---|---|
| 5.1 | Examine the implications of strategic marketing decisions for implementation and control. |
| 5.2 | Explain the concept of, and evaluate methods such as balanced scorecard for, stakeholder value measurement. |
| 5.3 | Apply investment appraisal techniques to marketing investment decisions. |
| 5.4 | Examine alternative approaches to modelling potential investment decisions in the deployment of marketing resources. |
| 5.5 | Define performance measurement systems for the deployment of marketing assets and the implementation of marketing plans. |
| 5.6 | Define budgetary and planning control techniques for use in the control of marketing plans and explain the pitfalls of control systems and how they may be overcome. |

## Assessment

CIM will offer a single form of assessment based on the learning outcomes for this module. It will take the form of an invigilated, time-constrained assessment throughout the delivery network. Candidates' assessments will be marked centrally by CIM.

# Overview and rationale

The development of strategies that build upon and leverage an organisation's competitive position globally is fundamental to strategic marketing decisions made in organisations. However, in a fast changing and dynamic environment, senior marketing managers need the ability not only to develop problem solving strategies but also the mindset that enables them to reinvent periodically the basis on which an organisation can compete. The challenges of doing this across a spectrum of fast moving, geographically and culturally varied markets in an effective manner represent a significant intellectual challenge and requires the development and refinement of decision-making skills.

This module builds on the *Marketing Planning* module at Stage 2 and the *Analysis and Evaluation* module. It introduces the knowledge and skills needed by aspiring senior marketing managers if they are to contribute to the strategic marketing decisions to build a sustainable competitive advantage. It places strong emphasis on developing the insights needed to re think and re-orientate the marketing direction of an organisation at a strategic level and therefore provides a valuable foundation for both the *Managing Marketing Performance* module and the final module, *Strategic Marketing in Practice*.

## Approach

This module provides the knowledge and skills for the contributing to strategic marketing decisions in the formulation of a competitive strategy. The end point of the module is a set of strategic decisions for the organisation that may be built into a corporate or business plan. This is taken forward into implementation in the *Managing Marketing Performance* module. It incorporates the relevant knowledge and understanding of strategic decisions within domestic, international and global contexts. The knowledge and skills acquired are applied in the *Strategic Marketing in Practice* module.

This module focuses on the decisions needed to develop a more innovative approach to the strategic development of the organisation that will build competitive advantage by creating added value for customers and other stakeholders. In doing this it is necessary for participants to study in an integrated way the complete strategic decision process to identify new marketing opportunities, areas for innovation and value creation in an organisation. They will need to learn the lessons of good practice of other organisations from different contexts from their own. Participants will have the opportunity to build concentrated experience that comes from studying the management of a series of critical incidents and emerging trends that have led to leading edge developments in marketing.

Finally, the module recognises that there is no 'right' strategic marketing decision for an organisation. It encourages participants to explore and propose approaches that require the re-evaluation and re-formulation of the strategies of organisations to survive and grow in today's global competitive environment.

## Syllabus content

The balance of weighting allocated to each of the five elements reflects the importance of the area to the achievement of learning and performance outcomes, and the depth and breadth of the material to be covered. Although each area may be regarded as a discrete element, there are clear progressions and overlaps in the knowledge and skills requirements have important implications for the delivery of the module.

### Element 1: The changing dimensions of competitive advantage. (10%)

This element develops an understanding of the dynamics of the changing dimensions of competitive advantage and how, in order to sustain competitiveness, organisations must make strategic marketing decisions effectively to manage brand, product and market life cycles across fragmented and complex global markets. It then goes on to examine the role of competitive relationships and how organisations compete globally. The influence of an organisation's market position is also explored in the formation of

these alliances and relationships as well as the possible implications on their strategic positioning and performance.

### Element 2: Challenging traditional strategic thinking; innovation and the reorientation & reformulation of competitive marketing strategies. (25%)

This is a key element to this module in that it provides an understanding of how senior managers, in making successful strategic marketing decisions, need continuously to reflect and challenge the assumptions on which previous strategies have been built, both in their own organisations and elsewhere. Central to this element is the examination and application of new marketing thinking. In doing this, the element explores the alternative approaches to strategic decisions (e.g. formal/analytical approach v transformation approaches) and develops the knowledge and skills managers need to determine drivers for realignment in strategic thinking. The element then goes onto to evaluate the role of innovation management and risk-taking in organisations in achieving competitive advantage and what organisations need to do to create an innovative marketing culture. The conclusion of this element examines the innovative strategy making process as an emergent learning process and how organisations can encourage such a process within their organisations.

### Element 3: Strategic marketing decisions for the global marketplace. (25%)

This element aims to provide an understanding of the concepts that underpin strategic marketing decisions for the global marketplace. It addresses the factors that determine which strategic options firms might decide on to make an appropriate response to their competitive situation, whilst at the same time creating customer and stakeholder value. In doing so it examines the issues of competitive capability and decision approaches that can be used to leverage capability and create advantage. The element then goes onto examine different patterns of development and different ways of building relationships in the supply chain as well as giving consideration to the use of more innovative approaches to the development of competitive strategies that will be successful in the future. As such the leveraging of individual and organisational learning, knowledge management and the use of e-technology to exploit competitive advantage should be discussed.

### Element 4: Strategic marketing decisions in the management of the portfolio. (25%)

This element encourages participants to consider the practical application of the competitive strategy by addressing the management of the elements of the global portfolio of products and services. In doing this, strategic decisions are explored for branding, communications, pricing and distribution that are both innovative and integrated. The challenge is to add value and remove costs within the firm and from the supply chain, and there are a number of enabling technologies that support this goal. The role of integrated marketing communications in a competitive strategy, the concept of relationship marketing and its role in the creation of global competitive advantage through supply chain development are all explored.

### Element 5: Investment decisions & control. (15%)

The final element develops the structure for the evaluation and appraisal of the strategic options. Techniques are discussed for making decisions on investment to support new strategies and the risks involved. Assessment of the increase in stakeholder value and cost reduction of the new strategies key performance indicators that will indicate future success are examined. The application of capital investment appraisal techniques to marketing investment decisions and the use of performance measurement systems in relation to the deployment of marketing based assets and the implementation of marketing plans are central to this element as well as the use of budgetary and planning control techniques in the control of marketing plans.

## Delivery approach

Tutors will need to demonstrate the lessons of good practice of organisations from different sector contexts. Case study drawn from successful global companies as well as small organisations lends themselves to this task.

# Websites

## The Chartered Institute of Marketing

| | |
|---|---|
| www.cim.co.uk | CIM website with information and access to learning support for participants. |
| www.cim.co.uk/learningzone | Direct access to information and support materials for all levels of CIM qualification |
| www.cim.co.uk/tutors | Access for Tutors |
| www.shapetheagenda.com | Quarterly agenda paper from CIM |

## Publications on line

| | |
|---|---|
| www.ft.com | Extensive research resources across all industry sectors, with links to more specialist reports. (Charges may apply) |
| www.thetimes.co.uk | One of the best online versions of a quality newspaper |
| www.economist.com | Useful links, and easily-searched archives of articles from back issues of the magazine |
| www.mad.co.uk | Marketing Week magazine online |
| www.brandrepublic.com | Marketing magazine online |
| www.westburn.co.uk | Journal of Marketing Management online, the official Journal of the Academy of Marketing and Marketing Review |
| http://smr.mit.edu/smr/ | Free abstracts from Sloan Management Review articles |
| www.hbsp.harvard.edu | Free abstracts from Harvard Business Review articles |
| www.ecommercetimes.com | Daily enews on the latest ebusiness developments |
| www.cim.co.uk/knowledgehub | 3000 full text journals titles are available to members via the Knowledge Hub – includes the range of titles above - embargoes may apply |
| www.cim.co.uk/cuttingedge | Weekly round up of marketing news (available to CIM members) plus list of awards and forthcoming marketing events. |

## Sources of useful information

| | |
|---|---|
| www.1to1.com | The Peppers and Rogers One-to-One Marketing site which contains useful information about the tools and techniques of relationship marketing |
| www.balancetime.com | The Productivity Institute provides free articles, a time management email newsletter, and other resources to improve personal productivity |
| www.bbc.co.uk | The Learning Zone at BBC Education contains extensive educational resources, including the video, CD Rom, ability to watch TV programmes such as the News online, at your convenience, after they have been screened |
| www.busreslab.com | Useful specimen online questionnaires to measure customer satisfaction levels and tips on effective Internet marketing research |
| www.lifelonglearning.co.uk | Encourages and promotes Lifelong Learning through press releases, free articles, useful links and progress reports on the development of the University for Industry (UFI) |
| www.marketresearch.org.uk | The Market Research Society. Contains useful material on the nature of research, choosing an agency, ethical standards and codes of conduct for research practice |
| www.nielsen-netratings.com | Details the current levels of banner advertising activity, including the creative content of the ten most popular banners each week (within Top Rankings area) |
| www.open.ac.uk | Some good Open University videos available for a broad range of subjects |
| www.direct.gov.uk | Gateway to a wide range of UK government information |
| www.srg.co.uk | The Self Renewal Group – provides useful tips on managing your time, leading others, managing human resources, motivating others etc |
| www.statistics.gov.uk | Detailed information on a variety of consumer demographics from the Government Statistics Office |

| | |
|---|---|
| www.durlacher.com | The latest research on business use of the Internet, often with extensive free reports |
| www.cyberatlas.com | Regular updates on the latest Internet developments from a business perspective |
| http://ecommerce.vanderbilt.edu | eLab is a corporate sponsored research centre at the Owen Graduate School of Management, Vanderbilt University |
| www.kpmg.co.uk www.ey.com/uk www.pwcglobal.com | The major consultancy company websites contain useful research reports, often free of charge |
| http://web.mit.edu | Massachusetts Institute of Technology site has extensive research resources |
| www.adassoc.org.uk | Advertising Association |
| www.dma.org.uk | The Direct Marketing Association |
| www.theidm.co.uk | Institute of Direct Marketing |
| www.export.org.uk | Institute of Export |
| www.bl.uk | The British Library, with one of the most extensive book collections in the world |
| www.managers.org.uk | Chartered Management Institute |
| www.cipd.co.uk | Chartered Institute of Personnel and Development |
| www.emerald-library.com | Article abstracts on a range of business topics (fees apply) |
| www.w3.org | An organisation responsible for defining worldwide standards for the Internet |

## Case studies

| | |
|---|---|
| www.1800flowers.com | Flower and gift delivery service that allows customers to specify key dates when they request the firm to send them a reminder, together with an invitation to send a gift |
| www.amazon.co.uk | Classic example of how Internet technology can be harnessed to provide innovative customer service |
| www.broadvision.com | Broadvision specialises in customer 'personalisation' software. The site contains many useful case studies showing how communicating through the Internet allow you to find out more about your customers |
| www.doubleclick.net | DoubleClick offers advertisers the ability to target their advertisements on the web through sourcing of specific interest groups, ad display only at certain times of the day, or at particular geographic locations, or on certain types of hardware |
| www.facetime.com | Good example of a site that overcomes the impersonal nature of the Internet by allowing the establishment of real time links with a customer service representative |
| www.hotcoupons.com | Site visitors can key in their postcode to receive local promotions, and advertisers can post their offers on the site using a specially designed software package |
| www.superbrands.org | Access to case studies on international brands |

# The Exam Paper

## Assessment methods and format of the paper

*Number of marks*

Part A:     One compulsory question based on an industry scenario or a company mini-case study: this question will be broken down into parts, typically three     50

Part B:     Choice of two questions from four     50
                                                                  100

The examination will be based on the stated learning outcomes and every examination will cover at least 80% of the syllabus content.

Time allowed: 3 hours

**Note**. Earlier drafts of the assessment methodology for this paper spoke in terms of Parts A, B and C, with one question from a choice of two being answered in each of Parts B and C. This proposal has been superseded by the format described above.

## Analysis of past papers

### June 2007

*Part A (compulsory case study: 50 marks)*

1     Qualitative and numerical data are provided on Google, an Internet products company.

    (a)     Evaluate Google's method of formulating strategy.

    (b)     Explain financial and analytical tools that could be used by Google to select new ideas for commercialisation.

*Part B (two from four: 25 marks each)*

2     Discuss the segmentation of the Asian market for cosmetics and its implications for strategic marketing decisions.

3     Assess the key issues in developing a global strategy for a financial services company. Would learning gained in marketing engineering products be transferable to this role?

4     Explain value based marketing with reference to a chosen example organisation.

5     Discuss the view that e-business has failed to develop beyond being an additional distribution channel.

### December 2006

*Part A (compulsory case study: 50 marks)*

1     A major Taiwanese manufacturer of electronic consumer goods is attempting to establish its own brand in Western markets. Its customers are taking counter-measures and market conditions are affecting its profitability.

    (a)     Explain the issues and their implications for marketing strategy.

    (b)     Explain the criteria it should use to select strategic options.

    (c)     Evaluate strategic marketing options for building a global brand.

*Part B (two from four: 25 marks each)*

2      Explain how an innovative marketing culture can create value for both customers and shareholders.

3      Explain how a general engineering company can utilise its capabilities to exploit new opportunities.

4      Explain implementation and control measures to support acquisition and disposal of business units.

5      Explain the strengths and weaknesses of financial information for purposes of selecting major investment projects. Choose between two projects on the basis of NPV.

## June 2006

*Part A (compulsory case study: 50 marks)*

1      Charities are under pressure to increase the donations they receive. Marketing techniques such as segmentation, communication and new product development are important aids to achieving this.

      (a)      Advise on the strategic marketing decisions that should be considered in this context.

      (b)      Recommend an integrated communications strategy.

*Part B (two from four: 25 marks each)*

2      Report on key decision areas involved in moving from market follower to market leader.

3      Using an example sector, explain why co-operative strategies such as alliances and joint ventures are increasingly being used.

4      With reference to an example tourist destination, advise on the effect of environmental changes on marketing strategy, strategic options and strategic decisions.

5      Using numerical and other data provided, advise on specific proposed pricing decisions, brand building and project appraisal.

## December 2005

*Part A (compulsory case study: 50 marks)*

1      Wizzgames Ltd, a video games developer, is considering a number of options as to how they should strategically develop their future markets.

      (a)      Discuss the arguments for and against the two strategies suggested, in relation to Wizzgames Ltd: product innovation to develop its own global brand, and obtaining the licence to develop games (and sequels) based on movies and sports.

      (b) (i)  Using cost volume profit analysis (CVP), evaluate the two options outlined, and advise Wizzgames Ltd of the strategic implications they need to consider in making their decision.

          (ii) Comment on the limitations of CVP analysis as an aid to strategic marketing decision making.

*Part B (two from four: 25 marks each)*

2      In high technology markets, many products and services very quickly reach the mature phase of the life cycle and effectively become commodities. Using appropriate examples, explain what options are available to firms to manage the situation and build a competitive advantage that can be maintained.

3      Explain the major barriers to the integration of knowledge management (KM) and learning activities for strategic marketing decisions. Using examples, show how companies have overcome these barriers.

4       Morita Ltd manufacture stainless steel kitchen utensils for major retail stores' own brands, and have traditionally used an absorption cost based approach to pricing. They are finding it increasingly difficult to compete with low priced imports.

   (a)    Critically evaluate the impact of their pricing strategy on achieving a competitive advantage.

   (b)    Explain what strategic options they have and the factors they should consider if they are to compete more effectively against low priced imports.

5       'A Corporate Social Responsibility (CSR) policy should be viewed as an investment in a strategic asset rather than an expense and, in assessing performance, companies should take a broader view and not simply concentrate on one aspect, such as shareholder/owner value.'

   Using examples, critically evaluate this statement, discussing how following a policy of CSR may conflict with the principle of shareholder value.

## June 2005

*Part A (compulsory case study: 50 marks)*

Dyson, the domestic appliance company, has recently suffered a reduction in sales.

   (a)    Critically evaluate the long-term sustainability of Dyson's global competitive advantage in view of the changing situation authored in the case study.

   (b)    In light of your answer to (a), advise Dyson on the strategic marketing decision they should take in order to secure a sustainable global competitive position.

*Part B (two from four: 25 marks each)*

2       It is said that market leaders exhibit the value disciplines of either operational excellence, product leadership or customer intimacy. Using examples, evaluate how each of these can be developed to achieve a sustainable competitive advantage. Examine the implications of your assessment for the strategic marketing decisions of the companies you have chosen.

3       Concepta Ltd has been successfully selling contemporary jewellery in several countries through small specialist retailers. However, the company is now experiencing slow growth in sales and declining profits, and fears their current markets have reached maturity. Advise the managing director on the opportunities for innovation in the marketing process the company might exploit, in order to rebuild its competitive advantage.

4       A supplier of office equipment that currently uses traditional promotion and distribution methods is considering moving to a web-only strategy to improve efficiency. As a consultant appointed to help the company make the appropriate decision, explain the advantages and disadvantages of the options the company has and recommend a course of action to them.

5       Pelican drinks supply a range of soft drinks to supermarkets, suppliers of vending machines and a range of smaller retailers. In search of further growth they are trying to decide whether they should:

   –      Adopt a programme of product development and expand their range of products

   **OR**

   –      Consolidate their market position with their current products but further develop their sales through new distribution outlets

   Advise the company on how they should financially appraise the two options.

## December 2004

*Part A (compulsory case study: 50 marks)*

1   Lego, the toy manufacturer, has posted disappointing results and has problems with its product line.

    (a)   Critical evaluation of Lego's branding strategy

    (b)   Consider choice of locations and propose a suitable market research programme

*Part B (two from four: 25 marks each)*

2   Appraisal of market factors and implementation issues in a B2B market

3   Organisational, operational and marketing differences between a large global business and a small niche player

4   Rational and emergent strategy: comparison and suitability for a small B2B firm

5   Financial criteria and tools for evaluating new services; breakeven analysis of specific proposal

## Specimen paper

*Part A (compulsory case study: 50 marks)*

1   L'Oreal dominate the global beauty market but are experiencing both increased competition and changing social attitudes.

    (a)   Critical evaluation of the changing basis for competitive advantage

    (b)   Identification of the main strategic marketing issues and potential options for dealing with them

*Part B (two from four: 25 marks each)*

2   Explanation and evaluation of the shareholder value principle

3   Identification and evaluation of critical success factors for the development of global brands

4   Evaluation of customer relationship management

5   Identification of factors reflecting investment marketing decisions and financial evaluation of an investment proposal

# About this BPP Study Text

## The CIM qualification scheme

The CIM Professional Post-Graduate Diploma (PPGD) is very different from its predecessor. Like the Professional Certificate and the Professional Diploma, it is the result of an extensive research, consultation and course design project. As a result of this work, the three levels of qualification are embedded in a supporting **conceptual framework**.

## Statements of Marketing Practice

Statements of Marketing Practice (SOMPs) define what marketers actually do at various levels in organisations. They are based on research and provide the foundation for the examination syllabuses. You will find a section headed 'Related Statements of Practice' preceding the syllabus in each BPP Study Text. These are the SOMPs that that unit of study is intended to support. The knowledge and skill requirements given in the syllabus for each unit underpin the SOMPs.

## Strategic marketing and the PPGD

The PPGD is intended for the **aspiring strategic marketer**, that is, for the person who is moving or will shortly move into a role with influence at the strategic level. The primary role of strategic marketing is to identify and create value for the business through strongly differentiated positioning. It does this by influencing the strategy and culture of the organisation towards a strong customer focus.

## The PPGD

The PPGD is organised into four units: Analysis and Evaluation, Strategic Marketing Decisions, Managing Marketing Performance and Strategic Marketing in Practice. Just as at the lower levels of the CIM qualification, the fourth unit, Strategic Marketing in Practice, is an integrative unit that draws together the threads of the other three units. However, perhaps more than is the case at the lower levels, the first three units **are themselves highly integrated**. They proceed in a logical sequence, which is based on the well-known rational model of strategy. This is split into three consecutive parts that are accurately reflected in their titles. Between them, they cover the whole field of strategic marketing, but they are not separate from each other, because business strategy itself is not compartmentalised. The split is merely one of convenience. It is important that you understand this, because you must make appropriate connections in your understanding and not regard the units as hermetically sealed off, one from another.

There is, in fact a great deal of commonality of subject matter in the first three units; the distinction between them lies in the way the ideas and techniques are used and the purposes they serve. This is reflected in the syllabuses for the three units. Let us take an important example that appears in all three: the idea of **shareholder value**.

Creating, safeguarding and enhancing the wealth of shareholders are what business is about. For marketing to play its proper role it must be able to demonstrate that it generates a return on the assets it uses and that in specifically financial terms it is worthwhile. The only satisfactory way to do this is by using the techniques of financial appraisal, such as ratio analysis and discounted cash flow. Now the idea of shareholder value is important at all stages of strategic management. At the analysis stage it is used to measure the current and past success of the company and its competitors. At the stage of strategic choice, it is the yardstick by which competing future strategies are measured. And at the implementation stage it is the basis of the strategic control system, setting the desired standard for performance.

## Study Text coverage

As always, we have aimed to provide you with comprehensive coverage of your exam syllabus and the three Study Texts covering the first three units have been prepared with this aim in mind. This means that there is considerable repetition of material in these three Study Texts, reflecting as they do, the repetition in the syllabuses. This has the advantage that each Study Text is complete in its coverage. On the other hand, it also means that each one is perhaps rather larger than it otherwise might be. Nevertheless, we feel that completeness of coverage is more important than mere handiness.

# Part A
## The changing dimensions of competitive advantage

# The strategic background

## Syllabus content

- The role and strategic management of life cycles
- The influence of market position on strategy and performance
- The changing dimensions of strategic decisions made to sustain competitive advantage
- The concepts of project management

# Introduction

This chapter deals with the material that makes up Element 1 of the knowledge and skill requirements of your syllabus. The unifying theme of this Element is **change**: in particular, change in the business environment and the way in which organisations respond to it through their strategic decisions.

Section 1 is a brief introduction to the way change is affecting business and emphasises two vitally important drivers of strategic change: **globalisation** and the **Internet**.

Sections 2 and 3 deal with the strategic importance of the life cycle concept and how it may be applied to markets, brands and customers as well as to products.

Section 4 is about the effect of overall market position on strategic success. In particular, the influence of market share is discussed, with particular reference to experience effects and PIMS data.

Finally, Section 5 discusses project management, since your syllabus requires you to be able to apply the principles of this particular management discipline to limited life products and technologies.

# 1 The background to strategic decisions

## 1.1 The changing strategic environment

**FAST FORWARD**

Today's strategic business decisions are made against a background of accelerating change. Two very important aspects of the changing business environment are **globalisation** and the **Internet**.

This book is about **making strategic decisions to sustain competitive advantage**. Strategic decision-makers must contend with a very wide range of variables, including (among others) their own organisations, their financial resources, their products and their markets. This variety of influences alone makes corporate strategy a complex topic. The complexity involved is increased by the fact that strategy does not exist in isolation: it must relate to the conditions of the real world. These are constantly changing – and the pace of change appears to be increasing. All aspects of the business environment are subject to rapid and often profound **change**. The corporate strategist must be alive to these changes and their implications. A future orientation is an essential component of the strategic direction of any organisation. There are two particularly important drivers of strategic change: **globalisation** and the **Internet**.

**Globalisation**. Globalisation is a reality for businesses everywhere. Any organisation anywhere in the world, no matter how small, is likely to be affected in some way by globalisation. Customers, suppliers, regulators, providers of finance, governments and competitors are unlikely to be confined to one country.

(a)   Major international alliances are being formed and growth by takeover and merger is creating larger companies. These large organisations are taking advantage of the **increased market access** and opportunities that freer trade offers and of the **comparative and absolute cost advantages** it brings.

(b)   Some industries have managed to insulate themselves against international competition. This applies particularly to agriculture. However, the trend can only be against such special arrangements.

(c)   Industry standards are becoming internationalised.

(d)   High fixed costs and high R&D costs are leading to the wider marketing of individual technologies in order to gain volume.

(e)   Similar customer segments are emerging in different countries as a result of increased travel and the internationalisation of popular culture.

Boomer

(f)     The same global corporations are competing (and co-operating where appropriate) in the same major markets.

Foresighted strategists must **think globally, even if they act locally**.

**The Internet**. The commercial potential of the Internet is enormous; this is particularly true of the interactive features of its World Wide Web aspect. Much routine consumer and business purchasing can be done with little human intervention; information can be provided and exchanged; and a whole new industry of website design and maintenance has been created. However, notice that where physical products are concerned, **fulfilment** is as important and demanding as it ever was.

**All aspects of the business environment are subject to change** because of the effects of these two drivers. Here are some particularly salient examples.

(a)     **Technology**. *Moore's Law* tells us that the processing capability of silicon chips doubles every 18 months. The potential for more powerful and sophisticated products is immense; even more important is the potential for changing the way that business is done. The _WWW_ growth of the World Wide Web represents a quantum jump for those organisations that are able and willing to exploit it.

(b)     **Demographics**. In Europe, the population is aging as birth rates fall. The so-called 'boomer' generation, now in its 50s, continues to dominate markets and a youth orientation is becoming relatively less important. Extensive population movements and cultural integration are likely as the EU expands.

(c)     **Economic growth**. On the other side of the world, significant changes are taking place in Chinese society as its economy expands. Skiing, an expensive diversion, is becoming increasingly popular; Nanshan ski village was established in 2001, overcoming the lack of natural snow by making its own. _SNOW_

(d)     **Supply chain management**. Large manufacturing organisations are no longer defined by their production facilities. They are becoming organisers of sub-contract manufacturers and concentrating their efforts on design, marketing and service. This change arises from the fall in transaction costs of such arrangements arising from globalisation and the direct cost advantage of sourcing from technically sophisticated but relatively low-wage economies.

The rate at which new conditions emerge in the business environment is matched by the rate at which today's innovation becomes tomorrow's commonplace. The duration of the competitive advantage produced by any innovation is unlikely to last more than a few years; in many cases it will last only a few months, as is evidenced by the rate of new product development in the consumer electronics industry. The product life cycle concept is still useful, but more and more products are likely to suffer from a rather truncated period of maturity.

**Exam tip**

The draft specimen paper for this exam included as question 1 a scenario based on changing conditions in the global cosmetics markets. There were two requirements, each worth 25 marks.

*     The first asked you to evaluate the changes that had taken place, in strategic terms.

*     The second asked you to identify the three main strategic marketing issues and to develop suitable strategic options.

## 1.2 Implications for marketing managers

New challenges require new responses. For marketing managers this has important implications.

(a)     There is a need for **strategic innovation**. This implies not just the development of new strategies but also the development of **new ways of thinking** about how to develop them. We will look at the

5

variety of ways in which strategy can be developed later in this Study Text: for now you should note that **learning**, **agility** and **innovation** are to be preferred to repetitive and imitative processes of strategic development.

(b)   Organisations need to put the market at the heart of their strategies and marketing managers need to learn how to exercise **greater strategic influence**. This implies the acceptance of rigorous performance measurement for marketing activities and of the need for the marketing to create measurable **value** for the business. Marketing should have a direct and positive effect on profit and marketing managers should embrace this aim.

## 1.3 Strategy in the future

**FAST FORWARD**

Doyle suggests five main issues for strategic managers.

– Market participation
– Marketing strategy
– Operations strategy
– Global strategy
– Organisation structure

*Doyle* suggests that in the future organisations will have to deal with five main issues of strategic management.

(a)   **Participation**. There should be a continuing review of the markets in which a business participates. Withdrawal from old markets, continuation in them and entry to new ones should be undertaken in order to maximise potential future return. A decision about an individual market should be based on its **attractiveness** (that is, its profit potential) and the company's own **competitive potential** when operating within it.

(b)   **Marketing strategy**. The profound influence of the **Internet** is affecting many aspects of normal marketing practice.

   – **Distribution** via retail outlets is being replaced by web services such as online banking and shopping.

   – **Pricing** is becoming more transparent as customers shop around.

   – **Promotion** can be entirely web-based.

(c)   **Operations strategy**. The **direct business model**, as used by *Dell*, is built around close co-operation with suppliers and **mass-customisation** for customers. Retailers are by-passed, distribution costs cut and inventories reduced.

(d)   **Global strategy**. The globalisation trend already outlined is bringing greater efficiencies and lower costs. Companies must seize these advantages while staying in touch with their widely varying markets.

(e)   **Organisation structure**. The new global, Internet enabled business has a number of characteristics.

   – There are more information workers and fewer unskilled ones.

   – These workers are more mobile and employable: they must be managed and motivated differently.

   – Delayering, empowerment and cross-functional team-working have destroyed the traditional hierarchy and management career.

   – They have also brought increased flexibility and responsiveness as information is better managed and used.

# 2 The product life cycle

The profitability and sales of a product can be expected to change over time. The **product life cycle (PLC)** is an attempt to recognise distinct stages in a product's sales history. Marketing managers distinguish between product class, form and brand.

The PLC applies in differing degrees to each of the three cases. A **product class** (eg washing machines) may have a long maturity stage, but a particular make or brand within the class might have an erratic life cycle. **Product forms**, however, tend to conform to the classic life cycle pattern, which is illustrated by the diagram below. Within the product class 'washing machines' forms such as top loaders, front loaders, twin tubs and automatics have existed.

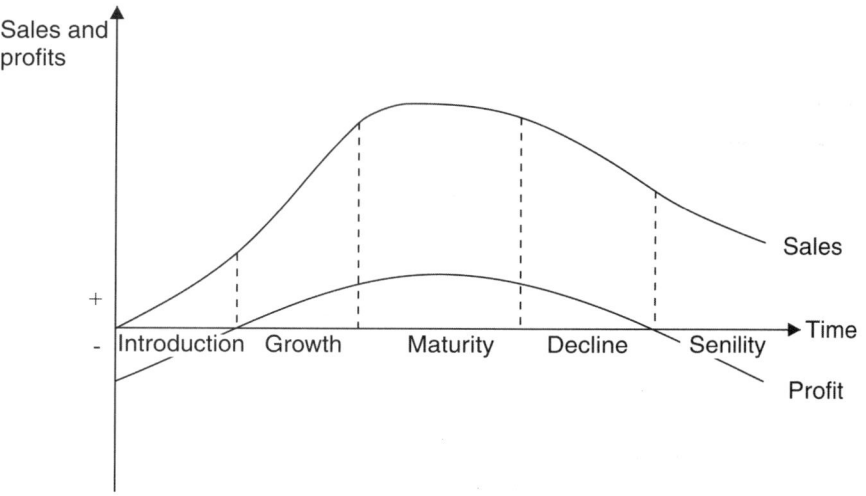

### Introduction

(a)  A new product takes time to find acceptance by would-be purchasers and there is a slow growth in sales. Unit costs are high because of low output and expensive sales promotion.

(b)  There may be early teething troubles with production technology.

(c)  The product for the time being is a loss-maker.

### Marketing at Work

In February 2005, *Anheuser-Busch* launched a new drink called $B^E$ ('B to the E'). This is beer spiked with caffeine, ginseng and guarana; the extra ingredients are intended to reduce the depressant effect of the alcohol in the beer. Response was mixed.

### Growth

(a)  If the new product gains market acceptance, sales will eventually rise more sharply and the product will start to make profits.

(b)  Competitors are attracted. As sales and production rise, unit costs fall.

**Maturity**. The rate of sales growth slows down and the product reaches a period of maturity which is probably the longest period of a successful product's life. Most products on the market will be at the mature stage of their life. Profits are good.

**Decline**. Some products reach a stage of decline, which may be slow or fast. Eventually, sales will begin to decline so that there is over-capacity of production in the industry. Severe competition occurs, profits fall and some producers leave the market. The remaining producers seek means of prolonging the product life by modifying it and searching for new market segments. Many producers are reluctant to leave the market, although some inevitably do because of falling profits.

## 2.1 The relevance of the PLC to strategic planning

**FAST FORWARD**

The PLC concept is still a useful input to strategic management but it must be used with caution and discretion.

In reviewing outputs, planners should assess the following.

(a) The **stage of its life cycle** that any product has reached.

(b) The **product's remaining life**, ie how much longer the product will be able to contribute significantly to profits.

(c) How **urgent is the need to innovate**, to develop new and improved products in time?

### 2.1.1 Difficulties of the PLC concept

(a) **Recognition**. How can managers recognise where a product stands in its life cycle?

(b) **Not always true**. The traditional curve of a PLC does not always occur in practice. Some products have no maturity phase, and go straight from growth to decline. Some never decline if they are marketed competitively (eg certain brands of breakfast cereals).

(c) **Changeable**. Strategic decisions can change or extend a product's life cycle.

(d) **Competition varies** in different industries. The financial markets are an example of markets where there is a tendency for competitors to copy the leader very quickly, so that competition has built up well **ahead** of demand.

 Marketing at Work

**Airbus 1**

*Airbus* is a consortium of four partners, and commands about 30% of the airliner market outside the EU. Airbus has launched a range of aircraft which compete with Boeing in every sector of the market, save the Boeing 747, and it is now going to build a 'super-jumbo'.

Airbus is expected to be very profitable. It has a relatively modern range of aircraft in an industry with product life cycles of 25 years or more.

The carrot Airbus offers to potential partners is that it will be able to introduce new technology. Almost as a spoiler, Boeing has suggested an oxygen-burning plane flying at supersonic speeds.

It is perhaps easy enough to accept that products have a life cycle, but it is not so easy to sort out how far through its life a product is, and what its expected future life might be.

(a) **Sources of PLC predictions**

- An analysis of past sales and profit trends
- The history of other products
- Market research
- If possible, an analysis of competitors
- A review of technological developments

(b) The future of each product should be estimated in terms of both sales revenue and profits.

It is plausible to suggest that products have a life cycle, but it is not so easy to sort out how far through its life a product is, and what its expected future life might be. To identify these stages, the following should be carried out.

(a) There ought to be a **regular review** of existing products.

(b) The future of each product should be estimated in terms of both **sales revenue and profits**.

(c) **Estimates of future life and profitability should be discussed with any experts available** to give advice, for example, R & D staff about product life, management accountants about costs, and marketing staff about prices and demand.

Once the assessments have been made, decisions must be taken about what to do with each product. There are three possibilities.

(a) **To continue selling** the product, with no foreseeable intention of stopping production.

(b) To initiate action **to prolong a product's life**, perhaps by advertising more, by trying to cut costs or raise prices, by improving distribution, or packaging or sales promotion methods, or by putting in more direct selling effort.

(c) To plan **to stop producing the product** and either to replace it with new ones in the same line or to diversify into new product-market areas.

Costs might be cut by improving productivity of the workforce, or by redesigning the product slightly, perhaps as a result of a value analysis study.

Strategic and marketing mix decisions are considered in Part C of this Study Text.

## 2.2 The product life cycle and the marketing orientation

FAST FORWARD

The PLC concept can be extended to encompass demand and technology.

Does the PLC promote a product orientated focus when in fact a 'market orientated' focus is necessary? Ansoff extends the PLC concept to encompass the **demand/technology life cycle**. The diagram below illustrates how a **demand life cycle** (DLC) is made up of a number of **technology life cycles** (TLC) which in turn are composed of PLCs.

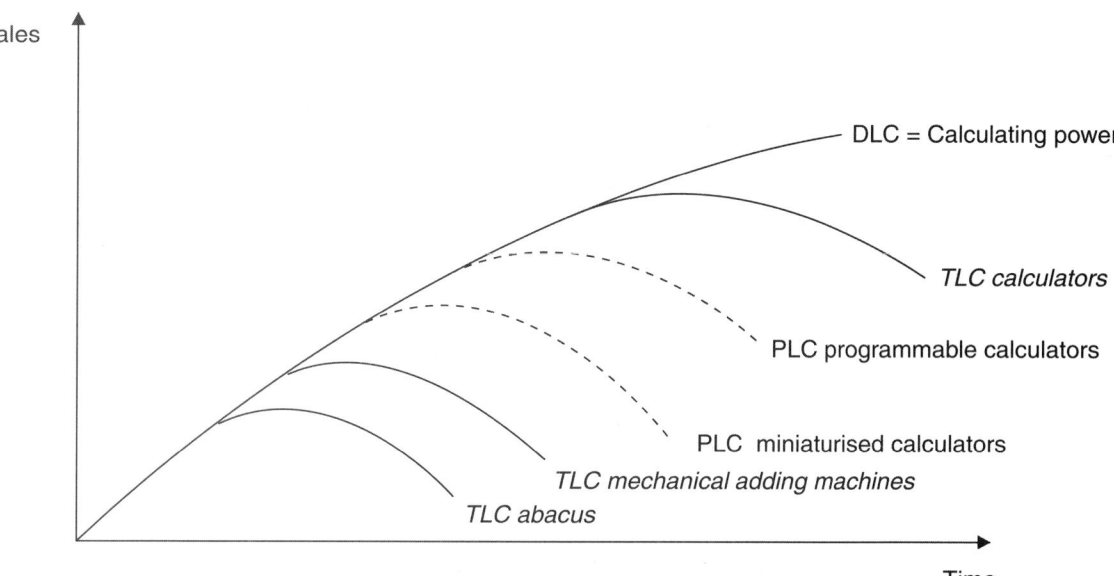

For example, 'calculating power' represents a human demand that is probably in the growth stage of the DLC. This has been composed of a number of TLCs – finger counting, abacuses, slide rules, adding machines, calculators, computers. Each new technology usually satisfies the **generic need** in a **superior way**. A new technology will, however, be likely to display its own life cycle, with discernible stages of

growth and maturity. Decline will set in when it reaches the limit of its development. It is then likely to be supplanted by a new technology in the early phase of its life cycle.

The rate of technological progress varies from continuous gradual improvement to rapid and radical change. Steady improvement may be taken as the most common route to progress, but strategists and marketers in particular must be alert to the emergence of developments with revolutionary potential. A recent example of such development is the cell phone, which has created a vast new industry that did not previously exist.

The TLC indicates that for many products, death will eventually transpire through **technology** and **competitive innovation**.

## Marketing at Work

**Airbus 2**

Going back to the Airbus example, Airbus assumed continued demand for long-haul air travel when developing its super jumbo, and believes that this is best satisfied by large planes flying to major destination hubs. Much of this is deemed accounted for by growth in long-haul tourism, although this theory is likely to be tested by the worldwide downturn in travel (caused for example by terrorism and the SARS virus) that has affected some of the international carriers so badly.

The PLC concept probably has more value as a **control tool** than as a method of **forecasting** a product's life. Control can be applied to speeding up the growth phase, extending the maturity phase and recognising when to cease making a product altogether.

We will return to the PLC concept later in this Study Text when we consider the management of the product portfolio.

## 2.3 The industry life cycle

**FAST FORWARD**   Industries may display a **life cycle**: this will affect and interact with the five forces.

The **industry life cycle** reflects changes in demand and the spread of technical knowledge among producers. Innovation creates the new industry, and this is normally product innovation. Later, innovation shifts to processes in order to maintain margins. The overall progress of the industry life cycle is illustrated below.

|  | Inception | Growth | Maturity/shakeout | Decline |
|---|---|---|---|---|
| **Products** | Basic, no standards established | Better, more sophisticated, differentiated | Superior, standardised | Varied quality but fairly undifferentiated |
| **Competitors** | None to few | Many entrants Little concentration in industry | Competition increases, weaker players leave | Few remain. Competition may be on price |
| **Buyers** | Early adopters, prosperous, curious must be induced | More customers attracted and aware | Mass market, brand switching common | Enthusiasts, traditionalists, sophisticates |
| **Profits** | Negative – high first mover advantage | Good, possibly starting to decline | Eroding under pressure of competition | Variable |
| **Strategy** | Dominate market, build quality | React to competitors with marketing spend | Cost reductions sought | Control costs |

The life cycle model of an industry is of particular strategic significance since it incorporates a number of particularly significant variables, including those of competitors and customers.

# 3 The PLC and market dynamics

An important issue to planners is how quickly a new product will be adopted by the market; that is to say, what sort of time scale is expected along the horizontal axis of the PLC.

## 3.1 Influences on the diffusion rate of new ideas

(a)  The **complexity** of the new product

(b)  The **relative advantages** it offers

(c)  The degree to which the innovation fits into **existing patterns** of behaviour/needs

(d)  The **ability to try** the new product, samples, test drives or low value purchases entailing little risk

(e)  The ease with which the product's benefits can be **communicated** to the potential customer

## 3.2 Diffusion and the consumer

**FAST FORWARD**

Consumers' attitudes to **innovation** vary and this is a major influence on the rate of diffusion.

These factors affect the rate at which different segments and sub-segments of the chosen market will adopt the product. The growth phase of the PLC, for instance, involves a slightly different group of customers from those who adopted it during the launch phase. A simple example arises from the use of a price skimming strategy: in the early part of the product life cycle a relatively high disposable income defines the target segment. Later, when price has fallen, a larger group of customers – effectively a different market – may be targeted.

In *Consumer Behaviour, Schiffmann and Kanuk* offer a modified version of *Everett Rogers'* analysis in *Diffusion of Innovation* (1995).

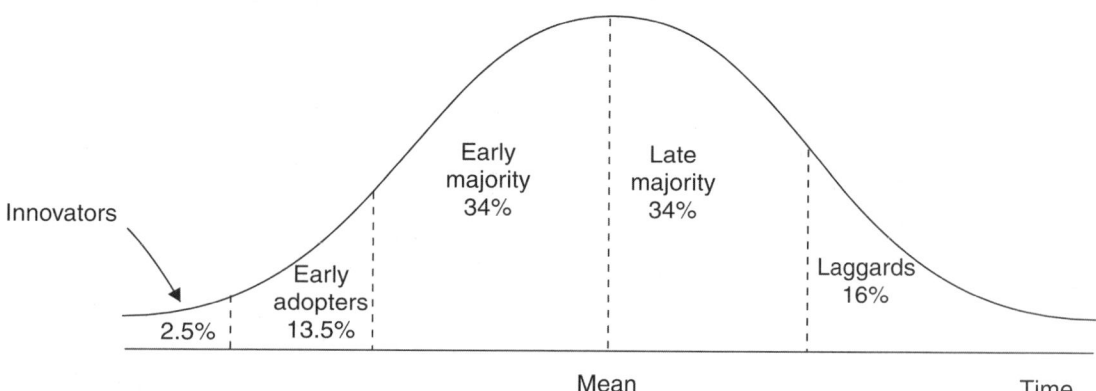

The characteristics of consumers in these adopter categories varies and so the marketing planner wishing to get the best from a new product, encourage its diffusion and avoid wasting budget, will focus market attention on these different segments, as the product passes through the life cycle.

(a)  **Innovators**

These are eager to try new ideas and products and often in close contact with change agents like sales staff and other opinion leaders. Often perceived to be risk takers, prepared to try and willing to pay often premium prices for 'being the first'.

(b)   **Early adopters**

They too are willing to change and are often opinion leaders themselves. They are likely to have greater exposure to the mass media than later adopters and certainly more willing to change. They are likely to seek out information actively about new products in specialist journals etc.

(c)   **Early majority**

A more conservative segment who tend to purchase a new product just ahead of the average time, but who will have given it some thought before the purchase.

(d)   **Late majority**

These are slower than the average and sceptical about new products. They are very cautious purchasers likely to need some persuading.

(e)   **Laggards**

These are the smaller group of traditionalists actually unwilling to change. They may actually be forced to change only when their previous choice is obsolete and no longer available.

**Diffusion and marketing strategy**. Marketers usually want to ensure a rapid diffusion or rate of adoption for a new product. This allows them to gain a large share of the market prior to competitors responding.

(a)   A **penetration strategy** associated with low introductory pricing and promotions designed to facilitate trial are associated with such a strategy.

(b)   However in some markets, particularly where R & D cost has been high, where the product involves new technology or where it is protected from competition perhaps by patent, a **skimming** policy may be adopted. Here price is high initially usually representing very high unit profits and sales can be increased in steps with price reductions, in line with available capacity or competitors' responses.

## 3.3 Other influences

Needless to say, different products get adopted at different speeds. The marketer will want rapid acceptance, to forestall competition. Here is a list of issues which influence the speed of market penetration.

| Issue | Comment |
|---|---|
| **Network externalities** | The product is only of value if other people have it – such as telephones, the Internet. |
| **Common standards** | CD and DVD players operate to a common standard. Mobile phones operate to two standards globally. Digital TV in the UK is delivered by competing intermediaries. |
| **Complementary products** | Computer games consoles need computer games to play on them. |
| **Switching costs** | It will cost a lot to change to certain products. |
| **Experimentation** | For groceries, it is easy to try something new, as the expense is small. Film companies introduce 'trailers' as part of a marketing campaign to give potential audiences a feel for the film. |

The introductory stage represents the highest risk in terms of purchasing a new and, as yet, untested product. Buyers reflect this: they typically consist of the relatively wealthy, to whom the risk of a loss is relatively small, and the young, who are more likely to make risky purchases.

In the growth and mature stages the mass market needs to be attracted. By the time decline sets in the product is well tested with all its faults ironed out. At this stage enter the most risk-averse buyers, termed **laggards**. These are the mirror image of those who participated in the introductory stage, being the poorer and older sections of the community.

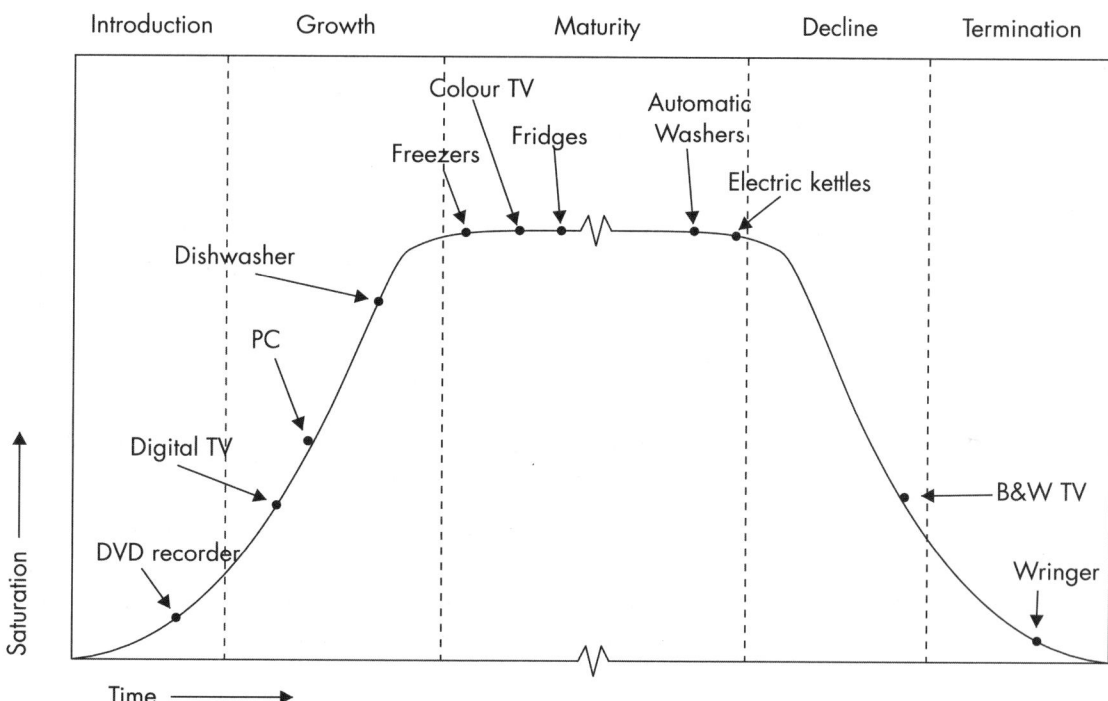

*Comparing products at different PLC stages*

The above display of products, at various stages through the PLC, represents the USA in the late 1960s and early 1970s. Studies were conducted to establish whether or not there were significant differences in the purchasers of refrigerators in the mature stage and compacters (waste disposal units) in the introductory stage.

The high income group with a family income of $10,000 or more made up some 90% of those purchasing compactors. There was also a noticeable lack of 65+ year olds. In contrast, the mature refrigerator market appeared to reflect the complete population range.

# 4 Experience, market share and PIMS

**FAST FORWARD**

**PIMS** data indicate that profit increases with market share. This appears to be for a set of reasons relating to **economies of scale**. High levels of production also allow **experience effects** to take place.

## 4.1 Economies of scale

There is a relationship between the quantity of products produced and the cost per unit.

**Key concept**

**Economy of scale**. The more you produce and sell, the cheaper each successive unit will be.

### 4.1.1 Example

Let us take an example of a publisher contracting with a printer to print Study Texts. (Note: the prices below are notional only. Printers' charges vary according to paper prices, paper quality, turnaround times, volume of work and so on.)

| Quantity printed | Cost | Cost per book |
|---|---|---|
| 100 | £500 | £5.00 |
| 1,000 | £2,500 | £2.50 |
| 2,000 | £4,720 | £2.36 |

The reason for the difference is that there are the same **fixed costs** incurred (for example, in setting up the press) no matter how many or few books you print.

This shows that the quantity produced affects the cost per unit. From the above example, if customers were unwilling to pay more than £3 for their books, and the publishers wanted to make £0.50p profit on top of print cost, then the publisher would have to sell **at least** 1,000 books.

How is this relevant to market share? It shows that high market share can, by spreading fixed costs over many units of production, be more profitable. Higher sales volumes can mean lower costs per unit, hence higher profits. The Boston Consulting Group (BCG) estimated that as production volume doubles, cost per unit falls by up to 20%. **High market share therefore gives cost advantages**.

**Key concept**

> **Market share** is 'one entity's sales of a product or service in a specified market expressed as a percentage of total sales by all entities offering that product or service'. Thus, a company may have a 30% share of a total market, meaning that 30% of all sales in the market are made by that company.

**Relative market share** is the share of the market relative to that of the manufacturer's largest competitor.

(a)    An evaluation of market shares helps to identify **who the true competitor really is**, and avoids trying to outdo the wrong competitor.

(b)    The approach serves as a basis for marketing strategy, with a firm seeking as a target to build up an x% share of a particular market.

## 4.2 Experience curves

The experience curve takes this further. The more units **over time** that a firm produces, the cheaper will each unit be to produce. Why?

(a)    **Economies of scale**, as identified above.

(b)    **Learning**: the more people do a task, the more efficient they become (up to a point), and it takes them less time.

(c)    **Technological** improvements: firms can improve their production operations and make better use of equipment.

(d)    **Simplifying products can cut costs**. For example, car manufacturers are cutting costs by ensuring that the same components can be used in different marques.

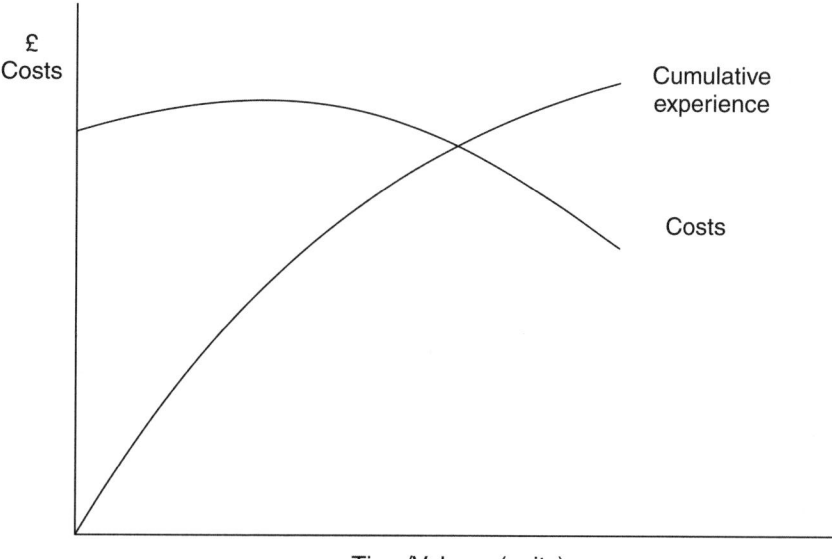

You will recall that the BCG portfolio analysis matrix uses relative market share as one of its axes. This is, in fact, an application of both economies of scale and the experience curve: relative market share is a surrogate measure used to estimate the cost advantages conferred by these two phenomena. Relative market share is used rather then absolute market share since it relates directly to the degree of advantages possessed by competitors.

**Working with the experience curve**

(a) The experience curve is not automatic.

(b) Technological changes can render a particular process obsolete.

(c) Low costs do not have to mean lower prices, although many firms have used the experience curve to buy market share.

(d) Marketing people should focus on the customer not on the process, and so the experience curve should not detract from **customer focus**.

 Marketing at Work

Japanese firms pioneered target costing. They identified a customer need and specified a product to satisfy that need.

The production department and its accountants then worked out:

- How the product could be built
- The volume needed to reach the market price
- How quickly costs could be driven down.

## 4.3 Profit Impact of Market Strategies (PIMS)

The Strategic Planning Institute in the USA has been accumulating data on the performance of thousands of firms. This data has been assembled in the PIMS databank and exclusively analysed. **PIMS analysis** attempts to establish the profitability (ie return on capital) of various marketing strategies, and identifies a link between the size of **return on capital** and **market share** so that companies in a strong competitive position in the markets for their base products would be earning high returns.

In general, **profits increase in line with market share**.

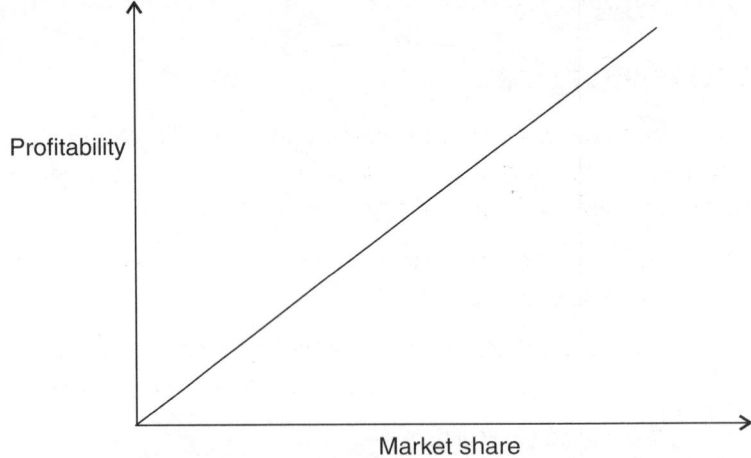

Three possible reasons were put forward for this correlation.

(a)     **Economies of scale** and experience curve effects enable a market leader to produce at lower unit costs than competitors, and so make bigger profits. A company with the highest market share, especially if this company is also the innovator with the longest experience, will enjoy a considerable competitive advantage. This is referred to as the experience curve.

(b)     **Bargaining power**. A strong position in the market gives a firm greater strength in its dealings with both buyers and suppliers.

(c)     **Quality of management**. Market leaders often seem to be run by managers of a high calibre.

The linear relationship above does not always hold true. Some industries display a V-shaped relationship.

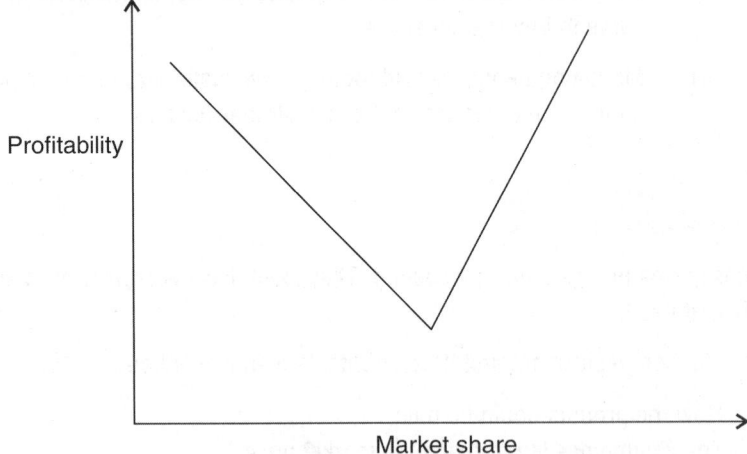

Profitability falls until a certain critical market share is reached, which makes it more likely that there will be a polarisation between large firms and small players. SME's (small and medium sized enterprises) find it very difficult to maintain their position.

PIMS researchers would argue that since profitability is a key objective, and since profitability depends on market share, companies should formulate market share objectives. There are four broad groups of market share strategies.

(a)     **Build**. This requires further investment to be made in order to achieve an increased market share. Management must be convinced that product and market have good potential.

(b)     **Harvest**. Only the minimum is invested: the product is a cash cow.

(c)     **Withdraw**. The product has little potential and is discontinued.

(d)   **Hold**. Steady as she goes: the aim is to grow with the market or industry. Investment is made as essential.

## 4.4 Low market share

Low market share does not **inevitably** mean poor returns. If this were so, small businesses would always make low returns, and this is simply not true. However, certain **conditions must exist for a low market share to be compatible with high returns**.

(a)   **Niche marketing**. Create new market segments which are a small but profitable proportion of the total market.

(b)   **Premium price strategy**. Emphasising product quality, and charging higher prices. (Efficient use would have to be made of R & D in manufacturing industries.)

(c)   Strong **management**.

(d)   When there is a **large, stable market**, where product innovations and developments are uncommon, and where **repeat-buying by customers is frequent**, a company can earn good profits with only a low market share.

There are clear implications for small- and medium-sized businesses.

## 4.5 Problems with PIMS

(a)   **Identifying each market segment properly**. An up-market producer is in a different market segment to a down-market cheap-goods producer, and it would be wrong to classify them as competitors in the same market. In Porter's terminology, they may not exist in the same **strategic group**.

(b)   **Measuring the actual size of the market**, and so the company's own market share in proportional terms.

(c)   **Establishing what returns** are available from a particular market share.

It has also been argued that **PIMS analysis is more relevant to industrial goods markets** than to consumer goods markets, where the correlation between high market share and high returns is not as strong.

**Exam tip**

An old syllabus question asked why market share is important and when it might not be appropriate as an objective. Consider for example market leaders with near monopolies. Increasing market share and driving out competitors would lead to government action and regulation. Furthermore, the cost of increasing market share might exceed its value in profit terms.

## 4.6 Strategic implications of market share

Implications of market share should be considered in product-market development planning.

(a)   **How easy will it be to build up a market share?** This will depend on the rate of sales growth in the market. Obviously, it is easier to penetrate a growing market than a static one.

(b)   **What share of the market will be needed to earn the target profit and return on capital?** Depending on costs, sales prices and total sales volume in the market, the size of market share needed to make a profit will vary.

Marketing at Work

**Reebok**

*Reebok* was a best-selling trainer brand but competition from *Nike* and *Adidas* saw its market share plummet and its share price fall from over $50 in 1997 to $7 at the start of 2001.

Reebok is seeking to bounce back as a 'sports brand that operates' in a fashion market, and has designed advertising to appeal to 16-24 year olds.

Other outdoor brands, such as *Timberland* and *Caterpillar*, have also eaten away Reebok's market share. In 2000, Timberland had 2.9% of the US trainer market (2.1% in 1999). Fashion brands such as *Hermes* and *DKNY* have also entered the market.

# 5 Project management

**FAST FORWARD**

**Project management** concepts may be useful in the management of limited life products and technologies.

**Key concept**

A **project** is 'an undertaking that has a beginning and an end and is carried out to meet established goals within cost, schedule and quality objectives' (Haynes, *Project Management*, 1997).

## 5.1 Characteristics of projects

- Specific start and end points
- Well-defined objectives
- The project endeavour is to a degree unique
- The project usually contains costs and time schedules
- A project cuts across many organisational and functional boundaries

**Marketing projects**. Projects (and hence the need to deploy project management skills) are common in marketing management at all levels. This is because marketing and business strategy are not generally matters of routine procedure. Products come and go; campaigns are launched and managed; markets are entered and abandoned, Much of the work is inevitably of a project nature. This is particularly the case with the management of products in fast moving markets, such as those for fashion goods, consumer electronics, publishing and holidays. It is therefore appropriate to familiarise yourself with the basics of project management.

Marketing at Work

**Examples of projects**

| Project | Comment |
|---|---|
| **Management** | • Development of MkIS |
| **Marketing** | • Developing and launching a new product<br>• Implementing a promotional campaign with defined objectives |

### 5.1.1 Special management problems with projects

| Problem | Comment |
| --- | --- |
| Teambuilding | The work is carried out by a team of people usually assembled for one project, who must be able to communicate effectively and immediately with each other. |
| Expected problems | There can be many novel **expected** problems, each one of which should be resolved by careful design and planning prior to commencement of work. |
| Unexpected problems | There can be many novel **unexpected** problems, particularly with a project working at the limits of existing and new technologies. There should be mechanisms within the project to enable these problems to be resolved during the time span of the project without detriment to the objective, the cost or the time span. |
| Delayed benefit | There is normally no benefit until the work is finished. The 'lead in' time to this can cause a strain on the eventual recipient who feels deprived until the benefit is achieved (even though in many cases it is a major improvement on existing activities) and who is also faced with increasing expenditure for no immediate benefit. |
| Specialists | Contributions made by specialists are of differing importance at each stage. Assembling a team working towards the one objective is made difficult due to the tendency of specialists to regard their contribution as always being more important than other people's and not understanding the interrelationship between their various specialities in the context of the project. |
| Stakeholders | If the project involves several parties with different interests in the outcome, there might be disputes between them. |

### 5.1.2 The objectives of project management

| Objective | Comment |
| --- | --- |
| Quality | The end result should conform to the proper specification. In other words, the result should achieve what the project was supposed to do. |
| Budget | The project should be completed without exceeding authorised expenditure. |
| Timescale | The progress of the project must follow the planned process, so that the result is ready for use at the agreed date. As time is money, proper time management can help contain costs. |

## 5.2 The project life cycle  —40

A typical project has a **project life cycle**.

- **Define** the project: identify what has to be done to meet specified needs
- **Design** the project: plan how the needs will be met and show benefits
- **Deliver** the project: assemble resources, carry out plan, deliver output
- **Develop** the process: review outcomes, document lessons for future use

## 5.3 The role of the project manager ← Time money staff

The project manager has resources of time, money and staff. These have to be co-ordinated effectively. The project manager's duties are summarised below.

| Duty | Comment |
|---|---|
| Outline planning | Project planning (eg targets, sequencing)<br><br>• Developing project targets such as overall costs or timescale needed (eg project should take 20 weeks).<br><br>• Dividing the project into activities (eg questionnaire design, review etc), and placing these activities into the right sequence, often a complicated task if overlapping.<br><br>• Developing a framework for the procedures and structures, managing the project (eg decide, in principle, to have weekly team meetings, performance reviews etc). |
| Detailed planning | Work breakdown structure, resource requirements, network analysis for scheduling. |
| Teambuilding and delegation | The project manager has to meld the members into an effective team. |
| Communication | The project manager must let superiors know what is going on, and ensure that members of the project team are properly briefed. |
| Co-ordinating project activities | Between the project team and users, and other external parties (eg suppliers of hardware and software). |
| Monitoring and control | The project manager should estimate the causes for each departure from the standard, and take corrective measures. |
| Problem resolution | Even with the best planning, unforeseen problems may arise, and it falls upon the project manager to sort them out, or to delegate the responsibility for so doing to a subordinate. |
| Quality control | This is a problematic issue, as there is often a short-sighted trade-off between getting the project out on time and the project's quality. |

## 5.3.1 Project planning tools

The project manager thus needs to **schedule the activities** in the most efficient way given:

(a) The **dependency** of some activities on others (the foundations of a house are **always** laid before the roof is constructed). Alternatively, some tasks may be carried out in **parallel** to save time.

(b) **Constraints on resources**. Some resources will not be available at the ideal time or at the lowest price.

The project manager will have been given a broad-brush time estimation for any activity. For this you need:

- The **duration** of each sub-unit of work
- The **earliest time** work in a particular unit must be started
- The **latest time** it must be started

## 5.3.2 Gantt charts

A simple plan for a project can use a **bar line chart** (sometimes called a **Gantt chart**).

(a) It can be used as a **progress control chart** with the lower section of each bar being completed as the activity is undertaken.

(b)    A delay in a particular piece of work and its knock on effect on other work can be shown in a **linked bar chart**. This shows the links between an activity and preceding activities which have to be completed before this particular activity can start.

Here is an example of a progress control chart.

| No. | DESCRIPTION OF WORK OR ACTIVITY | TIME (DAYS) | | | | | | | | | | | | | |
|---|---|---|---|---|---|---|---|---|---|---|---|---|---|---|---|
| | | 1 | 2 | 3 | 4 | 5 | 6 | 7 | 8 | 9 | 10 | 11 | 12 | 13 | 14 |
| 1 | Excavate for foundations and services (drainage) | | | | | | | | | | | | | | |
| 2 | Concrete foundations | | | | | | | | | | | | | | |
| 3 | Build walls and soakaways for drainage | | | | | | | | | | | | | | |
| 4 | Construct roof | | | | | | | | | | | | | | |
| 5 | Fit garage doors | | | | | | | | | | | | | | |
| 6 | Provide services (electric) | | | | | | | | | | | | | | |
| 7 | Plaster | | | | | | | | | | | | | | |
| 8 | Decorate | | | | | | | | | | | | | | |

- **Advantage**: easy to understand

- **Disadvantage**: limited when dealing with complex projects. They only display a restricted amount of information and the links between activities are fairly crude.

## Chapter Roundup

- Today's strategic business decisions are made against a background of accelerating change. Two very important aspects of the changing business environment are **globalisation** and the **Internet**.

- Doyle suggests five main issues for strategic managers.

    - Market participation
    - Marketing strategy
    - Operations strategy
    - Global strategy
    - Organisation structure

- The PLC concept is a useful input to strategic management but it must be used with caution and discretion.

- The product life cycle concept can be extended to encompass demand and technology.

- Industries may display a **life cycle**: this will affect and interact with the five forces.

- Consumers' attitudes to **innovation** vary and this is a major influence on the rate of **diffusion**.

- **PIMS** data indicate that profit increases with market share. This appears to be for a set of reasons relating to **economies of scale**. High levels of production also allow **experience effects** to take place.

- **Project management** concepts may be useful in the management of limited life products and technologies.

## Quick Quiz

1    Give two particularly important drivers of strategic change.

2    What does Moore's Law say?

3    What five main issues does Doyle identify as crucial for strategic management?

4    Which customer group buys a new product after the innovators but before the early majority?

5    What is the effect of learning upon costs?

6    Does profitability always increase as market share rises?

7    What are the objectives of project management?

## Answers to Quick Quiz

1    Globalisation and the Internet

2    The processing capability of silicon ships doubles every 18 months

3    Market participation, marketing strategy, operations strategy, global strategy, organisation structure

4    Early adopters

5    They fall

6    No. It may be necessary to reach a critical level of market share before profitability increases

7    Quality, budget, timescale

# Part B
## Competitive marketing strategies

# 2

# Models of strategic management

## Syllabus content

- Approaches to strategic marketing decisions
- Marketing strategy as an emergent or learning process

# Introduction

Element 2 of your syllabus requires you to have a good grasp of the evolving nature of strategic processes. In this chapter we discuss ways in which strategy is made in organisations. There are many approaches, each with something to offer.

We start by reviewing the **rational model**. This is the classic approach; it has its weaknesses, but its great strength is that it is thorough. As a result, this method actually forms a good checklist of the things that strategists should consider, if only briefly.

The rest of this chapter is about other approaches to strategy. These are, generally speaking, **descriptive** rather than **prescriptive**; that is to say, they are based on observation of what real world organisations actually do when making their strategies.

# 1 The rational model

## 1.1 An outline of the model

**FAST FORWARD**

The rational model is a formal approach to achieving a stated objective.

In this chapter we discuss different approaches to making strategies.

First we outline the rational model. This is classic form of strategic management, all encompassing, top down and likely to be ponderous. Here is a case example as to how it applies in practice.

## Marketing at Work

**Ciba-Geigy**

*Goold and Quinn* (in *Strategic Control*) cite Ciba-Geigy, a Swiss-based global firm with chemicals and pharmaceuticals businesses, as an example of formal strategic control and planning processes.

(a)    Strategic planning starts with the identification of strategic business sectors, in other words, areas of activity where there are identifiable markets and where profit, management and resources are largely independent of the other sectors.

(b)    Strategic plans are drawn up, based on a 'comprehensive analysis of market attractiveness', competitors and so on. There are three important aspects to these plans.

–    Long term objectives
–    Key strategies
–    Funds requirements

(c)    At corporate level, these plans are reviewed. Head office examines all the different plans, and, with a 7-10 year planning horizon, the total risk, profitability, cash flow and resource requirements are assessed. Business sectors are allocated specific targets and funds.

**Key concept**

**Planning**: 'the establishment of objectives and the formulation, evaluation and selection of the policies, strategies, tactics and action required to achieve these objectives. Planning comprises long-term/strategic planning, and short-term operations planning.'

Characteristics of strategic plans using the rational model

- Documented (written down)

- The result of a formal, systematised process with a start and end point

- Determined or endorsed by senior managers, with little direct involvement from operational managers, although they may be consulted

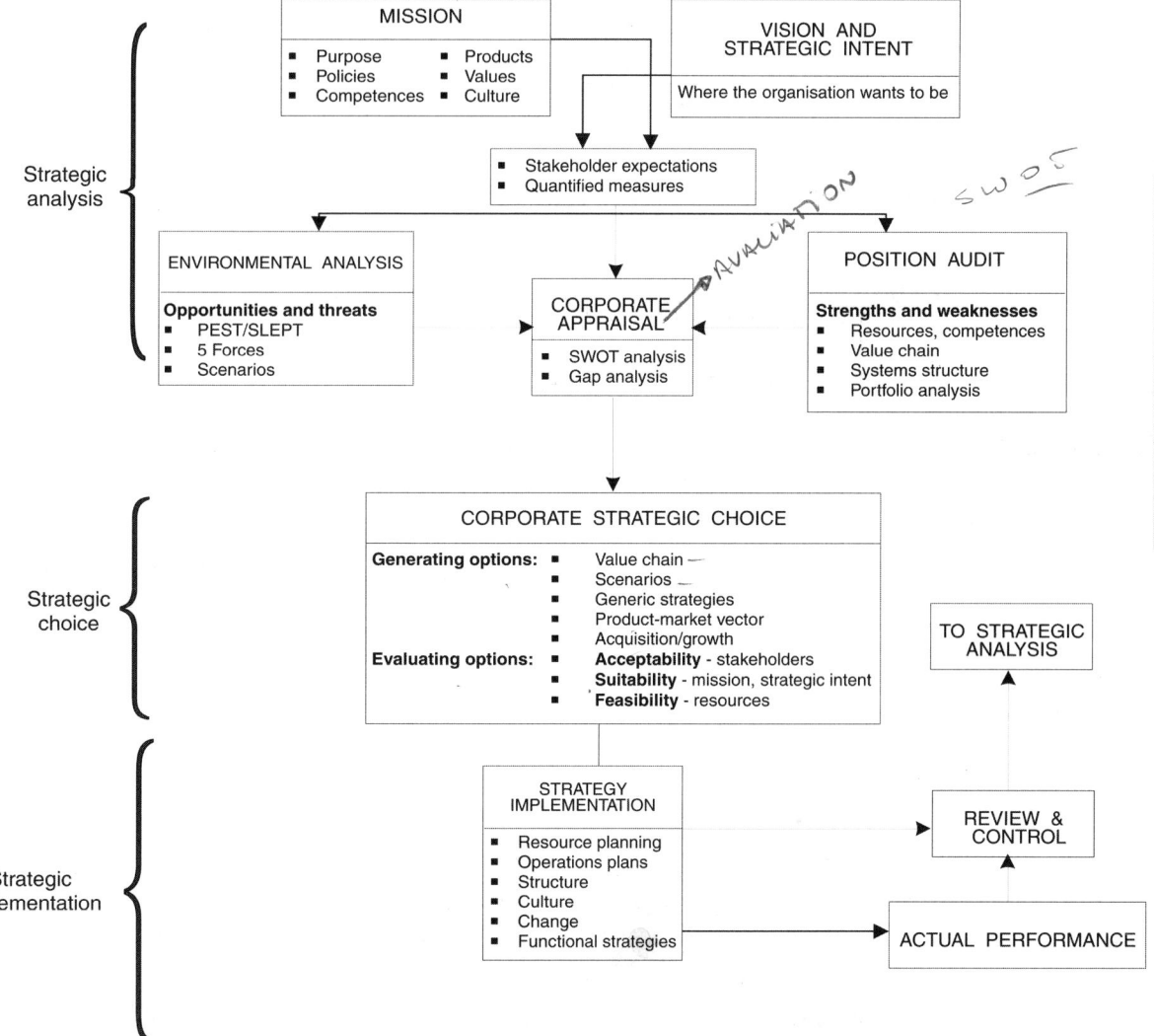

The diagram above outlines the process of strategic planning. At each stage, the process involves the use of various techniques, tools and **models** to make sense of the situation.

The rational model of strategic planning moves from the theoretical to the practical; from thinking about what the organisation exists for to doing something concrete about it. It is also an iterative process: it is **not** done once and for all. In large organisations there may be a planning department which produces a revised plan at regular intervals; work will continue on some or all of the processes at all times. It is a process of refinement, of **adaptation to the environment**.

We now summarise each of the three main parts of this continuing process.

_EVALUATION :_
_- FEASIBILITY : RESOURCE_
_- SUITABILITY : MISSION, STRATEGIC INTENT_
_- ACCEPTABILITY : STAKEHOLDERS._

## 1.1.1 Strategic analysis

| Stage | Process | Comment | Key tools, models, techniques |
|---|---|---|---|
| 1 | Mission and/ or vision | Mission denotes values, the business's rationale for existing; vision refers to where the organisation intends to be in a few years time | • Mission statement |
| 2 | Goals | Interpret the mission to different stakeholders | • Stakeholder analysis |
| 3 | Objectives | Quantified embodiments of mission | • Measures such as profitability, time scale, deadlines |
| 4 | Environmental analysis | Identify opportunities and threats | • PEST analysis<br>• Porter's 5 force analysis and competitive advantage of nations<br>• Scenario building |
| 5 | Position audit or situation analysis | Identify strengths and weaknesses<br>Firm's **current** resources, products, customers, systems, structure, results, efficiency, effectiveness | • Resource audit<br>• Distinctive competence<br>• Value chain<br>• Product life cycle<br>• Boston (BCG) matrix<br>• General Electric business screen<br>• Shell directional policy matrix<br>• Marketing audit<br>For IT:<br>• Nolan's stage model<br>• McFarlan's grid<br>• Awareness frameworks |
| 6 | Corporate appraisal | Combines Stages 4 and 5 | • SWOT analysis charts |
| 7 | Gap analysis | Compares outcomes of Stage 6 with Stage 3 | • Gap analysis |

## 1.1.2 Strategic choice

| Stage | Comment | Key tools, models, techniques |
|---|---|---|
| **Strategic options generation** | Come up with new ideas<br>• How to compete (competitive advantage)<br>• Where to compete<br>• Method of growth | • Value chain analysis<br>• Scenario building<br>• Porter's generic strategic choices<br>• Ansoff's growth vector<br>• Acquisition vs organic growth |
| **Strategic options evaluation** | Normally, each strategy has to be evaluated on the basis of<br><br>• Acceptability<br>• Suitability<br>• Feasibility | • Stakeholder analysis<br>• Risk analysis<br>• Decision-making tools such as decision trees, matrices, ranking and scoring methods<br>• Financial measures (eg ROCE, DCF) For IT: Opportunity Frameworks |

### 1.1.3 Implementation and functional strategies

| Stage | Comment | Key tools, models, techniques |
|---|---|---|
| **Resource planning** | Deploying the resources to achieve the strategy | • Critical success factors<br>• Outsourcing |
| **Operations plans** | General intentions; co-ordination of cross-functional plans | • Activity schedules<br>• Budgets<br>• Project management<br>• For IT, systems development methodologies |
| **Organisation structure and culture** | Designing the organisation to implement the strategy | • Mintzberg's five element model<br>• Departmentation |
| **Change** | Implement changes | • Force field analysis<br>• Unfreeze-change-refreeze<br>• Negotiation |
| **Functional strategies** | HRM<br>Production<br>Marketing | • Personnel planning<br>• Motivation (eg Maslow)<br>• Appraisal schemes<br>• TQM<br>• Marketing information systems<br>• Marketing mix<br>• Segmentation<br>• Product life cycle (again) |

### 1.1.4 Control

| Stage | Comment | Key tools, models, techniques |
|---|---|---|
| **Control** | Review performance and amend<br><br>Performance indicators | • Critical success factors<br>• Balanced scorecard<br>• Marketing information system<br>• Budgets |

You can use these tables as checklists. Many of the models can be used in all phases of the strategic management process.

### 1.1.5 Contents of a strategic plan

Context

• Results of environmental appraisal
• Results of position audit

Long-term plan

• Mission statement
• Long-term objectives (eg market share, volume sales, position in industry)
• Critical success factors

The year ahead

• Annual goals
• Major strategic projects (eg new organisation structure, IT systems)

Implementation

- Schedules
- Budgets
- Performance measures

## 1.2 Assessing the rational model

### 1.2.1 For the rational model

**Assumptions of the rational model**

(a) **Top down**. Senior managers, or planning departments, 'think great thoughts'. The results of their deliberations are documented in a plan, and are refined into greater and greater detail.

(b) **Corporate first**. Strategies for the organisation as a whole are developed prior to strategies for individual business units or functions.

(c) **Breakdown**. Strategic planning can be broken down into its subcomponents, in the same way as manual work can be.

(d) **Objective evaluation**. Strategies are evaluated objectively on their merits, unclouded by bias.

**FAST FORWARD** ▶▶ The rational model is less popular than it was. It is possible to advance strong arguments for it and against it.

## Marketing at Work

Oil firms typically have long lead times between deciding to invest in a new field and bringing the investment on stream so that it can earn money.

Therefore, they must think 20 years ahead, in order to maintain supplies in future and keep in business at present.

Some oil firms are investing in renewable energy sources such as solar power, because they assume that pressure to reduce $CO_2$ emissions (for which petrol usage is responsible) will hit demand.

### 1.2.2 Advantages of a formal system of strategic planning

| Advantages | Comment |
|---|---|
| **Identifies risks** | Strategic planning helps in managing these risks. |
| **Forces managers to think** | Strategic planning can encourage creativity and initiative by tapping the ideas of the management team. |
| **Forces decision-making** | Companies cannot remain static – they have to cope with changes in the environment. A strategic plan draws attention to the need to change and adapt, not just to 'stand still' and survive. |
| **Better control** | Management control can be better exercised if targets are explicit. |
| **Enforces consistency at all levels** | Long-term, medium-term and short-term objectives, plans and controls can be made consistent with one another. Otherwise, strategies can be rendered ineffective by budgeting systems and performance measures which have no strategic content. |

| Advantages | Comment |
|---|---|
| **Public knowledge** | Drucker has argued that an entrepreneur who builds a long-lasting business has 'a theory of the business' which informs his or her business decisions. In large organisations, that the theory of the business has to become public knowledge, as decisions cannot be taken only by one person. |
| **Time horizon** | Some plans are needed for the long term. |
| **Co-ordinates** | Activities of different business functions need to be directed towards a common goal. |
| **Clarifies objectives** | Managers are forced to define what they want to achieve. |
| **Allocates responsibility** | A plan shows people where they fit in. |

## 1.3 Against the rational model

Criticisms of the rational model concern how it has worked in **practice**, and more fundamental problems of **theory**. *Mintzberg* is prominent among the critics.

### 1.3.1 Criticisms of strategic planning in practice

| Problem | Comments |
|---|---|
| **Practical failure** | Empirical studies have not proved that **formal planning** processes ('the delineation of steps, the application of checklists and techniques') contribute to success. |
| **Routine and regular** | Strategic planning occurs often in an **annual cycle**. But a firm 'cannot allow itself to wait every year for the month of February to address its problems.' |
| **Reduces initiative** | Formal planning discourages **strategic thinking**. Once a plan is locked in place, people are unwilling to question it. Obsession with particular performance indicators mean that managers focus on fulfilling the plan rather than concentrating on developments in the environment. |
| **Internal politics** | The assumption of **objectivity** in evaluation ignores political battles between different managers and departments. |
| **Exaggerates power** | **Managers are not all-knowing**, and there are **limits** to the extent to which they can control the behaviour of the organisation. |

### 1.3.2 Criticism of the rational model in theory (Mintzberg, John Kay)

| Criticism | Comment |
|---|---|
| **Formalisation** | 'We have no evidence that any of the strategic planning systems – no matter how elaborate – succeeded in capturing (let alone improving on) the messy informal processes by which strategies really do get developed.' |
| **Detachment: divorcing planning from operations** | This implies that managers do not really need day to day knowledge of the product or market. But strategic thinking is necessary to detect the strategic messages **within** the nitty gritty of operations (eg like finding gold dust in a stream). |

| Criticism | Comment |
|-----------|---------|
| **Formulation precedes implementation** | A strategy is planned – then it is implemented. But **defining** strengths and weaknesses is actually very difficult in advance of **testing** them. 'The detached assessment of strengths and weaknesses may be unreliable, all bound up with aspirations, wishes and hopes'. Discovering strengths and weaknesses is a **learning process**. Implementing a strategy is necessary for learning – to see if it works. |
| **Predetermination** | Planning assumes that the environment can be forecast, and that its future behaviours can be controlled, by a strategy planned in advanced and delivered on schedule. In conditions of stability, forecasting and extrapolation make sense. But forecasting cannot cope with discontinuities (eg the change from mainframe computing to PCs). |
| **The military analogy (John Kay)** | An army's objective is to beat the enemy; the strategy describes how. This analogy is easy to grasp, but it may not be particularly relevant to **business** organisations. Their objectives are more complex and perhaps more ill-defined than an army's. They compete with other organisations for customers. They are less able to **command** resources than an army. Their employees want the organisation (and their jobs in it) to remain in permanent existence. |

## 1.4 Where do we go from here?

Mintzberg's critique has not been fully accepted. Although the idea that planning is the only means by which strategies can be made is flawed, planning does have many uses. These are supporting roles; they cannot fully account for the making of strategy itself.

- It can force people to **think**.
- It can **publicise** strategic decisions.
- It can help **direct** activities in some cases.
- It can **focus debate**.

**Exam tip**

> The great thing about the rational model is that it is **comprehensive**. Even if it is unrealistic to think of a given organisation moving with stately deliberation through an annual planning cycle, the rational model does give us a checklist that can be used to identify areas in which a company's strategy-making may be capable of improvement. You may well find it a useful source of ideas, especially in longer scenario questions.

## 1.5 The need for new models

The case example below illustrates a radically different approach to marketing strategy.

 Marketing at Work

### Honda

Honda is now one of the leading manufacturers of motorbikes. The company is credited with identifying and targeting an untapped market for small 50cc bikes in the US, which enabled it to expand, trounce European competition and severely damage indigenous US bike manufacturers. By 1965, Honda had 63% of the US market. But this occurred by accident.

On entering the US market, Honda's **planned strategy** was to compete with the larger European and US bikes of 250ccs and over. These bikes had a defined market, and were sold through dedicated motorbike dealerships. Disaster struck when Honda's larger machines developed faults – they had not been designed for the hard wear and tear imposed by US motorcyclists. Honda had to recall the larger machines.

Honda had made little effort to sell its small 50 cc motorbikes – its staff rode them on errands around Los Angeles. Sports goods shops and ordinary bicycle and department stores had expressed an interest, but Honda did not want to confuse its image in its 'target' market of men who bought the larger bikes.

The faults in Honda's larger machines meant that reluctantly, Honda had no alternative to sell the small 50cc bikes just to raise money. They proved very popular with people who would never have bought motorbikes before. Eventually the company adopted this new market with enthusiasm with the slogan: 'You meet the nicest people on a Honda.'

The strategy had **emerged**, against managers' conscious intentions, but they eventually responded to the new situation.

# 2 Patterns, competences and emergent strategies

## 2.1 Strategies as patterns of management decisions

FAST FORWARD

> According to Andrews, strategy is a **pattern of senior management decisions.**

*Andrews* does not separate **objectives** from the **strategies** designed to achieve them, as strategy arises out of the **general management process** whereby **senior** managers direct and control the business. This general management process generates **consistent** decisions. For example, a firm's managers may prefer certain types of market opportunities (eg low risk) than others.

For Andrews, **corporate strategy** is: 'the **pattern** of decisions in a company that determines and reveals its objectives, purposes, or goals, that produces the principal policies and plans for achieving those goals, and defines the range of business the company is to pursue, the kind of economic and human organisation it is or intends to be, and the nature of the economic and non economic contribution it intends to make to its shareholders, employees, customers and communities'.

## 2.2 Strategy as the exploitation of competences

Strategic opportunities must be related to the firm's resources. A strategic approach involves identifying a firm's **competences**. The **distinctive competence** of an organisation is what it does well, uniquely, or better than rivals. *Andrews* says that, for a relatively undifferentiated product like cement, the ability of a maker to 'run a truck fleet more effectively' than its competitors will give it competitive strengths (if, for example, it can satisfy orders quickly). These competences may come about in a variety of ways.

- **Experience** in making and marketing a product or service
- The talents and potential of **individuals** in the organisation
- The **quality of co-ordination**

Competences are a kind of resource and the idea of strategy as being based on competences is one aspect of the resource-based view promoted by *Hamel and Prahalad*.

**Key concept**

> **Core competences** critically underpin the organisation's competitive advantage.
>
> *Johnson & Scholes*

*Johnson & Scholes* divide competences into two types. An organisation must achieve at least a **threshold** level of competence in **everything** it does. The organisation's **core competences** are those where it **outperforms competitors** and that are **difficult to imitate**.

Competitiveness depends on **unique resources** or core competences. The organisation's level of performance in its core competences may be judged in three ways.

- Comparison with past results
- Comparison with industry norms
- Bench marking

### 2.2.1 Tests for identifying a core competence

(a) **It provides potential access to a wide variety of markets.** GPS of France developed a core competence in 'one-hour' processing, enabling it to process films and build reading glasses in one hour.

(b) **It contributes significantly to the value enjoyed by the customer.** For example, for GPS, the waiting time restriction was very important.

(c) **It should be hard for a competitor to copy.** This will be the case if it is technically complex, involves specialised processes, involves complex interrelationships between different people in the organisation or is hard to define.

In many cases, a company might choose to combine competences.

Bear in mind that **relying on a competence is no substitute for a strategy.** However, a core competence can form a basis for a strategy.

## 2.3 Freewheeling opportunism

**Freewheeling opportunism** is a pattern of strategy that displays little apparent coherence or forethought. It is common among highly entrepreneurial individuals who are prepared to seize opportunities and back hunches. It can be present in larger, highly innovatory businesses, but is a high risk approach, depending for its success on a combination of experience, talent and market awareness.

## 2.4 Emergent strategies and how to craft them

**FAST FORWARD**

> The rational approach also fails to identify **emergent strategies**, or allow for them, according to Mintzberg. Operations level can be a source of strategic change. Emergent strategies arise out of **patterns of behaviour**. They are not the result of the conscious intentions of senior managers. They have to be shaped or **crafted**. **Realised strategies** include intended and emergent strategies.

In the Honda case example, we mentioned that the planned strategy of selling large bikes had to give way to a strategy which had emerged by accident, almost. *Mintzberg* develops this theme further.

**Emergent strategies** do not arise out of conscious strategic planning, but from a number of ad hoc choices, perhaps made lower down the hierarchy. They may not initially be recognised as being of strategic importance. Emergent strategies develop out of **patterns of behaviour**, in contrast to planned strategies or senior management decisions which are imposed from above. An exercise will make the point clearer.

Action Programme 1

Aldebaran Ltd is a public relations agency founded by an entrepreneur, Estella Grande, who has employed various talented individuals from other agencies to set up in business. Estella Grande wants Aldebaran Ltd

to become the largest public relations agency in North London. Management consultants, in a planning document, have suggested growth by acquisition. In other words, Aldebaran should buy up the other public relations agencies in the area. These would be retained as semi-independent business units, as the Aldebaran Ltd group could benefit from the goodwill of the newly acquired agencies. When Estella presents these ideas to the Board there is general consensus with one significant exception. Livia Strange, the marketing director, is horrified. 'How am I going to sell this to my staff? Ever since we've been in business, we've won business by undercutting and slagging off the competition. My team have a whole culture based on it. I give them champagne if they pinch a high value client. Why acquire these new businesses – why not stick to pinching their clients instead?'

What is the source of the conflict?

## 2.5 Deliberate and emergent strategies

The diagram below should help explain the point.

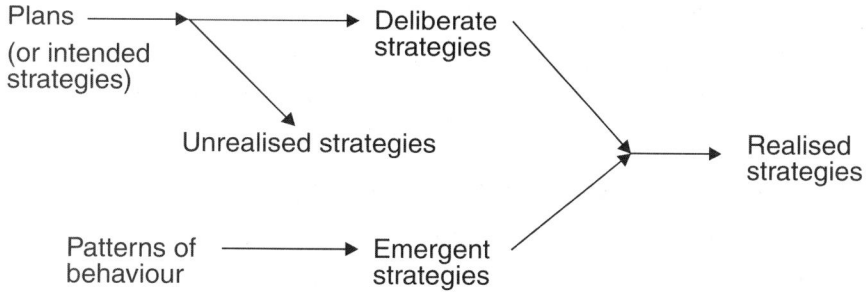

(a)    **Intended strategies** are plans. Those plans or aspects of plans which are actually realised are called **deliberate strategies**.

(b)    **Emergent strategies** are those that develop out of patterns of behaviour.

The task of **strategic management** is to control and shape these emergent strategies as they develop.

 Marketing at Work

**BPP**

BPP began life as a training company. Lecturers had to prepare course material. This was offered for sale in a bookshop in the BPP building. Owing to the demand, BPP began offering its material to other colleges, in the UK and world-wide. BPP Publishing, which began as a small offshoot of BPP's training activities, is now a leading publisher in the market for targeted study material for the examinations of several professional bodies. It is unlikely that this development was anticipated when the course material was first prepared.

No realised strategy will be wholly deliberate or wholly emergent. The line between deliberate and emergent elements within each strategy will be in part influenced by organisation structure and culture.

## 2.6 Implicit or explicit strategies

We already mentioned the fact that entrepreneurs have a theory of the business which they may or may not document.

- Implicit strategies may exist only in the chief executive's head.
- Explicit strategies are properly documented.

Some plans are more explicit than others.

## 2.7 Crafting emergent strategies

Managers cannot simply let emerging strategies take over. Why?

- **Direction**. The emergent strategy may be **inappropriate** for the long-term direction of the organisation and may have to be corrected.

- **Resources**. It may have future implications for **resource use** elsewhere: in most organisations, different parts of the business compete for resources.

- Managers might wish to build on the strategy by **actively devoting more resources** to it.

Mintzberg uses the metaphor of **crafting strategy** to help understand the idea. Strategies are shaped as they develop, with managers giving help and guidance, devoting more resources to some, exploiting new opportunities and **responding** to developments. For example, Honda's management reacted to the emergent strategy, eventually, and shaped its development.

Separating 'thinking' and 'doing' has the following result.

(a)  A **purely deliberate strategy hampers rapid learning from experience** (once the formulators have stopped formulating). For example it is hard with deliberate strategies stumble by accident into strategic growth.

(b)  A **purely emergent strategy defies control**. It may in fact be a bad strategy, dysfunctional for the organisation's future health.

Deliberate strategies introduce strategic change as a sort of quantum leap in some organisations. In this case, a firm undergoes only a few strategic changes in a short period but these are very dramatic.

 Marketing at Work

In other organisations, however, strategic change can be **haphazard**. Mintzberg mentions the example of the Canadian National Film Board. This used to make short documentaries but ended up by chance with a feature film. This forced it to learn the marketing of such films, and so it eventually became much more involved in feature length productions than before – strategy by accident.

The strategist must be able to **recognise** patterns and to manage the process by which emergent strategies are created. In other words, the strategist must be able to **find strategies** as well as **invent them**.

## 2.8 How to craft strategy

*Mintzberg* lists these activities in crafting strategy.

| Activity | Comment |
|---|---|
| **Manage stability** | <ul><li>Most of the time, managers should be implementing the strategies, not planning them.</li><li>Obsessions with change are dysfunctional. Knowing when to change is more important.</li><li>Formal planning is the detailed working out of the agreed strategy.</li></ul> |

| Activity | Comment |
|----------|---------|
| **Detect discontinuity** | • Environments do not change regularly, nor are they always turbulent, though managers should be on the lookout for changes. Some small environmental changes are more significant for the long term than others, though guessing which these are is a problem. |
| **Know the business** | • An intimate feel for the business has to include an awareness and understanding of operations. |
| **Manage patterns** | • Detect emerging patterns and to help them take shape. Some emergent strategies must be uprooted, others nurtured. |
| **Reconciling change and continuity** | • 'Crafting strategy .... requires a natural synthesis of the future, present and past.' Obsessions with change and/or continuity can be counterproductive. |

## 2.9 Section summary

- Strategy can emerge from patterns of behaviour, perhaps at operational level.

- Managers have to craft emergent strategies, accepting some and giving them resources, and rejecting others.

- An organisation's realised strategy will be a mix of emergent and intended strategies.

## Action Programme 2

Britannia Hospital has just appointed a new director, Florian Vole, imported from the private sector, where he had run 'Hanky House' a niche retail operation specialising in handkerchiefs and fashion accessories. The recession put the business into receivership, but Mr Vole was sought out to inject his private sector expertise in running a public sector institution. He calls a meeting of the hospitals senior managerial, medical and nursing staffs. 'What the public sector has been missing too long is vision, and when you're eyeball-to-eyeball with change, it's vision that you need, not planning documents and statistics. We need to be nimble and quick to adapt to our customer's ever changing needs. That is our strategy!'

What do think of Florian Vole's approach?

# 3 Strategy and managerial intent

**FAST FORWARD**

Johnson and Scholes suggest an approach which follows a similar outline to the rational model, but which accounts for the political and cultural influences on managers.

*Johnson and Scholes* discuss two other ways in which strategy can arise through deliberate management intent rather than simply emerging.

## 3.1 The command view

'Here strategy develops through the direction of an individual or group, but not necessarily through formal planning.' In this model there is a person or group with acknowledged strategic power and responsibility. The mechanisms by which this authority arises are reminiscent of Weber's analysis of **legitimate authority** into **legal-rational**, **charismatic** and **traditional**. Johnson and Scholes mention the autocratic leader; the charismatic leader whose reputation or personality gives control of strategic direction; and the making of economic and social strategy in the public sector by elected politicians.

## 3.2 Paradigm and politics

(a) The word **paradigm** may be used to signify the basic assumptions and beliefs that an organisation's decision-makers hold in common. Note that this is a slightly different concept from **culture**. The paradigm represents **collective experience** and is used to make sense of a given situation; it is thus essentially conservative and inhibiting to innovation, while an innovative **culture** is entirely feasible.

(b) The **politics** of the organisation may also influence strategy.

'The political view of strategy development is that strategies develop as the outcome of processes of bargaining and negotiation among powerful internal or external interest groups (or stakeholders).'

Johnson and Scholes describe the processes by which paradigm and politics influence the process of strategy development.

**Step 1**    **Issue awareness**

- Internal results, customer responses or environmental changes can make **individuals** aware of a problem.

- A **trigger** alerts the **formal** information system to the problem, so that organisational activity takes over from the individual's consideration of the problem.

**Step 2**    **Issue formulation**.
Managers try to analyse and get to the root of the problem. Information may be used to rationalise, rather than challenge, management's existing view of the situation. **Formal analysis** in practice plays a little role.

**Step 3**    **Solution development**.
Some possible solutions are developed and one is selected.

- **Memory search**: solutions which worked in the past.
- **Passive search**: wait for a solution to suggest itself.

Solutions begin with a vague idea, which is further refined and explored by internal discussion.

**Step 4**    **Solution selection**

- **Eliminate unacceptable plans**. This screening process involves bargaining, diplomacy and judgement rather than formal evaluation according to the business case. ('Unacceptable' might mean unacceptable in terms of organisational politics, rather than in terms of business sense.)

- **Endorsements**. Many strategic decisions **originate from management subsystems**, which senior managers authorise. Junior managers might filter strategic information, or ignore certain options, to protect themselves.

 Marketing at Work

### Enron

Enron is now notorious for its unethical practices. However, its collapse is traceable to a failure of strategic control. In the early 1990s, Enron was extremely successful as a market maker in the supply of gas and electricity. Its strategy was 'asset light': it did not produce gas, or very much electricity, but it

used its financial expertise and its control of gas pipe lines and electricity grids to make large profits from the integration of supply and demand.

Unfortunately, early success bred hubris and quite junior executives were allowed to make major investments in industries whose characteristics were totally different from the homogeneity of product and ease of distribution of gas and electricity. In each case, the strategies failed because they made large demands for capital and low utilisation of Enron's core trading competences.

Johnson and Scholes are less averse to planning than Mintzberg, but instead of assuming a rational objectivity, they anchor plans in the behaviour of the organisation and the people in it.

# 4 Incrementalism

The environment is uncertain and there are limits on what managers can achieve. Small steps may be a more practical way to move forward than to attempt to follow a grand plan.

## 4.1 Bounded rationality

In practice, managers are limited by time, by the information they have and by their own skills, habits and reflexes.

- Strategic managers do **not** evaluate all the possible options open to them in a given situation, but choose from a small number of possibilities.

- Strategy making necessitates compromises with interested groups through political bargaining. This is called **partisan mutual adjustment**.

- The manager **does not optimise** (ie get the best possible solution).

- Instead the **manager satisfices**. The manager carries on searching until he or she finds an option which appears tolerably satisfactory, and adopts it, even though it may be less than perfect. This approach Herbert Simon characterised as **bounded rationality**.

## 4.2 Incrementalism

*Lindblom* described another approach. **Incrementalism** involves small scale extensions of past practices.

- It avoids major errors.

- It is more likely to be acceptable, because consultation, compromise and accommodation are built into the process.

### 4.2.1 Disadvantages of incrementalism

- Incrementalism does not work where radical new approaches are needed, and it has a built-in conservative bias. Forward planning does have a role.

- Even as a descriptive model of the public sector, it does not always fit. Some changes do not seem incremental, but involve dramatic shifts.

- Incrementalism ignores the influence of corporate culture, as it filters out unacceptable choices.

- It might only apply to a stable environment.

**Action Programme 3**

Sir Humphrey Appleby pops in to see his boss, the Minister for Administrative Affairs. The Minister has a proposal. 'I've examined all the options, and I believe that strategy C is the best. My planners have done a great job, don't you agree?' 'Yes, Minister,' Sir Humphrey replies, 'But I'll have to run it past Horace in the Treasury, and of course, the Prime Minister's office – I hesitate to predict what the European Commissioner in Brussels will think ... do you want me to suggest to your planners that we try again'.

What models of strategic planning and management are discussed here?

## 4.3 A middle way? Logical incrementalism

**Key concept**

**Logical incrementalism**: managers have a general idea of where the organisation should go, but strategies should be tested in small steps, simply because there is too much uncertainty about actual outcomes.

Strategy is best described as a **learning process**. Logical incrementalism has the best of both worlds.

- The broad outlines of a strategy are developed by an in-depth review.
- There is still practical scope for day-to-day incremental decision making.

## 4.4 Contrasts

The implications of rationality and incrementalism can be expressed in diagrammatic form.

(a) *Rational planning model*

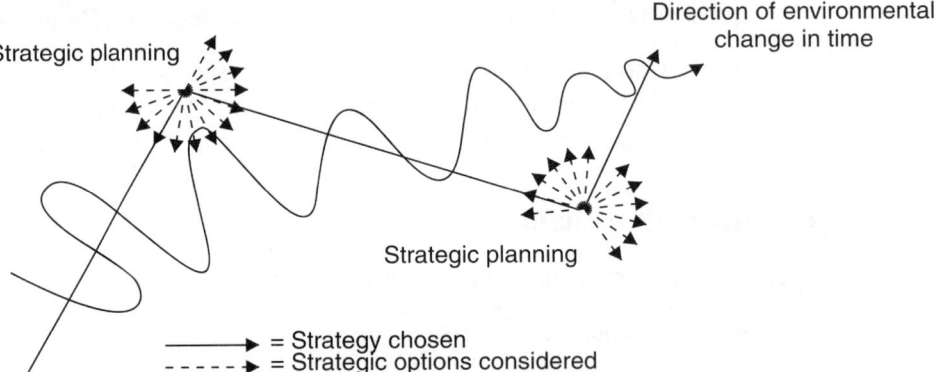

The dangers of the rational model are that the environment may change too quickly for the planning processes to react. All directions are considered, however.

(b)    *Incremental model*

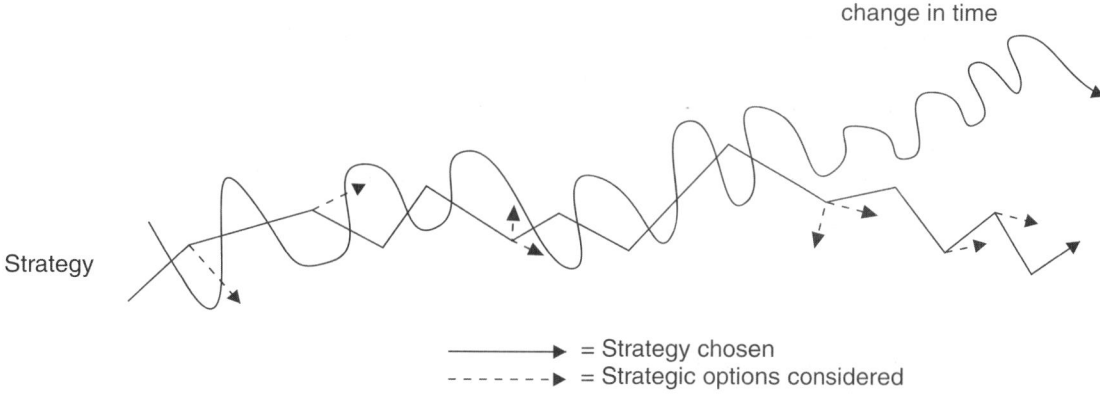

Direction of environmental
change in time

Strategy

⟶ = Strategy chosen
------▶ = Strategic options considered

Incremental change may not be enough as the number of strategic options considered may be insufficiently radical to cope with environmental shift.

## 4.5 Section summary

- Managers do not take optimal (ie the best) decisions but satisfactory ones (decisions which will 'do').

- Managers do not pursue the whole rational model, but take small-scale decisions, building on what has gone before (incrementalism).

# 5 Strategic thinking

Ohmae argues that successful strategic thinking involves a creative and intuitive approach to the business, not just logic.

## 5.1 Strategic thinking as an intuitive process

*Kenichi Ohmae* (in *The Mind of the Strategist*) argues that **formal strategic planning processes have withered strategic thinking**. Strategy is essentially a creative process.

- **Successful strategists** 'have an idiosyncratic **mode of thinking** in which company, customers and competition merge in a dynamic interaction out of which a comprehensive set of objectives and plans for action eventually crystallises'.

- 'Successful business strategies result not from rigorous analysis but from a **particular state of mind'**. For Ohmae, the challenge to strategic management is to try to reproduce this ability in organisational structures, forms and cultures.

A strategist should be able to see beyond the present. There are several aspects to **strategic thinking**.

- Flexible thinking (what if? questions).
- Avoiding wrongly-focused perfectionism.
- Keeping details in perspective (especially **uncertain details**).
- Focusing on key factors and the essentials (or **distinctive competences**) of a business.

### 5.1.1 How successful strategic thinking operates

(a) **Ask the right questions**. Find a **solution to a problem** rather than a **remedy to a symptom**. (Analogy: painkillers reduce a headache, they do not go to the underlying problem which may be poorly made spectacles, bad lighting or whatever.)

(b) **Observe the problems**.

(c) **Group** problems together by a process of **abstraction** (eg brainstorming) to see what they have in common (the **key factors**).

(d) Ohmae gives an example from an organisation's personnel system.

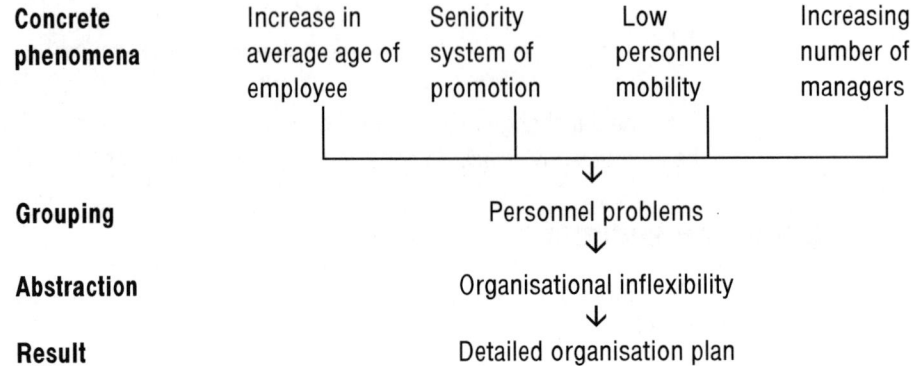

| **Concrete phenomena** | Increase in average age of employee | Seniority system of promotion | Low personnel mobility | Increasing number of managers |
|---|---|---|---|---|

**Grouping**           Personnel problems

**Abstraction**        Organisational inflexibility

**Result**             Detailed organisation plan

# 6 The environment and competition

The environment cannot be ignored. Strategy can be seen as a response to environmental forces.

**FAST FORWARD** ▶ Porter and Ohmae see business strategy in competitive terms. Competitive advantage is always relative to competitors. Possible future conditions must also be considered.

For *Hofer and Schendel*, a strategy secures a fit with the environment. Success flows from this fit.

(a) The environment is a key factor in the behaviour of any organisation, as organisations derive their **inputs** from it and distribute their **outputs** to it.

(b) **Fit or suitability** suggests that 'organisations are successful when they intentionally achieve internal harmony and external adaptation to their environment. Managers should use analytical techniques to identify the relationship between the organisation's internal capability and competences, and the external outputs. In very basic terms, the need for the fit is identified by the SWOT analysis and strategies are undertaken to secure the fit.'

(c) Hofer and Schendel suggest that strategy is a mediating force between the organisation and the environment.

Thus, although a strategy might be acceptable or feasible in principle, this does not necessarily make it the right one to choose. Arguably, the choice of strategy should follow a strategic logic.

**Key concept**

> According to *Stacey (Strategic Management and Organisational Dynamics)*, **strategic logic** requires that a proposed sequence of actions satisfy two conditions.
>
> - It must be consistently related to the objectives of the organisation.
>
> - It must match the organisation's capability (including its structure, control systems and culture) to its environment.
>
> The idea is that all the pieces of the strategic puzzle should fit together in a predetermined manner.

# 6.1 Competition

Most businesses face competitors. According to Ohmae, what counts is performance in **relative terms**. 'A good business strategy' is 'one by which a firm can gain significant ground on its competitors at an acceptable cost'.

| Method | Comment |
| --- | --- |
| **Re-adjust current resources** | Identify the key factors for success (or distinctive competence) and concentrate resources on these activities. |
| **Relative superiority** | A relative advantage can still be achieved by exploiting the competitors' actual or potential weaknesses. |
| **Challenge assumptions** | Challenge the accepted assumptions of doing business in a particular market (eg telephone banking challenges the need for branch networks in banks). |
| **Degrees of freedom** | Finding new ways of exploit markets (eg by segmentation, product/service differentiation etc). |

In all cases, direct competition on the competitors' own turf is avoided. Successful strategy is the interplay of three Cs: **customers**, **competitors** and the **corporation**. This Ohmae calls the **strategic triangle**.

*Porter* defines strategy in similar competitive terms.

**Key concept**

> **Competitive strategy** is 'the taking of offensive or defensive actions to create a defendable position within an industry ... and ... a superior return on investment'.

Porter highlights the importance of taking a competitive viewpoint. Porter suggests that over the past twenty years, firms have been learning to play to a new set of rules: benchmarking, outsourcing and the nurture of a few basic core competences. **The assumption is that rivals can easily copy any position, and so many companies are competing destructively** with each other in a state of **hyper-competition**. 'The root of the problem is the **failure to distinguish operational effectiveness and strategy**.

## 6.1.1 Creating a sustainable strategic position

| Task | Comment |
| --- | --- |
| **Operational effectiveness is not the same as strategy** | Operational effectiveness involves doing the **same** things better than other firms. Improvements here can be imitated. |
| **Strategy rests on unique activities** | Competitive strategy is about being **different** ... choosing to perform activities differently or to perform different activities than rivals.' |
| **A sustainable strategic position requires trade-offs** | Trade-offs limit what a company does. Trade-offs occur in three ways. <br> • When activities are not compatible (eg an airline can offer a cheap no-meals service, or offer meals; doing both results in inefficiencies). <br> • Where there will be inconsistencies in image and reputation. <br> • Where an activity is over or underdesigned for its use (eg overqualified staff in menial positions). |
| **Strategy is about combining activities** | This is hard to imitate. (Operational effectiveness is about being good at *individual* activities.) |

| Task | Comment |
|------|---------|
| **Strategy is about choices, not blindly imitating competitors** | Many firms operate inefficiently, and so can benefit by improving operational effectiveness, but industry leaders at productivity frontier need to make choices and trade-offs. |

Ohmae and Porter make three assumptions.

- The **survival** of a business is impossible without a **competitive strategy**.
- The **actual strategy chosen** will be **unique** to the organisation.
- The market place is sometimes like a **battlefield**.

## 6.2 The future orientation: Hamel and Prahalad

There are two approaches to the future.

- The future will change  incrementally (eg global warning, demographic trends).
- The future will be radically different (we do not know which inventions will succeed).

Obviously, both approaches are relevant and should be run in parallel.

*Hamel and Prahalad* make two suggestions.

- The future is not just something that happens to organisations.
- Organisations can create the future.

 Marketing at Work

**Coca-Cola**

In the 1980s, *Coca-Cola* decided to change its flavour to compete with Pepsi. Market research, taster tests and so forth elicited favourable responses to the change, and so the new formulation was introduced.

A small group of consumers vociferously opposed the change; and this opposition spread suddenly and rapidly like an epidemic, forcing Coca-Cola to re-introduce the old formula. It was hard to detect the reasons for this, but if some consumers perceived Coke to symbolise American values, then changing the formula appeared to be an assault on them.

This case illustrates four issues.

(a) The limitations of planning.

(b) The seemingly unpredictable behaviour of the environment (as it became fashionable not to drink the new formula).

(c) Small causes (a few disaffected Coke-drinkers) can generate major consequences, by amplification, almost.

(d) The limitations to organisational gathering of information.

Consumers, who had initially favoured the product, turned against it, for reasons that could not be predicted by market researchers.

*Stacey* outlines a very different view.

(a) **The environment is not always predictable**. The environment is a **feedback system**, in which some effects can be amplified such as the rapidly expanding boycott of new Coke.

(b)    Organisations can **shape their environment** (eg by moulding customer expectations) rather than just respond to it.

(c)    Too much of a **good thing can lead to failure**.

- Successful firms embody incremental and revolutionary change.

- Companies do not exist in a state of equilibrium, but instead exist between stability and instability, and it is this creative tension that enables innovation.

(d)    Managers' attempts to plan or impose a vision do not always shape up to the reality of emergent strategies. But too much emergent strategy leads to anarchy.

**Exam tip**

> Your examiner sees the concept of strategy as a competitive response to environmental forces as one of an opposing pair of dominant ideas about competitive strategy, the other of the pair being the suggestion that strategy is based on the exploitation of core competences. There is a question on this dichotomy in your BPP Practice and Revision Kit.

# 7 Learning based strategy

**FAST FORWARD**

> **Learning based** strategy-making recognises the need to exploit the input of the knowledge worker. The flow of fresh ideas challenges the **paradigm.**

There has been considerable theoretical attention paid to the concept of a **learning organisation**, but as yet there is no single coherent model available. In this section we shall attempt to draw together some of the ideas related to strategy.

The idea of strategy as the exploitation of unique core competences inevitably implies that there must be a continuing and effective process of organisational learning in order to maintain competitive edge. Competences must be kept up to date and new ones must be developed and exploited. Similarly, if competitive advantage is based on identifying opportunities in the environment, the company must keep up a constant scanning of existing and potential markets so that profitable segments may be identified. Learning based on this process of environmental scanning may be termed **signal learning**, since it is largely a process of monitoring and considering the signals that emerge from the business environment.

We mentioned the **paradigm** concept earlier in this chapter. A strong paradigm is developed as a result of success; if circumstances change, a strong paradigm may be a recipe for failure. Companies must be prepared to respond creatively to developments in the environment generally and particularly in their marketplaces.

## 7.1 Knowledge as a resource

With the transformation of advanced economies away from manufacturing and towards ever more complex service industries, there has been a growing awareness of the importance of the **knowledge worker**, whose input is based on a high degree of skill and learning, and of the **knowledge-intensive firm**, which employs large numbers of such workers. A firm of accountants is a good example of a knowledge-based firm.

There is an obvious requirement for such firms and workers to maintain, develop and exploit their knowledge, collectively and individually. With this requirement comes recognition of the human resource as a source of competitive advantage.

*Nonaka* identifies two types of knowledge.

(a)    **Tacit** knowledge may be compared to individual skills. It is personal and rooted in a specific context.

(b) **Explicit** knowledge is formal, systematised and easily shared. An example would be the specification for a technical process.

 Marketing at Work

*Liquidmetal Technologies* is a California-based company that specialises in high performance 'liquid metal' alloys. Liquidmetal® alloys are a revolutionary class of materials that redefines performance and cost paradigms. The superior properties of Liquidmetal alloys are made possible by revolutionary scientific and technological innovations. Liquidmetal alloys represent the first enabling materials technology since the creation of thermoplastics and possess characteristics that make them superior in many ways to other commercially-viable materials. First, they have an 'amorphous' atomic structure, which is unprecedented for structural metals. Second, they include a multi-component chemical composition, which can be optimised for various properties and processes. Finally, they lend themselves to process technology similar to that possessed by plastics.

## 7.2 Knowledge creation

The exploitation of knowledge requires that its acquisition or creation is organised in a rational fashion. *Argyris* was one of the early exponents of the need for business learning. He used the term **double loop learning** to describe this process. The term is derived from **control theory**, in which a feedback control system that incorporates the option of changing the target is called a double loop system.

In double loop learning, knowledge is not only acquired, organised, stored and retrieved, but the purposes for which this is done are constantly reviewed. This involves regular examination of the organisation's purpose and objectives in the light of the knowledge already acquired. Double loop learning may also be referred to as **3R learning**, since it incorporates processes of **reflection**, **re-evaluation** and **response** in order to bring about necessary development and change within the organisation.

## 7.3 The learning organisation

*Lynch* quotes *Garvin's* definition.

An organisation skilled at creating, acquiring and transferring knowledge, and at modifying its behaviour to reflect new knowledge and insights.

This clearly reflects Argyris's double loop approach. *Senge* has proposed that strategy development should be seen as a learning process. The essential nature of organisational learning in this sense is **active creativity**. Senge suggests that this is best undertaken by co-operative groups.

**Implications for strategy**. The learning organisation will generate a flow of fresh ideas and insights. This will promote renewal and prevent stagnation. Increased openness to the environment will enhance the quality of response to events. However, none of this will happen if there is a rigid, prescriptive, **top-down** approach to the strategy-making process. There must be a **wide range of inputs** and a commitment to **discussion and debate**. There must also be mechanisms for effective **knowledge sharing**. IT systems can be very useful in this process, but the essential precursor is an open minded commitment to effective learning, led from the top.

The potential advantages of the learning approach must not be allowed to seduce the organisation into endless, unfocused debate. Senior management must guide the process in order to keep it on track. They must also be prepared to take decisions without consultation when circumstances require them to do so.

# 8 Strategic decisions in smaller organisations

**FAST FORWARD** 》

The characteristics of **smaller organisations** and their limited resources tend to produce a particular pattern of strategic decision-making. Generally, this will be rather informal, entrepreneurial and customer oriented.

## 8.1 The strategic decision process

It is likely that a large company will be influenced by the rational model approach, since it is likely to have the resources to undertake more complex planning. Thus the main responsibility for the strategic marketing decisions lies with the top management. The implementation and the management of the strategy are seen as operational decisions that are carried out by the lower levels of the management.

However, in a smaller company the process may be much closer to the emergent approach, with strategic decisions being made as part of an iterative learning process. A small company would not have the same depth of information as a large company to carry out the same high level of detailed planning. It will not have the resources to employ specialist expertise and gather extensive information before a strategic marketing decision is made. It is more likely that the smaller company will initially make basic decisions about strategy and then, as learning progresses, further decisions will be made as seems appropriate.

### 8.1.1 The virtual organisation

The concept of the virtual organisation provides an alternative approach for small organisations to overcome their lack of internal expertise and other strategic resources. Such an organisation is generally defined as being geographically dispersed and therefore depending on electronic links to complete its production process. Using the concept more loosely, we can say that small organisations may develop a network of partnership relationships with other organisations in order to gain access to information and expertise that can provide benevolent influence on their strategic decisions.

This approach produces what is also known as a network organisation.

## 8.2 The B2B buying process

Another difference arises from the difference in the buying behaviour of B2B clients and the differing responses by the large and small firms. Where large customers are spending on major projects, they are likely to put contracts out to tender. It is the larger firms that will tender for these directly; smaller firms will not have the resources to do this, so they will sub-contract to the larger firm winning the contract. Thus the marketing decisions of the smaller company may be dependent on their relationships with the larger companies serving the same market and the amount of outsourcing they do. The smaller firm will aim to form close relationships with the larger contractors so that they are well positioned for sub-contracting opportunities.

## 8.3 Entrepreneurial v bureaucratic decision making

The smaller firm, because it is not subject to the strictures of formal planning processes, is much more able to be entrepreneurial in its decision-making. This means it is more likely to be innovative and be quicker to respond than its larger rivals. It also means the smaller firm is more able to be flexible in the decisions it makes and to respond more easily to market changes. Having less formal procedures makes them more able to take rapid customer focused decisions. Also, it may well have a different perception of risk and be more willing to take risks based on hunches and soundings in the market than the larger firm.

The smaller company, as already noted, has only limited resources. Often, it may be that the entire decision-making process has to be carried out by one person.

## Chapter Roundup

- The rational model is a formal approach to achieving a stated objective.

- The rational model is less popular than it was. It is possible to advance strong arguments for it and against it.

- According to Andrews, strategy is a **pattern of senior management decisions**.

- The rational approach also fails to identify **emergent strategies**, or allow for them, according to Mintzberg. Operations level can be a source of strategic change. Emergent strategies arise out of **patterns of behaviour**. They are not the result of the conscious intentions of senior managers. They have to be shaped or **crafted**. **Realised strategies** include intended and emergent strategies.

- Johnson and Scholes suggest an approach which follows a similar outline to the rational model, but which accounts for the **political** and **cultural influences** on managers.

- The environment is uncertain and there are limits on what managers can achieve. Small steps may be a more practical way to move forward than to attempt to follow a grand plan.

- Ohmae argues that successful strategic thinking involves a **creative and intuitive approach** to the business, not just logic.

- Porter and Ohmae see business strategy is **competitive terms**. Competitive **advantage is always relative** to competitors. Possible future conditions must also be considered.

- **Learning based** strategy-making recognises the need to exploit the input of the **knowledge worker**. The flow of fresh ideas challenges the **paradigm**.

- The characteristics of **smaller organisations** and their limited resources tend to produce a particular pattern of strategic decision-making. Generally, this will be rather informal, entrepreneurial and customer oriented.

## Quick Quiz

1   How does Andrews describe corporate strategy?

2   What is a distinctive competence?

3   How does strategy emerge?

4   How does Mintzberg suggest strategy is crafted?

5   According to Johnson and Scholes, what is the paradigm?

6   What is meant by satisficing and bounded rationality?

7   What is incrementalism?

8   What is Ohmae's view of the origin of successful strategy?

9   What is environmental fit?

10   What are the three sides of the strategic triangle?

## Answers to Quick Quiz

1   As a pattern of decisions

2   Something the organisation does well, uniquely or better than rivals

3   It develops out of patterns of behaviour

4   Managers respond to developments, exploit opportunities and allocate resources

5   Basic assumptions and beliefs held in common by an organisation's decision makers

6   Satisficing is accepting an imperfect but tolerable solution. Bounded rationality is the intellectual stance that accepts satisficing as an appropriate course of action

7   Small scale extensions of past practices

8   Strategy-making is a creative thought process

9   Adaptation of the organisation to its environment

10   Corporation, customers, competition

## Action programme review

1   Livia Strange's department has generated its own pattern of competitive behaviour. It is an emergent strategy. It conflicts directly with the planned strategy proposed by the consultants. This little case history also makes the additional point that strategies are not only about numbers, targets and grand plans, but about the organisational cultures influencing a person's behaviour.

2   Mr Vole hasn't quite made the transition from the fashion industry, where desire for silk handkerchiefs is relatively fickle, to an institution like Britannia Hospital. Here planning is necessary. Resources must be obtained to cope with future needs. Customer needs are likely to be fairly basic (ie security, comfort, medical attention, stimulation). However, in the actual delivery of care and services, Florian Vole has a point: experimentation with new care techniques might improve the hospital's service to its patients.

3   The Minister is a planner: he's describing the rational model. Sir Humphrey is advocating the partisan mutual adjustment model.

Now try Question 1 at the end of the Study Text

# Planning for the future

## Syllabus content

- The significance and application of new marketing thinking to strategic decisions
- The role of knowledge management in creating and sustaining competitive advantage
- The nature of innovation in marketing and factors affecting its development
- The role of innovation management in risk-taking in achieving competitive advantage
- The issues in creating an innovative marketing culture
- Strategic marketing decision making in SMEs

# Introduction

In the last chapter we examined ways in which strategic planning problems are tackled. An essential pre-condition for effective planning is considering the way future events might go. Marketing needs to be innovative if it is to be effective. Section 1 explores some of the cultural and organisational approaches that encourage innovation.

We then examine some of the techniques that may be used in planning for the future. Of course, there is no way of knowing just what the future holds, but this does not excuse us from doing our best to make sensible estimates. It is only if we have a forecast that we will be able to recognise the perturbing effects of unforeseen developments and take action to deal with them.

We conclude this chapter with a discussion of knowledge management. This is particularly relevant to the problem of dealing with the future. Corporate knowledge is akin to experience in the individual and, like experience, can help us to both plan and control our responses to developing situations.

# 1 Innovation

**FAST FORWARD**

**Innovation** is a major responsibility of modern management, particularly in commercial organisations. This is because both technology and society are developing extremely rapidly; new products must be matched with new market opportunities if businesses are to survive and prosper. Innovation in marketing is particularly important, since **marketing** provides much of the **interface** between the **organisation** and its **rapidly changing environment**.

We discussed the need for new strategic responses at the very beginning of this Study Text. **Innovation** will be a recurrent theme within it, since innovation is likely to be a major requirement for success in most commercial organisations. It will be an important part of the marketing manager's job to innovate, to recognise innovative ideas when they appear and to develop and manage the conditions and processes that support innovation.

It is important to remember that the need for innovation does not just relate to products and services: internal business processes are likely to be fertile ground for innovation and improvement. Innovation responses to the demands made of the marketing function will also be required and may prove to be particularly rewarding.

## 1.1 Innovation and the market orientation

A market orientation involves establishing customer needs and finding ways to satisfy them. Very obviously, innovation has a major role to play here. However, what of the kind of innovation that addresses no currently established need? Equally obviously, strategic management must take cognisance of such developments and investigate them carefully to see if they have the capacity to generate entirely new categories of demand. The *Sony Walkman* is the classic example of technical innovation of this type, but there are non-technological and service industry examples too. For example, before *Starbucks*, few people realised they needed a cup of coffee to take to work with them.

 Marketing at Work

Innovation can lead to major changes in the business model. In the UK, the major supermarket chains *Tesco* and *Sainsbury's* are moving into the convenience store sector, largely because of a shortage of sites for larger stores. Tesco acquired more than 800 convenience stores in 2002, while Sainsbury's may acquire 1200 stores from *TM Group*.

At the same time, *BP* continues to invest in its own chain of *Connect* convenience stores and *Wild Bean Cafés*. In an interesting move, BP has started direct marketing activity based on its involvement with the *Nectar* loyalty card scheme. Sainsbury's also uses Nectar as its loyalty card.

## 1.2 Innovation and control

*Peters and Waterman* found that one of the sources of innovation is increased **delegation**. In itself delegation has great value - morale and performance are improved, top management is freed for strategic planning and decisions are made by those closest to the problem concerned and therefore most informed about it. Most importantly, the organisation benefits from the imagination and thinking of its high flyers.

Warning bells ring, however, when delegation is confused with **lack of control**.

> 'The line between efficient corporate performance through delegation and anarchy resulting from a loss of total control is a very fine one.'                                             Alec Reed MD, Reed Accounting

**The dilemma then is between the need to be innovative so as to deal with a chaotic environment and the need to retain control so as to prevent anarchy**. This can be done simply by giving employees and managers parameters within which discretion can be exercised, and by ensuring that they know they are accountable for their actions.

To encourage innovation the objective for management should be to create a more outward-looking organisation. People should be encouraged to use their initiative to look for new products, markets, processes, designs and ways to improve productivity.

Innovation thrives best in an organisation when it is supported by its culture. *Thomas Attwood* suggests the following steps to encourage innovation.

- Ensure management and staff know what innovation is and how it happens.
- Ensure that senior managers welcome, and are seen to welcome, changes for the better.
- Stimulate and motivate management and staff to think and act innovatively.
- Understand people in the organisation and their needs.
- Recognise and encourage potential 'entrepreneurs'.

## 1.3 Company size

**FAST FORWARD**

**Small companies** appear to produce a disproportionate number of innovations because the sheer number of attempts by small-scale entrepreneurs means that some ventures will survive. The 90 to 99 per cent that fail are distributed widely throughout society and receive little attention.

On the other hand, **large companies** must absorb all potential failure costs; even if an innovation is successful, the organisation may face costs that newcomers do not have to bear, like converting current operations and customer-profiles to the new solution.

### 1.3.1 Small organisations and innovation

The research suggests that the following factors are crucial to the success of innovative small organisations.

(a) **Need orientation**. Lacking resources, successful small entrepreneurs soon find that it pays to approach potential customers early, test their solutions in the users' hands, learn from their reactions and adapt their designs rapidly.

(b) **Experts and fanatics**. Commitment allows the entrepreneur to persevere despite the frustrations, ambiguities and setbacks that always accompany major innovations.

(c)    **Long time horizons**. Time horizons for radical innovations make them essentially 'irrational' from a present-value viewpoint - delays between invention and commercial production/success can range from three to 25 years.

(d)    **Low early costs**. Innovators incur as few overheads as possible, their limited resources going directly into their projects. They borrow whatever they can and invent cheap equipment or processes, often improving on what is available in the marketplace.

(e)    **Multiple approaches**. Committed entrepreneurs will tolerate the chaos of random advances in technology, adopting solutions where they can be found, unencumbered by formal plans that would limit the range of their imaginations.

(f)    **Flexibility and quickness**. Undeterred by committees, the need for board approvals and other bureaucratic delays, the inventor/entrepreneur can experiment, recycle and try again, with little time lost. They quickly adjust their entry strategies to market feedback.

(g)    **Incentives**. Tangible personal rewards are foreseen if success is achieved and the prospect of these rewards (which may not be principally of a monetary nature) is a powerful driver.

## 1.3.2 Large organisations and innovation

Within large organisations, by contrast, the following **barriers to innovation and creativity** may typically be encountered.

(a)    **Top management isolation**. Financially-focused top managers are likely to perceive technological innovation as more problematic than, say, acquisitions or organic growth: although these options are just as risky, they may appear more familiar.

(b)    **Intolerance of fanatics**. Big companies often view entrepreneurial fanatics as embarrassments or trouble-makers.

(c)    **Short time horizons**. The perceived corporate need to report a continuous stream of upward-moving, quarterly profits conflicts with the long time-spans that major innovations normally require.

(d)    **Accounting practices**. A project in a big company can quickly become an exposed political target and its potential net present value may sink unacceptably. Also there is a tendency to apply false logic to **sunk costs**: it is important to remember that costs incurred in the past are not relevant to decisions taken in the present about the future. It is thus equally erroneous to cancel a project on the grounds that its forecast revenues do not offer an adequate return on its total costs as it is to persist with one on the grounds that a large amount has already been spent.

(e)    **Excessive rationalism**. Managers in large organisations often seek orderly advance through early market research studies or systematic project planning.

(f)    **Excessive bureaucracy**. Bureaucratic structures require many approvals that cause delays; the interactive feedback that fosters innovation is lost, important time windows can be missed and real costs and risks rise for the corporation.

(g)    **Inappropriate incentives**. When control systems neither penalise opportunities missed nor reward risks taken, the results are predictable.

Successful large organisations, have developed techniques that emulate or improve on the approaches used in small, fleet-of-foot companies.

(a)    **Atmosphere and vision**. Continuous innovation occurs largely because top managers appreciate innovation and atmosphere in order to support it. They project clear long-term vision for the organisation that go beyond simple economic measures.

**Marketing at Work**

A survey of innovative companies found that 81% said they had a vision for innovation; 82% said that innovative ideas were allowed to fail without penalty and 73% said they managed the pace of innovation in order to maintain focus. The correspondent scores for less innovative companies were 69%, 70% and 58%.

*Fortune, 7 March 2005*

(b) **Orientation to the market**. Within innovative organisations, managers focus primarily on seeking to anticipate and solve customers' emerging problems.

(c) **Small, flat hierarchies**. Development teams in large organisations normally include only six to seven key people; operating divisions and total technical units are kept below 400 people.

(d) **Multiple approaches**. Where possible, several prototype programmes are encouraged to proceed in parallel. Such redundancy helps the organisation to cope with uncertainties in development, motivates people through competition and improves the amount and quality of information available for making final choices on scale-ups or new-product/service introductions.

(e) **Development shoot-outs**. The most difficult problem in the management of competing projects lies in re-integrating the members of the losing team. For the innovative system to work continuously, managers must create a climate that honours high-quality performance whether a project wins or loses, reinvolves people quickly in their technical specialities or in other projects and accepts rotation among tasks and groups.

(f) **Skunkworks**. This is the name given the system in which small teams of engineers, technicians, designers and model makers are placed together with no intervening organisational or physical barriers, to develop a new product from idea to commercial prototype stage. This approach eliminates bureaucratic controls; allows fast, unfettered communications; permits rapid turnround times for experiments; and instils a high level of group identity and commitment.

(g) **Interactive learning**. Recognising that the random, chaotic nature of technological change cuts across organisational and even institutional lines, the big company innovators tap into multiple sources of technology from outside as well as to their customers' capabilities.

Many large companies seek to retain some of the innovation and flexibility supposedly characteristic of small firms. They are converging on a balance between bureaucracy (the old order) and entrepreneurship/ innovation (the new order) based on **synergies** and **alliances**.

(a) A **synergy** is a combination of businesses, internal services and organisation structures which means that the whole is worth more in value than the sum of the parts. People at all levels focus on doing what they do best.

(b) Organisations are also seeking to extend their reach without increasing their size by forming **strategic alliances** (closer working relationships) with other organisations. This involves partnerships and joint ventures as well as contracting out services to outside suppliers. It results in improved access to information and technology, and quicker responses. However, alliances are vulnerable to management failures and so must be carefully selected; in addition they involve genuine moves away from bureaucracy and hierarchy.

## 1.4 Encouraging innovation

> Companies can be organised and run in a way that stimulates innovation. This depends in large part on practical measures.

An innovation strategy calls for a management policy of giving encouragement to innovative ideas. This will require positive action.

(a) **Financial backing to innovation**, by spending on R & D and market research and risking capital on new ideas.

(b) **Giving employees the opportunity to work in an environment where the exchange of ideas for innovation can take place**. Management style and organisation structure can help here. Management can actively encourage employees and customers to put forward new ideas. Participation by subordinates in development decisions might encourage employees to become more involved with development projects and committed to their success. Development teams can be set up and an organisation built up on project team-work.

(c) Where appropriate, **recruitment policy should be directed towards appointing employees with the necessary skills for doing innovative work**. Employees should be trained and kept up to date.

(d) Certain managers should be made responsible for obtaining **information from outside the organisation about innovative ideas**, and for communicating this information throughout the organisation.

(e) Strategic planning should result in **targets being set for innovation**, and successful achievements by employees should if possible be rewarded.

### 1.4.1 Structure and culture

Interaction between structure and culture on the one hand and the promotion and management of innovation on the other was discussed at length by *Burns and Stalker* in their book *The Management of Innovation*. They described two approaches to managing organisations that may be thought of as opposite ends of a spectrum. One they called the **mechanistic** type of organisation, the other the **organic** or **organismic** type. The mechanistic type of organisation is very similar to the classic bureaucracy: very good at the efficient administration of routine business, but not very good at handling a rapidly changing environment, with its constant presentation of new problems. The organic approach, on the other hand, seemed to be very good at producing innovative solutions. The mechanistic structures and the organic structure are contrasted in the table below.

| Mechanistic | Organic |
|---|---|
| Tasks are specialised and broken down into subtasks. | Specialist knowledge and expertise is seen to contribute to the 'common task' of the concern. |
| Each individual task is 'abstract', pursued with techniques and purposes more or less distinct from that of the concern. People are concerned with task efficiency, not with how the task can be made to improve organisational effectiveness. | Each task is seen and understood to be set by the total situation of the firm: people are concerned with the task insofar as it contributes to organisational effectiveness. |
| Managers are responsible for co-ordinating tasks. | Each task is adjusted and redefined through interaction with others. This is rather like co-ordination by mutual adjustment. |
| There are precise job descriptions and delineations of responsibility. | Job descriptions are less precise: it is harder to 'pass the buck'. |

| Mechanistic | Organic |
|---|---|
| 'Doing the job' takes priority over serving the interests of the organisation. | 'The spread of commitment to the concern beyond any technical definition' |
| Hierarchic structure of control. An individual's performance assessment derives from a 'contractual relationship with an impersonal organisation.' | Network structure of control. An individual's job performance and conduct derive from a supposed community of interest between the individual and the organisation, and the individual's colleagues. (Loyalty to the 'team' is an important control mechanism.) |
| Decisions are taken at the top, where knowledge is supposed to reside. | Relevant technical and commercial knowledge can be located anywhere 'omniscience is no longer imputed to the head of the concern'. |
| Interaction is mainly vertical (up and down the scalar chain), and takes the form of commands and obedience. | Interaction is lateral and communication between people of different rank represents consultation, rather than command. |
| Operations and working behaviour are governed by instructions issued by superiors. | Communication consists of information and advice rather than instructions and decisions. |
| Insistence on loyalty to the concern and obedience to superiors. | Commitment to the concern's task (eg mission) is more highly valued than loyalty as such. |
| Internal knowledge (eg of the organisation's specific activities) is more highly valued that general knowledge. | 'Importance and prestige attach to affiliations and expertise valid in the industrial, technical and commercial milieux external to the firm.' |

**Four important points** to note

(a)  Although organic systems are not hierarchical in the way that bureaucracies are, there are **differences of status**, determined by people's greater expertise, experience and so forth.

(b)  The degree of **commitment to the concern** is more extensive in organic than mechanistic system. This is similar to the idea that an organisation's mission should motivate and inspire employees.

(c)  The reduced importance of hierarchy is replaced by 'the development of shared beliefs and values'. In other words, corporate culture becomes very powerful. **Control is cultural rather than bureaucratic**.

(d)  The two approaches represent **two ends of a spectrum**: there are intermediate stages between bureaucratic and organic organisations. Different departments of a business may be run on different lines. For example, the payroll department of a firm has a **well defined task** (eg paying salaries at the end of the month) with little variation. **Controls** are needed to ensure processing accuracy and to avoid fraud. A **mechanistic** system might be applied here. On the other hand, the '**creative** department' of an advertising agency, with a number of professional experts (copywriters, graphic designers, account executives), may be run on an **organic** basis.

*Burns and Stalker* recognised that organic systems would only suit individuals with a high tolerance for ambiguity and the personal stresses involved in being part of such an organisation - but the freedom of manoeuvre is considered worth this personal cost, for individuals who prize autonomy and flexibility.

## 1.4.2 The ambidextrous approach

A criticism levelled at organic organisations is that whilst they may be **good at creating ideas**, they might be **less good at exploiting them**. Decentralisation and loose structures encourage communication, but also perhaps make employees less likely to comply with a management instruction to exploit an innovation: in other words, there are problems of discipline at a basic level.

An organic structure might therefore be a drawback when certain types of things need to be done. For example, in warfare, a disciplined 'mechanistic' approach might be needed to fight certain kinds of battle: delays and indecision might be costly. (On the other hand, guerrilla warfare might be conducted organically.)

To get round this problem some organisations employ what might be termed an **ambidextrous approach to organisation structure**. By this is meant that organisations employ the elements of both the organic *and* mechanistic structures in their operations.

(a) **Creative departments** may be developed, to deal with R&D and so forth, often as part of an organisation's support staff in the configuration, possibly to offer new ideas to the technostructure. Their precise location in the structural configuration will obviously depend on circumstances.

(b) Instead of creating a permanent arrangement, a mechanistic company might designate certain occasions for employees to behave as if they were in organic companies. Such occasions include brainstorming sessions and quality circles.

# 2 The future orientation

**Future orientated** firms see the future as something that can be influenced and, in cases of industry transformation, created. A firm's activity to influence its future in part depends on the outlook of its management.

'Some management teams were simply more foresightful than others. Some were capable of imagining products, services and entire industries that did not exist and then giving them birth. These managers seemed to spend less time worrying about how to position the firm in existing competitive space and more time creating fundamentally new competitive space.' (*Hamel and Prahalad*, 1994)

In the previous chapter, we briefly mentioned that planning for the future must allow for elements of continuity **and** radical change.

*Hamel and Prahalad* suggest that:

- The future is not just something that happens to organisations
- Organisations can create the future

In practice, there is truth in both perspectives.

(a) Some trends are likely to continue indefinitely. In the physical environment, global warming will continue for the long term. In terms of demography, other than wars or famine, it is relatively easy to predict population trends. Forecasting techniques cover this.

(b) Other developments are harder to determine.

(i) In 1900, a long-term investor would have invested in railway shares.

(ii) In 1947, it was assumed that demand for computers would be no more than five worldwide.

(iii) Even now, nobody really knows which inventions or innovations will succeed.

Marketing at Work

*Japan Tobacco* licensed *Philip Morris International's Marlboro* brand for 30 years and captured 85% of Japan's cigarette market. However, the license will not be renewed when it expires in 2005.

To fill the gap, Japan Tobacco planned to launch 13 new cigarettes in 2004, including one that tastes of rum and another that smells of citrus fruit.

Hamel and Prahalad suggest, however, that **some companies are more prepared to shape the future** than others, and that this **future-orientated stance is somehow embodied in the corporate culture**. Hamel and Prahalad offer a diagnostic to indicate how future-orientated a company is.

| Diagnostic statement | Protect the past | Create the future |
|---|---|---|
| Senior management's viewpoint about the future is … | Conventional, reactive | Distinctive, far-sighted |
| Senior management spend most of their time on … | Re-engineering current processes | Regenerating core strategies |
| Within the industry, the company … | Follows the rules | Makes the rules |
| The company is better at … | Operational efficiency | Building new businesses |
| To what extent does the company pursue competitive advantage by … | Catching up with competitors? | Creating new sources of competitive advantage? |
| How is the company's agenda for change actually set? | By competitors | By a vision of the future |
| Are managers …. | Engineers of the present? | Architects of the future? |
| Are employees …. | Anxious? | Hopeful? |

 Action Programme

Undertake this diagnostic test for your own company. Carry it out alone and then get another member of staff to do it - from another department, say.

# 3 Gap analysis

**FAST FORWARD**

> Gap analysis is an important discipline for dealing with the future in very practical terms by directing attention to what needs to be done.

Strategic planners must think about the extent to which new strategies are needed to enable the organisation to achieve its **objectives**. One technique whereby this can be done is **gap analysis**. Gap analysis is based on establishing:

(a)     What are the **organisation's targets for achievement** over the planning period?

(b)     What would the organisation be expected to achieve if it **did not** develop any new strategies, but **simply carried on in the current way** with the same products and selling to the same markets?

There will be a difference between the targets in (a) and expected achievements in (b). New strategies will then have to be developed which **will close this gap**, so that the organisation can expect to achieve its targets over the planning period.

> **Gap analysis** is 'the comparison of an entity's ultimate objective with the sum of projections and already planned projects, identifying how the consequent gap might be filled'.

## 3.1 A forecast or projection based on existing performance: $F_0$ forecasts

The $F_0$ **forecast** is a forecast of the company's future results assuming that it **does nothing new**. The company is expected to continue to operate as at present without any changes in its products, markets, organisation, assets, human resources, research spending, financial structure, purchasing and so forth. Preparation of an $F_0$ forecast entails the following.

- The analysis of revenues, costs and volumes
- Projections into the future based on past trends
- Other factors affecting profits and return (eg in the environment, strikes, competitors)
- Finalising the forecast

The purpose of the $F_0$ forecast and gap analysis is to determine the **size of the task** facing the company if it wishes to achieve its target profits.

Forecasts can never be completely accurate. If possible, the error should be quantified in either of the following two ways.

(a) **Estimating likely variations**. For example 'in 2006 the forecast profit is £5 million with possible variations of plus or minus £2 million'.

(b) **Providing a probability distribution for profits**. For example 'in 2006 there is a 20% chance that profits will exceed £7 million, a 50% chance that they will exceed £5 million and an 80% chance that they will exceed £2$^1/_2$ million. Minimum profits in 2006 will be £2 million.'

## 3.2 The profit gap

The **profit gap** is the difference between the target profits (according to the overall corporate objectives of the company) and the profits on the $F_0$ forecast. Other forms of gap analysis (eg for sales revenue) can be developed.

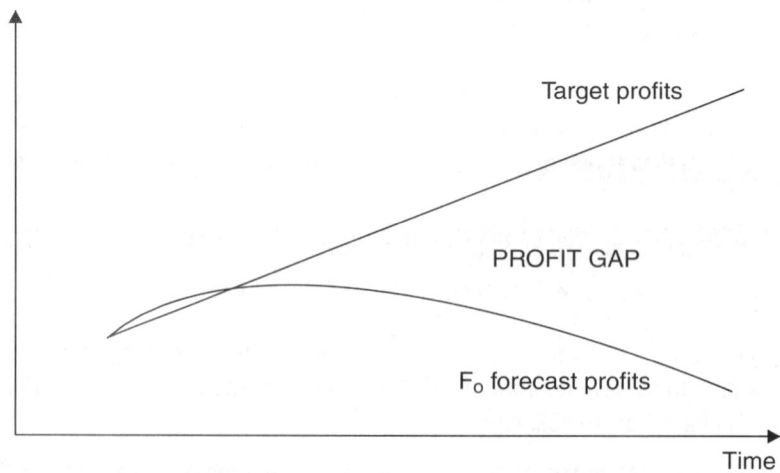

It is now that the company must decide what the **options are for bridging the gap**. This gap represents the extra task facing the company, in addition to just continuing the existing business. It indicates how much extra profit **has to be** generated by the decisions and the commitments to be made over the next few years. In deciding the size of the gap that must be closed, allowance must be made for errors in the forecast.

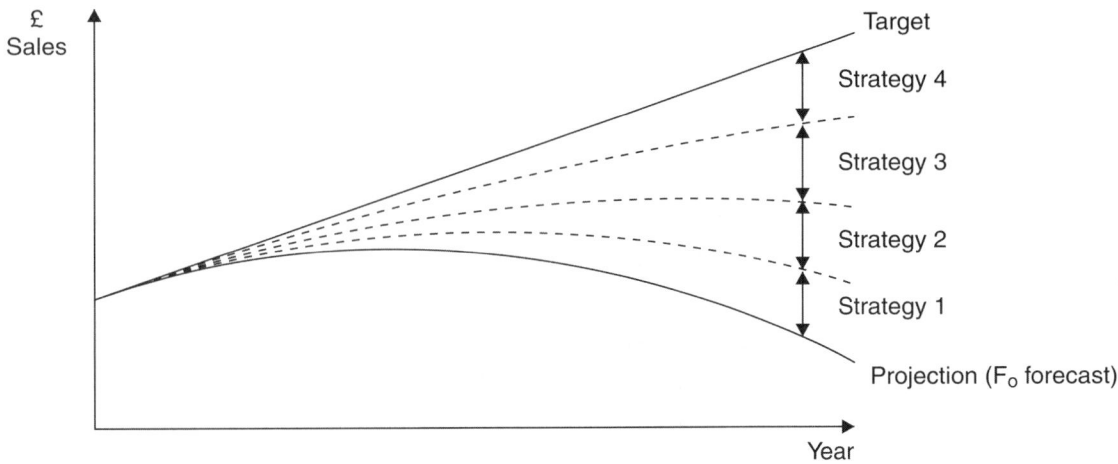

A key issue, however, is whether it is possible to forecast accurately.

# 4 Forecasting

**FAST FORWARD**

Conventionally, **forecasting techniques** can be used to predict demand in the short to medium term. However, such techniques depend on the reliability of past data. The uncertainties in using statistical forecasting to predict the future are considerable.

## 4.1 Types of forecast

**Key concepts**

**Forecasting** is 'the identification of factors and quantifications of their effect on an entity, as a basis for planning'.

**Projection**. A projection is 'an expected future trend pattern obtained by extrapolation. It is principally concerned with quantitative factors whereas a forecast includes judgements'.

**Extrapolation** is 'the technique of determining a projection by statistical means'.

## 4.2 Statistical forecasts

Statistical forecasts take past data and endeavour to direct it to the future, by **assuming** that **patterns or relationships which held in the past will continue to do so**. Many statistical techniques aim to reduce the uncertainty managers face. In **simple/static conditions the past is a relatively good guide** to the future.

### 4.2.1 Statistical forecasting techniques for static conditions

(a) **Time series analysis**. Data for a number of months/years is obtained and analysed. The aim of time series analysis is to identify:

- Seasonal and other cyclical fluctuations
- Long term underlying trends

For example, the UK's monthly unemployment statistics show a **headline figure** and the **underlying trend**. Time series analysis is covered in detail in your BPP Study Text for Analysis and Evaluation.

(b) **Regression analysis** is a quantitative technique to check any underlying correlations between two variables (eg sales of ice cream and the weather). Remember that the relationship between two variables may **only hold between certain values**. (You would expect ice cream consumption to rise as the temperature becomes hotter, but there is a maximum number of ice creams an individual can consume in a day, no matter how hot it is.)

(c)    **Econometrics** is the study of economic variables and their interrelationships, using computer models. Short-term or medium-term econometric models might be used for forecasting.

(i)    **Leading indicators** are indicators which change **before** market demand changes. For example, a sudden increase in the birth rate would be an indicator of future demand for children's clothes. Similarly, a fall in retail sales would be an indicator to manufacturers that demand from retailers for their products will soon fall.

(ii)    The firm needs the ability to **predict the span of time between a change in the indicator and a change in market demand**. Change in an indicator is especially useful for demand forecasting when they reach their highest or lowest points (when an increase turns into a decline or *vice versa*).

(d)    **Adoptive forecasts** change in response to **recent** data.

### 4.2.2 Problems with statistical forecasts

(a)    **Past relationships do not necessarily hold for the future.**

(b)    Data can be misinterpreted, and **relationships assumed where none exist**. For example, sales of ice cream rise in the summer, and sales of umbrellas fall - the link is the weather, not any correlation between them.

(c)    Forecasts do not account for special events (eg wars), the likely response of competitors and so on.

(d)    The variation and depth of business cycles fluctuate.

(e)    In practice statistical forecasters **underestimate uncertainty**.

## 4.3 Judgemental forecasts

**FAST FORWARD**

> **Intuitive** or **judgemental forecasting** is sometimes used. The **Delphi** technique aims to ensure that group dynamics do not take over from consideration of the issues.

Judgemental forecasts are used principally for the long term, covering several decades. However, because of the limitations of short-term forecasting they are used for the short term too. Effectively, they are based on **hunches or educated guesses**. Sometimes, these prove surprisingly accurate. At other times they are wide of the mark.

### 4.3.1 Modelling

At various points in this text, you have been given frameworks or models to structure your thinking.

**Key concept**

> A **model** is anything used to represent something else.
>
> - Descriptive: describing real-world processes
> - Predictive: attempting to predict future events
> - Control: showing how action can be taken

A model is a simplified representation of reality, which enables complex data to be classified and analysed.

## 4.3.2 Examples of models

| Type of model | Example |
|---|---|
| Descriptive | Value chain |
| | BCG analysis |
| | Five competitive forces |
| | Buyer behaviour |
| Predictive | Product life cycle |
| | Cost-volume profit analysis |
| Control | Input-process-output-feedback |
| | Sensitivity analysis |
| | Discounted cash flow |

Their relevance to building a future orientation depends on **how well they are used** and a **recognition of their limitations**.

## 4.3.3 Individual forecasting

(a) A company might forecast sales on the basis of the judgement of one or more executives.

    (i) **Advantages**

- Cheap
- Suitable if demand is stable or relatively simple

    (ii) **Disadvantage**

- Swayed most heavily by **most recent** experience rather than trend

(b) **Genius forecasting**

An individual with expert judgement might be asked for advice. This might be the case with the fashion industry; although demand might be hard to quantify, an ability to understand the mind of the customer will be very useful.

(c) In practice, forecasts might be prepared by an interested individual who has read the papers, say, and has promoted an item for management attention.

## 4.3.4 Consensus forecasts

**Jury forecasts**. A panel of experts and/or executives prepare their own forecasts and a consensus forecast emerges from this.

(a) **Advantages**: expert opinions are sought and obtained.

(b) **Disadvantages**. The jury might **dilute** the best. The **group dynamics** will interfere with the decision. Each expert might differ and, in a face-to-face situation, the more forceful or confident would win the argument.

**Delphi method**. This was developed to overcome problems relying on **known** experts or personalities in the jury.

(a) Participants remain **anonymous**, known only to the organiser.

(b) Participants respond to a **questionnaire** containing tightly-defined questions. The Delphi technique **retains anonymity**. The results are collated and statistically analysed, and are defined by the organiser to each expert. The experts respond again.

(c)     The Delphi technique is **time consuming**.

(d)     In practice, it seems to be the case that experts are **universally optimistic**.

## 4.4 Statistical versus judgemental and consensus forecasts

*David Mercer* identifies the relative advantages and disadvantages of each method.

| Use of forecasts | Statistical | Judgement |
|---|---|---|
| **Changes in established patterns** | Past data is no guide | Can be predicted but could be ignored |
| **Using available data** | Not all past data is used | Personal biases and preferences obscure data |
| **Objectivity** | Based on specific criteria for selection | Personal propensity to optimism/pessimism |
| **Uncertainty** | Underestimated | Underestimated, with a tendency to over-optimism |
| **Cost** | Inexpensive | Expensive |

### 4.4.1 Using both methods

Judgemental forecasting is **speculative**. However, speculation may be necessary to identify changing patterns in data or weak signals reflecting or presaging social changes.

 Marketing at Work

Many small enterprises lack even the most basic marketing skills, with seven out of ten start-ups failing to identify their market and potential customers. But simple marketing techniques can make the difference between failure and runaway success.

Some of Britain's most innovative entrepreneurs started their businesses as little more than cottage industries. Richard Branson founded his business empire - which now stretches from air travel to personal equity plans - by selling records to his school friends, and Anita Roddick started *The Body Shop* by bottling potions and lotions on her kitchen table. Both have eschewed the text book marketing techniques and the jargon favoured by their competitors because they are intuitive marketers and, crucially, they carefully identified their target markets.

Inevitably, not all those starting up a new enterprise have the innate talent of a Branson or a Roddick and some fail to embrace even the most basic marketing principles. John Stubbs, chief executive of the Marketing Council, says: 'Marketing for some remains obscure and is perceived as an expensive luxury.' Research from *Barclays Bank* indicated that only three in ten start-up businesses carry out initial research to identify their market and potential customers, increasing the likelihood of one of the most common causes of business failure: loss of market and sales.

## 4.5 Market forecasts and sales forecasts

 FAST FORWARD

Market forecasts and sales forecasts complement each other. The market forecast should be carried out first of all and should cover a longer period of time. The modelling of a demand function depends on quantifying complex relationships.

> **Market forecast**. This is a forecast for the market as a whole. It is mainly involved in the assessment of environmental factors, outside the organisation's control, which will affect the demand for its products/services.

   (a)   **Components of a market forecast**

      (i)   The **economic review** (national economy, government policy, covering forecasts on investment, population, gross national product, and so on).

      (ii)   **Specific market research** (to obtain data about specific markets and forecasts concerning total market demand).

      (iii)   Evaluation of **total market demand** for the firm's and similar products (for example profitability and market potential).

   (b)   **Sales forecasts** are estimates of sales (in volume, value and profit terms) of a product in a future period at a given marketing mix.

## 4.5.1 Research into potential sales

> **Sales potential** is an estimate of the part of the market that is within the possible reach of a product.

## 4.5.2 Factors governing sales potential

- The price of the product
- The amount of money spent on sales promotion
- How essential the product is to consumers
- Whether it is a durable commodity whose purchase is postponable
- The overall size of the possible market
- Competition

Whether sales potential is worth exploiting will depend on the cost which must be incurred to realise the potential.

## Example

Market research has led a company to the opinion that the sales potential of product X is as follows.

|  | Sales value | Contribution earned before selling costs deducted | Cost of selling |
|---|---|---|---|
| either | £100,000 | £40,000 | £10,000 |
| or | £110,000 | £44,000 | £15,000 |

In this example, it would not be worth spending an extra £5,000 on selling in order to realise an extra sales potential of £10,000, because the net effect would be a loss of £(5,000 − 4,000) = £1,000.

## 4.5.3 Estimating market demand

Estimating market demand is not necessarily as straightforward as you might at first think. Imagine you are the marketing manager of a company producing sports footwear. What is your market demand? Is it the volume of shoes purchased in the UK, or Europe, or the whole world? Should you be considering tennis shoes as well as running shoes? Shoes for children or only adults? And should you be forecasting demand for next year or over the next five years? The permutations seem endless.

**A demand function** is simply an expression which shows how sales demand for a product is dependent on several factors. These demand variables can be grouped into two broad categories.

(a) **Controllable variables or strategic variables**. These are factors over which the firm's management should have some degree of control, and which they can change if they wish. Controllable variables are essentially the marketing mix.

(b) **Uncontrollable variables**. These are factors over which the firm's management has no control.

    (i) **Consumer variables** depend on decisions by consumers, or the circumstances of consumers (for example their wealth).

    (ii) **Competitor variables** depend on decisions and actions by other firms, particularly competitors.

    (iii) **Other variables**. These include decisions by other organisations (for example the government) or factors which are outside the control of anyone (for example weather conditions, or the total size of the population).

A demand function can be set out as follows.

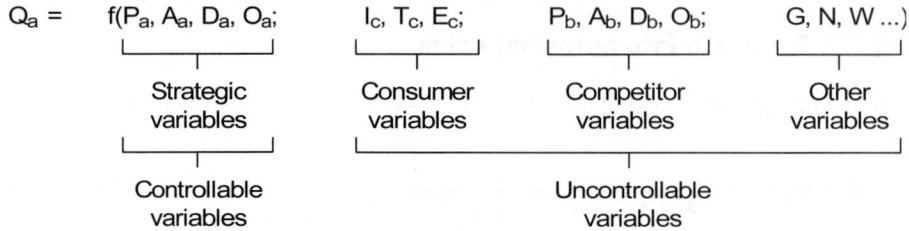

$$Q_a = f(P_a, A_a, D_a, O_a;\quad I_c, T_c, E_c;\quad P_b, A_b, D_b, O_b;\quad G, N, W \ldots)$$

| Strategic variables | Consumer variables | Competitor variables | Other variables |

Controllable variables | Uncontrollable variables

where

$Q_a$     is quantity demanded of a product A per period
$P_a$     is price of product A
$A_a$     is advertising and sales promotion for product A
$D_a$     is the design or quality of product A
$O_a$     is the number of retail outlets or other outlets for distribution of product A

$I_c$     is incomes of consumers/customers
$T_c$     is the tastes and preferences of consumers
$E_c$     is the expectation of consumers about future prices etc

$P_b$     is the prices of related goods (substitutes, complements)
$A_b$     is advertising/promotion for related goods
$D_b$     is design and quality of related goods
$O_b$     is the number of outlets for distribution of related goods

$G$     is government policy
$N$     is the number of people in the economy/potential market
$W$     represents the weather conditions

The demand function set out above is little more than common sense. But what firms should want to estimate or forecast is what future demand is likely to be. To do this, **an attempt should be made to quantify the relationship between demand for a product and the significant demand variables**. For example, a demand function might be measurable as

$$Q_a = 3{,}000 - 0.032\,P_a + 240\,A_a + 0.05\,O_a + 0.35\,P_b - 320\,A_b - 0.02\,O_b + 36\,I_b$$

There are two problems with measuring a demand function in this way.

(a) **Measurement**. There is the problem of deciding how to measure variables, especially qualitative variables such as product design, and consumer tastes.

(b)   **Valuation**. Then there is the mathematical problem of putting values to the 'constants' or coefficients for each variable (as in 4.19 above). This might be done using **regression analysis**.

# 5 Scenario planning

**Scenario building** is a more structured approach to developing views of the future. An individual scenario has to be internally consistent, but widely divergent scenarios may be equally relevant to strategic planning.

Because the environment is so complex, it is easy to become overwhelmed by the many factors. Firms therefore try to model the future and one technique is **scenario planning**.

**Key concept**

> **Scenario planning** is the development of a number of different views of the future to aid management decision-making.

## 5.1 Macro scenarios

**Macro scenarios** use macro-economic or political factors, creating alternative views of the future environment (eg global economic growth, political changes, interest rates). Macro scenarios developed because the activities of oil and resource companies (which are global and at one time were heavily influenced by political factors) needed techniques to deal with uncertainties.

## 5.2 Building scenarios

Keeping the scenario process simple is the way to get most out of scenarios.

(a)   Normally a **team** is selected to develop scenarios, preferably from diverse backgrounds. The team should include dissidents, who challenge the consensus, and some **reference outsiders** to offer different perspectives.

(b)   Most participants in the team draw on general reading and specialist knowledge.

### 5.2.1 Steps in scenario planning

Step 1   **Decide on the drivers for change**

- Environmental analysis helps determine key factors
- **At least** a ten-year time horizon is needed, to avoid simply extrapolating from the present
- Identify and select the **important** issues and **degree of certainty**

Step 2   **Bring drivers together into a viable framework**

- This relies almost on an intuitive ability to make patterns out of soft data, so is the hardest stage
- Items identified can be brought together as mini-scenarios
- There might be many possible trends, but these can be grouped together

Step 3   **Produce seven to nine mini-scenarios**. The underlying logic of the connections between the items can be explored.

**Step 4**     **Group mini-scenarios into two or three larger scenarios containing all topics.**

- This generates most debate and is likely to highlight fundamental issues

- More than three scenarios will confuse people

- The scenarios should be complementary not opposite. They should be equally likely. There is no good or bad scenario

- The scenarios should be tested to ensure they hang together. If not, go back    to Step 1

**Step 5**     **Write the scenarios**

- The scenarios should be written up in the form most suitable for managers taking decisions based on them

- Most scenarios are qualitative rather than quantitative in nature

**Step 6**     **Identify issues arising**

- Determine the most **critical outcomes**, or **branching points** which are critical to the long-term survival of the organisation

- Role play can be used to test what the scenarios mean to 'key actors' involved in the future of the business

## 5.3 Industry scenarios

An **industry scenario** is an internally consistent view of an **industry's** future structure. A set of industry scenarios is selected to reflect a range of possible futures. The **entire range**, not the most **likely** 'future', is used to design a competitive strategy. The process is as follows.

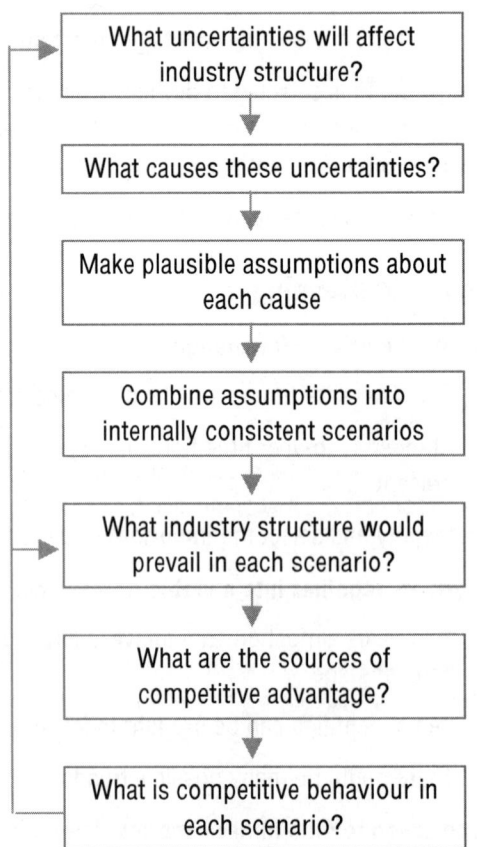

## 5.4 Using scenarios to formulate competitive strategy

(a)    A strategy built in response to only **one scenario is risky**, whereas one supposed to cope with them **all might be expensive**.

(b)    **Choosing scenarios as a basis for decisions about competitive strategy**. This is summarised in the table below.

| Approach | Comment |
|---|---|
| **Assume the most probable** | This appears to be common sense, but this choice puts too much faith in the scenario process and guesswork. A less probable scenario may be one whose **failure** to occur would have the **worst** consequences for the firm. |
| **Hope for the best** | A firm designs a strategy based on the scenario most attractive to the firm: wishful thinking. |
| **Hedge** | The firm chooses the strategy that produces **satisfactory** results under **all** scenarios. **Hedging, however, is not optimal**. The **low risk** is paid for by a **low reward**. |
| **Flexibility** | A firm taking this approach plays a wait and see game. This means that the firm waits to follow others. It is more secure, but sacrifices first-mover advantages. |
| **Influence** | A firm will try and influence the future, for example by influencing demand for related products in order that its favoured scenario will be realised in events as they unfold. |

**Exam tip**

> In 2000, an old syllabus exam asked you to advise how scenario planning could help an academic publishing company. Note you were not asked to develop the scenario itself but show how the process could benefit the firm. A similar question was asked in December 2001.

### Marketing at Work

**Scenario planning in the paper industry**

Extracts from the *Financial Times*, 21 March 2001

If there is one thing managers are confident they understand, it is their business. So imagine the shock when they discover their assumptions about its future are probably wrong.

That was the experience of senior managers from *UPM-Kymmene*, one of the world's largest papermakers, when they embarked on a scenario-planning project led by the University of Strathclyde Graduate School of Business.

What could change things most radically was the **Internet**, which was little understood when the project began in 1997. As managers drew up possible scenarios for the paper industry, the Internet emerged as a serious threat to future demand.

To add value to the project, UPM invited IPC Media, the biggest customer of its Caledonian mill, to join in. IPC, then part of Reed Elsevier, publishes UK magazines ranging from *TV Times* to *Woman's Own*, *Country Life* and *New Musical Express*. Seven managers from UPM and three from IPC were interviewed about their perception of outside forces and concerns about the industry. The researchers synthesised the interviews into broad themes and presented them to the managers, whose overriding preoccupation then was the **volatile price of paper**.

This preoccupation was challenged as they spent two days developing three scenarios, naming them 'The Godfather', 'The Party of Invaders' and 'The New Constellations'.

The first examined what would happen if industry consolidation gave fewer, larger companies greater control over how quickly paper capacity expanded. This scenario has been at least partially realised with the merger of Stora of Sweden and Enso of Finland in 1998 and more recent acquisitions by European groups in the Americas and Asia.

The Invaders scenario examined how the Internet would affect consumers and demand for paper. The New Constellations considered how tense relationships between paper manufacturers and publishers, based on price and volume, might be replaced by greater co-operation.

One thing that has changed is UPM's approach to its customers, says Mr Borthwick. 'We've recognised very clearly and are very focused on delivering value, rather than just using the traditional commodity-type selling approach'.

This shift led to the concept of 'synergy bank' through which UPM and its customers could benefit by helping each other. The paper manufacturer now offers customers advice on supply chain management, and they provide feedback on sales and readers.

Mr Burt is convinced, from his work with UPM and subsequently with a whisky company and a consulting firm in Scotland, that scenario planning leads to major changes in thinking.

Peter Barber, manufacturing director of IPC Media, says the publisher has reduced paper costs in a number of ways, partly thanks to the Strathclyde work. But he believes the big issues raised would have been better aimed at board directors.

Mr Borthwick does not expect demand for paper to slump in the foreseeable future. But he can imagine there might be a generational shift when children who have grown up with computers become decision-makers.

*Website address*: www.paperX.com

# 6 Market sensing

**FAST FORWARD**

Some market signals are hard to pick up, even though they may be of long-term significance. Managers thus need to be skilled in **market sensing**.

**Key concept**

**Market sensing**: 'how those ..... inside the company understand and react to the market place and the way it is changing' (Piercy, *Market-Led Strategic Change,* 1997).

**Market sensing** does **not** relate to the gathering and processing of information (**market research**) but how the information is **interpreted** and **understood** by decision makers in the company. It is related, therefore, to *Johnson and Scholes'* concept of the **recipe**.

**Exam tip**

The difference between market sensing and market research came up in December 1999 in an essay question.

 Marketing at Work

(a) *Piercy* cites the *Encyclopaedia Britannica*. Its managers simply did not believe that a small CD-ROM would replace the traditional book. In Autumn 1998, Encyclopaedia Britannica announced it was going to put its entire output on CD-ROM and abandon paper.

(b) In contrast, the horror novelist *Stephen King* decided in 2000 to publish a novel, chapter by chapter, on the Internet, for a 'voluntary' fee of $1. King abandoned the experiment because many people downloading the material did not pay, and there was not huge demand.

In short, market sensing failed. For reference, such as a dictionary or encyclopaedia, the ability to search is most important. People treat novels and narrative fiction in a different way, perhaps.

Piercy identifies the **myths of marketing information**.

- We need more information
- We need it quicker
- We can learn everything
- We know what our information needs are
- We know what we do **not** need to know
- We measure what matters
- We know what we know (and do not first accept what we are told)
- We know **who** decides what we know
- We know what this information means

These myths are countermanded by practical organisational realities.

(a) **Organisational culture controls how information is interpreted and how the company's 'picture of the world' is treated.**

(b) 'Knowledge is power'; **information is a weapon** in organisational politics.

(c) Defining the 'market' and forecasting sales is often a matter for **negotiation**. Marketing information can produce a lot of conflicting evidence. Where does a niche end and the market begin?

(d) The significance of information depends in part on the choices managers make.

Market sensing is a process in which managers can be drawn in to challenge their preconceptions and improve their understanding. Ideally, the process is one of discovery.

## 6.1 Process of market sensing

**Step 1**    **Capture** information by identifying the **environment** (eg five forces), the dimension (eg **substitute** products), the **time frame** and the **market**.

**Step 2**    **'Brainstorm'** the events in the environment that are currently developing and assess the probability of their occurrence and their likely effect.

**Step 3**    **Categorise** the event on the basis of probability and effect.

| | |
|---|---|
| Utopia: | likely, desirable |
| Dreams: | unlikely, desirable |
| Danger: | likely, undesirable |
| Future risks: | unlikely, undesirable |
| Things to watch: | medium likelihood, neutral effect |

| Effect of event | Probability of event | | |
|---|---|---|---|
| | High | | Low |
| | Utopia | | Field of dreams |
| | | Things to watch | |
| | Danger | | Future crises |

**Step 4** Answer the following questions

- Where are we planning for Utopia?
- Where are we planning for dangers?
- Where are we monitoring the factors in the MkIS?

It may be quite possible that managers have not made plans to deal with these eventualities or that the information systems do not report on these key issues.

**Step 5** **Link** conclusions from the sensing approach explicitly to **marketing plans**.

**Step 6** Encourage **participation** across **functions** and across **levels**. (Customer service staff have a very different perspective from the board of directors.)

**Step 7** Where necessary, change information provision to provide a richer or more relevant picture of the world, whilst avoiding:

- Information overload
- Confusion as the existing model appears outdated
- Fear of making any decisions at all
- Creating conflict between groups who may have shared a sense of direction

# 7 Knowledge management

> **FAST FORWARD**
>
> The aim of **knowledge management** is to organise and make available all the knowledge an organisation has, whether formally recorded or locked inside individuals' heads.

Knowledge management is a relatively new concept in business theory. It is connected with the theory of the **learning organisation** and founded on the idea that knowledge is a major source of competitive advantage in business. The aim of knowledge management is to exploit existing knowledge and to create new knowledge so that it may be exploited in turn. This is not easy. All organisations possess a great deal of data, but it tends to be unorganised and inaccessible. It is often locked up inside the memories of people who do not realise the value of what they know. Even when it is recorded in some way it may be difficult and time consuming to get at, as is the case with most paper archives.

Studies have indicated that 20 to 30 percent of company resources are wasted because organisations are not aware of what knowledge they already possess. *Lew Platt,* Ex-Chief Executive of *Hewlett Packard,* has articulated this, saying 'If only HP knew what HP knows, we would be three times as profitable'.

## 7.1 Data, information and knowledge

> **FAST FORWARD**
>
> **Data** is facts; **information** lies in the relationships between processed facts; **knowledge** is created when patterns are recognised in information.

There is an important conceptual hierarchy underpinning knowledge management. This distinguishes between **data**, **information** and **knowledge**. The distinctions are not clear-cut and, to some extent, are differences of degree rather than kind. An understanding of the terms is best approached by considering the relationships between them.

We start with **data**. Data typically consists of individual facts, but in a business context may include more complex items such as opinions, reactions and beliefs. It is important to realise that a quantity of data, no matter how large, does not constitute **information**.

**Information** is data that is **organised** in some useful way. For instance, an individual credit sale will produce a single invoice identifying the goods, the price, the customer, the date of the sale and so on. These things are data: their usefulness does not extend beyond the purpose of the invoice, which is to collect the sum due. Even if we possess a copy of every invoice raised during a financial year, we still only have data. However, if we **process** that data we start to create information. For instance, a simple combination of analysis and arithmetic enables us to state total sales for the year, to break that down into sales for each product and to each customer, to identify major customers and so on. These are pieces of information: they are useful for the **management** of the business, rather than just inputs into its administrative systems.

Nevertheless, we still have not really produced any **knowledge**. Information may be said to consist of the **relationships between** items of data, as when we combine turnover with customer details to discover which accounts are currently important and which are not. We need to go beyond this in order to create knowledge.

The conceptual difference between data and information is fairly easy to grasp: it lies chiefly in the **processes** that produce the one from the other. The difference between information and knowledge is more complex and varies from setting to setting. This is not surprising, since knowledge itself is more complex than the information it derives from.

A good starting point for understanding the difference is an appreciation of the importance of pattern: knowledge tends to originate in the **discovery of trends or patterns in information**. To return to our invoicing example, suppose we found that certain combinations of goods purchased were typical of certain customers. We could then build up some interesting customer profiles that would enhance our market segmentation and this in turn might influence our overall strategy, since we could identify likely prospects for cross-selling effort.

Another important aspect of the differences between data, information and knowledge is the relevance of **context**. Our sales invoice is meaningless outside its context; if you, as a marketing person, found an invoice in the office corridor, it would be little more than waste paper to you, though no doubt, the accounts people would like it back. However, if you found a list of customers in order of annual turnover, that would be rather more interesting from a marketing point of view. The information is **useful outside of its original context** of the accounts office.

This idea also applies to the difference between information and knowledge. If you were a visitor to a company and found a copy of the turnover listing, it would really only be useful to you if you were trying to sell the same sort of thing to the same customers. Its value outside its context would be small. However, if you found a marketing report that suggested, based on evidence, that customers were becoming more interested in quality and less interested in price, that would be applicable to a wide range of businesses, and possibly of strategic importance.

Here is a table that summarises the progression from data to knowledge.

| | Data | Information | Knowledge |
|---|---|---|---|
| **Nature** | Facts | Relationships between processed facts | Patterns discerned in information |
| **Importance of context** | Total | Some | Context independent |
| **Importance to business** | Mundane | Probably useful for management | May be strategically useful |

There is one final important point to note here and that is that the **progression** from data to knowledge is not the same in all circumstances. The scale is moveable and depends on the general complexity of the setting. Something may be **information** within its own context. Something similar may be **knowledge** in a different context. The difference will often be associated with the scale of operations. Take the example of a customer going into insolvent liquidation with £200,000 outstanding on its account. For a small supplier with an annual turnover of, say, £10 million, a bad debt of this size would be of strategic importance and might constitute a threat to its continued existence. Advance notice of the possibility would be valuable **knowledge**. However, for a company operating on a global scale, the bad debt write-off would be annoying but still only one item in a list of bad debts – **data**, in other words.

## 7.2 Knowledge management systems

Data, information and knowledge can be created, stored and manipulated with appropriate IT systems.

Recognition of the value of knowledge and understanding of the need to organise data and make it accessible have provoked the development of sophisticated IT systems.

**Office automation systems** are IT applications that improve productivity in an office. These include word processing and voice messaging systems.

**Groupware**, such as **Lotus Notes** provides functions for collaborative work groups. In a sales context, for instance, it would provide a facility for recording and retrieving all the information relevant to individual customers, including notes of visits, notes of telephone calls and basic data like address, credit terms and contact name. These items could be updated by anyone who had contact with a customer and would then be available to all sales people.

Groupware also provides such facilities as messaging, appointment scheduling, to-do lists, and jotters.

An **intranet** is an internal network used to share information using Internet technology and protocols. The **firewall** surrounding an intranet fends off unauthorised access from outside the organisation. Each employee has a browser, used to access a server computer that holds corporate information on a wide variety of topics, and in some cases also offers access to the Internet. Applications include company newspapers, induction material, procedure and policy manuals and internal databases.

(a)     Savings accrue from the elimination of storage, printing and distribution of documents that can be made available to employees online.

(b)     Documents online are often more widely used than those that are kept filed away, especially if the document is bulky (eg manuals) and needs to be searched. This means that there are improvements in productivity and efficiency.

(c)     It is much easier to update information in electronic form.

An **expert system** is a computer program that captures **human expertise** in a limited domain of knowledge. Such software uses a knowledge base that consists of facts, concepts and the relationships between them and uses pattern-matching techniques to solve problems. For example, many financial institutions now use expert systems to process straightforward loan applications. The user enters certain key facts into the system such as the loan applicant's name and most recent addresses, their income and monthly outgoings, and details of other loans. The system will then:

(a) Check the facts given against its database to see whether the applicant has a good previous credit record.

(b) Perform calculations to see whether the applicant can afford to repay the loan.

(c) Make a judgement as to what extent the loan applicant fits the lender's profile of a good risk (based on the lender's previous experience).

A decision is then suggested, based on the results of this processing.

IT systems can be used to store vast amounts of data in accessible form. A **data warehouse** receives data from operational systems, such as a sales order processing system, and stores it in its most fundamental form, without any summarisation of transactions. Analytical and query software is provided so that reports can be produced at any level of summarisation and incorporating any comparisons or relationships desired.

The value of a data warehouse is enhanced when **datamining** software is used. True datamining software **discovers previously unknown relationships** and provides insights that cannot be obtained through ordinary summary reports. These hidden patterns and relationships constitute **knowledge**, as defined above, and can be used to guide decision making and to predict future behaviour. Datamining is thus a contribution to organisational learning.

 Marketing at Work

**Wal-mart**

The American retailer *Wal-Mart* discovered an unexpected relationship between the sale of nappies and beer! Wal-Mart found that both tended to sell at the same time, just after working hours, and concluded that men with small children stopped off to buy nappies on their way home, and bought beer at the same time. Logically, therefore, if the two items were put in the same shopping aisle, sales of both should increase. Wal-Mart tried this and it worked.

Here is an amended version of our earlier table. This one includes the relevant IT systems.

|  | **Data** | **Information** | **Knowledge** |
|---|---|---|---|
| **Nature** | Facts | Relationships between processed facts | Patterns discerned in information |
| **Importance of context** | Total | Some | Context independent |
| **Importance to business** | Mundane | Probably useful for management | May be strategically useful |
| **Relevant IT systems** | Office automation<br>Data warehouse | Groupware<br>Expert systems<br>Report writing software<br>Intranet | Datamining<br>Intranet<br>Expert systems |

We will conclude this section with an example of the modern approach to knowledge management. You will notice that the IT system eventually developed looks like something half way between groupware and a database. However, the strategic impact of the system and its ability to create new corporate knowledge mean that it is properly described as a knowledge management system.

Notice also that the knowledge originates with people who are fairly low down in the hierarchy and who would not normally be described as knowledge workers. This illustrates the very important principle that valuable knowledge can be found at all levels and is not the prerogative of an elite.

 ## Marketing at Work

### Servicing *Xerox* copiers

Our story begins with researchers working on artificial intelligence who wanted to see if they could replace the paper documentation that Xerox technicians used on the road with an expert system.

The team found that it was indeed possible to build software that could do just that. But when they showed their first efforts to technicians, the response was underwhelming.

What kept technicians from finding fixes was not that the documentation was paper-based but that it didn't address all the potential problems. And not all problems were predictable. Machines in certain regions could react to extreme temperatures in different ways. A can of Mountain Dew overturned in one part of a machine could wreak havoc in another seemingly unconnected part. Technicians could handle these mishaps quickly only if they had seen them before or if another technician had run into a similar problem and shared the results.

Once the conversations with technicians revealed this gap in information sharing, the researchers realised that AI was the wrong approach. What Xerox needed instead was knowledge management. It wasn't a smart computer program that was going to fix these things, it was sharing the best ways to make these repairs.

When the researchers realised they needed to look at the way technicians work, they spent time in the field, following the technicians from call to call. What they observed proved invaluable – knowledge sharing was already unofficially ingrained in the organisation. Most striking was not how technicians solved common problems, but what they did when they came up against a tricky, intermittent one. Often they called one another on radios provided by the company. And in informal gatherings they shared vexing problems and their fixes.

Meanwhile, another researcher was busy comparing the way French and U.S. technicians worked. He discovered that, while French technicians appeared to work from immaculate, uniform documentation put out by headquarters, their real solutions also came from a second set of documentation – notes they carried with them detailing what they'd learned. It was from that database that researchers started building the first laptop-based knowledge-sharing system.

The researchers took the first iteration to France and began a series of exhaustive sessions with the French experts in the Xerox headquarters outside Paris. In those sessions, something magical happened: The system took on the shape of the people working on it, evolving with each suggestion from the actual users.

But the worldwide customer service group didn't take the project seriously. Nobody believed that the knowledge of the technicians was really valuable. So, working stealthily, outside the realm of worldwide management, the research team gave laptops and the fledging program to 40 technicians and matched them with a control group of technicians who relied solely on their own knowledge when fixing machines. After two months, the group with the laptops had 10 percent lower costs and 10 percent lower service time than those without – and the control group was jealous of those with the system.

By 1998, the system was officially deployed in the United States and began to make its way around the globe. Today it has more than 15,000 user tips, with more being added every day. The hope is that by 2002 it will be distributed worldwide to the company's 25,000 technicians. And already success stories abound. One technician in Montreal authored a tip about a 50-cent fuse-holder replacement that caused a chronic problem with a high-speed colour copier. A Brazilian technician had the same problem, and his customer wanted the $40,000 machine replaced. When he found the tip from Montreal, he fixed the machine in minutes. Current estimates have the system saving Xerox at least $7 million in time and replacement costs. It's tales like those that make senior management happy.

Adapted from Meg Mitchell, *www.darwinmag.com* February 2001

# 8 Small organisations

**FAST FORWARD**

**Small organisations** have their special problems of cost, cash flow, marketing and management.

## 8.1 Problems

Small organisations have their own problems.

(a) **Lack of economies of scale**: a small business will not qualify for the best purchasing terms from suppliers; will probably have to pay a higher rate of interest on its bank borrowings; and will not be able to afford to employ specialist staff, instead having to buy in their services at very high hourly rates.

(b) **External factors**. It is a constant complaint from businesses in the UK that there is an ever-increasing **burden of regulation and compliance** upon them. To the extent that this is true, this burden is likely to weigh most heavily on the small, owner managed business, with its very limited administrative capacity.

(c) **Over reliance** on a few key individuals can produce catastrophe if one of them leaves or is sick for a prolonged period.

(d) **Small market areas or a restricted range of products** mean that small businesses are particularly vulnerable to environmental changes. They tend to have all their eggs in one basket.

(e) **Cannot raise money**. Many small businesses complain they are unable to raise finance and rely heavily on bank loans. (Many proprietors, however, are unwilling to sacrifice control in order to raise bank finance.)

(f) Strategic decision making is likely to be heavily influenced by the experience and priorities of the owner(s) of small- and medium-sized businesses. These people not only tend to retain ultimate control of their businesses but tend to exert firm control over their more junior managers, partly by their recruitment policies and partly by their expressed preference.

## 8.2 The start up businesses

In addition to the problems that can affect small businesses generally, the **start-up** business has its own particular weaknesses.

(a) **Lack of profit**. A new venture is unlikely to turn an accounting profit for two to three years because significant investment has to be made in such things as premises, stocks, recruitment and business development before turnover starts to build up. It is essential, therefore, that start ups have the financial resources to run at a loss for several years.

(b) **Poor cashflow**. Managing cashflow is a demanding job: many owner managers do not possess the necessary skills. The problem is exacerbated when the business is under-capitalised, which is often the case with start ups. A further problem is that large firms often fail to pay their small business suppliers on time.

(c)    New owner managers are often **deficient in other skills** besides financial ones. New businesses are often founded by a person, or group of people, with expertise in only one or two business disciplines. Typically, these will be selling and/or technological expertise. Knowledge of procurement, logistics, personnel management, production engineering, marketing techniques and the essential detail of administration will often be missing. As a result, the aspiring sole trader or partnership is likely to find that unforeseen problems arise and consume an inordinate amount of time, hampering the deployment of the skills the managers do possess.

(d)    **Marketing expertise** is a particularly crucial requirement for the new business. Where the business is founded to exploit a new technical development, there is a long journey from the initial idea to market success. A fertile target market must be discovered by market research or created by promotional techniques; distribution systems must be set up and, perhaps most important of all, a suitable price must be set. Where distribution is to be through agents or wholesalers, as will often be the case, important discounts must be conceded without undermining either immediate cash flow or ultimate profitability.

(e)    Another important area of skill that is frequently lacking in new businesses is **personnel management**. Information technology applications have reduced the requirement for staff in terms of overall numbers but have increased the requirement for staff with a high level of specialised skills. Whether staff are engaged in large or small numbers, they must be managed carefully if they are to be motivated to support the firm's efforts. All too frequently, staff are taken for granted, poorly organised and even abused.

(f)    The effect of the **business cycle** should not be overlooked. A business started up at the peak of the cycle is likely to have only three or four years in which to establish itself and secure its position before the economic trend starts to decline. When times are hard, it will be difficult for most businesses even to maintain turnover and expansion will be a remote dream. Larger customers are likely to be merciless in their exploitation of small business's unwillingness to press them for payment, while suppliers will be equally merciless in demanding payment. During the trough of the cycle, larger businesses will cut costs by reducing their headcounts. The option of self-employment is likely to be quite attractive to some of those made redundant, but their prospects are not good: they will be starting up in a sluggish market and in the face of increased competition – from each other.

## 8.3 Developing the small business in the global market place

Many small businesses adopt a focus strategy simply because it is appropriate to the scale of their resources and the inclinations of their owner-managers. However, success in a niche business is as dependent on good marketing and strategic management as in any other strategy. The chosen segment must be understood in detail and its needs clearly served by the product offering. Standards of service must be kept high but costs must be carefully controlled. A particular problem of the niche business is the temptation to expand sales at the cost of cutting margins; this is particularly dangerous if the business is under-capitalised, as is often the case with smaller enterprises.

The forces of globalisation, enabled and amplified by the growth of Internet trading, have led many small businesses into international trade. There are several routes that seem particularly appropriate to such businesses.

(a)    Some small businesses gain global exposure and experience as **sub-contractors** to global companies.

(b)    Technologically highly sophisticated niche businesses may operate globally from their inception simply to find an adequate number of customers.

(c)     An expanding **network** of contracts and co-operation may link a small firm to the global market place.

## Chapter Roundup

- **Innovation** is a major responsibility of modern management, particularly in commercial organisations. This is because both technology and society are developing extremely rapidly; new products must be matched with new market opportunities if businesses are to survive and prosper. Innovation in marketing is particularly important, since **marketing** provides much of the **interface** between the **organisation** and its **rapidly changing environment**.

- **Small companies** appear to produce a disproportionate number of innovations because the sheer number of attempts by small-scale entrepreneurs means that some ventures will survive. The 90 to 99 per cent that fail are distributed widely throughout society and receive little attention.

- Companies can be organised and run in a way that stimulates innovation. This depends in large part on practical measures.

- **Future orientated** firms see the future as something that can be influenced and, in cases of industry transformation, created. A firm's activity to influence its future in part depends on the outlook of its management.

- Conventionally, **forecasting techniques** can be used to predict demand in the short to medium term. However, such techniques depend on the reliability of past data. The uncertainties in using statistical forecasting to predict the future are considerable.

- Gap analysis is an important discipline for dealing with the future in very practical terms by directing attention to what needs to be done.

- **Intuitive** or **judgemental forecasting** is sometimes used. The **Delphi** technique aims to ensure that group dynamics do not take over from consideration of the issues.

- Market forecasts and sales forecasts complement each other. The market forecast should be carried out first of all and should cover a longer period of time. The modelling of a demand function depends on quantifying complex relationships.

- **Scenario building** is a more structured approach to developing views of the future. An individual scenario has to be internally consistent, but widely divergent scenarios may be equally relevant to strategic planning.

- Some market signals are hard to pick up, even though they may be of long-term significance. Managers thus need to be skilled in **market sensing**.

- The aim of **knowledge management** is to organise and make available all the knowledge an organisation has, whether formally recorded or locked inside individuals' heads.

- **Data** is facts; **information** lies in the relationships between processed facts; **knowledge** is created when patterns are recognised in information.

- Data, information and knowledge can be created, stored and manipulated with appropriate IT systems.

- **Small organisations** have their special problems of cost, cash flow, marketing and management.

## Quick Quiz

1    Identify two views of the future.

2    What is gap analysis?

3    What do statistical forecasts do?

4    What problems underlie using a panel of experts to develop a forecast?

5    What is a model?

6    What is sales potential?

7    What is a scenario?

8    Outline a step process for building scenarios.

9    What is market sensing?

10    What characteristics distinguish knowledge from information?

## Answers to Quick Quiz

1    There are likely to be elements of **continuity** and **radical change**

2    The comparison of the sum of projections into the future with stated objectives

3    They attempt to predict the future, assuming it will resemble patterns established in the past

4    In group discussions, reputation and force of personality can bias the ultimate verdict

5    Anything used to represent anything else

6    An estimate of the part of a market that is within the possible reach of a product

7    The development of a number of different views of the future to aid management decision making

8    Decide on the change drivers; assemble them in a viable framework; produce mini-scenarios; group into larger scenarios covering all topics; write the scenarios; identify issues arising

9    The way people understand and react to the marketplace and the way it is changing

10    Knowledge discerns trends; is useful outside its original context and may be useful strategically

## Action Programme Review

The benefit of having someone from another department fill out the diagnostic is that you will get a different perspective on the business; Hamel and Prahalad talk about creating industries not markets.

Now try Question 2 at the end of the Study Text

# Part C

## Strategic marketing decisions

# Strategic advantage

## Syllabus content

- Building competitive capability and approaches to leveraging capability to create advantage across geographically diverse markets
- Porter's generic strategies
- Strategic marketing decisions for pioneers, challengers, followers and niche players
- Critical evaluation of strategic options in relation to shareholder value, using appropriate decision tools
- The contribution of value based marketing

# Introduction

Strategic choices are make in the context of an approach to strategic management. We have already discussed several possible approaches to marketing strategy. In this chapter we look in more detail at ways in which strategic advantage may be created. Note that these ideas are equally applicable to any basic strategic method, though they are most likely to be used in a more or less deliberate approach.

Any activity in any organisation should contribute in some way to the overall mission  of the organisation. For business organisations it is necessary that the strategy should be directed towards maintaining and enhancing **shareholder value** and this concept is discussed in Section 1. **Shareholder value is the overall measure of strategic success**. If you have already worked through the BPP Study Text for the *Analysis and Evaluation* module of the Stage 3 syllabus, this topic will already be familiar to you. Note also that shareholder value actually appears in Element 3 of your syllabus. We cover it here because it seems to us to be of sufficient importance to your background awareness to warrant an early introduction.

Shareholder value has been proposed as a suitable measure of business success to replace purely profit-related, accounting-based measures. Some feel that these measures do not give a sufficiently rounded picture of the strategic progress of an enterprise. Shareholder value is still an accounting concept, albeit a modern one, and a full understanding depends on some knowledge of the financial arithmetic involved in the **discounting** of future cash flows to a **net present value**. These are covered in an annex at the end of the chapter and, if you are at all unsure about these ideas, we would advise you to study the annex before you look at Section 1.

The remaining sections of this chapter discuss the development of competitive advantage and the means that can be used to achieve it. The context here is that the business mission is understood,  the environment has been studied and we are aware of the strengths and weaknesses of our organisation.

Having determined the extent of the gap that needs to be filled, we can now turn our attention to the strategies needed to fill it. The important point to recognise is that there will almost always be **alternatives**. Identifying these alternatives and carefully evaluating the options is an essential part of the planning process.

We identified three categories of strategic choice.

(a)     The **competitive strategies** are the strategies an organisation will pursue for competitive advantage (a condition which is proof against 'erosion by competitor behaviour or industry evolution'). They determine **how you compete**.

(b)     **Product-market strategies** (which markets you should enter or leave, which products you should sell) determine **where you compete** and the direction of growth.

(c)     Institutional strategies (ie relationships with other organisations) determine the **method of growth**.

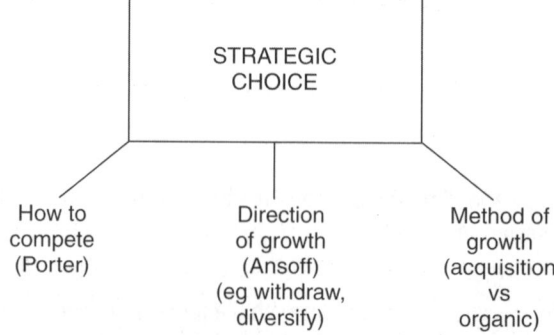

In some instances you might find it difficult to distinguish between **corporate strategy** and **marketing strategy**.

(a)     **Corporate strategy** will ultimately involve decisions and direction for all functions of the operation.

(b)     **Marketing strategy** incorporates decisions relating to the positioning of the marketing mix to exploit and develop product/market opportunities.

# 1 Shareholder value analysis

FAST FORWARD

Shareholder value analysis may be used to measure corporate (and hence management) performance in terms of benefit created for shareholders.

**Shareholder value analysis** (SVA) is a method of approaching the problem of business control by focusing on the **creation of value for shareholders**. Independent financial analysts measure the **value offered by a company's shares** by considering the **market value** of all the shares in existence (the **market capitalisation**), in the light of the **company's prospects** for generating both cash and capital growth in the future. If the current market capitalisation is less than the estimate of actual value, then the shares are undervalued. Investment is necessary to produce either assets that grow in value or actual cash surpluses, so the process of shareholder value analysis is essentially one of estimating the likely effectiveness of the company's **current investment decisions**. It is thus both a system for judging the worth of current investment proposals and for judging the performance of the managers who are responsible for the company's performance.

In the past, marketing managers have tended to pursue purely **marketing objectives**, such as sales growth, market share, customer satisfaction and brand recognition. None of these marketing objectives *necessarily* translates into increased shareholder value, and as a result, marketing has suffered from a lack of perceived relevance to true business value. An emphasis on profitability as a measure of success has led to a certain amount of **short-termism** in strategic management, with an emphasis on **containing and reducing current costs** in order to boost current profits. Unfortunately, this approach tends to underestimate the longer-term effect of such action and can lead to corporate decline. Investment in **intangible assets** such as brands can make a positive contribution to long-term shareholder value.

## 1.1 Computing value

FAST FORWARD

Shareholder value created by past performance is measured by **economic profit**. The **cashflow** approach is more appropriate for assessing plans for the future.

According to *Doyle* (2002), the extent of a company's success may be measured in two ways. The first is by using the concept of **economic profit** (trademarked by Stern Stewart and Company as **Economic Value Added**®). The expression *economic profit* is used to distinguish the measure from **accounting profit**, which is computed according to the strict rules of accountancy. These feature, in particular, the principle of **prudence**. This makes it impossible for accounting profit to recognise spending on pure research, for instance, as an investment in an asset, since there is no guarantee that it will ever produce anything worth having; the same would be true of much marketing spending on building long-term effectiveness.

**Economic profit** is created when the return on a company's capital employed exceeds the cost of that capital.

Economic profit = NOPAT − (capital employed × cost of capital)

where NOPAT is net operating profit after tax.

Cost of capital is, effectively, the return that has to be made to providers of capital in the form of interest on loans and dividends on shares. It may be calculated as a **weighted average**, which takes account of both the expectations of shareholders and lenders who have provided loans. (Buying shares generally entails greater risk than making a loan, so shareholders generally demand higher returns than lenders. This is why a weighted average figure must be used.)

Economic profit is related to capital employed by **return on capital employed** (ROCE). This is a percentage and may thus be compared directly with cost of capital. When ROCE exceeds the cost of capital (r), economic value is created: under these circumstances (ROCE > r), the company is offering a greater return on capital than is available elsewhere.

Economic profit is useful for examining the company's **current and past performance**, but is less useful for assessing **future prospects**. For that purpose it is more appropriate to use the **cash flow approach**. Be aware that both the economic profit method and the cash flow method should produce the same result when applied to a particular company.

The **cash flow approach** may be used to estimate the degree of economic value a company may be expected to create in the future. It is based on an estimation of likely future **cash flows**, both positive and negative, as indicated in the corporate plans. (A cash flow is simply a sum of money paid or received by the company.) This is easier to do than to compute future NOPAT, because it is far less complex and depends on far fewer variables.

### 1.1.1 Discounting cash flows

Because the SVA technique depends very much on the estimation of future cash flows arising from current investments, it is necessary to use **discounting arithmetic** in order to make the necessary judgements. You may be asked to do some simple discounting in your exam, so we provide an explanation in the Annex to this chapter.

### 1.1.2 Business risk

**Business risk**. Some businesses are inherently **riskier** than others: the degree of risk can be measured by the degree of predictability that attaches to its expected cash flows. A low risk business will have steady income from period to period, without any unexpected highs and lows. A high-risk business will have returns that vary wildly and unexpectedly from period to period, though its total long-term return may be as great or greater than the low-risk operation. Generally, **investors are risk averse** and, as a result, they demand higher returns from high-risk businesses than from low-risk ones. The high-risk business must therefore use a **higher cost of capital** in its shareholder value analysis than the low-risk business.

## 1.2 Value based management

**FAST FORWARD**

> Purely marketing objectives are no longer acceptable; value based management aims always to **maximise shareholder value** by developing competitive advantage.

*Doyle* (2003), tells us that business success should be measured by shareholder value analysis because of the property rights of shareholders and the 'pressures to oust management that does not deliver competitive returns'. Purely marketing objectives are no longer acceptable to investors or the analysts whose reports they rely on. What Doyle calls **value based management** is based on three elements.

(a)   A **belief** that maximising shareholder returns is the objective of the firm

(b)   The **principles**, or strategic foundations of value are first, to target those market segments where profits can be made and second, to develop competitive advantage 'that enables both the customer and the firm to create value'.

(c)   The **processes** 'concern how strategies should be developed, resources allocated and performance measured'.

SVA is particularly appropriate for judging strategic investment decisions and applies the same principles that have been used for appraising investment in such tangible assets as premises and plant for many years. It is necessary to consider both the **cash costs** of the strategic investment to be made, and the **positive cash flows** that are expected to be produced by it. These may then be discounted to a net present value (NPV) using an appropriate cost of capital, and a judgement made on the basis of the NPV. Any specifically marketing proposal, such as an enhanced advertising spend or a new discount structure may be assessed in this way, though it will almost certainly be necessary to take advice from the finance function on the process.

Estimating the value of such investments forms one part of basic shareholder value analysis. Doyle also recommends that when considering the total value of a business, it is also necessary to consider the probable **residual value** of the business. This is the present value of cash flows in the more distant future, outside the normal planning horizon, which Doyle suggests is five years. This assumes no special competitive advantage from current investments and simply uses the cost of capital as an estimate of the rate of return on investments.

### 1.2.1 Marketing assets

Value based management means that purely marketing investment proposals will be judged as described above. It will be necessary for marketing managers to justify their spending requests in such terms, on the basis that such spending is not a cost burden to be minimised but an investment in intangible assets such as the four that Doyle suggests.

- Marketing knowledge
- Brands
- Customer loyalty
- Strategic relationships with channel partners

The obstacle that lies in the path of this approach to marketing use of SVA is the common perception that marketing spending is merely a cost to be controlled and minimised. The onus is on marketing managers to demonstrate that their budgets do in fact create assets that provide competitive advantage for the business and that the benefits exceed the costs.

**Exam tip**

> The draft specimen paper for this exam included a 25 mark question on the theory of shareholder value. No computations were called for and the question was essentially an opportunity to explain what the shareholder value principle is, how it works and why it should be used.

### Reference

Strategy as Marketing, Doyle, P in *Images of Marketing* ed Cummings S and Wilson D, Blackwell Publishing Limited, 2003.

## 1.3 Value drivers

**FAST FORWARD**

> The creation of value depends on three categories of value driver: **financial**, **marketing** and **organisational**.

*Doyle* suggests that it is possible to identify the factors that are critical to the creation of shareholder value. These he calls **value drivers**; he divides them into three categories.

- **Financial**
- **Marketing**
- **Organisational**

It is important to remember that **the financial drivers should not be targeted directly**: they are objectives, not the components of strategy. The company influences them by the proper management of the **marketing** and **organisational** drivers.

### 1.3.1 Financial value drivers

There are four drivers of financial value.

- **Cash flow volume**
- **Cash flow timing**
- **Cash flow risk**
- **Cash flow sustainability**

### 1.3.2 Cash flow volume

Clearly, the higher that positive cash flows are and the lower negative cash flows are, the greater the potential for creating value.

**Profitability**. In the most simple terms, profit margin is measured by net operating profit after tax (NOPAT). NOPAT can be increased in three ways.

(a)    **Higher prices**. Marketing strategies such as building strong brands can enable the charging of premium prices. A particularly powerful route to higher prices is **innovation**, since desirable new products will normally justify increased prices.

(b)    **Reduced costs**. Cost reduction depends on increased efficiency in all aspects of the business operation.

(c)    **Volume increases**. Other things being equal, volume growth increases the absolute profit margin and may increase the profit rate as well

**Sales growth**. If increases in sales volume can be achieved without disproportionate increases in costs or, in particular, excessive discounting, positive cash flows will naturally increase. Increased sales can also bring increased **economies of scale**, which will take the form of reduced costs of all types. Overheads are spread over greater volumes and purchasing discounts reduce the cost of sales.

**Investment**. Investment provides the resources necessary to do business. These include premises, equipment, stocks, transport and well-trained, experienced staff. However, ill-advised investment can destroy value faster than profitable investment can create it, so any proposal for investment must be judged on its potential for generating acceptable returns. The **net present value** (NPV) approach (described in the Annex to this chapter) is the investment appraisal method best suited to the shareholder value principle, in that any project that has a NPV greater than zero provides a return greater than the cost of capital used in the discounting arithmetic.

### 1.3.3 Cash flow timing

The further into the future a cash flow occurs, the lower its present value. If positive cash flows can be achieved in the near future and negative ones put off until later, the company benefits. This is why companies and individuals put off paying their bills for as long as possible. Buying on credit and selling for cash is another approach.

Doyle gives five examples of ways that marketing managers can accelerate cash flows.

(a)    **Faster new product development** processes, including the use of cross-functional teams and conducting projects concurrently rather than consecutively.

(b)    **Accelerated market penetration** through pre-marketing campaigns, early trial promotions and word-of-mouth campaigns using early adopters.

(c)    **Network effects**: that is, achieving market status as the industry standard. This is a self-reinforcing, feedback effect in which success leads to even greater success. It was seen, for instance, in the videotape market when *VHS* displaced the technically superior *Betamax*. Aggressive marketing measures to build the installed base are required.

(d)    **Strategic alliances** speed market penetration, normally by providing extra distribution effort.

(e)    **Exploiting brand assets**: new products launched under a suitable, established brand are likely to be more successful than others.

### 1.3.4 Cash flow risk

The higher the degree of **risk** associated with future cash flows, the greater the proportion of them that will not actually come to pass. High risk can produce low returns as easily as high ones. Apart from this overall averaging effect, there is the disadvantage associated with **infrequent large cash flows**: failure of such a cash flow to occur can have catastrophic consequences. Risk is also associated with timing: the further into the future that a cash flow is expected to occur, the greater the risk associated with it, since there is a greater likelihood of **changed conditions** affecting its eventual value and even whether or not it actually occurs.

Doyle suggests that the most effective marketing route to reduced cash flow risk is 'to increase customer satisfaction, loyalty and retention' by deploying such techniques as loyalty programmes and measures to increase satisfaction. Building **good channel relationships** also helps, both by building an element of loyalty based on good service and by sharing information on demand patterns to smooth stock fluctuations.

### 1.3.5 Cash flow sustainability

A single positive cash flow is useful. A positive cash flow that is repeated at regular intervals is much more useful. Quite apart from the extra cash involved, sustainable cash flows make it easier to plan for the future. Positive cash flows derive from the creation of competitive advantage and a sustainable advantage will lead to sustainable cash flows.

There are many **threats to sustainable profits**, including aggressive competition from copies and substitutes and, particularly in B2B markets, the bargaining power of customers. Part of the role of marketing management is to counter such threats using techniques such as those outlined above in connection with reducing risk.

Sustainable advantage also offers a benefit in the form of **enhanced options** for future development. Just as financial options to buy and sell securities and currency have their own value, so a strategy that creates **real options** for future activity has a value over and above any immediate competitive advantage it may offer. A simple example is the development of a completely new product for a given market that can also be made viable in other markets at low incremental cost. *Richard Branson's* ability to use his brand *Virgin* with almost any consumer product is another example. There are network effects here too, in that as more and more dissimilar *Virgin* products become available, the brand's suitability for use with even more types of product grows.

### 1.3.6 Marketing value drivers

Doyle analyses four marketing value drivers. The first, choice of markets, is only applicable to the large, diversified organisation, but the remaining three apply to all companies.

### 1.3.7 Choice of markets

A large organisation operating a number of strategic business units (SBUs) must apply a continuing **portfolio analysis** to them. You will be familiar with such portfolio analysis tools as the BCG matrix and the GE business screen from your earlier studies, but you may only have considered their use at **the product level**. Nevertheless, it is both feasible and proper to apply the concept at **the SBU level** in order to determine priorities for investment and policies for exploitation. Doyle suggests a very simple, one-dimensional classification of SBUs.

(a) **Today's businesses** generate the bulk of current profits and cash, but probably have only modest growth potential. If successful, they attract modest investment for incremental developments; if performing badly they are put right rapidly or sold off.

(b) **Tomorrow's businesses** have high potential and require major investment.

(c)   **Options for growth** are the seeds of more distant businesses; such as research projects, market trials and stakes in new, small businesses that are a long way from success. Recognising the worth of such ventures is a difficult task; in the world of venture capital, it is recognised that many good ideas will come to nothing in the end.

A large company needs a suitable mix of the three types of SBU each with its own appropriate strategic objectives, though there may be opportunities for **synergy**, such as the use of common brand names. SBUs that do not fit into one of the categories should be divested.

## 1.3.8 Target markets

Most customers are not worth selling to. The loyal, long-term customer that pays full price and requires little special service attention is the ideal – but very few fall into this category. Nevertheless, it is appropriate to target this class of customer specifically rather than simply to aim for a large customer base. Desirable customers display four important characteristics.

- They are **strategic** in that their needs match the company's core capabilities.
- They are **significant** in terms of their size or potential for growth.
- They are **profitable**.
- They are **loyal**.

## 1.3.9 Differential advantage

For other than convenience purchases, customers must have a reason for buying from a particular supplier. **Differential advantage** is created when target customers decide to buy and to remain loyal. Doyle proposes four types of customer, each of which is suited by a particular strategic approach to creating differential advantage.

A strategy of **product leadership** is based on innovation and speed to market. It is the differential advantage that enables a company to sell to **customers who want the latest, most fashionable products**. A good example is *Sony*, with its continuing development of well-designed, expensive customer electronics.

**Operational excellence** is needed to offer a combination of **customer convenience** and the **lowest prices**. *Wal-Mart* and *Toyota* are good examples of this approach.

**Brand superiority** is based on careful marketing research and strong and consistent marketing communication. This approach works with customers who identify with the **brand's values** or seek the **reassurance** that brands provide.

A growing segment is made up of customers seeking customised solutions to their specific wants. The appropriate strategy here is **customer intimacy**. This approach is becoming more feasible as information technology developments improve the ability of companies to store and access details of customer habits, needs and preferences.

Note that concentration on one particular strategy does not mean that the others can be neglected. A level of **threshold competence** must be achieved in all four, with one being established as the field of **core competence**.

## 1.3.10 Organisational value drivers

Doyle declares that 'in most situations organisational capabilities and culture are more important than strategy', and goes on to make several comparisons between pairs of companies that use similar strategies in the same industries but with markedly differing degrees of success. The differences arise from the extent to which the companies involved are able to develop and deploy appropriate **core competences** and this in turn is highly conditional upon the **culture** of the organisation and the **attitudes** of the people working in it.

## Marketing at Work

One of the examples Doyle gives is the contrast between the relative performance of *Singapore Airlines* and *Sabena*. Both 'target business travellers travelling between major international hubs with a value proposition based on service. But Singapore Airlines has been much more successful in delivering high levels of customer service and achieving extraordinary customer satisfaction and loyalty.'

An important variable is **organisational structure**. In the days of mass marketing, a vertically organised hierarchical form was appropriate for achieving economies of scale and expertise. Companies now seeking to cut overheads, achieve fast response to changing markets and competition and exploit the advantages of a mass customisation approach need something better. Increasingly, advances in IT are producing organisations based on **networks**.

(a) **Internal networks** take the form of horizontally oriented, cross-functional teams with responsibility for processes that deliver customer satisfactions. Communication flows freely, making the best use of resources whatever their functional label. This style of working reduces costs, speeds response and improves motivation.

(b) **External networks** are created when companies withdraw from activities that are not fundamental to their specific value-creating strategy and **concentrate on their core competences**. They buy in the services they no longer perform for themselves, using the core competences of other companies to support their own. This type of organisation arises under the pressure of new technologies, new markets and new processes that make it difficult for any organisation to do everything well.

We introduced the **McKinsey 7S** model in an earlier chapter. It was designed to show how the various aspects of a business relate to one another. It is a useful illustration of the way culture fits into an organisation. In particular, it shows the links between the organisation's behaviour and the behaviour of individuals within it.

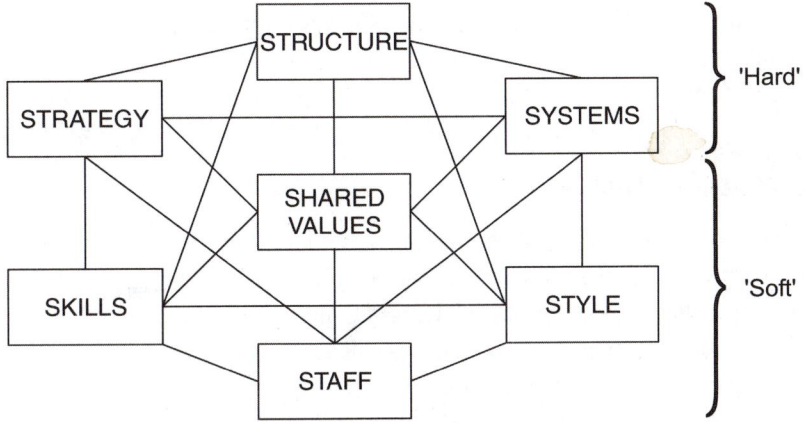

Three of the elements were considered 'hard' originally, but in today's context they are becoming more flexible.

(a) **Structure**. The organisation structure determines division of tasks in the organisation and the hierarchy of authority from the most senior to junior. As discussed above, today's company is likely to be made up of flat, empowered networks.

(b) **Strategy**. Strategy is way in which the organisation plans to outperform its competitors; it will be market-led.

(c) **Systems**. Systems include the technical systems of accounting, personnel, management information and so on, with particular emphasis on how market-related information is distributed and used.

The McKinsey model suggests that the 'soft' elements are equally important.

(a) **Shared values** lie at the heart of the organisation and are the guiding principles for the people in it. They are vital for developing the motivation to drive the organisation to achieve.

(b) **Staff** are the people in the organisation. They have their own complex concerns and priorities. The successful organisation will recruit the right staff and develop their motivation to pursue the right goals.

(c) **Style** is another aspect of the corporate culture, and includes the shared assumptions, ways of working and attitudes of senior management.

(d) **Skills** are the core competences that enable the company to create value in a particular way.

The importance of the 'soft' elements for success was emphasised by *Peters and Waterman* in their study of 'excellent' companies.

## 1.4 Limitations of SVA

**FAST FORWARD** ⟩⟩ The SVA approach is subject to limitations that managers should be aware of.

Doyle says that the 'essence of the shareholder value approach is that managers should be evaluated on their ability to develop strategies that earn returns greater than their cost of capital'. He goes on to assert that this approach is superior to traditional performance measures because it avoids emphasis on short-term results and is more appropriate than financial accounting measures for valuing businesses when intangibles such as brands and relationships with customers and suppliers are the primary assets. However, **SVA has its limitations** and managers should be aware of them.

### 1.4.1 Forecasting

SVA depends absolutely on the accuracy with which future cash flows can be forecast and these in turn depend on the normal parameters of planning such as sales forecasts. The danger is always that the managers responsible for these forecasts will display conscious or unconscious bias, either building slack into their forecasts to produce easily attainable targets or being over-optimistic to please their seniors.

### 1.4.2 Cost of capital

Calculating an accurate cost of capital is very difficult and the subject of much debate and research by financial management professionals. While the level of **loan interest** is clearly easily available, it can vary from loan to loan and in the case of overdraft finance may vary from time to time. The **cost of share capital** is much more difficult to compute since it is really only accessible through an examination of stock market behaviour and that is extremely complex. A further complication is the issue of **risk premium**. To some extent this is built into the cost of loan and share capital, but where money is allocated internally, management must make up their own minds. All these factors mean that choice of discount rate is very much a matter of judgement and the 'correct' rate may be unknowable to an accuracy of better than plus or minus several percentage points.

### 1.4.3 Estimating terminal value

When SVA is applied to a business strategy or project, two time periods are considered, divided by the normal planning horizon, which Doyle suggests should be five years. During the first five years, returns greater than the cost of capital are sought; thereafter, it is assumed that initial competitive advantage will have been eroded away and returns are expected to cover the cost of capital and no more. For this approach to work, it is necessary to estimate the present value of the cash flows from the five-year point onwards. There is no single, accepted way of doing this; business and financial judgement are needed and widely differing estimates can result.

### 1.4.4 Baseline business value

To calculate the **extra value** created by a given strategy it is necessary to compare two figures: the present value of the company if the strategy is pursued, and the present value if no change is made to current strategy. The latter is the baseline value. Once again, judgement is required in calculating this value, particularly since it may not be possible to maintain the current flow of profit simply by doing more of the same. Indeed, new strategies may be essential if the business is to avoid eventual liquidation.

### 1.4.5 Options for the future

Options to buy and sell securities, commodities and currencies have been a feature of financial markets for many years. Such options have prices and the way their value changes with time has also been the subject of much debate and research among finance professionals. Companies can create **real options** for themselves by their strategic decisions, but the valuation of such options is not currently possible using the techniques of SVA. A simple example of such an option would arise if a company decided to enter a new foreign market by means of direct exports. The market knowledge and contacts thus generated might well put the company in a strong position to undertake local manufacturing, should it wish to do so. The basic strategy of direct exporting could itself be valued by means of SVA, but it would not be possible to assign a value to the extra value created in the form of the option to manufacture locally.

### 1.4.6 Market valuation

The aim of the shareholder value approach to strategic management is to reward shareholders for providing financial resources to the company. These rewards take two forms: **dividends** and **capital appreciation**. Dividends are directly affected by the positive cash flows generated by successful strategies; capital appreciation, however, in the form of a rising share price, is not so clearly subject to this effect in the short term. Longer term future prospects for positive cash flows explain about 80 per cent of market price movement, but in the shorter term, markets are heavily influenced by a variety of other extraneous environmental influences. To reduce short-term share price volatility, company senior management must both investigate strategic forecasts very carefully and communicate their longer-term plans to the market.

## 2 Competitive strategy: how to compete

**FAST FORWARD**

**Competitive strategies** require actions to create a defendable position. They include cost leadership, differentiation and focus.

**Competitive advantage** is anything which gives one organisation an edge over its rivals in the products it sells or the services it offers.

A firm should adopt a **competitive strategy** to secure a **competitive advantage**.

**Key concept**

> **Competitive strategy** means 'taking offensive or defensive actions to create a defendable position in an industry, to cope successfully with ... competitive forces and thereby yield a superior return on investment for the firm. Firms have discovered many different approaches to this end, and the best strategy for a given firm is ultimately a unique construction reflecting its particular circumstances'. (Porter, *Competitive Advantage,* 1998)

## 2.1 The choice of competitive strategy

*Porter* suggests there are **three generic strategies** for competitive advantage.

**Cost leadership** means being the lowest-cost producer in the industry as a whole.

**Differentiation** is the exploitation of a product or service which the **industry as a whole** believes to be unique.

**Focus** involves a restriction of activities to only part of the market (a segment) through:

- Providing goods and/or services at lower cost to that segment (**cost-focus**)
- Providing a differentiated product or service to that segment (**differentiation-focus**)

**Cost leadership and differentiation are industry-wide strategies. Focus involves segmentation** but involves pursuing, **within the segment only**, a strategy of cost leadership or differentiation.

## 2.2 Cost leadership

A cost leadership strategy seeks to achieve the position of lowest-cost producer in the **industry as a whole**. By producing at the lowest cost, the manufacturer can compete on price with every other producer in the industry, and earn higher unit profits, if the manufacturer so chooses.

### 2.2.1 How to achieve overall cost leadership

(a)   Set up production facilities to obtain **economies of scale**

(b)   Use the **latest technology** to reduce costs and/or enhance productivity (or use cheap labour if available)

(c)   In high technology industries, and in industries depending on labour skills for product design and production methods, exploit the **learning curve effect**. By producing more items than any other competitor, a firm can benefit more from the learning curve, and achieve lower average costs.

(d)   Concentrate on **improving productivity**

(e)   **Minimise overhead costs**

(f)   **Get favourable access to sources of supply**

(g)   **Relocate to cheaper areas**

 Marketing at Work

**IKEA**

More and more, for manufactured goods, cost advantage is based on cheap labour in the developing world. Example is IKEA's expansion of manufacturing in Vietnam, from where it sourced more than $100 million in products in 2003. It expects its Vietnamese business to triple in value over the next four years.

Such trade speeds development and growth in less developed countries, allowing them to make use of their main source of economic advantage, and provides cheap goods to consumers in more developed countries.

In IKEA's case, it expects to work closely with its Vietnamese partners, providing advice on purchasing, productivity and expansion. Despite some privatisation, the market-based approach to production is not widely understood in this still largely planned economy.

## 2.3 Differentiation

A differentiation strategy assumes that competitive advantage can be gained through **particular characteristics** of a firm's products. Products may be categorised as:

(a) **Breakthrough products** offering a radical performance advantage over competition, perhaps at a drastically lower price.

(b) **Improved products** which are not radically different from their competition but are obviously superior in terms of better performance for a similar price.

(c) **Competitive products** which derive their appeal from a particular compromise of cost and performance. For example, cars are not all sold at rock-bottom prices, nor do they all provide immaculate comfort and performance. They compete with each other by trying to offer a more attractive compromise than rival models.

### 2.3.1 How to differentiate

- Build up a brand image
- Give the product special features to make it stand out
- Exploit other activities of the value chain

 Marketing at Work

We all know about branding and product modification in food. Organic food is increasing in popularity, as it is differentiated on the basis of:

- Possible health benefits (disputed by some nutritionists)
- Kindliness to the environment (and to animals)

The end product may be the same (eg pasta) but the ingredients and process by which it is made are a source of differentiation. Retailers and manufacturers of branded goods charge more for organic variants of standard products.

*The Economist* (21 April 2001) reported that Japanese buyers of American soya beans 'are willing to pay a premium for quality – and for knowing exactly where their food came from. By preserving [the] crop's identity [farmers] can fetch over 25% more per bushel.' A number of companies provide tracking services.

Ultimately this is about differentiating a commodity – in short, decommodifying it. The advantage for retailers is that, with tens of thousands of new food products introduced to US supermarkets each year, the right agricultural pedigree provides further differentiation.

### 2.3.2 Advantages and disadvantages of industry-wide strategies

| Advantages | Cost leadership | Differentiation |
|---|---|---|
| **New entrants** | Economies of scale raise entry barriers | Brand loyalty and perceived uniqueness are entry barriers |
| **Substitutes** | Firm is not so vulnerable as its less cost-effective competitors to the threat of substitutes | Customer loyalty is a weapon against substitutes |
| **Customers** | Customers cannot drive down prices further than the next most efficient competitor | Customers have no comparable alternative |

| Advantages | Cost leadership | Differentiation |
|---|---|---|
| **Suppliers** | Flexibility to deal with cost increases | Higher margins can offset vulnerability to supplier price rises |
| **Industry rivalry** | Firm remains profitable when rivals go under through excessive price competition | Brand loyalty should lower price sensitivity |

| Disadvantages | Cost leadership | Differentiation |
|---|---|---|
| **New entrants** | Technological change will require capital investment, or make production cheaper for competitors | New entrants can differentiate too |
| **Substitutes** | Substitutes with improved features or marketing may 'undercut' even a cost leadership strategy if customers use them as better products, making the strategy redundant (and expensive) | Sooner or later, customers become price sensitive |
| **Customers** | Cost concerns ignore product design or marketing issues | Customers may not value the differentiating factor |
| **Suppliers** | Increase in input costs can reduce price advantages | Differentiation might require specialist inputs |
| **Industry rivalry** | Competitors can benchmark their processes or cut costs | Competitors can copy |

## 2.4 Focus (or niche) strategy

In a focus strategy, a firm concentrates its attention on one or more particular segments or niches of the market, and does not try to serve the entire market with a single product.

(a)    A **cost-focus strategy**: aim to be a cost leader for a particular segment. This type of strategy is often found in the printing, clothes manufacture and car repair industries.

(b)    A **differentiation-focus strategy**: pursue differentiation for a chosen segment. Luxury goods are the prime example of such a strategy.

### 2.4.1 Advantages of a focus strategy

- A niche is more secure and a firm can insulate itself from competition.
- The firm does not spread itself too thinly.

### 2.4.2 Drawbacks of a focus strategy

(a)    The firm **sacrifices economies of scale** which would be gained by serving a wider market.

(b)    **Competitors can move into the segment**, with increased resources (eg the Japanese moved into the US luxury car market, to compete with Mercedes and BMW).

(c)    The **segment's needs may eventually become less distinct** from the main market.

**Exam tip**

Exams in 2000 and 2002 examined niche strategies in the car industry. The example of MG Rover was used in 2002 in the context of a strategic alliance with a Chinese automotive group.

## Marketing at Work

In 2005, *The Financial Times* reported on Tyrrells' Potato Chips, a niche manufacturer of crisps that uses potatoes produced on its own farm. William Chase, owner of the company, set it up in part to escape from dependence on the major supermarkets and in part to add extra value to his basic product, potatoes. Major feature of his strategy is to sell mainly though small retailers at the upper end of the grocery and catering markets. The *Financial Times* summarises the Tyrells' strategy under six headings.

- **Branding**. Tyrrells' marketing taps into the public's enthusiasm for 'authenticity' and 'provenance'. Its crisp packets tell the story of Tyrrells'. Pictures of employees growing potatoes on the Herefordshire farm and then cooking them illustrate the journey from 'seed to chip'.

- **Quality**. Tyrrells' chips are made from traditional varieties of potato and 'hand-fried' in small batches.

- **Distribution**. Tyrrells' sells directly to 80 per cent of its retail stockists. Students from a local agricultural college are employed to trawl through directories and identify fine-food shops to target with samples. After winning their business, Tyrrells' develops the relationship though personal contact.

- **Diffusion strategy**. Selling to the most exclusive shops cerates a showcase for Tyrrells' to target consumers who are not sensitive to price, allowing it to grow profitably.

- **New product development**. Tyrrells' is constantly bringing out new flavours and products. Experimental recipes are produced in sample runs and given free to shops to test with customers. Recent introductions include apple chips, honey glazed parsnips and Ludlow sausage with wholegrain mustard.

- **Exporting**. This has created a further sales channel through fine-food stores. Yet it has also forced greater dependency on distributors, introducing an unwelcome layer between itself and its customers.

## 2.5 Which strategy?

Although there is a risk with any of the generic strategies, Porter argues that a firm **must** pursue one of them. A **stuck-in-the-middle** strategy is almost certain to make only low profits. 'This firm lacks the market share, capital investment and resolve to play the low-cost game, the industry-wide differentiation necessary to obviate the need for a low-cost position, or the focus to create differentiation or a low-cost position in a more limited sphere.'

## Action Programme 1

The managing director of Hermes Telecommunications plc is interested in corporate strategy. Hermes has invested a great deal of money in establishing a network which competes with that of Telecom UK, a recently privatised utility. Initially Hermes concentrated its efforts on business customers in the South East of England, especially the City of London, where it offered a lower cost service to that supplied by Telecom UK. Recently, Hermes has approached the residential market (ie domestic telephone users) offering a lower cost service on long-distance calls. Technological developments have resulted in the possibility of a cheap mobile telecommunication network, using microwave radio links. The franchise for this service has been awarded to Gerbil phone, which is installing transmitters in town centres and stations etc.

What issues of competitive strategy have been raised in the above scenario, particularly in relation to Hermes Telecommunications plc?

In practice, it is rarely simple to draw hard and fast distinctions between the generic strategies as there are conceptual problems underlying them.

(a)   **Problems with the cost leadership concept**

(i)   **Internal focus**. Cost refers to internal measures, rather than the market demand. It can be used to gain market share: but it is the **market share which is important**, not cost leadership as such.

(ii)   **Only one firm**. If cost leadership applies cross the whole industry, only one firm will pursue this strategy successfully.

(iii)   **Higher margins can be used for differentiation**. Having low costs does **not** mean you have to charge lower prices or compete on price. A cost leader can choose to 'invest higher margins in R & D or marketing'. Being a cost leader arguably gives producers more freedom to choose other competitive strategies.

(b)   **Problems with the differentiation concept**

Porter assumes that a differentiated product will always be sold at a **higher price**.

(i)   However, a **differentiated product** may be sold at the same price as competing products in order to **increase market share**.

(ii)   **Choice of competitor**. Differentiation from whom? Who are the competitors? Do they serve other market segments? Do they compete on the same basis?

(iii)   **Source of differentiation**. This can include **all** aspects of the firm's offer, not only the product. Restaurants aim to create an atmosphere or 'ambience', as well as serving food of good quality.

**Focus** probably has fewer conceptual difficulties, as it ties in very neatly with ideas of market segmentation. In practice most companies pursue this strategy to some extent, by designing products/services to meet the needs of particular target markets.

'Stuck-in-the-middle' is therefore what many companies actually pursue quite successfully. Any number of strategies can be pursued, with different approaches to **price** and the **perceived added value** (ie the differentiation factor) in the eyes of the customer.

## 2.6 Section summary

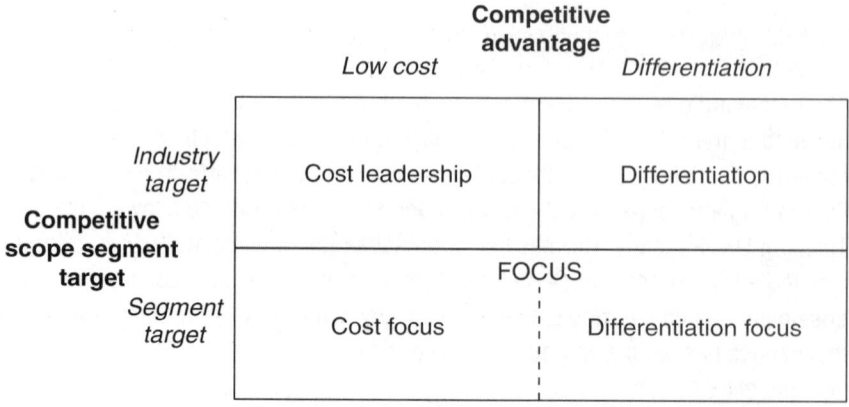

# 3 Sustainable competitive advantage

**Competitive advantage** has to be sustained. It can come from better products, customer perceptions, costs, competencies, assets, economies of scale, attitudes and relationships, offensive and defensive.

A key issue in competitive advantage is ensuring it is **sustained**.

(a) Competitive advantage only really exists in the customer's mind.

(b) Competitive advantage can be **lost easily** as a result of **market changes** or **new ways of doing business**. The advantage of Marks & Spencer (covered in more detail later in this text) comes to mind.

Competitive advantage will be lost, gradually or rapidly, if the organisation's chosen strategy loses its relevance. Customers' needs are no longer met and market share declines. This is termed **strategic wear-out**. Strategic wear-out is dealt with in more detail later in this chapter.

In an earlier chapter, we identified some key issues regarding competitor orientation.

- Operational effectiveness is not the same as strategy
- Strategy rests on unique activities
- A sustainable strategic position requires trade-offs
- Strategy involves making choices not blindly imitating competitors

## 3.1 Different types of advantage

| Competitive advantage | Example/comment |
|---|---|
| **Better product** in some way | Renault – safest car in its class |
| **Perceived advantage** or psychic benefit | Exclusivity (eg Harrods) |
| **Global skills** | BA |
| **Low costs**, via high productivity or focus | Discount retailers or supermarkets such as Lidl or Aldi |
| **Better competences** | Some firms are 'better' at marketing or aligning technologies to markets than others |
| **Superior assets** | Property, cash or brands |
| **Economies of scale** | Size can be a source of competitive advantage |
| **Attitude** | This is partly related to culture and management abilities |
| Superior **relationships** | Companies can exploit business alliances and develop personal relationships |

The most important competitive advantages depend on the market and existing competitors. *Davidson* suggests that the best advantages are the hardest to copy.

 Marketing at Work

*Ratners* sold low-cost jewellery, cleverly developing a 'low cost' position for a luxury indulgent item tied up with people's self-image.

Ratners destroyed this advantage when its managing director publicly announced that the products were 'crap'.

# 4 Competitive positions

Firms can choose a variety of strategies to **attack or defend** their position. Different strategies are appropriate to challengers, followers, leaders and nichers.

The broad generic strategies outlined above have some flaws, as we have seen. We suggested a number of approaches to price and value. In this section we describe how marketing activities can be used against **competitors**.

Considering strategic options from a competitor rather than customer orientation is referred to as **competitive marketing strategy**. *Kotler and Singh* in the *McKinsey Quarterly* (1981) identified **five offensive** and **six defensive** competitive strategies named after military strategies.

## 4.1 Offensive warfare

Offensive strategies can be used by all companies. In order to ensure success, a company must be able to gain an advantage over the competition in the segment or area of attack. Kotler describes the following **attack strategies**.

| Strategy | Comment |
|---|---|
| **Frontal attack** | This is the direct, head-on attack meeting competitors with the **same product line, price, promotion and so on**. Because the attacker is attacking the enemy's strengths rather than weaknesses, it is generally considered the riskiest and least advised of strategies. |
| **Flanking attack** | The aim is to engage competitors in those product markets where they are weak or have no presence at all. Its overreaching goal is to build a position from which to launch an attack on the major battlefield later without waking 'sleeping giants'. |
| **Encirclement attack** | Multi-pronged attack aimed at diluting the defender's ability to retaliate in strength. The attacker stands ready to block the competitor no matter which way he turns in the product market.<br><br>(i) An attacker can encircle by **product proliferation** as Seiko did in the watch market, supplying 400 watch types in the UK out of 2,300 models worldwide.<br><br>(ii) **Market encirclement** consists of expanding the products into all segments and distribution channels. |
| **Bypass attack** | This is the most indirect form of competitive strategy as it **avoids confrontation** by moving into new and as yet uncontested fields. Three types of bypass are possible; develop **new products**, diversify into **unrelated products** or diversify into **new geographical markets**. |
| Guerrilla warfare | Less ambitious in scope, this involves making small attacks in different locations whilst remaining mobile. Such attacks take several forms: law suits, poaching personnel, interfering with supply networks and so on. The overriding aim is to **destabilise** by prods rather than blows. |

## 4.2 Defensive warfare

It is generally agreed that **only a market leader** should play defence in an attempt to hold on to its existing markets in the face of competitive attack.

| Strategy | Comment |
|---|---|
| **Position defence** | Static defence of a current position, retaining current product-markets by consolidating resources within existing areas. **Exclusive reliance** on a position defence effectively means that a business is a **sitting target** for competition. |
| **Mobile defence** | A high degree of **mobility prevents the attacker's chances of localising defence** and accumulating its forces for a decisive battle. A business should seek market development, product development and diversification to create a stronger base. |
| **Pre-emptive defence** | **Attack is the best form of defence**. Pre-emptive defence is launched in a segment where an attack is **anticipated** instead of a move into related or new segments. |
| **Flank position defence** | This is used to occupy a position of **potential** future importance in order to deny that position to the opponent. Leaders need to develop and hold secondary markets to prevent competitors using them as a spring board into the primary market. (For example, Japanese manufacturers used the upper–end executive and coupe market to break into the volume car sector in the US.) |
| **Counter-offensive defence** | This is attacking where one is being attacked. This requires **immediate response** to any competitor entering a segment or initiating new moves. Examples are price wars, where firms try to undercut each other. |
| **Strategic withdrawal** | May be a last resort, but 'cutting your losses' can be the best option in the long run. Management resistance to what is seen as a drastic step is likely to be the biggest barrier. |

The five attacking strategies for challenging market leaders and the six defensive strategies used to fight off challenges are not mutually exclusive. As contingent factors change, a successful company will reconsider and revise its core strategies

## Action Programme 2

Hester Bateman plc (HB plc) is a manufacturing cutler: that is, the company makes knives, forks and spoons. HB is based in Sheffield in the United Kingdom which has been the centre of the UK cutlery industry for at least one hundred years. When the industry was first established, it was very fragmented and there were many small entrepreneurial businesses making cutlery. Often, these businesses were organised around a family and they usually employed between six and ten people. Hester Bateman was one such entrepreneur. The industry began to consolidate, in the late nineteenth century and early twentieth century, as a series of mergers were effected.

HB plc was constituted in its present form in the 1920s when it obtained its market listing on the Stock Exchange. It now consists of a large factory which employs 500 people and a Head Office employing 200 people. These are both in Sheffield.

In 1990 HB plc made a rights issue to finance a modernisation programme in its factory. At that time the Board reviewed the company's objectives. A statement was issued by the Board which said:

'HB plc is a UK manufacturing cutler based in Sheffield, the home of the cutlery industry. Our success is due to harnessing local skills in production and design and using these to deliver the finest quality product to our customers across the world. They know that the finest cutlery in the world is stamped "Made in Sheffield". We intend to continue with our fine traditions.'

HB plc has always made all its cutlery in Sheffield and attaches great importance to the fact that it can, therefore, be marked 'Made in Sheffield'.

HB plc usually spends approximately £150,000 a year on research and development. Five per cent of this spending is on new designs for the export market and the remainder is evenly split on designs for the home market and on improvements in production systems.

*BQ plc*

There is another UK manufacturing cutler of a similar size to HB plc, BQ plc, which is based in Birmingham.

Since 1991 BQ plc has followed a different production policy to HB plc. Approximately half of its cutlery is made in Korea and imported to the UK and marketed under BQ plc's brand names.

*Markets*

From the date of its formation until the late 1980s HB plc did very good business with countries across the world.

Since 1990 HB plc has experienced increasing competition from countries of the Pacific Rim – Korea, Taiwan, Hong Kong and Singapore. This competition has been conducted on the basis of cost. This has been possible because the production technology involved in making cutlery is a mature one. It is also comparatively cheap and readily available. Further, for many users cutlery has become a generic product.

Generics are unbranded, plainly packaged, less-expensive versions of products, purchased in supermarkets, such as spaghetti, paper towels and canned peaches.

HB plc has experienced a growing loss of market share in the UK to imports from the Pacific Rim. HB plc's export markets have largely disappeared. The only export business which it does is an annual sale of about £200,000 of very high quality cutlery to a department store in New York. HB plc makes a gross margin of 45% on this business.

Estimated market data at December 2002:

|  | UK market share | |
| --- | --- | --- |
|  | by quantity % | by value % |
| HB plc | 35 | 45 |
| BQ plc* | 30 | 35 |
| Imports | 35 | 20 |

* These percentages include all cutlery sold by BQ plc whether made in the UK or in Korea.

*Financial performance*

The increasingly competitive environment has had a marked effect on HB plc's profitability and stock market performance. After the publication of its latest annual results the following comment was made in an influential UK financial newspaper:

'HB plc's latest results which show a profit after tax of £2.25 million look deceptively good. However, these are flattered by the fact that HB plc has not made any major investments since the 1980s.

Its ROCE is about 4% and this could be beaten by any fixed return risk-free deposit investment. There seems to be little prospect of growth in any direction. These shares are really only a HOLD for the sentimental; otherwise SELL.'

*Required*

(a)     How can Porter's classification of generic strategies be used by HB plc to analyse its current competitive position?

(b)     Discuss the extent to which you believe that the statement of objectives made in 1990 is still applicable today.

(c)    Recommend possible marketing strategies for HB plc. Discuss the advantages and disadvantages of your recommendations.

We can apply these strategies to firms with different positions in the market.

- Pioneers
- Followers
- Challengers
- Nichers

### 4.2.1 Strategies for pioneers

- Position defence
- Mobile defence
- Flanking defence
- Contraction defence (withdrawal)
- Pre-emptive defence
- Counter-offence

### 4.2.2 Strategies for challengers

Challenges can either attack lenders, accept the status quo, or try and win market share from other smaller companies in the market.

- Frontal attack
- Flank attack
- Encirclement attack
- Bypass attack
- Guerrilla attack

 Marketing at Work

**Dolls**

Between 2001 and 2004, *Mattel* lost 20% of its share of the worldwide fashion-doll segment to smaller rivals such as *MGA Entertainment*, creator of a hip new line of dolls called *Bratz*. MGA recognized what Mattel had failed to – that preteen girls were becoming more sophisticated and maturing more quickly. At younger ages, they were outgrowing *Barbie* and increasingly preferring dolls that looked like their teenage siblings and the pop stars they idolized. As the target market for Barbie narrowed from girls aged three to 11 to girls about three to five, the Bratz line cut rapidly into the seemingly unassailable Mattel franchise. Mattel finally moved to rescue Barbie's declining fortunes, launching a brand extension called *My Scene* that targeted older girls, and a line of hip dolls called *Flavas* to compete head-on with Bratz. But the damage was done. Barbie, queen of dolls for over 40 years, lost a fifth of her realm almost overnight – and Mattel didn't see it coming.

*GS Day and PJH Shoemaker, Harvard Business Review, November 2005*

### 4.2.3 Strategies for followers

Many firms succeed by imitating the leaders. This is common in financial services markets where the basic functionality of a product is similar. Given that there are controls over monopoly status, most markets will have at least two players. Followers can follow:

- **Closely**, by imitating the marketing mix, and targeting similar segments
- **At a distance**, with more differentiating factors
- **Selectively** to avoid direct competition.

Kotler makes the important point that 'followership is not the same as being passive or a carbon copy of the leader'. The follower has to define a path that does not invite competitive retaliation. He identifies three broad followership strategies.

(a)    **Cloner**. This is a parasite that lives off the investment made by the leader in the marketing mix (such as in products or distribution). The **counterfeiter** is an extreme version of the cloner, who produces fakes of the original (eg fake Rolex watches for sale in the Far East).

(b)    **Imitator**. This strategy copies some elements but differentiates on others (such as packaging).

(c)    **Adapter**. This involves taking the leader's products and adapting or even improving them. The adapter may grow to challenge the leader.

### 4.2.4 Market nichers

This is associated with a **focus** strategy and relies partly on segmentation, and partly on specialising. There are several specialist roles open to market nichers.

(a)    **End user specialist**, specialising in one type of customer

(b)    **Vertical level specialist**, specialising at one particular point of the production/ distribution chain

(c)    **Specific customer specialist**, limiting selling to one or just a few customers

(d)    **Geographic specialist** selling to one locality

(e)    **Product or service specialist**, offering specialised services not available from other firms

(f)    **Quality/price specialist** operating at the low or high end of the market

(g)    **Channel specialist**, concentrating on just one channel of distribution

# 5 Products and markets

**FAST FORWARD**

> **Product-market strategy** includes market penetration, market development, product development and diversification.

*Ansoff* drew up a **growth vector matrix**, describing a combination of a firm's activities in current and new markets, with existing and new products.

**Key concept**

> **Product-market mix** is a short-hand term for the products/services a firm sells (or a service which a public sector organisation provides) and the markets it sells them to.

*Ansoff's product-market growth matrix*

|  | Existing products | New products |
|---|---|---|
| Existing markets | *Market penetration strategy*<br><br>1 More purchasing and usage from existing customers<br>2 Gain customers from competitors<br>3 Convert non-users into users (where both are in same market segment) | *Product development strategy*<br><br>1 Product modification via new features<br>2 Different quality levels<br>3 'New' product |
| New markets | *Market development strategy*<br><br>1 New market segments<br>2 New distribution channels<br>3 New geographic areas eg exports | *Diversification strategy*<br><br>1 Organic growth<br>2 Joint ventures<br>3 Mergers<br>4 Acquisition/take-over |

## 5.1 Current products and current markets: market penetration

**Market penetration**. The firm seeks to:

(a) **Maintain or to increase its share** of current markets with current products, eg through competitive pricing, advertising, sales promotion

(b) Secure dominance of growth markets

(c) Restructure a mature market by driving out competitors

(d) Increase usage by existing customers eg airmiles, loyalty cards

### Marketing at Work

Good examples of strategies for market penetration are air miles and 'frequent flier' services. A decision to fly with an airline gives the customer air miles, which can be redeemed on later flights, and which will encourage the customer to fly again.

## 5.2 Present products and new markets: market development

**Market development** is when the firm seeks new markets for its **current** products or services. It is appropriate when its products are strengths which can be matched by opportunities in new markets. Ways of developing markets include:

(a) **New geographical areas** and export markets (eg a radio station building a new transmitter to reach a new audience).

(b) **Different package sizes** for food and other domestic items so that both those who buy in bulk and those who buy in small quantities are catered for.

(c) **New distribution channels** to attract new customers (eg organic food sold in supermarkets not just specialist shops).

(d) **Differential pricing policies** to attract different types of customer and create **new market segments**. For example, travel companies have developed a market for cheap long-stay winter breaks in warmer countries for retired couples.

## 5.3 New products and present markets: product development

Product development is the launch of new products to existing markets.

(a) **Advantages**

- Product development forces competitors to innovate
- Newcomers to the market might be discouraged

(b) The **drawbacks** include the expense and the risk.

## 5.4 New products: new markets (diversification)

**Diversification** occurs when a company decides to make **new products for new markets**. It should have a clear idea about what it expects to gain from diversification. There are two types of diversification, related and unrelated diversification.

(a) **Growth**. New products and new markets should be selected which offer prospects for growth which the existing product-market mix does not.

(b)  **Investing surplus** funds not required for other expansion needs: but the funds could be returned to shareholders.

(c)  The firm's strengths match the opportunity if:

(i)  Outstanding new products have been developed by the firm's research and development department

(ii)  The profit opportunities from diversification are high.

## Marketing at Work

Japan's Tu-Ka mobile phone network has had its recent poor performance rescued by the success of its new S-Phone model.

The S-phone has been designed to appeal to Japan's rapidly growing – and largely technophobe – elderly population. Its buttons are large and perform only one function each. The volume is set high. There are no text messages and definitely just the one ring tone.

The battery is designed so that if the owner forgets to charge it for days on end and fails to use the phone in the intervening time, it will still happily receive a call a month later.

A spokesman for Tu-Ka said that perhaps the most attractive feature of the S-Phone was that, unlike its complicated rivals, it does not come with an instruction manual of intimidating thickness.

Fumie Ochiai, a 68-year-old shopper in Tokyo's Shinjuku district, said, 'My daughter worries about me because I live on my own now. She tried buying me a normal mobile phone but it made so many noises during the night that I turned it off and hid it in a drawer. I find the microwave a bit complicated, but my daughter said that this phone could even be used by idiots.'

Tu-Ka has achieved great competitive advantage by targeting a large, growing and neglected market segment with a very carefully specified new product.

*The Times, 17 February 2005*

## 5.5 Related diversification

**Key concept**

**Related diversification** is 'development beyond the present product market, but still within the broad confines of the industry ... [it] ... therefore builds on the assets or activities which the firm has developed' (*Johnson and Scholes*). It takes the form of vertical or horizontal integration.

**Horizontal integration** refers to development into activities which are competitive with or directly **complementary** to a company's present activities. *Sony*, for example, started to compete in computer games, building on its presence in consumer electronics.

**Vertical integration** occurs when a company becomes its own:

(a)  **Supplier** of raw materials, components or services (**backward vertical integration**). For example, backward integration would occur where a milk producer acquires its own dairy farms rather than buying raw milk from independent farmers.

(b)  **Distributor** or sales agent (**forward vertical integration**), for example where a manufacturer of synthetic yarn begins to produce shirts from the yarn instead of selling it to other shirt manufacturers.

### 5.5.1 Advantages of vertical integration

(a) A **secure supply of components** or raw materials with more control. Supplier bargaining power is reduced.

(b) **Strengthen the relationships** and contacts of the manufacturer with the 'final consumer' of the product.

(c) Win a share of the **higher profits**.

(d) Pursue a **differentiation strategy** more effectively.

(e) Raise **barriers to entry**.

### 5.5.2 Disadvantages of vertical integration

(a) **Overconcentration**. A company places 'more eggs in the same end-market basket' (Ansoff). Such a policy is fairly inflexible, more sensitive to instabilities and increases the firm's dependence on a particular aspect of economic demand.

(b) The firm **fails to benefit from any economies of scale or technical advances** in the industry into which it has diversified. This is why, in the publishing industry, most printing is subcontracted to specialist printing firms, who can work machinery to capacity by doing work for many firms.

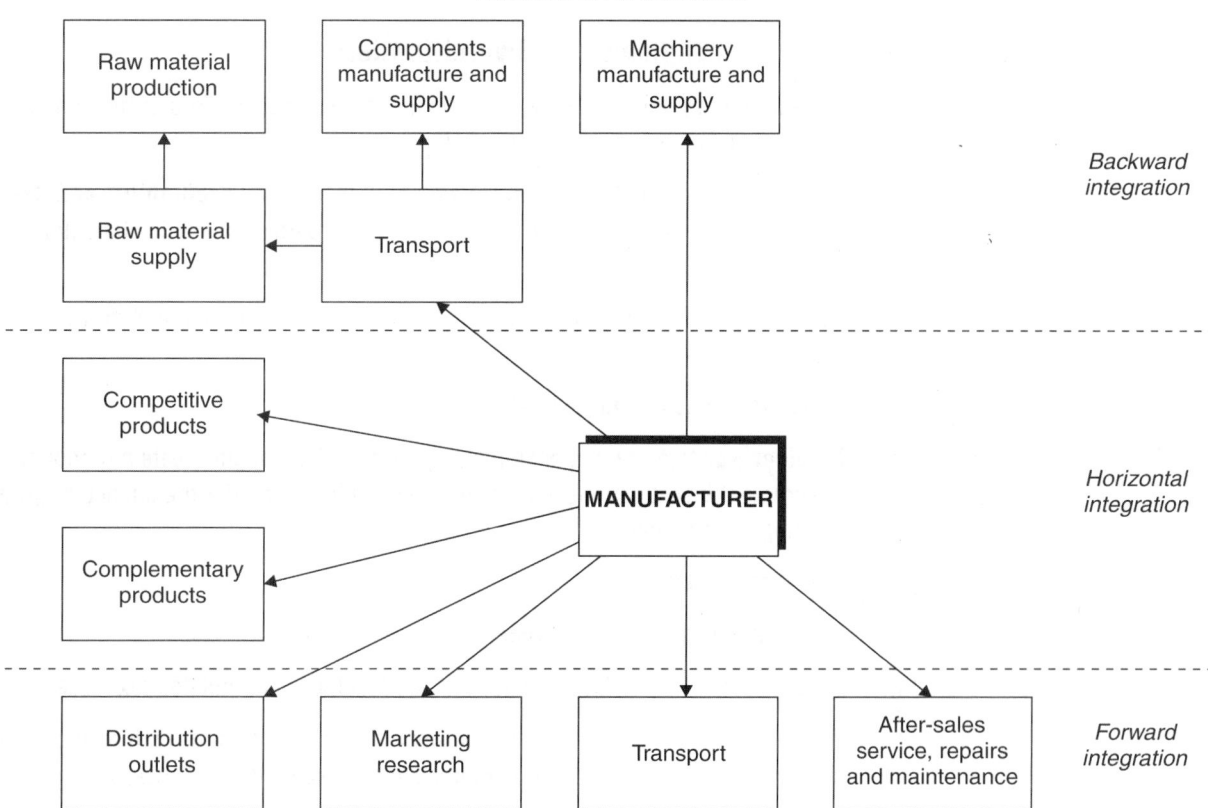

*Related diversification*

*Source: Johnson and Scholes*

## Marketing at Work

(a)   An example of horizontal integration has been cited earlier in this text. In the UK, deregulation of energy supplies means that gas suppliers can sell electricity and electricity suppliers can sell gas. They are complementary and also, when it comes to heating, competitive products.

(b)   Two good examples of forwards vertical integration are Laura Ashley and Benetton, both clothing manufacturers with dedicated retail outlets and a distinct brand identity. Vertical integration does not only apply to the retail sector.

(c)   An example of backwards vertical integration is from the pharmaceuticals sector, when big pharmaceuticals have acquired small-product biotech companies.

# 5.6 Unrelated diversification

**Key concept**

**Unrelated or conglomerate diversification** 'is development beyond the present industry into products/markets which, at face value, may bear no close relation to the present product/market.'

Conglomerate diversification is now very unfashionable. However, it has been a key strategy for companies in Asia, particularly South Korea.

## 5.6.1 Advantages of conglomerate diversification

(a)   **Risk-spreading**. Entering new products into new markets offers protection against the failure of current products and markets.

(b)   **High profit opportunities**. An improvement of the **overall profitability and flexibility** of the firm through acquisition in industries which have better economic characteristics than those of the acquiring firms.

(c)   **Escape** from the present business. For example, Reed International moved away from paper production and into publishing.

(d)   **Better access to capital** markets.

(e)   **No other way to grow**. Expansion along existing lines might create a monopoly and lead to government investigations and control. Diversifications offer the chance of growth without creating a monopoly.

(f)   **Use surplus cash**.

(g)   **Exploit under-utilised resources**.

(h)   **Obtain cash**, or other financial advantages (such as accumulated tax losses).

(i)   **Use a company's image and reputation** in one market to develop into another where corporate image and reputation could be vital ingredients for success.

## 5.6.2 Disadvantages of conglomerate diversification

(a)   The **dilution of shareholders' earnings** if diversification is into growth industries with high P/E ratios.

(b)   **Lack of a common identity and purpose** in a conglomerate organisation. A conglomerate will only be successful if it has a high quality of management and financial ability at central headquarters, where the diverse operations are brought together.

(c) **Failure in one of the businesses will drag down the rest**, as it will eat up resources. **British Aerospace** was severely damaged by the effect of a downturn in the property market on its property subsidiary, **Arlington Securities**.

(d) **Lack of management experience** in the business area. **Japanese steel companies** have diversified into areas completely unrelated to steel such as personal computers, with limited success.

(e) **No good for shareholders**. Shareholders can spread risk quite easily, simply by buying a diverse portfolio of shares. They do not need management to do it for them.

## Action Programme 3

A large organisation in road transport operates nation-wide in general haulage. This field has become very competitive and with the recent down-turn in trade, has become only marginally profitable. It has been suggested that the strategic structure of the company should be widened to include other aspects of physical distribution so that the maximum synergy would be obtained from that type of diversification.

(a) Name three activities which might fit into the suggested new strategic structure, explaining each one briefly.

(b) Explain how each of these activities could be incorporated into the existing structure.

(c) State the advantages and disadvantages of such diversification.

**Exam tip**

> Arguably, vertical integration is the opposite of outsourcing some activities – do you buy them in or make your own? A problem with the integration model is that it is focused on a simple manufacturer rather than the service sector.

## 5.7 Withdrawal

It might be the right decision to cease producing a product and/or to pull out of a market completely. This is a hard decision for managers to take if they have invested time and money or if the decision involves redundancies.

**Exit barriers** make this difficult.

(a) **Cost barriers** include redundancy costs, the difficulty of selling assets.

(b) **Political barriers** include government attitudes. Defence is an example.

(c) **Marketing considerations** may delay withdrawal. A product might be a loss-leader for others, or might contribute to the company's reputation for its breadth of coverage.

(d) **Psychology**. Managers hate to admit failure. Furthermore, people might wrongly assume that carrying on is a low risk strategy, especially if they (wrongly) feel bound to carry on, as they have spent money already.

### 5.7.1 Reasons for exit

(a) The **company's business** may be in buying firms, selling their assets and improving their performance, and then selling them at a profit.

(b) **Resource limitations** mean that less profitable businesses have to be abandoned. A business might be sold to a competitor, or occasionally to management (as a buy-out).

(c) A company may be forced to quit, because of **insolvency**.

(d) **Change of competitive strategy**. In the microprocessor industry, many American firms have left high-volume DRAM chips to Asian firms so as to concentrate on high value added niche products.

(e) **Decline in attractiveness of the market**.

(f) **Funds can earn more elsewhere**.

## 5.8 Section summary

Product-market strategy can be:

- **Penetration**: same products, same markets
- **Product development**: new products, same markets
- **Market development**: same products, new markets
- **Diversification**: new products, new markets
- **Withdrawal**
- Any **combination** of the above, depending on the product portfolio

# 6 Methods of growth: alliances and networks

**FAST FORWARD**

Many firms are growing by **alliances** with other firms, short of a full scale merger or acquisition. These are supposed to offer synergies and mutual benefits.

**Growth** can involve:

(a) **Building up new businesses** from scratch and developing them (sometimes called organic growth)

(b) **Acquiring** already existing businesses from their current owners via the purchase of a controlling interest in another company

(c) A **merger** is the joining of two or more separate companies to form a single company

(d) Spreading the costs and risks (**joint ventures**, **alliances** or other forms of **co-operation**)

## 6.1 Acquisitions

**The purpose of acquisitions**

(a) **Marketing advantages**

   (i) Buy in a new product range

   (ii) Buy a market presence (especially true if acquiring a company with overseas offices and contacts that can be utilised by the parent company)

   (iii) Unify sales departments or to rationalise distribution and advertising

   (iv) Eliminate competition or to protect an existing market

(b) **Production advantages**

   (i) Gain a higher utilisation of production facilities and reap economies of scale by larger machine runs

   (ii) 'Buy in' technology and skills

   (iii) Obtain greater production capacity

   (iv) Safeguard future supplies of raw materials

   (v) Improve purchasing by buying in bulk

(c)   **Finance and management**

    (i)    Buy a high quality management team, which exists in the acquired company

    (ii)   Obtain cash resources where the acquired company is very liquid

    (iii)  Gain undervalued assets or surplus assets that can be sold off ('asset stripping')

    (iv)  Obtain tax advantages (eg purchase of a tax loss company)

(d)   **Risk-spreading**

(e)   **Independence**. A company threatened by a take-over might take over another company, just to make itself bigger and so a more expensive 'target' for the predator company.

(f)   **Overcome barriers to entry**

## Marketing at Work

**Acquisitions research**

Acquisitions are a financial disaster for shareholders, new research suggests.

A study of the performance of large takeovers completed between 1977 and 1994 has found that in the five years after a deal, the total return on investment underperformed by an average of 26 per cent, compared with shares in companies of similar size.

The research, by Alan Gregory and John Matako, of the University of Exeter's new Centre for Finance and Investment, showed that the effect of acquisitions on share price and dividends varied according to whether the bids were hostile or non-hostile and whether they were equity–financed or cash backed.

The underperformance on share-based deals is 36 per cent over five years, relative to unacquisitive companies.

Agreed bids also generated negative returns, with shareholders doing 27 per cent less well. Agreed share-based deals led to underperformance of 37 per cent.

Cash financing or bidder hostility were not enough on their own to make a profit likely, the report found However, bids that are cash-backed and hostile have a better chance of creating, rather than destroying, shareholder value.

On a low sample, the academics found that a successful hostile cash bids generated an average 50 per cent increase in the profitability of shares in the five years after the bid. Share-based bids perform poorly because shares in the acquiring companies are overvalued in the first place, Dr Gregory suggested.

He added that the process of gaining co-operation from the target board might also increase the cost, as executives might have to be persuaded to agree only if the acquirer offers over-generous terms. Unnecessary cost may be incurred if executives in an acquired company retain their jobs after completion of deals, he said.

*The Times, 18 October 2004*

## 6.2 Organic growth

Organic growth (sometimes referred to as internal development) is the primary method of growth for many organisations, for a number of reasons. Organic growth is achieved through the development of internal resources.

### 6.2.1 Reasons for pursuing organic growth

(a)   **Learning**. The process of developing a new product gives the firm the best understanding of the market and the product.

(b)    **Innovation**. It might be the only sensible way to pursue genuine technological innovations, and exploit them. (Compact disk technology was developed by Philips and Sony, which earns royalties from other manufacturers licensed to use it.)

(c)    There is **no suitable target for acquisition**.

(d)    Organic growth can be **planned more meticulously** and offers little disruption.

(e)    It is often **more convenient** for managers, as organic growth can be financed easily from the company's current cash flows, without having to raise extra money on the stock market (eg to fund an acquisition).

(f)    The **same style of management and corporate culture** can be maintained.

(g)    **Hidden or unforeseen losses are less likely** with organic growth than with acquisitions.

(h)    **Economies of scale** can be achieved from more **efficient use of central head office functions** such as finance, purchasing, personnel, management services and so on.

### 6.2.2 Problems with organic growth

(a)    **Time** – sometimes it takes a long time to climb a **learning curve**.

(b)    Barriers to entry (eg distribution networks) are harder to overcome: for example a brand image may be built up from scratch.

(c)    The firm will have to **acquire the resources independently**.

(d)    Organic growth may be **too slow for the dynamics of the market**.

 Marketing at Work

**Easy Rentacar**

*Stelios Haji-Ioannou* of *EasyJet* launched *easyRentacar.com*, an Internet-only car rental business aimed at the private consumer, charging lower prices thanks to a low cost base.

To the initial surprise of industry watchers, the company offered just one model, the small Mercedes A-class. Stelios signed the deal for 5,000 cars with Daimler-Chrysler at the Geneva Motor Show.

## 6.3 Alliances

**Alliances are becoming more popular**. An alliance is a business arrangement whereby firms share data, resources and activities to achieve mutually beneficial objectives. Alliances can take a number of forms.

- Agreements to co-operate on various issues
- Shared research and development
- Joint ventures, in which the partners create a separate business unit
- Supply chain rationalisation
- Licensing and franchising
- Purchase of minority stakes

### 6.3.1 Alliances and synergy

> **Synergy** is achieved when combining resources results in a better rate of return than would be achieved by the same resources used independently in separate operations.

### 6.3.2 Obtaining synergy from alliances

(a) **Marketing synergy**: use of common marketing facilities such as distribution channels, sales staff and administration, and warehousing. Petrol stations can double as burger outlets.

(b) **Operating synergy**: arises from the better use of operational facilities and personnel, bulk purchasing, a greater spread of fixed costs whereby the firm's competence can be transferred to making new products.

(c) **Investment synergy**: the joint use of plant, common raw material stocks, transfer of research and development from one product to another – ie from the wider use of a common investment in fixed assets, working capital or research.

(d) **Management synergy**: the advantage to be gained where management skills concerning current operations are easily transferred to new operations because of the similarity of problems in the two industries.

Hooley *et al* (1998) give an overview of some of the environmental factors that are stimulating the need for alliances.

- Scarce resources
- Increased competition
- Higher customer expectations
- Pressures from strong distributors
- Internationalisation of markets
- Changing markets and technologies
- Turbulent and unpredictable markets

 Marketing at Work

Iceland, with a population of 280,000, has several million surplus telephone numbers. *Mint* is a British company pioneering technology enabling mobile phone users to log on from network to network when abroad. Mint has acquired 50% of *Itallo*, an Icelandic mobile phone firm, in order to issue Mint's customers with an Icelandic mobile phone number, using Iceland as a hub from which to track users. (On arriving at their destination, users swap their usual SIM card for an Icelandic one: their calls are diverted via Iceland at a cheaper flat rate.)

**Exam tip**

> An exam in 2000 asked about strategic choices. The partnership was between a bank and a mobile phone company, to provide customers with home banking, bill paying and smart cards.

## 6.4 Consortia

**Consortia**: organisations co-operate on specific business prospects. Airbus is an example, a consortium including British Aerospace, Dasa, Aerospatiale and Casa (of Spain). However, it does have an unusual financial structure, and it will soon turn into a normal company.

## 6.5 Joint ventures

Two firms (or more) join forces for manufacturing, financial and marketing purposes and each has a share in both the equity and the management of the business. A joint venture is a separate business unit set up for the reasons outlined below.

(a) **Share funding**. As the capital outlay is shared, joint ventures are especially attractive to smaller or risk-averse firms, or where very expensive new technologies are being researched and developed (such is the civil aerospace industry).

(b) **Cut risk**. A joint venture can reduce the risk of government intervention if a local firm is involved (eg Club Méditerranée pays much attention to this factor).

(c) Participating enterprises **benefit from all sources of profit**.

(d) **Close control** over marketing and other operations.

(e) Overseas, a joint venture with an indigenous firm provides **local knowledge, quickly**.

(f) **Synergies**. One firm's production expertise can be supplemented by the other's marketing and distribution facility.

(g) **Learning** can also be a 'learning' exercise in which each partner tries to learn as much as possible from the other.

(h) **Technology**. New technology offers many uncertainties and many opportunities. Such alliances provide funds for expensive research projects, spreading risk.

(i) **The joint venture itself can generate innovations**.

(j) The alliance can involve **'testing' the firm's core competence** in different conditions, which can suggest ways to improve it.

### 6.5.1 Disadvantages of joint ventures

(a) Conflicts of interest between the different parties.

(b) Disagreements may arise over profit shares, amounts invested, the management of the joint venture and the marketing strategy.

(c) One partner may wish to withdraw from the arrangement.

## 6.6 Licensing

A **licensing agreement** is a commercial contract whereby the licenser gives something of value to the licensee in exchange for certain performances and payments. The licenser may provide, in return for a royalty:

- Rights to produce a patented product or use a patented production process
- Manufacturing know-how (unpatented)
- Technical advice and assistance
- Marketing advice and assistance
- Rights to use a trademark, brand and so on.

**Subcontracting** is also a type of alliance. Co-operative arrangements also feature in supply chain management, JIT and quality programmes.

## 6.7 Franchising

**Franchising** is a method of expanding the business on less capital than would otherwise be possible. For suitable businesses, it is an **alternative business strategy to raising extra capital** for growth. Franchisers include Budget Rent-a-car, Dyno-rod, Express Dairy, Holiday Inn, Kall-Kwik Printing, KFC, Prontaprint, Sketchley Cleaners, Body Shop and even McDonald's.

(a)   The **franchiser** offers its:

- Name, and any goodwill associated with it
- Systems and business methods
- Support services, such as advertising, training, help with site decoration etc

(b)   The **franchisee**:

- Provides capital, personal involvement and local market knowledge
- Pays the franchiser for being granted these rights and services
- Has responsibility for the running and profitability of his franchise

## 6.8 The virtual firm

An extreme example of an alliance is the so-called **virtual firm**. A virtual firm is created out of a **network of alliances** and subcontracting arrangements: it is as if most of the activities in a particular value chain are conducted by different firms, even though the process is loosely co-ordinated by one of them. It is outsourcing taken to its greatest extent.

For example, assume you manufacture small toys. You could in theory **outsource**:

- The design to a consultancy
- Manufacturing to a subcontractor in a low-cost country
- Delivery arrangements to a specialist logistics firm
- Debt collection to a bank (factoring)
- Filing, tax returns, bookkeeping to an accountancy firm

Virtual corporations effectively put market forces in all linkages of the value chain – this has the advantage of creating **incentives** for suppliers, perhaps to take risks to produce a better product, but can lead to a loss of control.

# 7 Hostile and declining markets

**FAST FORWARD**

Markets decline because of **environmental factors**. Some can be revitalised. In others, a firm has to choose whether it wants to stay in the market or withdraw.

Many of the portfolio models assume that markets are growing. However, this is certainly not the case in many markets and firms within them still have to survive.

## 7.1 Declining markets

### 7.1.1 Why do markets decline?

- Obsolete technology
- Change in customer needs, leading to fall in demand
- Alternative satisfactions

**Strategic alternatives** include:

- Revitalising the market
- Becoming a profitable survivor
- Harvest and withdraw

### 7.1.2 Revitalising the market

- Identify new market segments or submarkets
- Introduce new products
- Introduce new applications of existing products
- Change the market

 Marketing at Work

Since the 1950s, cinema attendances were in virtual decline in the movie market, having competed unsuccessfully with TV. However, cinema reinvented itself in the 1980s and 1990s.

(a) New action-packed features, supported by intensive marketing campaigns, brought in a new audience. Similarly, the digital technology makes for enhanced special effects, such as those shown in Gladiator.

(b) In the UK, the experience of cinema-going has been revolutionised with easily accessible multiplex cinemas open all day, in complexes with a variety of leisure activities, bars and restaurants.

(c) New formats, such as IMAX, are now available.

(d) Merchandising has significantly improved profits.

### 7.1.3 Becoming a profitable survivor

(a) Make a visible commitment to the market, as a signal to other competitors.

(b) Encourage competitors to leave by aggressive competition or by making it easier for them to quit.

(c) Purchase the competitor's capacity, close it down and carry on in a smaller niche.

**Harvest and withdraw**. Reduce investment and operating resources in order to make a graceful exit. Profits may still be made. However employees and customers may fear the lack of commitment and go elsewhere. A milking or harvesting strategy can be reversed, as the firm still has a market presence.

## 7.2 Hostile environments

*Aaker* describes a six-phase cycle for hostile markets.

| Phase 1: Margin pressure | Overcapacity leads to predatory pricing, benefiting large customers |
|---|---|
| Phase 2: Share shift | Each year, up to 5% of market share will shift under price pressure |
| Phase 3: Product proliferation | Firms create excess value by adding new lines |
| Phase 4: Self-defeating cost reduction | Firms cut costs but, in doing so, weaken themselves |
| Phase 5: Shakeout | Closures, mergers |
| Phase 6: Rescue | Some markets recover with fewer companies competing |

### 7.2.1 Winning in hostile markets

- Focus on **large customers**, to benefit from economies of scale
- **Differentiate on intangible factors** such as reliability and relationships
- Offer a broad **array of products** at a variety of prices
- Turn price into a commodity by **removing price from the customer's buying criteria**
- **Control cost** structures

# 8 Wear-out and renewal

**FAST FORWARD**

**Strategic wear-out** occurs when firms continue with old strategies that are no longer viable.

**Key concept**

Strategic and tactical **wear-out** is the problem that any organisation will face if it retains its current strategies and tactics without any review or consideration of changed circumstances.

The following factors give rise to wear-out.

(a) **Market changes**

- Customer requirements
- Distribution requirements

(b) **Competitor innovations**

(c) **Internal factors**

- Poor cost control
- Lack of consistent investment
- Ill-advised tinkering with successful strategies

Some organisations still continue to pursue marketing programmes long after their effectiveness has diminished. Many reasons can be put forward to explain this.

| Reason | Comment |
|---|---|
| **Fear of change** | Most people are afraid of change, preferring to stay in their own comfort zone. |
| **Change is becoming harder to forecast** | Many organisations opt to stay with what is familiar. |
| **'If it ain't broke, don't fix it!'** | Market leaders, having developed a successful strategy, are understandably reluctant to change it. |
| **Change too late** | The need for change often only becomes apparent when the gap between what a company is doing and what it should be doing increases to a point at which performance suffers in an obvious way. |
| **Failure to learn** | Companies fail because managers' **theory of the business** no longer works. A theory of the business contains the assumptions (about markets, technology etc) that shape any organisation's behaviour. |
| **The wrong customers** | Keeping *too* close to existing customers, rather than thinking about future customers, can also result in strategic wearout: 'an industry's leaders are rarely in the forefront of commercialising new technologies that do not initially meet the functional demands of mainstream customers'. **New technologies** are developed and take industry leaders unawares. |

| Reason | Comment |
|--------|---------|
| **Failure to look** | Some organisations do not have environmental monitoring and strategic review procedures embedded within their marketing planning systems. |

Four interlinked avenues of action are required to overcome the danger of strategic wear-out.

(a)   Regular and detailed reviews of each of the significant elements of the external environment
(b)   Identification of the ways these elements are changing
(c)   Evaluation of the implications of these changes on the organisation
(d)   Internal audit to establish the appropriateness of actions both currently and for the future

In order to avoid strategic wear-out a multi-functional perspective is required. A combination of strategic, organisational and cultural change is required. Companies are likely to be unsuccessful in maintaining change unless five demanding criteria are met.

- **Coherence** of direction, actions and timing
- **Environmental** assessment of competitors, customers and regulatory climate
- **Leading** change by creating the correct climate
- **Linking** strategic with operational change (communication and reward systems)
- Treating **people as assets** and investments rather than costs

**Exam tip**

> Companies need to recognise the danger of strategic wear-out, to plan for it, to be constantly on their guard against it. From an examination viewpoint, be able to point to examples of it in the marketplace. When were your company's systems last reviewed? How long have these systems been in place? Do you frequently review your marketing strategies and those of your major competitors and, having reviewed them, are they changed?
>
> A December 1999 exam offered a straightforward question – to be answered in report format – about the dangers, causes and preventative measures of strategic wearout. A similar question appeared two years later, in December 2001.

 Marketing at Work

*Marks & Spencer*, an icon of British retailing, had lost its way. When its profitability started to fall, there were hints that this was to do with positioning and product designs.

- A number of other retailers had set up, offering competitive or lower prices (ie better value for money) with different designs

- *Matalan* stores offered designer goods at low cost (eg even mannequins are too expensive for Matalan)

- M&S took a number of control actions

  - New advertising (based on real sizes for women)
  - New designers
  - Concept stores

More radical steps were then taken – to close overseas stores to concentrate on the UK.

After several years of rebuilding effort, M&S appeared to be emerging from its slump.

*Website:* www.marksandspencer.com

The Smalltown Horticulture Society is a non-profit-making organisation with 300 members. It is owned by its members who each pay an annual subscription of £7 a year, and it has £12,000 in the bank. It has no debts and its only assets are an old PC and printer and some stationery. It rents its premises. The society's purpose is to 'promote a greater understanding of Horticulture'.

*Note*. Horticulture: 'the art or science of cultivating gardens' *(Collins English Dictionary)*.

The society has held an annual flower show since 1905. Until 1980 the show was very well supported. It was held on the Wednesday and Thursday of the final week in September and attracted an attendance of around 8,000 people. Such a level of attendance enabled the society to cover the costs of the show and also to make a surplus. It used the surplus to finance its other activities, for instance providing free seeds to local elderly people.

Since 1980 the attendances have declined, and in 2002 the show was put on to a single-day basis as the admission receipts were insufficient to pay for the hire of the premises for two days. However attendances have continued to decline and the latest show was 'very disappointing' (Society Chairman).

Following this, the chairman made a statement in which he called for 'the ladies of Smalltown to become involved with the show like they used to be'. He observed that at the same time as the Smalltown show was being held, another society held a much bigger show in a town some sixty miles away. This show made a profit and was very well attended. Some Smalltown residents travelled to the other show but did not attend the Smalltown one.

The chairman concluded that 'unless we get better support in future, we will not be able to continue with the show and the people of Smalltown will lose out'.

*Required*

(a)   Comment on the extent to which the marketing concept has been utilised effectively, if at all, by the Society.

(b)   Recommend strategies which would enable the society to fulfil its purpose in the future.

# 9 International competitive strategy

Standard strategic models may be applied to international business but must be applied in a suitable way.

## 9.1 Competitive strategy

As we have already established, **competitive strategies** are the strategies an organisation will pursue for competitive advantage. They determine **how you compete**. Competitive advantage is anything which gives one organisation an edge over its rivals in the products it sells or the services it offers. This is equally applicable to global strategic decisions.

Porter's generic strategies may be applied in global operations, but they must be managed in a way that takes account of the international business environment. Here is  a summary of Porter's strategies as a reminder.

(a)   **Cost leadership** means being the lowest cost producer in the industry as a whole.

(b)   **Differentiation** is the offer of a product or service which is unique or in some way different from other products.

(c)   **Focus** involves a restriction of activities to a segment through:

(i)   providing goods and or services at lower cost to that segment (a cost-focus);

(ii)   providing a differentiated product or service for that segment (differentiation-focus).

**Cost leadership** and **differentiation** are industry-wide strategies. **Focus** involves market segmentation, but involves pursuing, **within the segment only**, a strategy of cost leadership or differentiation.

Although there is a risk with any of the generic strategies, Porter argues that a firm must pursue one of them. A **stuck-in-the-middle** strategy is almost certain to make only low profits, he says. Recent research has indicated that this is too simplistic. Being the lowest cost producer does not mean you have to compete on price.

It is, of course, fairly easy to see how such competitive strategy decisions can be taken in a large domestic market, such as the US, where many economies of scale are readily available. But IM involves recognising differences between country markets, the barriers to entry caused by national and cultural borders, and the global market.

Is it hard to achieve overall **cost leadership**. In terms of international and global marketing it perhaps only applies to a few companies, and even they might face restrictions on market entry.

(a)   Only a few companies are available to take advantage of global sourcing and the economies this offers.

(b)   Cost leadership is a dangerous strategy, as companies from developing countries might, for a short time, benefit from those countries' comparative advantages in lower labour costs. (Generally speaking higher productivity in advanced economies neutralises many of the gains from cheap labour. Thus, the NAFTA agreement has not led to a collapse in US employment. US workers are far more productive than Mexican ones and there is some evidence that as workers become more productive, their wages increase.)

(c)   Domestic producers might have substantial cost advantages owing to their proximity to the local markets.

(d)   A firm's ability to compete as the lowest cost producer in certain markets will be hampered.

- **Tariffs** raise the price of your goods in relation to competitors (eg producers of Scotch whisky trying to export to Japan)

- **Exchange fluctuations** can render your efficiently-made products more expensive than a those of local producers

(e)   Many of the costs of goods can be increased by factors outside management control, such as intricacies of the distribution system.

Clearly, then, a strategy of **differentiation** or **focus** can be more realistic.

(a)   Products can be **differentiated** for the international market, whilst keeping the same brand name (eg coffee).

(b)   The fact that, despite trade liberalisation, there are real differences between markets might suggest that focus is appropriate. Use national boundaries as a means of segmentation, or, as has been suggested, concentrate on those consumers in the international market who share characteristics **across** national segments.

**Beximco Pharmaceuticals**

An example of having the right 'product' for emerging markets is provided by the Bangladeshi firm, *Beximco Pharmaceuticals*, which pursues a differentiation-focus strategy.

Western firms, such as *Glaxo*, invest heavily in research and development, producing sophisticated but expensive products. Beximco, which sells to poorer markets, makes simple products cheaply. In developing countries, such as Vietnam and Iran, and even in Russia, a good supply of basic drugs is what is required. It is felt that there will be less emphasis on vertical expansion, which involves growing sales of sophisticated products to a small section of the population at ever-increasing prices.

Beximco has low wages and low research. Although tighter patent rules may make things worse, western drugs may go out of patent and can be copied.

## 9.2 Product-market strategies

Models such as the **Ansoff matrix** can also be applied, although its application might be more complex than in the single domestic market. To remind you, here follows a diagram.

*Product*

|  |  | Present | New |
|---|---|---|---|
| *Market* | *Present* | Market penetration; (for growth) or consolidation (to maintain position) or withdrawal | Product development |
|  | *New* | Market development | Diversification |

How can this be applied to international marketing strategy? Unfortunately the categories tend to shift.

(a) It is obviously easy to suggest what the **new market** might be: another country.

(b) What, however, do we mean by '**new product**'? Is the product new to the company? Has it only been developed? Is the company still on a learning curve in its domestic market? In this case there might be a choice.

    (i) Introduce the new product **simultaneously** in domestic and overseas markets.

    (ii) Have a continuing rolling programme.

        **Year 1**: the domestic market is dealt with first
        **Year 2**: existing overseas markets are serviced
        **Year 3**: genuinely new overseas markets are addressed

        By year 3, the decision to introduce new products into new markets has effectively become one of market development, on the grounds that product has already been on sale at home and in existing overseas markets.

(c) It would appear **unlikely** that a company would set up abroad in a completely unfamiliar market with a completely new product, when there are easy opportunities to minimise the risk.

Other strategic models such as the BCG matrix may also be applied to global operations.

The Ansoff matrix above can be applied equally to a company looking for new international development or to an established global player. Many strategic developments are concerned with building on where the organisation currently sits in global market, via current products and competences and stretching them to improve competitive position. There are a number of options for expanding or contracting operations.

## Chapter Roundup

- Shareholder value analysis may be used to measure corporate (and hence management) performance in terms of benefit created for shareholders.

- Shareholder value created by past performance is measured by **economic profit**. The **cash flow** approach is more appropriate for assessing plans for the future.

- Purely marketing objectives are no longer acceptable; value based management aims always to **maximise shareholder value** by developing competitive advantage.

- The creation of value depends on three categories of value driver: **financial**, **marketing** and **organisational**.

- The SVA approach is subject to limitations that managers should be aware of.

- **Competitive strategies** require actions to create a defendable position. They include cost leadership, differentiation and focus.

- **Competitive advantage** has to be sustained. It can come from better products, customer perceptions, costs, competencies, assets, economies of scale, attitudes and relationships, offensive and defensive.

- Firms can choose a variety of strategies to **attack or defend** their position. Different strategies are appropriate to challengers, followers, leaders and nichers.

- **Product-market strategy** includes market penetration, market development, product development and diversification.

- Many firms are growing by **alliances** with other firms, short of a full scale merger or acquisition. These are supposed to offer synergies and mutual benefits.

- Markets decline because of **environmental factors**. Some can be revitalised. In others, a firm has to choose whether it wants to stay in the market or withdraw.

- **Strategic wear-out** occurs when firms continue with old strategies that are no longer viable.

- Standard strategic models may be applied to international business but must be applied in a suitable way.

## Quick Quiz

1   Identify three categories of strategic choice.

2   What are Porter's three generic strategies?

3   Give some examples of means of obtaining competitive advantage.

4   Identify five offensive strategies.

5   Identify strategies for market followers.

6   Identify possible approaches to market development.

7   What are exit barriers?

8   What method of growth would be most suitable for a strategy based on learning?

9   How can growth be created in declining markets?

10  What is wear-out?

## Answers to Quick Quiz

1   How to compete; direction of growth; method of growth

2   Cost leadership; differentiation; focus

3   Better product; perceived advantage; global skills; low costs; better competencies; superior assets; economies of scale; attitude; superior relations

4   Frontal; flanking; encirclement and bypass attacks and guerrilla warfare

5   Cloning, adaptation and imitations

6   New geographical areas; different package sizes; new distribution channels; differential pricing

7   Exit barriers make it difficult for a firm to withdraw from a market. An example of a cost barrier would be redundancy costs

8   Organic growth

9   Market and product development

10  A failure to keep business strategy up to date with changed circumstances

## Action Programme Review

1   (a)   Arguably, Hermes initially pursued a cost-focus strategy, by targeting the business segment.

    (b)   It seems to be moving into a cost leadership strategy over the whole market although its competitive offer, in terms of lower costs for local calls, is incomplete.

    (c)   The barriers to entry to the market have been lowered by the new technology. Gerbil phone might pick up a significant amount of business.

2   (a)   In Hester Bateman's (HB's) case, the issues are not particularly clear cut. The size of the market is changing. From being strictly demarcated on national lines, the market has become global. This trend is certain to continue. In this new global market, what strategies can HB pursue?

(i)    Cost leadership would seem out of the question, in the short term at least. This is because cutlery making technology can be easily imitated by countries in the Pacific. At the moment, their labour costs are much lower; how long this will remain is a different question.

(ii)   Differentiation. HB could differentiate the product on a global basis, on the basis of quality (by using special alloys) or by designing products that are attractive to users, or by introducing a range of new designs.

(iii)  Focus. HB could decide to serve the UK or European market only, but it will still be vulnerable to cheaper competition. On the other hand it could position itself as a luxury brand to serve wealthier consumers.

Clearly, differentiation or focus are the way forward, as HB will always be vulnerable to lower cost competition, from Pacific Rim countries first of all, and then from other countries as they industrialise.

(b)    *Statement of objectives*

The statement of objectives contains remarkably few of them! Nothing has been quantified. As a mission statement it addresses the past not the future, on the assumption that past traditions can be preserved as a guarantee for future success.

To some extent, having survived the recessions of the early 1980s and 1990s, HB is in a strong position, having obviously taken steps to maintain its competitiveness. It is still able to trade on is quality image, as it has 45% of the market by value, as opposed to only 35% by volume. This is still significantly more than its competitors from overseas, suggesting that they are fighting over a niche that is relatively unprofitable for UK companies. Concentrating on the higher end of the market, rather than battling over market share for cheap generic items has been a sound strategy.

However, can this strategy be continued? It is possible that competitors will do their best to raise quality and HB's premium position will no longer be secure. Furthermore, the lack of investment will begin to tell. Finally, although the firm has maintained its market position in the short term, it has lost the confidence of investors in its ability to deliver long-term improvements.

HB therefore needs to update its objectives with a proper mission statement to satisfy the needs of its various stakeholders.

- To what extent can it continue to trade on its quality image?
- What customers is it looking to satisfy?
- What does it intend to do to address the concerns of its investors?

Clearly, the survival of the firm itself as an independent entity is in doubt. Investors are being advised to sell, yet the firm is still profitable and has a large share of the UK market. An argument perhaps is that it has failed to capitalise on the competitive strengths it has. If it is exporting to a New York department store, it is clear that there might be further export opportunities, which are not being satisfied, in the luxury goods market.

HB's position is therefore confused. On the one hand, it has survived two recessions, no mean feat. It has a commanding position in the British market, and its designs satisfy choosy US customers. Investors however have another viewpoint. The firm seems vulnerable to a take-over.

(c)    *Marketing strategies*

HB must first of all decide which generic strategy it is to pursue. We have suggested that cost leadership is out of the question, and so either differentiation or focus should be pursued. Once this is decided, a suitable marketing mix must devised. We can suggest a focus strategy, exploiting product differentiation (ie a differentiation-focus strategy). HB already produces cutlery of a different quality (eg the highest quality is exported to the US). In order to improve profits, HB first of all needs to identify which product markets are the most profitable, and deal with them in a suitable way. Different strategies might be suggested for different market niches to ensure profit streams.

Furthermore, the firm needs to undertake a programme of market research to find out what its customers (both retailers such as the New York department store, and the end-consumer or user) think about HB, and how it can better satisfy their needs.

*Product*

'Made in Sheffield' goods enable the firm to charge a premium price. The firm should concentrate on exploiting the international luxury market for high quality 'designer' goods. For example, scotch whisky is exported to Japan, and HB can skew its R and D towards producing a variety of innovative designs that can combine premium prices at the high end of the market.

At the same time it needs to enhance the profits earned from the UK market where it is facing cheap generic competition. It has little scope for cutting prices, and so it might be a good idea to maintain its position but at a lower price. It could set up, therefore, a brand of cheap imported cutlery, to compete with BQ and the other importers. This would release resources to concentrate on higher quality premium-priced products which could still have the Made in Sheffield tag. HB can therefore set up two brands. There are obviously profits to be earned from the generic end of the market, and HB still has the opportunity to deliver.

Many firms sell low and high-quality versions of a product under different brand names. It is not so much the company that has to be positioned appropriately in the market, as its brands.

The firm could also use its expertise in quality metal work to expand its product range (using Ansoff's product development strategy) into the same market. Suggestions might include:

- Related products such as silver (soup tureens, trays, silver goblets)
- Less plausibly, perhaps, ornaments, jewellery, even cufflinks

*Price*

The price element of the mix is implicit in the product. To increase its profitability, HB is to manufacture premium products at premium prices. This is in order to increase the ROCE: the New York business earns a gross margin of 45%.

Under a different brand name, HB is to import cheap generic products from Pacific Rim or cheaper countries, and use its existing networks to take on the competition. This will hopefully generate more profits, or at least cover costs, as the expensive manufacturing capability will be directed elsewhere. HB will be able to compete more effectively.

*Place*

The distribution system is an important element of the marketing mix. HB has obviously no problem in the UK, but perhaps it needs to consider whether it is as effective and efficient as it could be. We are told little about HB's existing distribution and logistics systems.

However, the twin pronged strategy does require some new expertise.

(i)     If the company is importing its generic products from overseas, it will need to have suitable warehousing and storage facilities, and to have systems which can predict likely demand, so customers do not have to wait too long.

(ii)    It is hoped that many of the premium priced products will be exported. The US department store is a model for strategies that can be adopted in other countries in the EU and over the world. HB will need assistance, perhaps from one of the UK government's export advisory services, to find distributors for its product. The distributors will inevitably have a significant say in how the goods are to be positioned and sold. In a market such as Japan, HB will need a suitable partner to negotiate the thickets of the distribution system; in a country that uses chopsticks, demand for cutlery will be limited, but it can be sold as a luxury item.

However, the main markets would be the US where further expansion is obviously possible and the EU.

The company might consider offering an enhanced service to customers, for example a just-in-time delivery system.

*Promotion*

Promotional strategies will be an essential feature of HB's repositioning itself as a premium priced quality product. This means finding a suitable advertising agency, and researching the communications messages the company wishes to pursue. It might mean advertising in media it has not used before (eg magazines promoting luxury goods, or lifestyle magazines such as *The World of Interiors*).

Finally the firm needs to promote itself to another audience: investors, who have to be convinced that the new strategy will work. At the moment they are critical, and will sell to a bidder. To keep their jobs, the existing managers must work to convince investors that the company's existing and potential strengths can be better exploited in future.

3 The first step in a suggested solution is to think of how a company operating nation-wide in general road haulage might diversify, with some synergistic benefits. Perhaps you thought of the following.

- Moving from nation-wide haulage to international haulage.
- Moving from general haulage to 'speciality' types of haulage (eg large items).
- Providing a despatch service for small items (although this too is a very competitive business).
- Hiring smaller vehicles to customers for 'self-drive'.
- Moving into warehousing.

Only three suggestions are required by the question. You may have thought of different ideas to those in the list. You should appreciate however, that the principles of diversification need to be applied in a specific situation and there are no obvious ready-made and off-the-peg answers to such problems.

(a) To move from nation-wide to international haulage, the company might be able to use its existing contacts with customers to develop an international trade. Existing administration and depot facilities in the UK could be used. Drivers should be available who are willing to work abroad, and the scope for making reasonable profits should exist. However, international road haulage might involve the company in the purchase of new vehicles (eg road haulage in Europe often involves the carriage of containerised products on large purpose-built vehicles). Since international haulage takes longer, vehicles will be tied up in jobs for several days, and a substantial investment might be required to develop the business. In addition, in the event of breakdowns, a network of overseas garage service arrangements will have to be created. It might take some time before business builds up sufficiently to become profitable.

(b) The same broad considerations apply to speciality types of haulage. Existing depot facilities could be used and existing customer contacts might be developed. However, expertise in specialist work will have to be 'brought in' as well as developed within the company and special vehicles might need to be bought. Business might take some time to build up and if the initial investment is high, there could be substantial early losses.

In the same way, you should be able to consider the other means of diversification suggested earlier in the solution. Although items (a) and (b) above do not cover all of the following items, the factors which need to be considered in a policy of diversification are as follows.

- Potential synergy
- The size of the initial investments
- The potential for growth and profits
- Facilities required
- Manpower required and expertise needed

- The difficulties in building up customer contacts
- Contingency planning: what happens if things do not go as well as expected?
- Risk
- To what extent are the products and services new, and to what extent are the markets new?

4    (a)    *Background*

There is considerable public interest in horticulture and gardening generally, as witnessed by the variety of television programmes on the subject, and the success of flower shows generally. The Society should be able to flourish in such a setting, as there appears to be no dearth of public interest.

Although the Society should be flourishing, it has not succeeded in tapping the wealth of public interest. This is shown in the slow decline of people attending the annual flower show.

This decline has prevented the Society from pursuing some of its traditional activities in the local community, such as providing seeds for the elderly. The club is not paying its way.

*Possible causes*

There have been significant social changes since the Society was founded. One significant change, identified by the Chairman's plea to the ladies of the town, is the changing role of women. Perhaps women are just not available to carry out the Society's functions any more. Reasons for this might include the increase in female employment.

Another significant change is the overall increase in car ownership. This has meant it is a easier than before for people to travel the distance to the next town with its competing flower show. This means that the catchment area of any show has grown larger, and people's activities may not be restricted to the strictly local environment.

*The marketing concept*

Although the Society is not a business seeking to make a profit, the marketing concept is still relevant to the past and future of the society. There has been no decline in public interest in horticulture, but it is clear that the Society is failing to tap the interest that does exist in the subject.

It is clear that the marketing concept has not applied to any significant degree.

(i)    The chairman believes the Society is of benefit to the local townsfolk, but the declining interests and attendances would indicate that this is definitely not the case. Fewer people are attending the shows, and this implies that people are being put off.

(ii)   The chairman is simply trying to carry on with the existing practices. This is at best a sales or a production orientation.

(b)    *Suggested strategies*

In order to address the slow decline in public interest, first of all an analysis should be carried out as to why there is a decline in interest.

(i)    Existing members of the society should be asked for their views, as those who are not on the committee of the society may have their own ideas on the situation.

(ii)   The society should conduct a survey to identify the population profile of Smalltown, how this relates to the Association's traditional membership, interest in horticulture amongst residents, and residents' knowledge of and opinions about the society and its activities.

The research is quite important. It may suggest that the society is simply not publicising itself or the show properly; perhaps it needs to arrange advance coverage in the local news media or local BBC or commercial radio station.

On the other hand, the society may have a poor but unjustified image; perhaps people perceive it as being run by a clique, who are out of touch with current demand. Certainly the chairman's plea to the ladies of the town to perform their traditional duties suggests he is out of touch.

The study might reveal other activities that the society could carry out (eg evening classes).

The Society should also consider how to promote the annual flower show more effectively, as this is its main source of funds.

(i)     Ensure that the show does not clash with larger ones held elsewhere.

(ii)    Give proper notice in local papers, or indeed by leafleting local people, or buy advertising at local garden centres, DIY stores.

(iii)   Try and obtain sponsorship from local businesses. Such funds might be used for advertising.

(iv)    Most importantly, address the identified deficiencies in the show, so that people are not disappointed.

(v)     Try to reach out to new, younger members, eg by a simple web page.

Now try Question 3 at the end of the Study Text

# Annex: Discounting cash flows

Discounting is a basic tool of financial analysis that is also widely used in other business techniques, so we will start off by showing you how it works.

The **basic principle of compounding** is that if we invest £X now for n years at r% interest per annum, we should obtain £S in n years time, where £S = £X$(1+r^n)$.

Thus if we invest £10,000 now for four years at 10% interest per annum, we will have a total investment worth £10,000 × $1.10^4$ = £14,641 at the end of four years (that is, at year 4 if it is now year 0).

**Key concept**

> The basic principle of **discounting** is that if we wish to have £V in n years' time, we need to invest a certain sum *now* (year 0) at an interest rate of r% in order to obtain the required sum of money in the future.

For example, if we wish to have £14,641 in four years' time, how much money would we need to invest now at 10% interest per annum? This is the reverse of the situation described in Paragraph 3 and, fairly obviously, the answer is £10,000. We can prove this.

Using our formula, S = X$(1 + r)^n$

| where | X | = | the original sum invested |
|---|---|---|---|
| | r | = | 10% |
| | n | = | 4 |
| | S | = | £14,641 |

| £14,641 | = | X$(1 + 0.1)^4$ |
|---|---|---|
| £14,641 | = | X × 1.4641 |
| ∴ X | = | $\dfrac{£14,641}{1.4641}$ = £10,000 |

£10,000 now, with the capacity to earn a return of 10% per annum, is the equivalent in value of £14,641 after four years. We can therefore say that £10,000 is the **present value** of £14,641 at year 4, at an interest rate of 10%.

**Key concept**

> The **present value** of a future sum is obtained by discounting the future sum at an appropriate discount rate.

The discounting formula is

$$X = S \times \frac{1}{(1+r)^n}$$

| where | S | is the sum to be received after n time periods |
|---|---|---|
| | X | is the present value (PV) of that sum |
| | r | is the rate of return, expressed as a proportion |
| | n | is the number of time periods (usually years). |

The rate r is sometimes called a cost of capital.

## Example: discounting

(a) Calculate the present value of £60,000 at year 6, if a return of 15% per annum is obtainable.

(b) Calculate the present value of £100,000 at year 5, if a return of 6% per annum is obtainable.

(c) How much would a person need to invest now at 12% to earn £4,000 at year 2 and £4,000 at year 3?

## Solution

The discounting formula, $X = S \times \dfrac{1}{(1+r)^n}$ is required.

(a)  $S = £60,000$
$n = 6$
$r = 0.15$

$PV = 60,000 \times \dfrac{1}{1.15^6}$

$= 60,000 \times 0.432$

$= £25,920$

(b)  $S = £100,000$
$n = 5$
$r = 0.06$

$PV = 100,000 \times \dfrac{1}{1.06^5}$

$= 100,000 \times 0.747$

$= £74,700$

(c)  $S = £4,000$
$n = 2 \text{ or } 3$
$r = 0.12$

$PV = (4,000 \times \dfrac{1}{1.12^2}) + (4,000 \times \dfrac{1}{1.12^3})$

$= 4,000 \times (0.797 + 0.712)$

$= £6,036$

This calculation can be checked as follows.

| | £ |
|---|---:|
| Year 0 | 6,036.00 |
| Interest for the first year (12%) | 724.32 |
| | 6,760.32 |
| Interest for the second year (12%) | 811.24 |
| | 7,571.56 |
| Less withdrawal | (4,000.00) |
| | 3,571.56 |
| Interest for the third year (12%) | 428.59 |
| | 4,000.15 |
| Less withdrawal | (4,000.00) |
| Rounding error | 0.15 |

## Project appraisal

Discounted cash flow techniques can be used to evaluate expenditure proposals such as the purchase of equipment or marketing budgets.

**Key concept**

**Discounted cash flow (DCF)** involves the application of discounting arithmetic to the estimated future cash flows (receipts and expenditures) from a project in order to decide whether the project is expected to earn a satisfactory rate of return.

**BPP**
LEARNING MEDIA

## The net present method value (NPV) method

> The **net present value (NPV) method** works out the present values of all items of income and expenditure related to an investment at a given rate of return, and then works out a net total. If it is positive, the investment is considered to be acceptable. If it is negative, the investment is considered to be unacceptable.

## Example: the net present value of a project

Dog Ltd is considering whether to spend £5,000 on an item of equipment. The excess of income over cash expenditure from the project would be £3,000 in the first year and £4,000 in the second year.

The company will not invest in any project unless it offers a return in excess of 15% per annum.

*Required*

Assess whether the investment is worthwhile.

## Solution

In this example, an outlay of £5,000 now promises a return of £3,000 **during** the first year and £4,000 **during** the second year. It is a convention in DCF, however, that cash flows spread over a year are assumed to occur **at the end of the year**, so that the cash flows of the project are as follows.

|  | £ |
|---|---|
| Year 0 (now) | (5,000) |
| Year 1 (at the end of the year) | 3,000 |
| Year 2 (at the end of the year) | 4,000 |

The NPV method takes the following approach.

(a) The project offers £3,000 at year 1 and £4,000 at year 2, for an outlay of £5,000 now.

(b) The company might invest elsewhere to earn a return of 15% per annum.

(c) If the company did invest at exactly 15% per annum, how much would it need to invest now to earn £3,000 at the end of year 1 plus £4,000 at the end of year 2?

(d) Is it cheaper to invest £5,000 in the project, or to invest elsewhere at 15%, in order to obtain these future cash flows?

If the company did invest elsewhere at 15% per annum, the amount required to earn £3,000 in year 1 and £4,000 in year 2 would be as follows.

| Year | Cash flow £ | Discount factor 15% | Present value £ |
|---|---|---|---|
| 1 | 3,000 | $\frac{1}{1.15} = 0.870$ | 2,610 |
| 2 | 4,000 | $\frac{1}{(1.15)^2} = 0.756$ | 3,024 |
|  |  |  | 5,634 |

The choice is to invest £5,000 in the project, or £5,634 elsewhere at 15%, in order to obtain these future cash flows. We can therefore reach the following conclusion.

- It is cheaper to invest in the project, by £634.
- The project offers a return of over 15% per annum.

The net present value is the difference between the present value of cash inflows from the project (£5,634) and the present value of future cash outflows (in this example, £5,000 × $1/1.15^0$ = £5,000).

An NPV statement could be drawn up as follows.

| Year | Cash flow £ | Discount factor 15% | Present value £ |
|------|------|------|------|
| 0 | (5,000) | 1.000 | (5,000) |
| 1 | 3,000 | $\dfrac{1}{1.15} = 0.870$ | 2,610 |
| 2 | 4,000 | $\dfrac{1}{(1.15)^2} = 0.756$ | 3,024 |
| | | Net present value | +634 |

The project has a positive net present value, so it is acceptable.

## Project comparison

**The NPV method can also be used to compare two or more investment options**. For example, suppose that Daisy Ltd can choose between the investment outlined above *or* a second investment, which also costs £28,000 but which would earn £6,500 in the first year, £7,500 in the second, £8,500 in the third, £9,500 in the fourth and £10,500 in the fifth. Which one should Daisy Ltd choose?

**The decision rule is to choose the option with the highest NPV**. We therefore need to calculate the NPV of the second option.

| Year | Cash flow £ | Discount factor 11% | Present value £ |
|------|------|------|------|
| 0 | (28,000) | 1.000 | (28,000) |
| 1 | 6,500 | 0.901 | 5,857 |
| 2 | 7,500 | 0.812 | 6,090 |
| 3 | 8,500 | 0.731 | 6,214 |
| 4 | 9,500 | 0.659 | 6,261 |
| 5 | 10,500 | 0.593 | 6,227 |
| | | NPV = | 2,649 |

Daisy Ltd should therefore invest in the second option since it has the higher NPV.

## Limitations of using the NPV method

There are a number of problems associated with using the NPV method in practice.

(a)   **The future discount factors** (or interest rates) which are used in calculating NPVs can only be **estimated** and are not known with certainty. Discount rates that are estimated for time periods far into the future are therefore less likely to be accurate, thereby leading to less accurate NPV values.

(b)   Similarly, NPV calculations make use of estimated **future cash flows**. As with future discount factors, cash flows which are estimated for cash flows several years into the future cannot really be predicted with any real certainty.

(c)   When using the NPV method it is common to assume that all cash flows occur **at the end of the year**. However, this assumption is also likely to give rise to less accurate NPV values.

There are a number of computer programs available these days which enable a range of NPVs to be calculated for different circumstances (best-case and worst-case situations and so on). Such programs allow some of the limitations mentioned above to be alleviated.

# Competitive positions

## Syllabus content

- Critical evaluation of strategic options in relation to shareholder value, using appropriate decision tools
- Formulation and evaluation of competitive strategies
- Appraisal of marketing strategies
- Building competitive capability and approaches to leveraging capability to create advantage across geographically diverse markets
- The incorporation of customer-led Internet marketing into marketing strategies
- The use of e-technology to build and exploit competitive advantage

# Introduction

In this chapter we look in detail at some further aspects of the creation of competitive advantage.

As an introduction we consider the evaluation of strategic options, since evaluations and choice are essential components of the strategic decision-making process. We then look in detail at the analysis of the market into segments and the selection of the segments that offer the best outcomes.

We complete this chapter with a detailed consideration of the marketing use of the Internet, a growing focus of business activity.

# 1 Evaluating options

**FAST FORWARD**

Strategies are evaluated according to their **suitability** to the firm's situation; their **feasibility** in terms of resources and competences; and their acceptability to key stakeholder groups, particularly shareholders and customers.

## 1.1 General evaluation criteria

According to the rational model, individual strategies have to be **evaluated**, according to a number of criteria, before a strategy or a mixture of strategies is chosen. Three criteria are **suitability**, **feasibility** and **acceptability**.

## 1.2 Suitability

**Suitability** relates to the **strategic logic** of the strategy. The strategy should fit the situation of the firm. It should satisfy a range of requirements.

- **Exploit** strengths: that is, **unique** resources and **core competences**
- **Rectify** company **weaknesses**
- **Neutralise** or deflect environmental **threats**
- Help the firm to **seize opportunities**
- **Satisfy the goals** of organisation
- **Fill the gap** identified by gap analysis
- Generate/maintain **competitive advantage**
- Involve an acceptable level of **risk**
- Suit the **politics** and corporate **culture**

A number of techniques can be used to assess suitability.

## 1.3 Life cycle analysis

The **product life cycle** concept may be used to assess potential strategies. This was discussed in Chapter 1.

The product life cycle approach may be combined with an appraisal of the company's strength in its markets using a **life cycle/portfolio matrix**. This was originally designed by consultants **Arthur D Little**.

STAGES OF INDUSTRY MATURITY

| | Embryonic | Growth | Mature | Ageing |
|---|---|---|---|---|
| **Dominant** | Fast grow<br>Start up | Fast grow<br>Attain cost leadership<br>Renew<br>Defend position | Defend position<br>Attain cost leadership<br>Renew<br>Fast grow | Defend position<br>Focus<br>Renew<br>Grow with industry |
| **Strong** | Start up<br>Differentiate<br>Fast grow | Fast grow<br>Catch up<br>Attain cost leadership<br>Differentiate | Attain cost leadership<br>Renew, focus<br>Differentiate<br>Grow with industry | Find niche<br>Hold niche<br>Hang in<br>Grow with industry<br>Harvest |
| **Favourable** | Start up<br>Differentiate<br>Focus<br>Fast grow | Differentiate,<br>focus<br>Catch up<br>Grow with<br>industry | Harvest, hang in<br>Find niche, hold niche<br>Renew, turnaround<br>Differentiate, focus<br>Grow with industry | Retrench<br>Turnaround |
| **Tenable** | Start up<br>Grow with industry<br>Focus | Harvest, catch up<br>Hold niche, hang in<br>Find niche<br>Turnaround<br>Focus<br>Grow with industry | Harvest<br>Turnaround<br>Find niche<br>Retrench | Divest<br>Retrench |
| **Weak** | Find niche<br>Catch up<br>Grow with industry | Turnaround<br>Retrench | Withdraw<br>Divest | Withdraw |

The position of the company on the **industry maturity** axis of this matrix depends on the assessment of eight factors including market growth rate, growth potential and number of competitors. Each stage has its own strategic implications. For instance, an ageing market will be subject to falling demand, so heavy marketing expenditure is unlikely to be justified.

### 1.3.1 Competitive position

(a) A **dominant** position allows the company to exert influence over the behaviour of competitors. It is rare in the private sector.

(b) A **strong** position gives considerable freedom of choice over strategy.

(c) A **favourable** position arises in a fragmented market, often when the company has strengths to exploit.

(d) A **tenable** position is vulnerable to competition and profitability may depend on specialisation.

(e) A **weak** position arises from inability to compete effectively. Firms of any size can find themselves in this condition.

## 1.4 Business profile analysis

In **business profile analysis** the expected effects of a strategy on the corporation are forecast. A business profile is then created by scoring the forecast state against the favourable parameters established by the empirical findings of PIMS research. There are eleven of these parameters; they relate to market position, financial strength, quality and operational efficiency. The forecast profile may be compared with the current profile in order to assess the proposed strategy for suitability.

## 1.5 Strategy screening

It is not enough merely to assess strategies for suitability. Eventually choices must be made. Such choices may be assisted by **strategy screening** methods, which include **ranking** and **scenario planning**. Ranking is dealt with later in this chapter. Scenarios have been described earlier in this Study Text. Potential strategies may be screened by assessing their suitability against each potential scenario. This leads not so much to a choice as to the establishment of a series of **contingency plans**.

## 1.6 Screening market opportunities

Kotler summarises the stages in evaluating a marketing opportunity as follows.

### Evaluating Market Opportunities

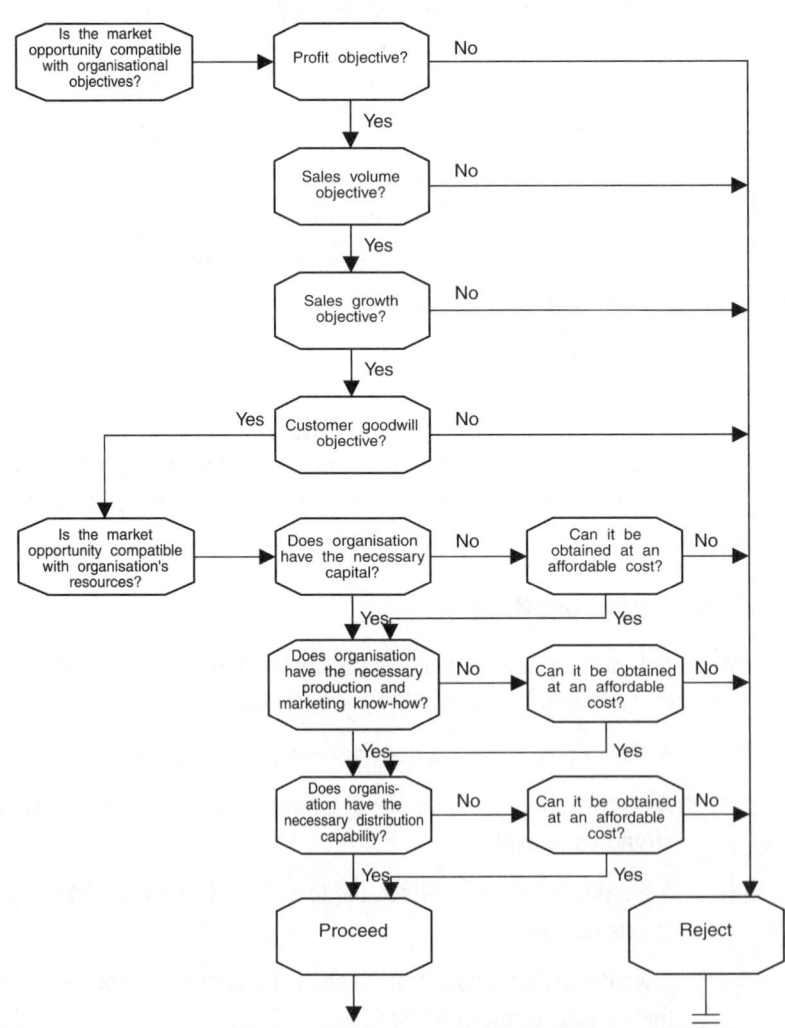

Adapted from Kotler: *Marketing Management Analysis, Planning and implementation and Control*

# 1.7 Feasibility

**Feasibility** asks whether the strategy can be implemented and, in particular, if the organisation has adequate **resources**.

- Enough **money**
- The **ability** to deliver the goods/services specified in the strategy
- The ability to deal with the likely **responses that competitors** will make
- Access to **technology, materials and resources**
- Enough **time** to implement the strategy

Strategies that do not make use of existing competences and therefore call for new competences to be acquired, might not be feasible, since gaining competences takes time and can be costly.

Two important financial approaches to assessing the feasibility of particular strategies are **funds flow** analysis and **breakeven** analysis. Funds flow analysis examines the way money flows into the business and out of it; where it comes from, where it goes, what it is committed to and how much of it is available. Breakeven analysis is dealt with in detail later in this Study Text.

**Resource deployment analysis** makes a wider assessment of feasibility in terms of **resources** and **competences**. The resources and competences required for each potential strategy are assessed and compared with those of the firm. A two stage approach may be followed.

(a) Does the firm have the necessary resources and competences to achieve the **threshold** requirements for each strategy?

(b) Does the firm have the core competences and **unique resources** to maintain **competitive advantage**?

When assessing feasibility in this way, it is important to remember that it may be possible to acquire new competences and resources or to stretch existing ones. Such innovation is likely to be difficult to imitate.

## 1.7.1 Feasibility studies

Very little appears to have been written specifically on this aspect in marketing literature. The following guidelines should therefore be found useful in the event of a future question on this matter. The guidelines are based on a specimen answer to a specific question on feasibility in a previous CIM case study.

## 1.7.2 The form and content of a feasibility study

| 1 | Corporate audit |
| --- | --- |
| | • Objectives, five year plan |
| | • Key criteria for project appraisal/evaluation |
| 2 | The scenario or project |
| 3 | Assumptions |
| 4 | Feasibility research |
| | (a) Experimental/technical research |
| | Design studies, performance specification, timings, costs. |
| | (b) Market research |
| | Demand analysis, competition, buying motives, pricing etc. |

> (c)   *Commercial potential* (to include analysis of the feasibility research in terms of timing, cost, human resource needs). Outline income and expenditure analysis.
>
> - Venture capital required
> - Cost of capital at current interest rate
> - Working capital
> - Short-term loans/overdraft requirements
> - Cash flow projections - funding periods
> - Contingencies
> - Payback periods and net gains

## 1.8 Acceptability

The **acceptability** of a strategy depends on the views of **stakeholders**.

**Financial considerations**. Strategies will be primarily evaluated by considering how far they contribute to meeting the dominant objective of increasing shareholder value. A wide range of measures is available to help assess financial viability.

| | |
|---|---|
| • Return on investment | • Cash flow |
| • Profits | • Price/Earnings |
| • Growth | • Market capitalisation |
| • EPS | • Cost-benefit analysis |

Specific projects and ventures can be assessed using a variety of financial techniques. The most satisfactory is the NPV approach explained in the Annex to Chapter 4. However, other techniques are also used, some of them rather crude in concept. We examine these other techniques later in this Study Text.

There are several important **stakeholder groups**.

(a)   The **workforce** constitutes an important stakeholder group that typically has an interest in the financial implications of strategy because of its links to **job security**. Successful strategies tat enhance shareholder value tend to reduce or put on hold the search for economies in head count. However, the success of some strategies may derive from cost reductions achieved partly by reducing the need for labour.

(b)   **Customers** may object to a strategy if it alters the perceived value they receive. Such an approach is likely to be followed rapidly by failure of the strategy in the targeted market segment.

(c)   **Banks** are interested in the implications for cash resources, debt levels and so on.

(d)   **Government**. A strategy involving a takeover may be prohibited under competition legislation.

(e)   **The public**. The environmental impact may cause key stakeholders to protest. For example, out of town superstores are now frowned upon by national and local government in the UK.

(f)   **Risk**. Different shareholders have different attitudes to risk. A strategy which changed the risk/return profile, for whatever reason, may not be acceptable.

How stakeholders relate to the management of the company depends very much on what **type of stakeholder** they are - internal, connected or external - and on the **level in the management hierarchy** at which they are able to apply pressure. Clearly a company's management will respond differently to the demands of, say, its shareholders and the community at large.

The way in which the relationship between company and stakeholders is conducted is a function of the parties' **relative bargaining strength** and the philosophy underlying **each party's objectives**. This can be shown by means of a spectrum.

|  | Weak | Stakeholders' bargaining strength | | | Strong |
|---|---|---|---|---|---|
| Company's conduct of relation- ship | Command/ dictated by company | Consultation and consideration of stakeholders' views | Negotiation | Participation and acceptance of stakeholders' views | Democratic voting by stakeholders | Command/ dictated by stakeholders |

## 1.9 Stakeholder mapping

*Mendelow* classifies stakeholders on a matrix whose axes are power held and likelihood of showing an interest in the organisation's activities. These factors will help define the type of relationship the organisation should seek with its stakeholders.

Level of interest

|  | Low | High |
|---|---|---|
| **Low** Power | A | B |
| **High** | C | D |

(a) **Key players** are found in segment D: strategy must be *acceptable* to them, at least. An example would be a major customer.

(b) Stakeholders in segment C must be treated with care. While often passive, they are capable of moving to segment D. They should, therefore be **kept satisfied**. Large institutional shareholders might fall into segment C.

(c) Stakeholders in segment B do not have great ability to influence strategy, but their views can be important in influencing more powerful stakeholders, perhaps by lobbying. They should therefore be **kept informed**. Community representatives and charities might fall into segment B.

(d) Minimal effort is expended on segment A.

## 1.10 Stakeholder response

**Stakeholder analysis** identifies the interest groups in an enterprise. Different stakeholders will have their own views as to strategy. As some stakeholders have **negative power,** in other words power to impede or disrupt the decision, their likely response might be considered. An analysis of **stakeholder risk** has two elements.

(a) The risk that any particular strategic option poses to the **interests of the different stakeholders**.

(b) The **risk that stakeholders might respond** in such a way as to make a proposed strategy less attractive.

| Stakeholder | Interests at stake | Response risk |
|---|---|---|
| **Management** | Pay, status, power, promotion | Subtle sabotage, procrastination, internal politics |
| **Employees** | Pay, security, expertise | Strike action, resignation |
| **Shareholders** | Return on investment | Sell shares, leaving the firm vulnerable to take over; refuse to invest more |
| **Bankers** | Loan security; profits | Refusal to continue lending arrangements; call in liquidator |
| **Customers** | Product | Switch to another supplier |
| **Suppliers** | Business | Will fail to deliver |
| **Government** | The public interest; election success; tax | Will regulate or tax |

## 1.11 The strategic value of stakeholders

**FAST FORWARD**

Analysing stakeholders by their power held and their degree of interest helps to understand their influence.

**The firm can make strategic gains from managing stakeholder relationships**. This was highlighted by a recent report by the Royal Society of Arts on **Tomorrow's Company**. 'Failure to manage such relationships can carry heavy penalties.' Studies have revealed:

(a) **Correlation between employee retention and customer loyalty** (eg low staff turnover in service firms generally results in more repeat business).

(b) **Continuity and stability** in relationships with employees, customers and suppliers is important in enabling organisations to **respond to certain types of change**.

These soft issues are particularly pertinent for industries where creativity is important and for service businesses. Knowledge based and service industries are likely to be the growth industries of the future.

In *Power In and Around Organisations*, *Mintzberg* identifies groups that not only have an interest in an organisation but power over it.

| The external coalition | The internal coalition |
|---|---|
| • Owners (who hold legal title) <br>• Associates (suppliers, customers, trading partners) <br>• Employee associations (unions, professional bodies) <br>• Public (government, media) | • The chief executive and board at the strategic apex <br>• Line managers <br>• Operators <br>• The technostructure <br>• Support staff <br>• Ideology (ie culture) |

Each of these groups has three basic choices.

• **Loyalty**. They can do as they are told.

• **Exit**. For example by selling their shares, or getting a new job.

- **Voice**. They can stay and try to change the system. Those who choose voice are those who can, to varying degrees, influence the organisation. Influence implies a degree of power and willingness to exercise it.

## 1.12 Strategy selection

**FAST FORWARD**

Whether or not a formal approach to strategy is taken, strategic managers must think flexibly and be prepared to respond to changing situations.

### 1.12.1 Planning and enforced choice

The techniques dealt with in this chapter are appropriate to the use of the rational model and may be useful when less formal approaches are taken. They also have a role when strategic developments are **imposed from outside** the organisation. This may come about, for instance, as a result of a major change in the environment, as when the oil shocks of the 1970s stimulated off-shore production, or because of the influence of a dominant stakeholder. A good example of the second possibility was the effect of Marks and Spencer's decision to cease buying from William Baird, a UK clothing manufacturer. This led to plant closures, reorganisation and a management buyout offer.

### 1.12.2 Formal evaluation of imposed strategy

(a) The first role of formal evaluation is to assess the degree of **risk** inherent in the imposed strategy. This may indicate that a medium-term programme to reduce risk is required; this could be incorporated into the overall plan.

(b) Secondly, techniques such as **scenario planning** can be used to establish contingency plans in case the imposed strategy leads to unacceptably low performance.

### 1.12.3 Learning from experience

The rational model is a heavily top-down approach. We have discussed the alternative, **emergent** or **incremental** approaches earlier in this Study Text. The danger associated with these approaches is **strategic drift**: the tendency for strategy to lose direction and coherence. This is especially likely in the divisionalised conglomerate, where SBU managers may strive for and attain increasing degrees of independence.

It is a desirable feature of the strategic apex of such a company that it is able to promote, nurture and exploit developments at the periphery as part of its strategic process. This combines bottom-up creativity with an element of control.

### 1.12.4 Real options

The option concept is very useful in the context of selecting strategies. The selection of a particular course of strategic action may offer **options for future strategy**. The availability of such an option should be considered when evaluating strategies.

A possible course of action may open up further possibilities: one important case is the possibility of making further, follow-on investments. This is equivalent to a **call option** in financial strategy. For example, if a manufacturing business decides to open a retail outlet, it acquires the option to stock complementary products from other manufacturers. If the NPV of the basic outlet strategy is assessed as negative, this negative sum represents the price of the option to expand the range at a future date.

Using this type of conceptual approach allows more subtle evaluation of possible strategies to be undertaken and permits more sophisticated choices to be made between alternatives. In particular, the option to abandon a chosen strategy at low cost will make that strategy more attractive than one with a high cost of abandonment. This choice might rise where there are two possible approaches to manufacturing a new product.

(a) Purchase of high efficiency, highly specialised machinery
(b) Purchase of lower efficiency, general purpose machinery

Option (a) may offer lower costs if the venture succeeds, but the ability to use option (b)'s machinery for another purpose reduces its cost of abandonment should the venture fail.

A strategy can be assessed on how it achieves the organisation's objectives, but some **objectives may conflict** and the choice may not be clear cut.

### 1.12.5 Ranking and scoring

**Ranking and scoring methods** are best illustrated by means of a simple example. The **objectives are weighted** in relative **importance** (eg minimising competitive threats may be more important than other objectives). We assume for the example below that the strategic options cannot be realistically combined.

| Objectives<br><br>Strategic option | Growth in profit by over 10% | Reduce dependence on suppliers | Minimise competitive threats | Score | Rank |
|---|---|---|---|---|---|
| Objective weighting | 4 | 3 | 5 | | |
| Do nothing | ✗ | ✗ | ✗ | – | – |
| Cut costs by subcontracting | ✓ | ✗ | ✗ | 4 | 3rd |
| Expand product range | ✓ | ✗ | ✓ | 9 | 1st |
| Offer discounts to customers for fixed term contract | ✗ | ✗ | ✓ | 5 | 2nd |

In the above example, expanding the product range would be chosen as the firm believes it will enhance profits and minimise competitive threats.

In many cases, the strategies may not be mutually exclusive, or it might be possible to implement all the strategic options above (other than doing nothing).

# 2 Risk evaluation

 **FAST FORWARD**

Risk must be managed and to do this, it must be quantified and its implications considered.

## 2.1 Types of risk

**Key concept**

**Risk** relates to uncertainty about the future. Any forward looking strategy is risky, because events might not turn out as anticipated.

(a) **Physical risk**, such as fire, earthquakes, computer failure.

(b) **Economic risk.** The strategy might be based on assumptions as to the economy which might turn out to be wrong.

(c) **Financial risk** relates to the type of financial arrangement in the decision, and the quality of the cash flows.

(d) **Business risk.** These risks relate to commercial and industry factors. In other words, there is the possibility that the strategy will fail because of new technology, competitors, customer reaction, operational failures.

(e)    **Political or country risk** includes nationalisation, sanctions, civil war, political instability, if these have an impact on the business.

(f)    **Exchange risk**. Changes in exchange rates affect the value of a transaction in a foreign currency.

(g)    **Information risk**. The data may not be reliable.

### Marketing at Work

The *Financial Times* reported an interesting aspect of the takeover of *Safeway* by *Wm Morrison Supermarkets*.

'Integrating the faltering Safeway with Wm Morrison Supermarkets (like-for-like sales over Christmas up by more than 10 per cent) is going to be quite a headache. And that makes the news that the group has failed to find a role for the two Safeway board members that it had agreed to take on very worrying.

'Lawrence Christensen may be staying on for three months. But that will make little difference in the three year integration process. Sir Ken and Bob Stott, one of his two managing directors, had always made big play of the fact that Mr Christensen and his colleague Jack Sinclair were going to join. It was usually the first thing they mentioned when asked about the integration risk.

'Apparently the two men felt there was not enough of a role for them. For that read that Morrison's current board members were not prepared to give up any of their responsibilities.

'It certainly increases the risk profile of the deal. It makes it more important then ever that Sir Ken gets quickly on with his much-promised (but yet-to-be-delivered) appointment of two non-executive directors.'

Martin Dickson, *Financial Times, 20 January 2004*

## 2.2 Risk appraisal in strategy evaluation

**Some strategies will be more risky than others**. One of the problems arising when evaluating alternative strategies is the reliability of the data used. Since the figures are compiled on estimates of the future, there must be considerable uncertainty about the final accuracy of the figures. Business planners frequently use the following.

- **Operational research** techniques to measure the degree of uncertainty involved
- **Probability theory** to express the likelihood of a forecast result occurring

### 2.2.1 Risk and evaluating strategies

(a)    If an individual strategy involves an **unacceptable amount of risk** it should be eliminated from further consideration in the planning process.

(b)    However, the risk of an **individual strategy** should also be considered in the context of the **overall 'portfolio' of investment strategies** and products adopted by the company.

**Risk can be quantified in statistical terms**. In decision trees, a variety of possible outcomes are developed. Each is given an **expected value (EV),** based on probabilities. The EVs at each decision point are then aggregated to produce an EV for the decision as a whole. However, the EVs do not deal in the relative riskiness of each project.

(a)    Project A might offer **profits** of £1,000,000 and **losses** of £500,000. If the probability of each is 50:50, the EV is (£1,000,000 × 50%) − (£500,000 × 50%) = £250,000.

(b)   Project B offers a 75% probability of a £300,000 profit and a 25% probability of a loss of £100,000. The EV is thus £200,000 ie (£300,000 × 0.75%) – (£100,000 × 25%)

Project A would be favoured, on a basis of EV **alone**, which is £250,000. There is a much higher prospect of **large** profits or **large** losses compared to project B. However, A is much more **risky** as the spread of outcomes is diverse.

**Sensitivity analysis involves asking 'what if?' questions**. By changing the value of different variables in the model, a number of different **scenarios** for the future will be produced. Price rises can be altered to 10% from 5%, demand for a product can be reduced from 100,000 to 80,000, the introduction of new processing equipment can be deferred by six months, on the revised assumption that there will be delays, and so on. Sensitivity analysis can be formalised by identifying **key variables** in the model and then changing the value of each, perhaps in progressive steps. For example, prices might be increased in steps by 5%, 7½%, 10%, 12½% and 15% and the effect on demand, profits and cash flows under each of these assumptions can be tested.

Sensitivity analysis would show which were the **key variables**.

### 2.2.2 Example

A company is producing a new product and a key variable is time to market. If it launches on time, it will sell 1,000 units at £10 each. If it is a month late, demand will fall by 50%. Each unit costs £5 to make. The company has learned that a material supplier has gone out of business. It can get the material for the same price, at the expense of being a month late, or it can pay £1 per unit more for the material and keep to the original deadline.

|  | Original plan £ | Month delay £ | Pay more for material £ |
|---|---|---|---|
| Revenue | 10,000 | 5,000 | 10,000 |
| Costs | 5,000 | 2,500 | 6,000 |
| Profit | 5,000 | 2,500 | 4,000 |

In this example we can see that profits are more sensitive to **demand** than to costs, so the firm would pay more for the new material.

A firm has a choice.

- Apply the most stringent controls to the most critical variables
- Alter the plans so that the most critical variables are no longer as critical
- When different planning options are available, choose a lower-risk plan

# 3 Segmentation

**Market segmentation** is based on different needs and different buying behaviour. Different products are not segments in themselves; rather it is consumer needs for fast cars, commercial needs that determine segments. Each market segment, providing it is large and profitable enough, can become a **target market** for a firm. Market segmentation is increasing because marketing, economic and technological advances have made it possible to address a greater variety of customer needs.

**Exam tip**

The purpose of segmentation is to identify target markets in which the firm can take a position. It is a popular topic for exam questions.

The whole process of segmentation, targeting and positioning was covered in a December 2000 mini-case – interestingly, the firm's initial segmentation, targeting and positioning strategy was not borne out by actual experience, so re-segmentation was necessary. Repositioning also came up in the same exam.

Geodemographic and psychodemographic segmentation were covered in June 2001 in the context of a new consumer service – positioning chocolate houses as an alternative to coffee houses such as Starbucks.

A December 2002 paper asked a question on the advantages of lifestyle segmentation techniques, and the difficulties associated with them when operating in a global market.

## 3.1 Segmentation, targeting and positioning

**Segmentation** of the market, **targeting** chosen segments and **positioning** the value offering through careful design of the marketing mix are the core processes in strategic marketing and the subject of key strategic marketing decisions.

**Steps in segmentation, targeting and positioning identified by Kotler**

| | | |
|---|---|---|
| **Step 1** | Identify **segmentation** variables and segment the market | ⎤ Segmentation |
| **Step 2** | Develop segment profiles | |
| **Step 3** | Evaluate the attractiveness of each segment | ⎤ Targeting |
| **Step 4** | Select the **target** segment(s) | |
| **Step 5** | Identify **positioning** concepts for each target segment | ⎤ Positioning |
| **Step 6** | Select, develop and communicate the chosen concept | |

We will look at these three vitally important strategic activities in this chapter, beginning in this section with **segmentation**.

A market is not a mass, homogeneous group of customers, each wanting an identical product. Market segmentation is based on the recognition that every market consists of potential buyers with different needs, and different buying behaviour. It is relevant to a **focus strategy**.

**Key concept**

> **Market segmentation** may therefore be defined as 'the subdividing of a market into distinct and increasingly homogeneous subgroups of customers, where any subgroup can conceivably be selected as a target market to be met with a distinct marketing mix'. (Kotler)

There are two important elements in this definition of market segmentation.

(a) Although the total market consists of widely different groups of consumers, each group consists of people (or organisations) with **common needs and preferences**, who perhaps react to market stimuli in much the same way.

(b) Each market segment can become a **target market for a firm**, and would require a unique marketing mix if the firm is to exploit it successfully.

## 3.2 Reasons for segmenting markets

| Reason | Comment |
|---|---|
| **Better satisfaction of customer needs** | One solution won't satisfy all customers |
| **Growth in profits** | Some customers will pay more for certain benefits |
| **Revenue growth** | Segmentation means that more customers may be attracted by what is on offer, in preference to competing products |
| **Customer retention** | By targeting customers, a number of different products can be offered to them |
| **Targeted communications** | Segmentation enables clear communications as people in the |

| Reason | Comment |
|---|---|
| | target audience share common needs |
| Innovation | By identifying unmet needs, companies can innovate to satisfy them |
| Segment share | Segmentation enables a firm to implement a focus strategy successfully |

## Action Programme 1

Jot down possible segmentation variables for adult education, magazines, and sports facilities.

### 3.2.1 Identifying segments

(a)   **One basis will not be appropriate in every market**, and sometimes **two or more bases might be valid** at the same time.

(b)   One basis or 'segmentation variable' might be 'superior' to another in a hierarchy of variables. Here are thus **primary and secondary segmentation variables**.

## Marketing at Work

**Capital One**

Capital One's competitive advantage comes not from the brand strength of American Express, or the economies of scale that Citibank enjoys, or from its links with affinity groups such as those that benefit MBNA Bank. Its strength is in gathering and using data. 'It is the best data mining shop anywhere in the US', is the assessment of Eric Clemons, professor of marketing at Wharton Business School at the University of Pennsylvania.

Its special skill is spotting the patterns that identify 'micro-segments' in the market for consumer credit. Last year, the company offered thousands of variations of credit card. It also conducted 64,000 marketing tests on small groups of customers to gauge how new varieties would be received.

The ability to segment the credit card market more finely than its competitors, and customise products accordingly, is what sets Capital One apart. Many companies talk about mass customisation. The Virginia-based company really does it.

*Financial Times, 14 May 2002*

## 3.3 Geographic segmentation

At its simplest, this involves dividing the market into regions and tailoring the marketing mix accordingly.

(a)   An example is **commercial radio stations**, which broadcast local news.

(b)   The market for educational material in the UK segments geographically: Scotland has a different system to England.

# 3.4 Demographic segmentation

Demographic segmentation involves classifying people according to objective variables about their situation.

## 3.4.1 Geodemographic segmentation

The ACORN system divides the UK into 17 groups which together comprise a total of 54 different types of areas, which share common socio-economic characteristics.

(a)     The 17 ACORN groups are as follows.

| The ACORN targeting classification: abbreviated list | | % of population |
|---|---|---|
| A | *Thriving (19.7%)* | |
| A1 | Wealthy achievers, suburban areas | 15.0 |
| A2 | Affluent greys, rural communities | 2.3 |
| A3 | Prosperous pensioners, retirement areas | 2.4 |
| B | *Expanding (11.6%)* | |
| B4 | Affluent executives, family areas | 3.8 |
| B5 | Well-off workers, family areas | 7.8 |
| C | *Rising (7.8%)* | |
| C6 | Affluent urbanites, town and city areas | 2.3 |
| C7 | Prosperous professionals, metropolitan areas | 2.1 |
| C8 | Better-off executives, inner city areas | 3.4 |
| D | *Settling (24.1%)* | |
| D9 | Comfortable middle agers, mature home-owning areas | 13.4 |
| D10 | Skilled workers, home-owning areas | 10.7 |
| E | *Aspiring (13.7%)* | |
| E11 | New home-owners, mature communities | 9.7 |
| E12 | White collar workers, better-off multi-ethnic areas | 4.0 |
| F | *Striving (22.7%)* | |
| F13 | Older people, less prosperous areas | 3.6 |
| F14 | Council estate residents, better-off homes | 11.5 |
| F15 | Council estate residents, high unemployment | 2.7 |
| F16 | Council estate residents, greatest hardships | 2.8 |
| F17 | People in multi-ethnic, low-income areas | 2.1 |

(b)     As an example of a more detailed breakdown, group E ('Aspiring') contains the following groups.

| E | *Aspiring (13.7% of population)* | |
|---|---|---|
| *E11* | *New home-owners, mature communities (9.7%)* | |
| 11.33 | Council areas, some new home-owners | 3.8 |
| 11.34 | Mature home-owning areas, skilled workers | 3.1 |
| 11.35 | Low rise estates, older workers, new home-owners | 2.8 |
| *E12* | *White collar workers, better-off multi-ethnic areas (4.0%)* | |
| 12.36 | Home-owning multi-ethnic areas, young families | 1.1 |
| 12.37 | Multi-occupied town centres, mixed occupations | 1.8 |
| 12.38 | Multi-ethnic areas, white collar workers | 1.1 |

Unlike geographical segmentation, which is fairly crude by area, geodemographics enables similar groups of people to be targeted, even though they might exist in different areas of the country. These various classifications share certain characteristics, including:

- Car ownership
- Unemployment rates
- Purchase of financial service products
- Number of holidays
- Age profile

### 3.4.2 The family life cycle

The **family life cycle (FLC)** is a summary demographic variable that combines the effects of age, marital status, career status (income) and the presence or absence of children. It is able to identify the various **stages through which households progress**. The table on the next page shows features of the family at various stages of its life cycle. Particular products and services can be target-marketed at specific stages in the life cycle of families.

It is important to remember that the model of the family life cycle shown in the table displays the **classic route** from young single to older unmarried. In contemporary society, characterised by divorce and what may be the declining importance of marriage as an institution, this picture can vary. It is possible and not uncommon to be young, childless and divorced, or young and unmarried with children. Some people go through life without marrying or having children at all. Individuals may go through the life cycle belonging to more than one family group. At each stage, whether on the classic route or an **alternative path**, needs and disposable income will change. Family groupings are, however, a key feature of society.

There has been some **criticism** of the traditional FLC model as a basis for market segmentation in recent years. (See, for example, Rob Lawson, 'The Family Life Cycle: a demographic analysis', *Journal of Marketing Management* (Summer 1988).)

(a)   It is modelled on the **demographic patterns of industrialised western nations** - and particularly America. This pattern may not be universally applicable.

(b)   As noted above, while the FLC model was once typical of the overwhelming majority of American families, there are now **important potential variations** from that pattern, including:

| | | | |
|---|---|---|---|
| (i) | Childless couples | - | because of choice, career-oriented women and delayed marriage |
| (ii) | Later marriages | - | because of greater career-orientation and non-marital relationships: likely to have fewer children |
| (iii) | Later children | - | say in late 30s. Likely to have fewer children, but to stress quality of life |
| (iv) | Single parents | - | (especially mothers) because of divorce |
| (v) | Fluctuating labour status | - | not just in work or retired, but redundancy, career change, dual-income |
| (vi) | Extended parenting | - | young, single adults returning home while they establish careers/financial independence; divorced children returning to parents; elderly parents requiring care; newly-weds living with in-laws |

(vii)    Non-family households   -   unmarried (homosexual or heterosexual) couples

- divorced persons with no children

- single persons (often due to delaying of first marriage and the fact that there are more women than men in the population)

- widowed persons (especially women, because of longer life-expectancy)

*Note:* The summary table can be found on the next page.

| | I | II | III | IV | V | VI | VII | VIII | IX |
|---|---|---|---|---|---|---|---|---|---|
| | *Bachelor Stage* | *Newly married couples* | *Full nest I* | *Full nest II* | *Full nest III* | *Empty nest I* | *Empty nest II* | *Solitary survivor in labour force* | *Solitary survivor(s) retired* |
| | Young single people not living at home | Young, no children | Youngest child under six | Youngest child six or over | Older married couples with dependent children | Older married couples, no children living with them, head of family still in labour force | Older married couples, no children living at home head of family retired | | |
| | Few financial burdens. | Better off financially than they will be in the near future. | Home purchasing at peak. | Financial position better. | Financial position still better. | Home ownership at peak. | Significant cut in income. | Income still adequate but likely to sell family home and purchase smaller accommodation. | Significant cut in income. |
| | Fashion/ opinion leader led. | High levels of purchase of homes and consumer durable goods. | Liquid assets/ savings low. | Some wives return to work. | More wives work. | More satisfied with financial position and money saved. | Keep home. | Concern with level of savings and pension. | Additional medical requirements. Special need for attention, affection and security. |
| | Recreation orientated. | Buy cars, fridges, cookers, life assurance, durable furniture, holidays. | Dissatisfied with financial position and amount of money saved. | Child dominated household. | School and examination dominated household. | Interested in travel, recreation, self-education. | Buy medical appliances or medical care, products which aid health, sleep and digestion. | Some expenditure on hobbies and pastimes. | May seek sheltered accommodation. |
| | Buy basic kitchen equipment, basic furniture, cars, equipment for the mating game, holidays. | Establish patterns of personal financial management and control. | Reliance on credit finance, credit cards, overdrafts etc. | Buy necessities foods, cleaning material, clothes, bicycles, sports gear, music lessons, pianos, holidays etc. | Some children get first jobs; others in further / higher education. | Make financial gifts and contributions. | Assist children. Concern with level of savings and pension. Some expenditure on hobbies and pastimes. | Worries about security and dependence. | Possible dependence on others for personal financial management and control. |
| | Experiment with patterns of personal financial management and control. | | Child dominated household. | | Expenditure to support children's further / higher education. | Children gain qualifications; move to Stage I. | | | |
| | | | Buy necessities washers, dryers, baby food and clothes, vitamins, toys, books etc. | | Buy new, more tasteful furniture, non-necessary appliances, boats etc holidays. | Buy luxuries, home improvements e.g. fitted kitchens etc. | | | |

An alternative or modified FLC model is needed to take account of consumption variables such as:

(a) Spontaneous **changes** in brand preference when a household undergoes a **change of status** (divorce, redundancy, death of a spouse, change in membership of a non-family household)

(b) **Different economic circumstances** and extent of consumption planning in single-parent families, households where there is a redundancy, dual-income households

(c) **Different buying and consumption roles** to compensate/adjust in households where the **woman works**. Women can be segmented into at least four categories - each of which may represent a distinct market for goods and services:

- Stay-at-home homemaker
- Plan-to-work homemaker
- 'Just-a-job' working woman
- Career-oriented working woman

## 3.5 Psychographic segmentation

Psychographic segmentation is not based on objective data so much as how people see themselves and their **subjective** feelings and attitudes towards a particular product or service, or towards life in general.

| Lifestyle dimensions | | | |
|---|---|---|---|
| *Activities* | *Interests* | *Opinions* | *Demographics* |
| Work | Family | Themselves | Age |
| Hobbies | Home | Social issues | Education |
| Social events | Job | Politics | Income |
| Vacation | Community | Business | Occupation |
| Entertainment | Recreation | Economics | Family size |
| Club membership | Fashion | Education | Dwelling |
| Community | Food | Products | Geography |
| Shopping | Media | Future | City size |
| Sports | Achievements | Culture | Stage in lifecycle |

Source: Joseph Plummer,
'The Concept and Application of Lifestyle Segmentation',
*Journal of Marketing* (January 1974), pp 33-37

Riesman identified three **distinct types of social behaviour**.

- **Tradition directed** behaviour is easy to predict and changes little
- **Other directedness** is behaviour influenced by the action and views of peer groups
- **Inner directedness** is behaviour uninfluenced by views of others

**Taylor Nelson** also identifies three main groups with sub groups.

(a) **Sustenance driven group**

(i) **Belongers**. What they seek is a quiet undisturbed family life. They are conservative, conventional, rule followers. Not all are sustenance driven.

(ii) **Survivors**. Strongly class-conscious, and community spirited, their motivation is to get by.

    (iii)    **Aimless**. Comprises two groups, (a) the young unemployed, who are often anti-authority, and (b) the old, whose motivation is day-to-day existence.

(b)    **Outer directed group**

    (i)    The balance of the belongers.

    (ii)    **Conspicuous consumers**. They are materialistic and pushy, motivated by acquisition, competition, and getting ahead. Pro-authority, law and order.

(c)    **Inner directed group**

    (i)    **Self-explorers**. Motivated by self-expression and self-realisation. Less materialistic than other groups, and showing high tolerance levels.

    (ii)    **Social resistors**. The caring group, concerned with fairness and social values, but often appearing intolerant and moralistic.

    (iii)    **Experimentalists**. Highly individualistic, motivated by fast moving enjoyment. They are materialistic, pro-technology but anti-traditional authority.

Variations on the lifestyle or psychographic approach have been developed, analysing more precisely people's attitudes towards **certain goods or services**. The value of this approach is that it isolates potential consumer responses to particular product offerings.

 ## Marketing at Work

The Henley Centre for Forecasting has outlined four different kinds of consumers in the market for technological and media products.

(a)    *Technophiles* (24% of the population) 'are enthusiastic about technology in a general sense and also show a high level of interest in applications of new technology. They are concentrated among the under-35s, are more likely to be male than female, and are more likely to belong to social grade C1 than AB'.

(b)    *Aspirational technophiles* (22% of the population) 'are excited in a general sense about technology but are much less interested in its applications. They are more likely to be male than female, and are concentrated in the AB social grade'.

(c)    *Functionals* (25% of the population) 'claim to be uninterested in technology but are not hostile to its applications, especially those areas which offer an enhancement of existing services. These consumers are more likely to be family ... and are most numerous among the over 45s'.

(d)    *Technophobes* (28% of the population) 'are hostile to technology at all levels and are sceptical about whether technology can offer anything new. Technophobes are concentrated in the over-60 age group, are more likely to be female than male, and are distributed fairly evenly through the social grades'.

**Exam tip**

> Lifestyle and geographic segmentation has featured in past questions. There are connections between the two. Some lifestyle segmentation approaches suggest that there are connections between demographic characteristics and lifestyles. Geodemographic segmentation extends this further to particular geographic areas.

**BPP** LEARNING MEDIA

### 3.5.1 The VALs framework

This framework was the result of a survey in the USA, identifying nine lifestyle groups in the population passing through various developmental stages. It is presented below.

| Developmental stage | Grouping (% of US population) |
|---|---|
| **Need-driven** | **Survivors**. This is a disadvantaged group who are likely to be withdrawn, despairing and depressed (4%). |
| | **Sustainers** are another disadvantaged group, but they are working hard to escape poverty (7%). |
| | These groups have relatively little purchasing power. |
| **Outer-directed** | **Belongers** are characterised as being conventional, nostalgic, reluctant to try new ideas and generally conservative (33%). |
| | **Emulators** are upwardly mobile, ambitious and status conscious (10%). |
| | **Achievers**. This group enjoys life and makes things happen (23%). |
| | These groups are affluent and interested in status products. |
| **Inner-directed** | **'I-am-me'** tend to be young, self engrossed and act on whims (5%). |
| | **Experientials** wish to enjoy as wide a range of life as possible (7%). |
| | **Societally** conscious have a clear sense of social responsibility and wish to improve society (9%). |
| | These groups are more concerned with individual needs. |
| **Nirvana** | **Integrateds** are completely mature psychologically and combine the positive elements of outer and inner directedness (2%). Very few individuals reach this stage. |

### 3.5.2 Social class

Age and sex present few problems but social class has always been one of the most dubious areas of marketing research investigation. Class is a highly personal and subjective phenomenon, to the extent that some people are class conscious or class aware and have a sense of belonging to a particular group. JICNAR's social grade definitions (A-E), which correspond closely to what are called Social Classes I-V on the Registrar General's Scale, are often used in quota setting.

| Registrar General's Social classes | JICNAR Social grades | Social status | Characteristics of occupation (of head of household) |
|---|---|---|---|
| I | A | Upper middle class | Higher managerial/professional eg lawyers, directors |
| II | B | Middle class | Intermediate managerial/administrative/ professional eg teachers, managers, computer operators, sales managers |
| III (i) non-manual | $C_1$ | Lower middle class | Supervisory, clerical, junior managerial/ administrative/professional eg foremen, shop assistants |
| (ii) manual | $C_2$ | Skilled working class | Skilled manual labour eg electricians, mechanics |
| IV | D | Working class | Semi-skilled manual labour eg machine operators |

| Registrar General's | JICNAR | | Characteristics |
|---|---|---|---|
| Social classes | Social grades | Social status | of occupation (of head of household) |
| V | | | Unskilled manual labour eg cleaning, waiting tables, assembly |
| | E | Lowest level of subsistence | State pensioners, widows (no other earner), casual workers |

From 2001 UK Office for National Statistics used a new categorisation system, reflecting recent changes in the UK population.

| New social class | Occupations | Examples |
|---|---|---|
| 1 | Higher managerial and professional occupations | |
| 1.1 | Employers and managers in larger organisations | Bank managers, company directors |
| 1.2 | Higher professional | Doctors, lawyers |
| 2 | Lower managerial and professional occupations | Police officers |
| 3 | Intermediate occupations | Secretaries/PAs, clerical workers |
| 4 | Small employers and own-account workers | |
| 5 | Lower supervisory, craft and related occupations | Electricians |
| 6 | Semi-routine occupations | Drivers, hairdressers, bricklayers |
| 7 | Routine occupations | Car park attendants, cleaners |

## 3.6 Behavioural segmentation

Behavioural segmentation segments buyers into groups based on their attitudes to and use of the product, and the **benefits** they expect to receive.

*Benefit segmentation of the toothpaste market*

| Segment Name | Principal benefit sought | Demographic Strengths | Special behavioural characteristics | Brands disproportionately favoured | Personality characteristics | Lifestyle characteristics |
|---|---|---|---|---|---|---|
| The sensory segment | Flavour, product appearance | Children | Users of spearmint flavoured toothpaste | Colgate, Stripe | High self-involvement | Hedonistic |
| The Sociables | Brightness of teeth | Teens, young people | Smokers | Macleans, Ultra-Brite | High sociability | Active |
| The Worriers | Decay prevention | Large families | Heavy users | Crest | High hypochondriasis | Conservative |
| The Independent Segment | Price | Men | Heavy users | Brands on sale | High autonomy | Value-oriented |

### 3.6.1 Risk reduction

A benefit of a product is that it **reduces risk**. Toothpaste reduces the risk of tooth decay, for example. This is relevant to the worriers in the table above. **Perceptions** of risk are often very subjective. **Attitudes to risk** are useful in that they **offer segmentation opportunities**.

(a)   Research has indicated high, medium, and low risk segments for producers of professional services by organisations such as consultants and market research agencies.

(b)   **Risk can also affect how a product is positioned**. According to *Marketing Business* (January 1997), certain 'food studies identified the feminine image of wine as a risk inhibiting the drinking of wine in certain segments'.

### 3.6.2 Occasion

Buyers can be segmented according to the occasion, when they use a product. The best example is business and leisure travel packages. *Kellogg's* has been trying to increase consumption of cornflakes by suggesting that cornflakes can be eaten at any time of the day, not only breakfast.

### 3.6.3 User status

The markets can be segmented according to types of users.

- Heavy users
- Medium users
- Rare users

In addition, the degree of loyalty can be estimated. Some customers are more loyal than others. Many firms mistake inertia for loyalty, however.

### Marketing at Work

The credit card market in the UK is becoming increasingly fragmented. Newcomers tend to offer lower interest rates than the mainstream competitors such as *Barclaycard*. The newcomers target or cherry-pick certain groups of customers with a good credit history, and who are motivated mainly by price.

Other card operators offer different customer benefits, by linking their cards to charitable organisations, so that some of the commission on each transaction goes to charity.

## 3.7 Segmentation of the industrial market

Segmentation may apply more obviously to the consumer market, but it can also be applied to an industrial market.

Industrial markets can be segmented with many of the bases used in consumer markets such as geography, usage rate and benefits sought. Additional, more traditional bases include customer type, product/technology, customer size and purchasing procedures.

(a)   **Geographic location**. Some industries and related industries are clustered in particular areas. Firms selling services to the banking sector might be interested in the City of London.

(b)   **Type of business** (eg service, manufacturing)

(i)   **Nature of the customers' business**. Accountants or lawyers, for example, might choose to specialise in serving customers in a particular type of business. An accountant may choose to specialise in the accounts of retail businesses, and a firm of solicitors may specialise in conveyancing work for property development companies.

(ii) **Components manufacturers** specialise in the industries of the firms to which they supply components.

(iii) **Type of organisation**. Organisations in an industry as a whole may have certain needs in common. Employment agencies offering business services to publishers, say, must offer their clients personnel with experience in particular desktop publishing packages. Suitable temporary staff offered to legal firms can be more effective if used to legal jargon. Each different type of firm can be offered a tailored product or service.

(iv) **Size of organisation**. Large organisations may have elaborate purchasing procedures, and may do many things in-house. Small organisations may be more likely to subcontract certain specialist services.

(c) **Use of the product**. In the UK, many new cars are sold to businesses, as benefit cars. Although this practice is changing with the viability of a 'cash alternative' to a company car, the varying levels of specification are developed with the business buyer in mind (eg junior salesperson gets a Focus, Regional Manager gets a BMW).

*Wind and Cardozo* developed a two-stage framework.

(a) *Stage 1* calls for the formation of macrosegments based on organisational characteristics such as size, SIC (Standard Industrial Classification) code and product applications.

(b) *Stage 2* involves dividing these macrosegments into microsegments based on the distinguishing characteristics of decision making units. They identify five general segmentation bases moving from the outer next towards the inner in the following sequence: demographic, operating variables, purchasing approaches, situational factors and personal characteristics of the buyer.

Less research has been carried out in industrial markets as compared with consumer markets. Moreover, consumer goods companies have, generally, applied marketing theory more rigorously in practice.

**Reference**

Wind, Y and Cardozo, R Industrial Marketing Segmentation, *Industrial Marketing Management*, March 1974 pp 153 - 166

## 3.8 Conjoint analysis

Conjoint analysis is a tool for implementing segmentation strategies, in NPD, repositioning exercises and pricing.

**Key concept**

> **Conjoint analysis** describes each product/service as a series of attributes, to which consumers ascribe different values. Consumers choose the offer that has the highest total value to them from the product attributes.

This involves developing a picture of a product in terms of its **attributes** and the **level** of each attribute. For example, motor cars have attributes of speed, safety, comfort, interior space, driving experience, price, style and reliability. Customers will ascribe different values to these attributes.

## 3.9 Trends in segmentation techniques

In *Mastering Marketing* (FT), the following trends have been identified.

- Greater use of 'softer' variables (eg lifestyles, attitudes)

- The segmentation variables are used for different purposes
- Data-mining: patterns in statistical data speak for themselves
- Greater use of primary and secondary segmentation variables
- A close connection between segmentation and NPD
- Computer modelling to discern the optimal addition to product lines
- Consideration of the segment's response to competitors' products

**Exam tip**

The CIM is keen to internationalise the paper, and so you may have to consider segments in overseas markets.

- To what extent are these segments equivalent to their buying behaviour to the segments in the home market?

- How much adaptation to the mix will be needed?

Do not assume the Russian market, say, or the Sri Lankan market or the UK market to be any more or less complex than each other.

# 4 Segment validity and attractiveness

**FAST FORWARD**

**Segment validity** depends upon size, availability, measurability and differentiation. **Segment attractiveness** can be assessed by analysing marketing, competitive and financial factors. Sometimes sales and markets forecasts can be used to assess the attractiveness of a market.

## 4.1 Segment validity

A market segment will only **be valid if it is worth designing and developing a unique** marketing mix for that specific segment. The following questions are commonly asked to decide whether or not the segment can be used for developing marketing plans.

| Criteria | Comment |
|---|---|
| **Can the segment be measured?** | It might be possible to conceive of a market segment, but it is not necessarily easy to measure it. For example for a segment based on people with a conservative outlook to life, can conservatism of outlook be measured by market research? |
| **Is the segment big enough?** | There has to be a large enough potential market to be profitable. |
| **Can the segment be reached?** | There has to be a way of getting to the potential customers via the organisation's promotion and distribution channels. |
| **Do segments respond differently?** | If two or more segments are identified by marketing planners but each segment responds in the same way to a marketing mix, the segments are effectively one and the same and there is no point in distinguishing them from each other. |
| **Can the segment be reached profitably?** | Do the identified customer needs, cost less to satisfy than the revenue they earn? |
| **Is the segment suitably stable?** | The stability of the segment is important, if the organisation is to commit huge production and marketing resources to serve it. The firm does not want the segment to 'disappear' next year. Of course, this may not matter in some industries. |

*Steps in the analysis of segmentation*

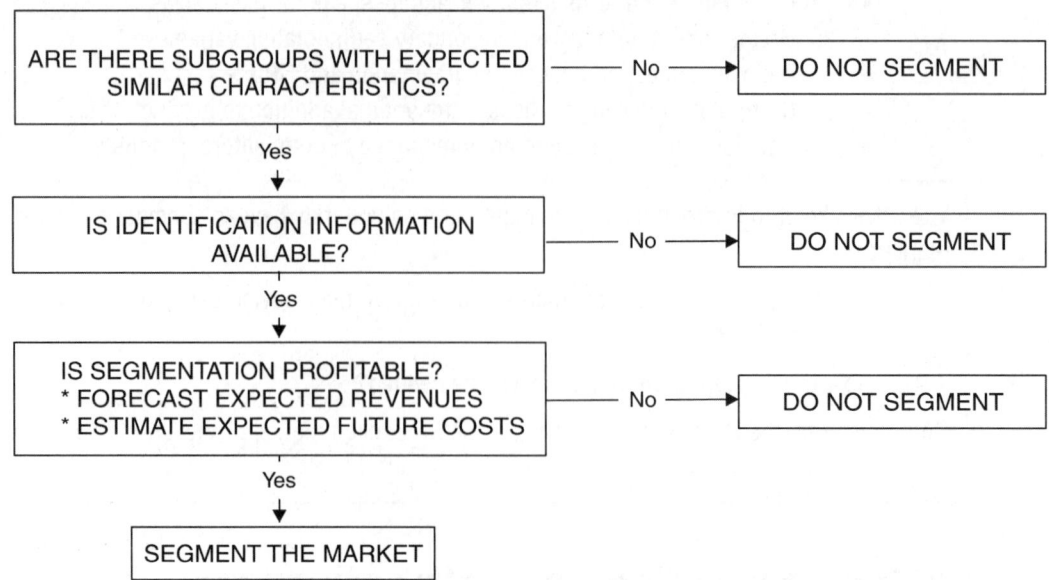

## 4.2 Segment attractiveness

A segment might be valid and potentially profitable, but is it potentially **attractive**?

(a)   A segment which has **high barriers to entry** might cost more to enter but will be less **vulnerable to competitors**.

(b)   For firms involved in **relationship marketing**, the segment should be one in which **viable relationship** between the firm and the customer can be established.

Segments which are most attractive will be those whose needs can be met by building on the company's strengths and where forecasts for demand, sales profitability and **growth** are favourable.

**Exam tip**

> You may be required to identify new segments and to take a strategic approach to positioning your offer to them.

### 4.2.1 A checklist of factors to consider when evaluating segment attractiveness

Hooley *et al* give a comprehensive list of factors for evaluating market attractiveness.

| Factors | Characteristics to examine |
|---|---|
| **Market factors** | • Size of the segment<br>• Segment growth rate<br>• Stage of industry evaluation<br>• Predictability<br>• Price elasticity and sensitivity<br>• Bargaining power of customers<br>• Seasonality of demand |

BPP
LEARNING MEDIA

| Factors | Characteristics to examine |
|---------|---------------------------|
| Economic and technological factors | • Barriers to entry<br>• Barriers to exit<br>• Bargaining power of suppliers<br>• Level of technology<br>• Investment required<br>• Margins available |
| Competitive factors | • Competitive intensity<br>• Quality of competition<br>• Threat of substitution<br>• Degree of differentiation |
| Environmental factors | • Exposure to economic fluctuations<br>• Exposure to political and legal factors<br>• Degree of regulation<br>• Social acceptability |

It is important to assess company strengths when evaluating attractiveness and targeting a market. This can help determine the appropriate strategy, because once the attractiveness of each identified segment has been assessed it can be considered along with relative strengths to determine the potential advantages the organisation would have. In this way preferred segments can be targeted.

Market segment attractiveness →

| Current and potential company strengths in serving the segment | | Unattractive | Average | Attractive |
|---|---|---|---|---|
| | Weak | Strongly avoid | Avoid | Possibilities |
| | Average | Avoid | Possibilities | Secondary targets |
| | Strong | Possibilities | Secondary targets | Prime targets |

# 5 Target markets

Having analysed the attractiveness of a segment, the firm will choose one or more **target markets**. Marketing policy may be **undifferentiated** (mass), **concentrated** or **differentiated**. The extreme form of differentiated marketing is **micromarketing**.

**Key concept**

A **target market** is a market or segment selected for special attention by an organisation (possibly served with a distinct marketing mix).

## 5.1 Policy options

Having identified distinct market segments, it is necessary to choose which ones to target and how to go about it. Careful consideration must be given to the criteria by which segments will be chosen. **Profitability** is clearly an important consideration but so are **accessibility**, **resources** required and

**potential for growth**. Targeting is a continuing process, since segments change and develop and so do competitors. The company is, to some extent, able to plan and control its own development also and it must respond to changes in the market place.

The marketing management of a company may choose one of the following policy options.

| Policy | Comment |
|---|---|
| **Undifferentiated marketing** | This policy is to produce a single product and hope to get as many customers as possible to buy it; segmentation is ignored entirely. This is sometimes called **mass marketing**. |
| **Concentrated marketing** | The company attempts to produce the ideal product for a single segment of the market (for example, *Rolls Royce* cars, *Mothercare* mother and baby shops). |
| **Differentiated marketing** | The company attempts to introduce several product versions, each aimed at a different market segment (for example, the manufacture of different styles of the same article of clothing). |

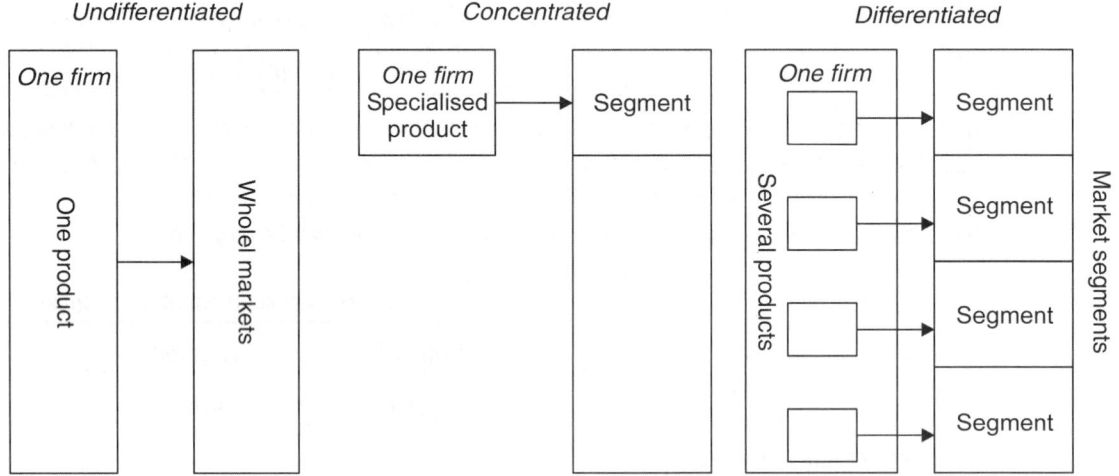

The major **disadvantage of differentiated marketing** is the additional costs of marketing and production (more product design and development costs, the loss of economies of scale in production and storage, additional promotion costs and administrative costs and so on). When the costs of differentiation of the market exceed the **benefits** from further segmentation and target marketing, a firm is said to have **over-differentiated**.

The major **disadvantage of concentrated marketing** is the business risk of relying on a single segment of a single market. On the other hand, specialisation in a particular market segment can give a firm a profitable, although perhaps temporary, competitive edge over rival firms.

The choice between undifferentiated, differentiated or concentrated marketing as a marketing strategy will depend on the following factors.

(a) The extent to which the product and/or the market may be considered **homogeneous**. **Mass marketing** may be sufficient if the market is largely homogeneous (for example, for safety matches).

(b) The **company's resources** must not be over extended by differentiated marketing. Small firms may succeed better by concentrating on one segment only.

(c) The product must be sufficiently **advanced in its life cycle** to have attracted a substantial total market; otherwise segmentation and target marketing is unlikely to be profitable, because each segment would be too small in size.

## 5.2 Micromarketing

Segmentation, as part of target marketing, looks certain to play an even more crucial role in the marketing strategies of consumer organisations in the years ahead. The move from traditional mass marketing to **micro marketing** is rapidly gaining ground as marketers explore more cost-effective ways to recruit new customers. This has been brought about by a number of trends.

(a) The **ability to create large numbers of product variants without the need for corresponding increases in resources** is causing markets to become overcrowded.

(b) The **growth in minority lifestyles** is creating opportunities for niche brands aimed at consumers with very distinct purchasing habits.

(c) The **fragmentation of the media** to service ever more specialist and local audiences is denying mass media the ability to assure market dominance for major brand advertisers.

(d) The **advance in information technology** is enabling information about individual customers to be organised in ways that enable highly selective and personal communications.

Such trends have promoted the developments in benefit, lifestyle and geodemographic segmentation techniques outlined. Consumer market segmentation has developed so much in the last few years that the vision of multinational marketers accessing a PC to plan retail distribution and supporting promotional activity in cities as far apart as Naples, Nottingham and Nice is now a practical reality.

## 5.3 Mass customisation

Micro-marketing is made possible by **mass customisation**, which features:

- The huge economies of scale of mass production
- The tailoring of products precisely to the customer's requirements

New manufacturing technology makes this possible. There is less need for a standard product if people's individual preferences can be catered for.

Marketing at Work

*Levi Jeans* in the US has offered a service whereby customers' measurements are fed through to an automated garment cutting process.

# 6 Positioning

**FAST FORWARD**

**Positioning** can be 'psychological' and 'real'. **Perceptual maps** enable users to identify positioning options. The foundation of a **positioning strategy** is to align what the company can do with what customers want. Repositioning is a risky and expensive response to poor performance.

## 6.1 Steps in positioning

**Step 1**  Identify differentiating factors in products or services in relation to competitors

**Step 2**  Select the most important differences

**Step 3**  Communicate the position to the target market

The value of positioning is that it enables **tactical marketing mix decisions to be made**.

**Key concept**

> **Positioning** is the act of designing the company's offer and image so that it achieves a distinct and valued place in the target customer's mind.

 Marketing at Work

In 2001, the car industry faced four challenges.

- A slump in demand (down perhaps by 20%) in the US and Europe, the two biggest markets
- Financial weakness
- Falling prices
- 21% overcapacity

In Europe, the biggest losers have been GM, Ford, Toyota, Nissan and Honda.

- GM – 'quality problems and tired designs' exacerbated by having four bosses in three years
- Japanese firms' 'product weakness' aggravated by exchange rate difficulties

The three American manufacturers are vulnerable because their profits have come from too narrow a model range. 'Car makers must dream up some exciting new vehicles to entice jaded and cautious consumers to open their wallets in a downturn.'

The article suggests that the 'recent success of European companies such as Volkswagen, Renault and PSA Peugeot Citroen, all of which have bounced back from near-death experiences, is instructive.'

Although they have improved efficiency, 'the secret of their success has been innovative products ... . It is ironic that the Europeans, notably the French, are showing the way as the car market fragments and branding becomes crucial ... . Today the cut is to have engineering skills and product development combined with a flair for brand management that Europeans only usually deploy for luxury goods.'

In the past, with five body styles, you could cover all of Europe's product segments. Now that would only cover half.

*The Economist, 31 March 2001*

## 6.2 Problems with positioning

How much do people remember about a product or brand?

(a) **Many products are, in fact, very similar**, and the key issue is to make them **distinct in the customer's mind**.

(b) People remember 'number 1', so the product should be positioned as 'number 1' in relation to a valued attribute.

(c) **Cosmetic changes** can have the effect of repositioning the product in the customer's mind. To be effective, however, this **psychological positioning** has to be **reinforced by real positioning**.

As **positioning is psychological as well as real**, we can now identify **positioning errors**.

| Mistake | Consequence |
| --- | --- |
| **Underpositioning** | The brand does not have a clear identity in the eyes of the customer |
| **Overpositioning** | Buyers may have too narrow an image of a brand |
| **Confused positioning** | Too many claims might be made for a brand |
| **Doubtful positioning** | The positioning may not be credible in the eyes of the buyer |

### 6.2.1 Positioning strategy checklist

| Positioning variable | Comment |
|---|---|
| • Attributes | • Size, for example |
| • Benefit | • What benefits we offer |
| • Use/application | • Ease of use; accessibility |
| • User | • The sort of person the product appeals to |
| • Product category | • Consciously differentiated from competition |
| • Quality/price | • One should support and validate the other, so that it makes sense to the customer and he understands what he is buying. For example, low quality at a high price is unlikely to sell. |

### Action Programme 2

Identify examples of positioning strategies in the table above.

## 6.3 Perceptual maps

One simple perceptual map that can be used is to plot brands or competing products in terms of two key characteristics such as price and quality.

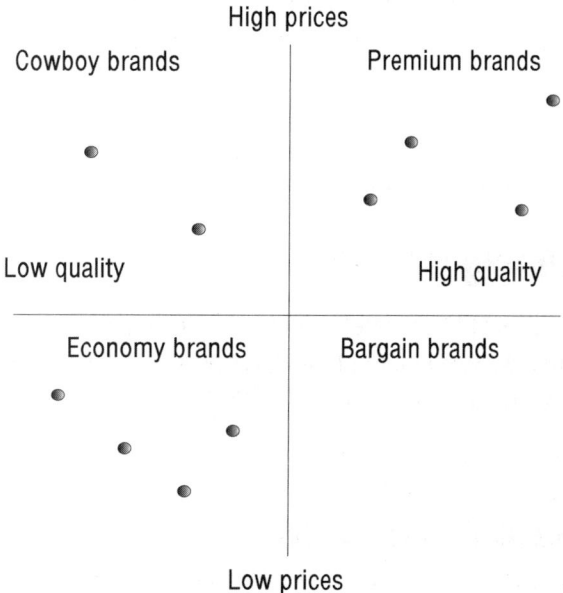

A perceptual map of market positioning can be used to **identify gaps in the market**. This example might suggest that there could be potential in the market for a low-price high-quality 'bargain brand'. A company that carries out such an analysis might decide to conduct further research to find out whether there is scope in the market for a new product which would be targeted at a market position where there are few or no rivals.

## 6.4 Mapping positions

*Kotler* identified a 3 × 3 matrix of nine different competitive positioning strategies.

| Product price | | | |
|---|---|---|---|
| *Product quality* | | | |
| | *High price* | *Medium price* | *Low price* |
| *High* | Premium strategy | Penetration strategy | Superbargain strategy |
| *Medium* | Overpricing strategy | Average-quality strategy | Bargain strategy |
| *Low* | Hit-and-run strategy | Shoddy goods strategy | Cheap goods strategy |

Once selected, the needs of the targeted segment can be identified and the marketing mix strategy developed to provide the benefits package needed to satisfy them. Positioning the product offering then becomes a matter of matching and communicating appropriate benefits.

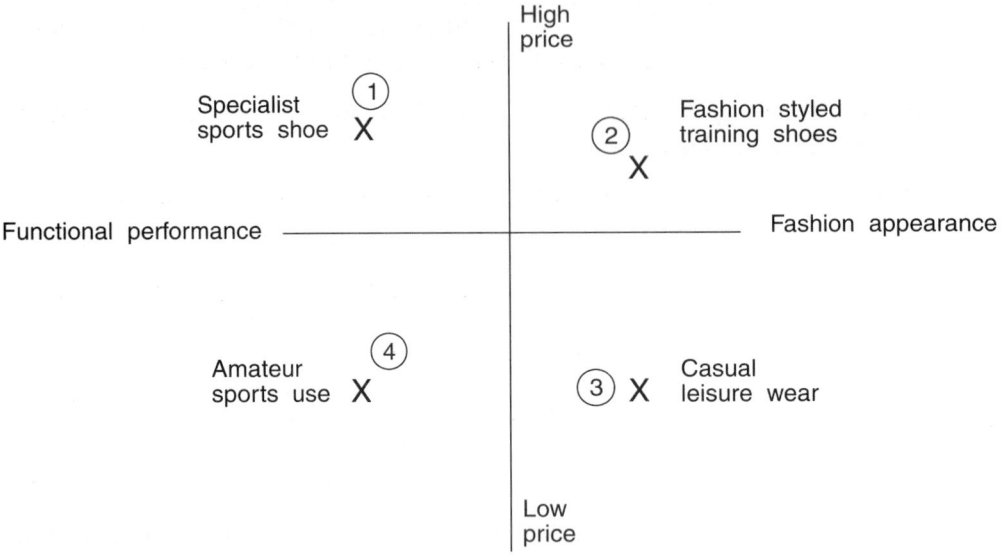

**Exam tip**

> The 'position map' approach can be applied to a number of areas, to brands for example, as in the December 2000 exam, in a question that also touched on non-profit marketing.

## 6.5 Repositioning

Strategic managers must be prepared to deal with under performance and failure. One possible response is repositioning of the market offering. However, this is a difficult and expensive process, since it requires the extensive remoulding of customer perceptions. The danger is that the outcome will be confusion in the mind of the customer and failure to impress the selected new segments.

# 7 Electronic commerce

**FAST FORWARD**

> **Electronic commerce** includes a wide range of applications and techniques based on the integration of computers and telephone networks.

**Key concept**

> **Electronic commerce** means conducting business electronically via a communications link.

## 7.1 Electronic Data Interchange (EDI)

EDI is a form of computer-to-computer data transfer. For example, instead of sending a customer a paper invoice through the post, the data is sent over telecommunications links. This offers savings and **benefits** to organisations that use it.

(a) It reduces the **delays** caused by postal paper chains.

(b) It avoids the need to **re-key** data and therefore saves time and reduces errors.

(c) It provides the opportunity to reduce administrative **costs** eg the costs associated with the creation, recording and storage of paper documents.

(d) It facilitates shorter **lead times** and reduced stock holdings which allow reductions in working capital requirements (eg Just-In-Time policies).

(e) It provides the opportunity to improve **customer service**.

The general concept of having one computer talk directly to another might seem straightforward enough in principle, but **difficulties** may arise.

(a) Businesses hold records in computer files to their own **file structure** specifications. A translation mechanism may be required to allow transfer between the systems.

(b) The problem of **compatibility** between different makes or types of computer was a serious one in the past, and some form of interface between the computers had to be devised to enable data interchange to take place.

(c) Businesses often work to differing **time** schedules and time-zones. Organisations may conduct system maintenance late at night thinking this will not affect business. However, an overseas company in a different time zone, may need to access the system.

(d) As the number of trading partners grows the number of one-to-one links eventually becomes **unmanageable**.

## 7.2 E-commerce and the web

**FAST FORWARD**

**E-commerce** is the process of trading on the Internet. Many business processes can be undertaken using e-commerce techniques.

The Internet allows businesses to reach potentially millions of consumers worldwide and extends trading time to seven days, around the clock. The OECD forecast global e-commerce to be worth $1 trillion by 2007-08.

An e-business **start-up** has a considerable advantage over more established companies working in the same business area, because it does not have to take existing systems into account. This gives the start-up the agility and flexibility to launch new services far more quickly and cheaply than established rivals.

For established companies e-commerce reduces expensive sales and distribution workforces, and offers new marketing opportunities.

### 7.2.1 Distribution

The Internet can be used to get certain products **directly into people's homes**. Anything that can be converted into **digital form** can simply be uploaded onto the seller's site and then **downloaded** onto the customer's PC at home. The Internet thus offers huge opportunities to producers of text, graphics/video, and sound-based products. Much computer software is now distributed in this way.

### 7.2.2 Electronic marketing

Besides its usefulness for tapping into worldwide information resources businesses are also using it to **provide information** about their own products and services.

For **customers** the Internet offers a **speedy and impersonal** way of getting to know about the services that a company provides. For **businesses** the advantage is that it is much cheaper to provide the information in electronic form than it would be to employ staff to man the phones on an enquiry desk, and much more effective than sending out mailshots that people would either throw away or forget about when they needed the information.

Companies will need to develop new means of promoting their wares through the medium of the Internet, as opposed to shop displays or motionless graphics. Websites can provide **sound and movement** and allow **interactivity**, so that the user can, say, drill down to obtain further information or watch a video of the product in use, or get a virtual reality experience of the product or service.

For many companies this will involve a rethink of current promotional activity.

 Marketing at Work

**Peapod.com**

Peapod.com is an online supermarket and one of the more sophisticated recorders and users of customers' personal data and shopping behaviour. With over 200,000 customers in various US cities, Peapod's website sells groceries that are then delivered to customer's homes. a list of previous purchases (including brand, pack size and quantity purchased) is kept on the site, so the customer can make minor changes from week to week, saving time and effort.

Peapod creates a database on each shopper that includes their purchase history (what they bought), their online shopping patterns (how they bought it), questionnaires about their attitudes and opinions, and demographic data (which Peapod buys from third parties). A shopper's profile is used by the company to determine which advertisement to show and which promotions/electronic coupons to offer. Demographically identical neighbours are thus treated differently based on what Peapod has learned about their preferences and behaviours over time.

Shoppers seem to like this high-tech relationship marketing, with 94% of all sales coming from repeat customers. Manufacturers like it too. the more detailed customer information enables them to target promotions at customers who have repeatedly bought another brand, thereby not giving away promotion dollars to loyal customers.

### 7.2.3 Collecting information about customers

People who visit a site for the first time may be asked to **register**, which typically involves giving a name, physical address and post code, e-mail address and possibly other demographic data such as age, job title and income bracket.

When customers come to the site on subsequent occasions they either type their (self-chosen) username and password or more usually now, if they are using the same computer, the website recognises them using a **cookie**, which is a small and **harmless** file containing a string of characters that uniquely identify the computer.

From the initial registration details the user record may show, say, that the user is male, aged 20 to 30 and British. The **website can respond** to this by displaying products or services likely to appeal to this segment of the market.

### 7.2.4 Clickstreams

As users visit the site more often, more is learned about them by **recording what they click on**, since this shows what they are really interested in. On a news site for instance, one user may always go to the sports pages first, while another looks at the TV listings. In a retail sense this is akin to physically following somebody about the store recording everything they do (including products they pick up and put back) and everything they look at, whether or not they buy it.

### 7.2.5 Virtual companies and virtual supply chains (VSC)

**Key concepts**

A **virtual company** is a collection of separate companies, each with a specific expertise, who work together, sharing their expertise to compete for bigger contracts/projects than would be possible if they worked alone.

A traditional **supply chain** is made up of the physical entities linked together to facilitate the supply of goods and services to the final consumer.

A **Virtual Supply Chain (VSC)** is a supply chain that is enabled through e-business links (eg the web, extranets or EDI).

The **virtual company** concept has been around since the mid-1990s. Initially, companies attempted to work together using fax and phone links. The concept only really became a reality when technology such as extranets came into common usage. Companies are now able to work together and exchange information online. For example, engineers from five companies could design a product together on the Internet.

Many companies have become, or are becoming, more virtual. They are developing into looser affiliations of companies, organised as a supply network.

Virtual Supply Chain networks have two types of organisation: producers and integrators.

(a) **Producers** produce goods and services. They have core competencies in production schedule execution. Producers must focus on delivery to schedule and within cost. The sales driver within these companies is on ensuring that their capacity is fully sold through their networking with co-ordinators. Producer are often servicing multiple chains, so managing and avoiding capacity and commercial conflicts becomes key.

(b) **Integrators** manage the supply network and effectively own the end customer contact. The focus of the integrating firms is on managing the end customer relationship. Their core competence is in integrating and controlling the response of the company to customer requirements. This includes the difficult task of synchronising the responses and performance of multi-tiered networks, where the leverage of direct ownership is no longer available, and of often outsourced services such as warehousing and delivery.

Many of the most popular Internet companies are integrators in virtual companies such as *Amazon.com* and *Lastminute.com*. These organisations 'own' customer contact and manage customer relationships for a range of producers.

## 7.3 The impact of e-commerce

**FAST FORWARD**

There are several features of the Internet that make it radically different from what has gone before.

E-commerce **challenges traditional business models** - because, for example, it enables product/service suppliers to interact directly with their customers, instead of using intermediaries (like retail shops, travel agents, insurance brokers, and conventional banks).

Although the Internet is global in its operation, its benefits are not confined to large (or global) organisations. **Small companies** can move instantly into a global market place, either on their own initiative or as part of what is known as a 'consumer portal'. For example, Ede and Ravenscroft is a small outfitting and tailoring business in Oxford: it could easily promote itself within a much larger 'portal' called OxfordHighStreet.com, embracing a comprehensive mixture of other Oxford retailers.

A **new economics of information** has arisen because, with the Internet, much information is free. Those with Internet access can view all the world's major newspapers and periodicals without charge.

An almost incredible **level of speed** is achieved, giving virtually instant access to organisations, plus the capacity to complete purchasing transactions within seconds. This velocity, of course, is only truly impressive if it is accompanied by equal speed so far as the delivery of tangible goods is concerned.

E-commerce has created **new networks of communication** - between organisations and their customers (either individually or collectively), between customers themselves (through mutual support groups), and between organisations and their suppliers.

The Internet stimulates the appearance of **new intermediaries** and the disappearance of some existing ones. Businesses are finding that they can cut out the middle man, with electronic banking, insurance, publishing and printing as primary examples.

**New business partnerships** have been established, through which small enterprises can gain access to customers on a scale which would have been viewed as impossible a few years ago. For example, a university can put its reading list on a website and students wishing to purchase any given book can click directly through to an online bookseller such as Amazon.com. The university gets a commission; the online bookseller gets increased business; the student gets a discount. Everyone benefits except the traditional bookshop.

**Transparent pricing** has been promoted, because potential customers can readily compare prices not only from suppliers within any given country, but also from suppliers across the world.

**Personalised attention** is facilitated even if such attention is actually administered through impersonal (yet highly sophisticated) IT systems and customer database manipulation.

E-commerce provides sophisticated **market segmentation** opportunities. Approaching such segments may be one of the few ways in which e-commerce entrepreneurs can create **competitive advantage**. As *Management Today* (March 2000) puts it:

> 'The starting point must be a neat niche, a funky few, a global tribe. You need to understand your particular tribe better than anyone else. The tribe is the basic unit of business... The good news is that there are lots of tribes out there - and some are enormous. It's just a question of identifying them, understanding them and meeting their needs better than anyone else.'

The web can either be a **separate** or a **complementary** channel.

A new phenomenon is emerging called **dynamic pricing**. Companies can rapidly change their prices to reflect the current state of demand and supply.

These new trends are creating **pressure** for companies. The main threat facing companies is that **prices will be driven down by consumers' ability to shop around**.

 Marketing at Work

**Airlines**

The impact of the web is seen clearly in the transportation industry. Airlines now have a more effective way of bypassing intermediaries (ie travel agents) because they can give their customers immediate

access to flight reservation systems. In the UK, EasyJet, has become the first airline to have over half of its bookings made on-line.

### Travel agents

The web has also produced a new set of on-line travel agents who have lower costs because of their ability to operate without a High Street branch network. Their low-cost structure makes them a particularly good choice for selling low margin, cheap tickets for flights, package holidays, cruises and so forth.

These low-cost travel agents have been joined, furthermore, by non-travel-agents who simply specialise in opportunistic purchasing (eg lastminute.com).

### Tesco

In another arena, Tesco is already the UK's largest Internet grocery business, but other companies are rapidly developing new initiatives. Waitrose@work allows people to order their groceries in the morning (typically through their employer's Intranet communication system) and then have them delivered to the workplace in the afternoon: this approach achieves significant distribution economies of scale so far as Waitrose is concerned.

### Financial services

The impact of the Internet is especially profound in the field of financial services. New intermediaries enable prospective customers to compare the interest rates and prices charged by different organisations for pensions, mortgages and other financial services. This means that the delivering companies are losing control of the marketing of their services, and there is a downward pressure on prices, especially for services which can legitimately be seen as mere commodities (eg house and contents insurance).

## 7.4 Disadvantages of e-commerce

**FAST FORWARD**

E-commerce involves its own mix of difficulties and disadvantages. These generally revolve around issues of security and convenience.

E-commerce involves an unusual mix of people – security people, web technology people, designers, marketing people – and this can be very difficult to manage. The e-business needs supervision by expensive specialists.

In spite of phenomenal growth the market is still fuzzy and undefined. Many e-businesses have only recently reported making any **profit**, the best-known example being *Amazon*, the Internet book-seller.

Unless the e-business is one started completely from scratch, any new technology installed will **need to link up with existing business systems**, which could potentially take years of programming. Under-estimating the time and effort involved is a common obstacle.

The international availability of a website means that the laws of all countries that transactions may be conducted from have to be considered. The legal issues surrounding e-commerce are complex and still developing.

### 7.4.1 Lack of trust

Above all, however, the problem with e-commerce is one of **trust**. In most cultures, consumers grant their trust to business parties that have a close **physical presence**: buildings, facilities and people to talk to. On the Internet these familiar elements are simply not there. The seller's reputation, the size of his business, and the level of customisation in product and service also engender trust.

Internet merchants need to elicit consumer trust when the level of **perceived risk** in a transaction is high. However, research has found that once consumers have built up trust in an Internet merchant such concerns are reduced.

Internet merchants need to address issues such as fear of **invasion of privacy** and abuse of customer information (about their **credit cards**, for example) because they stop people even considering the Internet as a shopping medium.

## 7.4.2 Cryptography, keys and signatures

The parties involved in e-commerce need to have confidence that any communication sent gets to its target destination **unchanged**, and **without being read by anyone else**.

One way of providing electronic signatures is to make use of what is known as **public key** (or asymmetric) **cryptography**. Public key cryptography uses **two keys – public and private**. The **private key** is only known to its owner, and is used to scramble the data contained in a file.

The 'scrambled' data is the electronic signature, and can be checked against the original file using the **public key** of the person who signed it. This confirms that it could only have been signed by someone with access to the private key. If a third party altered the message, the fact that they had done so would be easily detectable.

An alternative is the use of encryption products which support **key recovery**, also known as **key encapsulation**. Such commercial encryption products can incorporate the public key of an agent known as a **Key Recovery Agent (KRA)**. This allows the user to recover their (stored or communicated) data by approaching the KRA with an encrypted portion of the message. In both cases the KRA neither holds the user's private keys, nor has access to the plain text of their data.

 Marketing at Work

**E-commerce dangers and benefits**

For some the Internet is a necessary evil - others browse and surf the net with that obsessive drive that is peculiar to any new technology. But the Internet is not just any new technology. It is the most important communications development since the advent of the telephone, and like the telephone it has created its own culture and given birth to new businesses and new possibilities.

Early confusion about the Internet meant that many companies came to us having built their own websites after learning the rudiments of HTML. They had registered their company name and done everything by the book. The website went on-line and they all waited with baited breath. Nothing happened. No new business arrived and nothing changed, and they couldn't understand why.

E-commerce is a tidal wave; if you choose to participate you either 'sink or swim'. You must be daring enough in design to achieve something quite different from the ways things have been done in the past.

A website is a shopfront that must be located in the centre of town in the full gaze of everyone. A good one can make a small business as powerful and competitive as some of the largest players. It just needs flair and commitment to succeed. But to do so there are some measures that must be used. Marketing outside the web, in the press or even on the radio can alert the market to the website. The site itself should be properly identified by name, registered competently with the appropriate search engines and it must look good.

WEBSITE ESSENTIALS

- Integration with all company systems (ie back office)

- Speedy implementation

- Quick and easy updating by own staff to retain topicality

- Self producing audit records

- Promotion via the internet

- Press and PR for website

- Attractive design but appropriate for the web

- Scope to interact with visitors

- Planned structure to include profitable business concept

- Control and maintenance by owner, without developer involvement

The appearance of a website is extremely important. Attractive and easy to fill interactive forms can lure a sales prospect into being a buyer. One has seconds in which to achieve this end. Too many graphics slow down the procedure. The experience of visiting and browsing through the shop and responding to the goods on offer must be clever, intriguing, quick and efficient. Millions of pounds worth of business is lost on the Internet every day as a result of so-called interactive websites that are difficult to operate and dull.

The **key to success**, and the true working system is to be found in the **back office**. This invisible component is frequently overlooked. You can have the most seductive website in the world, but without a robust, secure, integrated back office system it's worth nothing. The website designer makes the shop window look good but cannot be expected to address the back office system.

Installing e-commerce can bring about overall improvements in accounting and management systems across the board. One bookseller never realised that he had fundamental problems in terms of dispatching stock and warehouse management. This is now being solved by the introduction of an integrated website that will interact with his financial and accounting system.

There are so many new possibilities and ventures created by this new technology, and the most inspired e-commerce enterprises will empower small and medium sized concerns to compete as never before.

Adapted from *Management Accounting, February 2000*

## 7.5 Customer service

Effective, competent and acceptable customer service through the web is a combination of the following factors:

(a) **Rapid response time**. If the website is not fast, the transient potential shopper will simply click on to another. These 'fickle' visitors to a website will only allow around five to eight seconds: if the site has not captured their attention in that time-frame, they will move elsewhere.

(b) **Response quality**. The website must be legible, with appropriate graphics and meaningful, relevant information supplied. Generally speaking, website visitors are not interested in the company's history and size: they are much more concerned about what the company can offer them.

(c)   **Navigability**. It is important to create a website which caters for every conceivable customer interest and question. Headings and category-titles should be straightforward and meaningful, not obscure and ambiguous.

(d)   **Download times**. Again, these need to be rapid, given that many Internet shoppers regard themselves (rightly or otherwise) as cash-rich and time-poor.

(e)   **Security/Trust**. One of the biggest barriers to the willingness of potential Internet customers actually to finalise a transaction is their fear that information they provide about themselves (such as credit card details) can be 'stolen' or used as the basis for fraud.

(f)   **Fulfilment**. Customers must believe that if they order goods and services, the items in question will arrive, and will do so within acceptable time limits (which will generally be much faster than the time limits normally associated with conventional mail order). Equally, customers need to be convinced that if there is a subsequent need for service recovery, then speedy and efficient responses can be secured either to rectify the matter or to enable unsatisfactory goods to be returned without penalty.

(g)   **Up-to-date**. Just as window displays need to be constantly refreshed, so do websites require frequent repackaging and redesign.

(h)   **Availability**. Can the user reach the site 24 hours a day, seven days a week? Is the down-time minimal? Can the site always be accessed?

(i)   **Site effectiveness and functionality**. Is the website intuitive and easy to use? Is the content written in a language which will be meaningful even to the first-time browser (ie the potential customer)?

 Action Programme 3

Up to now, many companies have ignored e-commerce. They have watched as a succession of much-publicised ventures have failed to get off the ground and even the best have struggled to translate success into profits. This has created an impression that the Internet is a confusing and dangerous sales channel that can, for now, be left to others.

Why, do you think, is this view increasingly untenable?

Net pioneers secured important advantages over latecomers. They used information about their customers to tailor their offerings and to foster a sense of community among users. For example, part of the appeal of *Amazon.co.uk* (the Internet bookseller) is the book reviews posted by other readers.

# 8 Developing a strategy for e-commerce

**FAST FORWARD**
> Within its limitations, the Internet can form the basis for a wide variety of value propositions. The aim remains the same: to create competitive advantage.

There are four broad approaches that a company may adopt towards the Internet.

(a)   Do not sell products through the Internet at all, and if distribution is conducted through resellers, prevent them from doing so. Provide only product **information** on the Internet. This may be an appropriate strategy where products are **large, complex and highly customised**, such as aircraft manufacturing.

(b)     **Leave the Internet business to resellers** and do not sell directly through the Internet (ie do not compete with resellers). This can be appropriate, for instance, where manufacturers have already assigned exclusive territories to resellers.

(c)     The manufacturer can **restrict Internet sales exclusively to itself**. The problem with this is that most large manufacturers do not have systems that are geared to dealing with sales to end users who place numerous, irregular small orders.

(d)     Open up Internet sales to everybody and **let the market decide** who it prefers to buy from.

On a more detailed level, in an article for *IT Consultancy* magazine, *Laurence Holt* offered 18 potential strategies for e-commerce.

| Strategy | Comment |
|---|---|
| **Outsource to your customers** | What do we do for our customers that they would rather do for themselves and could probably do better? Examples: *www.cisco.com*, *www.dell.com*. |
| **Cannibalise your own business** | If there were an Amazon.com in our market, what would it be doing? Examples: *www.egghead.com*. |
| **Host your competitors** | How can we create a marketplace that includes our competitors, but that we own? Examples: *www.sabre.com*, *www.jewellery.com*. |
| **Build one-to-one customer relationships** | How can we make each customer feel that we built our organisation just for them? Examples: *www.my.yahoo.com*, *www.firefly.com*, *www.netgrocer.com*. |
| **Make first contact** | What is the first step our customers take in the chain of events that leads them to buy from us? How can we make contact with them? Examples: *www.autobytel.com*. |
| **Be a process integrator** | What other things do customers need or do when they buy from us? Examples: *www.autobytel.com*. |
| **Catch rites of passage** | What major life changes are customers going through when they come into contact with us? How can we help? Examples: *www.usnews.com*, *www.citibank.com*. |
| **Create a community** | What interests do our customers share? How can we create a place that people with those interests will keep coming back to? Examples: *www.yahoo.com*. |
| **Create a niche portal** | How can we make our site the portal our customers go to first? Examples: *www.ft.com*. |
| **Pirate your value network** | How can we take over the roles of others in our value network? Examples: *www.dell.com*. |
| **Re-intermediate on information value** | How can we boost the value we add through information? Examples: *www.britannica.com*. |
| **Go pure cyberspace** | What if we made the digital world our first priority and the physical world second? Examples: *www.tiscali.com*. |
| **Be a fast follower** | What are our competitors doing that looks likely to be successful? How can we do the same thing faster? Examples: *www.barnesandnoble.com*. |
| **Think dream not transaction** | What dream do our customers start with that leads them to buy from us? How can we realise that dream? Examples: *www.expedia.com*. |
| **Beat the physical world** | What can we do in the digital world that would be impossible or not feasible in the physical world? Examples: *www.benjerry.com*. |

| Strategy | Comment |
|---|---|
| **Leverage the froth** | What simple ideas would capture most media and public attention, even if short-lived? Examples: *www.travelocity.com*, *www.lastminute.com*. |
| **Change the pricing model** | Would our customers benefit from a different way of pricing, perhaps micro-payments or auctions? Examples: *www.priceline.com*. |
| **Convert atoms to bits** | What physical world core competencies do we have that could be applied to the digital world? Examples: *www.ups.com*. |

If the decision is made to enter into e-commerce, an e-business venture needs **support and long-term commitment from high-level management**. Ideally such a project should be 'sponsored' by the chief executive or a board-level director.

## 8.1 Strategic issues

**FAST FORWARD**

The Internet's main opportunities lie in communication and distribution.

The development of an interactive facility requires a major shift away from conventional commercial activities. It has been suggested that this is often achieved in three phases.

| Phase | Comment |
|---|---|
| **Presentation** | The use of a website to enable visitors/customers to **access information** provides an opportunity to stand out from competitors and **enhance corporate image**. It is an opportunity to illustrate the organisation's products and services. This facility is often referred to as **brochureware**. |
| **Interaction** | This phase is characterised by **two-way communication**. Questions and answers flow between the system and the user. Visitors to the site are able to enquire more deeply than at the presentation stage and **information about the visitor** is logged and stored on a **database** for future reference and for both on and offline communications. |
| **Representation** | When this phase is reached the organisation will have replaced parts of its commercial activities with **full online transactions**. The organisation's traditional commercial trading methods and channels may still be in place and the new interactive facility provides a **complementary** and/or alternative method for **particular market segments**. |

It should not be assumed that all organisations move through each of these phases. If they do, it is at different speeds. Those that do migrate do so according to a number of variables, including, the **nature of the markets in which they operate**, their strategy, technical resources, attitude to risk and competitive pressures.

Internet technology can also be used strategically to enable communication with particular audiences.

(a) The **Internet** itself enables public access to an organisation's website.

(b) An **Intranet** refers to a private internal network which is normally used to enable communication with employees.

(c) **Extranets** allow particular external audiences such as distributors, suppliers and certain customers access to an organisation's facilities.

**Exam tip**

Extranets are important elements to consider when discussing communications with marketing channel partners, as featured in a question in the December 2002 exam.

The Internet offers two main marketing opportunities, namely **distribution and communication**. The ability to **reach customers directly** and so avoid many channel intermediaries reduces transaction costs and is a prime goal for most organisations.

## Marketing at Work

Digital Lifestyles (a company) has launched 'the first teen-lifestyle computerised entertainment system' and called it the **hip-e-mode**. This is a computer integrated into a 17 inch widescreen flat panel display. It has a built-in TV tuner, a hard drive that will record TV shows and a combination DVD/CD drive. With a broadband link it can download music and video from the Internet. Prices start at US$1,699 but the device is only available online at hip-e.com or by phone.

*Fortune, 7 March 2005*

The use of the Internet as a communications medium is equally attractive. It is more than a medium as it **facilitates interactivity and a two-way dialogue** that no other method of communication can support. Unlike other forms of communication, **dialogue is induced by the customer**, the speed and duration of the communication is **customer controlled** and the intensity of the relationship (with the on-line brand), is again customer managed. All the traditional tools of the promotional mix can be deployed over the Internet, with varying degrees of success, but it appears that **off-line marketing communications are required to support** the on-line communications and facilities. A combination of off and on-line communications need to be determined if the overall communications are to fulfil the **DRIP** roles (Differentiate, Remind/Reassure, Inform and Persuade).

The use of the Internet can perhaps be best observed when set alongside the **purchase decision process**. See the table below.

*Use of the Internet to support stages in the buying process*

> **Awareness**
>
> Not very effective at generating awareness and needs the support of offline communications to drive visitors to the site.
>
> **Positioning**
>
> As a means of presenting features and benefits the web is very good once a prospective customer has determined a need for a supplier search and is looking to compare offerings.
>
> **Lead generation**
>
> Once an active search commences leads can be obtained and used to reach prospects in the future.
>
> **Purchase decision support**
>
> By carrying vast amounts of information at low cost websites provide good opportunities to impress visitors and build credibility.
>
> **Facilitate purchase**
>
> Through the provision of basic transaction facilities (credit card payment) sales should not be lost once a decision to buy has been made.
>
> **Post purchase support and retention**
>
> Through the provision of free customer support and advice, levels of cognitive dissonance in customers can be reduced. Feedback from customers, email updates about product developments and the use of sales promotions to stimulate repeat site visits can improve reputation, enable cross selling and promote favourable word of mouth recommendations.
>
> Adapted from Chaffey, Mayer, Johnston and Ellis-Chadwick, *What's New in Marketing?* (2000)

## 8.2 E-commerce and website management

Management need to attend to three main decisions concerning their Internet and digital related facilities. These are their **development, maintenance and promotion**. All of these use resources and management need to be clear about the level of support that is appropriate. One of the key concerns is the web site itself. To be successful the web site should do the following.

(a) **Attract visitors** – with on-line and off-line methods

(b) **Enable participation** – interactive content, and suitable facilities to allow for transactions

(c) **Encourage return visits** – design targeted at needs of particular segments, free services and added value facilities

(d) **Allow for two-way information sharing** – personalisation reflecting visitor preferences, direct marketing and information retrieval provide visitors with the information they are seeking

 Marketing at Work

**Brand or business?**

'It is all very well spending millions on marketing so every person in the country knows about your company. But if none of them are actually buying your products or services, it is money down the drain.'

It has been suggested that the brief flourish of the 'dotcom' revolution ended largely because those responsible for marketing concentrated too many resources on "brand blazing" rather than looking after customers. Few dotcom businesses bothered to analyse, profile or even contact their website visitors.

Adapted from *Marketing Business October 2001*

**Exam tip**

> This came up in June 2000. You had to develop briefing notes.

Many observers are taking the view that the future of Internet marketing lies in the **business-to-business (B2B)** sector. The belief is based on the premises that:

(a) Selling low value items to **consumers** requires significant **spending on advertising and promotion**, and costly **back up systems**

(b) Consumers expect **free content**

(c) Businesses which look for quotes can massively **increase their source of suppliers**, nationally and globally

(d) Suppliers have a **wider market** to appeal to

B2B is therefore expected to break down barriers and enhance supply chain management.

 Marketing at Work

*Worldwidetender.com* is an online B2B marketplace which allows businesses to buy and sell excess stock. Customers include retail chains, supermarket chains, convenience store groups, bulk catering companies and restaurant chains. Average sales are around £10,000 but can reach £250,000. With these higher value transactions, communications rely on the telephone and e-mail to encourage trading.

Many similar middle market companies are following the worldwide tender approach. The E-Business Report published recently by Birmingham Business School shows only some 25% of middle market firms

are using the Internet for marketing and sales to consumers and almost 50% involved in B2B activity. Surveys by Forrester Research suggest the online market will account for approximately half of all B2B sales by 2007.

 **Marketing at Work**

**Otis**

*Otis* is the world's largest company in the manufacture, sales and service of people moving products such as elevators, escalators, shuttle systems and moving walkways. They have taken a dynamic and innovative approach to e-business.

Services include 24 hour access to maintenance records, an Internet-enabled flat-panel display elevator communication and entertainment system and the facility for customers to plan, price and track new equipment projects online. The global website can be accessed in more than 51 countries and in 26 languages. These initiatives have led to a re-evaluation of customer relationships and generation of new business. The process for ordering a new elevator had previously been based on the completion of 300 technical questions taking one to three months to complete. This now consists of 15 questions and an online ordering system that can be completed in 20 minutes. These changes now allow sales people to deliver excellent customer service.

From an article in *The Times 11 April 2001*

### 8.2.1 Benefits of using the Internet in e-commerce

| Benefit | How generated |
|---|---|
| Loyalty | Faster response |
| Productivity | Better management of the supply chain |
| Reputation | Depends on competition and ability of web-based strategies to offer real customer benefit |
| Costs | Generally lower, easier for customers to obtain information |

Organisational buying behaviour is generally more complex that consumer purchases. The Internet enables transparency. Moreover, a **website can be accessed by more people in the DMU**.

## 8.3 Establishing an Internet marketing capability

An organisation's sales/marketing Internet capability may, at the outset, solely **dispense information** (operating like a product catalogue), but may eventually become transactional (so that individuals can place orders) and/or **interactive** (dealing with queries, complaints and other kinds of customer communications). There are ten key steps to constructing an effective e-commerce strategy.

### 8.3.1 The context

To put these guidelines into context, a survey in 2000 by *Booz Allen & Hamilton* and the *Economist Intelligence Unit*, involving 600 executives, sought views on the strategic significance of the Internet.

    (a)    61 per cent believed the Internet would help them to achieve business goals.

    (b)    30 per cent said the Internet had already forced them to overhaul their existing business strategies.

(c)    On the other hand, only 28 per cent had generated income from the Internet.

The same survey highlighted seven **megatrends** which, coupled with the Internet, are changing the face of organisations.

(a)    New **distribution channels**, revolutionising sales and brand management.

(b)    The continued **shift of power** towards the consumer.

(c)    **Growing competition** locally, nationally, internationally and globally.

(d)    An acceleration in the **pace of business**.

(e)    The **transformation of companies** into 'extended enterprises' involving 'virtual teams of business, customer and supplier' working in collaborative partnerships.

(f)    A re-evaluation of how companies, their partners and competitors **add value** not only to themselves but in the wider environmental and social setting.

(g)    Recognition of **'knowledge'** as a strategic asset.

Most observers and experts agree that a successful strategy for e-commerce cannot simply be bolted on to existing processes, systems, delivery routes and business models. Instead, management groups have, in effect, to start again, by asking themselves such **fundamental questions** as:

(a)    What do customers want to buy from us?
(b)    What business should we be in?
(c)    What kind of partners might we need?
(d)    What categories of customer do we want to attract and retain?

In turn, organisations can visualise the necessary changes at three interconnected levels.

**Level 1**    The simple **introduction of new technology** to connect electronically with employees, customers and suppliers (eg through an intranet, extranet or website).

**Level 2**    **Re-organisation** of the workforce, processes, systems and strategy - in order to make best use of the new technology.

**Level 3**    **Re-positioning** of the organisation to fit it into the emerging e-economy.

So far, very few companies have gone beyond levels (1) and (2). Instead, pure Internet businesses such as Amazon and *AOL* have emerged from these new rules: unburdened by physical assets, their competitive advantage lies in knowledge management and customer relationships.

### 8.3.2 Ten key steps to constructing an effective strategy for e-commerce

**Step 1**    **Upgrade customer interaction**
The first thing for the organisation to do is to **upgrade the interaction with its existing customers**.

(a)    Create automated responses for the FAQs (Frequently Asked Questions) posed by customers, so that customers become conditioned to electronic communication. Automated responses, perhaps surprisingly in view of their impersonal nature, can help to improve customer confidence and trust.

(b)    Set fast response standards, at least to match anything offered by the competition.

(c)    Use e-mail in order to confirm actions, check understanding, and reassure the customer that their business is being taken forward.

(d)    Establish ease of navigation around your website and enhance the site's 'stickiness' so that there is a measurably reduced likelihood that actual or potential customers will migrate elsewhere.

A study conducted by Rubic Inc in the USA ('Evaluating the 'Sticky' Factor of E-Commerce Sites') found that the majority of websites fail to communicate effectively with customers. Only 40 per cent had a strategy of personalisation for their e-mail messages to customers; when customers responded to follow-up offers, only one quarter of websites recognised the fact that they were dealing with a repeat customer; 40 per cent of e-mail enquiries went unanswered despite promises of replies within two days.

**Step 2**  **Understand customer segments**

The organisation preparing its e-commerce strategy should **understand its customer segments** and classify each segment against the likelihood that it will be receptive to an Internet business route.

(a)    Some will be eager to transfer to the new technology, others will do so if persuaded (or incentivised), and residual groups will prefer to remain as they are.

(b)    Once the degree of profitability-per-customer has been established, efforts should be made to automate the provision of customer service and transaction capability so far as low-value customers are concerned.

(c)    The organisation may establish personalised service relationships with key (ie high profit-generating) customers.

**Step 3**  **Understand service processes**

The organisation must **understand its customer service processes** in order to disentangle those processes which can safely be put on to the Web and those which have to be delivered in other ways.

(a)    Typically, organisations serving customers may find that there are between five and ten generic transaction types which describe their relationships with these customers (eg information query, complaint, and so forth).

(b)    This analysis is essential for addressing such questions as: Which of these processes is appropriate for automation? Which of these processes will work better, from the customer's standpoint, if put on the web?

(c)    Transaction costs also need to be investigated, again from the perspective of the organisation and its overheads, and also taking into account the transaction costs incurred by the customer. These may involve money, but customers are often more conscious about time and timeliness. Getting on to the Internet takes longer than a telephone call (though this may not always be the case), so the customer, behaving rationally, will want more value from the process.

(d)    On the other hand, a short simple transaction is often better conducted over the telephone.

**Step 4**  **Define the role**

The organisation needs to **define the role for live interaction with its customers**.

(a)    Live interaction may be very useful if there is scope for cross-selling and the conversion of enquiries into sales.

(b)    The availability of service supplied by human intervention can also be appropriate if the organisation needs to build trust (eg it is a new brand which must work hard to establish confidence) and secure diagnostic information from the customer before any product or service can be delivered.

(c)    E-mail may not be sufficient as a communications route, especially if it involves a delay before replies or acknowledgements are forthcoming.

(d)    Live interaction can be essential for customers who have a strong preference for human contact.

**Step 5**   **Decide technology**

**Making the key technology decisions** involves some tough choices. Given the pace of change and innovation in this arena, it is difficult to know whether to initiate a pilot programme immediately, with the full IT and people investment scheduled for later, or whether to go for full integration at once. The risk with a pilot programme is that the organisation can be overtaken by pioneering competitors; the risk with full integration is that new systems can be inadequate or may even collapse completely, causing irretrievable havoc with customers.

**Step 6**   **Deal with the tidal wave**

There is much evidence that offering an Internet-based service can lead to a major increase in customer interaction, and so organisations need to develop strategies for **dealing with the tidal wave**. This might involve:

(a)   Ensuring sufficient capacity is available for worst-case scenarios
(b)   Using user-friendly technologies and system design
(c)   Setting targets for low-touch interaction
(d)   Ensuring facilities are scaleable if demand rapidly outstrips supply.

**Step 7**   **Create incentives**

The organisation may have to **create incentives for use of the lowest-cost channels**, with savings passed on the customer through discounts. The alternatives are:

(a)   To create **incentives** to switch to the lowest-cost channels, through financial inducements, training and additional benefits.

(b)   To introduce **disincentives** for continuing to use existing channels. Thus Abbey National has implemented a £5 charge for customers who pursue over-the-counter cash transactions in their branches. Such tactics almost invariably generate very hostile reactions from customers themselves and from consumer groups.

**Step 8**   **Decide on channel choices**

The eighth consideration involves the decision about **which channel choices to offer**, and whether, for instance, to confine operations to the 'click' route or whether to simultaneously maintain the 'brick' presence through a branch network. There are two crucial questions:

(a)   **Whether to offer the customer a choice of channels**, eg face-to-face, post, phone and Internet. Many banks offer all four; some have single-channel accounts (phone or Internet only), whilst others (like **egg**) allow constrained choice: **egg** (the Internet and telephone banking arm of the Prudential Assurance Company) will allow telephone and Internet customer interaction, but only permits new customers to enrol via the web.

(b)   **How to balance the costs of different channels whilst managing the Customer Relationship Management (CRM) database.** In most customer service environments, the quality and scope of the CRM database is central to the successful delivery of service, so it becomes desirable not to operate each customer-communication channel separately, but to integrate existing channels around a single CRM database.

(c)   One reason why Charles Schwab (specialists in stock and share dealing) is able to charge much bigger fees than some of its rivals is that it combines an online service with a low-cost branch network and a telephone service. They have recognised the web has certain virtues and weaknesses. The web is lousy if you have a complex question. Likewise, it does not allow for people's need for relationships. Not everyone feels happy about sending a cheque to a broker they have never seen.

**Step 9**  **Exploit the Internet**

The organisation should **exploit the Internet in order to create new relationships and experience**.

(a) It is desirable to create **tailor-made service** sites for significant customers.

(b) Proactive **product/service offerings** should be regularly incorporated into the website architecture.

(c) **Communities of users** and/or customers (depending on whichever is appropriate) should be facilitated, since these generate additional business through referral and may well undertake a large proportion of the customer-service activity among themselves. Such communities may also stimulate product/service innovation, new uses for existing products and services, and product/service extensions.

(d) Deliberate mechanisms need to be developed in order to **turn browsers into buyers**, and transform one-off customers into repeat purchasers.

(e) Any successful e-commerce strategy presupposes the likelihood that the product/ service supplier can engage the potential customer **emotionally** despite the technology which surrounds Internet availability.

It is necessary for the strategist to visualise the **extended experience** that customers encounter when they carry an Internet transaction through from initiation to completion. It is vital for organisations to place themselves in the shoes of customers and ask the question: what are our customers really buying? The answer, 99 times out of 100, is that customers are buying benefits whilst companies are selling features. Further, if the transaction lacks any emotional commitment, then it also lacks any real likelihood of voluntary customer retention.

**Step 10**  **Implement**

No strategy is worth the paper is written on if it simply remains a document, gathering dust: as Peter Drucker once pointed out, 'Strategy is nothing until it degenerates into work'.

## 8.4 Important aspects of strategy implementation for e-commerce

**Organisation and culture**. When organisations move into an electronic age, some people (and functions) increase their corporate influence, whilst others move into the shadows. The increasing use of technology is unsettling, especially for senior people (ironically, employees lower down the hierarchy are likely to be much more comfortable about technological innovation). The Internet promotes freedom of information, both upwards and downwards; this, for some managers, is equated with a loss of authority.

**Systems and infrastructure**. Implementation of e-commerce often requires integration of service systems, particularly call centres, the web, and CRM processes. This in turn may require a company to review its whole decision-making patterns and make some difficult choices about existing legacy procedures.

**Training**. Effective e-commerce implementation requires both staff and customers to be trained. Dealing with electronic interaction demands different skills from those which are appropriate to staff who focus on voice communications. Dealing simultaneously with written and verbal interaction is likely to call for a new skill set.

**Looking to the customers**. This is well summarised by Mike Harris, Chief Executive of *Egg*, explaining the need to avoid rehearsed, scripted and bureaucratic approaches which give the impression that technology is driving the interaction rather than the need to relate to people.

Conventional thinking says that a company should pay no more to bring in a customer than the net present value of the stream of profits that the customer will subsequently generate. Yet in the e-commerce context, investors have often rewarded companies for customer acquisition without asking any questions about how quickly those customers may disappear.

Similar turbulence is affecting the B2B world. Traditional manufacturing companies around the world, sensing the potential benefits from automating transactions with suppliers and customers, have rushed into e-commerce. Many have formed alliances to create their own on-line market place, especially in the automobile, aerospace and chemicals industries. By pooling their buying power, the organisations behind these alliances hope to have more control over their activities - and this leaves the small, purely Internet-based commodity/component exchanges struggling to attract the volume of transactions needed to make them viable.

 ## Marketing at Work

### E-technology - fuelling or fooling customer strategies?

One of the most important challenges the modern enterprise has is to find ways to increase value from its customers, rather than from its products, so as to get long-lasting growth rather than short-term gains. Research and practice forcefully demonstrate that e-technology can facilitate this - but not if e-technology is simply used to cut costs in order to drive market share of core products or services and so perpetuate past strategies.

Increased and sustained growth from customers can only come to firms that know how to 'lock-in' their customers. This means customers want them as their dominant or sole choice because they get ongoing superior value at low cost.

Enterprises get this lifelong customer value when they push boundaries to create new 'market spaces' which link benefits otherwise separated by industry or companies providing users with results or outcomes rather than just what they happen to make, have in stock, or be promoting at a moment in time. Contrast for instance: cars v personal mobility; books v information and knowledge discovery; PCs v global networking capability; audio-visual equipment v integrated home 'edutainment' - to see the difference.

In new market spaces, working together with a network of partners, the object is to provide an integrated experience for customers over their activity cycles: 'pre' the experience, when customers are deciding what to do; 'during' the experience, when they are doing it, and 'post' the experience, when they are keeping it going, reviewing, updating, and renewing. If value gaps or discontinuities happen in the customer activity cycle, companies (even industries) become vulnerable: other players (usually outsiders) get in, build relationships and capture the new wealth. Which is what happened to *IBM* in the late 1980s and why Amazon took the book retailers by storm.

There are four levels for which e-technology is currently being used.

**Level 1: Tell**. At its most basic, the object here is to create presence on the web for customers who come to the site in search of information about the company and its products or services. The result is a website catalogue or brochure.

**Level 2: Sell**. Here the Internet is used as an alternative channel or tool to promote and sell a firm's wares on-line, typically what food retailers are doing, or alternatively to sell others' wares. The problem here is that the enterprise is playing the same game: frequently what is delivered is just what is kept in stock, and emphasis often goes to supply management to save costs. When combined with savings on conventional infrastructures, price competition is created - resulting in a commodity spiral which inevitably ends up in poor service where no-one gains, including customers.

**E-technology customer strategy map**

| | | |
|---|---|---|
| **Integrate** | Level 4 | Become gateway to integrated personalised customer experience |
| **Augment** | Level 3 | Offer information and services to facilitate sales of more core items |
| **Sell** | Level 2 | Alternative channel to sell products/services |
| **Tell** | Level 1 | Website catalogue information about company/products/services |

*Degree of customer lock-in* (vertical axis)

*Potential for growth* (horizontal axis)

**Level 3: Augment.** At a more advanced level, through e-technology a firm can offer information, choice or services like remote diagnostics, as Dyson Appliances is doing. But the goal is still transactional - sell more core items, either directly or through distributors or retailers. The offering is augmented to differentiate the company in order to get customer loyalty and retention, to increase transactions and decrease transactional costs. This is often accompanied by customer relationship management tools: using databases to learn about what customers buy, in what quantities, where, and how often, as well as promotional devices like loyalty cards, typical of banks and airlines, but all too easy to emulate. Such CRM approaches do not really consider who these customers are, or interact with them to deliver ongoing, superior, personalised value.

**Level 4: Integrate.** In order to achieve that value, we need to move to level 4 on the e-technology customer strategy map. Here the enterprise becomes the gateway to customers, providing them with an integrated experience across product, industry, company, country and even brand, over time - sometimes lifetime. Customer relationships are managed interactively in a highly personalised way so as to achieve the 'lock-in', which happens because the enterprise knows more about the customer than anyone else and uses this information and knowledge to build offerings which are proactive and precise.

The intangibles - ideas, information and knowledge - which become the key component of the offering -are easy to assimilate, codify and disseminate using e-technology. And while the internet is a mass medium, customers can be handled in a highly personalised way at extremely low, if not zero, marginal cost.

What protects the enterprise here is that, once Level 4 has been reached, customer lock-in becomes self-reinforcing: the more information and knowledge customers share with the firm, the more proactive and precise offerings become, the more customers lock-in, and the more ideas, information and knowledge they share.

With its powerful and pervasive effects, e-technology allows the enterprise to excel with customers in ways never before imagined. The e-technology strategy map may help managers position themselves and make better decisions so that e-technology can fuel, rather than fool, their customer strategy.

*Strategy Magazine, May 2000*

## 8.5 Building an investment case for e-commerce

There is still opposition in some organisations to the necessary investment required for e-commerce. Reasons for this opposition often include:

(a)   Straightforward **resistance to change**, coupled with **fear of the unknown**. Even stories about Internet successes elsewhere may be viewed with caution on the grounds that they may not easily be transferable.

(b)   Existence of the belief that even if new entrants were able to take advantage of the fashionable popularity of the Internet, others coming along behind - 'laggards' - will not be able to do so.

(c)   The evidence that many 'dot.com' enterprises remain **unable to achieve sustained profitability** or indeed any profitability at all.

On the other hand, companies still experiencing doubts should put themselves in the shoes of a potential Internet competitor - and ask themselves: *How might they attack us?* The evidence from experience gained so far in the field of electronic commerce suggests the following scenarios:

(a)   They would ignore the unattractive, expensive channels through which your product or service is currently delivered. If your business is banking, they will not establish a branch network; if you are a retailer, they will not operate a chain of shops.

(b)   They will **cherry-pick** the more profitable customer segments. Again, if you are a bank, the new entrant will seek to entice away your credit-worthy customers with expensive tastes and unrestricted consumption habits.

(c)   They will create highly **differentiated customer segments**, possibly customised for specific individuals. In other words, they will offer a degree of personalised attention which you may find difficult to match.

(d)   They will deliberately choose to supply products and services where their presence on the World Wide Web will **add value** - both for themselves and for their customers.

(e)   They will offer **shared services** - so that they operate, in effect, as a one-stop shop for, say, a whole repertoire of financial services or in-home entertainment products.

(f)   They will capture **intermediary roles** - and benefit from the savings because their costs will not include commission paid to travel agents.

(g)   They can use the strength of their website as a **portal** - generating even more business for themselves through the provision of allied, complementary or even virtually identical services.

(h)   They can create **affiliate programmes** - equipping them with the capacity for organising comprehensive options. Thus, for example, an online grocer may develop relationships with up-market catering companies which cook and serve meals for dinner parties in customers' own homes.

(i)   They may **offer incentives** - in the form of reduced prices, discounts, cashback offers, lower interest rates, or higher investment returns. Some of these incentives may be tax-free if they are operated outside any given country's tax regime.

### E-business

Electronic business refers to aspects of business being conducted electronically throughout the entire value chain. Figures suggest companies that have commenced trading electronically with their supplies are experiencing a 20% reduction in costs.

Businesses around the world are on the verge of a revolution, as the web shifts the power from the firm to the customer. Products and services are now being purchased by consumers who are able to obtain more information, and thereby becoming more discerning.

The electronic communication revolution will mean that distance will no longer determine the price of communicating electronically. Adept use of e-commerce will become arguably the most important form of competitive advantage for businesses. It has the potential to create new business models and to find new ways of doing things. The benefits of e-commerce come not only from speeding up and automating a firm's internal processes but also from its ability to spread the benefits to other members of its supply chain.

E-business will eventually be deployed throughout an entire industry's supply chain, linking manufacturers, assemblers, distributors, marketers and customers. A single press of a button will trigger many processes throughout the chain. Table 1 provides a summary of the strategic implications of e-business. The provision of services will increasingly become more important than mere products. Web pages will deliver bespoke services, such as help for consumers in making their choices or stock management for business partners. Fixed prices will give way to reflect true market worth, and firms will join together to make convenient packages for the customer.

**Table 1 Strategic implications for e-business**

| | E-commerce | Strategic implications |
|---|---|---|
| **Communication** | The falling costs and increases in capacity of communications. | Death of distance. Virtual firms can become a reality. |
| **Business model** | The traditional business model is inappropriate for e-business. | Virtual organisations will be used to capture cost savings and overthrow established practices. |
| **IT** | Existing IT systems have not adequately dealt with the customer. | Traditional IT systems will have to complement the Internet. |
| **E-revolution** | Commoditisation will make it extremely difficult for firms to differentiate their products. | Need to refine and implement new e-business strategies. |
| **Value** | The finance function does not currently provide much added value in the current e-business environment. | Redesign traditional financial planning, control and evaluation techniques. |

*King and Clift* assert that most businesses will migrate to e-business in four stages.

- **Website:** Organisations make their presence in e-business. Attempts will be made to integrate their site's buying and selling processes into the organisation's back office, customer and marketing systems.

- **Connect website to supply chain:** Involves connecting the web site's capabilities to supply chains. For example, it is anticipated that the reduction in paperwork will reduce costs.

- **Form alliances:** Alliances will be formed to operationalise the new business model. Electronic share dealing on the internet is an example of this.

- **Industrial convergence:** E-business makes it possible for industries to combine expertise and produce package solutions.

The massive scale changes taking place in global markets now make it imperative that organisations (private and public sector) fully understand the business applications of e-commerce and are able to formulate, implement and evaluate corporate, business and operational strategies.

Adapted from *Management Accounting, February 2000*

## Chapter Roundup

- Strategies are evaluated according to their **suitability** to the firm's situation; their **feasibility** in terms of resources and competences; and their acceptability to key stakeholder groups, particularly shareholders and customers.

- Analysing stakeholders by their power held and their degree of interest helps to understand their influence.

- Whether or not a formal approach to strategy is taken, strategic managers must think flexibly and be prepared to respond to changing situations.

- Risk must be managed and to do this, it must be quantified and its implications considered.

- **Market segmentation** is based on different needs and different buying behaviour. Different products are not segments in themselves; rather it is consumer needs for fast cars, commercial needs that determine segments. Each market segment, providing it is large and profitable enough, can become a **target market** for a firm. Market segmentation is increasing because marketing, economic and technological advances have made it possible to address a greater variety of customer needs.

- **Segment validity** depends upon size, availability, measurability and differentiation. **Segment attractiveness** can be assessed by analysing marketing, competitive and financial factors. Sometimes sales and markets forecasts can be used to assess the attractiveness of a market.

- Having analysed the attractiveness of a segment, the firm will choose one or more **target markets**. Marketing policy may be **undifferentiated** (mass), **concentrated** or **differentiated**. The extreme form of differentiated marketing is **micromarketing**.

- **Positioning** can be 'psychological' and 'real'. **Perceptual maps** enable users to identify positioning options. The foundation of a **positioning strategy** is to align what the company can do with what customers want.

- Repositioning is a risky and expensive response to poor performance.

- **Electronic commerce** includes a wide range of applications and techniques based on the integration of computers and telephone networks.

- **E-commerce** is the process of trading on the Internet. Many business processes can be undertaken using e-commerce techniques.

- There are several features of the Internet that make it radically different from what has gone before.

- E-commerce involves its own mix of difficulties and disadvantages. These generally revolve around issues of security and convenience.

- Within its limitations, the Internet can form the basis for a wide variety of value propositions. The aim remains the same: to create competitive advantage.

- The Internet's main opportunities lie in communication and distribution.

- An organisation's sales/marketing Internet capability may, at the outset, solely **dispense information** (operating like a product catalogue), but may eventually become transactional (so that individuals can place orders) and/or **interactive** (dealing with queries, complaints and other kinds of customer communications). There are ten key steps to constructing an effective e-commerce strategy.

## Quick Quiz

1   State three criteria for evaluating strategic options.

2   Which groups make up the external coalition?

3   What is country risk?

4   How should acceptable risk be dealt with in strategic decisions?

5   To which generic competitive strategy is segmentation particularly relevant?

6   What is the importance of having a number of segmentation bases?

7   Which segmentation deals with the stages households pass through?

8   What categories have been traditionally used to segment industrial customers?

9   What criteria must be satisfied if a market segment is to be valid?

10   How do barriers to entry affect segment attractiveness?

11   What are the three policy options in selecting target markets?

12   What is positioning?

13   Define a 'virtual supply chain'.

## Answers to Quick Quiz

1   Suitability, feasibility, acceptability

2   Owners, associates, employee associations and the public

3   Risk of government action, war or insurrection that might affect the business

4   If should form part of a portfolio of projects with varying degrees of risk

5   Focus strategy

6   One basis will not be valid for every market and sometimes two or more bases might be valid at the same time

7   The family life cycle

8   Location, type of business, use made of the product, type and size of organisation

9   Measurability, size, accessibility, response, profitability, stability

10   Entry might require significant investment, but the barriers then provide some protection against other potential entrants

11   Differential, indifferential and concentrated marketing

12   Designing the offer to achieve a distinct and valued place in the customer's mind

13   A supply decision that is enabled through e-business links such as websites, extranets or electronic data interchange

# Action Programme Review

1    (a)    Adult education

- Age
- Sex
- Occupation
- Social class
- Education
- Family life cycle
- Lifestyle
- Leisure interest and hobbies

(b)    Magazines and periodicals

- Sex (Woman's Own)
- Social class (Country Life)
- Income and class aspirations (Ideal Home)
- Occupation (Marketing Week, Computer Weekly)
- Leisure interests (Railway Modeller)
- Political ideology (Spectator, New Statesman)
- Age

(c)    Sporting facilities

(i)    Geographical area (rugby in Wales, skiing in parts of Scotland, sailing in coastal towns)

(ii)    Population density (squash clubs in cities, riding in country areas)

(iii)    Occupation (gyms for office workers)

(iv)    Education (there may be a demand for facilities for sports taught at certain schools, such as rowing)

(v)    Family life cycle or age (parents may want facilities for their children, young single or married people may want facilities for themselves)

2

| Positioning strategy | Example |
|---|---|
| Attributes | Ads for PCs emphasise 'speed', what sort of chip they have (eg Pentium III) |
| Benefit | Holidays are advertised as offering relaxation or excitement |
| Use/application | 'Easy to use' products (eg hair tints that can be 'washed' in) |
| User | Reflect user characteristics, to appeal to the target audience and confirm their choice. May use celebrity endorsement, such as David Beckham in Vodafone advertisements |
| Product category | The Natural History Museum is fundamentally educational, but is moving towards a 'theme park' image for the schools market |
| Quality/price | 'Value for money' advertisements |

3    Relevant points include:

(a)    The likely scale and speed of development is immense.

(b)    Every part of the value chain is up for grabs. Any participant in the value chain could usurp the role of any other participant.

(i)    The free flow of information about buyers and sellers undermines the role of intermediaries.

(ii)    A book publisher could bypass retailers or distributors and sell directly.

(iii)    A book seller could decide to publish books, based on the information it has obtained about readers' interests.

Now try Questions 4A and 4B at the end of the Study Text

# Market entry methods

**6**

## Syllabus content

- Building competitive capability and approaches to leveraging capability to create advantage across geographically diverse markets
- Determining the lessons of best practice from strategic decisions made by successful global companies
- Appraisal of innovative marketing strategies in small and large companies operating in global markets

# Introduction

When a decision has been taken to seek competitive advantage by entering international markets, a **method of market entry** must be chosen. The method of entry to the overseas market has a number of wide reaching implications for the marketing mix, and is a critical indicator of a firm's depth of involvement in, and vulnerability to, the overseas market. Why might this be so?

A product might be manufactured at home or abroad. If the product is manufactured at home and exported, the firm is vulnerable to **exchange rate fluctuations**. On the other hand, a substantial investment might be needed for overseas operations.

Mode of entry also has implications for the **distribution channel**. Although, in domestic markets, firms often give some control over distribution to intermediaries, this problem is magnified in international terms. In some cases, a firm has no choice but to enter into a joint venture. For many firms, overseas operations means they are forced into meeting the **aims of intermediaries**, even though this may not be the ideal means of the satisfying the needs of the end consumer.

The method of market entry is of strategic importance. A market may not appear so attractive as in the initial assessment if the mode of entry requires unusual effort. So although method of entry decides 'how' a firm goes about international marketing it has strategic implications as it affects the **risk** a firm encounters. It is therefore important that you recognise that market entry **strategies** and market entry **methods** must be consistent and complementary. The latter is the way to achieve the goals of the former.

# 1 Entry strategies for overseas markets

**FAST FORWARD**

It is possible to identify **three methods of entry** to foreign markets.

- Indirect exports
- Direct exports
- Overseas manufacture

If an organisation has decided to enter an overseas market, its entry strategy is of crucial strategic importance. The mode of entry affects a firm's entire marketing mix and its control over the mix elements.

Broadly, three ways of entering foreign markets can be identified: direct exports, indirect exports and overseas manufacturing.

**Key concepts**

**Indirect exports**. These are sales to intermediary organisations at home which then resell the product to customers overseas. It is the outsourcing of the exporting function to a third party.

**Direct exports**. These are sales to customers overseas without the use of export houses etc. These customers may be intermediary organisations based abroad or end-users.

**Overseas manufacture**. A firm may set up its own production operation overseas or enter into a joint venture with an enterprise in the overseas market. As an example, a number of Japanese companies have established factories in the UK to manufacture for the UK and European markets.

Each of these methods is discussed in more detail below, but here is a diagram in outline.

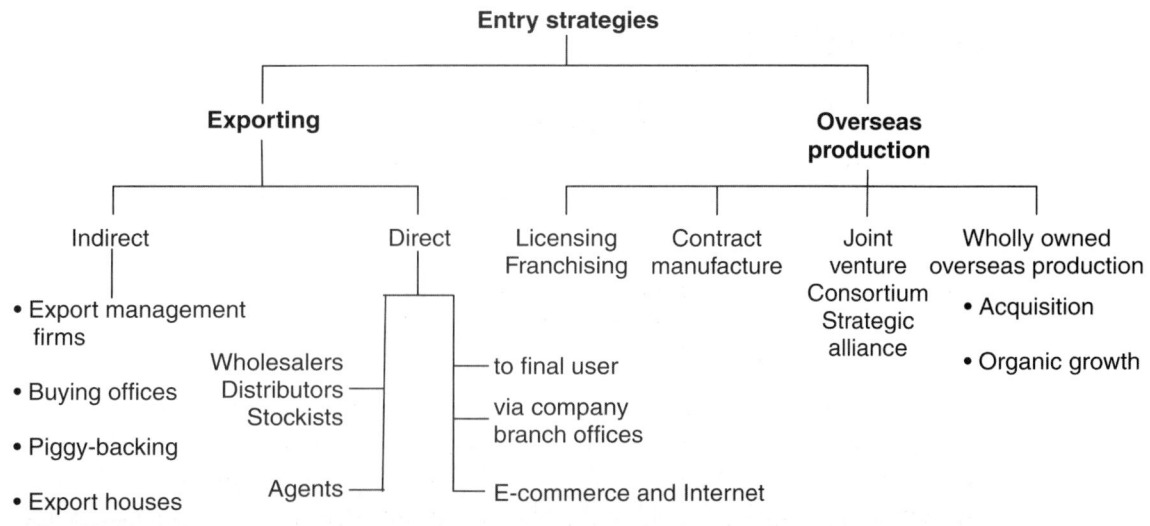

| | **Exporting** | **Overseas production** |
|---|---|---|
| **Advantages** | Concentrates production; small start possible; minimises overheads | Lower distribution costs; overcomes trade barriers; possibly lower production costs |
| **Key issues** | Exchange rates; protectionism | Political risk; partnership; managing overseas facilities; more risky |
| **Involvement** | Usually less involved, but an exporter might depend on the **overseas** market | Usually more involved, but overseas subsidiaries might act independently; varying levels of control and risk |

# 2 The criteria for selecting a method of entry

**FAST FORWARD**

The **choice** of method of entry is affected by:

- the firm and its products and history
- the foreign market
- the degree of involvement the firm wants in the foreign market

**The most suitable method of entry varies.**

(a) Among firms in the same industry (eg a new exporter as opposed to a long-established exporter)

(b) According to the market (eg some countries limit imports to protect domestic manufacturers whereas others promote free trade)

(c) Over time (eg as some countries become more, or less, hostile to direct inward investment by foreign companies)

To choose a method of entry to a particular market, a firm should consider the following issues.

(a) **Firm's marketing objectives**, in relation to volume, timescale and coverage of market segments. Thus setting up an overseas production facility would be inappropriate if sales are expected to be low in volume, or if the product is only to be on sale for a limited period.

(b) **Firm's size**. A small firm is less likely than a large one to possess sufficient resources to set up and run a production facility overseas. Not only would the firm have to provide investment capital and organisational ability, but it would also have to support the costs of continuing operations.

(c) **Mode availability**. A firm might have to use different methods of entry to enter different markets. Some countries only allow a restricted level of imports, but will welcome a firm if it builds manufacturing facilities which provide jobs and limit the outflow of foreign exchange. In this case, overseas manufacture is a better option than direct export.

(d) **Method quality**. In some cases, all modes may be possible in theory, but some are of questionable quality or practicality. The lack of suitably qualified distributors or agents would preclude the export, direct or indirect, of high technology goods needing installation, maintenance and servicing by personnel with specialist technical skills.

(e) **Human resources requirements**. These vary according to which method of entry is used. When a firm is unable to recruit suitable staff either at home or overseas, indirect exporting or the use of agents based overseas may be the only realistic option.

(f) **Market information feedback**. In some cases a firm can receive feedback information about the market and its marketing effort from its sales staff or distribution channels. In these circumstances direct export or joint ventures may be preferred to indirect export.

 Marketing at Work

One small UK company manufacturing and selling a range of leather goods decided to set up a direct export model using a sales subsidiary in France. Having done so they discovered from closer contact with the customers that the reason that one of their best selling lines in the UK was a flop in France was that French customers thought the regal red lining to their wallets was 'too vulgar'. A modest product change using a muted brown lining made the product very acceptable to French customers and sales rocketed.

(g) **Learning curve requirements**. Firms which intend a heavy future involvement might need to learn from the experience that close involvement in an overseas market can bring. This argues against the use of indirect exporting as the method of entry.

(h) **Risks**. Some risks, such as political risk or the risk of the expropriation of overseas assets by foreign governments, might discourage firms from using overseas production as the method of entry to overseas markets. Instead, firms might prefer the indirect export mode as it is safer. On the other hand, the risk of losing touch with customers and their requirements would encourage either direct export or overseas production.

(i) **Control needs**. Control over the marketing mix and the distribution channel varies greatly by method of entry. Production overseas by a wholly owned subsidiary gives a firm absolute control while indirect exporting offers virtually no control to the exporter.

**Exam tip**

The exam may feature a question on choice of entry criteria. You could have used the list above as a starting point to your answer.

## 2.1 Make or buy?

For a global organisation, this is a critical decision. Does it get a **better future return** from **investing in fixed assets**, to create manufacturing facilities, or will future returns be higher from **developing brands** and managing suppliers more effectively?

If the decision is to make, then all the **costs and risks** of establishing manufacturing facilities have to be shouldered, in return for total **control** over the downstream **supply chain** from the point of manufacture, including quality and delivery, and all the profits.

**Exam tip**

> The question surrounding the 'make or buy?' decision is one of whether the company offers more value to its customers (and shareholders) from making its own products.

In contrast, the **buy decision** avoids incurring the costs and risks of establishing manufacturing facilities. However, there will be costs involved in **managing suppliers** to ensure that they supply to agreed quality and delivery standards. The question surrounding the buy decision is one of whether companies offer more **value to customers and shareholders** from **outsourcing** the manufacture of the products that they sell.

As an example, Nike outsource all the manufacturing of their ranges and concentrate solely on the **design and development** of their products, and the development of their brand. The press reports of the Nike suppliers in low cost labour areas of the world, exploiting their employees, appears not to have damaged the Nike brand. The Nike example tends to demonstrate the case for the buy decision.

Product design and **brand development** do add value. Each person who wears a Nike product does so because they want to be associated with the imagery that surrounds the Nike brand. Any investment in brand development rather than manufacturing facilities could have a much higher future pay-off.

In view of the periodic concern raised in the press regarding the outsourcing of products from low cost labour areas – and no global organisation is immune from these allegations – a company may be better advised to consider a **strategic partnership** with selected suppliers. This would enable the company to be specific about who makes its products and where they are made, and perhaps even gain some additional brand value from being viewed as an active supporter of economic development. Also, the strategic partner will gain from being closely linked to a global organisation. There is more about strategic alliances in Section 4.

## 2.2 Financial implications

**FAST FORWARD**

> There are three important considerations affecting the market entry decisions: capital required, risk involved and repatriation of profit.

In order to contrast the financial implications of different methods of market entry, we can look in more detail at the use of **distributors** in the market place of a company's choice and compare this with the costs associated with creating its own manufacturing and marketing subsidiary.

Let us examine the two options in terms of the **capital required**, the **financial risk** and the possibility of **repatriation of profit**.

### 2.2.1 Capital required

In the case of using a distributor overseas, the level of **investment capital** is going to be very small. If we think of a motor manufacturer, it may be that there would be some need to support distributors with finance to bring the quality of showrooms to an acceptable minimum level, but for very many other manufacturers the expectation would be that the distributor bears most of the financial responsibility for premises, showrooms, warehousing and the like.

In the case of a manufacturing and marketing subsidiary, a substantial amount of **investment capital** would be required, either if building a new plant from scratch or buying out a pre-existing company. If it is a case of building a new plant, the investment capital will be **at risk** for a long period of time until the plant comes into operation and starts delivering a **return**.

There will also be a considerable need for **working capital** even when the plant is complete and this will be a **continuing commitment**.

### 2.2.2 Financial risk

There are a number of factors to be taken into account here, the two key issues being the risk of **currency fluctuations** and any **political risks** contingent upon the country within which the company is operating. If using distributors, the risk is limited to the amount of goods in the pipeline which have yet to be paid for. The level of this risk is dependent upon the **terms of trading** agreed with distributors. This risk can be offset by buying sterling forward from the bank.

A wholly owned subsidiary may well have a lesser risk associated with currency fluctuations for goods, but it is likely to have a much higher risk associated with the **political situation** in the country of operation. At the extreme, there may even be a small risk of **appropriation of assets** if the local government lurches strongly to the left or the population becomes concerned about the disturbing effects of inward investment.

### 2.2.3 Repatriation of profits

Using a distributor will not bring a high level of risk under this heading because the profit is made at the **point of sale** which is likely to be in the home country. The profit will therefore be in the home currency.

For a company with a subsidiary, it may have to face **local taxation** of its profits in the country of operation, unless it is providing assembled parts from its home market at internally derived pricing levels. If this practice is too obvious, however, there may be more political factors to contend with, depending upon the rigour with which the host government monitors **transfer pricing** deals.

**Exam tip**

> Having outlined some of the financial implications associated with different methods of entry, it should be clearly understood that there will inevitably be a whole range of factors to take into account which might make one or other of these possible methods more, or less, appealing. There is never one right answer. It depends, amongst other factors, on the **stage of development** of a company and its **experience** of international marketing.

# 3 Exporting

**FAST FORWARD**

> **Indirect exporting** occurs when a firm uses an intermediary. **Direct exporting** does not.

**Exporting** is the easiest, cheapest and most commonly used route into a new foreign market. Many firms become exporters in an unplanned, haphazard and reactive way, simply by accepting orders from potential customers who happen to be based overseas. However, it is also common for a firm to take a proactive approach to exporting, by systematic planning and the identification and selection of target markets for its exports. This gives rise to several advantages over those entry methods which require greater involvement in the overseas market.

(a) The principal benefit is that exporters are able to concentrate production in a **single location**, giving economies of scale and consistency of product quality.

(b) Firms lacking international marketing experience can try international marketing on a small scale.

(c) Exporting enables firms to **develop and test** their plans and strategies.

(d) Exporting enables firms to minimise their **operating costs**, administrative overheads and personnel requirements.

The Shanghai Forever Bicycle Company, which has built 100m bicycles since 1949, is making low profits as China's bicycle market is oversupplied. To use the capacity, the firm is investing in new types of bike and, as importantly, has been exporting heavily to Africa and South America. Excess domestic capacity makes establishing overseas plants a waste of money.

*Financial Times*

Although exporting requires a **low involvement** in the overseas market, this does not necessarily imply that only low investment is needed. Exporting requires investment in **market research**, **strategy** formulation and careful **implementation of the marketing mix**. The initial success of Japanese car firms in the USA and Europe was based on research and strategic planning that was both extensive and costly.

## 3.1 Indirect exports

**Indirect exporting** is where a firm's goods are sold abroad by other organisations. There are four ways of indirect export.

- Export houses
- Specialist export managers
- UK buying offices of foreign stores and governments
- Complementary exporting

### 3.1.1 Export houses

**Export houses** are firms which facilitate exporting on behalf of the producer. There are three main types of export house.

(a) **Export merchants** act as export principals. They buy goods from a producer and sell them abroad.

(b) **Confirming houses** also act as principals. Their main function is to provide credit to customers when the producer is unwilling to do so.

(c) **Manufacturers' export agents** are based at home, but sell abroad for the producer. An agent will usually cover a particular sector or industry, (eg pottery). Remuneration is by commission.

**Advantages of export houses**

(a) The producer gains the benefits of the export house's market knowledge and contacts.

(b) Except in the case of export agents the producer is relieved of the need to do the following.

- **Finance** the export transaction
- Suffer the **credit risk**
- Prepare **export documentation**

(c) The producer does not bear the **overhead costs** of export marketing.

(d) In some cases export merchants receive preferential treatment from foreign institutional and organisational customers.

(e) Where export agents are used, the producer retains considerable **control** over the market.

**Disadvantages of export houses**

(a)    Ultimately, it is not the producer's but the merchant's decision to market a product, and so a producer is at the merchant's mercy.

(b)    Any goodwill created in the market usually benefits the merchant and not the producer.

(c)    As with all intermediaries, an export house or merchant might service a variety of producing organisations. An individual producer cannot rely on the merchant's exclusive loyalty.

(d)    Export houses are not normally willing to enter into long term arrangements with a producer.

### 3.1.2 Specialist export managers

Specialist **export management firms** (SEMs) offer a full export management service. In effect, they perform the same functions as an in-house export department but are normally remunerated by way of commission.

(a)    Advantages of using a specialist export manager are the same as those for export houses. In addition, the manufacturer (or service provider) immediately gains its own export department without incurring overheads, retains full market control and can normally expect a long term relationship with the export manager.

(b)    Disadvantages do exist however.

(i)     As the export manager is an independent organisation, it can leave the producer's service and the producer will have gained **no in-house exporting expertise**.

(ii)    As the producer does not learn from the experience of exporting, this may adversely affect future options by restricting those available.

(iii)   The SEM may not have sufficient knowledge of all the producer's markets.

### 3.1.3 UK buying offices of foreign stores and governments

Many foreign governments and foreign companies (eg department stores) have buying offices set up permanently in the UK. In addition, other foreign companies send representatives on buying expeditions to the UK.

### 3.1.4 Complementary exporting

**Key concept**

> **Complementary exporting ('piggy back exporting')** occurs when one producing organisation (the **carrier**) uses its own established IM channels to market the products of another producer (the **rider**) as well as its own. The carrier may act as:
>
> (a)    A simple transporter, using spare capacity in its distribution network
> (b)    An agent, selling the rider's goods for commission
> (c)    A merchant, buying and selling the rider's goods

**Advantages of complementary exporting**

(a)    The carrier earns increased profit from a better use of distribution capacity and can sell a more attractive product range.

(b)    The rider obtains entry to a market at low cost and low risk.

**Turnkey contracts** may also provide opportunities for complementary exporting. A single firm engaged on a particular project overseas (eg construction and civil engineering projects in the Middle East) will often acquire products and services from other firms in the home country for the project.

## 3.2 Direct exports

**Direct exporting** occurs where the producing organisation itself performs the export tasks rather than using an intermediary. Sales are made directly to customers overseas who may be the wholesalers, retailers or final users. Sales may increasingly be made via e-commerce on the Internet.

### 3.2.1 Sales to final user

In this case there are clearly no intermediaries. Typical customers include industrial users, governments or mail order customers. Marketing in this environment is similar to marketing in the domestic market, although there are the added problems of distance, product regulations, language and culture.

### 3.2.2 Overseas agencies

Strictly speaking an **overseas export agent** is an overseas firm hired to effect a sales contract between the principal (ie the exporter) and a customer. Agents do not take title to goods; they earn a commission. In practice, however, the phrase is often understood to include distributors (who do take title). Some agents merely arrange sales; others hold stocks and/or carry out servicing on the principal's behalf.

**Advantages of overseas agents**

(a) They have extensive knowledge and experience of the overseas market and the customers.

(b) Their existing product range is usually complementary to the exporter's. This may help the exporter penetrate the overseas market.

(c) The exporter does not have to make a large investment outlay.

(d) The political risk is low.

**Disadvantages**

(a) An intermediary's commitment and motivation may be weaker than the producer's.

(b) Agents usually want steady turnover. Using an agent may not be the most appropriate way of selling low volume, high value goods with unsteady patterns of demand, or where sales are infrequent.

(c) Many agents are too small to exploit a major market to its full extent. Many serve only limited geographical segments.

(d) As a market grows large it becomes less efficient to use an agent. A branch office or subsidiary company will achieve economies of scale.

As with all intermediaries, the use of an agent requires careful planning, selection, motivation and control.

**Regulation of agency agreements**

As part of Single European Market harmonisation, UK companies have to apply European Union-wide legislation to agency agreements. The difference is that what were in the past freely negotiated agreements, are now based on a structure of law.

EU regulations apply to all agency agreements **within** the EU (including the domestic market), through not agents outside the EU. The law draws on German law. Both sides, the principal and agent, have precise rights and duties.

(a) Agents have the right to commission on sales within a reasonable time after the agreement has ended. The length of the period is not specified, so it has to be negotiated at the outset.

(b) Principals cannot delay paying their agents simply because the principals themselves have not received payment from customers.

(c) To terminate a contract, written notice is required (one month in the first year, two months in the second, and three months subsequently).

(d) Provided the agent has not breached contract terms, the agent is liable for compensation for termination of the agreement.

Small businesses, especially, will have to pay attention to agency contracts.

### 3.2.3 Distributors/stockists

**Distributors** are customers with preferential rights to buy and sell a range of a firm's goods in a specific geographical area. Distributors earn profit, not commission. They differ from wholesalers only in that their selling and marketing activities on behalf of a producer are restricted geographically.

**Stockists** are distributors who receive more favourable financial rewards than distributors as they normally undertake to carry at least a certain minimum level of stock. The advantages and disadvantages of distributors and stockists are similar to those associated with overseas agents.

 Marketing at Work

In some markets, such as Japan which has a complicated distribution system of retailers, a knowledgeable local distributor is essential. Tie-ups with Japanese partners and expensive marketing are necessary before discussions can start.

### 3.2.4 Company branch offices abroad

A firm can establish its own office in a foreign market for the purpose of marketing and distribution.

**Advantages**

(a) When sales have reached a certain level, branch offices become more effective than agencies.

(b) Sales performance will improve, as the commitment and motivation of a producer's own staff should be more effective than those of an agent.

(c) The producer retains complete marketing control.

(d) The producer should be able to acquire more accurate and timely market information.

(e) Customer service should improve. Intermediaries are notorious for poor performance in this respect.

**Disadvantages**

(a) Higher investment, overhead and running costs are entailed.

(b) There can be a political risk, particularly expropriation of assets.

(c) The firm will be subject to local employee legislation (eg minimum number of local staff, dismissal, trade union membership) which it may not welcome.

# 4 Overseas production

Firms that are fully committed to international marketing may undertaken overseas manufacture. This gives rise to several major benefits.

## 4.1 Advantages of overseas production

(a) Location abroad can offer a better understanding of the problems and **needs of customers** in the overseas market.

(b) Some markets (eg the USA) are so large that **economies of scale** can still be gained from overseas production.

(c) **Production costs** are lower in some countries overseas than at home.

(d) For firms producing weighty or bulky products (eg brewers), overseas production can reduce **storage and transportation costs**.

(e) Overseas production can overcome the effects of **tariff and non-tariff barriers** to imports.

(f) Where an **overseas government** is a customer, manufacture in the overseas market may be a factor in winning orders.

For firms which are late entrants to a market, **taking over a firm** in the overseas market can be a more effective way of establishing a production facility overseas than building one from scratch. Alternatively the firm might enter into **co-operative agreements** with firms in the overseas market.

The figure below (adapted from Doole, Lowe and Phillips, *International Marketing Strategy*, 1995) shows the balance between **control** and **risk** of the key market entry methods. Clearly, the greater the level of involvement, the greater the risk.

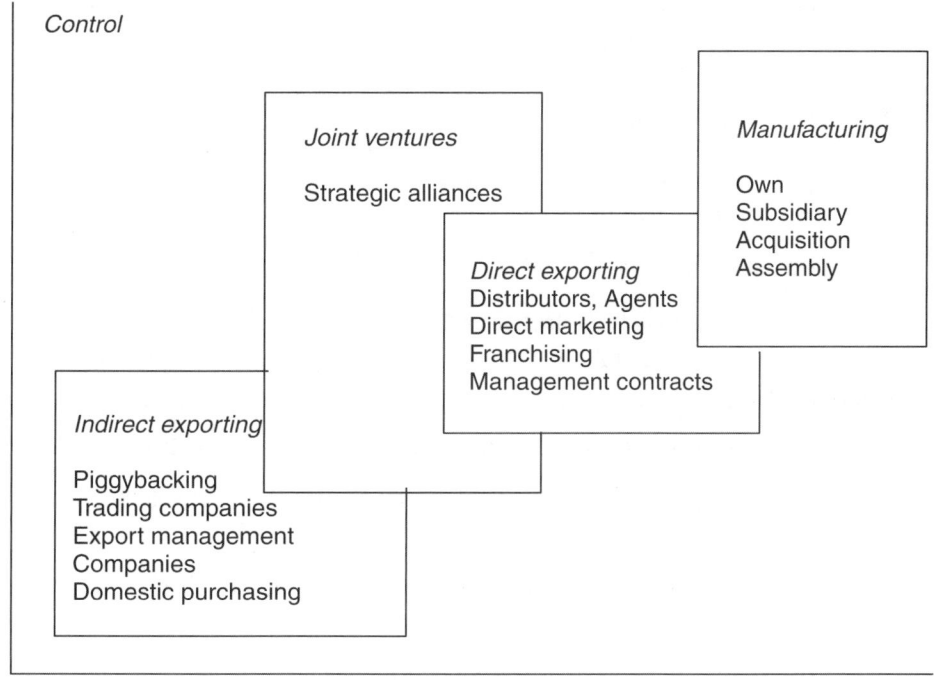

## 4.2 Methods of overseas production

A firm's strategic choice of overseas production method depends on its **objectives, resources and level of commitment** to international marketing. A wide range of co-operative approaches exists.

### 4.2.1 Licensing

**Key concept**

A **licensing agreement** is a commercial contract whereby the licenser gives something of value to the licensee in exchange for certain performances and payments.

The licenser may provide any of the following.

- Rights to produce a patented product or use a patented production process
- Manufacturing know-how (unpatented)
- Technical advice and assistance
- Marketing advice and assistance
- Rights to use a trademark, brand etc

**Licensing is growing** in extent and importance throughout the world. It is used by small, medium and large firms, as it has many **advantages**.

(a)    It requires **no investment**, save the continuing costs of monitoring the agreement.

(b)    It **enables entry** into markets that would otherwise be closed (eg by tariffs, government attitude and policies).

(c)    As a method of entry, it is relatively **simple and quick**.

(d)    The licenser gains access to **knowledge of local conditions**.

(e)    **New products** can be introduced to many countries quickly because of low investment requirements.

(f)    It provides all the usual **benefits of overseas production** (cheaper transport, lower import barriers and so on).

(g)    It can be a source of **competitive advantage**, if it spreads the firm's proprietary technology, giving it wider exposure than that of a rival.

**Drawbacks of licensing**

(a)    **Revenues from licenses are very low**, usually less than 10% of turnover. The significance of this naturally depends on the profit margins that might otherwise be expected.

(b)    A licensee may eventually become the licenser's **competitor**. During the license period, the licensee may gain enough know-how from the licensor to be able to operate independently.

(c)    Although the contract may specify a minimum sales volume, there is some danger that the **licensee will not fully exploit the market**.

(d)    Product quality might deteriorate if the licensee has a more lax attitude to **quality control** than the licenser.

(e)    **Governments may impose restrictions** or conditions on the payment of royalties to the licenser or on the supply of components.

(f)    It is often difficult to control the licensee effectively. The licensee's **objectives often conflict** with those of the licenser and disagreements are common.

Astute management of the license agreement is essential.

(a) Be **careful in the choice** of licensees (eg identify criteria that must be satisfied)

(b) **Design contracts** that protect both parties

(c) **Control the licensee**, by, say, having an equity interest in the licensee's business or by retaining control over key input components

(d) Take action to **motivate** the licensee

## Marketing at Work

**Consumer marketing**. Many beers are brewed under licence. For example, *Castlemaine XXXX*, an Australian beer, is brewed in the UK under licence.

**Industrial marketing**. *Pilkington's* developed the float glass process. It licensed the use of this process to other firms world-wide, and still collects revenue.

**Consumer and industrial applications**. The technology behind CDs was devised by *Philips*, but has been licensed world-wide.

### 4.2.2 Franchising

Franchising is a type of licensing.

**Key concept**

> The **franchise** agreement specifies, in more detail than a license agreement, exactly what is expected of the franchisee. In a franchise arrangement, the franchiser supplies a standard package of goods, components or ingredients along with management and marketing services or advice. The franchisee supplies capital, personal involvement and local market knowledge. *Avis*, *Holiday Inn*, *Pepsi Cola*, *Kentucky Fried Chicken*, the *Body Shop*, and *McDonald's* have franchise arrangements in many countries.

The **advantages and disadvantages of franchising** are largely the same as those of licensing.

(a) An extra benefit, however, is that it provides **some leverage for controlling the franchisee's activities**, as the franchiser supplies ingredients or components.

(b) A particular disadvantage of franchising is that the **search for competent candidates** is both costly and time consuming where the franchiser requires many outlets (eg *McDonalds* in the UK). This has led to decisions by *Burger King* and *Kentucky Fried Chicken* to reduce the number of franchised outlets in the UK.

### 4.2.3 Contract manufacture

In the case of contract manufacture a firm (the contractor) makes a contract with another firm (the contractee) abroad whereby the **contractee manufactures or assembles a product on behalf of the contractor**. The contractor retains full control over marketing and distribution whilst the manufacture is done by a local firm. Firms such as *Del Monte*, *Colgate*, and *Procter & Gamble* use this method of entry to overseas markets.

Advantages of contract manufacture include the following.

(a) There is **no need to invest** in plant overseas.

(b) Risk associated with **currency fluctuations** is largely avoided.

(c) The risk of **asset expropriation** is minimised.

(d)     A product manufactured in the overseas market may be **easier to sell**, especially to government customers.

(e)     Lower **transport costs** and, sometimes, lower production costs can be obtained.

**Contract manufacture is particularly suitable in the following conditions.**

- Countries where the **small size of the market** discourages investment in plant
- Firms whose main strengths are in **marketing** rather than production

Contract manufacture does involve some disadvantages, which include the following.

(a)     Overseas contractee producers who are **reliable and capable** cannot always be easily identified.

(b)     Sometimes the contractee producer's personnel must receive intensive and substantial **technical training**.

(c)     The contractee producer may eventually become a **competitor**.

(d)     **Quality control** problems in manufacturing may arise.

### 4.2.4 Joint ventures

**Key concept**

> A **joint venture** is an arrangement where two or more (often competing) firms join forces for **manufacturing, financial and marketing purposes** and each has a share in both the equity and the management of the business, sharing profits, risks and assets.

Forming a joint venture with a technologically advanced foreign company can lead to new product development, maybe at a lower cost.

Licensing, franchising and contract manufacture are loose forms of joint venture. However joint ventures are bound by much stronger formal ties. They essentially focus on a single national market. When based abroad, they usually involve partners of unequal strength, for example when a developed country multinational, contributing capital and technology joins forces with a local firm in a developing country, offering local market knowledge and contacts.

 Marketing at Work

*Ford* and *Mobil Oil* in the US announced a strategic alliance to work on new fuel systems for the automotive industry. Faced with threatened and actual new exhaust emission standards in California and, probably, the rest of the world, together with resource shortages in oil stocks possible in the foreseeable future, these two companies have chosen to pool R & D expertise to find a solution which can benefit both corporations.

US car manufacturers have acquired parts of Japanese firms to participate in small car development eg *Ford* and *Mazda*.

*Coca Cola* and *Cadbury Schweppes* bottle and distribute *Coca Cola* in Great Britain.

A joint venture is usually an alternative to seeking to buy or build a wholly owned manufacturing operation abroad and can offer substantial advantages.

(a)     As the **capital outlay is shared**, joint ventures are attractive to smaller or risk-averse firms, or where very expensive new technologies are being researched and developed (such as the civil aerospace industry).

(b)     When funds are limited, joint ventures permit **coverage of a larger number of countries** since each one requires less investment by each participator.

(c)     A joint venture can reduce the risk of **government intervention** as a local firm is involved (eg Club Mediterranean pays much attention to this factor). The strong role of government in China means that nearly all foreign ventures in China are alliances with Chinese partners.

(d)     Licensing and franchising often give a company **income based on turnover**, and any profits from cost reductions accrue to the licensee. In a joint venture, the participating enterprises benefit from **all sources of profit**.

(e)     Joint ventures can provide **close control** over marketing and other operations.

(f)     A joint venture with an indigenous firm provides **local knowledge**. This is a big advantage for firms seeking to do business in difficult markets, such as Russia. Political know-how, site selection expertise and business connections are important.

(g)     In **oligopolistic** markets, where a few firms are dominant, a foreign firm may find the cost of market entry too high, and seek an alliance with an established competitor.

 Marketing at Work

*Tesco* is to invest £130 million in developing a chain of hypermarkets in South Korea in partnership with *Samsung*. Tesco is to invest £80 million in cash, with Samsung contributing two hypermarkets and three development sites worth a similar amount.

Tesco said the move was part of a coherent long-term strategy of expanding into underdeveloped markets. It has acquired 13 hypermarkets in Thailand. Outside the UK, Tesco now operates in countries with a total population of 170 million people.

Partners in a joint venture do not necessarily hold equal shares, and the contribution from each partner may vary. Funding, technology, equipment and marketing organisation may be contributed. There are several forms of joint venture.

- **Spider's web**, which consists of many firms in a network
- **Go-together then split** after a period of time, either due to success or failure
- **Successive integration**

Peter Killing (*Strategies for Joint Venture* Success, 1983) categorises joint ventures into **dominant** and **shared** partnerships, depending upon which party's particular know-how or competencies are more critical.

The major disadvantage of joint ventures is that there can be major **conflicts of interest** between the different parties.

- **Profit** shares
- Amounts **invested**
- The **management** of the joint venture
- The **marketing strategy**

For these reasons firms such as IBM have, in the past, been reluctant to engage in joint ventures, although this policy has changed with the announcement of co-operative agreements with Apple (for work stations) Siemens and Dell.

Some protectionist **governments** discourage or even prohibit foreign firms setting up independent operations. Instead, they encourage joint ventures with indigenous firms.

(a)    Some governments regard uncontrolled investments from overseas as a type of colonial exploitation.

(b)    They are averse to sending foreign exchange outside the country.

(c)    Joint ventures generally involve a transfer of **know-how and technology** that benefits the local economy. Joint venturing between outside and local firms is encouraged, for example, in India, Nigeria and the former USSR.

There is always a potential for conflict. There are ways to minimise it.

- Careful selection of partners
- Formulation of jointly beneficial contracts
- Pre-arranging for arbitration to resolve any clashes that occur

## Marketing at Work

'*Bass*, the UK's second largest brewer, is set to pull out of a brewing joint venture that came to symbolise the intemperate expectations of some foreign companies in China's vast potential market.

The cultural chasm that divided the two partners was apparent at the 1996 launch. The Chinese tried to eat haggis and neeps and tatties with chopsticks, while the strains of bagpipes followed a Beijing opera performance.

Soon after the joint venture began production, growth in the local beer market, which had averaged over 20 per cent a year for more than a decade, began to decline.

As the market became over-supplied, local protectionism grew and road blocks went up across China to prevent deliveries to areas with one of the country's 850 breweries.

The Bass venture was in too isolated a location to command a large local market.

The cost of advertising in China's big cities was steep and largely failed to convince consumers to pay the extra price premium over local brands.

The market for premium beer remains limited in China, where fashionable bars are rarities beyond the large cities.'

*Financial Times, March 2000*

### 4.2.5 The consortium

Under this approach, member firms create a **working relationship**, but not a new entity. The aircraft industry offers several examples because the risks and costs associated with producing several hundred aircraft are so high.

The major jet engine companies have also been involved in this type of arrangement. Rolls Royce aero engines indulge in project specific ventures.

The consortium approach has the obvious advantage that the involvement of several high profile firms from several countries should ensure a certain level of sales.

### 4.2.6 Strategic alliances

These have become a popular model for global expansion. Some writers such as Kenichi Ohmae have argued that they are vital for survival in a world of fierce competition and shorter product life cycles.

'Globalisation is making the world too big for even the mightiest corporations to conquer alone.' (*Marketing Business*, September 2001). The channels to market have become so complicated that the only way to cope is through forming partnerships and alliances.

As an example, *Cable and Wireless* has formed an alliance with *Microsoft* and *Compaq* to launch A-Services, an application services provider which draws upon the skills of, and provides market benefits for, all three organisations.

- C & W: telecoms
- Microsoft: software
- Compaq: hardware

The participants tend to be **competing firms from different countries**, seeking to enhance their competencies by **combining resources**, but without sacrificing autonomy. The strategic alliance is usually concerned with gaining market entry, remaining globally competitive and attaining economies of scale. According to *Jeannet and Hennessey*, they can be categorised as follows.

- **Production** based alliances – improving manufacturing and production efficiency
- **Distribution** based alliances – sharing distribution networks
- **Technology** based alliances pooling R & D costs

Alliances may be **horizontal** (between two firms in the same industry) or **vertical**, involving collaboration between a supplier and a buyer. Sometimes, they involve firms with no such connection. Strategic alliances have mainly concentrated in manufacturing and high tech industries, and increasingly in services (notably airlines, such as the 'One World' alliance involving *British Airways*, *Qantas* and several other international collaborators).

A five-point checklist of 'Cs' has been suggested for **choosing an alliance partner**.

- **Complementary** skill sets and products
- **Capability** to enter new markets
- **Clear understanding** of the commercial arrangements
- **Chemistry** between the participants
- Shared intellectual **capital**

In summary, strategic alliances have the following features.

(a) They are **collaborations** between two or more competing companies of **similar strength**, generally from industrialised countries.

(b) The relative contributions by the companies are **balanced**.

(c) The **motivation** for the alliance is generally **broadly strategic or competitive**, rather than purely for market access or economies of scale.

(d) The **relationships are reciprocal** and provide the opportunity for learning.

(e) They have a **strategic and global focus**, and seek to enhance global competitiveness via gaining access to a whole series of resources and skills.

Factors for success are presented in an article in *Marketing Business,* (September 2001):

- Choose partners with **complementary skills**, products, markets
- Understand the **'strategic intent'** of the partnership
- Adopt the most appropriate partnership **structure**

- Resolve the **leadership** issue at the outset
- **Define the benefits** expected from the partnership
- Communicate the **purpose and intent** of the partnership internally
- Keep **communicating** with your partner and anticipate problems
- Define an **exit strategy** for failure at the outset
- **Monitor the benefits** the partnership delivers
- Recognise a company may need **multiple partnerships** in a global business market

### 4.2.7 Wholly owned overseas production

Establishing and running a **production facility** in an overseas market demonstrates the fullest commitment to that market. Production capacity can be built from scratch, or an existing firm acquired. It has the following **advantages**.

(a)     The firm does not have to **share its profits** with partners of any kind.

(b)     The firm does not have to **share or delegate decision making** and so there are no losses in efficiency arising from inter-firm conflict.

(c)     There are none of the **communication problems** that arise in joint ventures, license agreements etc.

(d)     The firm is able to operate a completely **integrated** and synergistic international system.

(e)     The firm gains more **experience** from overseas production.

There are also major disadvantages.

(a)     The **substantial investment** funding required prevents some firms from establishing operations overseas.

(b)     **Suitable managers**, whether recruited in the overseas market or posted abroad from home, may be difficult to obtain.

(c)     Some **overseas governments** discourage 100% ownership of an enterprise by a foreign company.

(d)     This method of entry forgoes the benefits of an **overseas partner's market knowledge, distribution system** and other **local expertise**.

     Action Programme

You are marketing chocolate for a large UK confectionery firm. The UK style of chocolate is not widely appreciated in Europe although a recent EU ruling has paved the way for British chocolate to be stocked on the continent. If you wished to expand into European markets, what method of entry would you use?

**Acquisition**, as a method of entry, is rapid and offers the benefits of an existing management team, market knowledge and all the other trappings of a 'going concern'. *General Motors*, for example, enjoyed these gains on entry to the UK market by the acquisition of *Vauxhall Motors*. At the same time, acquisitions which go wrong (eg the *Midland Bank's* purchase of the California based *Crocker Bank*) can have serious and long term penalties.

**Acquiring** a company can also be a way of ensuring a market presence in an overseas market or segment.

Acquiring an overseas subsidiary has the following justifications, in **marketing** terms.

- Shared **distribution networks** (ie getting more share out of your existing network)
- Access to **new markets**, in which the acquired company already has a presence
- Access to **new brands**, so that a variety of brands can be promoted

## Marketing at Work

Indian drug firms are becoming innovators as opposed to copycats, (*Economist*, September 2000). A Hyderabad-based company owned by Anji Reddy has set its sights on selling its own new drugs, and generics (those drugs whose patents have expired) to rich markets. Certain drugs with current sales of $40 billion are likely to lose patent protection by 2003, according to some observers.

*Ranbaxy*, the most ambitious Indian drugs firm, is following the strategy of buying an American company to gain access to the US market, and targeting difficult-to-make products in an attempt to protect itself against competition.

- Expansion of the **product range**.

The difficulties of **acquisitions** in international markets are expanded versions of their problems in the domestic markets, in other words problems with corporate culture, operational disruption and so forth.

**Organic growth** offers fewer of the 'quick' advantages of acquisitions: it involves building up a presence from scratch.

**Key concept**

> **Organic growth** is the expansion of a firm's size, profits and activities, achieved without taking over other firms.

(a) The disadvantages are the time and effort it takes to build a new market presence, especially in **mature** markets, where growth in market share involves a war of attrition, and where a firm has little **knowledge** of the market.

(b) However, it offers control over the process of growth, and there need be fewer clashes of corporate culture. For **new** products it might be better than acquisitions.

**Franchising**, discussed earlier might be a useful way of promoting 'organic growth', both with control and with a sharing of resources and local knowledge. After all, local franchisees can be bought out at a later stage.

Entry to an overseas market by creating new capacity can be beneficial if there are no likely candidates for takeover, or if acquisition is prohibited by the government.

(a) This entry method enables the use of the newest production technology.

(b) The investing company may also be able to start afresh with new forms of managing industrial relations.

These were major benefits for *Nissan Motors* when the company created new capacity in Sunderland and Tennessee. However, another reason for direct inward investment by Japanese companies in Europe is the threat of being excluded from the single European market. The UK has been a prime site because of government support and relatively low labour costs, for example when compared with Germany.

## Chapter Roundup

- It is possible to identify **three methods of entry** to foreign markets.

  - Indirect exports
  - Direct exports
  - Overseas manufacture

- The **choice** of method of entry is affected by:

  - the firm and its products and history
  - the foreign market
  - the degree of involvement the firm wants in the foreign market

- There are three important considerations affecting the market entry decisions: capital required, risk involved and repatriation of profit.

- **Indirect exporting** occurs when a firm uses an intermediary. **Direct exporting** does not.

- Firms that are fully committed to international marketing may undertaken overseas manufacture. This gives rise to several major benefits.

- A firm's strategic choice of overseas production method depends on its **objectives, resources and level of commitment** to international marketing. A wide range of co-operative approaches exists.

## Quick Quiz

1   What are the main ways of entering foreign markets?

2   What factors might affect the method of entry decision for a prospective international marketing company?

3   What are the advantages of exporting over methods of market entry requiring greater involvement?

4   What are the ways of exporting indirectly?

5   How are agents rewarded for their work?

6   What is the disadvantage of overseas manufacturing?

7   What are joint ventures and why are they so popular?

8   What is a consortium? Give an example.

9   What are the three principle types of alliance?

10   Why do some companies choose to enter overseas markets by acquisition?

## Answers to Quick Quiz

1   Direct exports, indirect exports and overseas manufacturing

2   Marketing objectives; firm's size; method availability and suitability; HR implications; availability of feedback

3   Concentrated production; possibility of starting small to gain international marketing experience

4   Export houses; specialist export managers; local buying offices; complementary exporting

5   By paying them commission on their sales

6   The greater the commitment of capital to plant and premises, the greater the risks

7   Two or more firms, possibly competitors, join forces in partnership for specific purposes such as manufacturing, marketing or finance: each has a share in equity and management

8   As opposed to a joint venture, a consortium, does not create a new business entity but merely a working relationship

9   Production based, distribution based and technology based

10  Acquisition is rapid and has the benefits of a going concern

## Action Programme Review

You would probably manufacture overseas, perhaps by buying an overseas company with the expertise and available brands.

> Now try Question 5 at the end of the Study Text

# Part D
# Managing the portfolio

# 7

# The marketing mix

## Syllabus content

- The nature and  dimensions of branding and brand decisions; their role in the development of advantage and their significance in global markets
- Product strategies and the role of new product development in competitive strategy
- The concept of relationship marketing and the role of long-term customer relationships in creating and delivering value
- The importance of managing marketing relationships in generating customer commitment
- The strategic management of the global portfolio and the expanded marketing mix

# Introduction

If you have sat any of the CIM's exams at previous levels, the elements of the marketing mix will be familiar to you, as they will if you come to this qualification with a career background in marketing. In this chapter, therefore, we do not go into detail about each area of the mix.

We provide you with an overview and then concentrate on:

- Areas specific to the syllabus
- The mix from a strategic viewpoint, highlighting key issues

# 1 An overview of the mix elements

**FAST FORWARD**

The exact components of the marketing mix need to be put together with judgement and creativity. Every product, market and every stage in the product's life will require a different balance of the marketing mix ingredients.

**Key concept**

Kotler defines the mix as follows. '**Marketing mix** is the set of controllable variables and their levels that the firm uses to influence the target market.'

The **marketing plan** is made up of decisions relating to the marketing mix for a product or service. In turn, each of these mix elements would be turned into a plan, at a more tactical level within the organisation. Each of these plans is prepared using the same basic framework that we have identified at both corporate and marketing level.

- Where are we now? (audit)
- Where are we going? (objectives)
- What are the alternative ways of getting there?
- Choosing the best option
- Developing an action plan (tactics)
- Implementation and control

You need to be prepared to understand and produce plans for these marketing mix elements in Diploma examinations.

The balance is often between a **push** and a **pull** strategy.

(a) A **push strategy** is concerned with moving goods out to wholesalers and retailers who then have the task of selling to customers, **ie getting dealers to accept goods**.

(b) A **pull strategy** is one of influencing final consumer attitudes so that a **consumer demand is created which dealers are obliged to satisfy**. A pull policy usually involves heavy expenditure on advertising, but holds the promise of stimulating a much higher demand.

(c) A proper balance between push and pull is necessary to optimise sales.

### 1.0.1 Stages in the formulation of a marketing mix

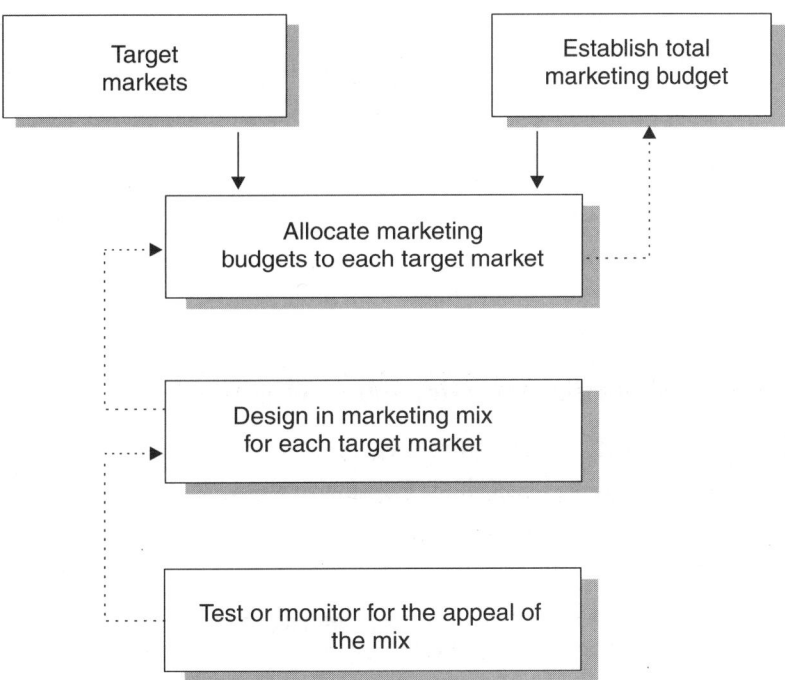

### 1.0.2 Design issues for the marketing mix

| Issue | Comment |
|---|---|
| **Profit/volume** | The sales response function shows how different areas of the mix affect volume sales and **profits**. All other things being equal, the mix design should maximise profits. |
| **Brand value** | The mix should, where relevant, support the brand value, if a strong brand is important. Not all firms depend on branding. |
| **Customers and distribution, segmentation** | The mix should satisfy customer needs, but note in many cases there are two customers to consider: the end-user and the intermediary or reseller. |
| **Life cycle** | The appropriate mix changes over the life cycle of the product. For example, a firm might adopt **penetration** or **skimming** prices at launch. |
| **Marketing environment** | This affects the optimal mix, but should be taken into account earlier in the planning process. |
| **Seasonality** | Clothes retailers are seasonally based, hence 'sales' after Christmas. |
| **Integration** | The elements of the marketing mix must support each other. There is no point promising the earth (promotion) if this cannot be delivered. |
| **Push/pull** | The mix can pull demand through the distribution chain or push it down. |
| **Competitive strategy** | The mix will support the competitive strategy. |

 Marketing at Work

You might like to contrast the marketing mix of these holiday firms. Each has been designed to appeal to a particular market segment.

(a) *British Museum Tours.* These are tours with an archaeological or cultural interest, and are accompanied by a leading academic. The tours are expensive and might include destinations such as Iran and Ethiopia. Hotels are the most comfortable available. Advertising is not high profile, and is often directed to those who are already members of the British Museum Society.

(b) *Explore.* This firm offers escorted holidays to small groups, in a variety of locations, which may involve some trekking and camping. Locations might include isolated villages in northern Thailand. The firm advertises itself on the basis of 'You'll see more'. The firm advertises in newspapers, but also likes to generate repeat business and word-of-mouth recommendation. Poster or TV advertising is not used.

### 1.0.3 Combining the marketing mix in practice

For high-selling products some firms prepare a demand function showing the relationship between price and quantity of demand. This is not always possible.

(a) It may not be possible to establish, scientifically, how the different elements of the mix might interact.

(b) Many smaller businesses do not have the resources to prepare complicated models in this way.

(c) Another problem, especially true of business-to-business markets, is that there might be relatively **few customers**, who might be able to dictate, quite precisely, product specifications and other arrangements. The price may be negotiated after the sort of hard bargaining rarely encountered in consumer markets.

We will now briefly identify some issues regarding each element of the mix. This section is partly revision and partly to get you thinking about key issues of each element of the mix, including the marketing mix for services. In the **UK and most of the developed world, services account for greater economic output than manufacturing**, so we will take a 7P rather than a 4P approach to this issue.

- Product
- Place
- Price
- Promotion

- People
- Processes
- Physical evidence

## 1.1 Product

> The conceptual nature of the product interacts with strategic issues such as branding and portfolio management.

### 1.1.1 What is a product?

**Key concept**

A **product** is a package of benefits meeting particular needs. It is anything that can be offered to a market, for attention, acquisition, use or consumption that might satisfy a want or need.

| Aspect | Example |
|---|---|
| **Physical aspect**: what the product is | Bank account |
| **Functional aspect**: what the product does | Keeps your money safe |
| **Symbolic aspect**: what the product means | If you bank with *Coutts*, you are a member of an exclusive set of people |

### 1.1.2 Levels of a product

| Level | Comment |
|---|---|
| Core benefit | A hotel offers rest and sleep away from home |
| Generic product | Any hotel is a building with rooms to rent |
| Expected product | Must expect cleanliness and quiet |
| Augmented product | Additional benefits (eg taxi service) |
| Potential product | Possible augmentations in the future (for example, fax machines for business travellers) |

(a) The augmented product in one country may, in a more prosperous country, be the expected product in a poor country.

(b) Most **competition** in the developed world is based around the **augmented product**.

### 1.1.3 Strategic issues for product

(a) **Defining the product**. Product is key in differentiation strategy, as the product can be manipulated to satisfy the needs of different market segments.

(b) **Selecting the product range**, in terms of **width** (how many segments) and **depth** (variety of options in each segment).

(c) Building a **brand**.

(d) Managing the **product portfolio** with new launches and deletions.

(e) **Quality**: this is fitness for use and can be analysed as quality of design, and quality of conformance (the product has been manufactured without defects).

## 1.2 Price

Price represents the revenue earning side of the mix. Influences on pricing policy are:

- The customer
- Competitors and the environment
- The company

Pricing involves a set of trade-offs between these three elements, more so, perhaps, than other aspects of the mix.

**Exam tip**

Many firms avoid competing on price if possible, but sometimes there is no alternative. Before responding on price alone, you should assess:

- Is the competitor offering the same combination of price and service?
- Is the price cut significant?
- What was the competitor's underlying justification for cutting the price?
- Effect on profitability
- Effect on overall marketing strategy

You are then offered a choice between maintaining prices, matching the lower prices, raising perceived quality and so on.

### 1.2.1 The customer

Price is the sacrifice the customer has to pay for the package of benefits, real or psychological, that the company has to offer.

(a) Traditional economics suggest a link between **pricing** policy and **quantity** ordered. For example, by lowering the price you would expect customers, within reason, to buy more. **Elasticity of demand** is where the extent to which demand is sensitive to price. If elasticity is low, raising or lowering the price will make little difference to the quantity bought.

(b) **Price sensitivity** affects elasticity. Price is only one influence on the buying decision. Piercy (1997) argues that **many firms under-price**, on the mistaken assumption that competitors will do the same and that consumers are highly price sensitive.

(c) **Raising prices and enhancing value** may be as **easy a way to raise profits** as **cutting prices to increase volumes**.

(d) Different price/value propositions succeed in different market segments.

(e) **Distributors and intermediaries** also have pricing objectives, so the price to the consumer may have to be set with the distributor's objectives in mind.

(f) Many customers have limited price awareness of prices in general, but they may notice sudden **fluctuations**.

(g) Many people think that pricing is an **ethical** issue.

### Marketing at Work

Developing drugs to combat AIDS has been expensive. The prices charged put the treatment way out of reach of sufferers in poorer countries where AIDS is prevalent. Some say that this pricing strategy is unethical. Others say that the money spent researching into drugs for AIDS could be spent on dealing with other life-threatening illnesses in poorer countries. Price does have 'ethical' connotations.

This has been highlighted very recently by events in South Africa, where there is a substantial problem with HIV.

The South African government intended to import cheap 'generic' copies of anti-AIDS drugs, as the price charged by the major pharmaceuticals companies was regarded as prohibitive.

The pharmaceuticals companies went to court, arguing that this breached their intellectual property rights and they needed to recover the development costs.

The court action turned into a PR disaster for the pharmaceuticals firm. They were perceived to have 'backed down' from the court action – especially when pressure groups started to ask difficult questions. They were portrayed in the (Western) media as being greedy and exploitative. However, the key issue for pharmaceuticals companies – getting a return on risky investments – will not go away.

### 1.2.2 The company

Pricing is a key decision as it can very easily affect margins and profits.

|  | A £ | B £ |
|---|---|---|
| Price | 10 | 9.50 |
| Cost | 8 | 8.00 |
| Profit | 2 | 1.50 |

B is priced at 5% cheaper than A, but is 25% less profitable. In other words, a 5% cut in price leads to a 25% cut in profits. Clearly more of the unit will have to be sold to make up the shortfall.

The problem is that the **cost of producing something is not determined by the price** charged. As firms aim to make profits for shareholders, prices are often set with costs in mind, as a floor. The marketer thus does not have complete freedom to determine prices.

### 1.2.3 Competitors

Price is also set by reference to other firms in the industry. Price can act as a differentiating factor, in line with other aspects of the mix.

(a)  In **commodity** markets, where differentiation is difficult, **price may be the only competitive tool**.

(b)  In some markets, a **firm acts as price leader**. Other firms follow the price leader if the leader raises, lowers or maintains the price level for a product.

Generally, price cuts to increase market share will be matched by competitors in some way. **If a rival firm cuts its prices in the expectation of increasing its market share**, a firm has the following options.

| Maintain its existing prices | This will work if only a little market share would be lost. Eventually, the rival firm may drop out of the market or be forced to raise its prices. However, this strategy may fail if the price cutter has a long-term advantage and can sustain lower prices. |
|---|---|
| Maintain prices but responding with a non-price counter-attack | The firm will be securing or justifying its current prices with a product change, advertising, or better back-up services, etc. |
| Reduce prices | This should protect the firm's market share so that the main beneficiary from the price reduction will be the consumer. |
| Raise prices and respond with a non-price counter-attack | The extra revenue from the higher prices might be used to finance an advertising campaign or product design changes. A price increase would be based on a campaign to emphasise the quality difference between the rival products. |

### 1.2.4 Current trends in pricing

Some trends in the **retail market** are worthy of note.

(a)  Consumers want **high quality at lower prices. 'Own-label' brands** are improving their quality.

(b)  Relatively **slow growth in consumer spending** means **greater competition** and **shrinking margins**.

(c)  National **brand owners** have to offer more benefits to the **retailer**.

(d)  The entry of US chains such as Wal-mart to Europe will put downward pressure on retail prices.

## 1.3 Place

Distribution (or place) provides the availability of the product to the customer and involves both logistical aspects, such as warehousing and transport and distribution channel choices and management.

**Logistics** is a significant problem for many companies, particularly if they provide 'just-in-time' services. Logistics, however, is something that it increasingly outsourced to specialist delivery firms such as *Eddie Stobart* (a brand in its own right) and specialist warehousing firms.

(a) The Channel Tunnel has changed some of the economics of long-term distribution.

(b) The UK and European governments would wish to encourage more use of rail on ecological grounds.

The **distribution channel** dilemma facing management is that of the trade-off between cost and control. The shorter the distribution channel the more control managers have over the marketing of the products, but the higher their distribution costs. Long distribution channels cut the costs but also reduce the firm's control. The various channels are outlined in the diagram below.

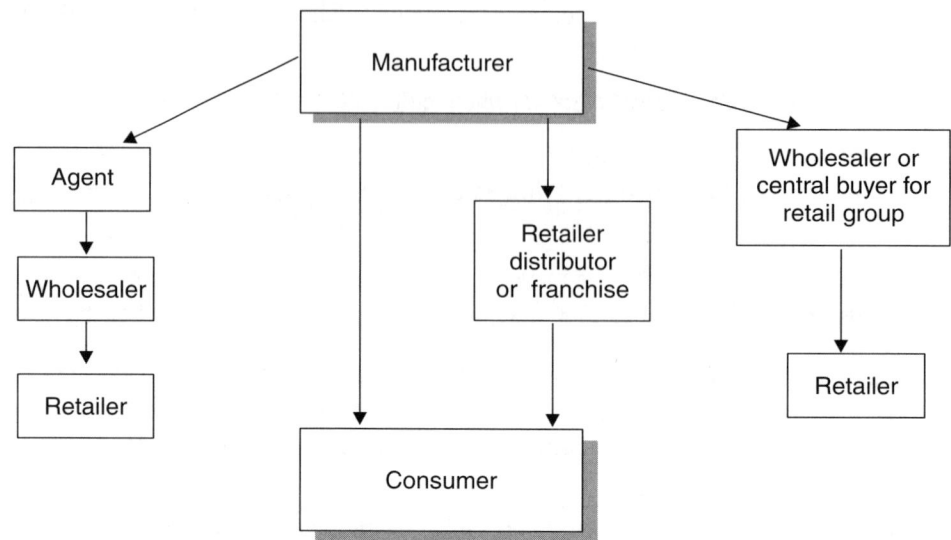

## Marketing at Work

### Parallel imports

In the US, a pair of *Levi Strauss* jeans costs £30. In the UK, you might pay £45. In the US, Levi Strauss jeans are a standard commodity, not a premium product (the positioning in the UK).

*Tesco* obtained Levis from elsewhere, selling them for £25, nearer the American price. Levi Strauss obtained a court order forbidding this.

The EU has pursued a policy supporting exclusive distributor arrangements, largely at the behest of luxury goods manufacturers. Some EU states are trying to outlaw them.

In 2004 Levi Strauss introduced a new brand, Levis Signature, specifically for distribution through supermarkets such as Tesco.

As consumers travel more, there may be a 'leaking' of perceptions of brand quality. With alcoholic drinks, a key price difference is caused by taxes.

### 1.3.1 Choosing or designing the distribution channel

Key issues relating to the choice of distribution channel

- Number of intermediaries
- Support given to distributors (eg technical advice)
- Control of distribution
- Integration of marketing effort throughout this chain
- Positioning of the product: the distribution should be aligned with this
- Possibility of direct marketing

**Why do firms use intermediaries?**

- Geography: customers may live too far away to be reached directly, or may be too dispersed
- Consolidation of small orders into large ones
- Better use of resources elsewhere
- Lack of retailing know-how
- Segmentation, with different segments for each market being reached by different distribution channels

## 1.3.2 Current strategic developments in distribution

The spurs to change are these.

(a) **Physical distribution costs** are increasing **relative** to other costs (ie as production costs fall). Sometimes these amount to 50% of the price the end-consumer pays.

(b) **Changing consumer lifestyles**: 'one small example is that those in work are time-poorer but money richer ... no wonder there's been a rapid rise in home delivery, from pizzas to wine to potatoes'.

(c) Long established discrete **distribution channels are beginning to leak** (eg beer-buyers can go to France and stock up with lower-taxed drinks).

(d) Offering EDI (**electronic data interchange**) enables a firm to cut lead times for orders. This can be a source of differentiation.

(e) **Distribution has a 'branding effect'**. 'Distribution can be a central and, explicit part of a brand's identity, such as First Direct (Midland Bank's telephone banking subsidiary).

(f) **Distribution channels' generation of customer information opens the door to marketing insight and power**. Retailers (through using EPOS) probably know more about customers than manufacturers. Distribution might become 'essentially an information system'.

(g) There has been a move towards a **concentration of retailer power** with large **retailers** tending to gain **power over the manufacturers in the distribution channel**. This shift in the balance of power has two consequences. Large multiples are able to **dictate product specifications**, and drive much harder bargains on matters of price and delivery. The large multiples' **own-label brands** are increasingly the major competition against branded goods.

(h) **Just-in-time** is a philosophy which applies to the whole production chain, but it is increasingly relevant to distribution, in satisfying the needs of demanding customers, particularly in business-to-business markets.

    (i) Manufacturers are seeking to reduce their stocks of components and raw materials, to eliminate stock holding costs and wasteful activities.

    (ii) Consequently they expect their suppliers to deliver in very small batches as and when demanded.

**Mail order**, in which goods are sold by catalogue, over the Internet, delivered by post or directly, is common in some markets.

(a) **Retailers do not have to be offered a mark-up**. This is why **book clubs** and internet bookshops such as *Amazon.com* are able to offer discounts on recommended retail prices.

(b) **Customers can be reached** who might not normally be able to purchase the product **from a shop**.

(c)   This makes it easier to sell to customers who **cannot do their shopping in normal shopping hours**.

(d)   **No large and expensive display area** in a shop.

(e)   Mail-order facilities can be **combined with an Internet website**.

## Action Programme 1

What social trends do you think might increase home delivery?

**Exam tip**

> You may be asked to identify direct marketing's contribution to marketing strategy. Do not just concentrate on the distribution aspect. Direct marketing also enables users to build up customer profiles, so information gleaned from successful direct marketing exercises can be input to the MkIS.

## 1.4 Promotion

There are four **categories of promotional activity**.

| Promotional | Comment |
|---|---|
| Advertising | Any **paid** form of non-personal presentation and promotion of ideas, goods or services by an identified sponsor. |
| Sales promotion | Encourage through incentives, over a short-term period, the purchase of the good or service. |
| Personal selling | The oral presentation of the goods or services, either to make a sale, or to create goodwill to improve the prospects of sales in the future. |
| Public relations | Unlike advertising, publicity cannot be bought and it might be thought of as unpaid advertising. Although organisations will spend large sums of money on publicity, they do not formally buy space in a newspaper or time on television or radio. Nor do they usually control the content of the publicity message, and so some publicity can be bad rather than good. However, they often try to manage publicity through the use of public relations. |

Marketing communications convey information about the product and the company. Recently, the trend is towards **integrated marketing communications**. In other words, the marketing communications should be integrated with the business strategy, the other elements of the marketing mix, and with each other. Few organisations practise an integrated communications approach in any systematic way. The various tools of marketing communications have traditionally been the exclusive preserve of different groups within the organisation.

**Promotion is the element of the mix most under control of the marketing department**. As far as managers are concerned, there are a number of issues which must be considered strategically for each form of communication.

| Issue | Comment |
|---|---|
| Role | Each form of communication has a different target. Media advertising is direct to the end user, whereas personal selling may be preferred for distributors. |

| Issue | Comment |
|---|---|
| **Objectives** | Each form of communication needs specific objectives:<br><br>• Advertising: raising awareness, repositioning<br><br>• Public relations: favourable press exposure<br><br>• Personal selling: sales targets, client relationships<br><br>• Sales promotion: sample rates |
| **Process management** | This covers relationships with external suppliers, budgeting, recruiting and personnel. |
| **Integration** | The elements of the mix should be integrated so that all customers get the appropriate message, and the different elements of the mix do not conflict with each other. |

### 1.4.1 Key strategic developments in promotion

| Development | Consequence |
|---|---|
| **Database marketing and data mining** | This enables targeting of promotional messages. |
| **Digital TV, many channels** | It will be harder to reach a single audience: rather like the trade magazine sector, fragmentation may cut advertising rates. |
| **Internet** | Ads that load before website content; banner ads; smart ads based on users' search terms and previous purchases |
| **Call centres** | Telephone call centres are mushrooming over the country. They provide sales and customer support activity. They tend to be rigid and bureaucratic in style. |
| **Sponsorship** | Sports and cultural organisations are seeking sponsors. Like all forms of activity, the sponsor has objectives to fulfil. This can be a difficult relationship. Sponsorship is not intrusive. |
| **Personal advice and loyalty** | As service industries develop, there will be greater scope for personal service such as financial services. |
| **Lobbying** | Some decisions regarding product standardisation and safety will be taken at EU level. Expertise in this area is necessary. |

 Marketing at Work

**Unofficial Internet sites**

The Internet offers firms the opportunity to create virtual communities. But it also offers dissatisfied customers or employees the chance to set up bulletin boards to discuss exactly what they think of the company, to publicise information companies would rather keep quiet, or to forward confidential price-sensitive information.

Specific anti-corporate websites have been set up to knock household names. *McSpotlight*, a site dedicated to campaigning against McDonalds, averages 1.5m hits a month. A large amount of the information may be biased, distorted or false.

From a PR point of view what should you do?

(a) Libel is hard to prove especially when people log on under assumed names, but some firms feel that suing is the only solution

(b)   Threats to close down a site would be seen as a threat to free speech, and anyhow would be hard to enforce

# 2 The service marketing mix

Services differ from physical products in that they are intangible, perishable and inherently variable, and their consumption cannot be separated in time from their production.

These factors complicate services marketing and make it necessary to manage three extra Ps: people, processes and physical evidence.

## 2.1 The importance of services

**Importance of services**

(a)   The service sector accounts for most economic activity in the UK, accounting for much more employment than manufacturing.

(b)   Competition has been introduced to service industries.

(c)   Many products contain a service element.

(d)   Service can be a differentiating factor in a firm's offer to the market.

(e)   Bad service is costly.

## Marketing at Work

A study by the Henley Centre indicated that 17% of a typical company's customers were affected by a range of service problems, such as poor information or inefficiency. 15% of people who switched bank account cited poor service as the reason. An unhappy customer tells up to nine others about bad service received.

## 2.2 Elements of services

Services differ from physical goods.

| | |
|---|---|
| **Intangibility** | A service cannot be seen, touched or displayed. The service is often difficult for the consumer to understand. |
| **Inseparability** | In general, it is impossible to separate the production and consumption of a service. (For example, a theatrical event is consumed when it is produced.) |
| **Perishability** | Services are perishable. They cannot be stored, they must be produced on demand and often can only be produced in the presence of the customer. Transport is a sort of service industry. A bus journey cannot be 'stored'. |
| **Variability** | The quality of the service product is typically highly dependent on the quality of the personnel conducting the transaction. |

## 2.3 Products and services combined

Many offers to the market have **both a product and a service element** to them.

- Teaching is almost entirely a service
- A restaurant meal is part product and part service
- A house is almost entirely a product, but it is acquired with the help of service firms

### 2.3.1 Dimensions of service quality

(a) **Technical quality** of the service encounter (what is received by the customer). For example, a customer is going to a bank about a pension. The quality of financial advice received can sometimes be evaluated by a customer. The dimension is based on the technical product training of the staff and their knowledge of the bank's services. It can be backed up by a range of sales aids, such as brochures and even computer based product illustrations which feed the customer's specific requirements into an interactive programme when then produces a customised quotation.

(b) The **functional quality** of the service encounter is how the service is provided. The dimension relates to the psychological interaction between the buyer and seller and is typically perceived in a very subjective way. It includes elements such as the following: the attitudes and behaviour of the employees, how they appear, how accessible the service is, the interrelationships between employees and customers.

(c) The **corporate image** dimension of service quality is a result of how consumers perceive the firm. This dimension can be affected by many factors including advertising and past experience with the firm.

### 2.3.2 Determinants of service quality

| Determinant | Quality |
|---|---|
| Tangibles | The physical evidence, such as the quality of fixtures and fittings of the company's service area, must be consistent with the desired image. |
| Reliability | Getting it right first time is very important, not only to ensure repeat business, but, in financial services, as a matter of ethics, if the customer is buying a future benefit. |
| Responsiveness | The staff's willingness to deal with the customer's queries must be apparent. |
| Communication | Staff should talk to customers in non-technical language which they can understand. |
| Credibility | The organisation should be perceived as honest, trustworthy and as acting in the best interests of customers. |
| Security | This is specially relevant to medical and financial services organisations. The customer needs to feel that the conversations with bank service staff are private and confidential. This factor should influence the design of the service area. |
| Competence | All the service staff need to appear competent in understanding the product range and interpreting the needs of the customers. In part, this can be achieved through training programmes. |
| Courtesy | Customers (even rude ones) should perceive service staff as polite, respectful and friendly. This basic requirement is often difficult to achieve in practice, although training programmes can help. |
| Understanding customers' needs | The use of computer-based customer databases can be very impressive in this context. The service personnel can then call up the customer's records and use these data in the service process, thus personalising the process. Service staff need to meet customer needs rather than try to sell products. This is a subtle but important difference. |
| Access | Minimising queues, having a fair queuing system and speedy but accurate service are all factors which can avoid customers' irritation building up. A pleasant relaxing environment is a useful design factor in this context. |

Marketing at Work

**Enterprise Rent-a-car**

Enterprise Rent-a-car is the market leader in car hire in the USA, with revenues of $6bn and a live car inventory worth $8bn. The company is 90% owned by the Taylor Family. Growth has come partly from targeting a specific sector: replacement for cars being serviced or off the road through accident or breakdown; partly from careful devolution of authority to 5000 branch managers; and partly from close attention to quality of customer service. The chosen market segment is not an easy one: customers may be distressed and agitated and insurance companies and garages must be involved in many of the hires.

Introduced in the 1990s, the Enterprise service quality index (ESQI) is the key: it has been refined over the years so that it is now based on just two questions to customers: are you satisfied with our service? And would you come back? Customers who say they are completely satisfied are three times more likely to come back for further hires. ESQI scores are sent to branch managers along with detailed financial performance information every month. ESQI scores are regarded as so important that no-one is ever promoted from a branch with below average ESQI results, no matter how good the branch's financial performance.

## 2.4 Deploying the marketing mix in services

As services differ from manufactured products, this causes potential **marketing problems**.

(a) The degree of **complexity** which characterises, for example, many financial products.

(b) **Inseparability**: the difficulty for consumers to distinguish between the service itself and its delivery system. The delivery system will be inextricably linked with the service itself and will often be considered as a component of that product. In this sense, there will be some aspects of the delivery system which must be seen as components of the core or tangible product while others may usefully be characterised as part of the augmented product.

### 2.4.1 Marketing services

(a) **Poor service quality in one case** (eg lack of punctuality of trains, staff rudeness, a bank's incompetence) **is likely to lead to widespread distrust of everything the organisation does**.

(b) If the service is intangible and offers a complicated future benefit, or is consumed 'on the spot', then attracting customers means promoting an attractive image and ensuring that the **service lives up to its reputation, consistently**.

(c) The **pricing of services is often complicated**, especially if large numbers of people are involved in providing the service.

(d) **Human resources management, not just customer care, is a key ingredient in the services marketing mix**, as so many services are produced and consumed in a specific social context. The human element cannot always be designed out of a service.

Service marketing involves three additional 'P's: people, processes and physical evidence.

### 2.4.2 People

That employees are relevant as an element in the marketing mix is particularly evident in service industries. After all, if you have had poor service in a shop or restaurant, you may not be willing to go there again. An American retailing firm estimated that there was an identifiable relationship between low staff turnover and repeat purchases. Managing front-line workers (eg cabin-crew on aircraft), who are the lowest in the organisational hierarchy but whose behaviour has most effect on customers, is an important task for senior management. It involves corporate culture, job design and motivational issues.

- Appearance
- Attitude
- Commitment
- Behaviour–

- Professionalism
- Skills
- Numbers
- Discretion

### 2.4.3 Processes

**Processes involve the ways in which the marketer's task is achieved.** Efficient processes can become a **marketing advantage** in their own right. For example, if an airline develops a sophisticated **ticketing system**, it can encourage customers to take connecting flights offered by allied airlines. Efficient processing of purchase orders received from customers can decrease the time it takes to satisfy them. Efficient procedures in the long term save money.

- Procedures
- Policies
- Mechanisation
- Queuing

- Information
- Capacity levels
- Speed/timing
- Accessibility

### 2.4.4 Physical evidence

**Physical evidence.** Again, this is particularly important in service industries, for example where the ambience of a restaurant is important. Logos and uniforms help create a sense of corporate identity.

| Environment | Facilities | Tangible evidence |
| --- | --- | --- |
| • Furnishings | • Vans/vehicles/aeroplanes | • Labels |
| • Colours | • Equipment/tools | • Tickets |
| • Layout | • Uniforms | • Logos |
| • Noise levels | • Paperwork | • Packaging |
| • Smells | | |
| • Ambience | | |

Marketing at Work

Telecommunications is a service, and an important aspect of physical evidence in telecommunications is the public phone box. BT replaced its old, expensive-to-maintain red phone boxes and introduced nondescript metallic kiosks, in which the phones actually worked. Scrapping the red phone boxes caused outrage.

# 3 Branding strategy

## 3.1 What is a brand?

FAST FORWARD

Much of the marketing mix activity goes to the development of **brands**, which are what the customers identify. Brands embody a set of expectations about the product. A brand image exists in the customer's mind.

**Key concept**

> - A **brand** is a collection of attributes which strongly influence purchase. (Davidson)
>
> - 'A name, term, sign, symbol or design or combination of them, intended to identify the goods or services of one seller or group of sellers and to differentiate them from those of competitors.' (Kotler)

Branding and a firm's reputation are linked. The important thing to remember is that a brand is something **customers** value: it exists in the customer's mind. A brand is the link between a company's marketing activities and the customer's perception.

## Marketing at Work

In suburban Philadelphia, not too many miles from Wharton's campus, is a retail establishment called *Ed's Beer Store*. It's a wonderfully prosaic name. Customers know what they can buy there, and if they have a complaint, they know whom to talk to.

But what about companies with names like *Agere*, *Agilent* or *Altria*? Or *Diageo*, *Monday* and *Verizon*? Or *Accenture*, *Cingular* and *Protiviti*?

Except for Monday, which may be a strange thing to call a company but it is nonetheless a real word, all these names are fabricated. What's more, none of them, even Monday, tells potential customers anything about the businesses they are in. Plus, they sound so contrived that you might conclude they will do nothing but elicit snickering and confusion in the market place.

According to marketing professors at Wharton, however, that is not necessarily the case. They say peculiar names, by themselves, may mean nothing to begin with. But if backed by a successful branding campaign, they will come to signify whatever the companies want them to mean.

*Website:* http://knowledge.wharton.upenn.edu

### 3.1.1 What makes up a brand?

- Effective product
- Distinctive identity
- Added values

supported by

**Visible**: Symbol, advertising, presentation (eg packaging)

**Invisible**: assets and competences, strong R&D, supply chain, effective selling, costs

### 3.1.2 Benefits of branding

| Beneficiary | Benefit of branding |
|---|---|
| **Customers** | • Branding makes it easier to choose between competing products, if brands offer different benefits. Brands help consumers cope with information overload<br>• Brands can support aspirations and self image<br>• Branding can confer membership of reference groups |
| **Marketers** | • Enables extra value to be added to the product<br>• Creates an impression in the consumer's mind; encourages re-purchase<br>• Differentiates the product, especially if competing products are similar<br>• Reduces the importance of price<br>• Encourages a pull strategy<br>• Other products/services can exploit the brand image (eg *Virgin*) |

| Beneficiary | Benefit of branding |
|---|---|
| Shareholders | • A brand is an intangible asset; even though it is not on the financial statements, a strong brand promises to generate future cash inflows and profits. This is called **brand equity**.<br><br>• Brands build market share, which can generate high profits through:<br>   - Higher volume<br>   - Higher value (higher prices)<br>   - Higher control over distributors |

**Evolution of brands**. Brands have evolved over time, to the extent that they satisfy customer needs.

(a) **Classic brands** (post World War II) were linked to a single goal (eg cleaner clothes).

(b) **Contemporary brands** meet functional needs but give associated benefits (eg *Volvo* and safety).

(c) **Post-modern brands**? Consumers use brands to attain a broad array of goals, as a result of 'time famine'.

    (i) Some marketers suggest that brands have an emotional content. Certainly, this might be the case for fashion items (eg trainers) where they confer status.

    (ii) Strangest of all is *Mercedes* (a subsidiary of *Daimler Chrysler*), previously known for luxury cars. Mercedes now has product offering that embraces small cars.

## 3.2 Brand strategies

**FAST FORWARD**

There are several basic branding strategies: company, umbrella, range and individual product.

### 3.2.1 Different types of brand strategy

(a) **Company brand**. The company name is the most prominent feature of the branding (eg Mercedes).

(b) **The company brand combined with an individual brand name** (eg Kellogg's: *Corn Flakes*, *Rice Krispies*). This option both legitimises (because of the company name) and individualises (the individual product name). It allows **new names to be introduced quickly and relatively cheaply**. Sometimes known as **umbrella branding**, firms might use this approach as a short-term way to save money.

(c) **Range brand**. Firms group types of product under different brands. For example, Sharwoods is a brand owned by *RHM Foods*. *Sharwoods* offers pickles, poppadums, sauces etc.

(d) **Individual name**. Each product has a unique name. This is the option chosen by *Procter & Gamble* for example, who even have different brand names within the same product line, eg *Bold*, *Tide*. The main advantage of individual product branding is that an unsuccessful brand does not adversely affect the firm's other products, nor the firm's reputation generally.

 Marketing at Work

*Penguin* is one of the oldest brands in UK paperback publishing and over the years has introduced brand extensions (*Puffin* for children, *Pelican* for academic) and sub-brands (*Penguin Classics*, *Penguin Modern Classics*) and indeed other products (*Penguin Classic CDs*).

A key issue for publishing is to identify the core of the brand.

(a)     The imprint or publisher?

(b)     The author? It appears to go without saying that people will buy a book by a recognised author, and that the author is at the heart of the brand.

In contrast, people buy '*Mills & Boon*' books - the core of the brand is the publisher, not the author.

The *Folio Society* publishes versions of classic literature, but markets its books partly as art objects, owing to the quality of the binding and paper, and the specially-commissioned illustrations.

### 3.2.2 Choice of brand strategy

(a)     **Company and/or umbrella brand name**

| Advantages | Disadvantages |
| --- | --- |
| • Cheap (only one marketing effort) | • Not ideal for segmentation |
| • Easy to launch new products under umbrella brand | • Harder to obtain distinct identity |
| | • Risk that failure in one area can damage the brand |
| • Good for internal marketing | • Variable quality |

For example, *Virgin* is a company brand name, supported by advertising, PR and the celebrity status of *Richard Branson*. (To what extent will the problems of *Virgin Trains* adversely affect the other brands?)

(i)     Service industries use umbrella marketing as customer benefits can cross product categories. *Marks & Spencer* diversified from clothes, to food and to financial services. *Tesco* and *Asda* have followed suit.

(ii)    Communication media are more diffuse and fragmented.

(iii)   One brand is supported by integrated marketing communications.

(iv)    Umbrella branding supports **database marketing** across the whole product range.

(v)     Distributor/retailer brands are umbrella brands in their own right, so **brand owners** have to follow suit.

(b)     **Range brands** offer some of the advantages of an umbrella brand with more precise targeting.

(c)     **Individual brand** name

| Advantages | Disadvantages |
| --- | --- |
| • Ideal for precise segmentation | • Expensive |
| • Crowds out competition by offering more choice | • Risky |
| • Damage limitation to company's reputation | |

## 3.3 Brand equity

The added value conferred by a brand is largely subjective. In blind testing many consumers cannot tell the difference between different products; however, they will exhibit a preference for a strong brand name when shown it. Apart from the quality and functionality of the product, brand equity is built on suggestion rather than substance.

**Key concept**

> **Brand equity** is the asset the marketer builds to ensure continuity of satisfaction for the customer and profit for the supplier.

Most consumer buying decisions, therefore, **do not depend on the functionality of the product**.

(a) Products are bought for **emotional reasons**. For example, most sports trainers are fashion products.

(b) Branding reduces the need for the intellectually challenging process of rational choice.

## Marketing at Work

**Factory equipment brands**

*MG Technologies* industrial group, the company that owns the *Tuchenhagen* brand, promotes the name as part of a multi-brand philosophy. At *Keyence*, one of the world's biggest producers of sensors and vision systems for factory processes, the brand management is somewhat simpler; the Keyence name, rather than specialist 'sub-brands', is the brand most heavily promoted by the company.

Another leader in running different brands within the same business is *Sandvik*, the world's biggest manufacturer of machine-tool devices.

Sandvik's tooling division has about 10 key brands. They include *Coromant*, which is associated with particularly hard cutting materials; *Valenite*, aimed at automotive applications; *Walter* (general machining); and *Titex* (drilling). Most of the company's advertising and marketing effort is aimed at establishing the value of these brands, rather than raising awareness of the Sandvik name itself.

Each of the main brands in the tooling division has its own employees in front-end fields such as marketing, sales and product development. They account for about a third of Sandvik's total 15,000 tooling employees. The rest are in back-end operations – which work on behalf of all the brands – such as research, manufacturing, distribution, finance and information technology.

According to Anders Thelin, the head of Sandvik's tooling activities, this approach means that customers with special requirements in a highly technical field feel their needs are addressed individually. 'By organising in this manner we can share best practices in fields such as manufacturing and research across all the brands, while ensuring that the selling operations are tailored directly to the specific customer's requirements,' he says.

*Financial Times, 8 February 2005*

### 3.3.1 Sources of brand equity

| Source | Comment |
|---|---|
| **Experience** | Customer's actual usage of a brand can give positive or negative associations. |
| **User associations** | Brands get an image from the type of people using them; brands might be associated with particular personalities. |
| **Appearance** | Design appeals to people's aesthetic sensibilities. |
| **Manufacturer's name** | The company reputation may support the brand. |
| **Marketing communication** | Building the brand by establishing its values is a major reason why marketing communication of all kinds is undertaken. |

### 3.3.2 Brand identity

Key concept

> **Brand identity**: 'the message sent out by the brand through its product form, name, visual signs, advertising. This is not the same as **brand image** which is how the target market perceives the brand.

### 3.3.3 Three aspects to a brand

| Aspect | Comment |
|--------|---------|
| Core | Fundamental, unchanging aspect of a brand. (Cider is an **alcoholic** drink made from apples.) |
| Style | This is the brand's culture, personality, the identity it conveys and so on. Compare the:<br>• Rustic personality of Scrumpy Jack<br>• Almost club-orientated personality of Diamond White |
| Themes | These are how the brand communicates through physical appearance of the product. |

Clearly, the **themes** are more easy to change than the **style**, which is more easy to change than the core.

Exam tip

> A June 2000 question asked about introducing a UK brand of soft drinks – with a distinct personality – into the Russian market. It showed how branding and segmentation can be applied to more complex problems.

## 3.4 How to build brands

  **FAST FORWARD**

> Brand building is a logical process that can proceed gradually, step by step towards a position of strength.

The process for building the brand is similar to that of building a product (core product, an expected product, an augmented product and a potential product). However, a product is, in some respects, purely functional, whereas a brand offers more.

### 3.4.1 A step approach to designing brands

**Step 1**   **Have a quality product** – but remember quality means **fitness for use** not the **maximum specification**. Functionality is only a starting point.

**Step 2**   **Build the basic brand**. These are the marketing mix criteria.

- They should support product performance
- They should differentiate the brand
- They should be consistent with positioning
- The basic brand delivers the core product in an attractive way

**Step 3**   **Augmentations** include extra services, guarantees and so on. (Expensive guarantees provide evidence that the firm takes quality seriously.)

**Step 4**   **Reaching its potential**, so that customers will not easily accept substitutes.

**Step 5**   Maintain **brand value** by using the marketing mix to persuade customers to re-buy.

**Step 6**   **Build brand loyalty**. Customers who rebuy and are loyal are valuable because:

- Revenue from them is more predictable
- Existing customers are cheaper than new customers

**Step 7** **Know where to stop in developing the brand**. (For example, an alcohol-free alcopop would be pointless.)

Brands that **reach their potential** have five key characteristics.

- A quality product underpinning the brand
- Being first to market, giving early mover advantages
- Unique positioning concept: in other words they are precisely positioned
- Strong communications underpinning the brand
- Time and consistency

## 3.4.2 The brand planning process

Brand strategy is one of the steps in the brand planning process just as marketing strategy is one step in the marketing planning process. *Arnold* (1992) in *The Handbook of Brand Management* offers a five stage brand planning process.

| Stage | Description |
|---|---|
| **Market analysis** | An overview of trends in the macro and micro environment and so includes customer and competitor analysis and the identification of any PEST factors which may affect our brand. For soft drinks, the explosion of competitive activity, particularly by own label, and new product introductions, such as Fruitopia, will be important. |
| **Brand situation analysis** | Analysis of the brand's personality and individual attributes. This represents the internal audit and questions such as, 'Is advertising projecting the right image?', 'Is the packaging too aggressive?', 'Does the product need updating?' need asking. This is a fundamental evaluation of the brand's character. |
| **Targeting future positions** | This is the core of brand strategy. Any brand strategy could incorporate what has been learnt in steps (1) and (2) into a view of how the market will evolve and what strategic response is most appropriate. Brand strategy can be considered under three headings. (1) Target markets (2) Brand positions (3) Brand scope |
| **Testing new offers** | Once the strategy has been decided the next step is to develop individual elements of the marketing mix and test the brand concept for clarity, credibility and competitiveness with the target market. |
| **Planning and evaluating performance** | The setting of the brand budget, establishing the type of support activity needed and measurement of results against objectives. Information on tracking of performance feeds into step (i) of the brand management process. |

 Marketing at Work

**Sunny Delight**

This is an example of what can go well – and – not well in planning, introducing and managing a new product. (Extracts from *The Guardian*, 11 April 2001.)

*Sunny Delight* burst upon Britain with its sunshine logo in April 1998. By August 1999, it was the country's third-largest-selling soft drink. Three years later, sales were down 36% by value and 28% by volume (moving annual totals to February 2001).

It was a textbook launch. Delight had been available in the US since 1964, it was sold as a downmarket drink competing for space alongside squashes and long-life drinks on ordinary shelves. The approach in the UK was to be different. *Procter and Gamble* (P&G), one of the world's most powerful grocery manufacturers, had acquired it at the end of the 80s and in 1996 began a long and thorough process of test marketing it for the UK in Carlisle.

Delight is 5% citrus juice, and a lot of sugar and water, with vegetable oil, thickeners, added vitamins and flavourings, colourings and other additives that make it look like fresh orange juice but appeal to the immature tastebuds of young children.

The ingredients were cheap but the price was set at a premium. P&G invested in a new filling plant costing about £12m, according to industry estimates, so that the drink could be packaged in the sort of frosted plastic bottles that fresh orange juice is usually sold in chill cabinets, next to fresh fruit juices.

P&G is one of the handful of companies that has the muscle to dictate where products are sold in supermarkets. All this was backed up by a huge direct marketing campaign and a £9.2m advertising campaign.

P&G's brands include Pampers, and it is thought to have built up a powerful database from offers over the years, which tells the company who we are and how old our children are ... it is also reported to have worked with retailers' data from loyalty cards to identify young, lower-income families. Teenagers were targeted with sponsorship of basketball.

This combined onslaught led to instant success. But the backlash came equally fast. The Food Commission condemned Sunny Delight as a con, accusing P&G of putting it in chill cabinets to mislead. Newspapers, the BBC's *Watchdog* programme and *Radio 4* all carried attacks on the brand and dubbed it 'The unreal thing'.

Then came the comic twist in the drama. In December 1999, a paediatrician, Dr Duncan Cameron, reported a new and alarming condition in the medical journals: Sunny Delight syndrome. A girl of five had turned bright yellow and orange after drinking 1.5 litres of the stuff a day. She was overdosing on betacarotene, the additive that gives the sugar-and-water drink its orange colour.

By a marketing man's nightmare of coincidence, the TV ads for the brand at the time showed two white snowmen raiding the fridge for Sunny Delight and turning bright orange. To add to the embarrassment, a leading consultant dermatologist, Professor John Hawks, said too much betacarotene could cause tummy upsets. As if to confirm its status as spawn of the devil, P&G was forced to join that happy band of cigarette manufacturers who put voluntary warnings on their products.

## 3.5 Brand extension

 **FAST FORWARD** A brand can be used on a wide range of products and services if its values are appropriate.

**Key concept**

> **Brand extension** uses a brand name successfully established in one market or channel to enter other. It is often termed **brand stretching** when the markets are very different.

### 3.5.1 Examples of brand extension

- **Retailers** such as *Dixons* and *Tesco* launching themselves as **Internet Service Providers**
- *Penguin Books* launching its own 'brand' of compact discs

- One of the greatest exponents of brand extension is Richard Branson. He has extended the *Virgin* brand, originally based on pop music, to cover mobile phones, trains and even financial services

### 3.5.2 Conditions for brand extension

(a) The **core values** of the brand must be **relevant to the new market**. EasyJet has transferred to car rental and internet cafes.

(b) The new market area must not affect the core values of the brand by association. Failure in one activity can adversely affect brand equity.

## Marketing at Work

*Mark Ritson*, assistant professor of marketing at the London Business School, wrote about two planned attempts at brand stretching in *Marketing* (April 2004). He did not expect either to succeed.

- *Stelios Haji–Ioannou*, founder of *Easyjet* has announced *easy4men*, a range of male grooming products. Ritson doubts this will succeed as *easyGroup* does not really have 'brand equity in the form of positive, valuable and extendable brand associations', it merely has 'an unusual business model built on a stripped-down product offering and dynamic pricing.'

- *The Daily Telegraph* is to launch a compact edition. Ritson expects this to fail because the Telegraph 'is tradition, it is conservatism, it is quality. It is all the things that a compact edition is not.' He contrasts the Telegraph's prospects with the successful launch of a compact edition of *The Independent*, 'a younger, different and more contemporary newspaper brand.'

### 3.5.3 Advantages of brand extension

| Advantage | Comment |
| --- | --- |
| **Cheap** | It is less costly to extend a brand then to establish a new one from scratch. |
| **Customer-perception** | Customer expectations of the brand have been built up, so this lower risk for the customer encourages 'trial'. |
| **Less risky** | Failure rate of completely new brands. |

### 3.5.4 Disadvantages of brand extension

| Disadvantage | Comment |
| --- | --- |
| **Segments** | The brand personality may not carry over successfully to the new segment. The brand values may not be relevant to the new market. |
| **Strength** | The brand needs to be strong already. |
| **Perception** | The brand still needs a differential advantage over competitors. |
| **Over-dilution** | Excessive extensions can dilute the values of the brand. |

## 3.6 Revitalising and repositioning

At times, the performance of a brand will falter and managers will attempt to rectify the situation by enhancing sales volume and improving profits in other ways.

**Revitalisation** means increasing the sales volume through:

- New markets (eg overseas)
- New segments (eg personal computers are being sold for family, as opposed to business, use)
- Increased usage (encouraging people to eat breakfast cereals as a snack during the day)

**Repositioning is more fundamental**, in that it is a **competitive strategy** aimed to change position to increase market share.

| Type of position | Comment |
|---|---|
| **Real** | Relates to actual product features and design |
| **Psychological** | Change the buyer's beliefs about the brand |
| **Competitive** | Alter beliefs about competing brands |
| **Change emphasis** | The emphasis in the advertising can change over time |

### 3.6.1 Success criteria for branding

**Beneficial qualities of a brand name**

- Suggest **benefits**, eg Schweppes' Slimline tonic
- Suggest qualities such as **action** or **colour** (eg easyJet, with an orange colour)
- Be **easy to pronounce**, recognise and remember
- Be **acceptable in all markets**, both linguistically and culturally
- Be **distinctive**
- Be **meaningful**

 **Marketing at Work**

Compare the following mobile phone brands.

- *Orange*
- *Vodafone*
- *Cellnet*
- *One-to-One*

Orange appropriates the colour orange, whereas Vodafone and Cellnet suggest aspects of the product, and One-to-One suggests the actual consumer benefit.

## 3.7 Brands in the global market place

**FAST FORWARD**

Brands, like most aspects of marketing practice, require a decision about standardisation or adaptation when taken into the global marketplace.

The most successful examples of worldwide branding occur where the brand has become **synonymous with the generic product** (eg Sellotape, Aspirin).

 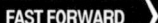

Brewing is an industry with significant economies of scale. Apart from *Heineken* and *Guinness*, it is only recently that big brewers have become 'international'. There are a variety of aspects of this development.

(a) Beers are branded across markets. *Stella Artois* is available in the UK as a premium product, whereas in Belgium it is 'a decent modestly price lager'.

(b) Other firms are expanding by acquisition. Interbrew, the brewer of Stella Artois has purchased *Labatt* of Canada, to gain access to markets in North and South America.

(c) Big brewing companies see many European and American markets are stagnant: they are trying to revive them with imported or foreign brands.

(d) Firms co-operate in some markets but compete in others. (*Guinness* distributes *Bass* in the US, whilst competing with Bass in the UK.)

(e) The greatest potential seems to be east Asia, where beer consumption is rising by 10% pa and South America, where growth is 4% pa.

Ultimately, even if the beer market eventually becomes truly global, it will remain fragmented for a long time to come.

**Blue Nun**

Blue Nun is being relaunched around the globe as an affordable, reliable and widely available bottle of wine. Having been in steady decline in the UK since 1985, sales are now healthy again. Half a million cases were sold in 2000. The target market in the UK is women over 35 who want to spend around £5 per bottle, while in Asia the core target market is slightly younger as they are newcomers to the wine market.

The wine is sold in over 80 countries. There is a 'brand book' with strict guidelines for local distributors on such matters as brand values and which fonts and colours to use. This should ensure consistency of brand message.

### 3.7.1 Global or local brand?

The key differences between a standardised global brand approach and an approach based upon identifying and exploiting local marketing opportunities are as described below.

(a) **Standardised global brand approach**

   (i) A standardised product offering to market segments which have exactly similar needs across cultures

   (ii) A common approach to the marketing mix and one that is as nearly standardised as may be, given language differences

(b) **Local marketing opportunities**

   (i) A recognition that the resources of the company may be adapted to fulfil marketing opportunities in different ways, taking into account local needs and preferences but on a global basis

   (ii) A willingness to sub-optimise the benefits of having a single global brand (eg advertising synergy) in order to optimise the benefits of meeting specific needs more closely

Marketing at Work

(a)     It is possible to move from a local brand to a global brand approach as demonstrated by the *Mars Corporation* with their *Snickers* brand. In the UK market, the biggest 'candy market' in Europe, Mars had decided to use the brand name *Marathon* for the chocolate bar known as Snickers in the US and elsewhere around the world. Reportedly, this was done to avoid confusion with the word knickers. There was a very distinctive brand identity in the UK to the extent that the company would sponsor the London Marathon and other sporting events to tie in with the brand name. Competition from *Nestlé* in Europe persuaded the company that they needed to take up the potential benefits of a standardised global brand approach rather than merely relying on a global marketing approach. They, therefore, changed the name to Snickers in the UK market at very considerable cost of advertising support.

(b)     *General Motors* who operate as *Opel* in Germany and elsewhere in Europe, and *Vauxhall* in the UK, chose to use the brand name *Vectra* for the 1996 update of the Vauxhall *Cavalier* in the UK market. This was done in order to standardise the name across the European market – since the 'Cavalier' model had been known as the Opel Vectra in most markets anyway. General Motors still use the Vauxhall company name in the UK market since it has strong brand equity in its own right.

For the international company marketing products which can be branded there are two further policy decisions to be made.

- The problem of deciding if and how to protect the company's brands
- Whether there should be one global brand or different national brands for a product

The major argument in favour of a single global brand is the economies of scale that it produces, both in production and promotion. But whether a global brand is the best policy (or even possible) depends on a number of factors, which address the two basic policy decisions above.

### 3.7.2 Legal considerations

(a)     Legal constraints may limit the possibilities for a global brand, for instance where the brand name has already been registered in a foreign country.

(b)     Protection of the brand name will often be needed, but internationally is hard to achieve.

- In some countries registration is difficult
- Brand imitation and piracy are rife in certain parts of the world

There are many examples of imitation in international branding, with products such as cigarettes, and denim jeans.

(c)     Worse still is the problem of piracy where a well known brand name is counterfeited. It is illegal in most parts of the world but in many countries there is little if any enforcement of the law. (Levis is one of the most pirated brand names.) Piracy is also a problem for intellectual property.

 Action Programme 2

Even with trademark protection the impact of a market leader's branding may be weakened by consumers who perceive the brand name as a generic term. Can you think of some examples?

**BPP**
LEARNING MEDIA

Marketing at Work

*Budweiser* is a US beer, but a beer with an identical name (though a very different taste) is made in the Czech Republic and is sold throughout Europe. *Anheuser-Busch*, the American owner, has been unable to buy the Czech beer's trademark.

### 3.7.3 Cultural aspects

Even if a firm has no legal difficulties with branding globally, there may be cultural problems, eg unpronounceable names or names with other meanings. There are many examples of problems in global branding, for example *Maxwell House* is *Maxwell Kaffee* in Germany, *Legal* in France and *Monky* in Spain. But sometimes a minor spelling change is all that is needed, such as *Wrigley Speermint* in Germany.

### 3.7.4 Other considerations

Many other influences affect the global branding decision.

(a) Differences between the firm's major brand and its secondary brands. The major brand is more likely to be branded globally than secondary brands.

(b) The importance of brand to the product sale. Where price, for example, is a more important factor, then it may not be worth the heavy expenditure needed to establish and maintain a global brand in each country; a series of national brands may be more effective.

(c) The problem of how to brand a product arising from acquisition or joint venture. Should the multinational company keep the name it has acquired?

**Exam tip**

Questions in this area often will specifically ask for examples, so you should keep your eyes on the business press. The draft specimen paper included a 25 mark question on developing a global brand and asked for examples of the way organisations have applied critical success factors in brand development.

## 4 Integrated marketing communications

**FAST FORWARD**

Integrated marketing communications encompasses all forms of communication between an organisation and its customers and potential customers. More broadly, it is **all forms of communication by an organisation with its environment**, including internal communication with employees and managers.

## 4.1 The need for consistency

Strategy must be communicated in such a way that the messages are **consistent** through time and **targeted accurately at appropriate stakeholder audiences**. Each organisation must constantly guard against the transmission of **confusing messages**, whether this is through the way in which the telephone is answered, the impact of sales literature, the way sales persons approach prospective clients or the transparency of an organisation's overall corporate activities.

Marketing communications is about the promotion of both **the organisation** and its **products and services.** An increasing number of managers recognise the growing role the organisation plays in the marketing process and the impact that organisational factors can have on the minds of consumers.

It appears logical to conclude that, if there are different audiences, they exist both inside and outside the organisation, and some of them actively contribute to the source of some communications (eg marketing communication agencies). It is important to bring corporate and business strategy together with marketing strategy so that all these elements can be integrated and marketing communication is effective.

A dictionary definition says that integration is 'combining parts into a whole'.

> Immediately it can be seen that **integration of marketing communications** is possible at three levels.
>
> - Integration with business strategy
> - Integration with marketing strategy
> - Integration of the promotional tools

### 4.1.1 Example

Thus a manufacturer of an exclusive and expensive perfume would have to take into account the **public relations aspects** of manufacturing using Third World labour or testing on animals; its **distribution policy** would support the image by selling through Harrods rather than Boots; its leaflets would fall out of *Vogue* and there would not be a 'win a body spray' competition in *Woman's Own*. Where would this company locate its main office? What would be the criteria for the recruitment of staff? Every aspect of the operation tells you something about the organisation and its product. **Integrated marketing communications is communication that delivers an utterly consistent message**.

Integrated marketing communications (IMC) means different things to different people, but is more likely to occur when organisations attempt to enter into a **co-ordinated dialogue with their various internal and external audiences**.

> **Marketing communications** is a management process through which an organisation enters into a dialogue with its various audiences. To accomplish this the organisation develops, presents and evaluates a series of co-ordinated messages to identified stakeholder groups.
>
> The objective of the process is to (re)position the organisation and/or their offerings, in the mind of each member of the target audience in a **consistent and likeable** way.

The word **dialogue** is used deliberately. Communication theory tells us that **feedback** is important. Of course, it is important to use feedback constructively and good marketing communications allows for the development of a **circle of information** between an organisation, its customers and interested stakeholders. Promotional messages should encourage target audiences to **respond** to organisations (or products/brands). This response can be immediate through, for example, **purchase behaviour**, registering on a **website**, using **customer care lines** or even through **storing information** in memory (or a file or desk) for future use.

The communication tools used in this dialogue and the messages conveyed should be **internally consistent with an organisation's strategies**. The target audiences should perceive the communication and associated cues as **co-ordinated, likeable and timely**. In addition, members of the target audience(s) should, at some time, be sufficiently motivated to want to respond to the communication and encourage future messages.

The word **positioning** is used in the definition as well. The manner in which an organisation (product or brand) is **perceived** relative to other competing products can be important to the level of success an organisation might enjoy.

Management pursuit and development of IMC involves the totality of an **organisation**, its **strategy** and all those with whom it **interacts**. IMC is too often depicted as just the co-ordinated impacts of the tools of the promotional mix, but it involves much more.

- **A range of activities**
- **Customer/audience focus**
- **The breadth of the organisation**
- **Cultural factors**

## 4.2 The development of IMC

There are a number of reasons why organisations are seeking to establish IMC. The following table sets out some of the drivers behind this growth (*Fill*, 1999).

| Organisational Drivers for IMC |
| --- |
| • Increasing profits through improved **efficiency** |
| • Increasing need for greater levels of **accountability** |
| • Rapid move towards **cross-border marketing** and the need for changing structures and communications |
| • Co-ordinated **brand development** and **competitive advantage** |
| • Opportunities to utilise **management time** more productively |
| • Provide **direction and purpose** |

| Market Based Drivers for IMC |
| --- |
| • Greater levels of **audience communications literacy** |
| • **Media cost** inflation |
| • Media and audience **fragmentation** |
| • **Stakeholders** need for increasing amounts and diversity of information |
| • Greater amounts of message **clutter** |
| • **Competitor activity** and low levels of brand differentiation |
| • Move towards **relationship marketing** from transaction based marketing |
| • Development of **networks, collaboration and alliances** |

| Communication Based Drivers for IMC |
| --- |
| • **Technological advances** (Internet, databases, segmentation techniques) |
| • Increased **message effectiveness** through **consistency** and reinforcement of core messages |
| • More effective **triggers** for brand and message recall |
| • More **consistent** and less confusing brand images |
| • Need to build **brand reputations** and to provide clear identity cues |

IMC is resisted for many reasons. Failure to establish IMC as a total concept may be for one or other of the following reasons.

- Financial structures and frameworks
- Reluctance to change
- Traditional hierarchical management and brand structures
- Attitudes and structure of suppliers and agencies
- Perceived complexity of planning and co-ordination
- Lack of experience

Overcoming these different forms of resistance can be tricky and partly because of the enormity of the task, especially in global organisations, there are few examples of truly rooted IMC. Here are some of the ways in which the restraints can be overcome.

- Adopting a customer focused philosophy
- Using training and development programmes

- Appointing change agents
- Planning to achieve competitive advantage
- Developing an incremental approach

The diagram below sets out a model of IMC and demonstrates the way in which the different elements of an organisation's activities need to be brought together if IMC is to flourish (Fill, 1999).

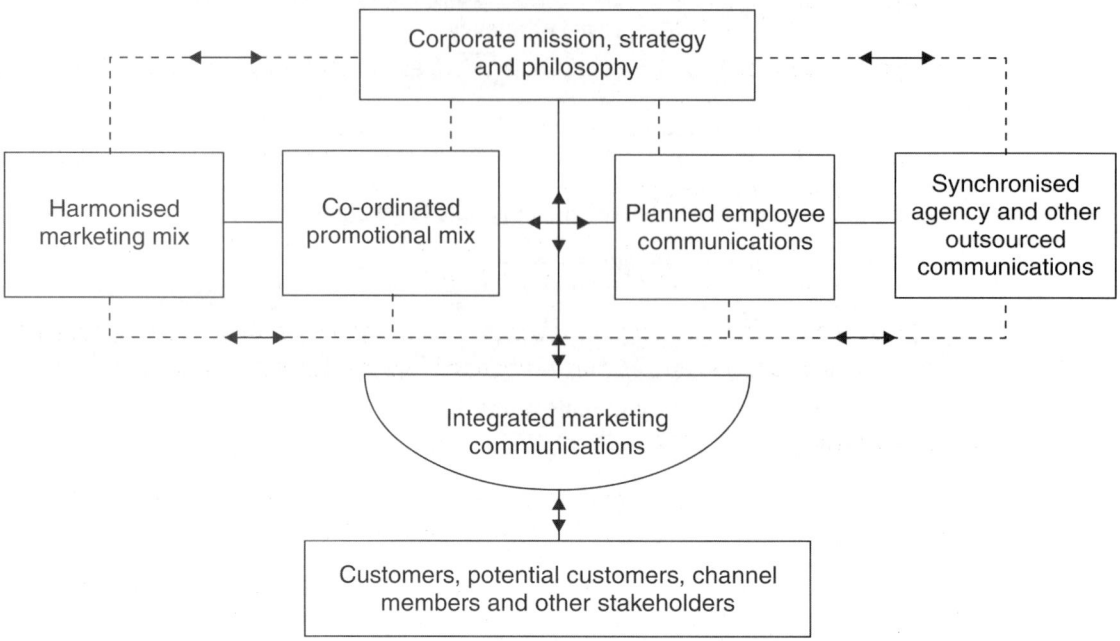

<table>
<tr><td>Key concept</td><td>**Integrated marketing communications** is a strategic approach to the management of an organisation's marketing communication activities.</td></tr>
</table>

## 4.3 Strategic marketing communications issues

FAST FORWARD

Strategic issues in marketing communication include, besides integration, media and audience fragmentation, ethics and the problem of measuring response.

Marketing communications is a fast moving discipline, not least due to the rapidly developing use of **newer technologies** such as the **Internet**. Organisations increasingly need to be aware of changes taking place and how these will affect their communications strategies. Lead times are short and competitors catch up quickly so anticipation of significant factors and their effects is vital.

Issues that might be considered to be currently affecting marketing communication strategy development are outlined below.

### 4.3.1 Integration

Not only must firms ensure that there is consistency in the delivery of messages to customers and other stakeholders, their **communications planning** needs to be an **integral part of their overall business and marketing planning**.

(a)   **Objectives** at all levels (business, marketing and communications) need to relate to each other.

(b)   **Strategies** have to relate to the objectives set.

(c)     Creative strategy and execution will ensure consumers and stakeholders receive **consistent messages** across all media.

(d)     This includes consistency between **strategic approaches**, push, pull and profile and the respective **communications mixes** selected.

### 4.3.2 Media fragmentation

The **increasing availability of different media** can to some extent make successful integration difficult to achieve, particularly on an international scale.

(a)     Cable, satellite and digital TV all provide media buyers with an increasing and complex **range of opportunities**.

(b)     Newsagent shelves are packed with new magazines and other products aimed at consumers with **differing and changing lifestyles**.

(c)     New media, including the Internet, present challenges for all communicators as **consumers look for new ways to gather information and make purchases**.

### 4.3.3 Audience fragmentation

Markets are also fragmenting. The process of segmentation becomes more difficult, with **smaller target groups** seeking product benefits to more closely match their individual needs.

(a)     This has led to developments in **relationship marketing**, with communications taking place on a one to one basis, even in fmcg sectors.

(b)     Companies are recognising the **lifetime value of customers**, with **retention** more effective than the constant demand for new business.

(c)     **Direct marketing**, led by sophisticated **database developments**, is taking over from traditional mass communication techniques.

### 4.3.4 Ethical issues

Marketing has long been criticised in some consumer quarters for creating unnecessary demand for products which consumers cannot afford to buy. The advent of the so-called 'sophisticated consumer' suggests that consumers are no longer so gullible. They will make choices based on information that they consider believable from companies that they trust.

### 4.3.5 Measuring response

In addition to the media fragmentation discussed above, marketers are seeking **measurable effectiveness from their communications budgets**. Agencies who have grown on the creation of expensive campaigns, which have been difficult to evaluate the success of, are now seeking new ways of demonstrating effectiveness. This has included a shift toward **direct response** advertising and the use of **TV programme sponsorship** where target audiences can be more closely identified with brands.

# 5 Customer relationships

**FAST FORWARD**

In recent times emphasis has increased on building and maintaining good long-term **relationships** with customers. This is because such relationships are more profitable than constantly searching for new customers owing to repeat purchasing, ease of service and so on.

The **customer** is central to the marketing orientation, but so far we have not considered this important concept in detail. Customers make up one of the groups of stakeholders whose interests management should address. The **stakeholder concept** suggests a **wider concern** than the traditional marketing approach of supplying goods and services which satisfy immediate needs. The supplier-customer relationship extends beyond the basic transaction. The customer needs to remain satisfied with his purchase and positive about his supplier long after the transaction has taken place. If his satisfaction is muted or grudging, future purchases may be reluctant or non-existent and he may advise others of his discontent. Customer tolerance in the UK is fairly high, but should not be taken for granted.

In deciding strategic direction and formulating marketing strategy, any company needs to address issues of customer care, because of:

(a)    **Legal** constraints

(b)    Industry **codes of conduct**

(c)    The recognition that keeping existing customers happy is cheaper than acquiring new ones

(d)    The **value chain**. Customer care is part of after-sales service and offers an opportunity for differentiation. It is also a valuable source of information.

**Not all customers are the same**. Some appear for a single cash transaction and are never seen again. Others make frequent, regular purchases in large volumes, using credit facilities and building up a major relationship. Yet another type of customer purchases infrequently but in transactions of high value, as for instance in property markets. This variation will exist to a greater or lesser extent in all industries, though each will have a smaller typical range of behaviour. However, even within a single business, customers will vary significantly in the frequency and volume of their purchases, their reasons for buying, their sensitivity to price changes, their reaction to promotion and their overall attitude to the supplier and the product. **Segmentation** of the customer base can have a major impact on profitability, perhaps by simply tailoring promotion to suit the most attractive group of customers.

Many businesses sell to intermediaries rather than to the end consumer. Some sell to both categories; they have to recognise that **the intermediary is just as much a customer as the eventual consumer**. Examples are manufacturers who maintain their own sales organisation but appoint agents in geographically remote areas and companies who combine autonomous operations with franchising. While it is reasonable to give the highest priority to the needs of the ultimate consumer and insist on some control over the activities of the intermediary, it must be recognised that he will only perform well if his own needs are addressed. For instance, a selling agent who has invested heavily in stock after being given exclusive rights in an area should be consulted before further demands are made on his cash flow by the launch of a new product.

## 5.1 Customer retention

Variation in customer behaviour was mentioned above. The most important aspect of this variation is whether or not the customer comes back for more. Customers should be seen as potentially providing a lifetime of purchases so that **the turnover from a single individual over time might be very large indeed**. It is widely accepted that there is a non-linear relationship between customer retention and profitability in that **a fairly small amount of repeat purchasing generates significant profit**. This is because it is far more expensive in promotion and overhead costs to convert a non-buyer into an occasional buyer than to turn an occasional buyer into a frequent buyer. The repeat buyer does not have to be persuaded to give the product a try or be tempted by special deals; he needs less attention from sales staff and already has his credit account set up. New customers usually have to be won from competitors.

The process of retaining customers for a lifetime is an important one and one in which integrated marketing communications has an important role to play. Instead of one-way communication aimed solely at gaining a sale it is necessary to develop an effective two-way communication process to turn a **prospect into a lifetime advocate**. This is shown in the following ladder of customer loyalty.

*Ladder of customer loyalty*

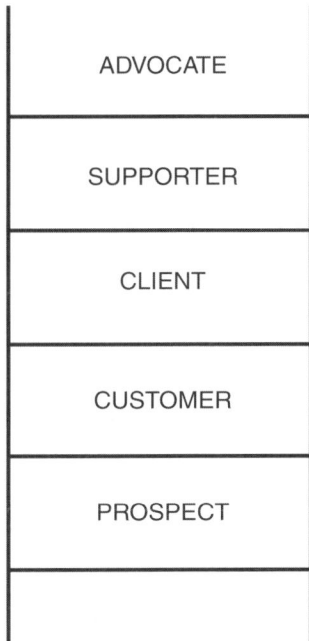

The purpose of relationship marketing is to establish, maintain and enhance relationships with customers and other parties so that the objectives of both parties involved are met.

(a) Because **service and industrial companies** have direct, regular and often multiple contacts with their customers (for example, the regular hotel guest who interacts with reception), the importance of 'part-time' marketers is increased. Customer contact with all employees is vital.

(b) **Trust and keeping promises**. To have an ongoing relationship, both parties need to trust each other and keep the promises they make. Marketing moves from one-off potentially manipulative exchanges towards co-operative relationships built on financial, social and structural benefits.

(c) **Network of exchange partners**. Customer relationships are important but so too are the relationships which organisations have with other parties such as suppliers, distributors, professional bodies, banks and trade associations.

## 5.2 Customers as assets

You might already be familiar with the concept of the customer as a **current asset** in financial terms – except in cash businesses eg, a customer is a debtor. **Goodwill** – or a company's reputation – is also considered an asset.

However, it will sometimes help you in evaluating strategic marketing decisions and persuading sceptical management accountants of your case if you consider the customer base as an **asset worth investing in**. After all, if you are looking for repeat business, you will expect future benefits from customers.

Today's highly competitive business environment means that customers are only retained if they are **very satisfied** with their purchasing experience. **Any lesser degree of satisfaction is likely to result in the loss of the customer**. Companies must be active in monitoring customer satisfaction **because very few will actually complain. They will simply depart**. Businesses which use intermediaries must be particularly active, since research shows that even when complaints are made, the principals hear about only a very small proportion of them.

## Marketing at Work

### Customer care

In the increasingly competitive service sector, it is no longer enough to promise customer satisfaction. Today, customer 'delight' is the stated aim for companies battling to retain and increase market share.

*British Airways*, which lists delighting customers among its new goals, says ensuring the safety of passengers and meeting all their needs drives everything it does. 'Other airlines fly the same routes using similar aircraft. What BA must do is provide a superior standard of efficiency, comfort and general service which persuades passengers to fly with us again and again,' says Mike Street, director of customer services at BA.

*Kwik-Fit*, the car repair group, is another company that has included customer delight in its mission statement. Its forecourt promises to deliver '100 per cent customer delight' in the supply and fitting of vehicle brakes, tyres and exhausts leaves little margin for mistakes – and none at all for making any customer unhappy. Staff attend courses at company-run centres covering 'all practical aspects of their work, customer care and general management techniques'. Commitment is encouraged by 'job security', opportunities for promotion and a reward package that includes profit-related pay and shares in the company.

Customer satisfaction is monitored via reply-paid questionnaires distributed after work is carried out and through a freephone helpline that is open 24 hours a day. Kwik-Fit also says its customer survey unit 'allows us to make contact with 5,000 customers a day, within 72 hours of their visit to a Kwik-Fit Centre.'

*Financial Times*

---

The most satisfactory way to retain customers is to offer them products which they perceive as providing **superior benefits** at any given price point. However, there are specific techniques which can increase customer retention. **Loyalty schemes** such as frequent flyer programmes, augment the product in the customer's eyes. The **club concept**, as used by *Sainsbury* and *Tesco*, offers small discounts on repeated purchases. The principal benefit of both these types of scheme, however, is the enhanced **knowledge of the customer** which they provide. Initial registration provides name, address and post code. Subsequent use of the loyalty card allows a detailed purchasing profile to be built up for individual customers. This enables highly targeted promotion and cross-selling later.

Research indicates that **the single largest reason why customers abandon a supplier is poor performance by front-line staff**. Any scheme for customer retention must address the need for careful selection and training of these staff. It is also a vital factor in **relationship marketing**.

## Marketing at Work

### Complaints

Complaints are among the best things that can happen to a company. They give managers the chance to rectify the situation over and above customer expectations; they give low cost feedback on how your products and services are perceived and handled properly, they create 'goodwill ambassadors' for your brand. In June, TMI, along with the Institute of Customer Service, the trade body, published research into how and why people in the UK complain and how they are dealt with. Among other findings, it confirmed the old management cliché that people tend not to complain they simply walk away. It is the expense of replacing customers that makes handling complaints well so cost-effective. 'We estimate that it costs five times as much to recruit a new customer as it does to keep an existing one,' says Julie Robinson, director of service delivery at *Virgin Atlantic*, the airline. 'As part of our staff training we need to show people that giving compensation when something goes wrong is not giving away the company's profits. Quite the opposite.' So what is the 'right' way to handle a complaint? Almost everyone agrees on step one: listen. 'You must listen to the customer,' says Ms Robinson, 'and not interrupt until you have under stood the problem.' But what then? Mr Brennan's company advocates an eight-step process. After saying 'thank you' comes explaining why you appreciate the complaint; apologising; promising you will do something about it straight away; asking for more information; correcting the mistake; checking customer satisfaction and, finally, preventing future mistakes. Mr Brennan is quick to point out the order of these steps. 'Many people ask for information first, such as name and address, making the customer feel as if they are somehow under suspicion. A complaint is a gift from a customer.' This unexpected generosity from the woman at the counter is confirmed by Stephen Walker, head of customer service at *Marks and Spencer*, the retailer, a UK company that is almost synonymous with handling complaints effectively. 'The information people give you when they complain,' he says, 'is invaluable to the organisation. We run a central database where complaints are logged, from which we can feed information back to the relevant buyer and suppliers, often on the same day. Customers are looking for a quick resolution of the problem and an assurance that we will do what we can to ensure it doesn't happen again.' Managers of big companies can also use complaints to develop one-to-one relationships with customers. 'Complaints offer an excellent chance to deal with customers face to face,' says Mr Walker. 'If you take a complaint seriously, and deal with it in a generous way, you can buy them for life.'

David Baker, *Financial Times, 2 August 2000*

## 5.3 Relationship marketing

**FAST FORWARD**

There is a move away from 'transactions' to **relationship marketing**. Firms aim to build loyalty, especially where switching costs are high and a lost customer is probably lost for a long time.

**Key concept**

**Relationship marketing** is defined very simply by *Grönroos* as the management of a firm's market relationships.

Much has been written in recent years on **relationship marketing**. *Gummesson* suggests it is a 'paradigm shift' requiring a **dramatic change** in marketing thinking and behaviour, not an add-on to traditional marketing.' In his book *Total Relationship Marketing*, he suggests that the core of marketing should no longer be the 4Ps, but 30Rs, which reflect the large number of complex relationships involved in business. *Kotler* says 'marketing can make promises but only the whole organisation can deliver satisfaction'. *Adcock* expands on this by remarking that relationship marketing can only exist when the marketing function fosters a customer-oriented **service culture** which supports the network of activities that deliver value to the customer. The metaphor of **marriage** has been used to describe relationship marketing, emphasising the nature of the necessary long-term commitment and mutual respect.

Relationship marketing is thus as much about **attitudes and assumptions** as it is about techniques. The marketing function's task is to inculcate habits of behaviour at all levels and in all departments that will enhance and strengthen the alliance. It must be remembered, however, that the effort involved in long-term relationship building is more appropriate in some markets than in others. Where customers are purchasing intermittently and **switching costs are low**, there is always a chance of business. This tends to be the pattern in **commodity markets**. Here, it is reasonable to take a **transactions approach** to marketing and treat each sale as unique. A **relationship marketing approach** is more appropriate where **switching costs are high** and a lost customer is thus probably lost for a long time. Switching costs are raised by such factors as the need for training on systems, the need for a large common installed base, high capital cost and the incorporation of purchased items into the customer's own designs.

The conceptual or philosophic nature of relationship marketing leads to a simple principle, that of **enhancing satisfaction by precision in meeting the needs of individual customers**. This depends on extensive **two-way communication** to establish and record the customer's characteristics and preferences and build a long-term relationship. *Adcock* mentions three important practical methods which contribute to this end.

- Building a **customer database**
- Developing **customer-oriented service systems**
- Extra **direct contacts with customers**

## 5.3.1 Databases

Modern **computer database systems** have enabled the rapid acquisition and retrieval of the individual customer's details, needs and preferences. Using this technology, relationship marketing enables telephone sales staff to greet the customer by name, know what he purchased last time, avoid taking his full delivery address, know what his credit status is and what he is likely to want. It enables new products to be developed that are precisely tailored to the customer's needs and new procedures to be established which enhance his satisfaction. It is the successor to **mass marketing**, which attempted to be customer-led but which could only supply a one-size-fits-all product. The end result of a relationship marketing approach is a mutually satisfactory relationship which continues indefinitely.

## 5.3.2 Customer care

Relationship marketing *extends* the principles of **customer care**. Customer care is about providing a product which is augmented by high quality of service, so that the customer is impressed during his transaction with the company. This can be done in ignorance of any detail of the customer other than those implicit in the immediate transaction. The customer is anonymous. **Relationship marketing is about having the customer come back for further transactions by ending the anonymity**. Adcock says 'To achieve results, it will be necessary to involve every department ... in co-ordinated activity aimed at maximising customer satisfaction'. The culture must be right; the right people must be recruited and trained; the structure, technology and processes must all be right.

It is inevitable that **problems** will arise. A positive way of dealing with errors must be designed into the customer relationship. *W Edwards Deming*, the prominent writer on quality, tells us that front line sales people cannot usually deal with the causes of mistakes as they **are built into the products, systems and organisation structure**. It is therefore necessary for management to promote vertical and horizontal interaction in order to spur changes to eliminate the **sources** of mistakes.

It is inevitable that there will be multiple contacts between customer and supplier organisations. Each contact is an opportunity to enhance or to prejudice the relationship, so staff throughout the supplier organisation must be aware of their marketing responsibilities. Two way communication should be encouraged so that the relationship can grow and deepen. There is a link here to the database mentioned above: extra contacts provide more information. Confidential information must, of course, be treated with due respect.

 Marketing at Work

### Customer Loyalty

The problem with profitable customers is retaining them, because they will attract the attention of your competitors. Building customer relationships may be the answer to both types of problem.

Relationship marketing is grounded in the idea of establishing a learning relationship with customers. At the lower end, building a relationship can create cross-selling opportunities that may make the overall relationship profitable. For example, some retail banks have tried selling credit cards to less profitable customers. With valuable customers, customer relationship management may make them more loyal and

willing to invest additional funds. In banking, these high-end relationships are often managed through private bankers, whose goals are not only to increase customer satisfaction and retention, but also to cross-sell and bring in investment.

In determining which customers are worth the cost of long-term relationships, it is useful to consider their lifetime value. This depends on:

- Current profitability computed at the customer level
- The propensity of those customers to stay loyal
- Expected revenues and costs of servicing such customers over the lifetime of the relationship

Building relationships makes most sense for customers whose lifetime value to the company is the highest. Thus, building relationships should focus on customers who are currently the most profitable, likely to be the most profitable in the future, or likely to remain with the company for the foreseeable future and have acceptable levels of profitability.

The goal of relationship management is to increase customer satisfaction and to minimise any problems. By engaging in 'smarter' relationships, a company can learn customers' preferences and develop trust. Every contact point with the customer can be seen as a chance to record information and learn preferences. Complaints and errors must be recorded, not just fixed and forgotten. Contact with customers in every medium, whether over the Internet, through a call centre, or through personal contact, is recorded and centralised.

Many companies are beginning to achieve this goal by using customer relationship management (CRM) software. Data, once collected an centralised, can be used to customise service. In addition, the database can be analysed to detect patterns that can suggest better ways to serve customers in general. A key aspect of this dialogue is to learn and record preferences. There are two ways to determine customers' preferences: transparently and collaboratively.

Discovering preferences transparently means that the marketer learns the customers' needs without actually involving them. For example, the Ritz Carlton Hotel makes a point of observing the choices that guests make and recording them. If a guest requests extra pillows, then extra pillows will be provided every time that person visits. At upmarket retailers, personal shoppers will record customers' preferences in sizes, styles, brands, colours and price ranges and notify them when new merchandise appears or help them choose accessories.

Barbara Kahn, *Financial Times, 9 October 2000*

## 5.3.3 Differences between transactional and relationship marketing

| Transactional | Relationship |
|---|---|
| Importance of single sale | Importance of customer relation |
| Importance of product features | Importance of customer benefits |
| Short time scale | Longer time scale |
| Less emphasis on service | High customer service |
| Quality is concern of production | Quality is concern of all |
| Competitive commitment | High customer commitment |
| Persuasive communication | Regular communication |

*Marketing, Principles and Practice:* Adcock, Bradfield, Halborg and Ross

Adcock *et al* point out that the most important issue in customer retention is focusing marketing effort on activities that promote a strong relationship rather than a single transaction.

### 5.3.4 The relationship marketing mix

By now you are familiar with the 4Ps of the basic marketing mix. Relationship marketing is highly dependent upon a fifth P: **people**. The features of the basic 4Ps must support the commitment to developing mutually beneficial  customer relationships. The **behaviour of the people** involved in the customer relationship is even more important, because relationship marketing success depends on their motivation to achieve it. In turn, that motivation depends to a great extent upon the leadership exercised by marketing managers. It is not enough to expect self-motivation because *all* staff are involved, not just those with a sales role.

### 5.3.5 Implementing relationship marketing programmes

*Kotler* suggests five steps, suitable for business-to-business or service markets.

**Step 1**   Identify **key customers**: (see below)

**Step 2**   Assign a **relationship manager** to each

**Step 3**   Develop clear **job descriptions**

**Step 4**   Appoint a manager to supervise the relationship managers

**Step 5**   Develop long-term plans for developing **relationships**

### 5.3.6 Sustaining the relationship

(a)   Offer **superior customer value** by personalising the interaction, involving two-way communication. This is essential for service industries such as life assurance. Hotels have systems that remember guests' preferences.

(b)   Be trustworthy and **reliable**, for example by offering a replacement.

(c)   **Tighten the connection**. Once the relationship is established, it must be nurtured to make it harder for the customer to defect.

(d)   **Co-ordinating capabilities**. The more successful the relationship, the greater the risk of imitation.

Kotler's approach is suitable for business-to-business markets or personal services such as financial advice. Some firms, however, have sought through data mining techniques to get a long-term view of the customer.

**Loyalty cards** are designed to reward customers for repeat purchase. They:

- Collect information about customer purchasing habits, enabling targeted marketing communication

- Reward customers for repeat purchase, to encourage sales volumes

Loyalty schemes vary in the benefit they offer.

(a)   Recent UK research indicates that owners of 'loyalty' cards spend more, but they are not necessarily loyal.

(b)   Furthermore, most customers still shop around and have one or more loyalty cards.

(c)   **Loyalty cards may prove to be an expensive failure**. Safeway in the UK has abandoned its UK loyalty card, preferring to invest in other forms of promotional activity determined by stores individually.

## 5.3.7 Key accounts

So far we have considered the retention of customers as an unquestionably desirable objective. **However, for many businesses a degree of discretion will be advisable**. 'Key' does not mean large. A customer's **potential** is very important. The definition of a key account depends on the circumstances. Key account management is about managing the future.

Customers can be assessed for desirability according to such criteria as the profitability of their accounts; the prestige they confer; the amount of non-value adding administrative work they generate; the cost of the selling effort they absorb; the rate of growth of their accounts and, for industrial customers, of the turnover of their own businesses; their willingness to adopt new products; and their credit history. Such analyses will almost certainly conform to a Pareto distribution and show, for instance that 80% of profit comes from 20% of the customers, while a different 20% generate most of the credit control or administrative problems. Some businesses will be very aggressive about getting rid of their problem customers, but a more positive technique would be to concentrate effort on the most desirable ones. These are the **key accounts** and the company's relationship with them can be built up by appointing **key account managers**.

Key account management is often seen as a high level selling task, but should in fact be a business wide team effort about relationships and customer retention. It can be seen as a form of co-operation with the customer's supply chain management function. The key account manager's role is to integrate the efforts of the various parts of the organisation in order to deliver an enhanced service. This idea has long been used by advertising agencies and was successfully introduced into aerospace manufacturing over 40 years ago. It will be the key account manager's role to maintain communication with the customer, note any developments in his circumstances, deal with any problems arising in the relationship and develop the long-term business relationship.

The key account relationship may progress through several stages.

(a) At first, there may be a typical adversarial sales-purchasing relationship with emphasis on price, delivery and so on. Attempts to widen contact with the customer organisation will be seen as a threat by its purchasing staff.

(b) Later, the sales staff may be able to foster a mutual desire to increase understanding by wider contacts. Trust may increase.

(c) A mature partnership stage may be reached in which there are contacts at all levels and information is shared. The key account manager becomes responsible for integrating the partnership business processes and contributing to the customer's supply chain management. High 'vendor ratings', stable quality, continuous improvement and fair pricing are taken for granted.

**Exam tip**

Customer relationship management (CRM) was the subject of a Part B question in the draft specimen paper for this exam. The question called for a critical evaluation of CRM, illustrated by examples.

## Chapter Roundup

- The exact components of the marketing mix need to be put together with judgement and creativity. Every product, market and every stage in the product's life will require a different balance of the marketing mix ingredients.

- The conceptual nature of the product interacts with strategic issues such as branding and portfolio management.

- Price represents the revenue earning side of the mix. Influences on pricing policy are:

    – The customer
    – Competitors and the environment
    – The company

    Pricing involves a set of trade-offs between these three elements, more so, perhaps, than other aspects of the mix.

- Services differ from physical products in that they are intangible, perishable and inherently variable, and their consumption cannot be separated in time from their production.

    These factors complicate services marketing and make it necessary to manage three extra Ps: people, processes and physical evidence.

- Much of the marketing mix activity goes to the development of **brands**, which are what the customers identify. Brands embody a set of expectations about the product. A brand image exists in the customer's mind.

- There are several basic branding strategies: company, umbrella, range and individual product.

- The added value conferred by a brand is largely subjective. In blind testing many consumers cannot tell the difference between different products; however, they will exhibit a preference for a strong brand name when shown it. Apart from the quantity and functionality of the product, brand equity is built on suggestion rather than substance.

- Brand building is a logical process that can proceed gradually, step by step towards a position of strength.

- A brand can be used on a wide range of products and services if its values are appropriate.

- At times, the performance of a brand will falter and managers will attempt to rectify the situation by enhancing sales volume and improving profits in other ways.

- Brands, like most aspects of marketing practice, require a decision about standardisation or adaptation when taken into the global marketplace.

- Integrated marketing communications encompasses all forms of communication between an organisation and its customers and potential customers. More broadly, it is **all forms of communication by an organisation with its environment**, including internal communication with employees and managers.

- Strategic issues in marketing communication include, besides integration, media and audience, ethics and the problem of measuring response.

- In recent times emphasis has increased on building and maintaining good long-term **relationships** with customers. This is because such relationships are more profitable than constantly searching for new customers owing to repeat purchasing, ease of service and so on.

- There is a move away from 'transactions' to **relationship marketing**. Firms aim to build loyalty, especially where switching costs are high and a lost customer is probably lost for a long time.

## Quick Quiz

1   What is the marketing mix?

2   What is meant by the terms 'push' and 'pull' strategy?

3   What is a product, defined from the customer's point of view?

4   Identify the basic influences on price.

5   What is the main concept underpinning integrated marketing communications?

6   What are the four characteristics distinguishing most services from most products?

7   What constitutes a brand?

8   Who benefits from branding?

9   Identify two strategies for NPD.

10  Distinguish between penetration and skimming strategies.

11  What is integrated marketing communications?

12  What is relationship marketing?

## Answers to Quick Quiz

1   The marketing mix is the set of controllable variables that firm uses to influence the target market.

2   **'Push'** strategy is about influencing the distribution channel to accept the product so that it is available to consumers. **'Pull'** strategy is about influencing the consumer so that demand draws the product into the distribution channel.

3   A package of benefits meeting particular needs

4   Customer, competition, supplier

5   Marketing communications should be integrated with business strategy

6   Services, compared with physical goods are intangible, inseparable, perishable and variable in quality

7   A branded product has a distinctive identity and added values that exist in the consumer's mind

8   All parties to the transaction: the customers and the management and owners of the supplying company

9   Leader and follower

10  Penetration sets low prices to achieve high volumes rapidly. Skimming sets prices high to achieve high unit profits early on

11  Communication that delivers an utterly consistent message

12  The management of the company's marketing relationships

## Action Programme Review

1     (a)     Ageing population: people may be physically incapable of trawling the supermarkets

        (b)     Increased traffic congestion: people may resent taking longer to drive to the shops

        (c)     More time at work: less time for shopping

        (d)     Once Internet shopping takes off, mail order will have the benefits of e-mail. Tesco currently has around 400,000 customers for its Internet shopping service

2     The classic example in the UK is *Hoover*, which is now a generic term for any vacuum cleaner and is even used as a verb meaning 'to clean with a vacuum cleaner'. Words you may be surprised to know were once brand names include nylon, aspirin, cellophane and escalator: all have lost trade mark legal status. *Kleenex* and *Xerox* almost went the same way.

Now try Question 6 at the end of the Study Text

# The global product portfolio

## Syllabus content

- Product strategies and the role of new product development in competitive strategy
- The strategic management of the global portfolio and the expanded marketing mix

# Introduction

Product/market decisions are perhaps the most critical area in corporate planning, and the issue that sets international marketing apart from domestic marketing probably more than any other.

In this chapter we examine the management of the global portfolio. We have already looked at the interaction of the product and market life cycles: in Section 1 we examine the plc model in more detail and consider the overall management of the global product development.

The management of a product portfolio in a global setting presents further complications to do with the suitability of products for different international markets, as does new product development. These matters take up most of the rest of this chapter, which concludes with a consideration of services as products.

# 1 The product life cycle and portfolio analysis

**FAST FORWARD**

The essence of a product is the **satisfaction** purchased by the buyer. The same physical object, however, can have different uses and meanings.

## 1.1 The product

A product may be said to satisfy needs by possessing the following attributes.

(a) **Tangible attributes**

- Availability and delivery
- Performance
- Price
- Design

(b) **Intangible attributes**

- Image
- Perceived value

These features are interlinked. A product has a tangible **price**, for example, but for your money you obtain the **value** that you perceive the product to have. You may get satisfaction from paying a very high price for your wine glasses, because this says something about your status in life: the glasses become part of your self-image.

### 1.1.1 Product classification

The term consumer goods is used to distinguish goods that are sold directly to the person who will ultimately use them from goods that are sold to people that want them to make other products. The latter are known as industrial goods.

### 1.1.2 Classification of consumer goods

(a) **Convenience goods**. The weekly groceries are a typical example. There is a further distinction between **staple goods** like bread and potatoes, and **impulse buys**, like the unexpected bar of chocolate that you find at the supermarket checkout. Brand awareness is extremely important in this sector.

(b) **Shopping goods**. These are more durable items, like furniture or washing machines. This sort of purchase is usually only made after a good deal of **advance planning and shopping around**.

(c) **Speciality goods**. These are items like jewellery or the more expensive items of clothing.

(d) **Unsought goods**. These are goods that you did not realise you needed! Typical examples would be the sort of items that are found in catalogues that arrive in the post.

## Action Programme 1

Think of three products that you have bought recently, one low-priced, one medium-priced, and one expensive item. Identify the product attributes that made you buy each of these items and categorise them according to the classifications shown above.

### 1.1.3 Classification of industrial goods

- **Installations**, eg major items of plant and machinery like a factory assembly line
- **Accessories**, such as printers for PC
- **Raw materials**: plastic, metal, wood, foodstuffs chemicals and so on
- **Components**: the Intel microchip in most PCs
- **Supplies**: office stationery, cleaning materials and the like

There are very few **pure products** or **pure services**. Most products have some service attributes and many services are in some way attached to products. However, we shall consider some of the features that characterise service marketing later on in this chapter.

## 1.2 The product life cycle

**FAST FORWARD**

The product life cycle is most useful as a control tool and least useful as an aid to forecasting.

We discussed the topic of life cycles in some detail earlier in this Study Text. We return to the topic here, partly as a reminder and partly to introduce new material pertinent to this chapter.

**Key concept**

The **product life cycle** asserts that products are born (or introduced), grow to reach maturity and then enter old age and decline.

Despite criticisms, the product life cycle (PLC) has proved to be a useful control device for monitoring the progress of new products after introduction. As Professor Robin Wensley of Warwick University puts it:

'The value of the product life cycle depends on its use, ie **it has greater value as one goes down the scale** from a predictive or forecasting tool, through a planning tool to a control tool.'

The profitability and sales position of a product can be expected to change over time. The product life cycle is an attempt to recognise distinct stages in a product's sales history. Here is the classic representation of the PLC.

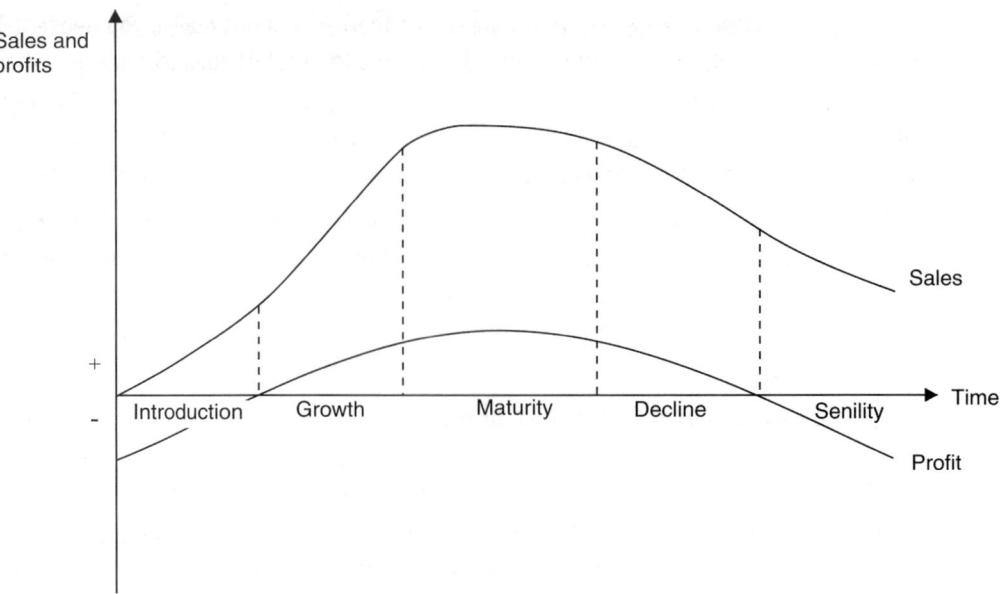

## Action Programme 2

Can you think of any products that have disappeared in your lifetime or are currently in decline?

## Action Programme 3

Where do you consider the following products or services to be in their product life cycle?

- Mobile telephones
- Baked beans
- Satellite television
- Cigarettes
- Carbon paper
- Mortgages
- Writing implements
- Car alarms
- Organically grown fruit and vegetables

### 1.2.1 Criticisms of the product life cycle

**FAST FORWARD**    With real products, the stages of the PLC can be difficult to recognise and may not conform to the basic model. Both internal strategic decisions and the state of competition in the market have an influence.

Although it is widely used, the PLC remains controversial. There have been contradictory papers directed at establishing or refuting the validity of the product life cycle by empirical tests. *Polli and Cook* concluded that the PLC is most likely to be relevant for products where consumer demand is high. From these results, Polli and Cook concluded that 'for given categories of goods the product life cycle can be a useful model for marketing planning'.

*Dhalla and Yuspeh* attempt to expose what they term the myth of the PLC. They point out that:

'in the absence of the technological breakthroughs *many product classes appear to be almost impervious to normal life cycle pressures, provided they satisfy some basic need*, be it transportation, entertainment, health, nourishment or the desire to be attractive.'

Whilst accepting the possibility of the existence of a **product** life cycle, the paper denies the existence of **brand** life cycles. The authors assert that any underlying PLC is a *dependent* variable which is **determined by marketing actions**; rather than an *independent* variable to which **companies should adapt**. In other words, if a brand appears to be in decline, this is not happening as a result of market changes, but because of either **reduced or inappropriate marketing** by the producer, or better marketing by competitors.

 Marketing at Work

### Ipana toothpaste

*Dhalla and Yuspeh* consider that this notion of the PLC as a binding constraint has led to many marketing errors. They cite the example of Ipana, an American toothpaste, that was marketed by a leading packaged goods company until 1968 when it was abandoned after entering decline. Two Minnesota businessmen who acquired the brand name, with hardly any promotion, generated 250,000 dollars sales in the first seven months of operations. Intelligent marketing, they point out, has kept such brands as Budweiser Beer, Colgate toothpaste and Maxwell House around long after competitive brands have disappeared.

The Marketing Science Institute examined over 100 product categories and concluded

> '.... Our results suggest strongly that the life cycle concept, when used without careful formulation and testing as an explicit model, is more likely to be misleading than useful.'

Dhalla and Yuspeh come to the general conclusion that managers adhering to the sequences of marketing strategies recommended for succeeding stages of the cycle are likely to do more harm than good. In particular, they cite the potential neglect of existing brands and wasteful expenditures on replacement 'me-too' products.

### 1.2.2 Criticisms of the practical value of the PLC

(a) Stages cannot easily be defined.

(b) Some products have no maturity phase, and go straight from growth to decline. Others have a second growth period after an initial decline. Some have virtually no introductory period and go straight into a rapid growth phase.

(c) **Strategic decisions can change a product's life cycle**: for example, by repositioning a product in the market, its life can be extended. If strategic planners decide what a product's life is going to be, opportunities to extend the life cycle might be ignored.

(d) **Competition** varies in different industries, and the **strategic implications** of the product life cycle will vary according to the nature of the competition. The traditional life cycle presupposes increasing competition and falling prices during the growth phase of the market and also the gradual elimination of competitors in the decline phase. This pattern of events is not always found in financial markets, where there is a tendency for competitors to follow-my-leader very quickly. Competition may build up well ahead of demand. The rapid development of various banking services is an example of this: for example, with bank cash dispenser cards, when one bank developed the product all the other major banks followed immediately.

## Action Programme 4

There must be many products that have been around for as long as you can remember. Companies like *Cadbury's* have argued that they spend so much on brand maintenance that they should be able to show a value for their brands as an asset in their accounts (though accountants find this hard to swallow).

Think of some examples of products that go on and on from your own experience and try to identify what it is about them that makes them so enduring.

### 1.2.3 The strategic implications of the product life cycle

**FAST FORWARD**    If specific PLC stages can be recognised, strategic control may be facilitated.

Having made these reservations about product life cycle planning, the strategic implications of the product life cycle might be as follows.

| | Phase | | | |
|---|---|---|---|---|
| | *Introduction* | *Growth* | *Maturity* | *Decline* |
| **Product** | Quality and functionality may be improvable. Product design and development are a key to success. No standard product and frequent design changes (eg DVD players and recorders). | Competitor's products have marked quality differences and technical differences. Quality and functionality improve. Product reliability may be important. | Products become more standardised and differences between competing products less distinct. | Products even less differentiated. Quality becomes more variable. |
| **Customers** | Initial customers willing to pay high prices. Customers need to be convinced about buying. | Customers increase in number. | Mass market Market saturation Repeat-buying Markets become segmented. | Customers are sophisticated buyers of a product they understand well. |
| **Marketing issues** | High advertising and sales promotion costs High prices possible Distribution problematic | High advertising costs still, but as a % of sales, costs are falling Prices falling More distributors | Segment specific Choose best distribution Brand image | Less money spent on advertising and sales promotion |

| Phase | | | | |
|---|---|---|---|---|
| | *Introduction* | *Growth* | *Maturity* | *Decline* |
| **Competition** | Few or no competitors | More competitors enter the market. Barriers to entry can be important. | Competition at its keenest: on prices, branding, servicing customers, packaging | Competitors gradually exit from the market. Exit barriers can be important. |
| **Profit margins** | High prices but losses due to high fixed costs | High prices, high contribution margins, and increasing profit margins High P/E ratios for quoted companies in the growth market | Falling prices but good profit margins due to high sales volume High prices in some market segments | Prices are still low and profits fall as sales volume falls, since total contribution falls towards the level of fixed costs. Some increases in prices may occur in the late decline stage. |
| **Manufacturing and distribution** | Overcapacity High production costs Few distribution channels High labour skill content in manufacture | Undercapacity Move towards mass production and less reliance on skilled labour Distribution channels flourish and getting adequate distribution is a key to marketing success. | Optimum capacity Low labour skills Distribution channels fully developed, but less successful channels might be cut. | Overcapacity because mass production techniques still used Distribution channels dwindling |

## 1.2.4 Control

The management of a product should fit its prevailing life cycle stage, as each stage has different financial and risk characteristics.

**Implications of each stage**

(a) **Development**. Money will be spent on market research and product development. Cash flows are negative and there is a high business risk.

(b) **Launches** require expensive promotion campaigns.

(c) **Growth**. The market grows, as does the demand for the product. Risks are competitor action.

    (i) The market price mix might turn out to be inappropriate for the product (eg the price is set too high).

    (ii) Competitors will enter, thereby reducing the profits that can be earned.

(d) **Maturity**. Few new competitors will enter the market. Risk is low, so the concentration is on profit.

At all stages, the **risk and return profile** of the product can be managed.

(a) Appropriate product-market strategies, such as innovation, new advertising, changing the product, finding new markets.

(b) Raising entry barriers.

Increased marketing expenditure may have the effect of reducing risk, commensurate with the decreased return.

**Each stage of the product life cycle has different needs in terms of information and financial control**

| | Launch | Growth | Maturity | Decline |
|---|---|---|---|---|
| **Characteristics** | High business risk. Negative net cash flow. DCF evaluation for overall investment | High business risk. Neutral net cash flow | Medium business risk. Positive cash flow | Low risk. Neutral-positive cash flow |
| **Critical success factors** | Time to launch | Market share growth. Sustaining competitive advantage | Contribution per unit of scarce resource. Customer retention. | Timely exit |
| **Information needs** | Market research into size and demand | Market growth, share. Diminishing returns. Competitor marketing strategies | Comparative competitor costs. Limiting factors | Rate of decline; best time to leave; reliable sale values of assets |
| **Financial and other controls** | Strategic 'milestones'. Physical evaluation. Mainly non-financial measures owing to volatility (eg rate of take up by consumers) | Discounted cash flow<br>Market share<br>Marketing objectives | ROI<br>Profit margin<br>Maintaining market share | Free cash flow (for investment elsewhere) |

## 1.3 Product portfolio planning

FAST FORWARD

**Product portfolio planning** aims to achieve a portfolio that works well in financial, marketing and production terms.

A company's product mix (or product assortment or portfolio) is all the product lines and items that the company offers for sale.

| Product mix | Characteristics of company's product line |
|---|---|
| **Width** | Number of product lines |
| **Depth** | Average number of items per product line |
| **Consistency** | Closeness of items in product range in terms of marketing or production characteristics. |

The product mix can be extended in a number of ways.

- Introducing **variations** in models or style
- Changing the **quality** of products offered at different price levels
- Developing **associated items**, such as a paint manufacturer introducing paint brushes
- Developing **new products** that have little technical or marketing relationships to the existing range

**Marketing at Work**

**Gum**

The market for functional gums, which deliver a real or imagined health benefit or stimulation, is growing fast. *Gumtech International's* US product portfolio ranges from the conventional, such as *Chew & Sooth*, for sore throats, to *Sugar Blocker* gum, which claims to reduce craving for sweets. Other US companies such as *Balchem Encapsulates*, which this month launched a vitamin C gum, and the *Quigley Corporation*, which markets *Cold-Eeze*, a homeopathic bubble gum have also carved out niche markets. Even *Wrigley's* – the world's largest chewing gum maker – has successfully launched *Ice White*, a teeth-whitening gum, and *Air-waves*, a decongestant, in Europe, and has test marketed a caffeine gum in the US. The company is reluctant to talk about its plans, but a spokesman confirms further research is taking place. One confectionery analyst says: 'I would expect gum manufacturers to start leveraging their existing products into different areas, taking advantage of gum's excellent properties as a pharmaceutical delivery mechanism. The growing interest in herbal remedies and anti-depressants such as St John's wort, could be an important driver.' It would be easy to dismiss functional gum as a bizarre niche product or the stuff of science fiction. But the latest predictions from *Datamonitor* show chewing gum in the fastest growing sector in the UK's moribund confectionery market. It is expected to grow by 8.3 per cent over the next four years, driven by sugar-free and functional ranges. If nothing else, this should give the UK's beleaguered sweet makers something to chew over.

*Marketing Week, 6 July 2000*

**Managing the product portfolio** involves broad issues such as what role should a product play in the portfolio, how should resources be allocated between products and what should be expected from each product. Maintaining balance between well-established and new products, between cash-generative and cash-using products and between growing and declining products is very important. If products are not suitable for the market or not profitable, then corporate objectives will be jeopardised. Equally, if potentially profitable products are ignored or not given sufficient support then crucial marketing opportunities will be lost.

It follows that there are benefits to be gained from using a **systematic approach to the management of the product range**. Marketing is not an exact science and there is no definitive approach or technique which can determine which products should remain, which should be pruned and how resources should be shared across the current product range. There are, however, techniques which can aid decision making.

### 1.3.1 Product-market matrices

**FAST FORWARD**

The product-market matrix is used to classify a product or a business **according to the features of the market and the features of the product**.

Matrices are often used at the level of corporate strategy to determine the relative positions of businesses and select strategies for resource allocation between them. The same techniques are equally valuable when considering products and the management of the product portfolio. The two most widely used approaches are the **Boston Consulting Group (BCG) growth-share matrix and the General Electric (GE) Business Screen**.

### 1.3.2 The BCG matrix

The BCG matrix, illustrated below, classifies products (or businesses) on the basis of their **market share relative to that of their competitors** and the **rate of growth in the market** as a whole. The split on the horizontal axis is based on a market share identical to that of the firm's **nearest competitor**, while the precise location of the split on the vertical axis will depend on the rate of growth in the market. Products

are positioned in the matrix as circles with a diameter proportional to their sales revenue. The underlying assumption in the growth-share matrix is that a larger relative market share will enable the business to benefit from economies of scale, lower unit costs and thus higher margins.

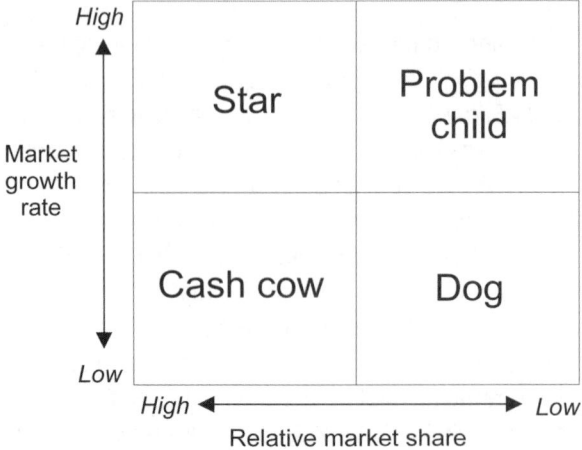

On the basis of this classification, each product (or, working at a higher level, each strategic business unit) will then fall into one of four broad categories.

(a)   A **problem child** has a small relative market share in a high growth industry. The generic product is clearly popular, but customer support for the company brand is limited. A small market share implies that competitors are in a strong position and that if the product is to be successful it will **require substantial funds**, and a new marketing mix. If the market looks good and the product is viable, then the company should consider a **build** strategy to increase market share. This would require the commitment of funds to permit more active marketing. If the future looks less promising then the company should consider the possibility of withdrawing the product. The problem child is sometimes referred to as the **question mark**.

(b)   A **star** is a product with a high relative market share in a high growth industry. By implication, **the star has potential for generating significant earnings** currently and in the future. However, at this stage it may still require substantial marketing expenditures to maintain this position, but would probably be regarded as a **good investment for the future**.

(c)   A **cash cow** has a high relative market share but in a mature slow growth market. Typically, it is a well established product with a high degree of consumer loyalty. Product development costs are low and the marketing campaign is well established. The cash cow will normally make a **substantial contribution to overall profitability**. The appropriate strategy will vary according to its precise position. If market growth is reasonably strong then a **hold** strategy will be appropriate, but if growth or share are weakening, then a **harvest** strategy may be more sensible, cutting back on marketing expenditure and maximise short-term cash flow.

(d)   A **dog** is a product characterised by low relative market share and low growth. Also, typically a well established product, it is apparently losing consumer support and may have cost disadvantages. The usual strategy would be to consider **divestment** unless cash flow position is strong, in which case the product would be **harvested** in the short term prior to deletion from the product range.

Implicit in the matrix is the notion that **markets are dynamic**. The typical new product is likely to appear in the problem child category to begin with; if it looks promising and is given effective marketing, it might be expected to become a star, then, as markets mature, a cash cow and finally a dog. The suggestion that most products will move through these stages does not weaken the role played by marketing. On the contrary, it strengthens it, since poor marketing may mean that a product moves from being a problem child to a dog without making any substantial contribution to profitability. Equally, of course, good marketing may enable the firm to **prolong** the star and cash cow phases, thus maximising **cash flow** from the product.

The framework provided by the matrix can offer guidance in terms of developing **appropriate strategies** for products and in maintaining a **balanced product portfolio**, ensuring that there are enough cash-generating products to match the cash-using products.

However, there are a number of **criticisms** of the BCG model.

(a) It **oversimplifies product analysis**. It concentrates only on two dimensions of product markets, size and market share, and therefore may encourage marketing management to pay too little attention to other market features.

(b) **Not all companies or products will be designed for market leadership**, in which case describing performance in terms of relative market share may be of limited relevance. Many firms undertaking this approach have found that all their products were technically dogs and yet were still very profitable, so they saw no need to divest. Firms following a **'niche' strategy** will commonly find their markets are (intentionally) small.

(c) The matrix **assumes a relationship between profitability and market share**. There is empirical evidence for this in many, but not all industries, particularly where there is demand for more customised products.

(d) The basic approach **may oversimplify the nature of products** in large diversified firms with many divisions. In these cases, each division may contain products that fit into several of the categories.

Despite these criticisms, the BCG matrix can offer guidance in achieving a balanced portfolio. However, given the difficulty of generalising such an approach to deal with all products and markets, its recommendations should be interpreted with care.

## 1.3.3 The General Electric Business Screen

The basic approach of the GE Business Screen is similar to that of the BCG matrix, but it includes a broader range of company and market factors in assessing the position of a product. This matrix classifies products (or businesses) according to **industry attractiveness** and **company strengths**. Typical examples of the factors that determine industry attractiveness and company strength are given below.

(a) **Industry attractiveness**: market size, market growth, competitive climate, stability of demand, ease of market entry, industry capacity, levels of investment, nature of regulation, profitability.

(b) **Company strengths**: relative market share, company image, production capacity, production costs, financial strengths, product quality, distribution systems, control over prices/margins, benefits of patent protection.

Although a broader range of factors are used in the classification of products, this is still a **highly subjective assessment**. Products are positioned on the grid with circles representing market size and segments representing market shares. The strategy for an individual product is then suggested on the basis of that position. It is interesting to note the apparent similarity in recommendations between the BCG matrix and the GE matrix; the basic difference arises from the method of classification.

|  | Attractive | Average | Unattractive |
|---|---|---|---|
| **Strong** | Invest for growth | Invest selectively for growth | Develop for income |
| **Average** | Invest selectively and build | Develop selectively for income | Harvest or divest |
| **Weak** | Develop selectively Build on Strengths | Harvest | Divest |

Company Strength (vertical axis) — Industry attractiveness (horizontal axis)

The broader approach of the GE matrix emphasises the attempt to match distinctive competences within the company to conditions within the market place. Difficulties associated with measurement and classification mean that the results of such an exercise must be **interpreted with great care** and not seen as a prescription for strategic decisions.

### 1.3.4 New and old products

The energy and effort placed into adding new products and brands to the portfolio is seldom mirrored by a similar effort in identifying and weeding out the weak or declining. One of the benefits of effective marketing strategy is to ensure the organisation's resources are directed to the most suitable market segments; this can easily be thrown away by a **proliferation of products**.

## Marketing at Work

**Product choice**

At one time, *Procter & Gamble* was selling 35 variations of *Crest* toothpaste and different nappies for girls and boys. The average supermarket in America devotes 20 ft of shelving to medicine for coughs and colds. Most of this choice is trumpery. New York-based Market Intelligence Service found that only 7% of the 25,500 new packaged products launched in America in 1996 really offered new or added benefits.

In fact, more choice does not translate into more sales. *Ravi Dhar*, of Yale University, examined how students decided what to buy, based on the number of versions of each product-category on offer. As the choice increased, so did the likelihood that students would not buy anything at all. *John Gourville* at Harvard Business School believes that some types of choice are more trouble than others. His – as yet incomplete – research suggests that consumers like to be offered choices in a single dimension: different sizes of cereal packet, say. If they are asked to make many trade-offs, such as whether to buy a computer with a modem or speakers, consumers start to feel anxious or even irritated.

*The Economist*

# 2 Product life cycles and international marketing mix decisions

A product's stage on the product life cycle may vary from country to country, and different marketing strategies will be appropriate in each case.

Many marketing mistakes have been made because firms have failed to take into account the fact that in different countries a product may be at different stages in its product life cycle.

Products, prices, marketing communications and channels of distribution need to be adapted as a product ages during its life cycle. The marketing mix programme for a new product should be fundamentally different from the mix programme for a mature product.

The product life cycle is relevant to international marketing management. Traditionally many firms have tended only to operate at home as long as performance there was satisfactory. Then, when domestic performance declined, they tried to close the gap by exporting. But this is possible only if there are **different product life cycle patterns** in different countries. In the diagram on the following page, the product is in the decline stage in the home market, in the growth stage in country X, and in the introduction stage in country Y.

*Product life cycles in different countries*

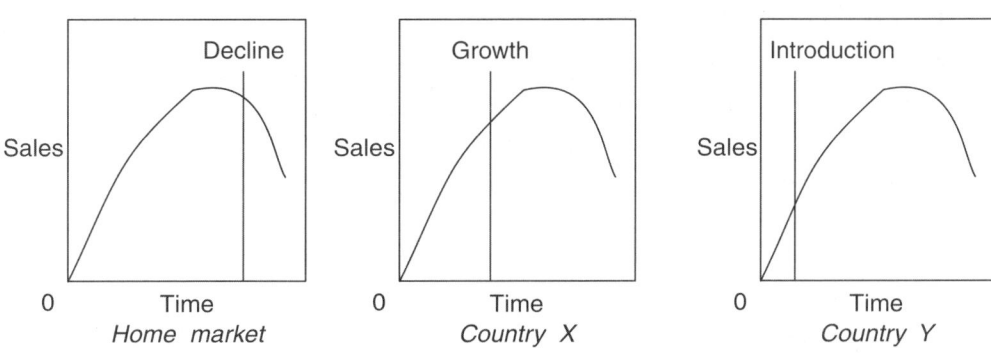

This approach was very convenient. Firms were simply able to classify markets according to their economic development and launch declining products in rapid succession into countries with progressively less market development. Nowadays, however, this type of strategy is less feasible, although not entirely impossible. The revolution in communications among countries during recent years has narrowed the time gap between when saturation occurs in the home market and the last overseas market entered. Hence, the **total** duration of the profit life cycle, aggregated across all the firm's markets, has shortened. For some products the profit life cycle pattern is exactly the same for home sales as for overseas markets.

As a result of these developments, international marketing must consider many markets simultaneously, with a view to implementing a global introduction.

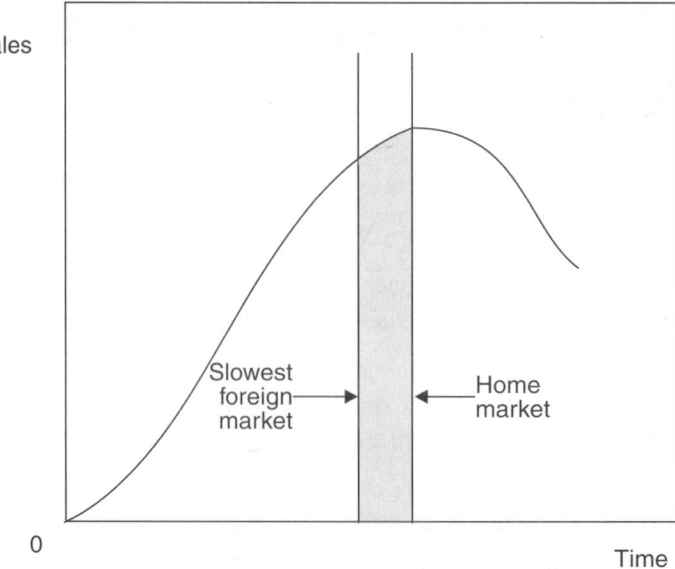

This is necessary to ensure that the product is launched in all potential markets before rivals have time to pre-empt the firm and to ensure that introduction everywhere coincides with the most appropriate demand conditions.

 Marketing at Work

The old *Volkswagen* Beetle car was manufactured and sold in Mexico, long after it ceased production in Germany, as a cheap means of transport. Production finally ceased in 2004.

## 2.1 Product life cycle and the market/country

**FAST FORWARD**

The ITLC is used in developing long-term product strategy. It postulates that many products pass through a cycle during which high income, mass-consumption countries are initially exporters but subsequently lose their export markets and ultimately become importers of the product.

**Key concept**

The **international trade life cycle** (ITLC) is the adaptation of the product life model to international conditions.

From the perspective of the initiator high income country, the pattern of development is as follows.

(a)   **Phase 1. The product is developed in the high income country** (eg the USA). There are two main reason for this.

    (i)    High income countries provide the greatest demand potential.

    (ii)    It is expedient to locate production close to the market during the early period so that the firm can react quickly in modifying the product according to customer preferences.

(b)   **Phase 2. Foreign production starts**. Firms in the innovator's export markets (such as the UK) start to produce the product domestically. Thus, for example, the UK market is then shared by the innovative US firm and the UK firms.

(c)   **Phase 3. Overseas producers compete in export markets**. The costs of the UK producers begin to fall as they gain economies of scale and experience. They may also enjoy lower

costs than the US firms. The UK firms now start to compete with the US producers in third-party export markets such as, say, Greece or Brazil.

(d) **Phase 4. Overseas producers compete in the firm's domestic market**. The UK firms become so competitive, due to their lower production costs that they start to compete with the US firms in the US domestic market. The cycle is now complete.

The cycle may well, however continue as firms in less developed countries enter and ultimately take over the market. The extent and speed of the process depends largely on the product's technical sophistication.

The major significance of the ITLC concept is in long-term strategic planning.

(a) A firm developing a new product in a high income country should try to penetrate foreign markets as quickly as possible so as to maximise early returns before lower-cost firms located elsewhere enter the market.

(b) Moreover, the innovator would do well to consider the benefits of establishing production capacity overseas as early as is technically feasible.

## 2.2 Product elimination

**FAST FORWARD**

Elimination (**divestment**) should be part of product portfolio analysis, where for each country a periodic review of product range is undertaken.

Factors to be taken into consideration during review would include the following.

- Current profitability
- Effects of elimination on the sale of other (complementary) products
- After-sales service implications
- Alternative product opportunities in each country
- The effect on sales/profits of product life extension/rejuvenation

All these factors become much more complex for the multinational company with overseas operations. The multinational company may be producing the product under consideration in a number of countries, under a number of different market conditions.

However, the multinational company's range of alternatives to product elimination for a marginal product is greater than for an exporter. A multinational company can export or license or arrange for contract manufacturing as an alternative to direct manufacturing abroad.

# 3 Standardisation versus adaptation

**FAST FORWARD**

Entry into foreign markets mandates decisions about whether or not to adopt the marketing mix to local conditions. The choice is between **standardising** the product in all markets to reap the advantages of scale economies in manufacture and, on the other hand, **adaptation** which gives the advantages of flexible response to local market conditions.

Marketing at Work

- The *Rolex* watch is the same all over the world. Its positioning as the watch for the high achiever is the same across the globe. It is an upmarket product and will be found in upmarket outlets.

- *Unilever's Lifebuoy* soap is positioned identically in India and East Africa, despite having different ingredients. It is promoted as an inexpensive soap that protects health.

Complete **global standardisation** would greatly increase the profitability of a company's products and simplify the task of the international marketing manager. The extent to which standardisation is possible is controversial in marketing. *Levitt* wrote:

'The global corporation operates with resolute constancy, at low relative cost, as if the entire world (or major regions of it) were a single entity; it sells the same things in the same way everywhere.'

At the other end of the spectrum, it has been argued that **adaptability** is the key ingredient for global success. Much of the decision making in an international marketing manager's role is concerned with taking a view on the necessity, or lack of it, of adapting the product, price and communications to individual markets.

**Factors encouraging standardisation**

(a)    **Economies of scale**

- Production
- Marketing/communications
- Research and development
- Stock holding

(b)    Easier management and **control**.

(c)    **Homogeneity** of markets, in other words world markets available without adaptation (eg denim jeans).

(d)    **Cultural insensitivity**, eg industrial components and agricultural products.

(e)    **Consumer mobility** means that standardisation is expected in certain products.

- Camera film
- Hotel chains

(f)    Where **'made in'** image is important to a product's perceived value (eg France for perfume, Sheffield for stainless steel).

(g)    For a firm selling a **small proportion** of its output overseas, the incremental adaptation costs may exceed the incremental sales value.

(h)    Products that are positioned at the **high end of the spectrum** in terms of price, prestige and scarcity are more likely to have a standardised mix.

Adaptation may be mandatory or discretionary.

**Mandatory product modification** normally involves either adaptation to comply with government requirements or unavoidable technical changes. An example of the former would be enhanced safety requirements, while the requirements imposed by different climatic conditions would be an example of the latter.

**BPP** )))
LEARNING MEDIA

**Discretionary modification** is called for only to make the product more appealing in different markets. It results from differing customer needs, preferences and tastes. These differences become apparent from market research and analysis; and intermediary and customer feedback.

(a) Levels of customer **purchasing power**. Low incomes may make a cheap version of the product more attractive in some less developed economies.

(b) **Levels of education** and technical sophistication. Ease of use may be a crucial factor in decision-making.

(c) Standards of **maintenance and repair** facilities. Simpler, more robust versions may be needed.

(d) **'Culture-bound' products** such as clothing, food and home decoration are more likely to have an adapted marketing mix.

These strategies can be exercised at global and national level, depending on the type of product.

 Marketing at Work

A current example of standardisation and adaptation issues relates to world markets for motor vehicles. In particular, the US government has taken up arms on behalf of the US car industry to increase US manufacturers' market share in Japan, claiming that there are structural barriers and non-tariff barriers.

In fact, Japan is one of the few countries (the others being the UK, the Republic of Ireland, Australia, New Zealand, South Africa and Sri Lanka) with right hand drive.

The real problem, according to the *Economist* is that the US car industry 'has never catered for those strange foreign markets, such as Japan and Britain, where cars are driven on the left and steered on the right ... *General Motors* doesn't sell a single car in Japan with the steering wheel where the drivers want it ... Meanwhile how about bashing those villainous Saudi Arabians for not buying American ski-equipment?'

Not all products are suitable for standardisation.

 Marketing at Work

Take the example of *Cadbury-Schweppes* which deals with chocolate and soft drinks.

(a) The UK consumer's taste in chocolate is not shared by most European consumers, who prefer a higher proportion of cocoa-butter in the final product. Marketing Cadbury's UK brands of chocolate on a Europe-wide basis would not seem to be appropriate: instead the acquisition of a European company would be the best way to expand into this market. The UK is thus a segment of a global market with its unique needs.

(b) The market for soft drinks on the other hand is different, with Schweppes tonic water well established as a brand across Europe.

## 3.1 Foreign trade orientation

FAST FORWARD ▶▶ There are three broad categories of approach to foreign trade: **ethnocentric**, **polycentric** and **geocentric**.

A firm's approach to this decision depends to a large extent on its attitude towards, and its level of involvement in, international marketing. There are broadly three types of approach in this context.

(a)    **Ethnocentrism**. Overseas operations are viewed as being secondary to domestic operations and are often simply a means of disposing of surpluses. Any plans for overseas markets are developed at home with very little systematic market research overseas. There is little or no modification of any aspects of the mix with no real attention to customer needs. This is the first step into international marketing and involves a centralised strategy.

(b)    **Polycentrism**. Subsidiaries are established, each operating independently with its own plans, objectives and marketing policies on a country by country basis. Adaptation will be at its most extreme with this approach. Polycentrism can be viewed as an evolutionary step and involves a decentralised strategy. It is easy to fall into a **multidomestic** pattern of operations that does not take advantage of co-ordinating actions across differential markets.

(c)    **Geocentrism**. The organisation views the entire world as a market with standardisation where possible and adaptation where necessary. It is the final evolutionary stage for the multinational organisation and involves an integrated marketing strategy.

## 3.2 Product considerations

In general terms, the extent to which the mix has to be adapted depends on the type of product. Some products are extremely sensitive to the environmental differences, which bring about the need for adaptation; others are not at all sensitive to these differences, in which case standardisation is possible.

A useful way of analysing products internationally is to place them on a continuum of **environmental sensitivity**. (We are referring to the social, legal, economic, political and cultural environments here.) The greater the environmental sensitivity of a product, the greater the necessity for the company to adapt the marketing mix.

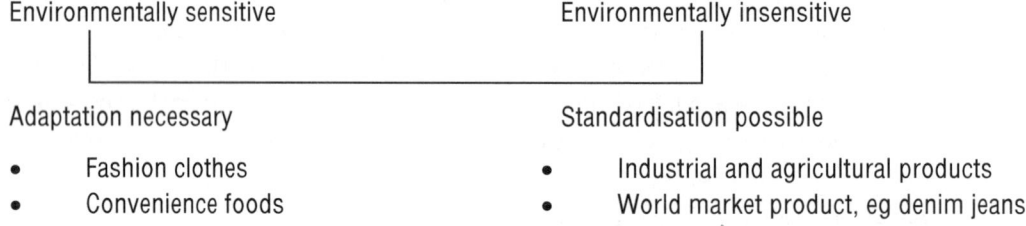

Environmentally sensitive                    Environmentally insensitive

Adaptation necessary                    Standardisation possible

- Fashion clothes
- Convenience foods

- Industrial and agricultural products
- World market product, eg denim jeans

A more sophisticated approach is a two-dimensional matrix. The vertical dimension measures the advantages of standardised marketing and the horizontal dimension takes the need for localised marketing into account. This is illustrated below.

## 3.3 Environmental forces

There are strong forces in the business environment drawing companies towards global marketing strategies, the most important of which are as follows.

(a)    **Demographic, cultural** and **economic convergence** among consumer markets and increasing homogeneity in the needs of industrial customers worldwide.

(b)    Increased need for **investment and research** to ensure long-term competitiveness, longer lead times involved in bringing products to market and the growing return needed for this process.

(c)    The growing importance of **economies of scale** (purchasing, manufacturing, distribution).

(d)    The **deregulation** of national markets, in areas such as air transport, financial services, telecommunications and power generation.

(e)    The impact of technology on manufacturing, transportation and distribution.

|  |  |  |
|---|---|---|
| **Sector 1**<br>**GLOBAL**<br><br>• Aircraft manufacturing<br>• Computers<br>• Industrial machinery<br><br><br>Automobiles | **Sector 3**<br>**BLOCKED GLOBAL**<br><br>• Telecommunications<br>• Generators<br><br><br><br>Pharmaceuticals | High |
| **Sector 2**<br>**MULTINATIONAL/**<br>**MULTIMARKET**<br>• Medical equipment<br>• Synthetic fibres<br>• Cash dispensers<br>• Electrical equipment | **Sector 4**<br>**NATIONAL/ LOCAL**<br><br>• Breweries<br>• Cement<br>• Retail trade<br><br><br>Processed food | Low |

*Advantages of standardised marketing*

Low                              High

*Need for localised marketing*

However, despite these strong worldwide forces, there are still many situations where the advantages of or need for local adaptation is high.

(a)     **Sector 1** contains true global marketing companies with a geocentric orientation. Local adaptation is inappropriate and globalising forces can be exploited to great advantage to the company. Examples include aircraft, computers and industrial machinery.

(b)     **Sector 2**. Multinational or multimarket companies with a polycentric orientation adopt this approach. Products require only a low degree of local adaptation. The world market for such multinational organisations is divided into regions or countries with different characteristics, such as W Europe, S America or the Far East. Products in this sector include electrical equipment.

(c)     **Sector 3**. Blocked global businesses are those in which both the need for local adaptation and the globalising factors discussed above are strong. This sector includes businesses that are dominated by economies of scale and would be global but for the influence of legal or political constraints (eg government purchasing policies) creating the need to adapt their products. Regional telephone networks offer a typical example.

(d)     **Sector 4** contains true local businesses. Strong local adaptation is necessary for success and there are no strong arguments in favour of globalisation (eg brewing and retail trade).

*Kenichi Ohmae* writes (in *The Borderless World*) that 'the lure of a universal product is a false allure', simply because local tastes are so different (eg American cars are generally too large and bulky for Europe's narrow streets). It is a similar story with brands. Some brands are global while many others are present in only one country.

Some products suit globalisation

•       Watches and cameras
•       Fashion-oriented, premium price branded goods including luxury items

To conclude, there are four possible decisions for products.

•       Sell products unmodified/standardised

- Modify or adapt products where necessary
- Develop new products for a specific market or group of markets
- Eliminate old/weak products

### Action Programme 5

What are the arguments in favour of product adaptation?

# 4 Product and communications

**FAST FORWARD**

The question of whether or not to adapt the product is often considered in conjunction with the **promotion/communication** issue. This gives four possible product and communication strategies.

|  | Product standardised | Product adapted |
|---|---|---|
| Communications standardised | Standardisation worldwide of both product and communications | Adaptation of product only |
| Communications adapted | Adaptation of communications only | Both product and communications adapted |

## 4.1 Standardised product and communications

This is the obvious strategy for the occasional exporter but also some major international companies seeking economies of scale.

*PepsiCo* has been successful with this strategy. Many perfumes and cosmetics are marketed in this way. *Polaroid*, however, failed in France with their instant picture camera because of failure to modify their product and communications activities from the successful USA version. This failure was due to the fact that the product was at a different stage in its product life cycle in France and the United States.

## 4.2 Standardised product and adapted communications

This strategy is used where a product meets different needs in different countries. Take bicycles for example. The product is the same, but communications can suggest different uses.

- France/Belgium    –    sport-recreation
- UK    –    recreation
- Third World    –    means of transport

## 4.3 Adapted product and standardised communications

This strategy is relevant where the product satisfies the same need (or solves the same problem) in many markets but conditions of use vary.

(a) Petrol companies adapt their fuel to climactic conditions but standardise their advertising and other promotional activities.

(b) Car manufacturers need different tyres and temperature control systems in Saudi Arabia than they do in the UK.

## 4.4 Adaptation of both product and communications

This strategy is the most costly one but may be necessary to exploit a market fully. For example, take these two stereotypes.

(a) US product – can be made or packaged in plastic and be disposable.

(b) German product – must be made or packaged in metal and must be durable and repairable because of German concern for environmental issues. Promotional activities must reflect these product attributes.

# 5 Other aspects of product decisions

Other aspects of the product decision principally concern packaging, labelling and after-sales service.

Standardisation vs adaptation is a major question about **packaging**. A problem might be the different sizes required in different countries. There are three aspects of packaging.

(a) **Protection**. Packaging may have to be adapted/modified if climate, handling facilities, time spent in distribution chain or usage rate vary.

(b) **Promotion**. Packaging will be adapted if package size, cost of packaging, colour preference, legal constraints, literacy, reputation/recognition varies from market to market.

(c) **Recyclability**. The issue of recyclability is becoming increasingly important. Germany, in particular, has a complex scheme for collecting and recycling household packaging materials. An EU directive has recently come into force in all European countries requiring a reduction in packaging use, greater re-use and recycling. This has had a significant impact on pack design and distribution channel management for some companies (**'reverse logistics'** for the return of packaging is now becoming standard in some industries).

Consumer needs and wants are not identical across markets.

 Marketing at Work

The market research agency, Research Business International, was commissioned to carry out some overseas work for its client, *Gillette*. Gillette wanted to know more about the market for its razor products in Africa. The agency discovered that in Nigeria, razors were used mainly for skinning animals, not for shaving. Gillette responded by developing a special holder which facilitated this product use.

**Labelling** is an example of mandatory modification required by government regulations.

(a) This usually concerns listing contents or use of appropriate language or languages

(b) Some countries have strict laws regarding describing the contents of each package

(c) Eco-labelling is now becoming important in some markets (primarily European markets at the moment) informing consumers of the environmental aspects of the product – for example the energy usage over the lifetime of refrigerators

**Servicing** is an increasingly important part of the augmented product (particularly in the developed economies) and is of great importance in international marketing. If the availability or quality of servicing is doubtful, consumers may choose to buy domestic products.

The service problem is a complex one for the exporter. It involves decisions about facilities, personnel and training. Should they use distributors which would involve training foreign staff and sending out HQ personnel to monitor or should they operate a direct servicing policy in which case they would fly out maintenance staff when required? The appropriate decision varies with the technical sophistication and value of the product.

# 6 New product development

New products feature in a firm's competitive and marketing strategies.

(a)    New and innovatory products can **lower entry barriers** to existing industries and markets, if new technology is involved.

(b)    The market for any product changes over time and its life. The interests of the company are therefore best met with a **balanced product portfolio**. Managers therefore must plan when to introduce new products, how best to extend the life of mature ones and when to abandon those in decline.

A firm should identify its **strategy underlying new product development**.

(a)    **Leader strategy**. Will the firm gain competitive advantage by operating at the leading edge of new developments? If yes, there are significant implications for the R&D activity and the likely length of product life cycles within the portfolio.

(b)    **Follower strategy**. Will the firm be more pro-active, adopt a follower strategy, which involves lower costs and less emphasis on the R&D activity? It sacrifices early rewards of innovation, but avoids its risks. A follower might have to license certain technologies from a leader (as in the case with many consumer electronics companies).

The term **new product development** encompasses a wide range of different types of activity ranging form the development of completely new products and technologies to repackaging of existing ones.

(a)    Bear in mind that new products can be:

- New to the market
- New to the company

(b)    *Booz, Allen and Hamilton* identified the following categories, in a survey of 700 firms.

| | |
|---|---|
| New to the world: new market | 10% |
| New product lines to enable a firm to enter a new sector | 20% |
| Additions to product line | 26% |
| Repositionings to new segments | 7% |
| Improvements/revisions | 26% |
| Cost reductions | 11% |

 Marketing at Work

When he conceived *NetJets* and the idea of fractional aircraft ownership more than 15 years ago, Richard Santulli launched a revolution. Today, fractional ownership is the hottest idea in business-jet acquisition and four major companies are competing in a market that continues to skyrocket.

For a fraction of the cost of a wholly-owned aircraft, a company receives all the full-ownership benefits including tax advantages and a great deal more. Operational concerns, overheads or inconveniences vanish. One phone call, wherever you happen to be, puts your travel department at the nearest of 5,000 airports across the nation.

Owners invest in a quarter– or an eighth-share of an aircraft and pay that fraction of the full cost. In turn, they receive a service guarantee that a plane will be available anywhere in the US and anytime it is needed, typically within four to six hours depending on the programme. Quarter-share owners receive 200 occupied flight hours annually, an eighth-share provides 100 hours and a one-sixteenth share accrues 50 annual flight hours. Each owner must also pay an apportioned monthly management fee for hangarage, crews, insurance, maintenance and administration. In addition, the owner pays a fixed rate per utilised hour for direct operating costs – largely fuel and engine-overhaul reserves. There are no charges for positioning flights or empty legs so the owner only pays when aboard, which makes one-way flights practical.

Fractional ownership also offers some unique benefits. Owners can trade hours for smaller or larger aircraft when the need exists, and many owners opt for multiple shares to add even greater flexibility. That means for the price of a share, the owner has full access to the entire fleet of aircraft and can choose one best suited to a task. Unlike owning a single aircraft, with fractional ownership you request aircraft in two different locations at once so you can fly a customer from one place while you send a marketing team to another. You can also call for your aircraft to be anywhere in the country without paying positioning charges. That is like having an aircraft based at some 5,000 locations across the country at all times.

Mark Patiky, *Harvard Business Review, June 2002*

## 6.1 The NPD process

**FAST FORWARD**

New product development includes the processes for bringing an idea to the stage of market launch, including product screening, test marketing and pricing. Marketing input is required at most stages.

### 6.1.1 Product research – new product development

**FAST FORWARD**

Cooper's Stage Gate™ approach to new product development incorporates idea generation, strategy formulation and a series of development stages, each preceded by a decision point. A development stage will only commence of the decision makers are satisfied that appropriate progress has been made.

The new product development process must be carefully controlled; new products are a major source of competitive advantage but can cost a great deal of money to bring to market. A screening process is necessary to ensure that resources are concentrated on projects with a high probability of success and not wasted on those that have poor prospects.

*Cooper* describes a typical modern screening process that he calls **Stage-Gate™**. This emphasises a cross-functional, prioritised, quality managed, project management approach consisting, typically, of five stages. Each stage begins with a **gate**; that is, a review meeting of managers who have the power either to kill the project or to allocate the resources necessary for it to progress to the next gate. Each gate incorporates the same three management elements.

(a) **Deliverables** are the results of the preceding stage's activity and are specified at its beginning.

(b) **Criteria** are applied by the decision makers to judge the progress of the project and decide whether or not to continue with it.

(c) **Outputs** are a **decision**, and such things as an **action plan**, a **budget** and a list of **deliverables** for the next gate.

A typical five stage process would look like this.

(a) The new idea is subjected to an initial screening to check such things as basic feasibility, strategic fit and marketability. Financial criteria are not usually applied at this stage. This is **Gate 1**.

**279**

(b) **Stage 1**. Preliminary investigation is likely to take less than a month and concentrates on preliminary assessment of market potential, technical implications and financial viability. Quick legal and risk assessments will also take place. This stage leads to **Gate 2**, which is similar to gate 1 in nature, but more rigorous. Gates 1 and 2 are probably operated by middle level managers since, in each case, the resources required to progress to the next stage are only moderate.

(c) **Stage 2**. It is now appropriate to **build a business case** for the project. The product is defined in detail and a full **marketing analysis** is carried out, featuring such processes as competitor analysis, user needs-and-wants studies, and value-in-use studies. There are also full **technical** and **manufacturing appraisals** and a detailed **financial analysis**. **Gate 3** assesses this business case and is probably operated by the company's senior management team, since approval at this stage will lead to heavy expenditure.

(d) **Stage 3**. The physical development of the product now proceeds, subject to a strict time schedule and budget of resources. Lengthy development phases may incorporate their own project management milestones to ensure control, but these are not formal gates in the Cooper sense. This stage leads to **Gate 4**, the **post development review**. The emphasis here is not on whether to proceed further but on ensuring that the project is on track and on reviewing the earlier work on feasibility using up to date information.

(e) **Stage 4**. This is the **testing and validation** stage and validates the entire commercial viability of the project. It may include **pilot production**, **field trials** and **test marketing**. **Gate 5** is **precommercialisation business analysis**. This gives top management the opportunity to check the work done in the testing and validation stage and apply final financial return and launch planning criteria.

(f) **Stage 5** is **full production** and **market launch**. Both must be carefully monitored and lead inexorably to the **post implementation review**, which considers the degree of success achieved by both the new product itself and the development process that led to its launch.

External to the **Stage-Gate™** management process are **idea generation** and **strategy formulation**.

(a) **Idea generation**, to be effective requires a system to promote, and reward creativity and innovative ideas. You will find lots of ideas elsewhere in this Study Text about how this can be done. Cooper suggests a four point plan.

    (i) Nominate one manager to be the **focal point for ideas**.
    (ii) That manager establishes where ideas may **arise**.
    (iii) Those sources are **encouraged**.
    (iv) The ideas they produce are **captured**.

(b) **Strategy formulation**. A business should have a detailed new product strategy, specifying goals, priorities, funding and methods. This is a top management responsibility.

Cooper suggests that the basic process outlined above can be improved using features he calls the **six Fs**.

(a) **Flexibility** is incorporated by routing projects through an abbreviated process if they are small or low risk.

(b) **Fuzzy gates** have other conditions than open or closed: for example, a project may be given a **conditional approval** that depends on some future achievement, such as the receipt of a favourable legal report that is not yet available.

(c) **Fluidity** means that the stages are not sealed off from each other by the gates. For example, it may be permissible to order some long lead-time supplies needed for the next stage before the current one is complete. Assessment of **risk** is crucial here.

(d)     **Focus** means considering portfolio management during the gate process, since resources saved by killing one project may then be redeployed to other, more promising ones.

(e)     **Facilitation** of the whole process should be the full time responsibility of a manager who is charged with making the process (not the project) work.

(f)     **Forever green**. The whole process can be used for other purposes than just new product development: it could, for instance be used on a proposal to extend premises.

Product research is not confined to dealing with new products. It has an important role in connection with **existing products**.

(a)     **Value engineering** may be used to continue the development of existing products so that they use less costly components or processes without compromising the perceived value of the market offer.

(b)     As products near the end of their **life cycle**, it may be possible to develop them for launch in a different market, or simply to extend their lives.

(c)     Where products are being replaced by new versions it may be advantageous to ensure that the new products are **backwards compatible** with the installed base. This is an important consideration in software engineering, for example.

## 6.1.2 Process research

Process research involves attention to how the goods/services are produced. Process research has these aspects.

(a)     **Processes** are crucial in service industries (eg fast food), where processes are part of the services sold.

(b)     **Productivity**. Efficient processes save money and time.

(c)     **Planning**. If you know how long certain stages in a project are likely to take, you can plan the most efficient sequence.

(d)     **Quality management** for enhanced quality.

An important aspect of process research is that advances are much more difficult to imitate then are product developments. Competitors can purchase and **reverse engineer** new products. With good physical security in place, they will find it much more difficult to imitate new processes.

**The strategic role of R&D**. R&D should support the organisation's chosen strategy. To take a simple example, if a strategy of **differentiation** has been adopted, it would be inappropriate to expend effort on researching ways of minimising costs. If the company has a competence in R&D, this may form the basis for a strategy of product innovation. Conversely, where product lifecycles are short, as in consumer electronics, product development is fundamental to strategy.

## 6.1.3 Identifying innovations likely to succeed

Arguably, the NPD process can start with looking at how an innovation can benefit the customers. One way of doing so is looking at customer benefits or buyer utility. (Wichai Kim & Renée Mauborgne, *Financial Times*, 25 January 2001.)

| Item | Comment |
|------|---------|
| **Customer productivity** | Does the innovation save time and effort? |
| **Simplicity** | Does the innovation reduce the complexity a customer faces? ('because life's complicated enough') |
| **Convenience** | Does innovation reduce the inconvenience the customer goes through? (eg speedier or automated check ins) |
| **Risk** | Does the innovation reduce risk? |
| **Fun image** | Can the innovation be enjoyed? |
| **Environmental friendliness** | Is it responsible? |

All these together add up to a 'utility proposition'. Clearly the firm has to price strategically, and deal with barriers to communication.

Speed in NPD can be facilitated by co-ordination between marketing and R&D throughout the design process. There are many good reasons why R&D should be more closely co-ordinated with marketing.

(a)   If the firm operates the marketing concept, then the 'identification of customer needs' should be a vital input to new product developments.

(b)   The R & D department might identify possible changes to product specifications so that a variety of marketing mixes can be tried out and screened.

### 6.1.4 Other measures to speed NPD

(a)   **Parallel engineering** (ie different aspects of the design are carried out simultaneously, rather than being shuffled to and fro in a sequence)

(b)   **Design for manufacture** (ie product design specification should, as far as possible, minimise new equipment or machine modification, which can be time consuming)

(c)   Setting up relationships with **distributors** early on to encourage rapid takeup

When it comes to launching a product, companies decide on different **launch strategies** for different product types. Arvind Sahay (Financial Times *Mastering Marketing* series) suggests that the following criteria apply when deciding upon the launch strategy (simultaneous launch, or one country at a time?) to be adopted.

(a)   Is the product purchased **separately** by the consumer, or as a component for another product or service?

(b)   How much **promotion** is required?

(c)   What is the **price** of the product? It has been suggested that a product which is satisfactory for its purpose and costs less than $300 is likely to be a mass market item. (This of course would not necessarily apply in developing economies.)

 Marketing at Work

### Johnson Wax

When you think 'platform,' you probably think 'software' – with *Microsoft Windows* dominating the pack. But *any* product, not just software, can become a platform. What's required is imagination. Consider how *SC Johnson & Son*, the multibillion-dollar consumer products company, managed to 'platform' its way from floors to shaving cream to candles – and much, much more.

Samuel Curtis Johnson started the company in 1886 when he purchased the parquet flooring division of the *Racine Hardware Company*. After laying floors, Johnson would finish the wood with a special wax of his own creation, which became very popular with customers. Their repeated requests to buy extra wax led Johnson to develop *Johnson's Prepared Wax* and move into consumer products.

Another product – a paste blended with wax that created a spectacular sheen – also looked very promising, but there seemed to be no convenient way for customers to use it. Then the company discovered aerosol can technology (first patented by Erik Rotheim of Norway in 1927), put the wax and paste mix into pressurized cans, and launched *Pledge* – the first sprayable furniture polish for home use.

The company soon realized it could fill aerosol cans with anything sprayable: Scented liquid became *Glade*, an air freshener now available in more than a dozen fragrances; DEET was combined with other to create an insect repellent *Off!*, which is still the category leader. Later, company scientists working on shaving technologies discovered that gel was a better lubricant for skin than traditional shaving cream. But how to dispense gel from an aerosol can? They solved this dilemma by introducing an expandable bladder in the bottom of the can; when the company launched *Edge*, it found a whole new market.

Meanwhile, *Off!* led to plug-in insect repellents and, through another route, to DEET-infused candles. Lanterns based on the candle technology now use Off! cartridges as well. In short, SC Johnson advanced from indoor parquet floors to outdoor insect-repelling lanterns by thinking of aerosol technology as a platform rather than simply as a way to put wax on wood.

*J Svikla and A Paoni, Harvard Business Review, October 2005*

## 6.1.5 Responsibility for NPD

At strategic level, NPD is ultimately the responsibility of the **board**. NPD requires, at different stages, the co-operation of R&D, marketing and production departments.

- The **marketing** department should identify the opportunity.
- The **designers** should, ideally, develop the product so that it satisfies customers' needs.
- The **products** should be produced in the most cost-effective way.

The ideal management structure for the NPD process involves:

- **Clear, realistic planning targets**
- A **project manager** to drive the project, perhaps with a sponsor at Board level

A key relationship is that between marketing personnel and R&D. The **danger** is that **NPD will be 'owned' by R&D**, so technically perfect products are produced which do not meet customer needs profitably.

The relationship of the R&D department with marketing personnel is sometimes problematic.

(a) **Cultural**. The R&D department may have an 'academic' or university atmosphere, as opposed to a commercial one.

(b) **Organisational**. If R&D consumes substantial resources, it would seem quite logical to exploit economies of scale by having it centralised.

(c) **Work**. Marketing work and R&D work differ in many important respects. R&D work is likely to be more open ended than marketing work.

## 6.1.6 Why R&D should be more closely co-ordinated with marketing

(a) If the firm operates the **marketing concept**, then the 'identification of customer needs' should be a vital input to new product development.

(b) The R&D department might identify possible changes to product specifications so that a **variety of marketing mixes** can be tried out and screened.

 Marketing at Work

**Nestlé**

*Nestlé* once had a central R&D function, with regional development centres. The central R&D function was involved in basic research. 'Much of the lab's work was only tenuously connected with the company's business... When scientists joined the lab, they were told "Just work in this or that area. If you work hard enough, we're sure you'll find something".' The results of this approach were:

- The research laboratory was largely cut off from development centres
- Much research never found commercial application

Nestlé reorganised the business into strategic business units (SBUs). Formal links were established between R&D and the SBUs. This means that research procedures have been changed so that a commercial time horizon was established.

**Exam tip**

You may be asked to improve the 'sequential' process of NPD. Suggestions include:

- Small product modifications more often than big one-off changes

- Improved MkIS and the use of focus groups early on

- Outsourcing some NPD work

- Use licensing arrangements

- Re-engineer the process, perhaps by using some of the project management techniques described at the end of the text

- Involving customers

- Drawing together a profit or venture team from elsewhere in the organisation

- Appoint managers dedicated to new products

- NPD development

## 6.1.7 New product development for overseas markets

Sometimes international marketing managers may need to develop new products for a specific overseas market or group of markets. If a product has been developed for one geographical market, taking it to other countries sometimes requires little extra developmental effort.

New product development (NPD) that co-ordinates efforts across national markets does tend to lead to better products. *Unilever* has four global research laboratories that develop products for different national markets while also investigating components for global products. The **Internet** has widened the potential for scouring the world for information for product design.

The success of new products in an international environment depends on a number of factors.

(a) It is important to have an appropriate **organisational structure**. An international division, responsive to international rather than purely domestic marketing concerns, is far more likely to introduce new products overseas successfully.

(b) There should be a commitment to **marketing research**. As we have seen, international market research is more complex than domestic market research.

(c)   Sources of **idea generation** should be as wide as possible: customers, intermediaries, competitors, research and development, sales staff and so on.

(d)   The new product development process should be implemented for **each country**.

 Marketing at Work

Designing a new version of one product for each market is prohibitively expensive, but a company may want more than one product covering all markets. *Nissan* has been a pioneer in finding the right balance. It reduced the number of different chassis designs from 40 to 8, for cars destined for 75 markets.

The development of new products for specific markets is especially relevant to developing nations, although if the market potential is not high a modification to an existing product may be more commercially viable.

Furthermore, there is increasing evidence of **time-based competition**. In other words many firms are reducing the time spent to get new products researched, designed and launched.

- It wrongfoots competitors (eg early mover advantages)
- It enables the firm to get the maximum return from patents
- It might enable the firm to set industry standards for new products
- It enables a premium or skimming pricing strategy

 Marketing at Work

*Microsoft* launched its *XBox* games console in March 2002 to 16 European territories, Australia and New Zealand. This followed launches in the US and Japan. At £299, many regarded it as too expensive to challenge *Sony's PS2*. The London launch was hosted by Richard Branson.

The games titles reflected a US bias, with no soccer title or Formula One game for European fans. However, the games 'Halo' and 'Project Gotham Racing' proved a hit with reviewers.

Relations with third party games publishers will need to be cultivated if Microsoft is to challenge Sony's dominance of the sector. It may be too much to hope that XBox will become the *de facto* market standard in the same way as the Windows operating system.

## 6.2 Test marketing

**FAST FORWARD**

The purpose of **test marketing** is to obtain information about how consumers react to a new product.

A test market involves testing a new consumer product in selected areas which are thought to be **representative** of the total market. In the selected areas, the firm will attempt to distribute the product through the same types of sales outlets it plans to use in the full market launch, and also to use the advertising and promotion plans it intends to use in the full market.

### 6.2.1 Characteristics of a good test marketing exercise

| Size of market | The test market area should be **large enough** to be representative of how the 'full' market might behave, but not so large as to be almost as expensive as a full national market launch. |
|---|---|
| Time | The test period should be sufficiently **long** to give customers time to become aware of the product, and to monitor not only initial sales demand but also repeat buying habits. |
| Representative | The test market must be as closely **representative** of the national market as possible. |
| Promotional facilities | One of the television regions could be used as a test area. |

### 6.2.2 Benefits of test marketing

(a) The company **can pre-test a planned marketing mix**. For example, they may be able to identify product faults not identified at the development stage, or they may discover potential distribution problems.

(b) Expensive product failure may be avoided.

(c) **Results** from the test market may enable the company to prepare more accurate **sales forecasts**.

(d) The costs and risks of a full-time launch are postponed.

### 6.2.3 Disadvantages of test marketing

(a) Unless the test market area is **typical** of the market as a whole, the information obtained about potential demand will be **biased** and misleading.

(b) A lengthy test market will **alert competitors** to what the firm is planning to do, and give them time to prepare their own response to the new product.

(c) Only a **small sample** will be used, which raises statistical problems.

(d) Consumers may be aware of the test and **distort their answers** accordingly.

(e) Estimates for the future cannot reliably be based on results recorded today.

(f) **Competitors** may decide to **sabotage** the test, for example by flooding the area with increased advertising activity.

(g) It is difficult to translate national media plans into local equivalents.

(h) Some goods, for example consumer goods such as household furniture, have lengthy repurchase cycles which would make test marketing far too lengthy to be of any practical forecasting value.

### 6.2.4 Other forms of experimentation

(a) **Simulated store technique (or laboratory test markets)**. In these tests, a group of shoppers are invited to watch a selection of advertisements for a number of products, including an advertisement for the new product. They are then given some money and invited to spend it in a supermarket or shopping area. Their purchases are recorded and they are asked to explain their purchase decisions (and non-purchase decisions).

(b) **Controlled test marketing**. In these tests, a research firm pays a **panel of stores to carry the new product for a given length of time**. This test helps to provide an assessment of in-store factors.

## 6.3 New product pricing: market penetration and market skimming

When a firm launches a new product on to the market, it must decide on a pricing policy which lies between the two extremes of market penetration and market skimming.

There are **three elements in the pricing decision for a new product**.

- Getting the product accepted
- Maintaining a market share in the face of competition
- Making a profit from the product

**Market penetration** pricing is a policy of low prices when the product is first launched in order to gain sales volume. It is therefore a policy of sacrificing short-term profits in the interests of long-term profits.

### 6.3.1 Conditions favouring penetration policy

(a)    The firm wishes to **discourage rivals** from entering the market.

(b)    The firm wishes **to shorten the initial period of the product's life cycle**, in order to enter the growth and maturity stages as quickly as possible. (This would happen if there is high elasticity of demand for the product.)

(c)    Significant economies of scale and experience effects are anticipated when high volumes are achieved.

(d)    The market is known to be price sensitive.

A firm might therefore deliberately build excess production capacity and set its prices very low; as demand builds up, the spare capacity will be used up gradually, and unit costs will fall; the firm might even reduce prices further as unit costs fall. In this way, early year losses will enable the firm to dominate the market and have the lowest costs.

The aim of **market skimming** is to gain **high unit profits very early** on in the product's life.

(a)    The firm charges **high prices** when a product is **first launched**.

(b)    The firm **spends heavily on advertising** and sales promotion to win customers.

(c)    As the product moves into the later stages of its **life cycle** (growth, maturity and decline) **progressively lower prices will be charged**. Profit is thus skimmed off in progressive stages until sales can only be sustained at lower prices.

### 6.3.2 Conditions suitable for a skimming policy

(a)    The **product is new and different**, so that customers are prepared to pay high prices.

(b)    **Demand elasticity is unknown**. It is better to start by charging high prices and then reducing them if the demand for the product turns out to be price elastic, than to start by charging low prices and then attempting to raise them substantially when demand turns out to be price inelastic.

(c)    High initial prices might not be profit-maximising in the long run, but they generate **high initial cash flows**. A firm with liquidity problems may prefer market-skimming for this reason.

(d)    Skimming may also enable the firm to identify **different market segments** for the product, each prepared to pay progressively lower prices.

The firm may lower its prices in order to attract more price-elastic segments of the market; however, these price reductions will be gradual. Alternately, the entry of competitors into the market may make price reductions inevitable.

**Marketing at Work**

**Reverse engineering**

Japanese consumer electronics companies are finding it more and more difficult to keep ahead of competitors from other countries. For example, Japanese companies had developed and commercialised DVD players in the late 1990s; by 2001, Chinese manufacturers were making them so cheaply that *Wal-Mart* could sell them for $US29. There was a boom in sales and the market was saturated much faster then the Japanese had expected. Protection lies in two areas: technical complexity and legal protection for intellectual property. Japanese companies are believed to maintain a three to five year lead in extremely high resolution TV pictures, while the large scale integrated circuits in DVD recorders are so complex that they may retain their lead until 2010. *Matsushita* filed the most patents in China each year from 1999 to 2002.

Michiyo Nakamoto, *Financial Times, 21 January 2004*

**Introductory offers** may be used to attract an initial customer interest. Introductory offers are temporary price reductions, after which the price is then raised to its normal commercial rate.

## 6.4 Success and failure of new products

**FAST FORWARD**

New products can fail in the short-term or in the long-term. The NPD process should improve success rates, but success is never guaranteed.

A successful new product or brand satisfies corporate objectives by:

- Gaining/sustaining market share
- Meeting profit targets
- Generating cash inflows
- Doing the above in the right timeframe

### 6.4.1 Reasons for failure

| Reason | Comment |
|---|---|
| **Poor commitment** | NPD is a sideline; managers want to do NPD, but are unwilling to risk the resources to develop the competences necessary |
| **Poor thinking** | Designers and promoters of NPD within the organisation have their own interests to pursue and downplay potential problems |
| **Poor execution** | Many NPD processes involve uncertain outcomes but the product is wanted in an unrealistic timescale |
| **Poor management** | The research process for NPD may not be run properly |
| **Poor marketing** | The product might fail because of poor marketing research or by poor marketing |
| **Poor analysis** | Both the process of NPD and the product can be more time consuming and expensive than anticipated |

## 6.5 Enhancing innovation

**FAST FORWARD**

Continuous innovation has become more or less essential to business success. It is important to promote a culture that supports new ideas. The learning organisation approach is based on *Senge's* five disciplines.

### 6.5.1 The need to speed up innovation is a key issue

'Innovation has become the religion of the late 20th century' (*The Economist*, 20 February 1999). Commonly cited spurs to innovation are:

- Shorter product life cycles
- Increasing prosperity
- New technology enabling new services

A *Marketing Business* survey of UK marketers offered the following findings.

(a) 71% of respondents considered innovation to be more important then marketing existing products and services.

(b) Whilst 59% of respondents believed strongly that innovation is 'key to British business', only 31% believed their companies shared this view.

(c) When asked to consider what would improve the potential for innovation, 71% said that 'the key to making their own companies more innovation-driven lay in **management initiatives**… The need for a **risk taking culture** and **better communications** were also mentioned.' Two-thirds identified lack of time as a constraint.

### 6.5.2 Seven types of opportunity for innovation

- The 'unexpected success': exploit it
- The difference between what did happen and what was supposed to happen: find out why
- Inadequacy in an underlying process: reforms to process
- Changes in industry or market structure
- Demographic changes
- Fashion
- New knowledge and technology

**Many businesses only concentrate on new technology,** rather than the other opportunities to innovate listed above. Many businesses feel that their future survival is at stake if they do not innovate. Companies are keen to find out a more **predictable way of emerging with winners**. There is no systematic way to encourage innovation but *The Economist* suggests these steps.

**Step 1**    **Imagining**: the initial insight about a market opportunity for a particular technology

**Step 2**    **Incubating**: nurturing the technology to gauge whether it can be commercialised.

**Step 3**    **Demonstrating**: building prototypes and getting feedback from potential customers

**Step 4**    **Promoting**: persuading the market to adopt the invitation

**Step 5**    **Ensuring** the product or process has **as long a life as possible**

Steps 1, 2 and 3 cannot be managed in a conventional way. Firms could:

- Create a culture in which innovation and learning exist throughout the organisation
- Designate separate teams, or individuals to come up with ideas.

An innovation culture can be considered in the context of a **learning organisation**.

### 6.5.3 Creativity and innovation

Creative ideas can come from anywhere and at any time, but if management wish to foster innovation they should try to provide an organisation structure in which innovative ideas are encouraged to emerge.

(a) **Innovation requires creativity**. Creativity may be encouraged in an individual or group by establishing a climate in which free expression of abilities is allowed.

(b)    Creative ideas must then be **rationally analysed** to decide whether they provide a viable proposition.

In an article in *Marketing Business* (April 2000), *Ty Francis* exposes ten myths about innovation.

(a)    Extensive **market research** is not essential: creativity is more important than collecting more data.

(b)    **Creative leaps** into the unknown are needed. They may change the entire company (there is no place in today's business environment for 'steady-as-she-goes incrementalism').

(c)    **The responsibility of the entire enterprise**. Focusing on existing products and customers will achieve nothing. Functional responsibilities need to be disregarded: 'if you do what you've always done you'll get the results you've always had'.

(d)    More than simply **intellectual** endeavour. **Core creative competencies** are needed, and a creative culture needs to be stimulated.

(e)    **Not just about NPD**. Innovation may simply mean a new process or a new component material for an existing product. The biggest returns came from **innovative strategy**.

(f)    **'The future is happening now'**. Organisations need to get away from a problem solving orientation, and become more involved in **creating their future** rather than simply planning for it.

(g)    **'Not just in a crisis'**. Innovation should not just occur quickly and under duress when a company is desperate. Real innovative breakthroughs need proper consideration and thought.

(h)    **'Not one best way'**. There is no such thing as a foolproof or faddish **toolkit** for innovation. Commercially viable innovations only come from a **proper knowledge** of the company's abilities and its industry.

(i)    'Not a **mechanistic business process**'. Innovation is a way of working that should colour everything the company does. 'In a very real sense, innovation is better approached as an art form rather than a science.'

(j)    Innovation does not live off **existing brands and products**. Companies must move on. Strong brands can actually stifle innovation, and in any case some competitors are always going to be able to copy what you do.

### 6.5.4 Organisational learning

*Ikujiro Nonaka* holds that the successful creation of **ideas**, as opposed to the mere processing of information, depends on a number of organisational factors.

(a)    'Creating new knowledge is not simply a matter of processing objective information. Rather it depends on tapping the highly subjective insights, intuitions, and hunches and making those insights available for testing and use by the company as a whole'. Basically, this means that:

(i)    no one individual or group of individuals can, even in principle, be the source of all knowledge about a firm's activities;

(ii)    there must be a way whereby all individuals can communicate their insights to other members of the organisation, so that these insights flow into a pool of knowledge from which the whole company can draw.

(b)    Furthermore, there is the idea that a company is 'a living organism'. This means that it can learn.

*Peter Senge* argues that to create a learning organisation, individuals and groups should be encouraged to learn five disciplines.

| Discipline | Comment |
|---|---|
| **Systems thinking** | This is the ability to see particular problems as part of a wider whole, and to devise appropriate solutions to them. |
| **Personal learning and growth** | Individuals should be encouraged to acquire skills and knowledge. |
| **Mental models** | These are deeply ingrained assumptions which determine what individuals think. This can be about the best way of managing people, about products (eg how a car looks is more important than how comfortable it is to drive) or marketing (price is more important than quality). Learning organisations can use a number of group techniques to make these models explicit, and to challenge them. An inability to question mental models can lead to strategic wear-out. |
| **Shared vision** | but not so forceful as to discourage organisational learning. |
| **Team learning** | Some tasks can only be done in groups. Teams, however, must be trained to learn, as there are factors in group dynamics which impede learning. |

**Key concept**

'A **learning company** is an organisation skilled at creating, acquiring, and transferring knowledge, and at modifying its behaviour to reflect new knowledge and insights.'

## 6.5.5 Characteristics of the learning company

| Characteristic | Comment |
|---|---|
| **The learning approach to strategy** | The strategy process is designed as a learning process with experimentation and feedback loops built into a system. *Pedler, Burgoyne and Boydell* cite as an example *Shell*, where a senior executive from another plant and/or country is invited to review the operation of a plant, to discover its hidden fundamentals and ways of doing business. As much information as possible is brought to bear on a problem. |
| **Participative policy making** | All members of a learning company have the chance to participate in the learning process. In practice it means that a variety of stakeholder influences are accepted. |
| **Informating** | Informating is the use of information as a resource for the whole organisation to exploit in order to develop new insights. |
| **Formative accounting** | Accounting and budgeting systems should be structured for the benefit of all their internal users to assist learning. Such systems might encourage individuals or departments to act as small businesses treating internal users as customers. |
| **Internal exchange** | Internal exchange develops the idea of the internal customer. Each unit regards the other units as customers, whose needs must be identified and satisfied, in the context of the company as a whole. |
| **Reward flexibility** | In a learning company, there is a flexible approach to remuneration. The underlying principles of the salary remuneration system should be brought out into the open. Changing the reward system might result in a change in the distribution of power within the company. Rewards are not only financial but relate to the pleasure, enjoyment, and social life that people get out of work. |

| Characteristic | Comment |
|---|---|
| **Enabling structures** | The notion of enabling structures implies the features of the organic organisation with indeterminate roles which alter to allow for growth. Organisation structures are temporary arrangements that must respond to changed conditions and opportunities. |
| **Boundary workers as environmental scanners** | In a learning organisation, environmental monitoring is not restricted to specialists or managers. All employees dealing with the boundary should try and monitor the environment. |
| **Intercompany learning** | **Benchmarking** is an example of intercompany learning. |
| **Learning climate** | Managers must encourage learning. |
| **Self development opportunities for all** | A variety of training resources should be offered, initiating courses, seminars, counselling, work experience. Training and development has a high priority in a learning organisation, as it increases the flow of information and ideas, and develops the skills which can make use of them. |

 Marketing at Work

*Daiichi*, a Japanese electronics appliance firm, offers three year warranties on its products. Before the warranty expires, it sends a repairman to service the customer's machine. Before he leaves, the repairman offers to check other appliances, whether or not the customer acquired them from Daiichi. This is a means of gathering product and market information. When the repairman returns to the office, he fills out a detailed report on the types of products in the home, their models and ages. This information is made available to Daiichi's sales force, who can offer the customer an appropriate mix of products.

# 7 Services and other product forms

## 7.1 Services

FAST FORWARD

Because of their characteristics of inseparability, intangibility and so on, services are harder to trade than goods, for obvious reasons: you cannot export haircuts or physiotherapy, for example. However, many services are produced and marketed on a global scale.

Here are some examples of services whose marketing can be conducted globally.

- Financial and banking services
- Transportation (eg airlines)
- Tourism
- Legal, accounting and consultancy services
- Telecommunications and media services
- Retailing
- Utilities, such as power generation
- Fast food

The marketing mix for services also includes people, processes and physical evidence but there are issues of overall service design, quality and delivery and management.

(a)    **Overall service design**. Some service ideas transport easily from one country to another. The classic example is the American hamburger bar, such as **McDonald's** or **Burger King** (owned by a British firm).

(b)    **Service quality and delivery**. Service improvements in one country can be introduced by a firm to another country, providing the market is open. The UK has a very competitive market in credit cards. Many American banks, including MBNA, Beneficial Bank and Advanta have entered the UK, offering tailored mixes of service and price to targeted segments in the UK market. This offers improvements and enhancement on existing offerings.

(c)    **Service management**. Service companies in one country can expand by buying up service facilities elsewhere, to provide resources of finance and expertise.

These have a number of implications for the marketing mix.

**People** are a key element in service delivery. Firms providing international services with high customer-contact, such as airlines, have been well aware for many years of the need to motivate service staff to give of their best.

(a)    Airline cabin crew can be trained to speak the languages relevant to the routes they fly.

(b)    If service quality depends on **consistency**, training is very important.

(c)    **Spatial zones** can communicate messages. In Western societies, we give work colleagues or acquaintances a large zone of personal space. Only family and close friends will enter an individual's near zone. If a colleague comes too close, our reaction is to back off, as our personal space is being invaded. This is not so in some Far Eastern countries, where space is at a premium and people have far less privacy. There, it is acceptable to stand far closer to others.

 Marketing at Work

*BAA* (formerly British Airports Authority) aims to be acknowledged 'as the best run airports company in the world'. It has ambitions to run airports in Italy, Australia and South Africa.

It has developed its own MBA (Master of Business Administration) course, with the University of Surrey, with special emphasis on the needs of running an airport. (Diploma of Management Studies courses are also available.) BAA says 'it wants to see employees from terminal duty managers to firefighters and security staff doing the courses'.

**Processes** describe the way the service is delivered. Of course, this is infinitely bound up with people, but well designed processes are essential to service design and delivery.

 Marketing at Work

Most business travellers like flexibility in a hotel. Important 'processes' in catering for business travellers might be:

* delivery of fax messages
* datapoints to enable laptop computers to work
* provision of town maps
* fast and responsive laundry service
* security at the check-in desk

Processes must also be **adapted** to the legal environment of each country, for example with legal or financial services. Failure to follow 'due process' might lead to a weak legal position in litigation.

**Physical evidence** in international marketing terms can include factors such as these.

(a)    Coherent **branding** across service outlets in the world. This will be reflected in packaging (of materials supplied with the service), staff uniforms and so on.

(b)    Attention to the design, layout and lighting of any physical environment, such as aircraft cabins, hotel rooms, restaurant.

(c)    People communicate both by using language and non verbal signs. A shake of the head to us means no and a nod yes. This convention is reversed in some cultures.

**Exam tip**

> Past questions have asked you to identify key characteristics of services which make them difficult to market internationally.

## 7.2 Commodities and semi-processed products

**FAST FORWARD**

> The key feature of a commodity is that it is impossible to differentiate the core product. Semi-processed products are similar to raw materials but have been taken beyond their basic form.

**Key concept**

> A **commodity** is an undifferentiated, generic product or service, especially raw materials, industrial products or agricultural products.

A key example of raw material commodities is provided by **agricultural produce**. Many countries do not have the population to consume all that they produce, so the export market is extremely important. Conversely, some countries do not have enough raw materials for their needs. Access to adequate **transport facilities** is key.

 Marketing at Work

In America, the Facility Guarantee Programme (FGP) has been set up to enhance facilities in emerging markets (such as Jamaica, Trinidad and Tobago, Costa Rica, El Salvador, Panama and Peru) that process, handle, store or transport agricultural products imported from the US. Improved and expanded grain handling and storage at a discharge port will ultimately increase efficiency and lower the costs.

The state of Oregon in the USA exports about 40% of its total agricultural production to overseas markets, chiefly to Pacific Rim countries which have been badly affected by the Asian economic crisis, so it can be important to **diversify markets** for commodities, as with other products.

Commodity marketing has been transformed by **communications technology** in much the same way as other product types. Print media has been overtaken by the Internet. Overseas marketing has been helped by the development of refrigerated containers and shipment tracking systems.

Commodity exporting often accounts for a significant proportion of a **developing country** economy. To take the example of Ethiopia, the export of hides, skins, meat, animals and leather products accounted for about 15% of 1997/98 exports. Coffee accounts for 62% and the remainder is taken up by textiles, fruit and vegetables and pulses and seeds.

The price of commodities can be set on the **commodity exchanges** of international stock exchanges or in **futures contracts**, eg cocoa futures.

## 7.3 Semi processed products

Semi-processed products are neither in their basic nor their final form, but have been processed by the producer to some extent. Examples include fruit harvested and frozen prior to further processing, the leather and animal skins exported by Ethiopia, perhaps to be made into handbags or clothing by factories in a more developed country, or industrial components that have been partly finished before transfer to another company for further processing and installation in industrial machinery.

Semi-processed products are sold to buyers who know they can **add value** to them by further processing. This further processing may not be possible in the country of origin due to lack of skilled labour or other resources.

## Chapter Roundup

- The essence of a product is the **satisfaction** purchased by the buyer. The same physical object, however, can have different uses and meanings.

- The product life cycle is most useful as a control tool and least useful as an aid to forecasting.

- With real products, the stages of the PLC can be difficult to recognise and may not conform to the basic model. Both internal strategic decisions and the state of competition in the market have an influence.

- If specific PLC stages can be recognised, strategic control may be facilitated.

- The management of a product should fit its prevailing life cycle stage, as each stage has different financial and risk characteristics.

- **Product portfolio planning** aims to achieve a portfolio that works well in financial, marketing and production terms.

- The product-market matrix is used to classify a product or a business **according to the features of the market and the features of the product**.

- A product's stage on the product life cycle may vary from country to country, and different marketing strategies will be appropriate in each case.

- The ITLC is used in developing long-term product strategy. It postulates that many products pass through a cycle during which high income, mass-consumption countries are initially exporters but subsequently lose their export markets and ultimately become importers of the product.

- Elimination (**divestment**) should be part of product portfolio analysis, where for each country a periodic review of product range is undertaken.

- Entry into foreign markets mandates decisions about whether or not to adopt the marketing mix to local conditions. The choice is between **standardising** the product in all markets to reap the advantages of scale economies in manufacture and, on the other hand, **adaptation** which gives the advantages of flexible response to local market conditions.

- There are three broad categories of approach to foreign trade: **ethnocentric**, **polycentric** and **geocentric**.

- The question of whether or not to adapt the product is often considered in conjunction with the **promotion/communication** issue. This gives four possible product and communication strategies.

- Other aspects of the product decision principally concern packaging, labelling and after-sales service.

- New product development includes the processes for bringing an idea to the stage of market launch, including product screening, test marketing and pricing. Marketing input is required at most stages.

- Cooper's Stage Gate™ approach to new product development incorporates idea generation, strategy formulation and a series of development stages, each preceded by a decision point. A development stage will only commence of the decision makers are satisfied that appropriate progress has been made.

- Successful NPD is a rational, step-by-step process of submitting new ideas to a sequence of hurdles. Cooper's Stage-Gate technique is a modern example of how the process can be managed.

- The purpose of **test marketing** is to obtain information about how consumers react to a new product.

- When a firm launches a new product on to the market, it must decide on a pricing policy which lies between the two extremes of market penetration and market skimming.

- New products can fail in the short-term or in the long-term. The NPD process should improve success rates, but success is never guaranteed.

- Continuous innovation has become more or less essential to business success. It is important to promote a culture that supports new ideas. The learning organisation approach is based on *Senge's* five disciplines.

- Because of their characteristics of inseparability, intangibility and so on, services are harder to trade than goods, for obvious reasons: you cannot export haircuts or physiotherapy, for example. However, many services are produced and marketed on a global scale.

## Chapter Roundup Continued

- The key feature of a commodity is that it is impossible to differentiate the core product. Semi-processed products are similar to raw materials but have been taken beyond their basic form.

## Quick Quiz

1   What are the marketing implications of the growth phase of the PLC?

2   What is probably a good strategy for a 'dog'?

3   List three approaches to international marketing.

4   What forces encourage global marketing strategies?

5   Identify four international strategies for product and communications.

6   What are the aspects of packaging?

7   What factors govern success of new products in an international environment?

8   What is the consequence of reduced gaps between product life cycles in different markets?

9   What are the stages of the international trade life cycle?

10  What is a commodity?

## Answers to Quick Quiz

1   Advertising costs still high, but falling as a percentage of sales. Prices are falling and the number of distributors is increasing.

2   Divestment unless positive cash flow would permit harvesting in the short term

3   Ethnocentrism, polycentrism and geocentricism

4   Market convergence; need for increased investment; need for economies of scale; freer trade; impact of technology

5   Both product and communications may be standardised or adapted: this gives four possible combinations

6   Protection, promotion, recycleability

7   Organisation structure: marketing research: idea generation: NPD for each country

8   Simultaneous global introduction

9   Product development in a high income country: foreign production starts; overseas producers compete in export markets; overseas producers compete in the original home market

10  An undifferentiated, generic product or service

# Action Programme Review

1    This depends on your own experience.

2    Consider manual typewriters, audio cassettes and pre-recorded VHS video cassettes

3    Most of these are open to discussion, particularly in the context of global operations

4    This will depend on the examples you have chosen.

5    Arguments in favour of product adaptation include the following.

   (a)    **Greater sales potential**, where this also means greater profitability, which it may not!

   (b)    **Varied conditions of product use** which may force a company to modify its product.

   - Climatic variations (corrosion in cars produced for dry climates)

   - Literacy or skill levels of users (languages which can be used on a computer)

   - Cultural, social or religious factors (religious or cultural requirement for food products – Halal slaughtering of New Zealand lamb for Middle Eastern Markets, for instance, or dolphin-friendly tuna catching methods of Europe and the USA)

   (c)    **Variation in market factors**. Consumer needs are in their nature idiosyncratic, and there are likely to be distinctive requirements for each group not met by a standard product.

   (d)    **Governmental or political influence**. Political factors may force a company to produce a local product.

   - Taxation
   - Legislation
   - Pressure of public opinion

   (e)    **Local competition**

Now try Question 7 at the end of the Study Text

# 9

# Price and place

## Syllabus content

- How pricing policies and strategies can be used to build competitive advantage
- The role of alliances and the creation of competitive advantage through supply chain development and marketing partnerships

# Introduction

This chapter deals with two elements of the marketing mix: price and place.

Setting price is commonly seen as a particularly important and difficult process and is often controlled at the highest level. Section 1 covers both the economic theory of pricing and the methods used in practice. Price elasticity of demand is a theoretical concept of great importance for market segmentation. Pricing policy and strategies are dealt with in Section 2.

Section 2 introduces some cost accounting background and considers breakeven analysis and the associated computations.

Place, or distribution, is the final element of the mix to be considered. Section 3 looks at the nature of various distribution structures and discusses some of the influences which affect choice of channel.

# 1 Price

**FAST FORWARD**

**Price** is the only element of the mix which generates revenue rather than creating cost. It must be consistent with the other elements of the marketing mix and is particularly associated with **perceptions of quality**. Economic theory deals with price in terms of market forces; its most useful aspect for the marketer is the idea of **price elasticity of demand**, which measures the extent to which a change in **price** is reflected by a proportionate change in **demand**.

Price can be defined as a measure of the value exchanged by the buyer for the value offered by the seller. It might be expected, therefore, that the price would reflect the costs to the seller of producing the product and the benefit to the buyer of consuming it.

Pricing is the only element of the mix which generates revenue rather than creating costs. It also has an important role as a competitive tool to **differentiate** a product and an organisation and thereby exploit market opportunities. Pricing must also be **consistent** with other elements of the marketing mix since it contributes to the overall image created for the product. No organisation can hope to offer an exclusive high quality product to the market with a low price – the price must be consistent with the overall **product offer**.

## Action Programme 1

In what circumstances would you expect price to be the main factor influencing a consumer's choice?

Although pricing can be thought of as fulfilling a number of roles, in overall terms a price aims to produce the desired level of sales in order to meet the objectives of the business strategy. Pricing must be systematic and at the same time take into account the internal needs and the external constraints of the organisation.

The ultimate objective of pricing, as with other elements of the marketing mix, is to produce the required level of sales so that the organisation can achieve its specified objectives. **Two broad categories of objectives may be specified for pricing decisions**; they are not mutually exclusive, but they are different nonetheless.

(a)    **Maximising profits** is concerned with maximising the returns on assets or investments. This may be realised even with a comparatively small market share depending on the patterns of cost and demand.

(b) **Maintaining or increasing market share** involves increasing or maintaining the customer base which may require a different, more competitive approach to pricing, while the company with the largest market share may not necessarily earn the best profits.

Either approach may be used in specifying pricing objectives, and they may appear in some combination, based on a specified rate of return and a specified market share. It is important that stated objectives are consistent with overall corporate objectives and corporate strategies.

## 1.1 Price setting in theory

Key concept

Economic theory suggests that price for any good is set by market forces. Under conditions of perfect competition, an **equilibrium price** will exist such that demand and supply are perfectly matched and there is neither surplus nor shortage of the good in question.

Market pricing is illustrated in the diagram below. The upward sloping supply curve shows the natural tendency of manufacturers to enter a market if prices are high and to leave it if they are low. The downward sloping demand curve reflects the unwillingness of consumers to buy at a high price and their willingness to buy at a low one. The vertical co-ordinate of the point where the two curves cross is the prevailing equilibrium price; the horizontal co-ordinate shows the amount of the good in question bought and sold in the market. The equilibrium price is also called the **clearing price**, because it clears the market; there is neither unsatisfied demand nor unsold goods.

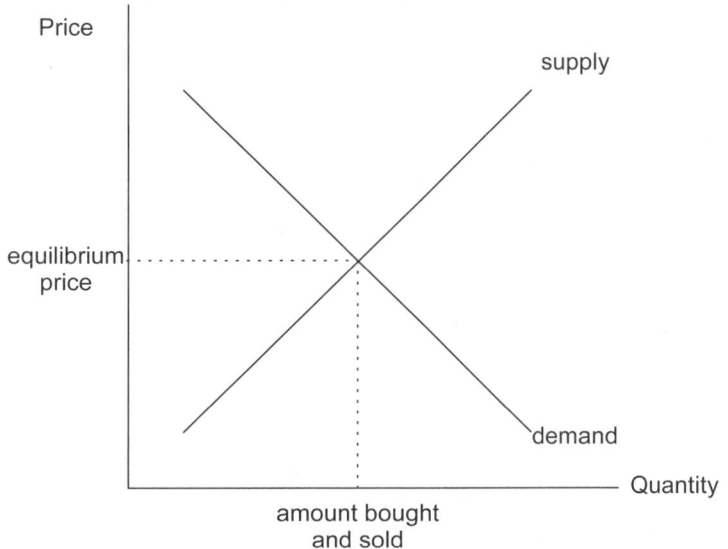

This simple mechanism gives a reasonable picture of **commodity markets**, in which there are many buyers and sellers and none has significant **market power**; that is, the ability to influence price **other than by buying and selling** relatively small quantities. More complex models are used to describe markets in which a supplier or group of suppliers has market power.

(a) A **monopolist** is the sole supplier in a market and is able to prevent other suppliers from entering. Monopolists are in a strong position to exploit the consumer and are frowned upon by government.

(b) **Oligopolists** are members of a small group who between them control supply in a market. Oligopoly is characterised by price 'stickiness'. That is to say, oligopolists typically compete with one another but only in matters **other than price**.

(c) Suppliers under **monopolistic competition** attempt to obtain some of the monopolist's market power by supplying a **differentiated** product. The success of this depends on the willingness of the consumer to accept that the product is, in fact, different. Clearly, this is a very important area for the marketer.

## 1.2 Price elasticity of demand

Key concept

> **Price elasticity of demand** is a measure of the degree of change in demand for a good when its price changes. If the change in demand is large in proportion to the change in price, demand is said to be **elastic**. If the change in demand is small in proportion to the change in price, demand is said to be **inelastic**.

Price elasticity of demand is measured as:

$$\frac{\text{The change in quantity demanded, as a \% of demand}}{\text{The change in price, as a \% of the price}}$$

Since the demand goes up when the price falls, and goes down when the price rises, the elasticity has a negative value, but it is usual to ignore the minus sign. Values greater than 1 indicate elastic demand, while values less than 1 indicate inelastic demand.

### 1.2.1 Example

The price of a product is £1.20 per unit and annual demand is 800,000 units. Market research indicates that an increase in price of 10 pence per unit will result in a fall in annual demand of 75,000 units. What is the price elasticity of demand?

## Solution

Annual demand at £1.20 per unit is 800,000 units.

Annual demand at £1.30 per unit is 725,000 units.

% change in demand $\qquad \frac{75,000}{800,000} \times 100\% = 9.375\%$

% change in price $\qquad \frac{10p}{120p} \times 100\% = 8.333\%$

Price elasticity of demand $= \dfrac{-9.375}{8.333} = -1.125$

Ignoring the minus sign, price elasticity is 1.125.

The demand for this product, at a price of £1.20 per unit, would be referred to as *elastic* because the price elasticity of demand is greater than 1.

### 1.2.2 Elastic and inelastic demand

The value of demand elasticity may be anything from **zero** to **infinity**. Where demand is **inelastic**, the quantity demanded falls by a **smaller** percentage than the percentage rise in price, and where demand is **elastic**, demand falls by a **larger** percentage than the percentage rise in price.

There are three special values of price elasticity of demand; 0, 1 and infinity.

(a)    **Demand is perfectly inelastic**. There is no change in quantity demanded, regardless of the change in price. The demand curve is a vertical straight line. Demand for tobacco is almost perfectly inelastic in the short term, for any reasonable increase in duty, as Chancellors of the Exchequer know.

(b)  **Perfectly elastic demand** (infinitely elastic). Consumers will want to buy an infinite amount, but only up to a particular price level. Any price increase above this level will reduce demand to zero. The demand curve is a horizontal straight line. This is illustrated by a market price in a **commodity market**.

(c)  **Unit elasticity of demand**. **Total revenue for supplies** (which is the same as total spending on the product by households) **is the same whatever the price**.

### 1.2.3 The significance of price elasticity of demand

The price elasticity of demand is relevant to **total spending** on a good or service. When demand is **elastic**, an increase in price will result in a fall in the quantity demanded, and the supplier's **total revenue will fall**. When demand is inelastic, an increase in price will still result in a fall in quantity demanded, but **total revenue will rise**.

Information on price elasticity of demand indicates how consumers can be expected to respond to different prices. Business people can make use of information on how consumers will react to pricing decisions as it is possible to trace the effect of different prices on total revenue and profits. Information on price elasticities of demand will be useful to a business which needs to know the price decrease necessary to clear a surplus (excess supply) or the price increase necessary to eliminate a shortage (excess demand).

### 1.2.4 Factors influencing price elasticity of demand for a good

The main factors affecting price elasticity of demand are as follows.

(a)  **The availability of close substitutes**. The more substitute goods there are, especially close substitutes, the more elastic will be the price elasticity of demand for a good. The elasticity of demand for a particular brand of breakfast cereal is much greater than the elasticity of demand for breakfast cereals as a whole, because the former have much closer substitutes. **This factor is probably the most important influence on price elasticity of demand**.

(b)  **The time period**. Over time, consumers' demand patterns are likely to change, and so, if the price of a good is increased, the initial response might be very little change in demand (inelastic demand). As consumers adjust their buying habits in response to the price increase, demand might fall substantially. The time horizon influences elasticity largely because the longer the period of time which we consider, the greater the knowledge of **substitution possibilities** by consumers and the provision of substitutes by producers.

(c)  **Competitors' pricing**. As mentioned earlier, market dominated by a small number of large suppliers is called an oligopoly. In an oligopoly, firms are very sensitive to price changes by their competitors. If the response of competitors to a price increase by one firm is to keep their prices unchanged, the firm raising its prices is likely to face **elastic** demand for its goods and **lose business**. If the response of competitors to a reduction in price by one firm is to match the price reduction themselves, the firm is likely to face **inelastic** demand but at lower prices. That is, all the firms in the market are likely to retain their market share, but **at a lower price**. As a result, oligopolists tend **not to compete on** price. The diagram below illustrates the kinked demand curve perceived by the individual oligopolist.

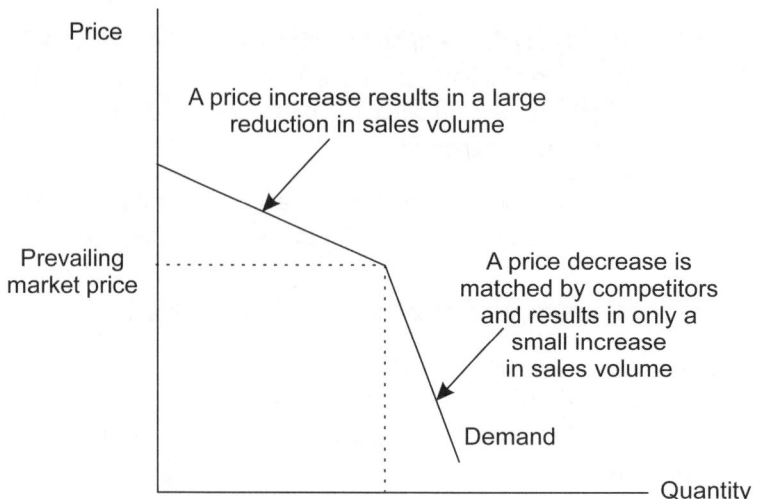

 Action Programme 2

What are the limitations of price elasticity as a factor in determining prices?

## 1.3 Price setting in practice

**FAST FORWARD**

**Cost-plus pricing** is widely used because it is fairly easy to do and should lead to profitable prices. It can take account of demand by adjusting the margin added for profit. **Competitor** action, whether actual or expected, influences real-world price setting, especially under conditions of oligopoly and competitive bidding. Some customers enjoy a **consumer surplus** because they are prepared to pay a higher price. **Differential pricing** enables the supplier to exploit this willingness.

There are three main types of influence on price setting in practice: **costs, competition and demand.**

### 1.3.1 Costs

In practice, cost is the most important influence on price. Many firms base price on simple **cost-plus** rules: in other words, costs are estimated and then a profit margin is added in order to set the price. This method is fairly easy to apply and ensures that costs are covered. Costs are usually available from accounting records, sometimes in great detail.

The price may be based on **direct costs** or **full costs**, the difference being that full cost includes overheads whereas direct cost does not. In either case, a suitable margin is added to cost; under the direct cost method this has to cover overheads as well as profit. Under the full cost method, the margin represents profit only. While appearing to ignore demand, this method can take account of market conditions by adjusting the margin applied.

A common example occurs with the use of **mark-up** pricing. This is used by retailers and involves a fixed margin being added to the buying-in price of goods for resale. This fixed margin tends to be conventional within product classes. In the UK, for example: fast moving items, such as cigarettes, carry a low 5-8% margin (also because of tax factors); fast moving but perishable items, such as newspapers, carry a 25% margin; while slow moving items which involve retailers in high stockholding costs, such as furniture or books, carry 33%, 50% or even higher mark up margins. If all the firms in the industry use the same pricing basis, prices will reflect efficiency; the lowest price firm will be the most efficient.

The problems with cost-plus pricing arise out of difficulties in defining direct costs and allocating overheads, and with over or underestimation of attainable production levels. Because the cost-plus

approach leads to price stability, with price changing only being used to reflect cost changes, it can lead to a marketing strategy which is **reactive** rather then **proactive**. In addition, there is very limited consideration of **demand** in cost-based pricing strategies. From a marketing perspective, cost-based pricing may lead to **missed opportunities** as little or no account is taken, particularly in the short run, of the price consumers are **willing** to pay for the brand, which may actually be higher than the cost-based price.

Particular problems may be caused by the use of cost-based pricing for a **new brand** as **initial low production levels** in the introduction stage may lead to a **very high average unit cost and consequently a high price**. A longer term perspective may thus be necessary, accepting short-term losses until full production levels are attained. Finally, if the firm is using a product line promotion strategy then there is likely to be added complexity in the pricing process.

### 1.3.2 Competition

We have already looked at price behaviour under oligopoly. In reality, the kinked demand curve theory would produce **going rate pricing** in which some form of average level of price becomes the norm, perhaps, in the case of a high level of branding in the market, including standard price differentials between brands.

In some market structures **price competition may be avoided by tacit agreement** leading to concentration on non-price competition; the markets for cigarettes and petrol are examples of this. Note that explicit agreement to fix prices is illegal. Price-setting here is influenced by the need to **avoid retaliatory responses by competitors** resulting in a breakdown of the tacit agreement and so to price competition. Price changes based on real cost changes are led in many instances by a representative firm in the industry and followed by other firms. From time to time tacit agreements break down leading to a period of price competition. This may then be followed by a resumption of the tacit agreement. Often such actions are the result of external factors at work on the industry. Industry level agreements do not necessarily preclude short-term price competition for specific brands, especially where sales promotion devices, such as special offers, are used.

### Action Programme 3

There is at least one service industry in which this practice is the norm and which is regularly reported in the headlines. Can you think of it?

### 1.3.3 Demand

Rather than cost or competition as the prime determinants of price, **a firm may base pricing strategy on the intensity of demand**. Cost and competition factors, of course, remain influences or constraints on its freedom to set price. **A strong demand may lead to a high price, and a weak demand to a low price**: much depends on the ability of the firm to segment the market price in terms of elasticity.

Whenever there is a single price for a good, some consumers enjoy a **consumer surplus**. This is because of the downward slope of the demand curve. **If price were to rise, there would be some purchasers who would pay the higher price**. The difference between the market price and the higher price a purchaser is prepared to pay is the consumer surplus enjoyed by that purchaser. In elasticity terms, the demand of that purchaser is price inelastic. If such consumers can be identified and a higher price charged to them, the supplier obviously benefits. This is called **price discrimination** or **differential pricing**.

In practice, measurement of price elasticity and, implementing differential pricing can be very difficult. There are a number of bases on which discriminating prices can be set. These distinctions reduce or remove altogether the possibility that customers expected to pay the higher price will be able to succeed in paying the lower one.

(a) **By market segment**. A cross-channel ferry company would market its services at different prices in England, Belgium and France, for example. Services such as cinemas and hairdressers are often available at lower prices to old age pensioners and/or juveniles.

(b) **By product version**. Many car models have 'add on' extras which enable one brand to appeal to a wider cross-section of customers. Final price need not reflect the cost price of the add on extras directly: usually the top of the range model would carry a price much in excess of the cost of provision of the extras, as a prestige appeal.

(c) **By place**. Theatre seats are usually sold according to their location so that patrons pay different prices for the same performance according to the seat type they occupy.

(d) **By time**. This is perhaps **the most popular type of price discrimination**. Off-peak travel bargains, hotel prices, telephone and electricity charges are all attempts to increase sales revenue by covering variable but not necessarily average cost of provision. British rail operators are successful price discriminators, charging more to rush hour rail commuters whose demand is inelastic at certain times of the day.

Price discrimination can only be effective if a number of conditions hold.

(a) The market must be **segmentable in price terms**, and different sectors must show different intensities of demand. Each of the sectors must be identifiable, distinct and separate from the others, and be accessible to the firm's marketing communications.

(b) There must be little or no chance of a **black market** developing so that those in the lower priced segment can resell to those in the higher priced segment.

(c) There must be little chance that competitors will **undercut** the firm's prices in the higher priced market segments.

(d) The cost of segmenting and administering the arrangements should not exceed the extra revenue derived from the price discrimination strategy.

The firm could use a **market test** to estimate the effect on demand of a price change. This would involve a change of price in one region and a comparison of demand for the brand with past sales in that region and with sales in similar regions at the old prices. **This is a high risk strategy**: special circumstances (confounding factors) may affect the test area (such as a competitor's advertising campaign) which could affect the results. Also customers may switch from the test brand if a price rise is being considered and become loyal to a competitive brand; they may not switch back even if the price is subsequently lowered.

Alternately, **a direct attitude survey** may be used with respondents. **Pricing research is notoriously difficult**, especially if respondents try to appear rational to the interviewer or do not wish to offend him or her. **Usually there is a lack of realism in such research**; the respondent is not actually faced with having to pay out hard earned income and therefore may give a hypothetical answer that is not going to be translated into actual purchasing behaviour. Nevertheless, pricing research is increasingly common as firms struggle to assess the perceived value customers attribute to a brand to provide an input to their pricing decisions.

## 1.4 Price sensitivity

**Pricing policy** is determined in the light of the customers' sensitivity to price, the objectives and actions of suppliers, competitors and intermediaries and the interplay of forces like inflation and income levels.

Price sensitivity will vary amongst purchasers. **Those who can pass on the cost of purchases will be least sensitive** and will respond more to other elements of the marketing mix.

(a) Provided that it fits the corporate budget, the **business traveller** will be more concerned about the level of service and quality of food in looking for an hotel than price. In contrast, a family on holiday are likely to be very price sensitive when choosing an overnight stay.

(b) In industrial marketing, the **purchasing manager is likely to be more price sensitive than the engineer** who might be the actual user of new equipment that is being sourced. The engineer and purchasing manager are using different criteria in making the choice. The engineer places product characteristics as first priority, the purchasing manager is more price oriented.

Research on price sensitivity has had some interesting results.

(a) Customers have a good concept of a 'just price' – **a feel for what is about the right price** to pay for a commodity.

(b) Unless a regular purchase is involved, **customers search for price information before buying**, becoming price aware when wanting to buy but forgetting soon afterwards.

(c) Customers will buy at what they consider to be a bargain price without full regard for need and actual price.

(d) For consumer durables it is the **down payment** and **instalment price** rather than total price which is important to the buyer.

(e) In times of rising prices the **price image tends to lag** behind the current price, which indicates a resentment of the price increase.

 Marketing at Work

### Luxury hi-fi

The luxury end of the hi-fi market caters for an elite band prepared to pay huge prices for audio systems. It accounts for $1 billion in sales, compared to $70 billion for US consumer electronics alone. But this market often pioneers features and products which later become standard in the mass market, for example, noise reduction systems and CDs. The latest craze, however, is raising some eyebrows, because it threatens to turn the clock back – it is for valve (vacuum tube) powered amplifiers, which were assumed to have died out when they were replaced by transistors in the 50s and 60s.

Why should this be happening? Transistors are smaller, cheaper and more reliable. By 1990, the sales of valve amplifiers had fallen to almost zero. But enthusiasts maintain that the tubes reproduce musical notes more accurately, that the sound is better. By 1996, half of all up-market hi-fi amplifiers in the US were powered by valves.

Further, the most sought after amplifiers use the most antediluvian technology, single end amplifiers using a single 'triode', the design which in 1906 first made amplification possible. Since they produce only a few watts of power, they must be used with ancient but efficient 'horn' loudspeakers – which are consequently, also making a comeback.

This is the equivalent of going back to the *Ford Model T* when modern cars are on the market. Manufacturers are being tempted in by the lure of fat margins. *Audio Note*, a pioneer of the single ended market in Japan, sells amplifiers that range from $1,700 to $252,500 for the *Gaku-On*. Speakers cost around $40,000 per pair. Philips subsidiary Marantz, a mass market organisation, has just launched a tube amplifier for $50,000 while also reissuing a tube amplifier it last made in the 1950s for $8,400. *Westrex*, a small Atlanta firm, has resumed production of the 300B triode, and hopes to sell 30,000 per year, giving it 40% of a market currently dominated by the Chinese and East European tube makers.

What effect will this have on the mass market? No-one really knows, but it seems likely that this will become an important segment within the audio market, although no-one can predict the potential size or profitability.

*The Economist*

## 1.5 Miscellaneous factors affecting price decisions

### 1.5.1 Intermediaries' objectives

If an organisation distributes products or services to the market through independent intermediaries, **the objectives of these intermediaries have an effect on the pricing decision**. Such intermediaries are likely to deal with a range of suppliers and **their aims concern their own profits rather than those of suppliers**. Also, the intermediary will take into account the needs of its customers. Thus conflict over price can arise between suppliers and intermediaries which may be difficult to resolve.

**Many industries have traditional margins for intermediaries**; to deviate from these might well cause problems for suppliers. In some industries, notably grocery retailing (as we have seen), the power of intermediaries allows them to dictate terms to suppliers. Some companies set a price to distributors and allow them to set whatever final price they wish. A variant involves publishing an inflated **recommended retail price** so that retailers can offer large promotional discounts. The relationship between intermediaries and suppliers is therefore complex, and price and the price discount structure is an important element.

### 1.5.2 Competitors' actions and reactions

An organisation, in setting prices, **sends out signals to rivals. These rivals are likely to react** in some way. In some industries (such as petrol retailing) pricing moves in unison; in others, price changes by one supplier may initiate a price war, with each supplier undercutting the others.

### 1.5.3 Suppliers

**If an organisation's suppliers notice that the prices for an organisation's products are rising, they may seek a rise in the price for their supplies** to the organisation, arguing that it is now more able to pay a higher price. This argument is especially likely to be used by the trade unions in the organisation when negotiating the 'price' for the supply for labour.

### 1.5.4 Inflation

In periods of inflation the organisation's prices may need to change in order to **reflect increases in the prices of supplies**, labour, rent and so on. Such changes may be needed to keep relative (real) prices unchanged (this is the process of prices being adjusted for the rate of inflation).

### 1.5.5 Quality connotations

**In the absence of other information, customers tend to judge quality by price**. Thus a price change may send signals to customers concerning the quality of the product. A rise may be taken to indicate improvements, a reduction may signal reduced quality, for example, through the use of inferior components or a poorer quality of raw material. Thus any change in price needs to take such factors into account.

### 1.5.6 New product pricing

Most pricing decisions for existing products relate to price changes. Such changes have a **reference point** from which to move (the existing price). But **when a new product is introduced for the first time there may be no such reference points**; pricing decisions are most difficult to make in such circumstances. It may be possible to seek alternative reference points, such as the price in another market where the new product has already been launched, or the price set by a competitor. Also, see below on penetration and skimming.

### 1.5.7 Income effects

In times of rising incomes, price may become a less important marketing variable than, for instance, product quality or convenience of access (distribution). When income levels are falling and/or unemployment levels rising, price will become a much more important marketing variable.

## Marketing at Work

**Supermarkets**

In the recession of the early 1990s, the major grocery multiples such as *Tesco*, *Sainsbury*, *Safeway* and *Waitrose*, who steadily moved up-market in the 1980s with great success suddenly found bargain stores such as *Foodgiant* and *Netto* a more serious threat.

This led the supermarkets to set up own label product ranges which undercut prices for branded products.

### 1.5.8 Multiple products

**Most organisations market not just one product but a range of products. These products are commonly interrelated, perhaps being complements or substitutes. The management of the pricing function is likely to focus on the profit from the whole range rather than that on each single product.** Take, for example, the use of **loss leaders**: a very low price for one product is intended to make consumers buy other products in the range which carry higher profit margins.

### 1.5.9 Strategic issues

**Price decisions are often seen as highly sensitive and as such may involve top management more clearly than other marketing decisions.** As already noted, price has a very obvious and direct relationship with profit. Ethical considerations are a further factor; whether or not to exploit short-term shortages through higher prices: illustrative of this dilemma is the outcry surrounding the series of petrol price rises following the outbreak of the Gulf crisis in 1990.

**Early cash recovery objective**: an alternative pricing objective is to recover the investment in a new product or service as quickly as possible, to achieve a minimum payback period. The price is set to facilitate this objective. This objective would tend to be used in three circumstances.

- The business is high risk.
- Rapid changes in fashion or technology are expected.
- The innovator is short of cash.

## 1.5.10 Rule of thumb methods

**Going rate pricing**. Try to keep in line with industry norm for prices, as discussed earlier.

**Quantum price**: in retail selling the concept of a **quantum point** is often referred to. When the price of an item is increased from, say, £9.65 to £9.95, sales may not be affected because the consumers do not notice the price change. However, if the price is increased from £9.95 to £10.05 a major fall in sales may occur, £10 acting as a quantum point which can be approached but not passed if the price is not to deter would be purchasers.

**Odd number pricing**: sometimes referred to as *psychological pricing*, the odd number pricing syndrome (pricing at £1.99, say, rather than £2) is said to have originated not as a marketing concept but in department stores in order **to ensure the honesty of sales assistants**. The customer has to wait for change from £1.95 when, as is usual, they offer £2 in payment, so the assistant has to use the till. If the price was £2 and the customer need not wait for the change, there was thought to be a greater temptation to shop assistants to pocket the money and not to enter it into the till.

**One coin purchase**: confectionery firms have used another **psychologically based concept** of a one coin purchase. Rather than change price to reflect cost changes, such firms often alter the quantity in the unit of the product and keep the same price. This is a case of 'price-minus' pricing. The firm determines what the market will bear and works backwards, planning to produce and market a brand which will be profitable to them, selling at the nominated retail price.

**Gift purchases**: gift purchasing is often founded on the idea of price which is taken to reflect quality. Thus if a gift is to be purchased in an unfamiliar product category, a price level is often fixed by the buyer and a choice made from the brands available at that price. Cosmetics are often priced at £4.99 and £9.99 to appeal to gift purchasers at the £5 and £10 price level. Importantly, **packaging is a major part of the appeal** and must reflect a quality brand image, an important part of the psychology of gift choice.

## 1.5.11 Product line pricing

When a firm sells a range of related products, or a product line, its theoretical pricing policy should be to set prices for each product in order to maximise the profitability of the line as a whole. A firm may therefore have a **pricing policy for an entire product line**.

(a) There may be a **brand name** which the manufacturer wishes to associate with high quality and high price, or reasonable quality and low price and so forth. All items in the line will be priced accordingly. For example, all major supermarket chains have an own brand label which is used to sell goods at a slightly lower price than the major named brands.

(b) If two or more products in the line are **complementary**, one may be priced as a **loss leader** in order to attract more demand for all of the related products. An example is selling razors at very low prices whilst selling the blades for them at a higher profit margin. People will buy many of the high profit items but only one of the low profit items – yet they are 'locked in' to the former by the latter. Loss leaders also attract customers into retail stores where they will usually buy normally priced products as well as the loss leaders.

(c) If two or more products in the line share joint production costs (**joint products**), prices of the products will be considered as a single decision. For example, if a common production process makes one unit of joint product A for each one unit of joint product B, a price for A which achieves a demand of, say, 17,000 units, will be inappropriate if associated with a price for product B which would only sell, say, 10,000 units. 7,000 units of B would be unsold and wasted.

## 1.6 Pricing under oligopoly

As discussed earlier under **oligopoly**, in established industries dominated by a few major firms, however, it is generally accepted that a **price initiative by one firm** will be countered by a **price reaction** by competitors. Here, prices tend to be fairly stable, unless pushed upwards by inflation or strong growth in demand. Consequently, in industries such as breakfast cereals (dominated in Britain by *Kellogg's*, *Nabisco* and *Quaker*) or canned soups (*Heinz*, *Crosse & Blackwell* and *Campbell's*) a certain **price stability might be expected** without too many competitive price initiatives, except when cost inflation pushes up the price of one firm's products with other firms soon following.

In the event that a **rival cuts prices** expecting to increase market share, a firm has several options.

(a) It will **maintain its existing prices** if the expectation is that only a small market share would be lost, so that it is more profitable to keep prices at their existing level. Eventually, the rival firm may drop out of the market or be forced to raise its prices.

(b) It may **maintain its prices** but respond with a **non-price counter-attack**. This is a more positive response, because the firm will be securing or justifying its current prices.

(c) It may **reduce its prices**. This should protect the firm's market share at the expense of profitability. The main beneficiary from the price reduction will be the consumer.

(d) It may **raise its prices** and respond with a **non-price counter-attack**. The extra revenue from the higher prices might be used to finance promotion on product changes. A price increase would be based on a campaign to emphasise the quality difference between the firm's own product and the rival's product.

### 1.6.1 Price leadership

Given that price competition can have disastrous consequences for all suppliers in conditions of oligopoly, it is not unusual to find that large corporations emerge as **price leaders**. A price leader will dominate price levels for a class of products; **increases or decreases by the price leader provide a direction to market price patterns**. The price dominant firm may lead without moving at all. This would be the case if other firms sought to raise prices and the leader did not follow, then the upward move in prices will be halted. The price leader generally has a large, if not necessarily the largest, market share. The company will usually be an efficient low-cost producer with a reputation for technical competence.

**The role of price leader is based on a track record of having initiated price moves that have been accepted by both competitors and customers**. Often, this is associated with a mature well established management group. Any dramatic changes in industry competition, (a new entrant, or changes in the board room) may endanger the price leadership role.

# 2 Cost accounting and breakeven analysis

**FAST FORWARD**

**Pricing decisions** should be based on detailed information including knowledge of costs. Cost accountants use two main approaches: **absorption costing** and **direct costing**. Because overheads are unaffected by pricing decisions, direct costs and **contribution** should always be used for making decisions about prices and assessing profitability. Contribution is also used in **breakeven analysis**. The extent by which budgeted sales exceed the breakeven point is called the **margin of safety**.

We looked briefly at the two main approaches to accounting for costs when we considered cost-plus pricing methods. The approaches are usually known as **absorption costing** and **direct costing**.

## 2.1 Classification of costs

**Key concept**

> We may regard costs of production as being divided into two main categories. These are **direct costs** and **overheads**.

**Direct costs** are also called **variable costs** or, very frequently, **marginal costs**. They are the **costs** which can be identified as **directly associated** with the process of producing an item of a good or service: in a manufacturing context they would include the material which goes into the product, the labour used to produce it and any expenses traceable to it, such as power for the machine which was used to make it. The point about these costs is that **they do not arise until a unit of product is made**. They are called variable costs because they vary with the **volume of production**. **Overheads**, on the other hand, are incurred **whether production takes place or not**. This category of cost includes such items as rent, heat and insurance and will probably be far larger than the direct costs. Cost accounting schemes in large organisations usually only concern themselves with **manufacturing overheads**, marketing and administrative overheads being dealt with separately – though some organisations will absorb them into product cost as well.

**Absorption costing** calculates a cost for a product **including overheads**. This method is widely used.

(a)   It is **required by law** for valuation of stock in the published accounts of limited companies and plcs.

(b)   It allows a very **simple cost-plus approach to price**. This is frequently used for one-off, special orders. Cost plus pricing should ensure that the company makes a profit.

(c)   It draws management attention to the **control of overheads**.

However, absorption costing has several disadvantages. We need to consider two in the context of pricing.

(a)   The process of **allocating overheads to products is extremely arbitrary**; two cost accountants working separately might arrive at quite different results.

(b)   Since overheads are fixed in the short term, they are **irrelevant for decision making in the short term**; no short term decision can affect them and so they should be ignored. **Pricing is a short-term decision**.

As a result, the **direct cost** of a product should be used when making decisions about prices or comparing the financial performance of different products. This requires the use of **contribution.**

**Key concept**

> **Contribution** is defined as sales value less all variable costs of sale. These will include direct manufacturing costs and any direct selling costs such as a sales promotion or distribution cost per item. Contribution is an abbreviation of **contribution to fixed costs and profit** and is widely used in product management. The **contribution/sales (c/s) ratio** is calculated as contribution divided by selling price. Contribution can be calculated per item or in total.

## 2.2 Breakeven analysis

Breakeven analysis is a useful application of marginal costing. Before a company starts to make a profit during a trading period, it must first earn **enough contribution to cover its fixed costs**. The volume of sales at which this occurs is known as the **breakeven point** and may be expressed in units or value. At this volume of sales, revenue just covers fixed costs plus variable costs and this implies that **contribution at this point equals fixed costs**. As total contribution equals contribution per unit times number of units sold, **the number of units of sales required to breakeven** is equal to:

$$\frac{\text{Total fixed costs}}{\text{Contribution per unit}}$$

## 2.2.1 Example 1

Expected sales      10,000 units at £8 = £80,000
Variable cost         £5 per unit
Fixed costs           £21,000

*Required*

Compute the breakeven point.

# Solution

The contribution per unit is £(8 − 5)    = £3
Contribution required to break even    = fixed costs = £21,000
Breakeven point (BEP)    = £21,000 ÷ £3 = 7,000 units
In revenue, BEP    = (7,000 × £8) = £56,000

Sales above £56,000 will result in profit of £3 per unit of additional sales, and sales below £56,000 will mean a loss of £3 per unit for each unit by which sales fall short of 7,000 units. In other words, profit will improve or worsen by the amount of contribution per unit.

|  | 7,000 units | | 7,001 units |
| --- | --- | --- | --- |
|  | £ | | £ |
| Revenue | 56,000 | | 56,008 |
| Less variable costs | 35,000 | | 35,005 |
| Contribution | 21,000 | | 21,003 |
| Less fixed costs | 21,000 | | 21,000 |
| Profit | 0 | (= breakeven) | 3 |

**The sales revenue required to break even** can be calculated by dividing fixed costs by the c/s ratio.

## 2.2.2 Example 2

In the example above the C/S ratio is $\dfrac{£3}{£8}$ = 37.5%

Breakeven is where sales revenue = $\dfrac{£21,000}{37.5\%}$ = £56,000

At a price of £8 per unit, this represents 7,000 units of sales.

The contribution/sales ratio is a measure of how much contribution is earned from each £1 of sales. The C/S ratio of 37.5% in the above example means that for every £1 of sales, a contribution of 37.5p is earned. Thus, in order to earn a total contribution of £21,000, and if contribution increases by 37.5p per £1 of sales, sales must be:

$$\dfrac{£1}{37.5p} \times £21,000 = £56,000$$

An important application of breakeven analysis is the determination of **margin of safety**. This is simply the extent to which budgeted sales exceed break even. Knowledge of the magnitude of the margin of safety enables a reasoned response when sales do not reach budget. A small incursion into the margin of safety can probably be dealt with by a policy of 'wait and see', but if sales fall, more drastic action may be needed. Any adjustment of price will, of course, require a re-computation of the breakeven point and must be made in the light of what is known about price elasticity of demand.

A **breakeven chart** records the amount of fixed costs, variable costs, total costs and total revenue at all volumes of sales, and at a given sales price.

(a)

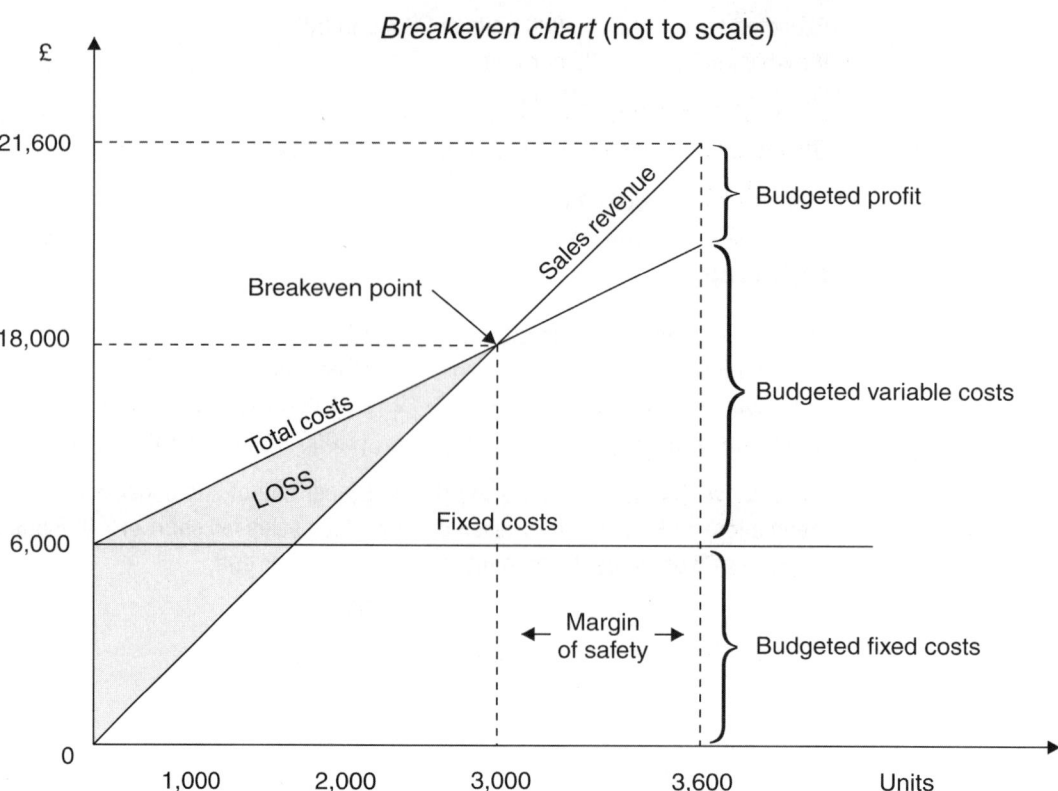

*Breakeven chart* (not to scale)

(b)   The breakeven point can also be calculated arithmetically as follows.

$$\frac{\text{Fixed costs (required contribution)}}{\text{Contribution per unit}} = \frac{£6,000}{£(6-3-1)}$$

$$= \quad £6,000 \div £2 \text{ per unit}$$

$$= \quad 3,000 \text{ units}$$

In other words, the firm needs to sell 3,000 units to cover its costs.

There are several **assumptions normally applied in CVP analysis**.

(a)   The **sale price per unit is constant** over the entire relevant range of output.

(b)   **Stock levels do not vary significantly**, so that production output and sales volumes are the same.

(c)   The **mix of products sold is constant** at all levels of activity, where more than one product is included in the analysis. In other words, the same proportion of each product will be sold whether total sales are, say, 100 units, or 1,000 units.

(d)   **Variable cost** per unit does not change, in the short run.

(e)   **Fixed costs are constant**. In practice many 'fixed cost' items are **step** cost in nature over a wide range of activity. For example, to increase output a new factory might have to be built. Fixed costs estimates should therefore apply within the relevant range of activity only.

(f)   **It ignores risk**.

(g)   It generally assumes that there are no **limiting factors** on production.

**Real-life pricing**

Before you get too worried about or carried away with the pricing methods and their technicalities described in this chapter, you should read the following extracts from an article by Vanessa Holder in the *Financial Times*.

'*Pricing is guesswork. It is usually assumed that marketers use scientific methods to determine the price of their products. Nothing could be further from the truth.*'

*David Ogilvy*
*Ogilvy on Advertising*

This view of pricing is widely held. 'There is very little we know about pricing and pricing research,' admitted one international company renowned for its premium pricing recently.

'Pricing is managers' biggest marketing headache,' noted Robert Dolan of the Harvard Business School in last September's Harvard Business Review. 'It's where they feel the most pressure to perform and the least certain that they are doing a good job.'

Yet managers are only too aware of the rewards of a better pricing strategy. It offers the seductive promise of an immediate – and possibly substantial – increase in profits, without heavy up front costs. It is an attractive lever for companies that want to put a renewed emphasis on expanding revenues after years of cost cutting.

Yet the problem is not usually a lack of familiarity with pricing options, according to Kalchas. Rather, the problem is the under-exploitation of these options as a result of roadblocks within the organisation. Many companies have a poor mechanism for setting prices; in addition, they make insufficient use of available data.

The article goes on to look at how this problem can be tackled, and indeed how some companies are already dealing with it. This is an article which is well worth reading in full (it is too long to reproduce here), so see if you can find it (perhaps in a good technical library).

# 3 Place

**FAST FORWARD**

**Distribution channels** provide transport, stockholding and storage, local knowledge, promotion and display. **Direct distribution** occurs when the product goes direct from producer to consumer.

**Downstream drift**

Companies are drifting downstream. That is, they are gradually losing interest in how they make their products, and focusing more on how those goods and services reach their ultimate customer.

The car industry's new obsession with what happens to its products once they leave the factory arises in part because it has already cut the costs of production substantially. So it is planning to take an axe to distribution costs, too. *Ford* is the company that is reshaping itself most radically. It is handing over more of the responsibility for manufacturing to sub-contractors. But at the same time it is acquiring automotive servicing companies, such as the UK's *Kwik-Fit* and a Florida-based car recycling business.

The trend is visible in other industries, too. Personal computer manufacturers have delegated most of the important technical decisions that shape their products to component suppliers such as *Intel* and *Microsoft*. They increasingly delegate the mundane task of making their products to third-party manufacturers.

But they are following *Dell Computer* in seizing back customer relationships from distributors and dealers. Indeed, by offering customers free internet access or free online training, they seek to infiltrate themselves into the customer's life.

*Peter Martin, Financial Times*

## 3.1 Distribution channels

Independently owned and operated distributors may well have their own objectives, strategies and plans. In their decision-making processes, these are likely to take precedence over those of the manufacturer or supplier with whom they are dealing. This can lead to conflict. Suppliers may solve the problem by buying their own distribution route or by distributing direct to their customers.

In order for a product to be distributed a number of basic functions usually need to be fulfilled.

| Transport | This function may be provided by the supplier, the distributor or may be sub-contracted to a specialist. For some products, such as perishable goods, transport planning is vital. |
|---|---|
| Stock holding and storage | For production planning purposes, an uninterrupted flow of production is often essential, so stocks of finished goods accumulate and need to be stored, incurring significant costs and risks. |
| | For consumer goods, holding stock at the point of sale is very costly; the overheads for city centre retail locations are prohibitive. A good stock control system is essential, designed to avoid stockouts whilst keeping stockholding costs low. |
| Local knowledge | As production has tended to become centralised in pursuit of economies of scale, the need to understand local markets has grown, particularly when international marketing takes place. The intricacies and idiosyncrasies of local markets are key marketing information. |
| Promotion | Whilst major promotional campaigns for national products are likely to be carried out by the supplier, the translation of the campaign to local level is usually the responsibility of the local distributor, often as a joint venture. |
| Display | Presentation of the product at the local level is often a function of the local distributor. Specialist help from merchandisers can be bought in but decisions on layout and display need to be taken by local distributors, often following patterns produced centrally. |

 Action Programme 4

For many goods, producers use retailers as middlemen in getting the product to the customer. Try to think of some of the disadvantages of doing this, from the producer's point of view.

### 3.1.1 Points in the chain of distribution

**Distributors**

(a) **Retailers**. These are traders operating outlets which sell directly to households. They may be classified in a number of ways.

   (i) Type of goods sold (eg hardware, furniture)

   (ii) Type of service (self-service, counter service)

   (iii) Size

   (iv) Location (rural, city-centre, suburban shopping mall, out-of-town shopping centre)

   (v) **Independent retailers** (including the local corner shop, although independents are not always as small as this)

   (vi) **Multiple chains**, some of which are associated with one class of product while others are 'variety' chains, holding a wide range of different stocks

   (vii) Still others are **voluntary groups** of independents, usually grocers.

(b) **Wholesalers**. These are intermediaries who stock a range of products from competing manufacturers to sell on to other organisations such as retailers. Many wholesalers specialise in particular products. Most deal in consumer goods, but some specialise in industrial goods, such as steel stockholders and builders' merchants.

(c) **Distributors and dealers**. These are organisations which contract to buy a manufacturer's goods and sell them to customers. Their function is similar to that of wholesalers, but they usually offer a narrower product range, sometimes (as in the case of most car dealers) the products of a single manufacturer. In addition to selling on the manufacturer's product, distributors often promote the products and provide after-sales service.

(d) **Agents**. Agents differ from distributors

   (i) Distributors **buy** the manufacturer's goods and **re-sell** them at a profit.

   (ii) Agents do not purchase the manufacturer's goods, but earn a commission on whatever sales they make.

(e) **Franchisees**. These are independent organisations which, in exchange for an initial fee and (usually) a share of sales revenue, are allowed to trade under the name of a parent organisation. Most fast food outlets are franchises.

(f) **Multiple stores** (eg **supermarkets**) buy goods for retailing direct from the producer, many of them under their 'own label' brand name.

 **Marketing at Work**

**Safeway's logistics**

*Safeway* has introduced a satellite tracking system in order to improve its distribution system. The company is to employ the system to track the movements of 600 trucks around the country and computers to check on drivers' techniques. It hopes to save at least £1m per year in fuel costs as well as improving the efficiency of its distribution system serving 420 supermarkets. The system could be used to tell, for example, whether a driver was over-revving in third gear, and using more fuel as a consequence; drivers could also be routed around traffic congestion, and stores warned of late deliveries. Safeway expect to recoup the costs (£1.5m installation and £350,000 per year operational) within the first year. Satellite tracking has already cut 10% off the full costs of one of the group's largest distribution depots at Warrington, and the savings could potentially be far greater in delay reduction and reduced labour costs.

Streamlining the system is felt to be an essential element in improving service to customers. According to a spokesman: 'By changing the warehouse process, we can add one day's life to fresh produce'.

The computer software involved will be integrated with Safeway's bar coding system for products, allowing managers to track the whereabouts of individual items as they move from depot to store. This control is felt to be essential in developing an effective marketing system.

*Financial Times*

### 3.1.2 Types of distribution channel

Choosing distribution channels is important for any organisation, because once a set of channels has been established, subsequent changes are likely to be costly and slow to implement. Distribution channels fall into one of two categories: **direct** and **indirect channels**.

**Direct distribution** means the product going directly from producer to consumer without the use of a specific intermediary. These methods are often described as **active** since they typically involve the **supplier** making the first approach to a potential customer. Direct distribution methods generally fall into two categories: those using **media** such as the press, leaflets and telephones to invite response and purchase by the consumer and those using a **sales force** to contact consumers face to face.

**Indirect distribution** is a system of distribution, common among manufactured goods, which makes use of intermediaries; wholesalers, retailers or perhaps both. In contrast to direct distribution, these methods are often thought of as being **passive** in the sense that they rely on consumers to make the first approach by entering the relevant retail outlet.

 Marketing at Work

**Thornton's chocolates**

The importance of place in marketing was borne out by the success of *Thorntons* in gaining a 13% rise in like-for-like sales, lifting interim profits by 30%. Roger Paffard, newly appointed chief executive, has seen his strategy of paying attention to the stores in which the company sells its chocolates pay off handsomely – in refitted stores, like-for-like sales were up by 22.5% he claimed. Pre-tax profits increased from £7.63m to £9.94m in the 28 weeks to 11 January. Christmas sales were up by 25%.

*Financial Times*

In building up efficient channels of distribution, a manufacturer must consider several factors.

(a)   How many **intermediate stages** should be used and how many dealers at each stage?

(b)   What **support** should the manufacturer give to the dealers? It may be necessary to provide an after-sales and repair service, and regular visits to retailers' stores. The manufacturer might need to consider advertising or sales promotion support, including merchandising.

(c)   To what extent does the manufacturer wish to **dominate a channel of distribution**? A market leader might wish to ensure that its market share is maintained, so that it could, for example, offer **exclusive distribution contracts** to major retailers.

(d)   To what extent does the manufacturer wish to **integrate its marketing effort** up to the point of sale with the consumer? Combined promotions with retailers, for example, would only be possible if the manufacturer dealt directly with the retailer (rather than through a wholesaler).

## 3.2 Channel design decisions

Channels are designed bearing in mind the characteristics of customers, the product, the available distributors and the methods used by competitors. There are factors encouraging both direct distribution and the use of intermediaries.

### Marketing at Work

**Airlines and travel agents**

Airlines are moving away from distributing their tickets via travel agents and towards the Internet. Travel agents' commission is being reduced or eliminated and the incentive payments they receive for making bookings with the global computer reservations systems are under threat. *Lufthansa*, for example, decided not to pay commission to travel agents after the end of August 2004.

Travel agents are responding by offering increased services, particularly to corporate clients, in return for direct charges.

In setting up a channel of distribution, the supplier must consider five things.

- Customers
- Product characteristics
- Distributor characteristics
- The channel chosen by competitors
- The supplier's own characteristics

### 3.2.1 Customers

The number of potential customers, their buying habits and their geographical locations are key influences. The use of mail order for those with limited mobility (rural location, illness) is an example of the influence of customers on channel design. Marketing industrial components to the car industry needs to take account of the geographic distribution of the car industry in the UK. The growth of Internet trading, both in consumer and business to business markets, has been built on the rapid spread of fast Internet access.

### 3.2.2 Product characteristics

Some product characteristics have an important effect on the design of the channel of distribution.

(a) **Perishability**

Fresh fruit and newspapers must be distributed very quickly or they become worthless. Speed of delivery is therefore a key factor.

(b) **Customisation**

Customised products tend to be distributed direct. When a wide range of options is available, sales may be made using demonstration units, with customised delivery to follow.

(c) **After-sales service/technical advice**

Extent and cost must be carefully considered, staff training given and quality control systems set up. Training programmes are often provided for distributors by suppliers.

(d)   **Franchising**

Franchising has become a popular means of growth both for suppliers and for franchisees who carry the set-up costs and licence fees. The supplier gains additional outlets quickly and exerts more control than is usual in distribution.

### 3.2.3 Distributor characteristics

The capability of the distributor to take on the distributive functions already discussed above is obviously an important influence on the supplier's choice.

### 3.2.4 Competitors' channel choice

For many consumer goods, a supplier's brand will sit alongside its competitors' products and there is little the supplier can do about it. For other products, distributors may stock one name brand only (for example, in car distribution) and in return be given an exclusive area. In this case, new suppliers may face difficulties in breaking into a market if all the best distribution outlets have been taken up.

### 3.2.5 Supplier characteristics

A strong financial base gives the supplier the option of buying and operating their own distribution channel. *Boots the Chemist* is a prime example. The market position of the supplier is also important: distributors are keen to be associated with the market leader but the third, fourth or fifth brand in a market is likely to find more distribution problems.

### 3.2.6 Factors favouring the use of direct selling

(a)   An expert sales force will be needed to demonstrate products, explain product characteristics and provide after sales service.

(b)   Intermediaries may be unwilling or unable to sell the product. For example, the ill-fated *Sinclair C5* eventually had to be sold by direct mail.

(c)   Existing channels may be linked to other producers, reluctant to carry new product lines.

(d)   The intermediaries willing to sell the product may be too costly, or they may not be maximising potential sales. This problem caused *Nissan* to terminate its contract with its sole UK distributor in 1991: Nissan believed that the distributor's pricing strategy was inappropriate.

(e)   If specialised transport requirements are involved, intermediaries may not be able to deliver goods to the final customer.

(f)   Where potential buyers are geographically concentrated the supplier's own sales force can easily reach them (typically an industrial market). One example is the financial services market centred on the City of London.

### 3.2.7 Factors favouring the use of intermediaries

(a)   There may be insufficient resources to finance a large sales force.

(b)   A policy decision to invest in increased productive capacity rather than extra marketing effort may be taken.

(c)   The supplier may have insufficient in-house marketing 'know-how' in selling to retail stores.

(d)   The assortment of products may be insufficient for a sales force to carry. A wholesaler can complement a limited range and make more efficient use of his sales force.

(e) Intermediaries can market small lots as part of a range of goods. The supplier would incur a heavy sales overhead if its own sales force took small individual orders.

(f) The existence of large numbers of potential buyers spread over a wide geographical area. This is typical of consumer markets.

### 3.2.8 Making the channel decision

Producers have a number of decisions to make.

(a) What types of distributor are to be used (wholesalers, retailers, agents)?

(b) How many of each type will be used? The answer to this depends on what degree of market exposure will be sought.

  (i) **Intensive distribution** involves concentrating on a segment of the total market, such as choosing limited geographical distribution rather than national distribution.

  (ii) Using **selective distribution**, the producer selects a group of retail outlets from amongst all retail outlets on grounds of the brand image, or related to the retailers' capacity to provide after sales service. *Rolls Royce's* image is safe in the hands of *H R Owen* but might be damaged if sold by an less established dealer.

  (iii) **Exclusive distribution** is an extension of selective distribution. Particular outlets are granted exclusive handling rights within a prescribed geographical area. Sometimes exclusive distribution, or franchise rights, are coupled with making special financial arrangements for land, buildings or equipment, such as petrol station agreements.

(c) Who will carry out specific marketing tasks?

  - Credit provision
  - Delivery
  - After sales service
  - Sales and product training
  - Display

(d) How will the performance of distributors be evaluated?

  - In terms of cost?
  - In terms of sales levels?
  - According to the degree of control achieved?
  - By the amount of conflict that arises?

To develop an integrated system of distribution, the supplier must consider all the factors influencing distribution combined with a knowledge of the relative merits of the different types of channel available.

### 3.2.9 Multi-channel decisions

A producer serving both industrial and consumer markets may decide to use intermediaries for his consumer division and direct selling for his industrial division. For example, a detergent manufacturer might employ salesmen to sell to wholesalers and large retail groups in their consumer division. It would not be efficient for the sales force to approach small retailers directly. The distribution channels appropriate for industrial markets may not be suitable for consumer markets.

### 3.2.10 Industrial and consumer distribution channels

**Industrial markets** may be characterised as having fewer, larger customers purchasing expensive products which may be custom built. It is due to these characteristics that industrial distribution channels tend to be more direct and shorter than for consumer markets. It has to be remembered, however, that the most appropriate distribution channels will depend specifically on the objectives of the company regarding market exposure. There are specialist distributors in the industrial sector, which may be used as well as, or instead of, selling directly to the companies within this sector.

There are fewer direct distribution channels, from the manufacturer to the consumer in the **consumer market**. Examples may be found in small 'cottage' industries or mail order companies. It is more usual for companies in consumer markets to use wholesalers and retailers to move their product to the final consumer.

(a)   **Wholesalers** break down the bulk from manufacturers and pass products on to retailers. They take on some of the supplier's risks by funding stock. Recently in the UK there has been a reduction in importance of this type of intermediary.

(b)   **Retailers** sell to the final consumers. They may give consumers added benefits by providing services such as credit, delivery and a wide variety of goods. In the UK, retailers have increased in power whilst wholesalers have declined. Retailing has also become more concentrated with increased dominance of large multiples.

### 3.2.11 Channel dynamics

Channels are subject to conflicts between members. This need not be destructive as long as it remains manageable. Manufacturers may have little influence on how their product is presented to the public. Conflicts are usually resolved by arbitration rather than judicial means.

(a)   In **corporate marketing systems** the stages in production and distribution are owned by a single corporation. This common ownership permits close integration and therefore the corporation controls activities along the distribution chain. For example, *Laura Ashley* shops sell goods produced in Laura Ashley factories.

(b)   **Contractual marketing systems** involve agreement over aspects of distribution marketing. One example of a contractual marketing system that has become popular over the last decade is franchising.

(c)   If a plan is drawn up between channel members to help reduce conflict this is often termed an **administered marketing system**.

Channel leadership gives power to the member of the channel with whom it lies. In industrial markets where channel lengths are generally short, power often lies with manufacturers of products rather than middlemen.

**Exam tip**

> Distribution is often not represented and easy to ignore, but is key to issues of speed and profitability. Each channel has different needs and requirements, as examined in December 2000. In December 2001 there was a question on the interesting topic of services distribution: in this case the distribution of package holidays.

## 3.3 Vertical marketing systems (VMS)

VMS have been developed to offer an alternative to traditional distribution channels. A VMS approach aims to integrate all the members in a chain of distribution into one cohesive and co-operative unit, all with a common objective and the ability to solve problems jointly.

The following diagram illustrates some of the various types of collaborative relationships that a company may get into. It may even be involved in several at once.

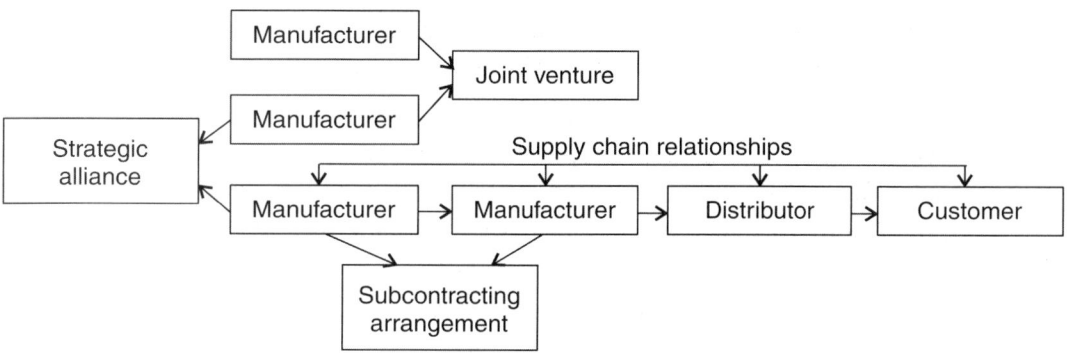

(Source: Hooley *et al*, *Marketing Strategy and Competitive Positioning*, 1998)

## 3.4 International channels

As markets open to international trade, channel decisions become more complex. A company can export using host country middlemen or domestic middlemen. These may or may not take title to the goods. Implications of channel management in the case of exporters include a loss of control over product policies like price, image, packaging and service. A producer may undertake a joint venture or licensing agreement or even manufacture abroad. All will have implications for the power structure and control over the product.

## 3.5 The supply chain

Many multinational enterprises (MNEs) have been getting larger. Some writers are arguing that the trend will continue – so that for many sectors there will be fewer players of world class dominating the field. We have seen this in the automobile industry for example, with many European companies merging to be able to compete effectively with US giants and the Japanese.

There have been, at the same time, much **closer links** with companies in the supply chain in order to extract best value for money and reduce stockholdings. This has had major consequences on the distribution methods of companies in these supply chains, delivering to their customers on a **just in time** (JIT) basis.

The change in supply chain linkage is demonstrated in the following model (taken from *Monczka*).

Historically, businesses in the supply chain have operated relatively independently of one another to create value for an ultimate customer. Independence was maintained by buffers of material, capacity and lead-times. This is represented in the 'Traditional' model shown below.

Market and competitive demands are now, however, **compressing lead times** and businesses are reducing inventories and excess capacity. Linkages between businesses in the supply chain must therefore become much tighter. This new condition is shown in the 'Integrated supply chain' model.

Monczka further claims that there seems to be increasing recognition that, in the future, it will be **whole supply chains** which will compete and not just individual firms. This will continue to have a great impact upon distribution methods.

*Supply chain models*

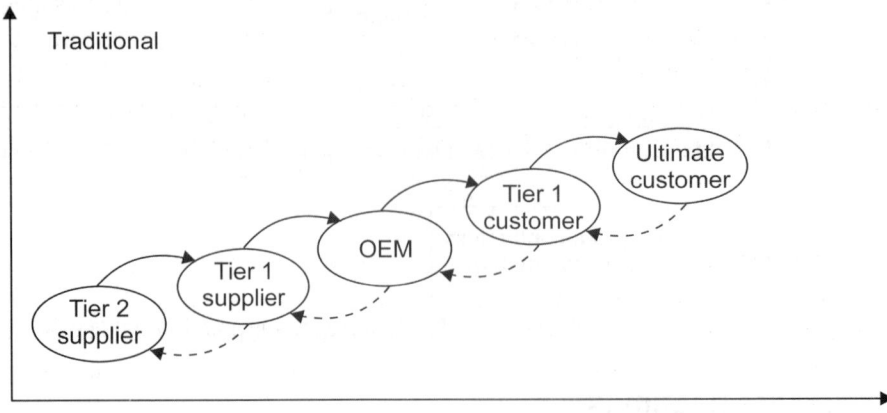

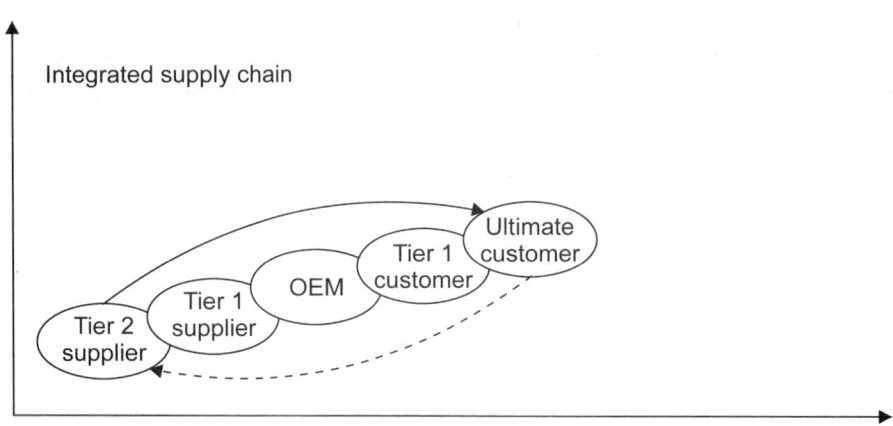

**Key concept**

> **Supply chain management** is about **optimising the activities** of companies working together to produce goods and services.

The aim is to co-ordinate the whole chain, from raw material suppliers to end customers. The chain should be considered as a **network** rather than a **pipeline** – a network of vendors support a network of customers, with third parties such as transport firms helping to link the companies.

## Marketing at Work

The Hong Kong based export trading company, *Li and Fung*, takes the following approach to its manufacturing supply chain.

'Say we get an order from a European retailer to produce 10,000 garments. It's not a simple matter of our Korean office sourcing Korean products or our Indonesian office sourcing Indonesian products. For the customer we might decide to buy yarn from a Korean producer but have it woven and dyed in Taiwan. So we pick the yarn and ship it to Taiwan. The Japanese have the best zippers and buttons, but they manufacture them mostly in China. Okay, so we go to *YKK*, a big Japanese zipper manufacturer and we order the right zippers from their Chinese plants. Then we determine that, because of quotas and labour conditions, the best place to make the garments is Thailand. So we ship everything there. And because the customer needs quick delivery, we may divide the order across five factories in Thailand. Effectively, we are customising the value chain to best meet the customer's needs.

'Five weeks after we have received the order, 10,000 garments arrive on the shelves in Europe, all looking like they came from one factory with colours, for example, perfectly matched. Just think about the logistics and the co-ordination.

'This is a new type of value added, a truly global product that has never been seen before. The label may say "Made in Thailand", but it's not a Thai product. We dissect the manufacturing process and look for the best solution to each step. We're not asking which country can do the best job overall. Instead, we're pulling apart the value chain and optimising each step – and we're doing it globally.... . The classic supply-chain manager in retailing is Marks & Spencer. They don't own any factories, but they have a huge team that goes into the factories and works with the management.'   *Harvard Business Review,* 1998

**Managing the supply chain varies from company to company**. A company such as *Unilever* will provide the same margarine to both *Tesco* and *Sainsbury*. The way in which the product is delivered, transactions are processed and other parts of the relationship are managed will be different since these competing supermarket chains have their own ways of operating. The focus will need to be on customer interaction, account management, after-sales service and order processing.

If the supplier 'knows' what his customers want, it does not have to guess or wait until the customer places an order. It will be able to better plan its own delivery systems. The potential for using the **Internet** to allow customers and suppliers to acquire up-to-date information about forecast needs and delivery schedules is a very recent development, but one which is being used by an increasing number of companies.

The greatest **changes in supply chain management** have taken place in the implementation of software applications. Managers today have a wider choice of systems with quick implementation times – important in a competitive market where a new supply chain system is required. Supply chains at local, regional and global level are often managed simultaneously, via a standardised infrastructure that nevertheless allows for local adaptation where this is important.

## Marketing at Work

- A leading European manufacturer has said: 'We must localise those part of our supply chain that face the customer and regionalise all other parts of our supply chain to lower costs and improve speed of operations'.

- *PricewaterhouseCoopers* has run full page newspaper advertisements promoting its supply chain consultancy services, which indicates the importance of supply chain management to most companies. The text of one such advertisement reads: 'When it come to supply chain management, there's one universal truth: every customer is unique. What may be right for one, may not be for another.... We're working on some of the toughest supply chain problems all around the world. Reinventing strategy, optimising processes and applying new technologies intelligently. All to help companies improve their ability to operate globally and serve customers locally. With 150,000 people working in 50 different countries, we can make the world seem like a pretty small place'.

This may contain more than its share of buzzwords but it does illustrate the issues involved: the importance of individual customers, strategy and technology, and the ability of a large company to deliver services on a global basis where it has the resources.

## Action Programme 5

One of the fastest growing forms of selling in the US over the past decade has been the *factory* **outlet centre**. Discount factory shops, often situated on factory premises, from which manufacturers sell off overmakes, slight seconds, or retailers' returns are already well-established in the UK, but in the US developers have grouped such outlets together in purpose-built malls.

What would you suggest are the advantages of this method of distribution for customers and manufacturers?

 Marketing at Work

### OTC Medicines

The supply chain is often a crucial element in the success or failure of a product. In the case of over-the-counter (OTC) medicines, because of the unique features of the product, the situation and the constraints on marketers, the supply chain plays a key role in consumer choice making.

Medicines satisfy a powerful and basic need – relief from pain. As a consequence, products tend to be evaluated in terms of their strict efficacy, and the functions of branding or advertising are far less prominent than usual. According to *Mellors Reay and Partners*, who work on the marketing of OTC medicines, this is compounded by regulations and restrictions on the advertising and retail promotion of products. These include:

(a)     strict regulation of claims and impact of advertising;

(b)     non-display of items on retailers shelves;

(c)     restrictions on merchandising, discounting, the use of personality endorsement, loyalty schemes, cross promotions and free trials;

(d)     huge price rises when products transfer from prescription to OTC;

(e)     similarity between brand names because of reference to ingredients (for instance, paracetamol based analgesics include *Panadeine*, *Panadol*, *Panaleve*, *Panerel*, *Paracets*, and so on); and

(f)     the influence of the pharmacist who can overcome or counter any promotional effect.

The role of the pharmacist is crucial, and is becoming more ambivalent, as the old semi-medical professional role is combined with one as an employee of commercial and market oriented enterprises. The increasing availability of OTC medicines previously only available on prescription only increases this power. Marketing OTC medicines directly to consumers must involve, to some extent, countering the respect and trust of consumers for pharmacists.

Yet brands can become established in spite of these problems. Nurofen, for example, an ibuprofen based analgesic, has established a powerful presence by building a brand which is distinctive by using advertising which suggests both power and empathy, and also by visualising and emphasising in an imaginative way the experience and relief of pain.

*Admap*

## Chapter Roundup

- **Price** is the only element of the mix which generates revenue rather than creating cost. It must be consistent with the other elements of the marketing mix and is particularly associated with **perceptions of quality**. Economic theory deals with price in terms of market forces; its most useful aspect for the marketer is the idea of **price elasticity of demand**, which measures the extent to which a change in **price** is reflected by a proportionate change in **demand**.

- **Cost-plus pricing** is widely used because it is fairly easy to do and should lead to profitable prices. It can take account of demand by adjusting the margin added for profit. **Competitor** action, whether actual or expected, influences real-world price setting, especially under conditions of oligopoly and competitive bidding. Some customers enjoy a **consumer surplus** because they are prepared to pay a higher price. **Differential pricing** enables the supplier to exploit this willingness.

- **Pricing policy** is determined in the light of the customers' sensitivity to price, the objectives and actions of suppliers, competitors and intermediaries and the interplay of forces like inflation and income levels.

- **Pricing decisions** should be based on detailed information including knowledge of costs. Cost accountants use two main approaches: **absorption costing** and **direct costing**. Because overheads are unaffected by pricing decisions, direct costs and **contribution** should always be used for making decisions about prices and assessing profitability. Contribution is also used in **breakeven analysis**. The extent by which budgeted sales exceed the breakeven point is called the **margin of safety**.

- **Distribution channels** provide transport, stockholding and storage, local knowledge, promotion and display. **Direct distribution** occurs when the product goes direct from producer to consumer.

- Channels are designed bearing in mind the characteristics of customers, the product, the available distributors and the methods used by competitors. There are factors encouraging both direct distribution and the use of intermediaries.

## Quick Quiz

1    What is price elasticity of demand?

2    How does a seller exploit consumer surplus?

3    What is the difference between market penetration and market skimming?

4    What is price leadership?

5    What is the formula for breakeven point in units?

6    What is the use of CVP analysis?

7    What assumptions does CVP analysis make about unit price?

8    Differentiate between wholesalers, distributors and agents.

9    How do product characteristics influence distribution?

## Answers to Quick Quiz

1   A measure of the degree of change in demand for a good when its price changes

2   By raising prices without hurting demand

3   Penetration sets low prices to achieve high volumes rapidly. Skimming sets prices high to achieve high unit profits early on.

4   A dominant player whose pricing strategy is likely to set a benchmark for the industry

5   $\dfrac{\text{Total fixed cost}}{\text{Contibution per unit}}$

6   To answer important questions about sales volume and profit

7   That it is constant over the relevant range of output

8   A full answer is given in Section 3.1.1

9   Characteristics include: perishability; customisation; level of after-sales support

## Action Programme Review

1   You might have identified a number of different factors here. Perhaps the most important general point to make is that price is particularly important if the other elements in the marketing mix are relatively similar across a range of competing products. For example, there is a very wide variety of toothpastes on the market, most of them not much differentiated from the others. The price of a particular toothpaste may be a crucial factor in its sales success.

2   The main problem is that, unless very detailed research has been carried out, the price elasticity of a particular product or service is likely to be unknown. As a theoretical concept, it is useful in gaining an understanding of the *effects* of price changes; but it is of little use as a practical tool in *determining* prices.

3   The industry referred to is the financial services industry. When economic factors cause alterations in interest rates (one of the main 'costs' borne by building societies and banks, because of their interest payments to investors), the societies reduce or increase their lending rates (the price of their mortgage products). It is usual to see one of the larger societies leading the way, after which the others fall into line.

4   Your answers might include some of the following points.

   (a)   The middleman's margin reduces the revenue available to the producer.

   (b)   The producer needs an infrastructure for looking after the retailers – keeping them informed, keeping them well stocked – which might not be necessary in, say, a mail order business.

   (c)   The producer loses some control over the marketing of the product. The power of some retailers (for example, W H Smith in the world of book publishing) is so great that they are able to dictate marketing policy to their suppliers.

5   Prices are up to 50% below conventional retail outlets and shoppers can choose from a wide range of branded goods, that they otherwise might not be able to afford. They can also turn a shopping trip into a day out, as factory outlet centres are designed as 'destination' shopping venues, offering facilities such as playgrounds and restaurants.

Manufacturers enjoy the ability to sell surplus stock at a profit in a controlled way that does not damage the brand image. They have also turned the shops into a powerful marketing tool for test-marketing products before their high street launch, and selling avant-garde designs that have not caught on in the main retail market.

Now try Question 8 at the end of the Study Text

# Ethical considerations

## Chapter topic list

1    Ethics and the organisation
2    Social responsibility
3    Corporate governance
4    Ethics and marketing

## Syllabus content

- The issues of corporate and social responsibility, sustainability and ethics in achieving competitive advantage, enhancing corporate reputation and creating stakeholder value

# Introduction

Organisations are part of human society and, like individual people, are subject to rules that govern their conduct towards others. Some of these rules are **law** and enforced by legal sanction. Other rules fall into the realm of **ethics** or morality and are enforced only by the strength of society's approval or disapproval. Under a system of government that enjoys a measure of political legitimacy, law is generally a matter of consensus. Legal rules are therefore largely a matter of enforcing broadly acceptable standards of behaviour in a practical way. Ethics is more concerned with **absolute standards** of **right and wrong** and, human nature being what it is, individuals have widely divergent views on what those standards should be. Inevitably, therefore, ethical conduct is a matter of continuing debate. The first section of this chapter is concerned with the strategic impact of ethical ideas on organisations.

The behaviour of organisations may also be considered in the light of notions of **corporate social responsibility**. This is a rather poorly defined concept. However, there does now seem to be widespread acceptance that commercial organizations should devote some of their resources to the promotion of wider social aims that are not necessarily mandated by either law or the rules of ethics.

The final section of this chapter is concerned with **corporate governance** and the mechanisms that may be installed to promote fair and honest behaviour at the strategic apex.

# 1 Ethics and the organisation

Ethics is not the same thing as law or the rules of religion. Ethical theory is not integrated: consequentialist, deontological and natural law based rules are capable of pointing to different conclusions. Partly as a result of this, **ethical dilemmas** can exist at all levels in the organisation.

## 1.1 Fundamentals of ethical theory

**Ethics** is concerned with **right and wrong** and how conduct should be judged to be good or bad. It is about how we should live our lives and, in particular, how we should behave towards other people. It is therefore relevant to all forms of human activity.

Business life is a fruitful source of **ethical dilemmas** because its whole purpose is material gain, the making of profit. Success in business requires a constant, avid search for potential advantage over others and business people are under pressure to do whatever yields such advantage.

### 1.1.1 Non-cognitivism, ethical relativism and intuitionism

The approach called **non-cognitivism** denies the possibility of acquiring objective knowledge of moral principles. It suggests that all moral statements are essentially subjective and arise from the culture, belief or emotion of the speaker.

Non-cognitivism recognises the differences that exist between the rules of behaviour prevailing in different cultures. The view that right and wrong are culturally determined is called **ethical relativism** or **moral relativism**. This is clearly a matter of significance in the context of international business. Managers encountering cultural norms of behaviour that differ significantly from their own may be puzzled to know what rules to follow.

### 1.1.2 Cognitivism

**Cognitivist** approaches to ethics are built on the principle that objective, universally applicable moral truths exist and can be known. There are four important cognitivist theories to consider after we have looked at **law** and **religion** in relation to ethics.

### 1.1.3 Ethics and religion

Religions are based on the concept of universally applicable principle. However, they not only provide endless examples to support the moral relativist approach, both in their rules and their statements of fundamental belief; they are also vulnerable to criticism on logical grounds. Specifically, how does God decide what is right and what is wrong? Presumably, it is not mere whim and **moral principles** are involved. The implication is that it is proper to seek to understand these reasons for ourselves and to use them as the basis of our moral code.

### 1.1.4 Ethics and law

Cognitivist ethics and law can be seen as parallel and connected systems of rules for regulating conduct. Both are concerned with right conduct and the principles that define it. However, ethics and law are not the same thing.

Law must be free from ambiguity. However, unlike law, ethics can quite reasonably be an arena for debate, about both the principles involved and their application in specific rules. The law must be certain and therefore finds it difficult to deal with problems of conduct that are subject to opinion and debate.

Another difference is that many legal rules are only very remotely connected with ethics, if at all, and some laws in some countries are of debateable moral stature, to say the least.

### 1.1.5 Consequentialist ethics: utilitarianism

The **consequentialist** approach to ethics is to make moral judgements about courses of action by reference to their outcomes or consequences. Right or wrong becomes a question of benefit or harm.

**Utilitarianism** is the best-known formulation of this approach and can be summed up in the **'greatest good'** principle. This says that when deciding on a course of action we should choose the one that is likely to result in the greatest good for the greatest number of people.

There is an immediate problem here, which is how we are to define what is good for people. *Bentham* considered that **happiness** was the measure of good and that actions should therefore be judged in terms of their potential for promoting happiness or relieving unhappiness. Others have suggested that longer lists of harmful and beneficial things should be applied.

The utilitarian approach may also be questioned for its potential effect upon minorities. A situation in which a large majority achieved great happiness at the expense of creating misery among a small minority would satisfy the 'greatest good' principle. It could not, however, be regarded as ethically desirable. A linked problem arises when we consider the nature of happiness and unhappiness, in that pain can be very much more intense than pleasure. We must therefore be very cautious in our netting-off of total happiness against total unhappiness.

However, utilitarianism can be a useful guide to conduct. It has been used to derive wide ranging rules and can be applied to help us make judgements about individual, unique problems.

### 1.1.6 Deontological ethics

**Deontology** is concerned with the application of universal ethical principles in order to arrive at rules of conduct, the word deontology being derived from the Greek for 'duty'. Whereas the consequentialist approach judges actions by their outcomes, deontology lays down *a priori* criteria by which they may be judged in advance. The definitive treatment of deontological ethics is found in the work of *Immanuel Kant*.

Kant's approach to ethics is based on the idea that facts themselves are neutral: they are what *is*; they do not give us any indication of what *should be*. If we make moral judgements about facts, the criteria by which we judge are separate from the facts themselves. Kant suggested that the criteria come from within ourselves and are based on a sense of what is right; an **intuitive awareness** of the nature of good.

Kant spoke of motivation to act in terms of 'imperatives'. A **hypothetical imperative** lays down a course of action to achieve a certain result. For instance, if I wish to pass an examination I must study the syllabus. A **categorical imperative**, however, defines a course of action without reference to outcomes. For Kant, moral conduct is defined by categorical imperatives. We must act in certain ways because it is right to do so – right conduct is an end in itself.

Kant arrived at two formulations of the categorical imperative with which we should be familiar.

(a)   'So act that the maxim of your will could hold as a principle establishing universal law.'

In other words, **never act in a way that you would condemn in others**. This is very close to the common sense maxim called the '**golden** rule' that is found in many religious teachings. It appears in the Bible as

'Therefore all things whatsoever ye would that men should do to you, do ye even so to them: for this is the law and the prophets' (Matthew 7:12)

(b)   'Do not treat people simply as means to an end but as an end in themselves.'

The point of this rule is that it distinguishes between **people** and **objects**. We use objects as means to achieve an end: a chair is for sitting on, for instance. People are different. Human dignity requires that we regard people differently from the way we regard objects, since they have unique intellects, feelings, motivations and so on of their own. Note, however, that this does not preclude us from using people as means to an end as long as we, at the same time, recognise their right to be treated as autonomous beings. Clearly, organisations and even society itself could not function if we could not make use of other people's services.

## 1.1.7 Natural law

Natural law approaches to ethics are based on the idea that a set of objective or 'natural' moral rules exists and we can come to know what they are.

At one time natural law theory time was concerned with the rights of the citizen against arbitrary acts by powerful rulers. This was subsequently developed into a more democratic concept of **government by consent**, with a prominent position occupied by what are now called '**human rights**'.

In terms of business ethics, the natural law approach deals mostly with **rights and duties**. Where there is a right, there is also a duty to respect that right. Clearly, this idea is not limited in its application to matters of law and government. It implies that we all must respect one another's rights of all kinds. For those concerned with business ethics there are undeniable implications for behaviour towards **individuals**. Unfortunately, the implications about duties can only be as clear as the rights themselves and there are wide areas in which disagreement about rights persists.

## 1.1.8 Duty and consequences

In their pure form, neither the duties of natural law nor Kant's categorical imperative will admit consideration of the consequences of our actions: we act in a certain way because we are obeying inflexible moral rules. Unfortunately, such an approach can have undesirable results. If people have **absolute rights** that we must respect whatever the circumstances, we may find that our actions in doing so harm the **common good**. An example is the accused person who commits an offence while on bail. The potential threat to public safety has to be balanced against the right of the individual to liberty. There is thus a **great potential for conflict** between courses of action based on the consequentialist approach and those based on deontology or natural law.

While individual cases are bound to provoke debate, it would be reasonable to suggest that an inflexible approach to rules of conduct is likely to produce **ethical dilemmas**. Deciding what to do when the arguments point in opposite directions is always going to be difficult. However, generally **we do not have the option of doing nothing**, and this is particularly true of business. We discuss some specific business related dilemmas later in this chapter.

### 1.1.9 Virtue ethics

The idea of pursuing a harmonious or virtuous life was first expressed by *Aristotle*. His approach was based on gentlemanly behaviour and a rational judgement about what constitutes good. To some extent this consists of **avoiding extremes** of any kind, since moderation will lead to virtue. For example, courage lies between cowardice at one end of the scale and foolhardiness at the other.

We need not concern ourselves too closely with the detail of Aristotle's approach, except to note that the cultivation of **appropriate virtues** has been proposed as a route to ethical behaviour in business. For example, managers might cultivate a range of virtues such as those listed below.

- Courage
- Fairness
- Empathy
- Persistence
- Honesty

- Politeness
- Receptivity to new ideas
- Determination
- Firmness

## 1.2 Ethics and strategy

FAST FORWARD

**Mission** should incorporate recognition of the ethical dimension. Corporate ethics has three contexts.

- Interaction with national and international society
- Effects of routine operations
- Behaviour of individuals

In this Study Text we have emphasised that what the organisation wishes to achieve – its **mission** – is fundamental to any focussed control of its activities. When we discussed the concept of mission we made passing reference to **policies and standards of behaviour**.

It is important to understand that if ethics is applicable to corporate behaviour at all, it must therefore be a fundamental aspect of **mission**, since everything the organisation does flows from that. Managers responsible for strategic decision making cannot avoid responsibility for their organisation's ethical standing. They should consciously apply ethical rules to all of their decisions in order to filter out potentially undesirable developments.

### 1.2.1 The scope of corporate ethics

Corporate ethics may be considered in three contexts.

- The organisation's interaction with **national** and **international society**
- The effects of the organisation's **routine operations**
- The behaviour of **individual members** of staff

**Influencing society**. Businesses operate within and interact with the political, economic and social framework of wider society. It is both inevitable and proper that they will both influence and be influenced by that wider framework. Governments, individual politicians and pressure groups will all make demands on such matters as employment prospects and executive pay. Conversely, businesses themselves will find that they need to make their own representations on such matters as monetary policy and the burden of regulation. International variation in such matters and in the framework of **corporate governance** will affect organisations that operate in more than one country. It is appropriate that the organisation develops and promotes its own policy on such matters.

**Corporate behaviour**. The organisation should establish **corporate policies** for those issues over which it has direct control. Examples of matters that should be covered by policy include health, safety, labelling, equal opportunities, environmental effects, political activity, bribery and support for cultural activities.

**Individual behaviour**. Policies to guide the behaviour of individuals are likely to flow from the corporate stance on the matters discussed above. The organisation must decide on the extent to which it considers it appropriate to attempt to influence individual behaviour. Some aspects of such behaviour may be of strategic importance, especially when managers can be seen as representing or embodying the organisation's standards. Matters of financial rectitude and equal treatment of minorities are good examples here.

 Marketing at Work

**Ethics panel assails Third World placebo studies**

It is unethical for US researchers to test expensive treatments on people in Third World countries who would be unable to afford those drugs, a bioethics commission warned on Thursday in a published report. In an article in the New England Journal of Medicine, the National Bioethics Advisory Commission also said it was unethical to give volunteers placebos instead of treatments that are known to work.

These warnings by Harold Shapiro and Eric Meslin, the chairman and executive director respectively of the presidential commission, mark the latest round in a debate over the rules for conducting studies in countries where ethical standards may be less stringent than in the United States.

The issue surfaced in the Journal in 1997 when Drs. Peter Lurie and Sidney M Wolfe of Public Citizen's Health Research Group cited 15 government-financed studies that, they said, were using unethical methods to test whether various treatments could block the spread of the AIDS virus from a woman to her newborn child. All were being done in developing countries.

Some of the women in those studies were given placebos, even though the GlaxoSmithKline drug AZT had been shown to prevent babies from contracting AIDS from their infected mothers. At the time, it was regarded as unethical in the United States and other countries to test alternative AIDS treatments by giving pregnant volunteers a placebo.

Supporters of the studies had argued that giving placebos was valid because the radically different economic conditions in developing countries, where AZT was not widely available, made it virtually impossible to do the type of research that had become the standard in developed countries.

Shapiro and Meslin, who lead the 17 member advisory council established by former President Bill Clinton in 1995, wrote in the Journal that the experimental treatment should be tested against the best established treatment, "whether or not that treatment is available in the host country."

Giving placebos when an effective treatment exists "is not ethically acceptable," they said.

Shapiro and Meslin also said it was important to "avoid the exploitation of potentially vulnerable populations in developing countries."

If an experiment is testing a drug or device that " is not likely to be affordable in the host country or if the health care infrastructure cannot support its proper distribution and use, it is unethical to ask persons in that country to participate in the research, since they will not enjoy any of its potential benefits," they said.

There have been suggestions that researchers or drug companies may be testing products in poor countries because the cost is less and the rules are less stringent.

"Conducting a trial in a developing country because it is more convenient or efficient or less troublesome to do is never a sufficient justification," said Shapiro and Meslin.

The two also said that if tests show that the experimental treatment turns out to be more effective, it should be made available to all the people who participated in the study.

Researchers should not abandon their volunteers after the study is completed, they said.

*Reuters*

# 2 Social responsibility

## 2.1 Corporate social responsibility

There is a fundamental split of views about the nature of corporate responsibility.

- The **stakeholder view** that a range of goals should be pursued
- The view that the business organisation is a purely **economic force**, subject to law

Businesses, particularly large ones, are subject to increasing expectations that they will exercise **social responsibility**. This is an ill-defined concept, but appears to focus on the provision of specific benefits to society in general, such as charitable donations, the creation or preservation of employment, and spending on environmental improvement or maintenance. A great deal of the pressure is created by the activity of minority action groups and is aimed at businesses because they are perceived to possess extensive resources. The momentum of such arguments is now so great that the notion of social responsibility has become almost inextricably confused with the matter of ethics. It is important to remember the distinction. Social responsibility and ethical behaviour are not the same thing.

In this context, you should remember that a business managed with the sole objective of maximising shareholder wealth can be run in just as ethical a fashion as one in which far wider stakeholder responsibility is assumed. On the other hand, there is no doubt that many large businesses have behaved irresponsibly in the past and some continue to do so.

### 2.1.1 Against corporate social responsibility

*Milton Friedman* argued against corporate social responsibility along the following lines.

(a) Businesses do not have responsibilities, only people have responsibilities. Managers in charge of corporations are responsible to the owners of the business, by whom they are employed.

(b) These employers may have charity as their aim, but 'generally [their aim] will be to make as much money as possible while conforming to the basic rules of the society, both those embodied in law and those embodied in ethical custom.'

(c) If the statement that a manager has social responsibilities is to have any meaning, 'it must mean that he is to act in some way that is not in the interest of his employers.'

(d) If managers do this they are, generally speaking, spending the owners' money for purposes other than those they have authorised; sometimes it is the money of customers or suppliers that is spent and, on occasion, the money of employees. By doing this, the manager is, in effect, both raising taxes and deciding how they should be spent, which are functions of government, not of business. There are two objections to this.

(i) Managers have not been democratically elected (or selected in any other way) to exercise government power.

(ii)    Managers are not experts in government policy and cannot foresee the detailed effect of such social responsibility spending.

Friedman argues that the social responsibility model is politically collectivist in nature and deplores the possibility that collectivism should be extended any further than absolutely necessary in a free society.

A second argument against the assumption of corporate social responsibility is that the **maximisation of wealth is the best way that society can benefit from a business's activities**.

(a)    Maximising wealth has the effect of increasing the tax revenues available to the state to disburse on socially desirable objectives.

(b)    Maximising shareholder value has a 'trickle down' effect on other disadvantaged members of society.

(c)    Many company shares are owned by pension funds, whose ultimate beneficiaries may not be the wealthy anyway.

## 2.1.2 The stakeholder view

The **stakeholder view** is that many groups have a stake in what the organisation does. This is particularly important in the business context, where shareholders own the business but employees, customers and government also have particularly strong claims to having their interests considered. This is fundamentally an argument derived from **natural law theory** and is based on the notion of individual and collective **rights**.

It is suggested that modern corporations are so powerful, socially, economically and politically, that unrestrained use of their power will **inevitably damage** other people's rights. For example, they may blight an entire community by closing a major facility, thus forcing long term unemployment on a large proportion of the local workforce. Similarly, they may damage people's quality of life by polluting the environment. They may use their purchasing power or market share to impose unequal contracts on suppliers and customers alike. And they may exercise undesirable influence over government through their investment decisions. Under this approach, the exercise of corporate social responsibility constrains the corporation to act at all times as a **good citizen**.

Another argument points out that corporations exist **within society** and are **dependent upon it** for the resources they use. Some of these resources are obtained by direct contracts with suppliers but others are not, being provided by government expenditure. Examples are such things as transport infrastructure, technical research and education for the workforce. Clearly, corporations contribute to the taxes that pay for these things, but the relationship is rather tenuous and the tax burden can be minimised by careful management. The implication is that corporations should recognise and pay for the facilities that society provides by means of socially responsible policies and actions.

*Henry Mintzberg* (in *Power In and Around Organisations*) suggests that simply viewing organisations as vehicles for shareholder investment is inadequate.

(a)    In practice, he says, organisations are rarely controlled effectively by shareholders. Most shareholders are **passive investors**.

(b)    Large corporations can **manipulate markets**. Social responsibility, forced or voluntary, is a way of recognising this.

(c)    Moreover, as mentioned above, businesses do receive a lot of **government support**. The public pays for roads, infrastructure, education and health, all of which benefits businesses. Although businesses pay tax, the public ultimately pays, perhaps through higher prices.

(d)    Strategic decisions by businesses always have wider social consequences. In other words, says Mintzberg, the firm produces two kinds of outputs: **goods and services** and the **social consequences of its activities** (eg pollution).

## 2.1.3 Externalities

If it is accepted that businesses do not bear the total social cost of their activities, then the exercise of social responsibility is a way of compensating for this. An example is given by the environment. Industrial pollution is injurious to health: if someone is made ill by industrial pollution, then arguably the polluter should pay the sick person, as damages or in compensation, in the same way as if the business's builders had accidentally bulldozed somebody's house.

In practice, of course, while it is relatively easy to identify statistical relationships between pollution levels and certain illnesses, mapping out the **chain of cause and effect** from an individual's wheezing cough to the dust particles emitted by Factory X, as opposed to Factory Y, is quite a different matter.

Of course, it could be argued that these external costs are met out of general taxation: but this has the effect of spreading the cost amongst other individuals and businesses. Moreover, the tax revenue may be spent on curing the disease, rather than stopping it at its source. Pollution control equipment may be the fairest way of dealing with this problem. Thus advocates of social responsibility in business would argue that business's responsibilities then do not rest with paying taxes.

Is there any justification for social responsibility outside remedying the effects of a business's direct activities? For example, should businesses give to charity or sponsor the arts? Several arguments have been advanced suggesting that they should.

(a)    If the **stakeholder concept** of a business is held, then the public is a stakeholder in the business. A business only succeeds because it is part of a wider society. Giving to charity is one way of encouraging the relationship.

(b)    Charitable donations and artistic sponsorship are a useful medium of **public relations** and can reflect well on the business. It can be regarded, then, as another form of **promotion**, which like advertising, serves to enhance consumer awareness of the business, while not encouraging the sale of a particular brand.

The arguments for and against social responsibility of business are complex ones. However, ultimately they can be traced to different assumptions about society and the relationships between the individuals and organisations within it.

# 2.2 The ethical stance

**FAST FORWARD**

An organisation's **ethical stance** is the extent to which it will exceed its minimum obligations to stakeholders. There are four typical stances.

–    Short-term shareholder interest
–    Long-term shareholder interest
–    Multiple stakeholder obligations
–    Shaper of society

**Key concept**

An organisation's **ethical stance** is defined by *Johnson and Scholes* as the extent to which it will exceed its minimum obligation to stakeholders.

*Johnson and Scholes* illustrate the range of possible ethical stances by giving four illustrations.

- **Short-term shareholder interest**
- **Long-term shareholder interest**
- **Multiple stakeholder obligations**
- **Shaper of society**

### 2.2.1 Short-term shareholder interest

An organisation might limit its ethical stance to taking responsibility for **short-term shareholder interest** on the grounds that it is for **government** alone to impose wider constraints on corporate governance. This minimalist approach would accept a duty of obedience to the demands of the law, but would not undertake to comply with any less substantial rules of conduct. This stance can be justified on the grounds that going beyond it can **challenge government authority**; this is an important consideration for organisations operating in developing countries.

### 2.2.2 Long-term shareholder interest

There are two reasons why an organisation might take a wider view of ethical responsibilities when considering the **longer-term interest of shareholders**.

(a)     The organisation's **corporate image** may be enhanced by an assumption of wider responsibilities. The cost of undertaking such responsibilities may be justified as essentially promotional expenditure.

(b)     The responsible exercise of corporate power may prevent a build-up of social and political **pressure for legal regulation**. Freedom of action may be preserved and the burden of regulation lightened by acceptance of ethical responsibilities.

### 2.2.3 Multiple stakeholder obligations

An organisation might accept the **legitimacy of the expectations of stakeholders other than shareholders** and build those expectations into its stated purposes. This would be because without appropriate relationships with groups such as suppliers, employers and customers, the organisation would not be able to function.

A distinction can be drawn between **rights** and **expectations**. The *Concise Oxford Dictionary* defines a right as 'a legal or moral entitlement'. One is on fairly safe interpretative ground with legal rights, since their basis is usually clearly established, though subject to development and adjustment. The concept of *moral* entitlement is much less well defined and subject to partisan argument, as discussed above in the context of **natural law**. There is, for instance, an understandable tendency for those who feel themselves aggrieved to declare that their *rights* have been infringed. Whether or not this is the case is often a matter of opinion. For example, in the UK, there is often talk of a 'right to work' when redundancies occur. No such right exists in UK law, nor is it widely accepted that there is a moral basis for such a right. However, there is a widespread acceptance that governments should make the prevention of large-scale unemployment a high priority.

Clearly, organisations have a duty to respect the **legal rights** of stakeholders other than shareholders. These are extensive in the UK, including wide-ranging **employment law** and **consumer protection law**, as well as the more basic legislation relating to such matters as contract and property. Where **moral entitlements** are concerned, organisations need to be practical: they should take care to establish just what *expectations* they are prepared to treat as *obligations*, bearing in mind their general ethical stance and degree of concern about bad publicity.

Acceptance of obligations to stakeholders implies that **measurement of the organisation's performance** must give due weight to these extra imperatives. For instance, as is widely known, *Anita Roddick* does not care to have the performance of *Body Shop* assessed in purely financial terms.

### 2.2.4 Shaper of society

It is difficult enough for a commercial organisation to accept wide responsibility to stakeholders. The role of **shaper of society** is even more demanding and largely the province of public sector organisations and charities, though some well-funded private organisations might act in this way. The legitimacy of this

approach depends on the framework of corporate governance and accountability. Where organisations are clearly set up for such a role, either by government or by private sponsors, they may pursue it. However, they must also satisfy whatever requirements for financial viability are established for them.

## 2.3 Ethical dilemmas

Businesses are very likely to be faced with ethical dilemmas. Custom and accepted practice may not be easily defensible when analysed using simple ethical ideas such as the duty and consequences rules.

There are a number of areas in which the various approaches to ethics and conflicting views of a business's responsibilities can create **ethical dilemmas** for managers. These can impact at the highest level, affecting the development of policy, or lower down the hierarchy, especially if policy is unclear and guidance from more senior people is unavailable.

Dealing with **unpleasantly authoritarian governments** can be supported on the grounds that it contributes to economic growth and prosperity and all the benefits they bring to society in both countries concerned. This is a consequentialist argument. It can also be opposed on consequentialist grounds as contributing to the continuation of the regime, and on deontological grounds as fundamentally repugnant.

**Honesty in advertising** is an important problem. Many products are promoted exclusively on image. Deliberately creating the impression that purchasing a particular product will enhance the happiness, success and sex-appeal of the buyer can be attacked as dishonest. It can be defended on the grounds that the supplier is actually selling a fantasy or dream rather than a physical article.

Dealings with **employees** are coloured by the opposing views of corporate responsibility and individual rights. The idea of a job as property to be defended has now disappeared from UK labour relations, but there is no doubt that corporate decisions that lead to redundancies are still deplored. This is because of the obvious impact of sudden unemployment on aspirations and living standards, even when the employment market is buoyant. Nevertheless, it is only proper for businesses to consider the cost of employing labour as well as its productive capacity. Even employers who accept that their employees' skills are their most important source of competitive advantage can be reduced to cost cutting in order to survive in lean times.

Another ethical problem concerns **payments by companies to officials** who have power to help or hinder the payers' operations. In *The Ethics of Corporate Conduct, Clarence Walton* discusses to the fine distinctions which exist in this area.

(a) **Extortion**. Foreign officials have been known to threaten companies with the complete closure of their local operations unless suitable payments are made.

(b) **Bribery**. This is payments for services to which a company is not legally entitled. There are some fine distinctions to be drawn; for example, some managers regard political contributions as bribery.

(c) **Grease money**. Multinational companies are sometimes unable to obtain services to which they are legally entitled because of deliberate stalling by local officials. Cash payments to the right people may then be enough to oil the machinery of bureaucracy.

(d) **Gifts**. In some cultures (such as Japan) gifts are regarded as an essential part of civilised negotiation, even in circumstances where to Western eyes they might appear ethically dubious. Managers operating in such a culture may feel at liberty to adopt the local customs.

Business ethics are also relevant to competitive behaviour. This is because a market can only be free if competition is, in some basic respects, fair. There is a distinction between competing aggressively and competing unethically. The dispute between *British Airways* and *Virgin* centred around issues of business ethics.

# 3 Corporate governance

> Abuses have led to a range of measures to improve **corporate governance**. Non-executive directors have a particular role to play.

**Key concept**

> The conduct of an organisation's senior officers constitutes its **corporate governance**.

*Lynch* says that the field of corporate governance includes the **selection** of the organisation's senior officers and 'their relationships with owners, employees and other stakeholders'. He points out that the influence of those officers over the future direction of the organisation makes corporate governance a matter of **strategic importance**.

Senior managers' influence amounts, in fact, to considerable power, and it is a matter of wide concern that power is wielded responsibly. Within the organisation, whatever the formal **ethical stance**, management decisions affect interests other than the purely financial. The effect on employment of short-term cost cutting is an example. Externally, the public interest may be affected. Lynch gives the example of the directors of privatised UK utility companies that awarded themselves large rewards, effectively at the taxpayer's expense.

Other recent examples include the deception and fraud committed by *Robert Maxwell* and, in the USA, the corrupt accounting policies pursued at *Enron Corporation*.

Extensive abuses have led to a variety of measures intended to improve the quality of corporate governance.

(a) The development of **accounting standards** has been driven in part by the need to prevent abuses in financial reporting.

(b) The various professional bodies all have their own **codes of professional conduct**.

(c) A series of major financial scandals has led to government intervention in the UK in the form of **commissions on standards of behaviour**, each producing its code of conduct.

**Corporate ethical codes**. Organisations often publish corporate codes of ethical standards. Fundamentally, this is a good idea and can be a useful way of disseminating the specific policies we have discussed above. However, care must be taken over such a document.

(a) It should not be over-prescriptive or over-detailed, since this encourages a legalistic approach to interpretation and a desire to seek loopholes in order to justify previously chosen courses of action.

(b) It will only have influence if senior management adhere to it consistently in their own decisions and actions.

Lynch points out that an important check on the abuse of power by senior managers is the **free flow of information to stakeholders**: 'wrongdoing will go unchecked as long as it remains unknown or unreported'. However, there are legitimate concerns about commercial confidentiality to be addressed here. The **auditor** has an important role to play, reviewing internal information on a confidential basis.

## 3.1 Two approaches to managing ethics

> A **compliance-based approach** highlights conformity with law and regulation. An integrity-based approach suggests a wider remit, incorporating ethics in the organisation's values and culture.

*Lynne Paine* (*Harvard Business Review*, March-April 1994) suggests that ethical decisions are becoming more important as penalties, in the US at least, for companies which break the law become tougher. (This might be contrasted with UK, where a fraudster whose deception ran into millions received a sentence of community service.) Paine suggests that there are two approaches to the management of ethics in organisations.

- **Compliance**-based
- **Integrity**-based

## 3.1.1 Compliance-based approach

A compliance-based approach is primarily designed to ensure that the company **acts within the letter of the law**, and that violations are prevented, detected and punished. Some organisations, faced with the legal consequences of unethical behaviour take legal precautions such as those below.

- Compliance procedures to detect misconduct
- Audits of contracts
- Systems for employees to report criminal misconduct without fear of retribution
- Disciplinary procedures to deal with transgressions

Corporate compliance is limited in that it relates only to the law, but legal compliance is 'not an adequate means for addressing the full range of ethical issues that arise every day'. This is especially the case in the UK, where **voluntary** codes of conduct and self-regulation are perhaps more prevalent than in the US.

An example of the difference between the **legality** and **ethicality** of a practice is the sale in some countries of defective products without appropriate warnings. 'Companies engaged in international business often discover that conduct that infringes on recognised standards of human rights and decency is legally permissible in some jurisdictions.'

The compliance approach also overemphasises the threat of detection and punishment in order to channel appropriate behaviour. Arguably, some employers view compliance programmes as an insurance policy for senior management, who can cover the tracks of their arbitrary management practices. After all, some performance targets are impossible to achieve without cutting corners: managers can escape responsibility by blaming the employee for not following the compliance programme, when to do so would have meant a failure to reach target.

Furthermore, mere compliance with the law is no guide to **exemplary** behaviour.

## 3.1.2 Integrity-based programmes

'An integrity-based approach combines a concern for the law with an **emphasis on managerial responsibility** for ethical behaviour. Integrity strategies strive to define companies' guiding values, aspirations and patterns of thought and conduct. When integrated into the day-to-day operations of an organisation, such strategies can help prevent damaging ethical lapses, while tapping into powerful human impulses for moral thought and action.

It should be clear to you from this quotation that an integrity-based approach to ethics treats ethics as an issue of organisation culture.

Ethics management has several tasks.

- To create and give life to an organisation's defining values.
- To create an environment that supports ethically sound behaviour
- To instil a sense of shared accountability amongst employees.

The table below indicates some of the differences between the two main approaches.

|  | Compliance | Integrity |
|---|---|---|
| **Ethos** | Knuckle under to external standards | Choose ethical standards |
| **Objective** | Keep to the law | Enable legal and responsible conduct |
| **Originators** | Lawyers | Management, with lawyers, HR specialists etc |
| **Methods (both includes education, and audits, controls, penalties)** | Reduced employee discretion | Leadership, organisation systems |
| **Behavioural assumptions** | People are solitary self-interested beings | People are social beings with values |
| **Standards** | The law | Company values, aspirations (including law) |
| **Staffing** | Lawyers | Managers and lawyers |
| **Education** | The law, compliance system | Values, the law, compliance systems |
| **Activities** | Develop standards, train and communicate, handle reports of misconduct, investigate, enforce, oversee compliance | Integrate values *into* company systems, provide guidance and consultation, identify and resolve problems, oversee compliance |

In other words, an integrity-based approach **incorporates** ethics into corporate culture and systems.

 Marketing at Work

*Charles Hampden-Turner* (in his book *Corporate Culture*) notes that attitudes to safety can be part of a corporate culture. He quotes the example of a firm called (for reasons of confidentiality) *Western Oil*.

Western Oil had a bad safety record. 'Initially, safety was totally at odds with the main cultural values of productivity (management's interests) and maintenance of a macho image (the worker's culture) ... Western Oil had a culture which put safety in conflict with other corporate values.' In particular, the problem was with its long-distance truck drivers (which in the US have a culture of solitary independence and self reliance) who drove sometimes recklessly with loads large enough to inundate a small town. The company instituted *Operation Integrity* to improve safety, in a lasting way, changing the policies and drawing on the existing features of the culture but using them in a different way.

The culture had five dilemmas.

(a)   **Safety-first vs macho-individualism.** Truckers see themselves as 'fearless pioneers of the unconventional lifestyle ... "Be careful boys!" is hardly a plea likely to go down well with this particular group'. Instead of trying to control the drivers, the firm recommended that they become *road safety consultants* (or design consultants). Their advice was sought on improving the system. This had the advantage that 'by making drivers critics of the system their roles as outsiders were preserved and promoted'. It tried to tap their heroism as promoters of public safety.

(b)   **Safety everywhere vs safety specialists.** Western Oil could have hired more specialist staff. However, instead, the company promoted cross functional safety teams from existing parts of the business, for example, to help in designing depots and thinking of ways to reduce hazards.

(c) **Safety as cost vs productivity as benefit**. 'If the drivers raced from station to station to win their bonus, accidents were bound to occur ... . The safety engineers rarely spoke to the line manager in charge of the delivery schedules. The unreconciled dilemma between safety and productivity had been evaded at management level and passed down the hierarchy until drivers were subjected to two incompatible injunctions, work fast and work safely'. To deal with this problem, safety would be built into the reward system.

(d) **Long-term safety vs short-term steering**. The device of recording 'unsafe' acts in operations enabled them to be monitored by cross-functional teams, so that the causes of accidents could be identified and be reduced.

(e) **Personal responsibility vs collective protection**. It was felt that if 'safety' was seen as a form of management policing it would never be accepted. The habit of management 'blaming the victim' had to stop. Instead, if an employee reported another to the safety teams, the person who was reported would be free of *official* sanction. Peer presence was seen to be a better enforcer of safety than the management hierarchy.

It has also been suggested that the following institutions can be established.

(a) An **ethics committee** is a group of executives (perhaps including non-executive directors) appointed to oversee company ethics. It rules on misconduct. It may seek advice from specialists in business ethics.

(b) An **ethics ombudsperson** is a manager who acts as the corporate conscience.

**Whistle-blowing** is the disclosure by an employee of illegal, immoral or illegitimate practices on the part of the organisation. In theory, the public ought to welcome the public trust: however, confidentiality is very important in the accountants' code of ethics. Whistle-blowing frequently involves **financial loss** for the whistleblower.

(a) Whistle-blowers may lose their jobs.

(b) A whistle-blower who is a member of a professional body cannot, sadly, rely on that body to take a significant interest, or even offer a sympathetic ear. Some professional bodies have narrow interpretations of what is meant by ethical conduct. For many the duties of **commercial confidentiality** are felt to be more important.

In the UK, the Public Interest Disclosure Act 1999 offers some protection to whistle-blowers, but both the subject of the disclosure and the way in which it is made must satisfy the requirements of the Act.

**Exam tip**

> The ethics codes described above can be related to mission, culture and control strategies. A compliance-based approach suggest that bureaucratic control is necessary; an integrity based approach relies on cultural control.

# 4 Ethics and marketing

**FAST FORWARD**

> The marketing function has its own specific areas of ethical responsibility as acknowledged in the societal marketing concept and the CIM Code of Professional Standards.

## 4.1 The societal marketing concept

*Kotler* (*Social Marketing,* 2002) suggests that a **societal marketing concept** should replace the marketing concept as a philosophy for the future.

**Key concept**

'The **societal marketing concept** is a management orientation that holds that the key task of the organisation is to determine the needs and wants of target markets and to adapt the organisation to delivering the desired satisfactions more effectively and efficiently than its competitors in a way that preserves or enhances the consumer's and society's well-being.'

**Exam tip**

In a past case study question, candidates were asked to consider what to do with a 'town centre': effectively being asked to advise a local authority. In this case a variety of stakeholder groups were interested: the general public, shopkeepers, drivers and so on.

In general, ethical issues – how companies behave – have become of more importance recently. Many companies are exploiting new found public concern with **ethical behaviour**. The Co-operative Bank developed a whole advertising campaign around avoiding investment in countries with oppressive regimes.

Responses to ethical concerns

- Introducing codes of **conduct** (eg to help and guide employees in difficult situations)
- Inviting outsiders to review ethical performance in some way.

Ultimately, however, ethics comes down to the individual behaviour of managers and employees. Acting ethically is often good business. *Which?* magazine alleged that BT employees had given misleading or inaccurate information about telephone services offered by cable firms. The poor publicity can hardly have helped BT's campaign to win back 'cable' customers.

## 4.2 Ethical issues and marketing

An August 1996 edition of *Marketing Success* briefly covered some issues of ethics which might be of relevance to marketers, using the 4Ps of the marketing mix as a framework.

(a) **Product/service**

(i) Failure to inform customers about risks associated with the use of the product: **dishonesty**. Currently, there are lawsuits in the US in which people are suggesting that the tobacco companies, despite their denials, have known for some time that nicotine is addictive.

(ii) Using materials of a poorer quality in a bid to cut costs.

(iii) Does manufacture involve an unacceptable environmental cost?

(b) **Pricing**. In economic terms, price is a matter of supply and demand and, in the pursuit of profit, prices are what the market will bear. Ethics come into the discussion when:

(i) Cartels attempt to fix prices by rigging the market
(ii) Consumers are sometimes charged extras, not officially disclosed

(c) **Promotion**

(i) Advertising: honest, legal, decent and truthful
(ii) Tastefulness of imagery (eg violence, sexual stereotyping)

(d) **Place**. Ethical concerns regarding relationships with intermediaries can involve the use of power, or delays in payment.

**BPP**
LEARNING MEDIA

## Marketing at Work

The Chartered Institute of Marketing's *Code of Professional Standards* is reproduced below.

1   A member shall at all times conduct himself with integrity in such a way as to bring credit to the profession of marketing and The Chartered Institute of Marketing.

2   A member shall not by any unfair or unprofessional practice injure the business, reputation or interest of any other member of the Institute.

3   Members shall, at all times, act honestly in their professional dealings with customers and clients (actual and potential), employers and employees.

4   A member shall not, knowingly or recklessly, disseminate any false or misleading information, either on his own behalf or on behalf of anyone else.

5   A member shall keep abreast of current marketing practice and act competently and diligently and be encouraged to register for the Institute's scheme of Continuing Professional Development.

6   A member shall, at all times, seek to avoid conflict of interest and shall make prior voluntary and full disclosure to all parties concerned of all matters that may rise to any such conflict. Where a conflict arises a member must withdraw prior to the work commencing.

7   A member shall keep business information confidential except: from those persons entitled to receive it, where it breaches this code and where it is illegal to do so.

8   A member shall promote and seek business in a professional and ethical manner.

9   A member shall observe the requirements of all other codes of practice which may from time to time have any relevance to the practice of marketing insofar as such requirements do not conflict with any provisions of this code, or the Institute's Royal Charter and Bye-laws; a list of such codes being obtainable from the Institute's head office.

10   Members shall not hold themselves out as having the Institute's endorsement in connection with an activity unless the Institute's prior written approval has been obtained first.

11   A member shall not use any funds derived from the Institute for any purpose which does not fall within the powers and obligations contained in the Branch or Group handbook, and which does not fully comply with this code.

12   A member shall have due regard for, and comply with, all the relevant laws of the country in which they are operating.

13   A member who knowingly causes or permits any other person or organisation to be in substantial breach of this code or who is a party to such a breach shall himself be guilty of such breach.

14   A member shall observe this Code of Professional Standards as it may be expanded and annotated and published from time to time by the Ethics Committee in the manner provided for below.

Transgressions of morality or ethics will quite rightly invoke the wrath and retaliation of **consumer watchdogs**, **ombudsmen** and last but by no means least, attract unfavourable **publicity in the media**. Gratifying needs and wants at the expense of others has become commercially if not politically incorrect. Matters such as smoking, litter, pollution, waste and noise have been issues of public concern.

There is increasing debate on the subject of **'ethical marketing'** and we are reading of the possibility of banks conducting 'environmental accounting' before agreeing to fund companies in industries which might have to conduct punitive environmental cleansing in response to future European legislation. In strategic marketing planning, therefore, ethical issues are of increasing concern.

## Chapter Roundup

- Ethics is not the same thing as law or the rules of religion. Ethical theory is not integrated: consequentialist, deontological and natural law based rules are capable of pointing to different conclusions. Partly as a result of this, **ethical dilemmas** can exist at all levels in the organisation.

- **Mission** should incorporate recognition of the ethical dimension. Corporate ethics has three contexts.

    – Interaction with national and international society
    – Effects of routine operations
    – Behaviour of individuals

- There is a fundamental split of views about the nature of corporate responsibility.

    – The **stakeholder view** that a range of goals should be pursued
    – The view that the business organisation is a purely **economic force**, subject to law

- An organisation's **ethical stance** is the extent to which it will exceed its minimum obligations to stakeholders. There are four typical stances.

    – Short-term shareholder interest
    – Long-term shareholder interest
    – Multiple stakeholder obligations
    – Shaper of society

- Businesses are very likely to be faced with ethical dilemmas. Custom and accepted practice may not be easily defensible when analysed using simple ethical ideas such as the duty and consequences rules.

- Abuses have led to a range of measures to improve **corporate governance**. Non-executive directors have a particular role to play.

- A **compliance-based approach** highlights conformity with law and regulation. An integrity-based approach suggests a wider remit, incorporating ethics in the organisation's values and culture.

- The marketing function has its own specific areas of ethical responsibility as acknowledged in the societal marketing concept and the CIM Code of Professional Standards.

## Quick Quiz

1    What is an organisation's ethical stance?

2    Why might an organisation act to secure long-term shareholder interests?

3    What is a right?

4    When should ethical considerations be included in performance measures?

5    What is bribery?

6    What is corporate governance?

7    What is the role of the auditor in corporate governance?

8    What is an externality?

9    What is whistle-blowing?

# Answers to Quick Quiz

1   The extent to which it will exceed its minimum obligation to shareholders

2   To improve corporate image and forestall legal regulation

3   A legal or moral entitlement

4   When moral expectations are accepted as obligations

5   Payment for services for which there is no entitlement

6   The conduct of the organisation's senior officers

7   The independent review of confidential information

8   A social or environmental cost of the organisation's activities not borne by the organisation

9   Informing outside agencies about transgressions by one's organisation

Now try Question 9 at the end of the Study Text

# Part E

## Investment decisions
## and control

# 11

# Control

## Syllabus content

- Investment appraisal techniques
- Stakeholder value measurement
- The implication of strategic marketing decisions for implementation and control
- Performance measurement systems for the deployment of marketing assets and the implications of marketing plans
- Budgeting and planning control techniques

# Introduction

We start this chapter with an account of some methods used in the financial appraisal of investment projects.

Strategic control has two aspects. It monitors and corrects current performance. Also, it feeds into the next planning cycle. Control in effect asks 'Where are we now?', the starting point of the planning process. Similarly, the measures used for control do bear some relationship with, and might be identical to, the detailed objectives and critical success factors determined earlier. Control involves a review of what we have achieved, or what we anticipate achieving in the light of our plans.

Performance measures include financial performance (as expressed in budgets), strategic performance (as monitored by strategic control systems – Sections 3 and 4) and various other measures (eg market share) and the effectiveness of the mix generally.

# 1 Investment appraisal

**FAST FORWARD**

> The best project appraisal method is net present value, but payback period and ROCE/ROI are also useful.

There are a number of ways of evaluating capital projects, the best of which is the **net present value** (NPV) method. This is dealt with in the annex to Chapter 4, which revises discounting arithmetic. This method is used by accountants because it is not subject to the errors that affect less sophisticated methods. However, it is a little complex to use and simpler methods are often employed for convenience. We will examine two of these simpler methods in this chapter. Note that all investment appraisal methods depend for their use on having reasonably accurate estimates of the cash flows associated with the proposal, both the immediate cost and the costs and revenues expected in the future.

We will look first at the **payback** method.

**Exam tip**

> Exam questions often ask about the pros and cons of the payback method.

**Key concept**

> **Payback** is the time it takes the cash inflows from a capital investment project to equal the cash outflows, usually expressed in years.

Payback is often used as a 'first screening method'. By this, we mean that when a capital investment project is being considered, the first question to ask is: 'How long will it take to pay back its cost?' The organisation might have a **target payback**, and so it would reject a capital project unless its payback period were less than a certain number of years.

However, a project should not be evaluated on the basis of payback alone. If a project gets through the payback test, it ought then to be evaluated with a more sophisticated investment appraisal technique.

## 1.1 Why is payback alone an inadequate investment appraisal technique?

The reason why payback should not be used on its own to evaluate capital investments should seem fairly obvious if you look at the figures below for two mutually exclusive projects (this means that only one of them can be undertaken).

BPP
LEARNING MEDIA

|  | Project P | Project Q |
|---|---|---|
| Capital asset | £60,000 | £60,000 |
| Profits before depreciation (a rough approximation of cash flows) | | |
| Year 1 | £20,000 | £50,000 |
| Year 2 | £30,000 | £20,000 |
| Year 3 | £40,000 | £5,000 |
| Year 4 | £50,000 | £5,000 |
| Year 5 | £60,000 | £5,000 |

Project P pays back in year 3 (about one quarter of the way through year 3). Project Q pays back half way through year 2. Using payback alone to judge capital investments, project Q would be preferred.

However the returns from project P over its life are much higher than the returns from project Q. **Project P** will earn total profits before depreciation of £140,000 on an investment of £60,000. **Project Q** will earn total profits before depreciation of only £25,000 on an investment of £60,000.

### 1.1.1 Disadvantages of the payback method

There are a number of serious drawbacks to the payback method.

(a) It **ignores** the **timing** of cash flows within the payback period, the cash flows after the end of payback period and therefore the total project return.

(b) It **ignores the time value of money** (a concept incorporated into more sophisticated appraisal methods). This means that it does not take account of the fact that £1 today is worth more than £1 in one year's time. An investor who has £1 today can either consume it immediately or alternatively can invest it at the prevailing interest rate, say 10%, to get a return of £1.10 in a year's time.

(c) Payback is **unable to distinguish between projects** with the same payback period.

(d) The choice of any **cut-off** payback period by an organisation is **arbitrary**.

(e) It may lead to **excessive investment** in **short-term projects**.

(f) It takes account of the risk of the timing of cash flows but not the **variability** of those cash flows.

### 1.1.2 Advantages of the payback method

In spite of its limitations, the payback method continues to be popular, and the following points can be made in its favour.

(a) It is **simple to calculate** and **simple to understand**. This may be important when management resources are limited. It is similarly helpful in communicating information about minimum requirements to managers responsible for submitting projects.

(b) It uses **cash flows** rather than accounting profits.

(c) It can be used as a **screening device** as a first stage in eliminating obviously inappropriate projects prior to more detailed evaluation.

(d) The fact that it tends to **bias** in favour of **short-term projects** means that it tends to minimise both financial and business risk.

(e) It can be used when there is a **capital rationing situation** to identify those projects which generate additional cash for investment quickly.

## 1.2 The return on capital employed method

The **return on capital employed** method (ROCE) (also called the **accounting rate of return** method or the **return on investment** ROI method) of appraising a capital project is to estimate the accounting rate of return that the project should yield. If it exceeds a target rate of return, the project will be undertaken.

Unfortunately, there are several different definitions of 'return on investment'. One of the most popular is as follows.

$$\text{ROCE} = \frac{\text{Estimated average profits}}{\text{Estimated average investment}} \times 100\%$$

The others include:

$$\text{ROCE} = \frac{\text{Estimated total profits}}{\text{Estimated initial investment}} \times 100\%$$

$$\text{ROCE} = \frac{\text{Estimated average profits}}{\text{Estimated initial investment}} \times 100\%$$

There are arguments in favour of each of these definitions. The most important point is, however, that the method selected should be used consistently. For examination purposes we recommend the first definition unless the question clearly indicates that some other one is to be used.

### 1.2.1 Example: the return on capital employed

A company has a target return on capital employed of 20% (using the first definition in Paragraph 1.2 above), and is now considering the following project.

| | |
|---|---|
| Capital cost of asset | £80,000 |
| Estimated life | 4 years |
| Estimated profit before depreciation | |
| Year 1 | £20,000 |
| Year 2 | £25,000 |
| Year 3 | £35,000 |
| Year 4 | £25,000 |

The capital asset would be depreciated by 25% of its cost each year, and will have no residual value. You are required to assess whether the project should be undertaken.

**Solution**

The annual profits after depreciation, and the mid-year net book value of the asset, would be as follows.

| Year | Profit after depreciation £ | Mid-year net book value £ | ROCE in the year % |
|---|---|---|---|
| 1 | 0 | 70,000 | 0 |
| 2 | 5,000 | 50,000 | 10 |
| 3 | 15,000 | 30,000 | 50 |
| 4 | 5,000 | 10,000 | 50 |

As the table shows, the ROCE is low in the early stages of the project, partly because of low profits in Year 1 but mainly because the net book value of the asset is much higher early on in its life.

The project does not achieve the target ROCE of 20% in its first two years, but exceeds it in years 3 and 4. So should it be undertaken?

When the ROCE from a project varies from year to year, it makes sense to take an overall or 'average' view of the project's return. In this case, we should look at the return as a whole over the four-year period.

|  | £ |
|---|---|
| Total profit before depreciation over four years | 105,000 |
| Total profit after depreciation over four years | 25,000 |
| Average annual profit after depreciation | 6,250 |
| Original cost of investment | 80,000 |
| Average net book value over the four year period $\dfrac{(80,000 + 0)}{2}$ | 40,000 |

ROCE = 6,250/40,000 = 15.6%

The project would not be undertaken because it would fail to yield the target return of 20%.

## 1.3 The ROCE and the comparison of mutually exclusive projects

The ROCE method of capital investment appraisal can also be used to compare two or more projects which are mutually exclusive. The project with the highest ROCE would be selected (provided that the expected ROCE is higher than the company's target ROCE).

### 1.3.1 Example: the ROCE and mutually exclusive projects

Arrow Ltd wants to buy a new item of equipment which will be used to provide a service to customers of the company. Two models of equipment are available, one with a slightly higher capacity and greater reliability than the other. The expected costs and profits of each item are as follows.

|  | Equipment item X | Equipment item Y |
|---|---|---|
| Capital cost | £80,000 | £150,000 |
| Life | 5 years | 5 years |
| Profits before depreciation | £ | £ |
| Year 1 | 50,000 | 50,000 |
| Year 2 | 50,000 | 50,000 |
| Year 3 | 30,000 | 60,000 |
| Year 4 | 20,000 | 60,000 |
| Year 5 | 10,000 | 60,000 |
| Disposal value | 0 | 0 |

ROCE is measured as the average annual profit after depreciation, divided by the average net book value of the asset. You are required to decide which item of equipment should be selected, if any, if the company's target ROCE is 30%.

**Solution**

|  | Item X | Item Y |
|---|---|---|
|  | £ | £ |
| Total profit over life of equipment |  |  |
| Before depreciation | 160,000 | 280,000 |
| After depreciation | 80,000 | 130,000 |
| Average annual profit after depreciation | 16,000 | 26,000 |
| (Capital cost + disposal value)/2 | 40,000 | 75,000 |
| ROCE | 40% | 34.7% |

Both projects would earn a return in excess of 30%, but since item X would earn a bigger ROCE, it would be preferred to item Y, even though the profits from Y would be higher by an average of £10,000 a year.

### 1.3.2 The drawbacks to the ROCE method of capital investment appraisal

The ROCE method of capital investment appraisal has the serious drawback that it does not take account of the **timing** of the **profits from an investment**. Whenever capital is invested in a project, money is tied up until the project begins to earn profits which pay back the investment. Money tied up in one project cannot be invested anywhere else until the profits come in. Management should be aware of the benefits of early repayments from an investment, which will provide the money for other investments.

There are a number of other disadvantages.

(a)    It is based on **accounting profits** and not cash flows. Accounting profits are subject to a number of different accounting treatments.

(b)    It is a **relative measure** rather than an absolute measure and hence takes no account of the size of the investment.

(c)    It takes **no account** of the **length of the project**.

(d)    Like the payback method, it **ignores** the **time value** of money.

There are, however, advantages to the ROCE method.

(a)    It is a **quick and simple calculation.**
(b)    It involves a familiar concept of a **percentage return.**
(c)    It looks at the **entire project life.**

# 2 Effective marketing feedback and control systems

**FAST FORWARD**

Special problems occur in marketing **feedback and control systems** because markets are made up of people and therefore are not very predictable.

**Marketing feedback and control systems need to recognise the volatile nature of human beings**. After all, **markets are people** or rather people's wants and needs, modified by affordability and availability. Problems of unsatisfactory feedback and control can occur.

(a)    People change

(b)    Reasons for change are not always apparent or identifiable

(c)    The same product can be bought by the same person for different purposes eg champagne to celebrate a win on the 3.30, or to drown sorrows after a loss on the 4.00.

(d)    Delays occur in the system due to suppliers being remote from consumers.

(e)    Competitor actions can seriously affect the systems.

(f)    Rarely is complete information affordable so that inadequacies occur in feedback.

(g)    Distortions inevitably occur in the data transfer between people. The more often the data is transcribed the more distortion will occur.

There is a need for **information feedback at each stage of the marketing process**.

(a)    Only if marketing managers are kept informed of what is happening and what is likely to happen, can they make sensible decisions. For example, **contingency planning depends upon 'what if' scenarios**. Only when managers receive information indicating a particular scenario is taking place can the right contingency plan be invoked. The information in this case acts as an identifier, a selector and a trigger.

(b)    The dimensions of marketing feedback and control systems are in fact wide-ranging and flexible. One of the most important marketing planning philosophies is to avoid a laissez-faire, complacent attitude to good news. We need to remember that **good sales figures represent the past situation**, so we need to worry about the future longer-term survival and growth.

Some items have greater immediacy than others. Failure to act on a serious complaint could lead to the loss of an important customer, adversely affecting future sales and profitability.

**Exam tip**

A question might ask about financial and other information in a marketing control system.

A four stage model is suggested.

(1)  Set targets
(2)  Measure achievement
(3)  Examine reasons
(4)  Take corrective action

This is similar to the control model we outline below.

# 3 Basic control concepts

**FAST FORWARD**

**Basic control systems** depend upon comparing results with plans: single loop feedback produces control action to modify performance, double loop feedback is used to modify the plan itself.

A good starting point in thinking about basic control concepts is to take the example of driving a car. In doing this we receive various **feedbacks** such as visual feedback to tell us if we are driving in the right direction, in the correct position on the road, at the right speed and so on. Instruments such as the speedometer and our senses – eyes, touch (vibration) provide the basic data. We measure this data against **standards** such as the speed limit, the highway code and laws and so on and, where necessary, take **corrective action** using control devices like the steering wheel and the accelerator.

The marketing planning and implementation process follows similar precepts. We cannot implement a plan in the first place until we know where we are going. In planning where we are going we need to know where we are now. It also helps if we know where we have come from.

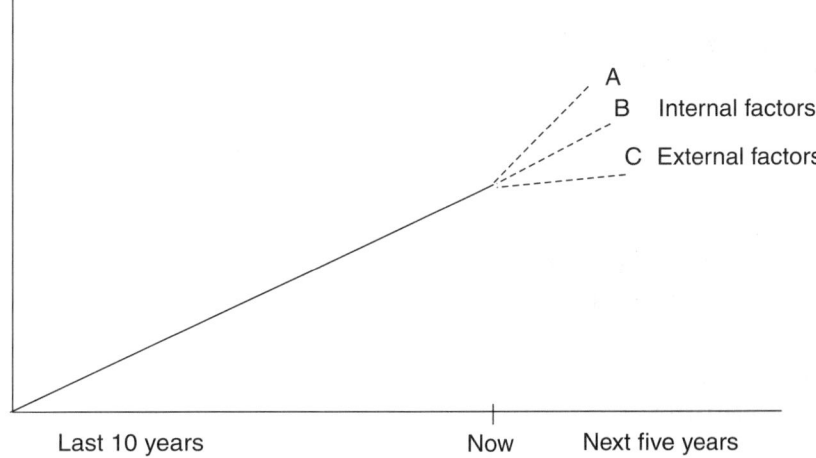

The past determines not only where we are now relative to it but out **future direction** (extrapolation of past trend assuming no change = position B). **Control is, however, only partial in marketing**.

(a)  We can change internal factors (the 7 Ps) positively so as to aim for position A.

(b)  However, external factors (political, economic, sociological, technological and competition) might act positively or negatively, in the latter case dragging us down to position C.

(c)  Nevertheless, the more information we have about the so called uncontrollable external factors, the more we can anticipate, ride or avoid the blows.

Here is a diagram of a **generic control system**.

# Control System

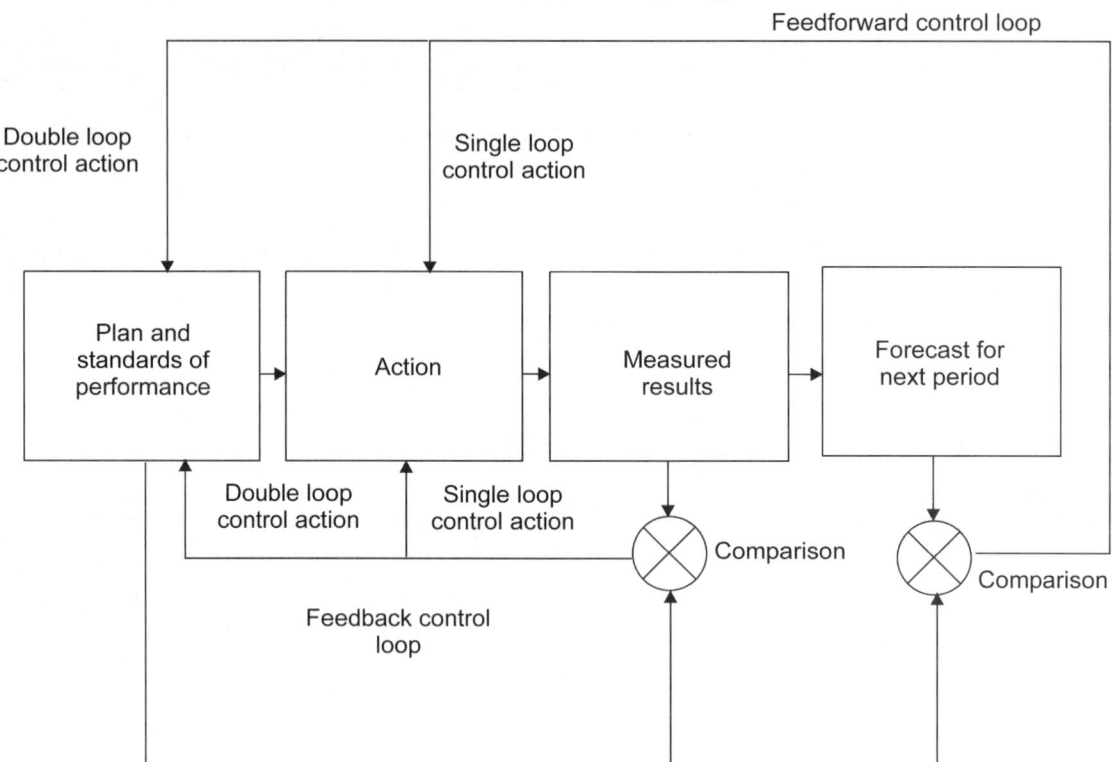

The essence of control is the measurement of results and comparison of them with the original plan. Any deviation from plan indicates that control action is required to make the results conform more closely with plan.

**Key concepts**

> **Feedback** occurs when the results (outputs) of a system are used to control it, by adjusting the input or behaviour of the system. Businesses use feedback information to control their performance.
>
> **Single loop feedback** results in the system's behaviour being altered to meet the plan.
>
> **Double loop feedback** can result in changes to the plan itself.

**Double loop feedback** is control information transmitted to a higher level in the system. Whereas single loop feedback is concerned with immediate task control, higher level feedback is concerned with overall control. The term double loop feedback indicates that feedback is used to indicate both divergence between the observed and expected results where control action might be required, and also the need for **adjustments to the plan itself**.

## 3.1 Feedforward control

(a) **Control delay**. A timelag may exist between the actual results and the corrective action. However, results can be anticipated.

(b) **Feedforward control** uses **anticipated** or forecast results, and compares them with the plan. **Corrective action** is thus taken **in advance**, before it is too late to do anything effective. Control is exercised before the results, rather than after the event.

*Emmanuel et al* describe **four necessary conditions that must be satisfied before any process can be said to be controlled**. These will help us to put control into a wider context still.

(a) **Objectives** for the process being controlled must exist, for without an aim or purpose control has no meaning.

(b)     The **output of** the process must be **measurable** in terms of the dimensions defined by the objectives.

(c)     A **predictive model** of the process being controlled is required so that causes for the non-attainment of objectives can be determined and proposed corrective actions evaluated.

(d)     There must be a **capability of taking action** so that deviations of attainment from objectives can be reduced.

It is important to understand that this concept of control involves more than just measuring results and taking corrective action. Control in the broad sense embraces **the formulation of objectives** – deciding what are the things that need to be done – as well as monitoring their attainment by way of feedback. Note two important points.

(a)     As *Drucker* pointed out, the most crucial aspect of management performance in business is economic success; that is, **financial targets are the vital ones**.

(b)     Targets are only useful if performance can be **measured**.

### 3.1.1 Examples

| Feedback | Standards | Control actions |
| --- | --- | --- |
| Sales figures | Against budget plus or minus | Stimulate/dampen down demand |
| Complaints | Number, frequency, seriousness | Corrective action |
| Competitors | Relative to us | Attack/defence strategies |
| Market size changes | Market share | Marketing mix manipulation |
| Costs/profitability | Ratios | Cost cutting exercises |
| Corporate image | Attribute measures | Internal/external communications |
| Environmental factors | Variances from norm | Invoke strategic alternatives |

## Action Programme 1

Sally Keene works for a large department store, as a manager.

(a)     At the beginning of each year she is given a yearly plan, subdivided into twelve months. This is based on the previous year's performance and some allowance is made for anticipated economic conditions. Every three months she sends her views as to the next quarter to senior management, who give her a new plan in the light of changing conditions.

(b)     She monitors sales revenue per square foot, and sales per employee. Employees who do not meet the necessary sales targets are at first counselled and then if performance does not improve they are dismissed. Sally is not unreasonable. She sets what she believes are realistic targets.

(c)     She believes there is a good team spirit in the sales force, however, and that employees, whose commission is partly based on the sales revenue earned by the store as a whole, discourage slackers in their ranks.

What kind of control, control system or control information can you identify in the three cases above?

# 4 Strategic control

A vast range of techniques is available for the purpose of strategic control. Strategic control may be based on critical success factors.

The **control measures and analytical techniques** that might be relevant for control at a strategic level are as follows.

| Type of analysis | Used to control |
|---|---|
| 1  *Financial analysis* | |
| Ratio analysis | Elements of profitability |
| Variance analysis | Costs or revenue |
| Cash budgeting | Cash flow |
| Capital budgeting and | |
| Capital expenditure audit | Investment |
| 2  *Market/sales analysis* | |
| Demand analysis | Competitive standing |
| Market share or penetration | |
| Sales targets | Sales effectiveness |
| Sales budget | Efficiency in use of resources for selling |
| 3  *Physical resource analysis* | |
| Capacity fill | Plant utilisation |
| Yield | Materials utilisation |
| Product inspection | Quality |
| 4  *Human resources analysis* | |
| Work measurement | Productivity |
| Output measurement | |
| Labour turnover | Workforce stability |
| 5  *Analysis of systems* | |
| Management by objectives | Implementation of strategy |
| Network analysis | Resource planning and scheduling |

## 4.1 Features of basic strategic control systems

Control must influence the behaviour of individuals and groups towards the implementation of the corporate strategy and towards progressive change.

(a) **Distinguish between control at different levels** in the management hierarchy (strategic, tactical, operational). Is the control measure intended to have an immediate impact (for example, 'firefighting', at an operational control or budgetary level) or will it take time for the measure to have a tangible effect?

    (i) Define **strategic objectives** (ie the organisation's eventual objectives in terms of competitive strategy).

(ii) Identify **strategic milestones** on the way to achieving strategic objectives. These could be the specific tasks by which strategic objectives are achieved. These are short-term steps along the way to long-term goals.

(iii) The **key assumptions** on which the strategy is based must also be monitored. A strategy drawn up from a position of limited competition (eg a protected national market) would have to be changed if the market was opened to foreign companies.

(b) **Individual managers** should be identified as having the responsibility for certain matters, and authority to take control measures.

(c) The **key factors for control** should be identified. Managers responsible for taking control action must be informed about what the key factors are, and why they are critical.

(d) **Control reporting should be timed sensibly.** Depending on the level of control, control reports should vary from occasional to regular and frequent.

(e) **Apply targets and standards**

- Targets for market share, in absolute and relative terms, compared with competitors
- Targets for relative product quality
- Timetables for strategic action programmes
- Targets for costs relative to the competitors' costs

(f) Control reports should only contain **relevant information** for the manager receiving the report.

(g) **Selective reporting**. Selective reporting means identifying **key points for control**.

(i) The **position of each product** in the product-market matrix or in its life cycle will suggest how much close watching the product needs.

(ii) A product which performs **inconsistently** might need close watching and control.

(iii) **Information and control reporting costs money**.

(iv) The **key item might be qualitative**. For example within the marketing function it might be considered vitally important that there should be a rapid and significant improvement in employee commitment and enthusiasm. Control reporting at the corporate planning level should therefore emphasise these points, and shift back to other matters when appropriate.

### 4.1.1 Example

Date: March 2006

Source: January 2003 planning document

Mission: Market share

1. *Long term targets, to be achieved by 2011*

   (a) X% value of market share
   (b) Y% profitability over the decade

   *Status: March 2003.* Market share lower than anticipated, owing to unexpected competition. Profits lower than expected because of loss of scale economies and increased marketing costs.

   *Outlook.* Profit will be improved thanks to cost-cutting measures. Market share target might be missed.

2. *Critical assumptions*

   The home market is growing only slowly, and is becoming mature. There are limited opportunities for segmentation.

   Overseas markets are likely to expand by Z% as some are reducing tariffs.

   *Status March 2006.* The home market has matured more quickly than expected. Overseas market growth can compensate for this.

3. *Critical success factors*

   - Exports increased by W%
   - Secure distribution arrangements

4. *Key tasks*

   - Launch of budget products for overseas markets

   - Setting up of a computerised distribution system to enhance speedy response to demand and to cut warehousing costs

   - Get ISO 9000 certification

Note the use of **critical success factors**. We discussed them briefly in the context of resource planning but they are also relevant to control.

*Day and Wensley* relate these to **advantages** and **outcomes** as follows.

(a) **Sources of advantage**

   - Superior skills
   - Superior resources

(b) **Positional advantages**

   - Superior customer value
   - Lower relative costs

(c) **Performance outcomes**

   - Customer satisfaction
   - Customer loyalty
   - Higher market share
   - Higher profits

**Marketing at Work**

*Freund* relates CSFs with strategies and performance indicators for a life insurance company as follows.

| CSF | Strategies | Performance indicators |
|---|---|---|
| Able to achieve critical mass volumes via existing brokers/ agents. | Develop closer ties with agents. Telemarket to brokers. Adjust agents' compensation. | Number of policies in force. Number of new policies written. Percentage of business with existing brokers. |
| Able to introduce new products within six months of industry leaders. | Underwrite strategic joint ventures. | Time taken to introduce. Percentage out within six months. Percentage of underwriters having extra certification. |
| Be able to manage product and product lines, profitably. | Segment investment portfolio. Improve cost accounting. Closely manage loss rate. | Return on portfolio segments. Actual product cost revenue versus budget. Loss ratio relative to competitors. |

### 4.1.2 CSFs which cover both financial and non-financial criteria

| Sphere of activity | Critical factors |
|---|---|
| **Marketing** | Sales volume <br> Market share <br> Gross margins |
| **Production** | Capacity utilisation <br> Quality standards |
| **Logistics** | Capacity utilisation <br> Level of service |

### 4.1.3 CSFs which relate to specific elements of the marketing mix

| Activity | CSF |
|---|---|
| **New product development** | Trial rate <br> Repurchase rate |
| **Sales programmes** | Contribution by region, salesperson <br> Controllable margin as percentage of sales <br> Number of new accounts <br> Travel costs |
| **Advertising programmes** | Awareness levels <br> Attribute ratings <br> Cost levels |

| Activity | CSF |
|----------|-----|
| **Pricing programmes** | Price relative to industry average |
| | Price elasticity of demand |
| **Distribution programmes** | Number of distributors carrying the product |

### 4.1.4 The trade off between short term and long term for control action

It is often the case that in order to rectify short-term results, control action will be at the expense of long-term targets. Similarly, controls over longer-term achievements might call for short-term sacrifices.

**Examples of the reasons for S/L trade-offs** are as follows.

(a) **Short-term losses**. A company has a target of building up its market share for a new product to 30% within four years. It has decided to do this with a low price market penetration strategy. As a short-term target, it wants the product to earn a small profit (£100,000) in the current year. Actual results after three months of the year indicate that the market share has already built up to 18%, but that the product will make a £50,000 loss in the year.

The S/L trade off involves a decision about what to do about short-term profitability (raise prices? cut back on advertising? reduce the sales force?) without sacrificing altogether the long-term market share target.

(b) **Capital expenditure**. K Bhattacharya has written as follows.

'This is one of the most vulnerable areas for detrimental S/L trade-offs. The horizon for returns is most certainly more than a year off, yet costs associated with the implementation of the programme can easily reduce short-term profits. Postponements can almost always release capital and manpower resources needed to generate immediate operating profit.'

(c) **Research and development**. This is another area where short-term profitability is boosted, by cutting back on R & D expenditure at the expense of the longer-term need to continue to develop new products.

(d) **Behaviour**. Very often managers are under pressure to produce good short-term results (for example immediate profitability) in order to get their next promotion.

### 4.1.5 Ensuring that the S/L trade off is properly judged and well balanced

(a) Managers should **recognise** whether or not S/L trade-offs in control action could be a serious problem.

(b) **Managers should be aware** that S/L trade-offs take place in practice.

(c) Controls should exist to prevent or minimise the possibility that short-term controls can be taken which damage long-term targets.

(d) Senior management must be given **adequate control information** for long-term as well as short-term consequences.

(e) The planning and review system should **motivate** managers to keep long-term goals in view.

(f) **Short-term goals should be realistic**. Very often, the pressure on managers to sacrifice long-term interests for short-term results is caused by the imposition of stringent and unrealistic short-term targets on those managers in the first place.

(g) **Performance measures should reflect both long-term and short-term targets**. There might be, say, quarterly performance reviews on the achievement of strategic goals.

# 5 Benchmarking and the market environment

**Key concept**

> **Benchmark**: an external target of performance against which a firm measures its activities.

**FAST FORWARD**

> **Benchmarks** can be set on a variety of key performance indicators as an objective form of control. Marketing research and competitor intelligence would be needed to establish benchmarks and to monitor progress.

The practice of benchmarking is becoming increasingly popular. There are two principal approaches.

(a) **Process benchmarking**, where data is exchanged between companies with similar administrative and manufacturing processes. For example, one of the factors affecting aircraft turnaround away from the home is the availability of spare parts required for routine maintenance. This process is very similar to the provision of field maintenance for office systems such as photocopiers and computers.

(b) **Competitor benchmarking** focuses on the performance and relative strengths of direct competitors using information from customer and supplier interviews and published data from any source available. A firm tries to be as good as its competitors.

## 5.1 Monitoring competitor performance

When an organisation operates in a competitive environment, it should try to obtain information about the financial performance of competitors, to make a comparison with the organisation's own results. It might not be possible to obtain reliable competitor information, but if the competitor is a public company it will publish an annual report and accounts.

### 5.1.1 Financial information that might be obtainable about a competitor

(a) Total profits, sales and capital employed.

(b) ROCE, profit/sales ratio, cost/sales ratios and asset turnover ratios.

(c) The increase in profits and sales over the course of the past twelve months (and prospects for the future, which will probably be mentioned in the chairman's statement in the report and accounts).

(d) Sales and profits in each major business segment that the competitor operates in.

(e) Dividend per share and earnings per share.

(f) Gearing and interest rates on debt.

(g) Share price, and P/E ratio (stock exchange information).

### 5.1.2 Advantages of benchmarking

(a) The comparisons are carried out by the managers who have to live with any changes implemented as a result of the exercise.

(b) Benchmarking focuses on improvement in key areas and sets targets which are challenging but achievable. What is really achievable can be discovered by examining what others have achieved: managers are thus able to accept that they are not being asked to perform miracles.

### 5.1.3 Disadvantages of benchmarking

(a)   Benchmarking is reactive; rather than imitating a competitor, another competitive strategy may be more focused.

(b)   It is not focused on the customer. The firm should set itself targets that customers value.

## 5.2 Market share performance

When a market manager is given responsibility for a product or a market segment, the product or market segment will be a profit centre, and measures of performance for the centre will include profits and cost variances etc. However, another useful measure of performance would be the **market share** obtained by the organisation's product in the market. A market share performance report should draw attention to the following.

(a)   The link between **cost and profit** and market performance in both the short term and the long term.

(b)   The performance of the **product or market segment** in the context of the product life cycle.

(c)   Whether or not the product is gaining or losing ground, as its market share goes up or down.

Changes in market share have to be considered against the change in the **market as a whole**, since the product might be increasing its share simply when the market is declining, but the competition is losing sales even more quickly. (The reverse may also be true. The market could be expanding, and a declining market share might not represent a decline in absolute sales volume, but a failure to grab more of the growing market.)

## 5.3 Monitoring customers

In some industrial markets or reseller markets, a producer might sell to a small number of key customers. The performance of these customers would therefore be of some importance to the producer: if the customer prospers, he will probably buy more and if he does badly, he will probably buy less. It may also be worthwhile monitoring the level of profitability of selling to the customer. **Key customer analysis** calls for seven main areas of investigation.

(a)   **Key customer identity**

- Name of each key customer
- Location
- Status in market
- Products they make and sell
- Size of firm (capital employed, turnover, number of employees)

(b)   **Customer history**

- First purchase date
- Who makes the buying decision in the customer's organisation?
- What is the average order size, by product?
- What is the regularity/periodicity of the order, by product?
- What is the trend in size of orders?
- What is the motive in purchasing?
- What does the customer know about the firm's and competitors' products?
- On what basis does the customer reorder?

- Were there any lost or cancelled orders? For what reason?

(c) **Relationship of customer to product**

- Are the products purchased to be resold? If not, why are they bought?
- Do the products form part of the customer's service/product?

(d) **Relationship of customer to potential market**

- What is the size of the customer in relation to the total end-market?
- Is the customer likely to expand, or not? Diversify? Integrate?

(e) **Customer attitudes and behaviour**

- What interpersonal factors exist which could affecting selling processes?
- Does the customer also buy competitors' products?
- To what extent may purchases be postponed?
- What emotional factors exist in buying decisions?

(f) **The financial performance of the customer**

How successful is the customer in his own markets? Similar analysis can be carried out as with competitors.

(g) **The profitability of selling to the customer**

# 6 Targets, budgets and ratios

FAST FORWARD

- **Planning** is not just an extension of **budgeting**, but there is a close link between them.
- A **budget** is a plan expressed in money terms, representing the resources needed to achieve the objective.

In terms of strategic marketing management, **planned** results often comprise:

(a) Targets for the overall **financial objective**, for each year over the planning period, and other financial strategy objectives such as productivity targets.

(b) Subsidiary **financial targets**

(c) Financial targets in the annual budget (including the sales budget and marketing expenditures budget)

(d) Product-market strategy targets

(e) Targets for each element of the **marketing mix**

## 6.1 Setting targets

**The organisation's objectives provide the basis for setting targets and standards**. Each manager's targets will be directed towards achieving the company objectives. Targets or standards do two things.

(a) They tell managers what they are **required to accomplish**, given the authority to make appropriate decisions.

(b) They indicate to managers **how well their actual results** measure up against their targets, so that control action can be taken where it is needed.

It follows that in setting standards for performance, **it is important to distinguish between controllable or manageable variables and uncontrollable ones**. Any matters which cannot be controlled by an individual manager should be excluded from their standards for performance.

## 6.2 Budgets

The **principal budget factor** should be identified at the beginning of the budgetary process. It is often sales volume and so the sales budget has to be produced before all the others.

**Key concept**

A **budget** is a consolidated statement of the resources required to achieve objectives or to implement planned activities. It is a planning and control tool relevant to all aspects of management activities.

### 6.2.1 Purposes of a budget

(a)   **Co-ordinates** the activities of all the different departments of an organisation; in addition, through participation by employees in preparing a budget, it may be possible to motivate them to raise their targets and standards and to achieve better results.

(b)   **Communicates** the policies and targets to every manager in the organisation responsible for carrying out a part of that plan.

(c)   **Control** by having a plan against which actual results can be progressively compared.

### 6.2.2 Preparing budgets

Procedures for preparing the budget are contained in the **budget manual**, which indicates:

- People responsible for preparing budgets
- The order in which they must be prepared
- Deadlines for preparation
- Standard forms

The preparation and administration of budgets is usually the responsibility of a **budget committee**. Every part of the organisation should be represented on the committee.

The preparation of a budget may take weeks or months, and the budget committee may meet several times before the master budget is finally agreed. Functional budgets and cost centre budgets prepared in draft may need to be amended many times over as a consequence of discussions between departments, changes in market conditions, reversals of decisions by management, etc during the course of budget preparation.

### 6.2.3 The budget period

A budget does not necessarily have to be restricted to a one year planning horizon. The factors which should influence the **budget period** are as follows.

(a)   **Lead times**. A plan decided upon now might need a **considerable time** to be put into operation. Many companies expect growth in market share to take a number of years.

(b)   **In the short-term some resources are fixed**. The fixed nature of these resources, and the length of time which must elapse before they become variable, might therefore determine the planning horizon for budgeting.

(c)   All budgets involve some element of **forecasting and even guesswork**, since future events cannot be quantified with accuracy.

(d)   Since **unforeseen events** cannot be planned for, it would be a waste of time to plan in detail too far ahead.

(e)   Most budgets are prepared over a one-year period to enable managers to plan and control **financial results for the purposes of the annual accounts**.

### 6.2.4 The principal budget factor

The first task in budgeting is to identify the principal (key, limiting) budget factor. This is the factor which puts constraints on growth. The principal budget factor could be:

(a)   Normally, sales demand, ie a company is restricted from making and selling more of its products because there would be no sales demand for the increased output at a price which would be acceptable/profitable to the company.

(b)   Resources machine capacity, distribution and selling resources, the availability of key raw materials or the availability of cash.

(c)   Once this factor is defined then the rest of the budget can be prepared.

## Action Programme 2

What do you think is the crucial difference between the principal budget factors of an organisation producing confectionery and a non-profit orientated organisation such as a hospital?

### 6.2.5 Budgets and forecasts

(a)   **A forecast is an estimate of what might** happen in the future.

(b)   In contrast, a **budget is a plan of what the organisation would like** to happen, and what it has set as a target, although it should be realistic and so it will be based to some extent on the forecasts prepared.

(c)   However, in formulating a budget, **management will be trying to establish some control over the conditions** that will apply in the future. (For example, in setting a sales budget, management must decide on the prices to be charged and the advertising expenditure budget, even though they might have no control **over other** market factors.)

(i)   Management might be able to take **control action** to bring forecasts back into line **with the budget**.

(ii)  Alternatively, management will have to accept that the budget will not be achieved, or it will be exceeded, depending on what the current forecasts include.

Budgets perform a dual role.

(a)   They **incorporate forecasting** and planning information.

(b)   They **incorporate control measures**, in that they plan how resources are to be used to achieve the targets, and they can be flexed for corrective action.

### 6.2.6 Problems in constructing budgets

(a)   Difficulties in identifying **principal budget factors**

- Sales demand may not be known
- Resources may not be known

(b)   **Unpredictability** in economic conditions or prices of inputs

(c) Because of **inflation**, it might be difficult to estimate future price levels for materials, expenses, wages and salaries.

(d) **Managers might be reluctant to budget accurately**.

(i) **Slack**. They may overstate their expected expenditure, so that by having a budget which is larger than necessary, they will be unlikely to overspend the budget allowance. (They will then not be held accountable in control reports for excess spending.)

(ii) They may **compete** with other departments for the available resources, by trying to expand their budgeted expenditure. Budget planning might well intensify inter-departmental rivalry and the problems of 'empire building'.

(e) **Inter departmental rivalries** might ruin the efforts towards co-ordination in a budget.

(f) Employees might resist budget plans either because the plans are not properly communicated to them, or because they feel that the budget puts them 'under pressure' from senior managers to achieve better results.

---

**Exam tip**

You will have come across budgets and budgeting in your earlier studies or work experience. It is important to recognise that Examiners are increasingly requiring that candidates demonstrate their appreciation of financial aspects and their implications for both marketing and business. You must be prepared to support plans with budgets both in the context of mini-cases and major case study exercises. These should:

- Indicate your awareness of the process of budgeting and its significance
- Identify key headings and inclusions.

---

## 6.2.7 Sales budget

(a) A **preliminary sales estimate**

- A study of normal business growth
- A forecast of general business conditions
- A knowledge of potential markets for each product
- The practical judgement of sales and management staff
- A realisation of the effect on sales of basic changes in company policy

(b) The **adjustment of the above preliminary sales estimate**

- Seasonal nature of the business
- The viewpoint of optimum selling prices
- Overall production or purchasing capacity
- Viewpoint of securing even manufacturing loads
- Overall selling expenses and net profits
- The financial capacity of the business

(c) The adjusted anticipated sales by value and quantity contained in the sales budget should then be classified by commodities, departments, customers, salesmen, countries, terms of sale, methods of sale, methods of delivery and urgency of delivery (rush or normal).

### 6.2.8 The expense budgets related to marketing

(a)   *Selling expenses budget*

- Salaries and commission
- Materials, literature, samples
- Travelling (car cost, petrol, insurance) and entertaining
- Staff recruitment and selection and training
- Telephones and telegrams, postage
- After-sales service
- Royalties/patents
- Office rent and rates, lighting, heating etc
- Office equipment
- Credit costs, bad debts etc

(b)   *Advertising budget*

- Trade journal – space
- Prestige media – space
- PR space (costs of releases, entertainment etc)
- Blocks and artwork
- Advertising agents commission
- Staff salaries, office costs, etc
- Posters
- Cinema
- TV
- Signs

(c)   *Sales promotion budget*

- Exhibitions: space, equipment, staff, transport, hotels, bar etc
- Literature: leaflets, catalogues
- Samples/working models
- Point of sale display, window or showroom displays
- Special offers
- Direct mail shots – enclosure, postage, design costs

(d)   *Research and development budget*

- Market research – design and development and analysis costs
- Packaging and product research – departmental costs, materials, equipment
- Pure research – departmental costs materials, equipment
- Sales analysis and research
- Economic surveys
- Product planning
- Patents

(e)   *Distribution budget*

- Warehouse/deposits – rent, rates, lighting, heating
- Transport – capital costs
- Fuel – running costs
- Warehouse/depot and transport staff wages
- Packing (as opposed to packaging)

### 6.2.9 A note on marketing communication

The theory behind setting an advertising budget is the theory of diminishing returns, ie for every extra £1 of advertising spent, the company will earn an extra £x of profit. Further expenditure on advertising is justified until the marginal return £x diminishes to the point where £x < £1. Unfortunately, the marginal return from additional advertising cannot be measured easily in practice for the following reasons.

(a)   Advertising is only one aspect of the overall marketing mix, and only one element of the promotions mix.

(b)   Advertising has some long-term effect, which goes beyond the limits of a measurable accounting period.

(c)   Where the advertising budget is fixed as a percentage of sales, advertising costs tend to follow sales levels and not vice versa.

### 6.2.10 Methods of setting the marketing budget

| Method | Comment |
|---|---|
| **Competitive parity** | Fixing promotional expenditure in relation to the expenditure incurred by competitors. (This is unsatisfactory because it presupposes that the competitor's decision must be a good one.) |
| **The task method (or objective and task method)** | The marketing task for the organisation is set and a promotional budget is prepared which will help to ensure that this objective is achieved. A problem occurs if the objective is achieved only by paying out more on promotion than the extra profits obtained would justify. |
| **Communication stage models** | These are based on the idea that the link between promotion and sales cannot be measured directly, but can be measured by means of intermediate stages (for example, increase in awareness, comprehension, and then intention to buy). |
| **All you can afford** | Crude and unscientific, but commonly used. The firm simply takes a view on what it thinks it can afford to spend on promotion given that it would like to spend as much as it can. |
| **Investment** | The advertising and promotions budget can thus be designed around the amount felt necessary to maintain a certain brand value. |
| **Rule-of-thumb, non-scientific methods** | These include the percentage of sales, profits etc. |

## 6.3 Budgetary control

**FAST FORWARD**

One of the purposes for which budgets are used is to provide an input into the corporate control system. Their use for control purposes is enhanced by detailed analysis of **variances** and **ratios**.

## 6.3.1 Variance analysis

It is fine to have a set of budgets and standards, but how do you apply them in practice? The use of budgets as a control device is often achieved through **variance analysis**. Quite complex variance analysis systems are applied to production costs: these need not concern us here, but a brief description of the technique might help, as it is relevant to marketing costs.

## 6.3.2 Example

Assume that, in a month, **budgeted** sales revenue amount to £1m. Actual sales amount to £960,000. The total **sales variance** is thus £40,000 (ie £1m – £960,000). It is adverse as we have sold less than planned. So far so good. But with a little bit more information we can find out a lot more.

Let us assume that, in our original budget, the £1m sales revenue was to result from selling 100,000 units at £10 each. However the cost of a key component rose suddenly, so we had to increase the selling price to £12 a unit. We sold only 80,000 units: total sales revenue amounted to £960,000. There is a total negative sales variance of £40,000 as actual sales are less than we anticipated (£1,000,000). This variance of £40,000 can be analysed into two elements.

(a) **Price variance**. We put up the prices to receive extra revenue from the actual sales

(£12 – £10) × 80,000 = £160,000, a positive or **favourable** price variance

(b) **Volume variance**. We sold fewer, so in volume terms, at the budgeted/standard price of £10 we have a negative or adverse volume variance of (100,000 – 80,000) × £10 or £200,000.

(c)

|  | £ |
|---|---|
| Budgeted sales revenue | 1,000,000 |
| Price variance | 160,000 |
| Volume variance | (200,000) |
| Actual sales revenue | £960,000 |

Other applications of sales variances include the **sales mix variance**. A firm might sell more of one product in a range and less of another than you anticipated, or there might have been some difference in prices. Variances can also be used in analysing other marketing costs, such as distribution expenditure.

## 6.3.3 Tolerance limits for variances at planning level

No corporate plan has the detail or accuracy that a budget has. Consequently, the tolerance limits giving early warning of deviations from the plan should be wider. For example, if tolerance limits in budgetary control are variance ± 5% from standard, then corporate planning tolerance limits might be set at ± 10% or more from targets.

Whatever the tolerance limits are, the reporting of results which go outside (either favourably or adversely) the limits must be prompt. If sales have dropped well below target, the reasons must be established quickly and possible solutions thought about. For example if a company's products unexpectedly gain second highest market share, the questions that should be asked are as follows.

- How did it happen?
- Has profit suffered?
- Can second place be made secure, and if so, how?
- Can the market leader be toppled? (And if so, is this profitable?)

## 6.3.4 Ratio analysis

Ratio analysis is a very important aspect of performance measurement. However, it is important to remember that the computation of ratios is in itself an almost worthless exercise: like most numerical information, ratios are only of value if they are **assessed for their significance**. Generally speaking, the value of ratios lies in the making of comparisons year on year and, sometimes, between comparable functions, projects or operations. **Financial ratios are explained in detail in your BPP Study Text for Paper 9: Analysis and Evaluation**.

## 6.3.5 Corporate ratios

The main corporate ratios are return on capital employed and, in the case of a quoted company, the price/earnings ratio. Marketing strategies **contribute** towards these, but they are at **too high a level of control** to be useful as control measures over marketing activities in particular.

(a)   **Profitability**. Marketing personnel have little direct control over the cost structure of the company, and so while they do contribute to profitability, they cannot control it.

(b)   **ROCE**, as conventionally measured, is a control measure for the company as a whole.

**Marketing relevant ratios** are a **mix of financial ratios and non-financial ratios**. For example:

(a)   **Financial ratio only**

(i)   Sales revenue or marketing expenditure can be compared: **over time**, against **budget** or against **competition**.

|  | 2005 | 2006 |
|---|---|---|
| Revenue | £10m | £15m |

2006/2005 gives an increase of 1.5:1.

(ii)   There may be relationships between different variables. For example

|  | 2005 | 2006 |
|---|---|---|
| Revenue | £10m | £15m |
| Bad debts | 0.5m | 1.2m |
| Bad debts/revenue | 1:20 or 5% | 2:25 or 8% |

Comparing these over time suggests that while **income has increased**, the **quality of sales** (in terms of **creditworthiness**) has fallen, as bad debts are 8% of revenue rather than 5%. Perhaps the sales force has been too generous.

(b)   **A mixture of financial ratios and non-financial data**

|  | 2005 | 2006 |
|---|---|---|
| Revenue | £10m | £15m |
| Sales personnel | 50 | 60 |

Revenue has increased by 50% whereas the sales force has increased by 20%.

|  | 2005 | 2006 |
|---|---|---|
| Revenue per sales employee | £0.2m | £0.25m |

The sales force is more productive in 2006 than in 2005.

(c)   **Non-financial data only**

This can refer to almost any aspect of a company's operations. We are concerned with marketing.

|  | 2005 | 2006 |
|---|---|---|
| Sales orders | 250 | 300 |
| Sales leads | 1,000 | 1,025 |
| Sales personnel | 50 | 60 |

In 2005, 25% of leads turned into orders, whereas in 2006 this has increased to 29%, so the sales force is more effective. The number of orders by sales person has stayed the same.

# 7 Marketing mix effectiveness

Marketing managers are responsible for monitoring their progress towards the agreed targets and objectives. To do this it is necessary to evaluate the effectiveness of the marketing mix.

This section will consider ways of controlling the effectiveness of four of the mix elements.

- Personal selling
- Advertising and sales promotions
- Pricing
- Channels of distribution

## 7.1 Personal selling

The effectiveness of personal selling can be measured for:

- The sales force as a whole
- Each group of the sales force (eg each regional sales team)
- Each individual salesperson

If there are telephone sales staff, their performance should be measured separately from the travelling sales staff.

**Measures of performance** would compare actual results against a target or standard.

- Sales, in total, by customer, and by product
- Contribution, in total, by customer and by product
- Selling expenses (budget versus actual) in relation to sales
- Customer call frequency
- Average sales value per call
- Average contribution per call
- Average cost per call
- Average trade discount
- Number of new customers obtained
- Percentage increase in sales compared with previous period
- Average number of repeat calls per sale
- Average mileage travelled per £1 sales

**It is not an easy task to decide what the standards should be**. It is important not to assume that the efficient sales person who makes ten calls a day is doing a better job than the colleague who makes fewer calls but wins more orders.

There can be a big difference between (a) net sales (ie sales after returns and discounts) and (b) profits or contribution. The costs of selling and distribution can be a very large proportion of an organisation's total costs, and so the performance of a sales force should be based on productivity and profitability, rather than sales alone.

## 7.2 The effectiveness of advertising

### 7.2.1 Performance measures for advertising

(a)  **Exposure**. Exposure can be measured in terms of frequency (eg the number of times a TV advertisement is screened) and the number of potential customers reached. One TV advertisement might reach two million people; by repeating the advertisement, the intention would be to reach people who missed the advertisement previously, but also to reinforce the message through repetition to people who have seen it before.

(b)  **Awareness**. Awareness of the existence of a product, or awareness of certain particular features of a product. Awareness could be measured by recall tests or recognition tests.

(c)  **Sales** (volume and/or revenue). Advertising is often intended to increase sales but the effect of advertising on sales is not easy to measure. Why should this be?

(i)   Advertising is only one part of a marketing mix. Other factors influencing sales might be price changes, whether intermediaries have stocked enough of the products to meet an increase in demand, and competitors' actions.

(ii)  Advertising might succeed in **maintaining** a firm's existing market share, without actually increasing sales.

(d)  **Profits**. The difficulties of measuring the effect of an advertising campaign on profits are therefore the same as those described in (c) above. Breakeven analysis might be used to calculate the volume of extra sales required to cover the (fixed) costs of the advertising. In monitoring the effects of a campaign, management might be able to judge whether this minimum increase in sales has or has not, in all probability, been achieved. However, advertising might be necessary to build a brand or for management to invest in it.

(e)  **Attitudes**. The aim of a campaign might be expressed in terms of 'x% of customers should show a preference for Product A over rival products'.

(f)  **Enquiries**. Advertising might be aimed at generating extra enquiries from potential customers. Where possible, enquiries should be traced to the advertisement. For example, a customer reply coupon in a magazine advertisement should be printed with an identification number or label, identifying the magazine and date of its issue.

It is difficult to measure the **success of an advertising campaign**, although volume of sales may be a short-term guide.

(a)  A campaign to launch a new product, however, may have to be judged over a longer period of time (ie to see how well the product establishes itself in the market).

(b)  Advertising's main purpose in the communication mix is to create **awareness** and **interest**.

(c)  The effectiveness of advertising is therefore usually measured by marketing researchers in terms of **customer attitudes** or **psychological response**. Most of the money is spent by agencies on **pre-testing** the given advertisement or campaign before launching it into national circulation. Relatively less tends to be spent on **post-testing** the effect of given advertisements and campaigns.

Post-testing involves finding out how well people can **recall** an advertisement and the product it advertises, and whether (on the basis of a sample of respondents) attitudes to the product have changed since the advertising campaign.

New financial service brands including *Virgin Direct* and *Goldfish* failed to convert high levels of awareness into new business.

The brands, supported by estimated ad budgets of about £5m and £10m respectively and featuring Richard Branson and Billy Connolly, were ever-present on TV at the end of 1996, with Goldfish securing 30 per cent brand awareness for its credit card and Virgin 13 per cent for its products. But neither converted that awareness into new business, according to exclusive research on new financial service and loyalty schemes conducted by the RSL Strategic Initiatives Monitor.

Its survey showed that less high-profile brands such as *MBNA's* credit card, which had an awareness of only ten per cent, achieved a holding of two per cent – outstripping its higher spending rivals.

Significantly the reasons for changing suggest that credit card holders are looking for immediate benefits rather than the promise of rebates in the future from their cards. Over a third of new cardholders mention low APR (annual percentage rate – broadly, interest rate) and a quarter 'no annual fee' as reasons for taking new cards. In contrast only six per cent were attracted by points or tokens offered, while five per cent claim to have switched because they banked with the card issuer.

### 7.2.2 Justifying advertising

It would seem sensible too, to try to consider the effectiveness of advertising in terms of **cost, sales and profit**, but only if the aim of an advertising campaign was directed towards boosting sales. If there is a noticeable increase in sales volume as a result of an advertising campaign, it should be possible to estimate the extent to which advertising might have been responsible for the extra sales and contribution, and the extra net profit per £1 of advertising could be measured.

### 7.2.3 The effectiveness of sales promotions

There is often a direct link between below-the-line advertising (sales promotions) and short-term sales volume.

(a) The **consumer sales response** to the following is readily measurable.

- Price reductions as sales promotions (for example introductory offers)
- Coupon 'money-off' offers
- Free sendaway gifts
- On-pack free gift offers
- Combination pack offers

(b) It might also be possible to measure the link between sales and promotions for industrial goods, for example special discounts, orders taken at trade fairs or exhibitions and the response to trade-in allowances.

(c) However, there are other promotions where the effect on sales volume is **indirect** and not readily measurable, for example sponsorship, free samples, catalogues, point-of-sale material and inducements.

(d) Promotions may go hand-in-hand with a direct advertising campaign, especially in the case of consumer products, and so the effectiveness of the advertising and the sales promotions should then be considered together.

A manufacturer can try to control sales promotion costs by:

(a)    Setting a **time limit** to the campaign (for example, money off coupons, free gift offers etc must be used before a specified date).

(b)    **Restricting the campaign** to certain areas or outlets.

(c)    Restricting the campaign to **specific goods** (for example, to only three or four goods in the manufacturer's product range, or only to products which are specially labelled with the offer).

## 7.3 Pricing

### 7.3.1 Aspects of pricing

(a)    There are two types of discounts.

    (i)    **Bulk purchase discount** that encourage higher sales and are justified by economies of scale.

    (ii)    **Settlement discounts**, which are given to encourage prompt payment of accounts, thus reducing the amount of working capital needed.

(b)    Sales prices are set with a view to the total **sales volume** they should attract.

    (i)    **New product pricing policy** might be to set high **skimming** prices or low **penetration** prices.

        (1)    For skimming prices, consider whether they have been too high, because the market has grown faster than anticipated, leaving the organisation with a low market share because of its high prices.

        (2)    For penetration prices, consider whether the price level has succeeded in helping the market to grow quickly and the organisation to grab its target share of the market.

    (ii)    Decisions to raise prices or lower prices will be based on assumptions about the **elasticity of demand**. Did actual increases or decreases in demand exceed or fall short of expectation?

(c)    An aspect of **product-market strategy** and positioning is the mixture of product quality and price. An organisation might opt for a **high price and high quality** strategy, or a **low price and average quality** strategy. Actual price performance can be judged:

    (i)    By comparing the organisation's prices with those of competitors, to establish whether prices were comparatively low, average or high, as planned

    (ii)    By judging whether the mix of product quality and price appears to have been effective

### Marketing at Work

Some of the most familiar ways to market consumer goods are proving to be costly failures.

Recent research has begun to tell the makers of consumer goods which types of marketing actually work. Marketing is not about to become a science, but it will henceforth be easier to tell one half of the marketing budget from the other.

One surprise concerns price cuts. Packaged-goods firms spend some $70 billion a year on various promotions. Among marketing men, however, price cuts remained as popular as ever. It is an article of faith that they both reward loyal customers and woo new ones. Now even this is in question.

(a)     For a start, consumers say they prefer incentives other than price.

(b)     Price cuts also appear to have little lasting effect on sales volumes. In an unpublished study, a team at Purdue University led by Doug Bowman spent eight years scrutinising how almost 1,600 households in America bought a typical household product such as detergent. The study found that consumers exposed to repeated price cuts learnt to ignore the usual price.

(c)     Neither do price cuts attract new customers. The unexpected explanation for this was that almost all the customers buying the discounted product had tried it before. It seems that brands are built in other ways: price cuts are simply a gift to loyal customers. Little wonder that only a third of all promotions pay for themselves.

Another trick is to dazzle the jaded consumer with variety. At one time, *Procter & Gamble* was selling 35 variations of *Crest* toothpaste and different nappies for girls and boys. The average supermarket in America devotes 20ft of shelving to medicine for coughs and colds. Most of this choice is trumpery.

In fact, more choice does not translate into more sales. Ravi Dhar, of Yale University, examined how students decided what to buy, based on the number of versions of each product-category on offer. As the choice increased, so did the likelihood that students would not buy anything at all. John Gourville at Harvard Business School believes that some types of choice are more troublesome than others. His research suggests that consumers like to be offered choices in a single dimension: different sizes of cereal packet, say. If they are asked to make too many trade-offs, such as whether to buy a computer with a modem or speakers, consumers start to feel anxious or even irritated.

The custom in marketing departments of moving managers off a brand within two years has rewarded those who boost sales, even if their favoured marketing strategy achieves no lasting good. Some firms, such as *Coca-Cola* and *AT&T*, now employ brand equity managers to oversee the long-term health of their brands.

There are also new ways of using detailed information to target promotions. Buzzwords abound – relationship marketing, key account management, and in the world of packaged goods, efficient consumer response (ECR).

## 7.4 Channels of distribution

Some organisations might use channels of distribution for their goods which are unprofitable to use, and which should either be abandoned in favour of more profitable channels, or made profitable by giving some attention to cutting costs or increasing minimum order sizes.

It might well be the case that an organisation gives close scrutiny to the profitability of its products, and the profitability of its market segments, but does not have a costing system which measures the costs of distributing the products to their markets via different distribution channels.

A numerical example might help to illustrate this point. Let us suppose that Biomarket Ltd sells two consumer products, X and Y, in two markets A and B. In both markets, sales are made through the following outlets.

- Direct sales to supermarkets
- Wholesalers

Sales and costs for the most recent quarter have been analysed by product and market as follows.

| | Market A | | | Market B | | | Both markets | | |
|---|---|---|---|---|---|---|---|---|---|
| | X | Y | Total | X | Y | Total | X | Y | Total |
| | £'000 | £'000 | £'000 | £'000 | £'000 | £'000 | £'000 | £'000 | £'000 |
| Sales | 900 | 600 | 1,500 | 1,000 | 2,000 | 3,000 | 1,900 | 2,600 | 4,500 |
| Variable production costs | 450 | 450 | 900 | 500 | 1,500 | 2,000 | 950 | 1,950 | 2,900 |
| | 450 | 150 | 600 | 500 | 500 | 1,000 | 950 | 650 | 1,600 |
| Variable sales Costs | 90 | 60 | 150 | 100 | 100 | 200 | 190 | 160 | 350 |
| Contribution | 360 | 90 | 450 | 400 | 400 | 800 | 760 | 490 | 1,250 |
| Share of fixed costs (production, sales, distribution, administration) | 170 | 80 | 250 | 290 | 170 | 460 | 460 | 250 | 710 |
| Net profit | 190 | 10 | 200 | 110 | 230 | 340 | 300 | 240 | 540 |

This analysis shows that both products are profitable, and both markets are profitable. But what about the channels of distribution? A further analysis of market A might show the following.

| | Market A | | |
|---|---|---|---|
| | Supermarkets | Wholesalers | Total |
| | £'000 | £'000 | £'000 |
| Sales | 1,125 | 375 | 1,500 |
| Variable production costs | 675 | 225 | 900 |
| | 450 | 150 | 600 |
| Variable selling costs | 105 | 45 | 150 |
| Contribution | 345 | 105 | |
| Direct distribution costs | 10 | 80 | 90 |
| | 335 | 25 | 360 |
| Share of fixed costs | 120 | 40 | 160 |
| Net profit/(loss) | 215 | (15) | 200 |

This analysis shows that although sales through wholesalers make a contribution after deducting direct distribution costs, the profitability of this channel of distribution is disappointing, and some attention ought perhaps to be given to improving it.

# 8 The balanced scorecard

At the strategic level it is necessary to form an overview of the business's progress towards its goals. To do this it is not enough to look at the performance of marketing alone, or even at summary financial results. A more rounded picture is needed. This is provided by the four **perspectives** of the **balanced scorecard**.

## 8.1 The balanced scorecard

**Key concept**

The **balanced scorecard** is:

'a set of measures that gives top managers a fast but comprehensive view of the business. The balanced scorecard includes financial measures that tell the results of actions already taken. And it complements the financial measures with **operational** measures on customer satisfaction, internal processes, and the organisation's innovation and improvement activities – operational measures that are the drivers of future financial performance.' (Robert Kaplan, January-February 1992, *Harvard Business Review.*)

The reason for using such a system is that 'traditional financial accounting measures like return on investment and earnings per share can give misleading signals for continuous improvement and innovation – activities today's competitive environment demands'. The balanced scorecard allows managers to look at the business from four important perspectives

- Customer
- Financial
- Internal business
- Innovation and learning

### 8.1.1 Customer perspective

**'How do customers see us?'** Given that many company mission statements identify customer satisfaction as a key corporate goal, the balanced scorecard translates this into specific measures. Customer concerns fall into four categories.

(a) **Time**. Lead time is the time it takes a firm to meet customer needs from receiving an order to delivering the product.

(b) **Quality**. Quality measures not only include defect levels – although these should be minimised by TQM – but accuracy in forecasting.

(c) **Performance** of the product. (How often does the photocopier break down?)

(d) **Service**. How long will it take a problem to be rectified? (If the photocopier breaks down, how long will it take the maintenance engineer to arrive?)

In order to view the firm's performance through customers' eyes, firms hire market researchers to assess how the firm performs. Higher service and quality may cost more at the outset, but savings can be made in the long term.

### Complaints

All businesses need systems for handling complaints since complaints are a most important aspect of the way their customers view them. Complaints indicate **dissatisfaction**: the degree of dissatisfaction a firm is willing to tolerate is an important strategic decision that should be informed by **analysis of the rate, severity and topic** of complaints. It is important to remember that complaints are not an accurate index of dissatisfaction since many of those dissatisfied will not bother to complain, they will vote with their purses and go elsewhere. In fact, willingness to complain may be encouraged by proper handling of complaints, while an absence of complaints may simply indicate customers' belief that complaining will be a waste of effort.

### 8.1.2 Internal business perspective

The **internal business perspective** identifies the **business processes that have the greatest impact on customer satisfaction**, such as quality and employee skills.

(a) Companies should also attempt to identify and measure their **distinctive competences** and the critical technologies they need to ensure continued leadership. Which processes should they excel at?

(b) To achieve these goals, **performance measures must relate to employee behaviour**, to tie in the strategic direction with employee action.

(c) An information system is necessary to enable executives to measure performance. An **executive information system** enables managers to drill down into lower level information.

### 8.1.3 Innovation and learning perspective

The question is **'Can we continue to improve and create value?'** Whilst the customer and internal process perspectives identify the *current* parameters for competitive success, the company needs to learn and to innovate to **satisfy future needs**.

- How long does it take to develop new products?
- How quickly does the firm climb the experience curve to make new products?
- What percentage of revenue comes from new products?
- How many suggestions are made by staff and are acted upon?
- What are staff attitudes?
- The company can identify measures for training and long-term investment.

### 8.1.4 Financial perspective

**'How do we appear to shareholders?'** Financial performance indicators indicate 'whether the company's strategies, implementation, and execution are contributing to bottom line management.'

### 8.1.5 Financial performance indicators

| Measure | For | Against |
|---------|-----|---------|
| **Profitability** | Easy to calculate and understand. | Ignores the size of the investment. |
| **Return on investment (profit/ capital)** | Accounting measure: easy to calculate and understand. Takes size of investment into account. Widely used. | • Ignores risk<br>• Easy to manipulate (eg managers may postpone necessary capital investment to improve ratio)<br>• What are 'assets'? (eg do brands count?)<br>• Only really suited to products in the maturity phase of the life cycle, rather than others which are growing fast. |
| **Residual income** | Head office levies an interest charge for the use of asset. | Not related to the size of investment except indirectly |
| **Earnings per share** | Relates the firm's performance to needs of its shareholders | Shareholders are more concerned about future expectations; ignores capital growth as a measure of shareholders' wealth |
| **DCF measures** | Relates performance to investment appraisal used to take the decision; cash flows rather than accounting profits are better predictors of shareholder wealth | • Practical difficulties in predicting future cash flows of a whole company<br>• Difficulty in separating cash flows for products which share resources |

### 8.1.6 Linkages

**Disappointing results** might result from a **failure to view all the measures as a whole**. For example, increasing productivity means that fewer employees are needed for a given level of output. Excess capacity can be created by quality improvements. However these improvements have to be exploited (eg by increasing sales). The **financial element** of the balanced scorecard 'reminds executives that improved quality, response time, productivity or new products, benefit the company only when they are translated into improved financial results', or if they enable the firm to obtain a sustainable competitive advantage.

**The balanced scorecard only measures performance. It does not indicate that the strategy is the right one**. 'A failure to convert improved operational performance into improved financial performance should send executives back to their drawing boards to rethink the company's strategy or its implementation plans.'

### 8.1.7 Example: a balanced scorecard

*Balanced Scorecard*

| Financial Perspective | |
|---|---|
| **GOALS** | **MEASURES** |
| Survive | Cash flow, net margin |
| Succeed | Monthly sales growth and operating income by division |
| Prosper | Increase market share and ROI |

| Customer Perspective | |
|---|---|
| **GOALS** | **MEASURES** |
| New products | Percentage of sales from new products |
| Responsive supply | On-time delivery (defined by customer) |
| Preferred supplier | Share of key accounts' purchases |
| | Ranking by key accounts |
| Customer Partnership | Number of cooperative engineering efforts |
| | Customer survey |
| Value for money | |

| Internal Business Perspective | |
|---|---|
| **GOALS** | **MEASURES** |
| Technology capability | Manufacturing configuration vs competition |
| Manufacturing excellence | Cycle time |
| | Unit cost |
| | Yield |
| Design productivity | Safety record |
| New product introduction | Engineering efficiency Actual introduction schedule vs plan |

| Innovation and Learning Perspective | |
|---|---|
| **GOALS** | **MEASURES** |
| Technology leadership | Time to develop next generation of products |
| Manufacturing learning | Process time to maturity |
| Product focus | Percentage of products that equal 80% sales |
| | New product introduction vs competition |
| Time to market | Staff survey |
| Staff empowerment | |

Many firms use profit or investment centre organisation to control the performance of different divisions. A profit centre is where managers are responsible for revenues and costs; an investment centre is a profit centre in which managers have some say in investment decisions. Always keep in mind the following.

(a) Different divisions may offer different risk/return profiles.

(b) Managers will take dysfunctional decisions if these put their performance in a better light.

(c) An economically efficient, fair transfer pricing system must be devised.

(d) There are problems in assessing how shared fixed assets or head office costs should be charged out.

## Chapter Roundup

- The best project appraisal method is net present value, but payback period and ROCE/ROI are also useful.

- Special problems occur in marketing **feedback and control systems** because markets are made up of people and therefore are not very predictable.

- **Basic control systems** depend upon comparing results with plans: single loop feedback produces control action to modify performance, double loop feedback is used to modify the plan itself.

- A vast range of techniques is available for the purpose of strategic control. Strategic control may be based on critical success factors.

- **Benchmarks** can be set on a variety of key performance indicators as an objective form of control. Marketing research and competitor intelligence would be needed to establish benchmarks and to monitor progress.

- **Planning** is not just an extension of **budgeting**, but there is a close link between them.

- A **budget** is a plan expressed in money terms, representing the resources needed to achieve the objective.

- The **principal budget factor** should be identified at the beginning of the budgetary process. It is often sales volume and so the sales budget has to be produced before all the others.

- One of the purposes for which budgets are used is to provide an input into the corporate control system. Their use for control purposes is enhanced by detailed analysis of **variances** and **ratios**.

- Marketing managers are responsible for monitoring their progress towards the agreed targets and objectives. To do this it is necessary to evaluate the effectiveness of the marketing mix.

- At the strategic level it is necessary to form an overview of the business's progress towards its goals. To do this it is not enough to look at the performance of marketing alone, or even at summary financial results. A more rounded picture is needed. This is provided by the four **perspectives** of the **balanced scorecard**.

## Quick Quiz

1    What is the special feature of marketing feedback and control systems?

2    What strategic  measures could be used to control competitive standing?

3    What are the disadvantages of benchmarking?

4    What areas should be investigated when undertaking an analysis of key customers?

5    What is the purpose of a budget?

6    What is the principal budget factor?

7    What is budgetary slack?

8    How may the cost of sales promotions be controlled?

9    What are possible aims of discount pricing?

10    What are the perspectives of the balanced scorecard?

## Answers to Quick Quiz

1   The need to recognise the complexity of human behaviour

2   Demand analysis and market share or penetration

3   It is reactive and imitative rather than innovative; and it is not focused on the customer

4   Identity; history; use of product; relationship to end-market, attitudes and behaviour, financial performance, profitability

5   To co-ordinate, to communicate and to control

6   The organisational factor that limits overall performance: usually sales

7   A margin for error inserted by a manager into his budget to buffer his performance

8   By restricting their availability by geography, by time or to specific goods

9   To increase sales volumes or to encourage prompt payment

10  Financial, customer, internal business, innovation and learning

## Action Programme Review

1   The plan has to be altered as a result of feedback.

   (a)   This is a **standard**, in other words, a measure of expected performance.

   (b)   Counselling is control action to improve the individual's performance. Dismissal is control action too, if the employee is replaced by someone who performs better, thus raising the performance of the department as a whole.

   (c)   This is feedforward control based on culture.

2   A sweet company's principal budget factor is likely to be demand, as expressed in sales forecasts. A hospital's principal budget factor is almost certainly going to be the funding allocation from the government.

Now try Question 10 at the end of the Study Text

# Part F

# Mini-cases in
# the examination

# 12

# Mini-cases in the examination

# Introduction

With the obvious exception of the dedicated case study paper, *Strategic Marketing in Practice*, each exam at Professional Post-Graduate diploma level incorporates a 50 mark mini-case study as Part A. Candidates often have difficulty with mini-cases, so this chapter offers detailed guidance on how to tackle them. Question practice can be found in the BPP *Practice & Revision Kit* for this subject – an order form can be found at the end of the Study Text.

# 1 What is a mini-case?

A mini-case in the examination is a 500-800 word long description of an organisation at a moment in time. You first see it in the examination room and so you have a maximum of 72 minutes to read, understand, analyse and answer the mini-case. The length of the mini-case is likely to be between one and two pages of A4.

The approach is the same for all the subjects and so practice in one area will benefit your other Diploma subjects.

The mini-case carries 50% of the available marks in the examination. Students who fail a Diploma paper are often found to have had difficulties with the mini-case. It is worth noting that a good result on the mini-case can be used to compensate for a weaker performance in part B of the paper.

As mini-cases are fundamental to your exam success, you should be absolutely clear about what mini-cases are, CIM's purpose in using them, what the examiners seek and then, in context, to consider how best they should be tackled.

## 1.1 The purpose of the mini-case

Diploma examiners require students to demonstrate not only their knowledge of marketing management, but also their ability to use that knowledge in a commercially credible way in the context of a real business scenario.

**You cannot pass this part of the paper by regurgitating theory**. You must be able to apply the theory to real problems. The mini-case is included to test your competence in analysing information and making clear and reasonable decisions.

## 1.2 The examiners' requirements

The examiners are the consumers of your examination script. You should remember first and foremost that they need a paper which makes their life easy. That means that the script should be well laid out, with plenty of white space and neat readable writing. All the basic rules of examination technique must be applied, but because communication skills are fundamental to the marketer, the ability to communicate clearly is particularly important.

The examination is your opportunity to market yourself to the examiner, in this case as a marketing professional competent in the skills of analysis and evaluation. As actions speak louder than words, a candidate who has failed to plan the answers or who has run out of the resource time, is unlikely to impress.

Management skills are commonly ignored by candidates who fail to recognise their importance. Management is more about thinking than knowing, more about decision than analysis. It is about achieving action through persuasive communication. It is about meeting deadlines. It is therefore about clear, logical analysis under time pressure, which leads to decisive recommendations presented in simple, clear business English.

The six key factors from the above paragraph are:

- Thinking
- Logical analysis
- Decision
- Action
- Persuasive communication
- Business English

All must be demonstrated to the examiners, especially in the case and mini-case study elements of the Diploma examinations.

If you are entering the Diploma by exemption, take particular note of the examiners' requirements. Certificate holders will have encountered mini-cases before. They should note the change in emphasis from the learning of marketing to its management.

Examiners' reports note the reasons why candidates fail. It makes depressing reading to go back over a series of reports because year after year the examiners make the same points and year after year many candidates ignore them! No examiner can understand why candidates refuse to take notice of their requirements. In everyday life we do what our manager instructs, or we leave the job (one way or another). If candidates would only think of the examiners as senior managers at work, and address them accordingly, the pass rate would shoot up.

## 1.3 Examiners' comments

Examiners' reports on mini-cases repeatedly stress the same points.

(a)     Relate the time allocated to the answer to the marks available.

(b)     Answer the question asked. Never use a question as a pretext to answer a different one.

(c)     Time planning is crucial to success.

(d)     Quality and insight are worth more than quantity and detail.

(e)     It is essential to write in role.

(f)     Intelligently apply knowledge of theory to a marketing problem.

(g)     Do not repeat chunks of the mini-case in the answer.

(h)     Do not show any analytical work (for example SWOT) unless specifically requested.

(i)     Presentation must be of management quality. Spelling and grammar are important, only a certain laxity will be allowed for the pressures of the exam room.

Direct quotes from examiners' reports reinforce the points made in the previous paragraph.

(a)     'The commonest 'self-destruct' faults

- Bad time management
- Using the question as a pretext to answer a different one
- Poor presentation'

(b)     'Your examiners regard badly constructed and unrealistic case solutions as a particularly serious failing among candidates for the professional diploma of a chartered institute.'

(c)     'The gap between question answering and case solving abilities continues to be very marked.'

(d)     'A wider spread of up-to-date knowledge (greater than Coca-Cola and McDonald's) would give the examiner greater confidence in your competence.'

(e) 'Management of any sort, and particularly marketing management, is about thinking rather than knowing. It is for example about selecting the best strategy rather than simply knowing the range of options available.'

(f) 'Preparation time should be spent in practising techniques as much as in learning content.'

(g) 'Diploma candidates not only need to demonstrate their ability to communicate succinctly as a subsidiary test of marketing awareness but in their own interests of scoring higher marks by getting more valid points across in the limited time available in the exam situation.'

(h) 'It is a shame that such basic mistakes mar what are often otherwise diligent and enthusiastic efforts.'

## 1.4 The expectations of examiners

Examiners are experienced marketing managers. They know that mini-cases give only limited information and that candidates are working under a tight time constraint. They do not, therefore, require considered, fully rounded answers. There is insufficient data and time. The successful candidate learns to work with what is available, to make reasonable assumptions that help in the decision making process, and to present an answer cogently and concisely.

The examiner can only mark within the criteria that have been established. The requirements are set out very clearly. It is not difficult to satisfy them. The well prepared candidate should not fail the mini-case. Since the information is limited, the time is very constrained, and the examiner is looking for evidence of a managerial approach, any candidate that makes reasonable assumptions about the case, takes clear and sensible decisions, and communicates these succinctly must pass.

Also remember that mini-cases are set for all candidates. Some will know absolutely nothing about the industry, some will work in it and be expert. Candidates take the examinations in centres across the world. Therefore the examiner will not ask technical questions about the industry, nor any tied to a specific culture or economy. Questions have to be more general, more open, less specific. However, you will be expected to have acquired a level of business appreciation and marketing knowledge from your other studies.

### 1.4.1 Summary

The requirements are as follows.

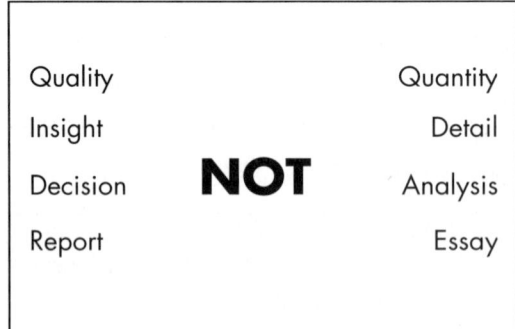

| Quality | | Quantity |
|---------|---|----------|
| Insight | | Detail |
| Decision | **NOT** | Analysis |
| Report | | Essay |

## 1.5 Management reports in CIM mini-cases

A management report is a specialised form of communication. It is the language used in business. It is not difficult to learn to write in report style, but it does require practice to become fluent. Mini-cases must always be answered in report style.

Management reports are action planning documents and are generally written in the third person. Their role is to make positive recommendations for action. Situational analysis is included only if it is needed to clarify an ambiguity. Examiners complain that many candidates do little more than produce a SWOT analysis as their response to a mini-case. Support material is often included, but as appendices to the body of the report. In CIM mini-case work it is exceptional to include an appendix.

Management reports: the basic rules

- Always head a report with the name of your organisation.
- State to whom it is addressed, from whom it comes, and give the date.
- Head the report (for example 'Marketing research plan for 2004/05').
- Number and sub-number paragraphs. Head them if appropriate.
- Present the contents in a logical order.
- Include diagrams, graphs, tables only if they have positive value.
- Include recommendations for action that are written as intention against time.

If you are forced to use appendices there are two further rules to remember.

- Refer to them within the body of the report (eg 'See Appendix A').
- Indicate when the report concludes (.../ends).

Management reports are written in crisp, no-nonsense business English. There is no room for superlatives, flowery adjectives nor flowing sentences. You are not trying to entertain, simply to present facts as clearly as possible. Think about the style you would adopt if writing a report to senior managers at work.

As we have already said, presentation is of key importance in CIM examinations. The rules are as follows.

- Use a black or a blue pen, never red or green.
- Start your first answer on the facing page of the answer book, never inside the cover.
- Make the first three pages as neat and well laid out as possible, to impress.
- Use plenty of space. Do not crowd your work.
- Number your questions above your answers. Never write in either margin.
- Leave space (four or five lines) between sections of your report.

# 2 An approach to mini-cases

Mini-cases are easy once you have mastered the basic techniques. The key to success lies in adopting a logical sequence of steps which with practice you will master. You must enter the exam room with the process as second nature, so you can concentrate your attention on the marketing issues which face you.

Students who are at first apprehensive when faced with a mini-case often come to find them much more stimulating and rewarding than traditional examination questions. There is the added security of knowing that there is no single correct answer to a case study.

You will be assessed on your approach, style, creativity and commercial credibility, but you will not be judged against a single 'correct' answer. Treat the mini-case as though it were happening in real life, at work or at a social meeting with a friend. Most of the mini-case is narrative; it tells a story or paints a picture. If a friend says over a drink 'I've got a problem at work' the most usual answer is 'Tell me about it'. The listener will need background information to establish frame reference and to understand the problem. That is what the case narrative is doing. Most of it is background, and it should be read just to grasp the context and flavour of the situation.

It helps to pretend to yourself that the examiner needs your advice. The questions posed indicate the advice which is being sought.

(a)    Just as your friend would not be impressed if you spent half an hour pontificating on how he or she got themselves into this situation, neither will the examiner reward you for analysis of how the situation arose.

(b)    Neither will the examiner be impressed with a long list of 'you could do this ....' 'but on the other hand....' Identify the alternatives, but make a clear recommendation if you want to win friends and influence examiners.

You will be faced with limited information, less than would be available to you in the real world. This is one of the limitations of case study examinations, but everyone is faced with the same constraint. You are able to make assumptions where it is necessary.

A reasonable assumption is logically possible and factually credible. You may need to make and clearly state two or three assumptions in order to tackle a case.

Some students feel uncomfortable that there is no bedrock (an easy, well defined question) on which to build. They feel all at sea and panic.

Preparation is the answer. It is important to practise the technique of handling a mini-case. There are three later in this chapter, and they should be taken individually. For each there are careful instructions and a time guide is given. After you have completed these it will still be necessary for you to develop speed, but the principles needed for success in the examination will have been established. Mini-case scenarios are also included as one of the data sheets in the CIM's *Marketing Success* and these will provide you with regular new material on which to practise.

## 2.1 An example of a mini-case

This mini-case example is worked through stage by stage to show you the process. This shows you the methodology.

## 2.2 Direct Lounge Furniture Ltd (DLF)

DLF is owned by two entrepreneurs each of whom built up a separate direct marketing business, one in the East Midlands and one in the West Midlands over a period of some 15 years, before merging three years ago. The main advantages of the merger were joint advertising, wider product ranges, more flexible production and less reliance upon one person. The two owners are good friends and work well together, meeting at least once a week.

Both the two constituent businesses comprise showrooms mainly featuring upholstered three-piece suites finished in Dralon cloth, in a wide variety of styles and colours. This furniture is manufactured in two small factories, each of which has an adjoining showroom.

Sales are achieved by advertising in free newspapers delivered to Midlands households. These advertisements illustrate the furniture on offer, strongly emphasise the lower prices available to the public by buying direct from the manufacturers and of course invite readers to visit the showrooms without obligation.

Upon visiting the showroom the public can look around the products on offer, discuss their individual requirements with a salesperson and be shown round the factory to emphasise the quality of the workmanship, wooden frames etc.

This marketing formula works very well and sales/profits are booming. Customers feel they are involved in the design of their own furniture and that they are getting good value. DLF enjoy high proportions of recommendations and repeat sales.

Buying behaviour patterns are however changing. People are tending to buy individual items rather than the standard three-piece suite (two armchairs plus a 2/3/4 seater settee) and to seek co-ordination with curtains, carpet etc. In partial response to this the East Midlands showroom offers made-to-measure curtains in Dralon to complement or match the upholstery. Another change in the industry is in the foam used for upholstering which was formerly highly flammable and when on fire gave out dense black smoke causing many deaths. Legislation has now been passed enforcing the use of safer foam.

The media exposure of the fire hazard has caused the public to be more careful when choosing furniture and increasing affluence has also resulted in a move up-market by more households.

DLF are well aware that their formula appeals mainly to the more price-conscious households, who have been tolerant of the somewhat less than sophisticated showroom and factory conditions associated with direct marketing of this nature.

## 2.2.1 Question

You have been called in by DLF as a consultant to advise on expansion options. After conducting a marketing audit and a SWOT analysis you are now evaluating the options for:

- Product development only
- Market development only
- A combination of both product and market development

Submit your report giving the advantages and disadvantages of each of these three options in more detail, stating what control techniques you would recommend in each case.

## 2.2.2 Analysis

You should immediately identify the following characteristics about the business.

- DLF is a small business.
- They operate in a local market.
- They specialise in the direct marketing of consumer durables.

These characteristics should start to inform your thinking about the case and the nature of the business, for example you can now make the following connections.

(a) *Small business:* may mean limited resources.

(b) *Local market:* local communication media.

(c) *Direct marketing:* control over marketing mix but cost of storage and delivery, credit provision etc.

(d) *Consumer durables:* infrequent purchase, influenced strongly by style, colour, not brand names etc.

The secret of case study questions is to really play the role you have been given. You need to be able to picture this business, its products and showrooms. As soon as you have a mental picture you will be able to fit easily into the role of marketing consultant.

Now read through the case again and identify the key points, strengths, weaknesses etc. You can do this on the examination paper to save time. You need to really think about the narrative and what it is telling you.

Alternatively, or in addition, you can convert the information onto a SWOT chart to help clarify the picture. Remember that you are not presenting this to the examiner, so use a page at the back of your answer book and do not waste too much time on it.

Remember that weaknesses can always be converted into strengths and that threats can usually be turned to opportunities. Do not waste time worrying about how to categorise an element. It is usually more important that you have identified it.

*SWOT of Direct Lounge Furniture Ltd*

| Strengths | Weaknesses |
|---|---|
| • Owners are friends | Could be a weakness if they fall out; may imply informal systems and procedures |
| • Established | Resources for expansion limited for a small business |
| • Financially strong; sales and profits high | Perceived as bottom end of market |
| • Good reputation<br>  –price<br>  –workmanship | • Limited geographic market<br>• Two unsophisticated showrooms<br>• Product oriented<br>• Limited product portfolio<br>• Little marketing activity |
| Opportunities | Threats |
| • Higher customer incomes<br>• Safety awareness pushing demand towards higher value products<br>• New materials and production techniques which may become available | • Legislation<br>• Changing customer needs and attitudes Increased standard of living amongst current customers<br>• Possibility of increased competition |

Marketing audit is an assessment of the current marketing activity of DLF. We have uncovered some clues when developing the corporate SWOT.

(a) The company is product oriented not marketing oriented.

(b) There is advertising activity but no evidence of a co-ordinated marketing function, therefore no marketing procedures, plans etc.

(c) We can do a SWOT on the marketing mix.

    (i) *Product*

        Strength: good workmanship, low prices, range of suites

        Weakness: not a varied product portfolio, one material used, traditional ideas of customer needs

    (ii) *Promotion*

        Weakness: limited to local advertising, not targeted or controlled. Product oriented by featuring pictures of products

        Strength: good local image and reputation for value for money

    (iii) *Place*

        Weakness: limited to two showrooms. No information on waiting lists etc

    (iv) *Price*

        Strength: current pricing policy is a strength while market is price conscious, but the market is changing

Marketing opportunities do exist and some have been identified for us.

(a)     To diversify into new products

- Curtains
- Other furniture

(b)     To develop a wider market

(c)     To develop new segments in the current geographic market

(d)     To reposition DLF as a quality product provider

Review the question carefully. We have done the SWOT and the marketing audit. Our response should be based on our analysis of the company. It should not be just a presentation of the analysis.

We are required to evaluate three options and to submit a report indicating the advantages, disadvantages and control techniques in each case.

---

It is important that you attempt all parts of this question if you want a chance to gain the maximum marks. In this case the question requirements give you an automatic structure to your report.

---

Before going further you will find it useful to spend 55 minutes preparing your own answer to the question. Compare it with the suggested solution we have provided. Remember that there is no single right answer. Use our solution only as a guide and as an indicator of the process involved.

## 2.2.3 Solution

---

Report to:     Managing Directors

Direct Lounge Furniture Ltd

From:     A Consultant

Date:     5 April 20XX

Subject:     Evaluation of product/market opportunities for DLF Ltd.

**1     Background**

1.1     Following our initial analysis of DLF's current situation we have found that although the company is in a secure financial position, with no doubt about short-term survival, the medium-term picture is rather bleak.

1.2     The DLF product range is limited to lounge suites, traditionally configured and covered in one fabric, Dralon. This type of lounge furniture is probably in the mature stage and possibly in the decline stage of its life cycle. The DLF position has been weakened by the following macroenvironmental changes.

- Changing customer needs and expectations in home furnishings.

- Higher incomes making demand increasingly price inelastic.

- Safety fears encouraging customers to trade up.

1.3     We would therefore confirm your personal assessment that for DLF to thrive in the medium and long term, positive action must be taken to develop new product/market strategies. It is important that this action is undertaken before declining demand has an adverse impact on profitability and erodes the resources necessary for exploiting a new opportunity.

---

*The options*

## 2 Product development only

2.1 Product development could cover any activity from modification of the existing product (lounge suites), to adding new products to the range. We will assume that the option is basically the former.

2.2 *Advantages*

    (a) This would be a market oriented development, allowing products to be designed to meet identified customer needs.

    (b) You are experienced in the business, its production and operational requirements, materials etc.

    (c) You have an established reputation in the business of lounge furniture.

    (d) Product development would allow ranges and lines to be developed to meet the needs of a variety of market segments and would provide a number of opportunities to develop and enhance the business. The workmen have the skills to develop a quality 'made to order' package.

2.3 *Disadvantages*

    (a) You are positioned at the value for money end of the market. Repositioning for a new segment of the market would require a considerable marketing effort and may be easier with a new kind of product, for example dining room furniture.

    (b) Proliferation of product choice would increase the costs of stockholding, requiring a greater variety of raw materials etc.

    (c) Existing showrooms may be unsuitable for attracting a different group of customers.

    (d) Product portfolio is limited. Recession and declining demand for lounge furniture affects the whole business.

2.4 *Controls*

    (a) Enquiry and sales data by product line would be important to assess the profitability of new products offered.

    (b) If the product range was extended to provide all lounge furnishings, for example curtains, cushions, and tables, it would be important to measure the scale of value added sales, by customers purchasing additional items.

    (c) Information on customers would help to identify whether target markets are being attracted. As most products will be delivered, it should be relatively easy to monitor geographic locations and possibly develop a simplified process for classifying residential neighbourhoods.

    (d) There should be controls on production activities such as average stock levels. Order times etc would also be important to monitor efficiency of the operations as a more customer oriented product policy was developed.

## 3 Market development only

3.1 This would involve looking for new customers for the existing product range. It would imply increasing the geographic spread of the business.

3.2 *Advantages*

    (a) It would require no change to the existing operation at production level.

(b) It would allow the profitable value for money target customer base to be extended. These are customers who DLF already know well.

(c) It would require no additional investment in the production resources.

### 3.3 Disadvantages

(a) It would leave the company product oriented, looking for customers for products, instead of developing products for customers. In the long run this approach will make DLF very vulnerable to competition.

(b) Although this strategy may boost sales in the short run, we know that customer needs and wants are changing and that this low price, traditional product is in decline.

(c) It would require investment in distribution to set up either showrooms or agencies in new areas. These may prove difficult to control.

### 3.4 Controls

(a) Controls would need to focus on any new distribution channels and salespeople established. Cost of sales and conversions of enquiries would help DLF establish the rate at which the new market became aware of their products.

(b) Given the indicators of general decline in DLF's market, control information would be needed to monitor average customer purchases (two sofas and no chairs), demand for matched curtains, average spend and other purchase patterns. This would provide valuable control information for sales forecasting.

## 4 Product and market development

4.1 At its extreme, for example moving into high quality kitchen units, product and market developments could be a major diversification, involving not only products but also customers with whom DLF is unfamiliar. However, diversifying into TV cabinets and coffee tables for a made to measure premium market would involve less risk.

### 4.2 Advantages

(a) It allows DLF to have an effective new start, researching the market to identify product/market opportunities which could be developed.

(b) Assuming that the current cash cow business will be retained at least in the short run, this strategy would diversify the business and so reduce the risk of sudden changes in demand caused by external variables.

(c) A product/market development would allow DLF to completely reposition themselves in the furniture market.

4.3 *Disadvantages*

(a) The strategy would be risky. The extent of the diversification would indicate how much risk is involved.

(b) It would be expensive, involving investment in both marketing and production.

(c) There is a danger of attempting to develop too many opportunities simultaneously, losing sight of the core business and over-extending resources.

4.4 *Controls*

(a) Such a major shift in strategy would require close control. New product sales levels would need to be monitored as would the value of business from new market segments.

(b) New distribution channels and promotional activities would probably be needed and these would also require evaluating to assess their effectiveness.

(c) Plans and budgets for the separate parts of the business would need establishing, together with administrative systems and procedures. These are unlikely to exist in the current small scale operation.

5 **Conclusions and recommendations**

(a) Action is needed to ensure the medium-term survival of DLF.

(b) The business has the strengths to extend its product range to meet the needs of new customer segments, in particular high quality, made to order products at premium prices. This extension of the product portfolio should be developed after careful research of the target market.

(c) The company should clearly review its mission and should establish financial objectives for the operation. Corporate and marketing plans must be developed as well as a management information system.

A Consultancy will be happy to offer any further assistance to DLF in this activity.

# 3 Other questions in the examination

Although the questions in Section B are of the more traditional examination style, you must still make certain that you do not answer them in a purely academic manner.

Ensure that you support theory with real world examples and illustrations, use the introductions and conclusions to comment on the value of the concept in question, disadvantages of a technique and so on. You should evaluate every question in terms not only of its content, but also the context in which it is being asked.

Most students will have the knowledge to pass the exam, it is using that information in the 'context' of the question which causes the downfall. A question about the role of planning in the public sector should be answered differently from the same question set in a private sector context.

Make sure you answer the questions set out and watch out for variations in mark allocation made within a question.

These suggested solutions which follow are just that. There is no single correct answer, but use them as a comparison for your own work and an example of the style, approach and the depth needed in the exam.

Remember to practise answers in exam conditions. You will have only 30 minutes per question in the exam room. After allowing planning and review time allow a little over 20 minutes writing time per question. Quality not quantity is required.

## Chapter Roundup

- This chapter has explained the nature and purpose of a mini-case. We have used examples from past examination papers to demonstrate how to use our recommended technique and extracts from examiners' reports have illustrated the examiners' requirements and common mistakes made by candidates.

# Question and answer bank

# 1 Empire Chemicals
**45 mins**

> **Tutorial note**. The data in this case is based on the experience of ICI; however, names and certain key details have been changed. You should concentrate on the data in the case study itself, rather than ICI's subsequent history. Remember that Empire Chemicals is a fictitious company, although based on a real one.

Empire Chemicals is one of the UK's largest companies with several divisions including paints, pharmaceuticals, bulk chemicals, and agrochemicals such as fertiliser. Empire Chemicals detected three years ago that the financial performance of its paints business was deteriorating. Profits were steady, but its return on capital was falling. Mr Matthew Black, the main board director responsible for paints, reacted quickly to cut costs. Despite a 6% fall in turnover in the last two years, profits of the division have been rising, albeit modestly. Unfortunately, not all the divisions had such foresight. Empire's total profits are falling sharply. Mr Scott Wallace, a chemical industry analyst, says that Empire neglected to keep its costs under control in the past. Management controls are 'relatively undisciplined'. This is the legacy of a complicated management structure, which divided financial responsibilities confusingly between territorial and business managers. The autonomy of divisional heads is considerable.

Sir Denis Mack Smith created Empire's first globally organised businesses – first a world-wide pharmaceuticals operation and then, in 1984, a global agrochemical division. An increasing number of Empire's operations were set up to operate on an international basis, to meet the trans-national requirements of so many of its clients. However, Sir Denis did not streamline the organisation completely. A parallel power structure, based on geography rather than products, has been kept in place. Because Empire is ahead of the pack in running divisions on a global basis, analysts believe that it must be careful not to neglect the differing needs of European, Japanese and US purchasers. A director points out that only 20% of Empire's business is purely domestic, but the Chairman and main board executives spend a disproportionate amount of time on UK matters.

Empire itself has long considered itself virtually bid-proof. It is one of the UK's biggest employers with 53,700 employees in Britain and it spends some 70% of its £679m R&D budget at home. However Cobb Holdings plc has purchased a stake with a view to a takeover.

Despite years of efforts by Empire to refashion itself, which did make it more international and produced a gush of profits when times were good, the company is still spread thinly across an array of separate products and markets ranging from research-intensive products to PVC (which goes to make plastic buckets). Empire has many products, in many different markets.

The company's embattled chairman, Sir Henry Sanderson has had to eat his words about the company being recession-proof. 'When I suggested that I saw no return to the dark days of recession, I was clearly wrong,' he acknowledges.

*Required*

To what extent do you think strategic planning has succeeded or failed at Empire Chemicals? Briefly outline an alternative model.
**(25 marks)**

# 2 Forecasting of sales
**45 mins**

You have been given the task of co-ordinating the forecasting of sales for your firm's budget preparation. Last year the sales forecast was overstated by more than thirty per cent against actual sales. As a result some profit centres budgeted to spend more than they actually achieved in revenue.

*Required*

Write a memo to the sales department which:

(a) explains the importance of having accurate forecasts

(b) discusses and evaluates the importance of having meaningful budgetary control information in the context of this example. **(25 marks)**

# 3 Franchise
**45 mins**

Your Taiwan based organisation has been approached by a major UK clothing retailer with a view to franchising their operation in your home market. Write a report outlining the information that is needed in order to make a management decision on this proposal. Show how you would acquire this data.

**(25 marks)**

# 4A Discount oriented competitor
**45 mins**

A major bank has declared that it is going to enter an already very competitive motor insurance market and offer highly competitive prices to customers. You have been asked to provide a briefing paper advising a financial services company, which is a well established direct insurer, on the options open to them when faced by this new discount orientated competitor. **(25 marks)**

# 4B Feasibility study
**45 mins**

### Organisational background

SJM is a long-established retail organisation operating 227 supermarkets nationally. It is a listed company which has expanded over its 60-year history. The company has attained distinctive competitive advantage by stocking and selling only high-quality products. SJM plc has enjoyed profitable trading and now ranks as one of the leading retailers in the country. It has not been affected by restructuring of the retailing industry and its Board is intent on maintaining the company's independence.

The Board of the company has set a clear aim of achieving profitability with efficient consumption of resources, whilst maintaining the sale of high-quality goods and delivering a courteous and efficient service to customers. This overall aim has been incorporated within the mission statement and forms a central part of the company's promotional advertising.

*Financial characteristics of the company*

The following information is supplied in respect of SJM plc for the last financial year.

| | £million |
|---|---|
| Turnover, | 2,400 |
| Earnings attributable to ordinary shareholders | 220 |

There were 1,200 million ordinary shares in issue at the end of the last financial year and the company's share price was £4.03.

SJM plc has established that its cost of capital is 12% per annum. Over the last year, the company's share price has varied between £3.30 and £4.05. SJM plc paid a dividend of £0.12 (12 pence) per share in the last financial year and has achieved steady dividend growth of 8.4% per annum over the last five years.

*'Out-of-town' stores*

The company has recognised that its customers are increasingly using personal transport and value the convenience of 'out-of-town' locations. 'Out-of-town' means that a store is located on a city's fringes rather than in the centre. The object of building stores in such a location is to provide customers with easier access to shopping facilities as this is often difficult within the busy city environment. Typical of the out-of-town location is a large car parking facility and good public transport links.

SJM plc established a plan five years ago to build a number of out-of-town superstores to an original design near four major cities. The first of these superstores has now been in operation for one year. The other superstores are in various stages of completion.

SJM has followed its competitors in developing out-of-town sites and is considering a partnership initiative with another retailer whose merchandise would not be a competitive threat. This would involve joint development of superstores on out-of-town sites. The only commitment to this initiative by SJM plc, so far, is a feasibility study of a single joint project with the other retailer. This will be completed before entering any contractual obligations.

*The superstore strategy*

SJM aims to provide a satisfactory return to its shareholders. The superstore which is already operational has achieved a high level of profitability in its first year of operation. The company has also experienced a simultaneous reduction in return obtained from other stores which it operates within the vicinity of the superstore. SJM plc is aware of growing governmental concern at the impact out-of-town developments are having on city centre retailing. These two factors have caused the company planners to pause before approving any other out-of-town developments. In addition, public transport provision has been established to service the operational superstore, but the transport providers are now objecting that there is insufficient demand to maintain frequent services as most customers travel to and from the site by car.

*Superstore developments*

The superstore developments are all built to a standard specification which comprises 40,000 square metres. The life of the project is fifteen years. Typically, the development takes place over a three-year period from planning stage to final commissioning. Each superstore is assumed, for investment appraisal purposes, to have a life of 12 years following completion. The cost of the first superstore development was £25 million with approximately 20% being incurred in the first year. The remaining costs are split evenly over the second and third years. Included within these costs was £500,000 for architects' fees which have reduced by half in subsequent developments. The architects' fees can be assumed to fall due for payment in direct proportion to the building costs.

The superstore developments are targeted to achieve a net cash inflow of £250 per square metre per annum from the commencement of operations. Experience has shown that the first superstore has achieved this target during the first year of operation. A total reduction in net cash inflow over the same period has occurred in other SJM plc stores which trade within the surrounding areas. This has been calculated as having the effect of reducing the superstore net cash inflow by £40 per square metre per annum.

Each superstore is assumed to have a net residual value of zero. All cashflows can be assumed to occur at the end of the year to which they relate. The cashflows and discount rate are in real terms (ie they have been adjusted for inflation).

*Financial appraisal of the first superstore*

| Year | | Discount factor @ 12% | Present value |
|---|---|---|---|
| | £'000 | | £'000 |
| Cost of development | | | |
| 1 £25m × 20% | 5,000 | 0.893 | (4,465) |
| 2 (£25m – £5m) × 50% | 10,000 | 0.797 | (7,970 |
| 3 (£25m – £25m) × 50% | 10,000 | 0.712 | (7,120) |
| Total | 25,000 | | (19,555) |

| | | Cumulative discount factor | |
|---|---|---|---|
| Revenue over 12 years | £'000 | | |
| Gross £250 × 40,000 sq metres | 10,000 | | |
| Less £40 × 40,000 sq metres | (1,600) | | |
| Net annual revenue per annum | 8,400 | 4.409 | 37,035 |
| Net present value | | | 17,480 |

*Required*

(a) Comment on the financial appraisal which justified the investment in the first superstore. **(5 marks)**

(b) Identify the market opportunities and threats which SJM plc will confront if it develops more out-of-town superstores. **(7 marks)**

(c) Describe and comment on the impact of the out-of-town developments by SJM plc on each of five groups of stakeholders. **(8 marks)**

(d) Discuss whether SJM plc should pursue other out-of-town developments completely on its own or jointly with the other retailer. Pay particular attention to potential planning and operational difficulties which may arise from these initiatives. **(5 marks)**

**(25 marks)**

# 5 Market entry
**45 mins**

Outline the market entry methods and the levels of involvement associated with the development of a company's globalisation process from initial exporting through to becoming a global corporation. Specify what you consider to be the important criteria in deciding the appropriate entry method. **(25 marks)**

# 6 Brand stretching
**45 mins**

As a Marketing Planner for a financial services company, identify the key elements of a brand strategy and the criteria which should be used in brand stretching decisions. **(25 marks)**

# 7 Standardisation
**45 mins**

In an ideal world, companies would like to manufacture a standardised product. What are the factors that support the case for a standardised product and what are the circumstances that are likely to prevent its implementation? Support your argument with examples. **(25 marks)**

# 8 Pricing policy

**45 mins**

Construct a report to marketing management that explains the factors that should be taken into consideration when pricing for a product line.

**(25 marks)**

# 9 Nadir products

**45 mins**

John Staples is the Finance Director of Nadir Products plc, a UK-based company which manufactures and sells bathroom products – baths, sinks and toilets – to the UK market. These products are sold through a selection of specialist shops and through larger 'do-it-yourself' stores. Customers include professional plumbers and also ordinary householders who are renovating their houses themselves. The company operates at the lower end of the market and does not have a strong reputation for service. Sales have been slowly declining whereas those of competitors have been improving. In order to encourage increased sales the Board of Directors have decided to pay senior staff a bonus if certain targets are achieved. The two main targets are based on profit levels and annual sales. Two months before the end of the financial year the Finance Director asks one of his staff to check through the orders and accounts to assess the current situation. He is informed that without a sudden improvement in sales before the year end the important sales targets will not be met and so bonuses will be adversely affected.

The Finance Director has proposed to other senior staff that this shortfall in sales can be corrected by taking one of the following decisions.

1. A significant discount can be offered to any retail outlet which takes delivery of additional products prior to the end of the financial year.

2. Scheduled orders due to be delivered at the beginning of the next financial year can be brought forward and billed before the end of this year.

3. Distributors can be told that there is a risk of price increases in the future and that it will be advisable to order early so as to circumvent this possibility.

The Board is not sure of the implications associated with such decisions.

*Required*

(a) As a consultant, prepare a report for the Board of Nadir Products examining the commercial and ethical implications associated with each of the proposed options mentioned above. **(10 marks)**

(b) Assess the significance of the corporate social responsibility model for Nadir Products. **(15 marks)**

**(25 marks)**

# 10 Feedback and control system

**45 mins**

What factors should be taken into account in the development of a marketing feedback and control system? In what ways might the information possibly be used? **(25 marks)**

# 1 Empire Chemicals

## Strategic planning at Empire Chemicals

Although Empire Chemicals has a large range of businesses, there is always the danger that like any conglomerate business it can lose its sense of direction.

Empire includes diverse product-market mixes such as paints, fertiliser and agrochemicals, pharmaceuticals, bulk chemicals. Each of these products has different characteristics. The synergies, between for example paints and pharmaceuticals are hard to see. However, it is probable that profits from bulk chemicals are much more volatile than, say, pharmaceuticals, which perhaps require a higher research base. The business synergies might be financial.

The question what business are we in? is therefore hard to answer, other than in the most general terms.

Sir Henry Sanderson's statement that at one time the business had been thought of as recession-proof seems complacent. Each individual business might have conducted SWOT analyses, but as the group operates in so many different environments, it might have been hard to conduct an analysis for the group as a whole. The fact that the effects of recession were not anticipated does indicate at group level at least, a failure of analysis.

The overall strategic choice for the group as a whole has obviously been made. It functions largely by conglomerate diversification, like Cobb. The admittedly poor cost control, and Cobb's bid, suggests that tactical plans allow for too much corporate flab. Possible economies of scale in accounting and other overheads are avoided.

The only way to judge the success or failure of strategic plans is with hindsight, which is not available to the planners.

Emergent strategies are those which develop out of patterns of behaviour. They do not develop from management's explicit control or from planning. The result from operational decisions and their unintended consequences exploiting sudden insights, and develop in the process of business itself, rather than as a separate planning exercise. Mintzberg holds that this is how many business strategies actually developed in practice.

The past history of the company suggests a freewheeling approach to entering different product-market areas. Freewheeling opportunism has perhaps seduced the company into spreading itself too thinly as a pattern of decision making. It is significant that the chairman and main board spend too much time on purely UK matters. Clearly, they have not achieved a global perspective.

The planning process failed to take the fluctuations of the business cycle into account. The existence of the business cycle is not an uncertainty, although the exact timing and severity of any down turn cannot be predicted. It is hard to see how any major environmental discontinuities have affected Empire. The bid by Cobb, however, could not be predicted. Perhaps the firm regarded itself as secure from any takeover.

Arguably, there is insufficient planning. An internal appraisal would have revealed the excess costs sooner. Bad planning, rather than an excess of planning, would seem to be evident.

# 2 Forecasting of sales

MEMO

To:       Sales Personnel
From:     Mike Jones
Date:     24 November 20XX
Subject:  Sales forecasts and budgetary control information

(a) **The importance of having accurate forecasts**

Annual forecasts, usually classed as medium-term forecasts, are **statements of the estimated volume of sales of an organisation's products and/or services in the next financial year**. They are used to assist the organisation's financial planning process since they are expressed in monetary amounts and thereafter feed into the annual budget. It is therefore only by estimating the following year's sales that an organisation can estimate how much money will be available to spend in the future.

It must be remembered, however, that forecasts are only estimates and it is very difficult to produce accurate ones. In being optimistic and **overstating** the forecasts, several problems can arise.

(i) High forecasts can lead to **high targets for the sales force**. This can be demoralising if the sales team do not achieve the target.

(ii) For a company quoted on the Stock Exchange, overstating the forecast could affect the **share price** if the City loses confidence.

(iii) Sales forecasts feed into **production plans**. Over-optimistic forecasts can lead to **excess stocks in the warehouse**. Not only does this tie up capital, it also increases the likelihood of damage and waste.

(iv) **Extra staff** may be taken on in sales or production to cope with the expected level of sales. If this does not materialise, there may need to be redundancies.

Although there are obvious problems with overstating the expected level of sales, **understatement** can lead to problems as well. Actual demand will then be greater than supply. This can lead to:

- **Competitors benefiting** from the organisation's lost sales
- An increase in the amount of **overtime** required and therefore **higher salary costs**
- An increase in **bonus payments** to sales people who exceed their targets

As both overstating and understating forecasts can lead to problems, it is clear that a balance is required. It is therefore important to ensure that forecasts are as accurate as possible. This entails having good, **up-to-date internal data and marketing intelligence**. Sales statistics should be available in a suitable format and all the factors affecting sales should be understood by the people involved in the forecasting process.

In some organisations these people will be accountants, although ideally sales and marketing managers and possibly sales representatives should be involved as they are closer to the market place. **Appropriate methods of forecasting** should be used, whether quantitative or qualitative or a mixture of the two.

Any **assumptions made** (such as rate of inflation, exchange rates, rate of adoption of a product, increase in a competitor's promotional activity and so on) should be clearly stated so that if any of these change markedly, adjustments can easily be made. It therefore follows that it is important to **review forecasts regularly** to take into account any new information and adjust the figures as appropriate. Although totally accurate forecasts cannot be guaranteed, at least the adverse effects of inaccurate forecasts will be minimised.

(b) **The importance of meaningful budgetary control information**

The budget sets out the company plan in a formal way and really only delivers benefits when it is **measured against actual performance**. Budgetary control information enables this process to take place. It consists of a report of actual performance set against details of what was expected to be achieved – the budget performance. The result is a formal **variance analysis report** for management. The variance analysis will contain important indicators as to the reasons for a discrepancy between budgeted and actual results.

Variance analysis information is complex and needs to be fully understood. At first sight it is tempting to dismiss minor variances as unimportant and this may be true. However, before dismissing small variances the cause as well as the effect has to be appreciated, to ensure that the events which gave rise to the variance do not imply serious problems in that particular budget.

In this case, the first step is to find the reason for the shortfall in the sales budget. Ways to produce more accurate information in future must be found.

With errors of such significance further questions also arise. If many of the firm's costs are fixed, the losses in some profit centres might be thought of as inevitable if sales are so far below expectations. However, **sensitivity analysis** could have been carried out; a thoughtful examination of a 'worst case' scenario could have anticipated the impact of such a large error and contingency plans (increased promotion, cost-cutting) could have been laid.

More importantly, as information was being collected the variances should have been seen as so significant that urgent action should have been taken. An important feature of all information is its **timeliness**, and that would appear to have been overlooked. Hence profit centres continued to spend their cost budgets, without taking account of the fact that the revenue planned to support the spending was not being achieved.

Budgets are **quantitative plans**, and as such should be based on the nature of a particular organisation as a system with a degree of integration. **One figure is likely to be the driver of other figures** in the planning process. In this case the errors in the sales forecast inevitably meant that there were related errors in the budgets for purchases, stocks and debtors. These will have further consequences for the company, as they drive the **payments and receipts** pattern which governs the amounts of **working capital** available.

There appears to be a lack of understanding about the way in which control information is used. For such a large error to exist, significant variances of actual to budget must have been evident early in the year (assuming the business is not a particularly seasonal one). It would appear that no action was taken and the reasons for that must be investigated.

Finally, **effective action should be taken in response to control information**, and that was clearly lacking. This could have been due to management weakness, or to a poor **reporting system** that simply recorded details without allowing investigation.

# 3 Franchise

### Franchising

Compared to a company owned outlet, which is operated by salaried employees, a franchised store is operated by a franchisee who is an independent legal entity. **Franchisees** pay their respective franchisers an initial fee as well as a monthly royalty fee, which is usually specified as a percentage of sales revenue.

In addition, franchisees are responsible for investment in the outlet and are expected to closely follow the franchiser's operating norms. Franchising's primary attributes (eg capital formation, motivated entrepreneurs, standard systems, brand recognition, and procedures to control operations) help to solve key challenges connected with services marketing firms (eg small size, intangibility of services, quality control).

(a)   **Information required**

As a Taiwan based organisation who has been approached by a UK clothing retailer with a view to franchising their operations in Taiwan certain information will be required before a decision can be made whether to take up this opportunity.

(i) **Marketing**

    (1)    How well recognised is the retail brand in its market and in our home market?

    (2)    What marketing support is provided by the franchiser: launch activity, on-going promotions, PR, advertising?

    (3)    What product range will be available and how much merchandising flexibility will be allowed?

    (4)    What happens in terms of stock ownership, returns, old stock etc?

    (5)    What pricing policies are involved in the contract?

    (6)    How quick and effective are the current logistics?

(ii) **Finance**

    (1)    What are the costs of implementing and maintaining the operation?

    (2)    What are the forecasted sales?

    (3)    What are the forecasted profit implications?

    (4)    What historical sales, cash flow and profit figures are available from current franchisees?

    (5)    Are there capital borrowing implications?

    (6)    What financial consulting support is offered by franchiser?

(iii) **Human resources**

    (1)    Is there any recruitment, selection, appraisal and disciplinary support offered?

    (2)    What training guidelines and workshops are provided?

    (3)    Are any HRM software systems available?

    (4)    Are there any employment policy principles which will need to be adopted from franchiser's operating philosophy?

(iv) **Retail operations**

    (1)    What systems are required and/or provided: tills, EPOS, procurement?
    (2)    What store location and design support is provided?
    (3)    What merchandising support/policies are stipulated?
    (4)    What information, monitoring and control procedures are required?

(b) **Acquiring this information**

As with any research activity, the use of all the elements of a **Marketing Information System** should be utilised.

### The marketing information system

A lot of information can be gathered from **internal records** in the form of franchisee information provided by the UK retailer. Meetings to discuss the questions outlined above should provide a lot of background data. As the UK retailer has approached us, the firm should be receptive to our information requirements and make the relevant personnel in marketing, finance, HR and operations available to us, perhaps via email or a visit to the UK head office. On this visit, it would also be possible to conduct primary research in regard to a retail audit in UK principal town centres to see the retailer in operation in their home country. It would also be important to visit current franchisers in other countries around the world.

In addition, from market **intelligence sources**, reports would be available on retailing trends in both countries, financial performance of the retailer and reports on the retailer's franchising operations.

**Meetings** with our own **financial advisors** and lawyers would be required to assess the franchise agreement.

Finally, consumer research in Taiwan should be conducted to test the appeal of the new retail concept, store design, merchandise and pricing strategy. This would allow verification of sales forecast data provided by the franchiser.

Once these questions have answers with a reasonable degree of confidence a decision on whether to accept the franchise proposal could be taken.

# 4A Discount oriented competitor

### Introduction

Price competition is a factor in many markets ranging from industrial air conditioning to FMCGs such as cat food to the specific case of this question, financial services and motor insurance. In fact the advent of direct insurers such as Direct Line changed the competitive forces in this market by rapidly increasing the direct writers' share of the market at the expense of higher priced insurance brokers.

(a) **Issues to consider in response to a price-based attack**

    (i)    **Service criteria**

        (1)    Is your service significantly different from the competitor initiating the price attack?

        (2)    Do you have a strong brand?

        (3)    Can you supply a different range of insurance packages?

        (4)    Can you add services to your current range?

(ii)     **Demand criteria**

    (1)     Is the price cut significant enough to attract consumer attention?

    (2)     Are there a number of market segments with different insurance requirements and price sensitivities?

    (3)     Do you have strong customer loyalty?

(iii)    **Competition criteria**

    (1)     Why did the competitor change the price?

- Take market share
- Utilise excess capacity
- Meet changing cost conditions
- Lead an industry-wide price change

    (2)     Is it likely to be a permanent price cut?

    (3)     What is the likely affect of the price cut on your market share?

    (4)     What are other competitors likely to do?

(iv)    **Cost criteria**

    (1)     What is the likely affect of the price cut on your profitability?
    (2)     Will the price cut take your price below your costs?
    (3)     Will a price cut increase demand and produce economies of scale effects?

(v)     **Strategy criteria**

    (1)     How will a change in price affect overall marketing strategy?

(b)    **Options available**

If the decision is taken, after considering the answers to the above questions, that the competitor is offering superior value to our customers and taking business away from us, we have several options to consider.

(i)    **Maintain price**: if it is decided that by dropping prices the company would lose too much margin, or the insurer would not loose much market share, or it could regain share when necessary, or it would retain the more profitable customers.

The Radio Times in the TV listings price war maintained its price at 50p when all others dropped theirs in response to price based attacks. At the end of six months a number of the new entrants left the market, unable to sustain an acceptable margin, and the prices stabilised. The Radio Times, whilst losing some market share, came out of the war maintaining higher levels of profitability.

(ii)    **Raise perceived quality**: if it is cheaper to maintain price but improve the actual or perceived quality of the insurance package. Improving the product, service and communications could do this.

(iii)   **Reduce price**: if the insurer's costs fall with volume, the market is price sensitive, it would be difficult to rebuild share once lost to the new entrant.

However, engaging in price wars can be very costly. When the price wars began in the supermarkets in the early 1990s, Sainsbury's responded to the price cutters such as Kwik Save and Aldi by trying to draw more customers in with their Essentials campaign, which cut the price of hundreds of own-label products. This wiped more than £850 million off the stock market value of Sainsburys and sales showed an underlying fall of 1%.

(i) **Increase price and improve quality**: if a target segment can be identified which values quality and is substantial enough to offset the reduction in volumes.

(ii) **Launch lower-price insurance package**: if the company has the resources to have a deeper product line, one higher priced, one the same as the competitors and one lower, this will signal a strong competitive reaction and may dissuade further price erosions or force the competitor to exit the market.

The right decision will be partly dependent on the reactions of the other players in the market. However, by considering the questions outlined above, the chances of making the wrong decision should be greatly reduced.

# 4B Feasibility study

(a) The **financial appraisal** does justify the investment. However, it has a number of deficiencies.

(i) It is unlikely that a superstore would have a residual value of nil. The land alone would be worth something for redevelopment, and its value might be high. Of course, this increases the attractiveness of the project still further.

(ii) As the cash flows and discount rates have been expressed in real terms, inflation has presumably been considered. The problem lies not so much in the discount rate but the fact that net cash inflow in real terms is supposed not to change. In fact, inflation rates differ on retail products, and so the sales mix of the superstore will have a significant impact. Is this likely to change?

(iii) The calculation seems to take no account of the **risk** that revenue might be less than expected. Were a competitor to open a similar store nearby, the sales per square metre could fall significantly. Many UK supermarkets have faced competition from discounters recently, which has forced price cutting. Political factors have been mentioned in the question; possible curbs on car usage suggested might reduce the stores' attractiveness as destinations. With current plans to revitalise high streets, customers might want a number of stores to visit.

(iv) No account has been taken of major changes in retail formats, and additional construction costs.

(v) As an exercise in strategic management there seems little external orientation or consideration of wider issues of the business environment. A scenario building approach could have integrated strategic and financial issues.

(vi) How will the development affect investors' view of the company over the next few years? Shareholders are expecting consistent dividend growth. The firm has to ensure sufficient resources of cash for this, as well as to fund its investment programmes, with dividend cover of 1.5 (£220 million earnings ÷ £144 million total dividend).

(b) **Market opportunities and threats**

**Opportunities**

Supermarkets make their profits on a high volume of transactions. (Earnings of £220m are 10% of revenue.) Any increase in the volume of transactions will bring significantly increased profits. The new superstores have been designed to increase the volume of transactions. They hope to attract new customers (market development):

(i) Who have cars and who like to do all their shopping in one go

(ii) From competitors with no out-of-town stores in the area

(iii)     From the city centre (in the USA, where out-of-town shopping has become more developed, some suburbs are said to have developed into 'edge cities' of their own)

(iv)     From other outlying areas, as the store's location will be convenient for people who are further afield

(v)     In other parts of the country, if SJM's geographical coverage is not evenly spread

The firm can generate additional sales to existing customers

(i)     Extend the range of products on offer (product development eg ASDA, who are selling books)

(ii)     Provide services which make shopping convenient (eg a crèche or a tea shop)

The superstores will enable the firm to retain its existing customers, who might otherwise go over to competitors. (This is a reason why many supermarkets now have loyalty card schemes.)

It is possible that there will be knock on effect. Some customers may visit the superstores only rarely but, if they are favourably impressed, they might use SJM's other stores at other times.

SJM's new stores offer an opportunity to save money, in that the logistics of stocking them are probably better than the city centre sites. They are probably more profitable. SJM already seems quite large; any increase in market share might enable the firm to strike even better bargains with suppliers.

**Threats**

In the UK, supermarkets have been expanding at the expense of smaller grocers and butchers, and against weaker chains, but there might come a point when the market is unable to support any more stores.

The danger is that SJM and its competitors may thus saturate the market, in which case SJM will be left with a large fixed capital investment with limited opportunity for growth.

However, competition in any area is partly restricted by planning regulations, in that most local authorities would not want too many out-of-town developments next to each other. Paradoxically, better transport links, especially roads, would enable customers to go even further afield, thus increasing competition.

New firms can enter the industry. In the UK, discount retailers have established useful niches, by concentrating on price. SJM might have to segment its stores differently. For example, people might change their habits and go to discount stores for essentials and specialist stores for other items.

The government is hoping to revive the city centres, although it is not clear what form this policy will take. If city centre shopping becomes more attractive, for whatever reason, out-of-town developments will suffer. (A number of the supermarket chains have returned to city centre sites; an example is *Tesco Metro*.) A problem might be that customers will visit a site with a **number** of stores, not just one.

The heavy use of funds might mean that other ways of increasing profitability (eg by investing in IT or making other service improvements) are not exploited.

Any curtailment on car usage (eg through road pricing, whereby people pay per mile travelled) will decrease the centre's attractiveness. Furthermore decreased bus service will discourage some shoppers (eg the elderly) from using the centre.

(c)     **Impact on stakeholders**

A stakeholder is a person or group with an interest in the activities of a business. The affect on stakeholder groups (five only required) is outlined below.

(i)     **Shareholders**

Shareholders expect dividend growth, and they probably hope that the 8.4% annual growth will be continued. In this they may be disappointed in the long term, as there are government restrictions on out-of-town shopping developments and there is the risk that the market will be saturated and that cheaper stores will take over. This might restrict profits growth. Furthermore, any investment programmes will need more resources. However, given management's track record so far, they should have no cause for concern. The short-term prospects seem bright, and given slow rises in living standards, customers will have more to spend.

The higher the P/E ratio, the greater investors' confidence. The prospect of enhanced profits and cash flows should raise the share price, and might enable SJM to raise more capital more cheaply to fund its programme.

(ii)    **Customers**

Serving customers more effectively is the rationale for the whole business. Their interests will be served by the convenience the store offers, its size and range of goods, the easy parking, and the possibility of one-stop shopping.

However, if city centre shops close, customers might feel forced to use the out-of-town site. The problems with public transport suggest that some customers might eventually be disadvantaged by the move. SJM must hope that the increased business deals with this problem.

(iii)   **Suppliers**. The out-of-town developments affect two groups of suppliers.

(1)     The investment will be a boon to construction firms which will be building the new developments. Firms which provide infrastructure (eg electricity and water) can expect increased revenue from the development.

(2)     Suppliers of the goods that SJM retails will welcome the opportunity for increased sales. Much of the immediate impact will depend on delivery arrangements: most supermarkets have central warehouses from which deliveries are made. The new store programme might involve improvements to SJM's existing logistics networks.

Suppliers might be concerned at increased concentration of bargaining power in the hands of a smaller number of large retailers, and to this extent such developments may not be entirely welcome in the long term. Retailers can more or less dictate terms to suppliers (especially small firms).

(iv)    Employees as suppliers of labour will benefit from available jobs, and the new sites may be more pleasant places to work. However, such jobs are not paid too well, and employees may have to rely on a decreasingly reliable public transport service. That said, if the firm was consistently loss making they'd lose their jobs anyway, whereas if the firm expands, this gives further opportunities for promotion.

Many firms have employee share ownership schemes (*ASDA* is an example); if SJM has one, employees will benefit from increased profits.

(v)     **The local community**. Local people will benefit from a major employment opportunity nearby, and better shops. It is local government's job to ensure that planning regulations are adhered to, but there may be drawbacks.

(1)     A massive change in traffic patterns may result, causing inconvenience and noise in previously quiet areas, and pressure on existing infrastructure

(2)     A loss of 'countryside' (although this is in theory protected by green belt policies), which spoils the environment

   (3) Some local businesses will suffer, both competitors and other firms in the city centre which benefited from passing trade

  (vi) **Central government**. The government aims to promote economic growth, and this economic activity will be welcome, as will the concomitant tax policy. Government policy covers many areas, however, including transport and the environment, and central government does not always speak with one voice.

(d) **Joint ventures**

  The first store was effectively an experiment which has succeeded well. If all future developments are going to do as well, why share the benefits with another firm?

  (i) We noted that the initial financial appraisal ignored risk. A joint venture is a way of sharing risk.

  (ii) Sites are not always easy to find, and will become more difficult if new developments are becoming less acceptable. A joint venture might afford more flexibility.

  (iii) Customers are probably familiar with shopping malls which contain a large number of major stores. Both stores would benefit from trade from each other's customers. In other words, as well as customers who drove specifically to shop at SJM, customers of the partner firm might also drop in.

  (iv) Costs might be saved on construction and legal costs. For example, the firms would share the costs of any roads that had to be built. There would be other economies of scale in managing the development.

If a joint venture with a supplier of non-competing products is attractive to SJM's customers, it should be attractive to SJM, in its search to maximise sales per square metre. Whether SJM should go ahead or not will depend on the results of the feasibility study.

  (i) The relationship between the partners' business should be genuinely complementary for both to benefit. The mere fact that they do not compete is not enough. A clothes retailer and a food retailer might go together. A food retailer and, say, a firm selling car spares is a less logical mix if both hope to benefit from their mutual proximity.

  (ii) Both will have to agree on the joint management of the site, and this includes things such as delivery times (so their respective delivery lorries do not get in each others' way).

  (iii) They need to agree common policies for security, fire safety and so forth, which become more pressing the larger the site. In addition, there needs to be a clear agreement as to running the site. They may appoint a site manager to look after the entire operation.

  (iv) Joint marketing arrangements might be needed to entice people to the site. For this to have maximum effectiveness, the partners will need to co-ordinate promotions. This implies that any incompatibilities in their business aims should be kept to a minimum. Furthermore, colour schemes, signage and so forth need to be acceptable to both parties. SJM might have to give the site a separate identity of its own.

# 5 Market entry

The principle methods of market entry are **indirect exporting, direct exporting, direct inward investment** and **co-operation** through the formation of alliances, partnerships and joint ventures.

**Indirect exporting** involves the company in very **low risk** since it will be selling its products to a domestic organisation who will then export the product to the final destination. These domestic intermediaries are either classified as **export houses/trading companies** or export management companies.

**Piggy-backing** is another indirect exporting method which involves another company acting as the carrier for the product.

Indirect exporting offers the exporter little or no control over market development, and although it is often used by many small companies to get started in the international market place it will not lead to a global corporation.

**Direct exporting** involves a higher level of risk and can result in a company having a global presence if properly managed. Direct exporting is relatively low cost and, subject to no entry barriers being present and the company having adequate resources, it can allow a rapid entry into many markets. The most usual form of direct exporting is either through the appointment of agents who will be paid a commission, or by appointing **distributors** who will hold stock but may or may not own it, depending on the terms of the distributorship.

For certain types of business, **franchising** is the equivalent of direct exporting. An overseas organisation will pay for the rights to use the business concept. As with direct exporting through agents or distributors, franchising would allow a company to operate globally in a very short space of time, providing it had the necessary human resources to support it.

An arrangement whereby a company has its products **manufactured under license** could be seen as similar to franchising. The issuing of licenses to have products made on a global scale will be constrained by human resources of the organisation.

**Direct inward investment** is a high risk strategy since it is subject to the acceptance of the host government. Examples of direct inward investment are the setting up of own facilities, or the acquisition of or merger with existing businesses in the host country. The advantages of direct inward investment are **total control** of market development and (because of the higher risks) greater profits can be expected. Due to the investment required, direct inward investment as a means of becoming global is **expensive** and usually takes a long time. It took Nissan 30 years to establish 24 plants in 18 countries. It took Ford and General Motors up to 40 years to establish their global presence.

**Co-operation strategies** can either involve direct inward investment such as the formation of joint ventures (which usually require the incoming partner to share the costs of establishing the new entity), or no inward investment as with strategic alliances. Globalisation via joint ventures can be expensive and slow due to the constraints of limited financial resources and possibly limited targets, whereas strategic alliances can lead to a fairly rapid global presence.

### Decision Criteria

These are likely to be based on any or all of the following.

- Company resources
- Company expectations and objectives
- Management expertise and attitude towards international expansion and development
- Existing involvement overseas
- The nature and features of the product
- Nature of the target markets
- Nature and size of competition in the target markets
- Barriers to entry

# 6 Brand stretching

> **Examiner's comments**. Not a popular question, and whilst many candidates identified brand strategy, they did not extend this to cover the specific issue of brand stretching.

## Introduction

Experts now view **brands** as the **link between** a company's marketing activities and consumers' perceptions of these activities. In the 1990s this brand revolution is particularly relevant to sectors such as financial services. The difficulties consumers have in understanding intangible products and the extent to which the service **becomes** the brand, both present marketing challenges together with the need to exploit brand equity through brand **stretching activities**.

## Elements of Brand Strategy

Arnold (1992) in *The Handbook of Brand Management*, outlines a five stage brand management process.

1.   **Market analysis**: Market definition, Market segmentation, Competitor positions, Trends: PEST and Micro factors

2.   **Brand situation analysis**: Brand personality, Individual attributes. Internal analysis = is advertising projecting the right image? Is the packaging too aggressive? Does the product need updating? Fundamental evaluation of the brand's character.

3.   **Targeting future positions**: Future developments. Brand strategy: any brand strategy should incorporate what has been learnt in steps 1 and 2 into a view of how the market will evolve and what strategic response is most appropriate. Target markets, brand positions and brand scope are the elements of brand strategy.

4.   **Testing new offers**: Individual elements of mix and test marketing the total offer.

5.   **Planning and evaluating performance**: Level of expenditure. Type of support activity. Measurement against objectives: awareness and availability, attitudes. Information on tracking of performance feeds into step 1 on analysis.

From this we see that brand strategy involves decision on three issues: target market(s), brand positioning and brand stretching.

## Brand stretching

Brand stretching refers specifically to the use of an existing, successful brand being used to launch products in an unrelated market. (Note: a brand extension is the use of an established brand name on a new product within the same broad market.)

The starting point for this activity is to identify the current brand's core values. Brands should only be **stretched** in these cases.

(a)   The **core values of the brand have relevance** to the new market into which it is to be launched. Marks & Spencer with its retail operations has established a strong brand image for quality, value and integrity. All these values are also important in the financial services market. This has allowed Marks & Spencer to stretch their brand successfully into the financial services sector.

(b)   The **new market area will not affect the value of the brand in its core market**. Virgin's brand name has been successfully stretched into a number of markets including financial services. However the brand may now be affected by the problems it is experiencing operating train services in the UK.

There is a school of thought that states that it may be easier for service companies to stretch umbrella brands across markets. Financial services companies using umbrella brands can also run into database marketing programmes across their whole service range, American Express being a good example. In general though, most financial service brands are currently too weak to support much brand stretching activity.

# 7 Standardisation

The factors encouraging and supporting **standardisation** of products are, principally, **economies of scale** in production, **research and development** and **marketing communications**. With standardised products, and a belief that an ethnocentric approach to the markets of the world is appropriate, then standardised marketing plans can be used in all markets.

**Standardised marketing communications** enable single images to be created, and for some products competitive advantage can be extracted from country of origin effect. With standardised products produced in a number of plants around the world, production can be shared amongst the plants and markets supplied from any or all of the plants to take advantage of prevailing favourable conditions.

The use of satellite broadcasting by advertisers encourages the use of standardised advertising due to the very large footprints of the satellite transmissions. Thus, in the medium term developments in global communications technology could give greater impetus to standardisation. In the recent past Ford have announced that the Mondeo is to be their first 'world car', and historically a number of product such as 35mm film, blank VHS tapes and certain designer goods have become standardised throughout the world.

The circumstances that prevent or hinder standardisation are legion. Differing **usage conditions** for example due to differing climates make standardisation of some products difficult. Differences in **taste, income and level of sophistication** will also impact on standardisation.

**Intervention** by government in the form of tariffs and non-tariff barriers together with pressure from **regulatory bodies** can prevent a standardisation strategy being effective. Markets will vary dramatically in their **development cycles**, and correspondingly, products will be at a different stage of their life cycles in differing markets. For instance, bicycles are leisure products in the developed world but vital transport products in the developing world. This demonstrates that the global standardisation of bicycles will be difficult, but regional standardisation may be practical.

**Technology differences** will also hinder standardisation. Computer users in the developed world are more likely to operate with the latest versions of micro processors in their PC's. Users in the developing world will invariably use the older technology. It is in the interests of both the micro processor manufacturers and the PC manufacturers to maintain these differentials, in order to re-coup the investments in the respective technologies.

The standardisation of **global brands** is a far more frequently encountered phenomenon with many brands being targeted at the emerging **world youth culture**, for instance Nike and Reebok. These companies appear to be exploiting the global communication of sport and the desire of young people world-wide to be associated with the brands worn by their sporting heroes.

# 8 Pricing policy

Report

To:    *The management*
From: *A Marketer*
Re:    *Pricing policy of a product line*

A product line can be defined in terms of a 'broad group of products whose uses and characteristics are basically similar'. Such products can be differentiated by:

(a)    Price
(b)    Packaging
(c)    Targeted customer
(d)    Distribution channel used

A firm may have a line of products because it wishes to target a number of segments of the market, all of whom require different benefits. The following are the considerations you might make when detailing the influences on pricing of a product line.

(a) *Product quality.* If the firm is seeking a niche upper market segment and a reputation for quality then it may decide a high price is necessary (for example, the Caribbean cruise holiday market). This price may hold for all products in the line, yet there may be special offers for block bookings or during certain times in the year when demand falls.

(b) *Company image.* The firm may be seeking an exclusive image in the market place and may use pricing strategy in conjunction with public relations to achieve this, for example Marks & Spencer.

(c) *Costs of production.* The firm will want to meet the full costs of production and make sustainable profits so pricing must reflect this. The bigger the operation, the bigger the scale economies available from production and marketing, particularly where products are very similar (thus permitting bulk manufacture/purchase of parts). This situation would help secure lower prices and increased competitiveness in a mass market.

(d) *Degree of standardisation of products.* An extension of (c) above, this implies that where products in a line are quite different in order to meet consumer needs, then the costs of the product and, therefore, the price, will have to be higher.

(e) *Desired level of profit.* A firm may willingly take losses on one line of product as long as the range of products meets the forecast profits target. It may price, therefore, to achieve this goal.

(f) *Desired level of market share.* A firm may set or alter prices as a promotional tool to realise market share goals.

(g) *To manage the portfolio effectively.* The firm may have a number of product lines in the market (or different markets) at the same times. Portfolio analysis may indicate that price changes to specific products in specific lines at specific times may realise more revenue from life-cycles; the firm is thus able to use pricing to manage profitability.

(h) *To market diversify.* The firm may be able, through lowering or increasing the price, to take its product line into a different market (upper or lower in income grouping). Some changes to the line (apart from price) would also probably be necessary in order to do this.

(i) *As a promotional tool.* A firm may use its pricing structure as a promotional tool to bring 'value for money' to the customer's attention. In order to increase added value it may additionally offer 'free servicing' as an added incentive.

(j) *To capitalise on novelty.* If the product line is new, and the market largely untapped, a firm may be able to harvest significant profits from the market over the short term by pricing up the whole line. Innovative products will command this competitive advantage until other, similar products enter the market, when the firm will need to reduce its profits to stay competitive. Such pricing up over the short term will additionally help cover the heavy research and development costs of innovation.

(k) *Price leadership.* Where a few suppliers dominate a market (an oligopoly), price competition is most unusual. Any reduction in price by one supplier is likely to be matched immediately by the others, so no benefit accrues. Price increases which are not matched rapidly erode sales. It is common in such markets for a price leader to emerge. This is likely to be a major player with a reputation for efficiency. The price leader indicates the current appropriate level of prices without using its leadership competitively.

Please raise any queries regarding this report with me.

A Marketer

# 9 Nadir Products: ethics

## Part (a)

---

**Tutorial note**. While this question clearly has an important ethical slant, it is important to deal with the commercial impact of the proposed courses of action. If you feel your experience has not prepared you to do this, think in terms of stakeholder theory and ask yourself what connected stakeholders like customers are reasonably entitled to expect and how *you* would react to these ploys.

Do not spend more than a minute on dealing with the report form requirement: a suitable heading and, perhaps, numbered paragraphs are all that are required. A short introductory paragraph giving the reason for the report is a good way to get started.

---

REPORT

To:       Board Members, Nadir Products plc
From:     A Consultant
Date:     December 200X
Subject:  Proposed adjustments to turnover reporting

You asked me to comment on the commercial and ethical implications of suggestions that had been made about the value of this year's turnover. There was concern that a current decline in sales will adversely affect the level of bonuses paid to senior staff.

My first comment is that the assumption behind the suggestions appears wrong. The aim of the bonus scheme was surely to provide an incentive for senior staff to take appropriate action to improve performance. If performance has not improved, it would be perverse to adjust the numbers so that they receive the bonuses anyway. There is an element of moral hazard here: if the bonuses are in effect guaranteed and not dependent on improved performance, the incentive effect disappears and the scheme might as well be abandoned.

I understand that there is concern that staff will be adversely affected by the downturn in sales value. However, I must point out the questionable nature of the suggestions from an ethical point of view. It is likely that the detailed proposals will create a conflict of interests since each has the potential to disadvantage shareholders. It would be ethically inappropriate to pursue any course of action that reduced shareholder value in order to enrich senior staff.

I will now examine the individual proposals.

Discount for additional sales. A discount is an unexceptional sales promotional device that may be used, for instance, to increase or defend market share or to shift excess stock. It has a cost, in the form of reduced margin, and it is a matter of commercial judgement to decide whether the benefit is greater than the cost. It may also have the effect of merely bringing sales forward in time, so that later trading periods suffer.

Of the three suggestions, this is the most defensible. However, it is quite *indefensible* if it is undertaken solely in order to boost bonuses, because of the conflict of interest discussed above.

Bringing forward scheduled orders is a form of window dressing. Your auditors will deploy checks on such activities as a matter of course, and may succeed in detecting this. The accounts would then have to be adjusted, since there is no commercial justification for the practice. It can be seen as detrimental to shareholders since the reported profit would be overstated and, while this may have a positive effect on share value in the short term, were it ever discovered, it would bring into question the company's corporate governance. Such a scheme is also likely to irritate customers who may respond by delaying payment and even seeking a new supplier. This would clearly disadvantage the company.

This suggestion is unacceptable on both ethical and practical grounds.

Warning of possible price rises. I take it as read that there are no actual plans to raise prices? If this is the case, to say that such plans exist is untruthful and therefore inappropriate for a company that wishes to maintain high ethical standards. Further, to hide behind a form of words such as 'there *may* be price rises' would be equally dishonest, since the intention would be to create a specific, incorrect impression in customers' minds. When the warning is eventually shown to be spurious, customers' estimation of the company will fall, with an eventual knock-on effect on turnover.

This ploy is comparable to the previous one in its potential effect on shareholders and customers but is even more unethical

Conclusion. None of the suggestions is acceptable ethically or commercially as a solution to the senior staff bonus problem.

### Part (b)

The stakeholder view is that many groups have a stake in what the organisation does. This is particularly important in the business context, where shareholders own the business but employees, customers and government also have particularly strong claims to having their interests considered. It is suggested that modern corporations are so powerful, socially, economically and politically, that unrestrained use of their power will inevitably damage other people's rights. Under this approach, the exercise of corporate social responsibility constrains the corporation to act at all times as a good citizen. Particular emphasis is laid on the preservation of employment and protection of the environment.

We are not told the extent of Nadir Products operations. If as seems likely, they are largely confined to the UK, or at least to the EU, the company's activities will be subject to fairly demanding legal requirements concerning such basic aspects of good corporate citizenship. They must conform or court legal sanctions.

Another argument points out that corporations exist within society and are dependent upon it for the resources they use. Some of these resources are obtained by direct contracts with suppliers but others are not, being provided by government expenditure. Examples are such things as transport infrastructure, technical research and education for the workforce. Clearly, Nadir Products contributes to the taxes that pay for these things, but the relationship is rather tenuous and the tax burden can be minimised by careful management. The company can do as much or as little as it cares to in this connection.

*Mintzberg* suggests that simply viewing organisations as vehicles for shareholder investment is inadequate, since in practice, he says, organisations are rarely controlled effectively by shareholders. Most shareholders are passive investors. We do not know whether or not this is the case with Nadir Products.

Many organisations regard the exercise of corporate social responsibility as valuable in promoting a positive corporate image. The management of Nadir Products therefore may feel that it is appropriate to take an instrumental approach to such matters as sponsorship and charitable giving. Charitable donations and artistic sponsorship are useful media of public relations and can reflect well on the business. They can be regarded as another form of promotion, which like advertising, serves to enhance consumer awareness of the business. It would be necessary for the company to ensure that the recipients of its generosity were appropriate to its operations at the bottom end of the market: grand opera would probably be inappropriate.

The arguments for and against social responsibility are complex ones. However, ultimately they can be traced to different assumptions about society and the relationships between the individuals and organisations within it. It is unlikely to be something that need occupy a great deal of the time of Nadir Products' directors.

# 10 Feedback and control system

> **Examiner's comments**. Too many answers concentrated specifically on the MkIS rather than broader issues of feedback and control, and the use to which this information can be put.

Planning can be defined as 'deciding what to do', whereas control can be defined as 'ensuring that the desired results are achieved'. The feedback and control process can be illustrated by a simple model.

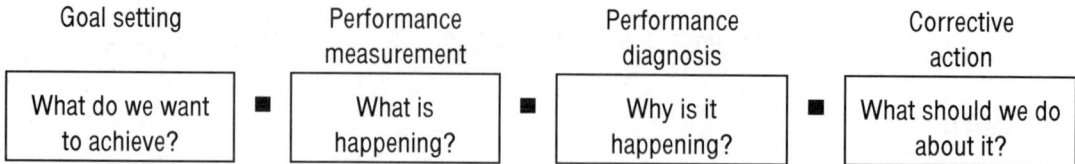

| Goal setting | Performance measurement | Performance diagnosis | Corrective action |
| :---: | :---: | :---: | :---: |
| What do we want to achieve? | What is happening? | Why is it happening? | What should we do about it? |

**Feedback and control** involves the following.

- Goal setting
- Performance measurement
- Performance diagnosis
- Taking corrective action

**Goal setting** is the role of the planning element of strategic marketing. Ideally, the standards set will have been developed within an understanding of what the organisation is able to deliver. Specifically, the factors which should be taken into account include the following.

(a) The **type of control information** required – financial and non-financial

(b) The **methods used to collect** the information – audits, budgets and variance analysis

(c) **Who** requires the information?

(d) What **form the information should take** – weekly, monthly annual reports, presentations, continuous computer based data

(e) The information **systems** required

(f) The **resource** implications

(g) The **behavioural implications** of controlling peoples' activities

This final point is less obvious, but very important if the control system is to work effectively. The involvement of a range of managers and personnel in the evaluation process is vital, together with the need for **good communication**, both within the marketing unit and between departments. Effective implementation of the feedback and control system will require **internal marketing** to employees, **motivation** of personnel and effective **co-ordination** of marketing activities.

Feedback and control information can be used in five distinct areas of operation.

- Financial analysis
- Market analysis
- Sales and distribution analysis
- Physical resource analysis
- Human resource analysis

**Market, sales and distribution analyses** are particularly relevant for marketing planning.

| Type of analysis | Used to control |
|---|---|
| Market/sales analysis to consider size and growth of market and market share | Competitive standing |
| Demand analysis | Sales effectiveness |
| Sales targets | Efficiency in use of resources for selling |
| Sales budget | |

Information on these areas can be gathered through **audits, budgeting or variance analysis**. Marketing audits allow for regular monitoring of the successful implementation of marketing plans. For example, a marketing manager might use the information from the mix audit to recognise that communication targets are not being reached. From this point, corrective action would be needed in the form of a campaign review and redevelopment.

**Budgeting is the most common form of control**. It is financial in nature and very useful when applied to marketing implementation. Budgets tend to be short-term and based on the annual plan for achievement of the year's **profit and sales forecasts**. Monthly deviations from the sales plan tend to require tactical alterations, for example in the form of price increases or decreases to influence demand.

Where budgeting is **longer-term**, this is more appropriate for **monitoring strategic decisions** such as product portfolio management. For example, in the product plan there will be products identified as question marks or potential stars. The position of each product in the matrix will suggest how much close monitoring and control is needed. Information on high-risk or high-potential new products would be used to manage the risk, and to ensure sales forecasts are accurate to avoid back order or production problems.

**Variance analysis** leads on from budgeting, and involves detailed analysis of the difference between actual and expected results. This sort of control information might possibly be used to consider sales-price variances, sales-quantity variances, profit variances and market share variances.

Many marketing activities are not evaluated or controlled but are assumed to be effective. Marketers tend to enjoy planning and tactical implementation but shy away from feedback on the results of their initiatives. This is short-sighted, as it severely limits learning from experience and can, at worst, result in inefficient and ineffective marketing plans.

# Further reading

P Doyle, *Value Based Marketing*, Wiley, 2000

J Johansson, *Global Marketing*, Irwin McGraw Hill, 2000

P Doyle, *Marketing Management and Strategy*, Pearson, 2002, 3rd ed

C Gilligan & R Wilson, *Strategic Marketing Management*, Butterworth Heinemann, 2003, 3rd ed

G Hooley, J Saunders and N Piercy, *Marketing Strategy and Competitive Positioning*, Prentice Hall, 1998, 2nd ed

I Doole & R Lowe, *International Marketing Strategy*, Thomson Learning, 2002, 3rd ed

O Walker, B Harper, J Mullins and J Larreche, *Marketing Strategy*, McGraw Hill, 2003

D Aaker, *Strategic Marketing Management*, J Wiley & Sons, 2000, 6th ed

S Mathur, *Creating Value*, Butterworth Heinemann, 2001, 2nd ed

H Davidson, *The Committed Enterprise*, Butterworth Heinemann, 2002

P Ahmed & M Kafiq, *Internal Marketing*, Butterworth Heinemann, 2002

H Mintzberg, J Quinn & S Ghoshal, *The Strategy Process*, Pearson, 1999

K Ohmae, *The Mind of the Strategist*, McGraw Hill, 1982

R Stacey, *Strategy Management and Organisational Dynamics*, FT Prentice Hall, 2000

G Hamel & C Prahalad, *Competing for the Future*, HBS Press, 1994

M Porter, *Competitive Advantage*, The Free Press, 1985

T Peters & R Waterman, *In Search of Excellence*, Profile Business, 2004

T Burns & G Stalker, *The Management of Innovation*, OUP, 1994

P Kotler, *Marketing Management*, Prentice Hall, 2002, 11th ed

H Ansoff, *Corporate Strategy*, Pan MacMillan, 1986

G Johnson & K Scholes, *Exploring Corporate Strategy*, Prentice Hall, 1999, 5th ed

N Piercy, *Marketing Budgeting*, Croom Helm, 1986

E Gummesson, *Total Relationship Marketing*, Butterworth Heinemann, 1999

D Adcock, *Marketing Strategies for Competitive Advantage*, Wiley, 2000

I Nonaka, *The Knowledge Creating Company*, Oxford Press, 1995

P Senge, *The Fifth Discipline*, Currency, 1994

C Emmanuel, D Otley & K Marchant, *Accounting for Management Control*, Chapman and Hall, 1990

P Drucker, *The Practice of Management*, Longman, 1993

S Dibb, L Simkin, W Pride, O Ferrel, *Marketing: Concepts and Strategies*, Houghton Mufflin, 2000

N Piercy, *Market-led Strategic Change*, Butterworth Heinemann, 2001

C Hofer, D Schendel, *Strategy Formulation*, South Western College Publishing, 1978

H Simon, *Administrative Behaviour*, Simon & Schuster, 1997

W French & C Bell, *Organizational Development*, Prentice Hall, 1995, 6th ed

J-P Jeannet, H Hennessey, *Global Marketing Strategies*, Houghton Mifflin, 1995, 3rd ed

# Key concepts & index

## REVIEW FORM & FREE PRIZE DRAW

All original review forms from the entire BPP range, completed with genuine comments, will be entered into one of two draws on 31 January 2008 and 30 July 2008. The names on the first four forms picked out on each occasion will be sent a cheque for £50.

**Name:** _____    **Address:** _____

_____

_____

**How have you used this Text?**
*(Tick one box only)*

☐ Self study (book only)

☐ On a course: college_____

☐ With BPP Home Study package

☐ Other _____

**Why did you decide to purchase this Text?**
*(Tick one box only)*

☐ Have used companion Kit

☐ Have used BPP Texts in the past

☐ Recommendation by friend/colleague

☐ Recommendation by a lecturer at college

☐ Saw advertising in journals

☐ Saw website

☐ Other _____

**During the past six months do you recall seeing/receiving any of the following?**
*(Tick as many boxes as are relevant)*

☐ Our advertisement in *Marketing Success*

☐ Our advertisement in *Marketing Business*

☐ Our brochure with a letter through the post

☐ Our brochure with *Marketing Business*

☐ Saw website

**Which (if any) aspects of our advertising do you find useful?**
*(Tick as many boxes as are relevant)*

☐ Prices and publication dates of new editions

☐ Information on product content

☐ Facility to order books off-the-page

☐ None of the above

**Have you used the companion Practice & Revision Kit for this subject?**     ☐ Yes     ☐ No

**Your ratings, comments and suggestions would be appreciated on the following areas.**

|  | Very useful | Useful | Not useful |
|---|---|---|---|
| Introductory section (How to use this text, study checklist, etc) | ☐ | ☐ | ☐ |
| Introduction | ☐ | ☐ | ☐ |
| Syllabus coverage | ☐ | ☐ | ☐ |
| Action Programmes and Marketing at Work examples | ☐ | ☐ | ☐ |
| Chapter roundups | ☐ | ☐ | ☐ |
| Quick quizzes | ☐ | ☐ | ☐ |
| Illustrative questions | ☐ | ☐ | ☐ |
| Content of suggested answers | ☐ | ☐ | ☐ |
| Index | ☐ | ☐ | ☐ |
| Structure and presentation | ☐ | ☐ | ☐ |

|  | Excellent | Good | Adequate | Poor |
|---|---|---|---|---|
| Overall opinion of this Text | ☐ | ☐ | ☐ | ☐ |

**Do you intend to continue using BPP Study Texts/Kits/Passcards?**     ☐ Yes     ☐ No

**Please note any further comments and suggestions/errors on the reverse of this page.**

**Please return to: Glenn Haldane, BPP Professional Education, FREEPOST, London, W12 8BR**

## REVIEW FORM & FREE PRIZE DRAW (continued)

**Please note any further comments and suggestions/errors below.**

**FREE PRIZE DRAW RULES**

1. Closing date for 31 January 2007 draw is 31 December 2006. Closing date for 31 July 2007 draw is 30 June 2007.

2. Restricted to entries with UK and Eire addresses only. BPP employees, their families and business associates are excluded.

3. No purchase necessary. Entry forms are available upon request from BPP Professional Education. No more than one entry per title, per person. Draw restricted to persons aged 16 and over.

4. Winners will be notified by post and receive their cheques not later than 6 weeks after the relevant draw date. List of winners will be supplied on request.

5. The decision of the promoter in all matters is final and binding. No correspondence will be entered into.